WITHDRAWN

RIVERSIDE TEXTBOOKS
IN EDUCATION

EDITED BY ELLWOOD P. CUBBERLEY

PROFESSOR OF EDUCATION
LELAND STANFORD JUNIOR UNIVERSITY

DIVISION OF SECONDARY EDUCATION
UNDER THE EDITORIAL DIRECTION
OF ALEXANDER INGLIS

ASSISTANT PROFESSOR OF EDUCATION
HARVARD UNIVERSITY

READINGS IN THE
HISTORY OF EDUCATION

A COLLECTION OF SOURCES AND READINGS TO
ILLUSTRATE THE DEVELOPMENT OF EDUCATIONAL
PRACTICE, THEORY, AND ORGANIZATION

BY

ELLWOOD P. CUBBERLEY

PROFESSOR OF EDUCATION
LELAND STANFORD JUNIOR UNIVERSITY

HOUGHTON MIFFLIN COMPANY

BOSTON   NEW YORK   CHICAGO

The Riverside Press Cambridge

The Riverside Press

CAMBRIDGE · MASSACHUSETTS

U · S · A

PREFACE

THE Readings which this volume reproduces have been collected, from time to time, by the author in connection with the instruction of university classes in the general history of education, and have been used with students as reading supplemental to a lecture course on the subject. They are now gathered together and organized into the present volume, and made to run parallel with and to supplement the author's textbook on the *History of Education*, published at this same time. The chapter arrangement of the two books is the same, and the different Readings are referred to by cross-reference (**R. 172,** etc.) throughout the *History* volume. At the same time the selections are of such a general nature, have been so organized and arranged, and their importance and significance are so explained in the chapter introductions, that the volume of *Readings* may be used as a reference volume of sources by instructors using other texts on the history of education.

The Readings have been selected and arranged primarily with a view to illustrating the history of educational practice and progress and organization, rather than the history of educational theory, though a number of typical and illustrative selections from the more important writers on educational theory, and particularly modern theory, have been included. They have also been selected with a view to illustrating that aspect of the history of educational progress which conceives of educational development as being a phase of the rise and preservation and spread of our western civilization. The Readings accordingly follow such great main lines as the foundation elements of our civilization, as laid by Greece, Rome, and the Christians; the almost extinction of the new civilization in the barbarian migrations, and the gradual reduction of these new peoples to order and a semblance of civilization; the preservation of the old learning and the foundation of schools during the dark period; the reawakening of scholarship, and the reëstablishment of learning in the new universities; the great period of the Revival of Learning, during which that human inquiry which first characterized Greek thought again arose in the western world; the continuation of this spirit of inquiry into matters of religion and world phenomena, giving rise to the religious revolts and the beginnings of modern science study; the educational consequences of the Protestant Revolts among the different religious sects, and the rise of the vernacular school; character of the schools as evolved by the middle of the eighteenth century; the rise of political inquiry, the formulation of a new individualistic and political theory for the school, and the transition of the school from the control of the Church to that of the State; the rise of modern state-school systems, and the adoption of the school as the great constructive tool of the State; the spread of western civilization and the state-school idea over the world; and some of the more important of the new expansions and conceptions of modern education.

It is hoped that the volume of *Readings* as organized may prove useful to teachers and students of the history of education generally, as well as to those who use the companion volume of Text. It is believed that this one volume will be found to contain sufficient supplemental reading to meet the needs of most classes studying the subject. It could be used as a library reference volume, almost to the exclusion of other collateral reading.

ELLWOOD P. CUBBERLEY

Stanford University, Cal.

September 4, 1920

CONTENTS

CONTENTS

CONTENTS

CONTENTS

CONTENTS

CONTENTS

CONTENTS   xvii

CONTENTS

CONTENTS

LIST OF FIGURES

READINGS IN THE
HISTORY OF EDUCATION

CHAPTER I
THE OLD GREEK EDUCATION

THE Readings in this chapter deal with Spartan education, as typical of the older tribal practices of the Hellenes, and with Athenian education before the Age of Pericles, as typical of the best evolved in Greece before its Golden Age. The Readings reproduced describe and compare both, and give a good basis for an understanding of the underlying motives and the character of each.

The selection from Plutarch (1) describes well the Spartan methods, purposes, and teachers, while the selection from Plato (2) gives a similar description for Athenian education. The selection from Lucian (3) pictures an Athenian schoolboy's day, and the one from Aristotle (4) describes well the care taken as to citizenship enrollment, the exclusion of foreigners and all others not of proper birth, and the nature of the training of the Ephebic years. The selection from Freeman (5) is an excellent comparison of the character and ideals of the Spartan and the Athenian types of education, and the usefulness of each for the progress of the State. The aim of the Athenian education which produced such large human results is well stated by Thucydides (6).

The degree to which Athens was able to evolve beyond the earlier tribal type of preparedness education, represented so well by Sparta, is evidence as to the wonderful ability of the Attic Greeks to make progressive changes in living and in government, and consequently to advance where others stood still. Far more than other Greeks, those of Attica were imaginative, original, versatile, adaptable, progressive, and endowed with rare mental ability. Only on such an assumption can we explain not only the very superior type of training for citizenship which they evolved, but also their marvelous achievements in art, philosophy, litera-

ture, and science at this early period in the development of the
civilization of the world.

1. Ancient Education in Sparta

(*Plutarch's Lives*, Lycurgus; selected passages)

Plutarch (46–120 A.D.), a Greek who lived an active public life,
largely in diplomatic service for Rome, has left us a number of
character sketches of historical personages in Greek and Roman
history which throw much light on ancient conditions.   The following extracts from his Life of Lycurgus, the Spartan lawgiver,
who is supposed to have lived in the ninth century B.C., describes
Spartan education.

As for the education of youth, which he looked upon as the greatest
and most glorious work of a lawgiver, he began with it at the very
source, taking into consideration their conception and birth, by regulating the marriages.   For he did not (as Aristotle says) desist from
his attempt to bring the women under sober rules.   They had, indeed,
assumed great liberty and power on account of the frequent expeditions
of their husbands, during which they were left sole mistresses at home,
and so gained an undue deference and improper titles; but notwithstanding this he took all possible care of them.   He ordered the virgins
to exercise themselves in running, wrestling, and throwing quoits and
darts; that their bodies being strong and vigorous, the children afterwards produced from them might be the same; and that, thus fortified
by exercise, they might the better support the pangs of childbirth, and
be delivered with safety.

It was not left to the father to rear what children he pleased, but he
was obliged to carry the child to·a place called *Lesche*, to be examined
by the most ancient men of the tribe, who were assembled there.   If
it was strong and well proportioned, they gave orders for its education,
and assigned it to one of the nine thousand shares of land; but if it was
weakly and deformed, they ordered it to be thrown into the place called
Apothetæ, which is a deep cavern near the mountain Taygetus; concluding that its life could be no advantage either to itself or to the public, since nature had not given it at first any strength or goodness of
constitution. . . . The Spartan children were not under tutors purchased or hired with money, nor were the parents at liberty to educate
them as they pleased: but as soon as they were seven years old, Lycurgus ordered them to be enrolled in companies, where they were all kept
under the same order and discipline, and had their exercises and recreations in common.   He who showed the most conduct and courage
amongst them, was made captain of the company.   The rest kept

their eyes upon him, obeyed his orders, and bore with patience the punishment he inflicted: so that their whole education was an exercise of obedience. The old men were present at their diversions, and often suggested some occasion of dispute or quarrel, that they might observe with exactness the spirit of each, and their firmness in battle.

As for learning they had just what was absolutely necessary. All the rest of their education was calculated to make them subject to command, to endure labor, to fight and conquer. They added, therefore, to their discipline, as they advanced in age; cutting their hair very close, making them go barefoot, and play, for the most part, quite naked. At twelve years of age, their undergarment was taken away, and but one upper one a year allowed them. Hence they were necessarily dirty in their persons, and not indulged the great favor of baths, and oils, except on some particular days of the year. They slept in companies, on beds made of the tops of reeds, which they gathered with their own hands, without knives, and brought from the banks of the Eurotas. In winter they were permitted to add a little thistle-down, as that seemed to have some warmth in it.

At this age, the most distinguished amongst them became the favorite companions of the elder; and the old men attended more constantly their places of exercise, observing their trials of strength and wit, not slightly and in a cursory manner, but as their fathers, guardians, and governors: so that there was neither time nor place, where persons were wanting to instruct and chastise them. One of the best and ablest men of the city was, moreover, appointed instructor of the youth: and he gave the command of each company to the discreetest and most spirited of those called *Irens*. An *Iren* was one that had been two years out of the class of boys: a *Milliren*, one of the oldest lads. This *Iren*, then, a youth twenty years old, gives orders to those under his command, in their little battles, and has them to serve him at his house. He sends the oldest of them to fetch wood, and the younger to gather pot-herbs: these they steal where they can find them, either slyly getting into gardens, or else craftily and warily creeping to the common tables. But if any one be caught, he is severely flogged for negligence or want of dexterity. They steal, too, whatever victuals they possibly can, ingeniously contriving to do it when persons are asleep, or keep but indifferent watch. If they are discovered, they are punished not only with whipping, but with hunger. Indeed, their supper is but slender at all times, that, to fence against want, they may be forced to exercise their courage and address. This is the first intention of their spare diet: a subordinate one is, to make them grow tall. . . .

The boys steal with so much caution, that one of them having conveyed a young fox under his garment, suffered the creature to tear out his bowels with his teeth and claws, choosing rather to die than to be detected. Nor does this appear incredible, if we consider what their young men can endure to this day; for we have seen many of them expire under the lash at the altar of Diana Orthia.

The *Iren*, reposing himself after supper, used to order one of the boys to sing a song; to another he put some question which required a judicious answer: for example, *Who was the best man in the city?* or, *What he thought of such an action?* This accustomed them from their childhood to judge of the virtues, to enter into the affairs of their countrymen. For if one of them was asked, Who is a good citizen, or who an infamous one, and hesitated in his answer, he was considered a boy of slow parts, and of a soul that would not inspire to honor. The answer was likewise to have a reason assigned for it, and proof conceived in a few words. He whose account of the matter was wrong, by way of punishment, had his thumb bit by the *Iren*. The old men and magistrates often attended these little trials, to see whether the *Iren* exercised his authority in a rational and proper manner. He was permitted, indeed, to inflict the penalties; but when the boys were gone, he was to be chastised himself, if he had punished them either with too much severity or remissness.

The adopters of favorites also shared both in the honor and disgrace of their boys: and one of them is said to have been mulcted by the magistrates, because the boy whom he had taken into his affections let some ungenerous word or cry escape him as he was fighting. This love was so honorable, and in so much esteem, that the virgins too had their lovers amongst the most virtuous matrons. A competition of affection caused no misunderstanding, but rather a mutual friendship between those that had fixed their regards upon the same youth, and a united endeavor to make him as accomplished as possible.

2. Description of an Athenian Schoolboy's Life

(Plato, *The Protagoras;* selected)

Plato (429–348 B.C.), the famous Greek philosopher, here describes in condensed form the training which an Athenian schoolboy received. The extract is from one of the Socratic dialogues in his *Protagoras*.

Education and admonition commence in the first years of childhood, and last to the very end of life. Mother and nurse and father and tutor are quarreling about the improvement of the child as soon as ever he is able to understand them; he cannot say or do anything without their setting forth to him that this is just and that is unjust; this is honourable, that is dishonourable; this is holy, that is unholy; do this and abstain from that. And if he obeys, well and good; if not, he is straightened by threats and blows, like a piece of warped wood. At a later stage they send him to teachers, and enjoin them to see to his manners even more than to his reading and music; and the teachers do as they are desired. And when the boy has learned his letters and is beginning to understand what is written, as before he understood only what was spoken, they put into his hands the works of great poets, which he reads at school; in these are contained many admonitions, and many tales, and praises, and encomia of ancient famous men, which he is required to learn by heart, in order that he may imitate or emulate them and desire to become like them. Then, again, the teachers of the lyre take similar care that their young disciple is temperate and gets into no mischief; and when they have taught him the use of the lyre, they introduce him to the poems of other excellent poets, who are the lyric poets; and these they set to music, and make their harmonies and rhythms quite familiar to the children's souls, in order that they may learn to be more gentle, and harmonious, and rhythmical, and so more fitted for speech and action; for the life of man in every part has need of harmony and rhythm. Then they send them to the master of gymnastic, in order that their bodies may better minister to the virtuous mind, and that they may not be compelled through bodily weakness to play the coward in war or on any other occasion. This is what is done by those who have the means, and those who have the means are the rich; their children begin education soonest and leave off latest. When they have done with masters, the state again compels them to learn the laws, and live after the pattern they furnish, and not after their own fancies; and just as in learning to write, the writing-master first draws lines with a style for the use of the young beginner, and gives him the tablet and makes him follow the lines, so the city draws the laws, which were the invention of good law-givers who were of old time; these are given to the young man, in order to guide him in his conduct whether as ruler or ruled; and he who transgresses them is to be corrected, or, in other words, called to account, which is a term used not only in your country, but also in many others.

3. Description of an Athenian Schoolboy's Day

The following description by Lucian of an Athenian schoolboy's life of a later period, but which Freeman thinks applies equally well to an earlier period, related to the details of schoolroom procedure rather than to the larger purposes, as did the preceding selection. It describes a long and a busy day for a boy, but one which must on the whole have been a very enjoyable one. It also seems to indicate that the boy attended different schools on the same day, a point which is not clear.

He gets up at dawn, washes the sleep from his eyes, and puts on his cloak. Then he goes out from his father's house, his eyes fixed on the ground, not looking at any one who meets him. Behind him follow attendants and pedagogoi, bearing in their hands the implements of virtue, writing tablets or books containing the great deeds of old, or, if he is going to a music school, his well-tuned lyre.

When he has labored diligently at intellectual studies, and his mind is sated with the benefits of the school curriculum, he exercises his body in liberal pursuits, riding, or hurling the javelin or spear. Then the wrestling school with its sleek, oiled pupils, labors under the midday sun, and sweats in the regular athletic contests. Then a bath, not too prolonged; then a meal, not too large, in view of afternoon school. For the school masters are waiting for him again, and the books which openly or by allegory teach him who was a great hero, who was a lover of justice and purity. With the contemplation of such virtues he waters the garden of his young soul. When evening sets a limit to his work, he pays the necessary tribute to his stomach and retires to rest, to sleep sweetly after his busy day.

4. Athenian Citizenship and the Ephebic Years

(Aristotle, Constitution of Athens; selected)

Aristotle (384–322 B.C.), the great organizing Greek mind, whom Eusebius called "Nature's private secretary, dipping his pen in intellect," here describes the constitutional requirements as to citizenship at Athens, and the training of the Ephebic years, which, by his time, had been extended to three years.

The present state of the constitution is as follows: Citizenship is a right of children whose parents are both of them citizens. Registration as a member of a deme or township takes place when eighteen years of age are completed. Before it takes place the townsmen of the deme find a verdict on oath, firstly, whether they believe the youth to be as old as the law requires, and if the verdict is in the negative he returns to the ranks of the boys. Secondly, the jury find whether he is freeborn and legitimate. If the verdict is against him he appeals to the Heliæa, and the municipality delegate five of their body to accuse him of illegitimacy. If he is found by the jurors to have been illegally proposed for the register, the State sells him for a slave; if the judgment is given in his favor, he must be registered as one of the municipality. Those on the register are afterwards examined by the senate, and if any one is found not to be eighteen years old, a fine is imposed on the municipality by which he is registered. After approbation, they are called *epheboi*, or cadets, and the parents of all who belong to a single tribe hold a meeting and, after being sworn, choose three men of the tribe over forty years of age, whom they believe to be of stainless character and fitted for the superintendence of youth, and out of these the commons in ecclesia select one superintendent for all of each tribe, and a governor of the whole body of youths from the general body of the Athenians. These take them in charge, and after visiting with them all the temples, march down to Piræus, where they garrison the north and south harbors, Munychia and Acte. The commons also elect two gymnastic trainers for them, and persons who teach them to fight in heavy armor, to draw the bow, to throw the javelin, and to handle artillery. Each of the ten commanders receives as pay a drachma [about twenty cents] per diem, and each of the cadets four obols [about thirteen cents]. Each commander draws the pay of the cadets of his own tribe, buys with it the necessaries of life for the whole band (for they mess together by tribes), and purveys for all their wants. The first year is spent in military exercises. The second year the commons meet in the theater and the cadets, after displaying before them their mastery in warlike evolutions, are each presented with a shield and spear, and become mounted patrols of the frontier and garrison the fortresses. They perform this service for two years, wearing the equestrian cloak and enjoying immunity from civic functions. During this period, to guard their military duties from interruption, they can be parties to no action either as defendant or plaintiff, except in suits respecting inheritances, or heiresses, or successions to hereditary priesthoods. When three years are completed they fall into the ordinary body of citizens.

5. Sparta and Athens compared

(Freeman, K. J., *The Schools of Hellas*, pp. 275–79, 281–82. London, 1907)

This is one of the most important books ever written on Greek educational practice, and in the extracts here presented the differences in the motives and practices of Sparta and Athens are well set forth.

The preceding chapters have sufficiently established, as it seems to me, that Hellenic education alike at Sparta and at Athens, in theory and in practice, aimed at producing the best possible citizen, not the best possible money-maker; it sought the good of the community, not the good of the individual. The methods and materials of education naturally differed with the conception of good citizenship held in each locality, but the ideal object was always the same.

The Spartan, with his schoolboy conception of life, believed that the whole duty of man was to be brave, to be indifferent to hardships and pain, to be a good soldier, and to be always in perfect physical condition; when his Hellenic instincts needed satisfaction, he made his military drill into a musical dance and sang songs in honour of valour. Long speaking and lengthy meditation he regarded with contempt, for he preferred deeds to words and thoughts, and the essence of a situation could always be expressed in a single sentence.   This Spartan conception of citizenship fixed the aim of Spartan education.   Daily hardships, endless physical training, perpetual tests of pluck and endurance, were the lot of the Spartan boy. He did not learn to read or write or count; he was trained to speak only in single words or in the shortest of sentences, for what need had a Spartan of letters or of chattering? His imagination had also to be subordinated to the national ideal: his dances, his songs, his very deities, were all military.

The Athenian's conception of the perfect citizen was much wider and much more difficult of attainment.   Pluck and harmony of physical development did not satisfy him: there must be equal training of mind and imagination, without any sacrifice of bodily health.   He demanded of the ideal citizen perfection of body, extensive mental activity and culture, and irreproachable taste.   "We love and pursue wisdom, yet avoid bodily sloth; we love and pursue beauty, yet avoid bad taste and extravagance," proclaims Perikles in his summary of Athenian ideals.   Consequently Athenian education was triple in its aims; its activities were divided between body, mind, and taste.   The body of the young Athenian was symmetrically developed by the scientifically designed exercises of the palaistra.   At eighteen the State imposed upon him two years of physical training at public cost.   In after life he could exercise himself in the public gymnasia without any payment; there was no actual compulsion, except the perpetual imminence of military service, which, however, almost amounted to compulsion.

As to mental instruction, every boy had to learn reading, writing, arithmetic, and gain such acquaintance with the national literature as these studies involved.   The other branch of primary education, playing and singing, intended to develop the musical ear and taste, was optional, but rarely neglected.   The secondary education given by the Sophists, rhetors, and philosophers was only intended for the comparatively few who had wealth and leisure.

Taste and imagination were cultivated in the music and art schools, but the influences of the theater, the Akropolis, the temples and public monuments, and the dances which accompanied every festival and religious occasion, were still more potent, and were exercised upon all alike.   This æsthetic aspect of education was regarded as particularly important in Hellas owing to the prevalent idea that art and music had a strong influence over character.

For the training of character was before all things the object of Hellenic education; it was this which Hellenic parents particularly demanded of the schoolmaster.   So strongly did they believe that virtue could be taught, that they held the teacher responsible for any subsequent misdemeanour of his pupils. . . .

Since the main object of the schools of Hellas was to train and mould the character of the young, it would be natural to suppose that the schoolmasters and every one else who was to come into contact with the boys were chosen with immense care, special attention being given to their reputation for virtue and conduct. At Sparta this principle was certainly observed. Education was controlled by a paidonomos, selected from the citizens of the highest position and reputation, and the teaching was given, not by hired foreigners or slaves, but by the citizens themselves under his supervision. But then the teaching at Sparta dealt mostly with the manners and customs of the State, or with bodily or military exercises, known to every grown man, and the citizens had plenty of leisure. The Athenians were in a more difficult position. There were more subjects for the boy to learn, and some of them the parents might have neither the capacity nor the time to teach. Owing also to the day-school system at Athens and the peculiarities of Hellenic manners, the boys needed some one always at hand to take them to and from school and palaistra. Thus both paid teachers and attendants were needed. But it was also necessary not to let education become too expensive lest the poor should be unable to afford it. Consequently the paidagogoi came often to be the cheapest and most worthless slaves, and the schoolmasters as a class to be regarded with supreme contempt. No doubt careful parents chose excellent paidagogoi, schoolmasters, and paidotribai for their sons, and made the choice a matter of much deliberation: the teachers at the best schools were often men of position and repute. But that the class as a whole was regarded with contempt there can be little doubt. The children went into school as they would have gone into any other shop, with a sense of superiority, bringing with them their pets, leopards and cats and dogs, and playing with them during lesson-times. Idlers and loungers came into the schools and palaistrai, as they came into the market-booths, to chatter and look on, seriously interrupting the work. The schoolmasters and paidotribai at Athens were, in fact, too dependent upon their public to take a strong line, and, in spite of their power, often exercised, of inflicting corporal punishment, they seem to have been distinctly at the mercy of the pupils and their friends. The paidagogoi too, though they seem to have kept their pupils in order, were often not the right people to control a boy's conduct; they were apt to have a villainous accent, and still more villainous habits. It must be confessed that the Athenians, in their desire to make education cheap, ran a very great risk of spoiling what in their opinion was its chief object, the training of character. . . .

It was the sense of duty to the State, the resolution to promote the happiness of the whole citizen-body, which made parents willing to undergo any sacrifice in order to have their sons educated in the way which would best minister to this ideal. The bills of the masters of letters and music and of the paidotribai, and the lengthy loss of the son's services in the shop or on the farm in Attica, the break-up of family life at Sparta, must have been a sore trial to the parents and have involved many sacrifices. Yet there is no trace of grumbling. The Hellene felt that it was quite as much his duty to the State to educate her future citizens properly as it was to be ready to die in her cause, and he did both ungrudgingly. If the laws which made the teaching of letters compulsory at Athens fell into desuetude, it was only because the citizens needed no compulsion to make them do their duty. Nor had the State to pay the school bills; for every citizen, however poor, was ready to make the necessary sacrifices of personal luxuries and amusements in order to do his duty by having his children properly taught. The State only interfered to make schooling as cheap and as easy to obtain as possible.

6. Athenian Education summarized

(Thucydides, book II, ¶ 40)

An excellent summary of the higher aims and accomplishments of Athenian education, at its best, is given by Thucydides (471–400 B.C.), the Athenian historian, when he puts into the mouth of Pericles the following words:

"If, then, we prefer to meet danger with a light heart but without laborious training, and with a courage which is gained by habit and not enforced by law, are we not greatly the gainers? Since we do not anticipate the pain, although, when the hour comes, we can be as brave as those who never allow themselves to rest; and thus, too, our city is equally admirable in peace and in war. For we are lovers of the beautiful, yet simple in our tastes, and we cultivate the mind without loss of manliness. Wealth we employ, not for talk and ostentation, but when there is real use for it. To avow poverty with us is no disgrace; the true disgrace is in doing nothing to avoid it. An Athenian citizen does not neglect the state because he takes care of his own household; and even those of us who are engaged in business have a very fair idea of politics. We alone regard a man who takes no interest in public affairs, not as a harmless, but as a useless character; and if few of us are originators, we are all sound judges of a policy. The great impediment to action is, in our opinion, not discussion, but the want of that knowledge which is gained by discussion preparatory to action. For we have a peculiar power of thinking before we act and of acting too, whereas other men are courageous from ignorance but hesitate upon reflection. And they are surely to be esteemed the bravest spirits who, having the clearest sense both of the pains and pleasures of life, do not on that account shrink from danger."

CHAPTER II
LATER GREEK EDUCATION

THE Readings in this chapter deal with Greek education and Greek educational influence in the period following the Persian Wars. The long-standing menace of Persian domination had been ended, and little democratic Attica, as well as Greece as a whole, was now free to develop according to its ability and native genius. In Attica a wonderful development took place almost at once, and Athens soon became the first city in the world in the arts of peace. The picture of Athens at the height of the Golden Age of Greece given by Wilkins (7) reveals something of her marvelous achievements in art and literature.

Such a development, together with the great expansion of Greek life and commerce and political relationships throughout the eastern Mediterranean world, naturally subjected the old education of the Ephebic class to serious strain, and remodeling had to take place. In the absence of any state educational system, all kinds of teachers opened schools of the newer type, offering to train for public speaking and eloquence and often making extravagant claims as to what they could accomplish. In time these new teachers organized and reduced their work to system, Isocrates being a leader in this work. In the selection given from his oration against these new-type teachers (8) we get some conception as to their pretensions, and also of his ideas as to the necessities for such training.

With the breakdown of the old training as a basis for developing virtue in the State, and the rise of the new teachers aiming to train for personal success without any basis of morality underlying their work, Athens faced a serious educational crisis. This Socrates attempted to solve by founding morality on personal knowledge as to right and wrong. His practice, well illustrated by the long dialogues in *The Republic* of Plato, which see, and by the selection given (9), was to lead men to correct ideas by asking them questions, and by a questioning method to draw men from unconscious ignorance to conscious ignorance, and from conscious ignorance to clear and reasoned truth. Knowledge of the right, he claimed, would be followed by doing the right. That such a sharp questioner would not be popular anywhere is easily understood, and the task of reforming education on a new philosophical and ethical basis naturally proved too large for any one man.

Of the two final selections, the first pictures Greek higher learning at Alexandria (10) and shows how Greek thought permeated the eastern Mediterranean world, though Greece politically was dead; while the second (11) gives a good idea of our great debt to the Greeks.

7. Athens in the Time of Pericles

(Wilkins, A. S., *National Education in Greece in the Fourth Century B.C.*
London, 1873; selected)

A brilliant picture of Athens in the days of her greatest glory — the Golden Age of Greece. The many non-school educational forces of the city are here well set forth.

But above all things the Athenian of the time of Pericles was living in an atmosphere of unequalled genius and culture. He took his way past the temples where the friezes of Phidias seemed to breathe and struggle, under the shadow of the colonnades reared by the craft of Ictinus or Callicrates and glowing with the hues of Polygnotus, to the agora where, like his Aryan forefathers by the shores of the Caspian, or his Teutonic cousins in the forests of Germany, he was to take his part as a free man in fixing the fortunes of his country. There he would listen, with the eagerness of one who knew that all he held most dear was trembling in the balance, to the pregnant eloquence of Pericles. Or, in later times, he would measure the sober prudence of Nicias against the boisterous turbulence of Cleon, or the daring brilliance of Alcibiades. Then, as the great Dionysia came round once more with the spring-time, and the sea was open again for traffic, and from every quarter of Hellas the strangers flocked for pleasure or business, he would take his place betimes in the theater of Dionysus, and gaze from sunrise to sunset on the successive tragedies in which Sophocles, and Euripides, and Ion of Chios, were contending for the prize of poetry. Or, at the lesser festivals, he would listen to the wonderful comedies of Eupolis, Aristophanes, or the old Cratinus, with their rollicking fun and snatches of sweetest melody, their savage attacks on personal enemies and merry jeers at well-known cowards or wantons, and, underlying all, their weighty allusions and earnest political purpose. As he passed through the market-place, or looked in at one of the wrestling schools, he may have chanced to come upon a group of men in eager conversation, or hanging with breathless interest on the words of one of their number; and he may have found himself listening to an harangue of Gorgias, or to a fragment of the unsparing dialectic of Socrates. What could books do more for a man who was receiving such an education as this? It was what the student gazed on, what he heard, what he caught by the magic of sympathy, not what he read, which was the education furnished by Athens. Not by her discipline, like Sparta and Rome, but by the unfailing charm of her gracious influence, did Athens train her children.

8. The Instruction of the Sophists

(Isocrates, *Against the Sophists;* selected)

Isocrates (436–338 B.C.), was an Athenian orator and rhetorician, who was educated in the schools of the Sophists Prodicus, Protagoras, and Gorgias. In 390 B.C., after a period as an advocate, he opened a school of his own, and organized the work of the preceding Sophists into what were afterwards known as the schools of Rhetoric. In his speech, *Against the Sophists*, written in this same year, he attacks those who attract pupils by low fees and big promises, and sets forth the principles underlying what he proposed to do in his school — a school which soon became famous throughout the Greek-speaking world.

FIG. 1

ISOCRATES (436–338 B.C.)

If all those who undertake instruction, would speak the truth, nor make greater promises than they can perform, they would not be accused by the illiterate. Now, those who inconsiderately have dared to boast, have been the cause that those men seem to have reasoned better, who indulge their indolence, than such as study philosophy: for, first, who would not detest and despise those who pass their time in sophistic chicanery? who pretend, indeed, that they seek truth, but, from the beginning of their premises, labour to speak falsities; for I think it manifest to all, that the faculty of foreknowing future things is above our nature: nay, we are so far from such prudence, that Homer, who, for his wisdom, has acquired the highest fame, has sometimes introduced gods in his poem, consulting about futurity; not that he knew the nature of their minds, but that he would show to us, that this was one of those things which are impossible for man. These men are arrived at that pitch of insolence, that they endeavour to persuade the younger, that, if they will be their disciples, they shall know what is best to be done, and thereby be made happy; and, after they have erected themselves into teachers of such sublime things, they are not ashamed to ask of them four or five minæ;[1] though did they sell any other possession for much less than its value, they would not hesitate to grant themselves mad. But now exposing to sale all virtue and happiness (if we will believe them), they dare argue, that, as being wise men, they ought to be the preceptors of others; yet they say, indeed, that they are not indigent of money, while, to diminish its idea, they call it pitiful gold and silver; though they require a trifling gain, and only promise to make those next to immortal, who will commence their disciples. . . .

When therefore some of the unlearned, considering all these things, see those who profess teaching wisdom and happiness, indigent themselves of many things, requiring a small sum of their scholars, and observing contradictions in silly sentences, though they see them not in actions; professing likewise, that they know futurity, yet not capable of speaking or deliberating properly of things present; and that those are more consistent with themselves, and do more things right who follow common opinions, than those who say they are possessed of wisdom: when they see this, I say, they think such disputations mere trifles, a loss of time in idle things, and not a real improvement of the human mind.

Nor is it just to blame these men only, but those likewise who profess to teach civil science to the citizens; for they also disregard truth; and think it artful, if they draw as many as possible, by the smallness of the recompense, and the greatness of their promises, and so receive something of them: and they are so stupid, and imagine others so, that though they write orations more inaccurate than some who are unlearned speak extempore, yet they promise they will make their disciples such orators, that they shall omit nothing in the nature of things; nay, that they will teach them eloquence, like grammar; not considering the nature of each, but thinking, that on account of the excellence of their promises, they will be admired, and the study of eloquence seem of higher value; not knowing, that arts render not those famous who insolently boast of them, but those who can find out and express whatever is in them. . . . Since I am advanced so far, I will speak more clearly of this topic; I say, then, it is no difficult matter to learn those forms or orders of things, by which we know how to compose orations, if any one puts himself under the care not of such as easily vaunt themselves, but such as have the real science; but, in regard of what relates to particular things, which we must first see, and mix together, and dispose in order, and, besides,

[1] About $80 to $100 in our money. Isocrates charged his pupils ten *minæ* for the course, extending over three or four years.

not lose opportunities, but vary the whole discourse with arguments, and conclude it in a harmonious and musical manner: these things, I say, require great care, and are the province of a manly and wise mind; and the scholar must, besides his having necessary ingenuity, perfectly instruct himself in the different kinds of orations, and be exercised in the practice: but it becomes the master to explain all these as accurately as possible, so as to omit nothing which may be taught. As for the rest, show himself such an example, that they who can imitate and express it, may be able to speak in a more beautiful and elegant manner than others. In whatever regard any thing of what I have mentioned is wanting, it must follow, that his disciples will be less perfect.

9. An Example of Socrates' Teaching

(Xenophon, *Memorabilia*, book IV, chap. II)

The following selection offers a good example of the work of Socrates (470–399 B.C.) in counteracting the teaching of his time, and in showing to those about him that there is a common morality and intelligence which guides the right acts of men, and that the reason that all do not see and follow the right is that they do not think carefully. The youth, Euthydemus, aspired to become a statesman and a ruler. Socrates, after first winning his confidence, finally sought him out one day and engaged him in conversation, as follows:

FIG. 2
SOCRATES (470–399 B.C.)

"Tell me, Euthydemus, have you really, as I hear, collected many of the writings of the men who are said to have been wise?" "I have indeed, Socrates," replied he, "and I am still collecting, intending to persevere until I get as many as I possibly can." "By Juno," rejoined Socrates, "I feel admiration for you, because you have not preferred acquiring treasures of silver and gold rather than of wisdom; for it is plain that you consider that silver and gold are unable to make men better, but that the thoughts of wise men enrich their possessors with virtue." Euthydemus was delighted to hear this commendation, believing that he was thought by Socrates to have sought wisdom in the right course. Socrates, observing that he was gratified with the praise, said, "And in what particular art do you wish to become skilful, that you collect these writings?"

As Euthydemus continued silent, considering what reply he should make, Socrates again asked, "Do you wish to become a physician? for there are many writings of physicians." "Not I, by Jupiter," replied Euthydemus. "Do you wish to become an architect, then? for a man of knowledge is needed in that art also." "No, indeed," answered he. "Do you wish to become a good geometrician, like Theodorus?" "Nor a geometrician either," said he. "Do you wish, then, to become an astronomer?" said Socrates. As Euthydemus said "No" to this, "Do you wish, then," added Socrates, "to become a rhapsodist, for they say that you are in possession of all the poems of Homer?" "No, indeed," said he, "for I know that the rhapsodists, though eminently knowing in all the poems of Homer, are, as men, extremely foolish." "You are perhaps desirous, then," proceeded Socrates, "of attaining that talent by which men become skilled in governing states, in managing households, able to command, and qualified to benefit other men as well as themselves." "I indeed greatly desire," said he, "Socrates, to acquire that talent." "By Jupiter," returned Socrates, "you aspire to a most honorable accomplishment, and a most exalted art, for it is the art of kings, and is called the royal art. But," added he, "have you ever considered whether it is possible for a man who is not just to be eminent in that art?" "I have certainly," replied he; "and it is not possible for a man to be even a good citizen without justice." "Have you yourself, then, made yourself master of that virtue?" "I think," said he, "Socrates, that I shall be found not less just than any other man." "Are there, then, works of just men, as there are works of artisans?" "There are, doubtless," replied he. "Then," said Socrates, "as artisans are able to show their works, would not just men be able also to tell their works?" "And why should not I," asked Euthydemus, "be able to tell the works of justice; as also, indeed, those of injustice; for we may see and hear of no small number of them every day?"

"Are you willing, then," said Socrates, "that we should make a *delta* on this side, and an *alpha* on that, and then that we should put whatever seems to us to be a work of justice under the *delta*, and whatever seems to be a work of injustice under the *alpha?*" "If you think that we need those letters," said Euthydemus, "make them." Socrates, having made the letters as he proposed, asked, "Does falsehood then exist among mankind?" "It does, assuredly," replied he. "Under which head shall we place it?" "Under injustice, certainly." "Does deceit also exist?" "Unquestionably." "Under which head shall we place that?" "Evidently under injustice." "Does mischievousness exist?" "Undoubtedly." "And the enslaving of men?" "That, too, prevails." "And shall neither of these things be placed by us under justice, Euthydemus?" "It would be strange if they should be," said he. "But," said Socrates, "if a man being chosen to lead an army, should reduce to slavery an unjust and hostile people, should we say that he committed an injustice?" "No, certainly," replied he. "Should we not rather say that he acted justly?" "Indisputably." "And if in the course of the war with them he should practice deceit?" "That also would be just," said he. "And if he should steal and carry off their property, would he not do what was just?" "Certainly," said Euthydemus; "but I thought at first that you asked these questions only with reference to our friends." "Then," said Socrates, "all that we have placed under the head of injustice, we must also place under that of justice?" "It seems so," replied Euthydemus. "Do you agree, then," continued Socrates, "that, having so placed them, we should make a new distinction, that it is just to do such things with regard to enemies, but unjust to do them with regard to friends, and that toward his friends our general should be as guileless as possible?" "By all means," replied Euthydemus. "Well, then," said Socrates, "if a general, seeing his army dispirited, should tell them, inventing a falsehood, that auxiliaries were coming, and should, by that invention, check the despondency of his troops, under which head should we place such an act of deceit?" "It appears to me," said Euthydemus, "that we must place it under justice." "And if a father, when his son requires medicine, and refuses to take it, should deceive him, and give him the medicine as ordinary food, and, by adopting such deception, should restore him to health, under which head must we place such an act of deceit?" "It appears to me that we must put it under the same head." "And if a person, when his friend was in despondency, should, through fear that he might kill himself, steal or take away his sword, or any other weapon, under which head must we place that act?" "That, assuredly, we must place under justice." "You say, then," said Socrates, "that not even toward our friends must we act on all occasions without deceit?" "We must not, indeed," said he, "for I retract what I said before, if I may be permitted to do so." "It is indeed much better that you should be permitted," said Socrates, "than that you should not place actions on the right side. But of those who deceive their friends in order to injure them (that we may not leave even this point unconsidered) which of the two is the more unjust, he who does so intentionally or he who does so involuntarily?" "Indeed, Socrates," said Euthydemus, "I no longer put confidence in the answers which I give; for all that I said before appears to me now to be quite different from what I then thought; however, let me venture to say that he who deceives intentionally is more unjust than he who deceives involuntarily." . . .

"Do you know any persons called slave-like?" "I do." "Whether for their knowledge or their ignorance?" "For their ignorance, certainly." "Is it, then, for their ignorance of working in brass that they receive this appellation?" "Not at all." "Is it for their ignorance in the art of building?" "Nor for that." "Or for their ignorance of shoemaking?" "Not on any of these accounts; for the contrary is the case, as most of those who know such trades are servile." "Is it, then, an appellation of those who are ignorant of what is honorable, and good, and just?" "It appears so to me." "It, therefore, becomes us to exert ourselves in every way to avoid being like slaves." "But, by the gods, Socrates," rejoined Euthydemus, "I firmly believed that I was pursuing that course of study by which I should, as I expected, be made fully acquainted with all that was proper to be known by a man striving after honor and virtue; but now, how dispirited must you think I feel, when I see that, with all my previous labor, I am not even able to answer about what I ought most of all to know, and am acquainted with no other course which I may pursue to become better!"

10. The Schools of Alexandria

(Draper, J. W., *History of the Intellectual Development of Europe*, vol. 1, pp. 187–92. New York, 1876)

An interesting description of the Alexandrian learning at its best is given in the following selection.

. . . A great state institution was founded at Alexandria. It became celebrated as the Museum. To it, as a centre, philosophers from all parts of the world converged. It is said that one time not less than fourteen thousand students were assembled there. Alexandria, in confirmation of the prophetic foresight of the great soldier who founded it, quickly became an immense metropolis, abounding in mercantile and manufacturing activity. As is ever the case with such cities, its higher classes were prodigal and dissipated, its lower only to be held in restraint by armed force. Its public amusements were such as might be expected — theatrical shows, music, horse-racing. In the solitude of such a crowd, or in the noise of such dissipation, any one could find a retreat — atheists who had been banished from Athens, devotees from the Ganges, monotheistic Jews, blasphemers from Asia Minor. . . .

The Alexandrian Museum soon assumed the character of a University. In it those great libraries were collected, the pride and boast of antiquity. Demetrius Phalareus was instructed to collect all the writings in the world. So powerfully were the exertions of himself and his successors enforced by the government that two immense libraries were procured. They contained 700,000 volumes. In this literary and scientific retreat, supported in ease and even in luxury — luxury, for allusions to sumptuous dinners have descended to our times — the philosophers spent their time in mental culture by study, or mutual improvement by debates. The king himself conferred appointments to these positions; in later times, the Roman emperors succeeded to the patronage, the government thereby binding in golden chains intellect that might otherwise have proved troublesome. . . . A botanical garden, in connection with the Museum, offered an opportunity to those who were interested in the study of the nature of plants; a zoölogical menagerie afforded like facilities to those interested in animals. . . . An anatomical school [was added], suitably provided with means for the dissection of the human body, this anatomical school being the basis of a medical college for the education of physicians. For the astronomers Ptolemy Euergetes placed in the Square Porch an equinoctial and a solstitial armil, the graduated limbs of these instruments being divided into degrees and sixths. There were in the observatory stone quadrants, the precursors of our mural quadrants. On the floor a meridian line was drawn for the adjustment of the instruments. There were also astrolabes and dioptras. Thus, side by side, almost in the king's palace, were noble provisions for the cultivation of exact science and for the pursuit of light literature. Under the same roof were gathered together geometers, astronomers, chemists, mechanicians, engineers. There were also poets, who ministered to the literary wants of the dissipated city — authors who could write verse, not only in correct metre, but in all kinds of fantastic forms — trees, hearts, and eggs. Here met together the literary dandy and the grim theologian. . . .

. . . The Museum made an impression upon the intellectual career of Europe so powerful and enduring that we still enjoy its results. That impression was twofold, theological and physical. The dialectical spirit and literary culture diffused among the Alexandrians prepared that people, beyond all others, for the reception of Christianity. . . .

But it was not alone as regards theology that Alexandria exerted a power on subsequent ages; her influence was as strongly marked in the impression it gave to science. Astronomical observatories, chemical laboratories, libraries, dissecting-houses, were not in vain. There went forth from them a spirit powerful enough to tincture all future times. Nothing like the Alexandrian Museum was ever called into existence in Greece or Rome, even in their palmiest days. It is the unique and noble memorial of the dynasty of the Ptolemies, who have thereby laid the whole human race under obligations, and vindicated their title to be regarded as a most illustrious line of kings. The Museum was, in truth, an attempt at the organization of human knowledge, both for its development and its diffusion. It was conceived and executed in a practical manner worthy of Alexander. And though, in the night through which Europe has been passing — a night full of dreams and delusions — men have not entertained a right estimate of the spirit in which that great institution was founded, and the work it accomplished, its glories being eclipsed by darker and more unworthy things, the time is approaching when its action on the course of human events will be better understood, and its influences on European civilization more clearly discerned.

Thus, then, about the beginning of the third century before Christ, in consequence of the Macedonian campaign, which had brought the Greeks into contact with the ancient civilization of Asia, a great degree of intellectual activity was manifested in Egypt. On the site of the village of Rhacotis, once held as an Egyptian post to prevent the ingress of strangers, the Macedonians erected that city which was to be the entrepôt of the commerce of the East and West, and to transmit an illustrious name to the latest generations. Her long career of commercial prosperity, her commanding position as respects the material interests of the world, justified the statesmanship of her founder, and the intellectual glory which has gathered round her has given an enduring lustre to his name.

11. What We Owe to the Greeks

(Butcher, S. H., *Some Aspects of the Greek Genius,* Essay I. London, 1891)

In the first Essay in the above-cited volume, entitled "What We Owe to Greece," Professor Butcher gives a very interesting picture of the Greek contribution to the life of the modern world. From it the following selections have been taken.

The Greeks, before any other people of antiquity, possessed the love of knowledge for its own sake. To see things as they really are, to discern their meanings and adjust their relations, was with them an instinct and a passion. Their methods in science and philosophy might be very faulty, and their conclusions often absurd, but they had that fearlessness of intellect which is the first condition of seeing truly. Poets and philosophers alike looked with unflinching eyes on all that met them, on man and the world, on life and death. They interrogated Nature, and sought to wrest her secret from her, without misgiving and without afterthought. Greece, first smitten with the passion for truth, had the courage to put faith in reason, and in following its guidance to take no count of consequences. . . .

At the moment when Greece first comes into the main current of the world's history, we find a quickened and stirring sense of personality, and a free play of intellect and imagination. The oppressive silence with which Nature and her unexplained forces had brooded over man is broken. Not that the Greek temper is irreverent, or strips the universe of mystery. The mystery is still there and felt, and has left many undertones of sadness in the bright and heroic records of Greece; but the sense of mystery has not yet become mysticism. . . . Greek thinkers are not afraid that they may be guilty of prying into the hidden things of the gods. They hold frank companionship with thoughts that had paralysed Eastern nations into dumbness or inactivity, and in their clear gaze there is no ignoble terror. Inroads, indeed, there were at times from the East of strange gods and fanatical rites; and half-lit spaces always remained in which forms of faith or ritual, lower as well as higher than the popular creed, took shelter; but, on the whole, we are henceforth in an upper and a serener air in which man's spiritual and intellectual freedom is assured. . . .

It was the privilege of the Greeks to discover the sovereign efficacy of reason. They entered on the pursuit of knowledge with a sure and joyous instinct. Baffled and puzzled they might be, but they never grew weary of the quest. The speculative faculty which reached its height in Plato and Aristotle, was, when we make due allowance for time and circumstance, scarcely less eminent in the Ionian philosophers; and it was Ionia that gave birth to an idea, which was foreign to the East, but has become the starting-point of modern science — the idea that Nature works by fixed laws. . . . The early poet-philosophers of Ionia gave the impulse which has carried the human intellect forward across the line which separates empirical from scientific knowledge; and the Greek precocity of mind in this direction, unlike that of the Orientals, had in it the promise of uninterrupted advance in the future — of great discoveries in mathematics, geometry, experimental physics, in medicine also and physiology. . . .

Again, the Greeks set themselves to discover a rational basis for conduct. Rigorously they brought their actions to the test of reason, and that not only by the mouth of philosophers, but through their poets, historians, and orators. Thinking and doing, "the spirit of counsel and might" — clear thought and noble action — did not to the Greek mind stand opposed. . . .

The East did not attempt to reconcile the claims of the state and the individual. The pliant genius of Greece first made the effort. In Greece first the idea of the public good, of the free devotion of the citizen to the state, of government in the interests of the governed, of the rights of the individual, took shape. The problem of the relation between the state and the individual was, indeed, very imperfectly solved in Greece. The demands, for instance, of the state were pitched too high, and implied a virtue almost heroic in its members. Even in Athens, where individual liberty was most regarded, certain urgent public needs were supplied mainly by the precarious method of private generosity instead of by state organisation. But though the Greeks may not have solved the political problem, they saw that there was a problem to solve, and set about it rationally; and they were the first to do so. They were gifted with a power, peculiarly Western, of delicate adjustment, of combining principles apparently opposite, of harmonising conflicting claims; they possessed a sense of measure, a flexibility, a faculty of compromise, opposed to the fatal simplicity with which Eastern politics had been stricken. Not tyranny, not anarchy, satisfied the Greek, but ordered liberty. . . .

This brief sketch may serve to indicate the qualities most distinctive of the Greek genius — the love of knowledge, the love of rational beauty, the love of freedom. In their first contact with the East — with Egypt and Assyria — during the period known as the Græco-Phœnician period of art, the Greeks had a trying ordeal to pass through. They came out of it, as we have seen, in a characteristic fashion.

1. Their political instinct was alien to Assyrian despotism.

2. Their lay instinct rose up against Egyptian priestcraft.

3. Their instinct for beauty and reason combined rejected in both arts — in Assyrian and Egyptian alike — what was monstrous and lifeless.

4. Their instinct for knowledge, their curiosity, their cosmopolitanism, led them to adopt the foreign *technique*, and to absorb all that was fruitful in the foreigners' ideas. They borrowed from every source, but all that they borrowed they made their own. The Phœnicians, it has been said, taught the Greeks writing, but it was the Greeks who wrote. In every department the principle holds good. They stamped their genius upon each imported product, which was to them but the raw material of their art. . . . Such, briefly, is our debt to Greece. And when we speak of Greece we think first of Athens. . . .

To Greece, then, we owe the love of Science, the love of Art, the love of Freedom: not Science alone, Art alone, or Freedom alone, but these vitally correlated with one another and brought into organic union. And in this union we recognise the distinctive features of the West. The Greek genius is the European genius in its first and brightest bloom. From a vivifying contact with the Greek spirit Europe derived that new and mighty impulse which we call Progress. . . .

From Greece came that first mighty impulse whose far-off workings are felt by us to-day, and which has brought it about that progress has been accepted as the law and goal of human endeavour. Greece first took up the task of equipping man with all that fits him for civil life and promotes his secular well-being; of unfolding and expanding every inborn faculty and energy, bodily and mental; of striving restlessly after the perfection of the whole, and finding in this effort after an unattainable ideal that by which man becomes like to the gods. . . .

CHAPTER III
THE EDUCATION AND WORK OF ROME

THE Readings in this chapter trace the education of a Roman boy from the earlier times, when the training given was simple and very practical, through the change in national ideals to the later period, when oratory had become the chief aim of Roman educational effort.

The principal early schoolbook was the Laws of the Twelve Tables. These have been lost in their original form, but the digest (12) gives an idea as to their nature, while Cicero tells us (13) of their importance in the education of youth. The Roman farmer's calendar (14) shows the farmer's duties and sacrifices, and from it one gets some idea of the simple rural life of the early Romans. The extracts from Polybius (15) and Mommsen (16) give us good pictures of the Roman citizen of the old school. The epitaph for a Roman matron (17) describes briefly the education of a girl in this same earlier period.

After Rome had expanded and had come to embrace all the Italian peninsula, and the State was being brought into increasing contact with the Hellenic world to the eastward, the need became manifest for a more extended education and a broader culture than the old education had afforded. Within two centuries the transition was accomplished, and the old educational training had been superseded by new types of schooling. At first Hellenic schools were set up, and the Hellenic school system was adopted at Rome; later a Roman modification of these schools was worked out, as better adapted to Roman life and more expressive of Roman character. That the change was resisted by the older and more conservative members of Roman society might naturally be supposed. Not only was much written against the new and in praise of the old education, of which the extracts from Marcus Aurelius (18) and Tacitus (19) were among the more temperate, but it was even attempted to prohibit the introduction of Greek teachers and schools by official edicts (20 a–b). Horace (22) gives a good picture of the solicitude of his father, in the transition period, to secure the best teachers of the time for his son.

The position of a schoolmaster at Rome, as in Greece, was that of a menial, and Martial (23 a–b) gives no very attractive picture of a Roman primary school.   Teaching, unenlivened by any ideas as to psychological procedure, was one long grind.   Both the teacher and the boy had a hard time.   The difficulties a boy faced in learning to read Latin, as had been the case with the Greek boy as well, are shown in the page reproduced from Vergil (21).   Cicero (24) and Quintilian (25) set forth the aim of the new education as finally evolved — oratory.   Though the position of the primary teacher always remained low, the teachers in the higher schools, under the later Empire, came to occupy an important social position, as is shown by the grant of privileges to physicians and teachers by Constantine (26).

The Roman system of instruction as finally evolved spread to all the provincial cities, and passed over to the Middle Ages as the basis for the Christian schools which later arose in the cathedral cities.   The Seven Liberal Arts of the Middle Ages were a direct descendant of the instruction in the Roman secondary schools.

12. The Laws of the Twelve Tables

What the laws of Moses were to the early Hebrews, the laws of Lycurgus to Sparta, the laws of Solon and the Homeric poems to Attica, the Laws of the Twelve Tables were to the early Romans. These were adopted in 451 and 450 B.C., being in part a codification of previous practices, and made in part as a concession to the plebes.   The first ten were adopted in 451, and the last two in 450. For several centuries these Laws formed the basis of instruction in reading and writing, and every boy was expected to know them and be able to explain their meaning.   They express both the spirit and the ideals of the old life and education at Rome.

The following is an analysis of their contents, as reconstructed by scholars, the originals being lost.

    I. Related to the Summons before a Magistrate.
    II. Described Judicial Proceedings.
    III. Execution, following Confession or Judgment.
    IV. The Rights of a Father.
    V. Related to Inheritance and Tutelage.
    VI. Related to Dominion and Possession.
    VII. The Law Concerning Real Property.
    VIII. The Law of Wrongs and Injuries (Torts).

IX. Public Law.
X. Sacred Law.
XI. Supplement to Tables I–V. Prohibiting inter-
marriage of the two classes of citizens.
XII. Supplement to Tables VI–X. Various matters.

To illustrate further the nature of these Laws, the main sub-
divisions of Table IV are given.

TABLE IV. THE RIGHTS OF A FATHER.

1. Provisions as to the immediate destruction of monstrous and
deformed children.
2. Relating to the control of a father over his children, the right
being given him, during their whole life, to scourge them, imprison,
keep rustic labor in chains, or sell or slay, even though they may
hold high office.
3. Three consecutive sales of a son by a father finally releases him
from his father's control.
4. Providing that no child born more than ten months after the
death of his reputed father to be held as a legitimate child.

13. Importance of the Twelve Tables in Education

(Cicero, *De Oratore*, book I, chap. XLIV)

Cicero, in his book on education for oratory, gives the following
comment on the importance of a knowledge of the Laws of the
Twelve Tables for those who would understand Roman law and
institutions. *De Oratore* was written in 55 B.C.

Though all the world exclaim against me, I will say what I think:
that single little book of the Twelve Tables, if any one look at the
fountains and sources of laws, seems to me, assuredly, to surpass the
libraries of all the philosophers, both in weight of authority, and in
plenitude of utility.   And if our country has our love, as it ought to
have in the highest degree, — our country, I say, of which the force
and natural attraction is so strong, that one of the wisest of mankind
preferred his Ithaca, fixed, like a little nest, among the roughest of
rocks, to immortality itself, — with what affection ought we to be
warmed toward such a country as ours, which, preëminently above all
other countries, is the seat of virtue, empire, and dignity?   Its spirit,
customs, and discipline ought to be our first objects of study, both
because our country is the parent of us all, and because as much wisdom
must be thought to have been employed in framing such laws, as in
establishing so vast and powerful an empire.   You will receive also
this pleasure and delight from the study of the law, that you will then
most readily comprehend how far our ancestors excelled other nations

in wisdom, if you compare our laws with those of their Lycurgus, Draco, and Solon. It is indeed incredible how undigested and almost ridiculous is all civil law, except our own; on which subject I am accustomed to say much in my daily conversation, when I am praising the wisdom of our countrymen above that of all other men, and especially of the Greeks. For these reasons have I declared, Scævola, that the knowledge of the civil law is indispensable to those who would become accomplished orators.

14. A Roman Farmer's Calendar

(Schreiber, *Atlas of Classical Antiquities*, Plate 62, Fig. 3)

A marble cube, two feet high and a foot square, of about 31–29 B.C. The translation of the space for May reveals the agricultural character of the Roman landowner, even at this late date.

FIG. 3. A MARBLE CALENDAR

(*Translation of the Space for May*)

THE MONTH OF MAY

XXXI days

The nones fall on the 7th day.
The day has $14\frac{1}{2}$ hours.
The night has $9\frac{1}{2}$ hours.
The sun is in the sign of Taurus.
The moon is under the protection of Apollo.
The corn is weeded.
The sheep are shorn.
The wool is washed.
Young steers are put under the yoke.
The vetch of the meadows is cut.
The lustration of the crops is made
Sacrifices to Mercury and Flora.

15. The Roman Character

(Polybius, book 1, chap. 37)

The following extract, taken from the historical writings of the Greek Polybius, who lived between 204 and 122 (?) B.C., and who spent much time in Rome, is a good description of the Roman point of view.

But it is a peculiarity of the Roman people as a whole to treat everything as a question of strength; to consider that they must of course accomplish whatever they have proposed to themselves; and that nothing is impossible that they have once determined upon. The result of such self-confidence is that in many things they do succeed, while in some few they conspicuously fail, and especially at sea. On land it is against men only and their works that they have to direct their efforts: and as the forces against which they exert their strength do not differ intrinsically from their own, as a general rule they succeed; while their failures are exceptional and rare.

16. The Grave and Severe Character of the Life of the Earlier Roman

(Mommsen, C. M. T., *History of Rome*, vol. II, pp. 4, 8)

The following passage from the German historian Mommsen gives a good picture of the life of a Roman citizen under the Republic.

Life in the case of the Roman was spent under conditions of austere restraint, and the nobler he was the less was he a free man. All-powerful custom restricted him to a narrow range of thought and action; and to have led a serious and strict life, or, to use a Latin expression, a grave and severe life, was his glory. Nothing more or less was expected of him than that he should keep his household in good order, and unflinchingly bear his part of counsel and action in public affairs. But while the individual had neither the wish nor the power to be aught else than a member of the community, the glory and the might of that community were felt by every individual burgess as a personal possession to be transmitted along with his name and his homestead to posterity; and thus, as one generation after another was laid in the tomb and each in succession added its fresh contribution to the stock of ancient honours, the collective sense of dignity in the noble families of Rome swelled into that mighty pride of Roman citizenship to which the earth has never, perhaps, witnessed a parallel, and the traces of which — strange as they are grand — seem to us whenever we meet them to belong, as it were, to another world. It was one of the characteristic peculiarities of this mighty pride of citizenship that, while not suppressed, it was yet compelled by the rigid simplicity and equality that prevailed among the citizens to remain locked up in the breast during life, and was only allowed to find expression after death; but it was displayed in the funeral of the man of distinction so intensely and so conspicuously that this ceremonial is better fitted than any other phenomenon of Roman life to give us who live in other times a glimpse of the wonderful spirit of the Romans.

17. The Education of Girls

(An ancient epitaph)

Women in Rome occupied a position of dignity and importance, but their place was in the home. For this they were carefully educated by their mothers, though many, in later times, also obtained some literary training. The following epitaph describes the simple history of one worthy matron.

Stranger, my tale is briefly told;
    O stay, and read with care.
This gloomy tomb contains the bloom
    Of one that once was fair.

Her name was Claudia.   To her lord
    Her heart's full love she paid.
Two sons she had, one left on earth
    And one beside her laid.

Her words were mild, her manners chaste;
    Her home she ruled in peace.
She plied the distaff and the loom.
    Now go away: I cease.

18. The Old Roman Education described

(Emperor Marcus Aurelius Antoninus, *The Thoughts*, chap. 1; trans. by George Long. London, 1873)

Marcus Aurelius, as he is commonly known, was born in 121 A.D., and was Emperor of Rome from 161 to 180. In the first chapter of his volume, *The Thoughts*, he has left us a good picture of old Roman family education. One sees from it the importance of the family life and training.

1. From my grandfather Verus [I learned] good morals and the government of my temper.

2. From the reputation and remembrance of my father, modesty and a manly character.

3. From my mother, piety and beneficence, and abstinence, not only from evil deeds, but even from evil thoughts; and further, simplicity in my way of living, far removed from the habits of the rich.

4. From my great-grandfather, not to have frequented public schools, and to have had good teachers at home, and to know that on such things a man should spend liberally.

5. From my governor, . . . I learned endurance of labour, and to want little, and to work with my own hands, and not to meddle with other people's affairs, and not to be ready to listen to slander.

6. From Diognetus (my tutor), not to busy myself about trifling things, and not to give credit to what was said by miracle-workers and jugglers about incantations and the driving away of dæmons and such things; and not to breed quails (for fighting), nor to give myself up passionately to such things; and to endure freedom of speech; and to have become intimate with philosophy; and to have been a hearer, first of Bacchius, then of Tandasis and Marcianus; and to have written

dialogues in my youth; and to have desired a plank bed and skin, and whatever else of the kind belongs to the Grecian discipline.

7. From Rusticus I received the impression that my character required improvement and discipline; and from him I learned not to be led astray to sophistic emulation, nor to writing on speculative matters, nor to delivering little hortatory orations, nor to showing myself off as a man who practices much discipline, or does benevolent acts in order to make a display; and to abstain from rhetoric, and poetry, and fine writing; and not to walk about in the house in ʌny outdoor dress, nor to do other things of the kind; and to write my letters with simplicity, like the letter which Rusticus wrote from Sinuessa to my mother; and with respect to those who have offended me with words, or done me wrong, to be easily disposed to be pacified and reconciled, as soon as they have shown a readiness to be reconciled; and to read carefully, and not to be satisfied with a superficial understanding of a book; nor hastily to give my assent to those who talk overmuch; and I am indebted to him for being acquainted with the discourses of Epictetus, which he communicated to me out of his own collection.

8. From Apollonius I learned freedom of will and undeviating steadiness of purpose; and to look to nothing else, not even for a moment, except to reason; . . .

9. From Sextus, a benevolent disposition, and the example of a family governed in a fatherly manner, and the idea of living conformably to nature; . . .

10. From Alexander the grammarian, to refrain from fault-finding, and not in a reproachful way to chide those who uttered any barbarous or solecistic or strange-sounding expression; but dexterously to introduce the very expression which ought to have been used, and in the way of answer or giving confirmation, or joining in an inquiry about the thing itself, not about the word, or by some other fit suggestion. . . .

14. From my brother Severus, to love my kin, and to love truth, and to love justice; . . . and from him I received the idea of a polity in which there is the same law for all, a polity administered with regard to equal rights and equal freedom of speech, and the idea of a kingly government which respects most of all the freedom of the governed; . . .

15. From Maximus I learned self-government, and not to be led aside by anything; and cheerfulness in all circumstances, as well as in illness; and a just admixture in the moral character of sweetness and dignity, and to do what was set before me without complaining. . . .

16. In my father I observed mildness of temper, and unchangeable resolution in the things which he had determined after due deliberation; and no vainglory in those things which men call honours; and a love of labour and perseverance; and a readiness to listen to those who had anything to propose for the common weal; and undeviating firmness in giving to every man according to his deserts; and a knowledge derived

from experience of the occasions for vigorous action and for remission.
. . . I observed too his habit of careful inquiry in all matters of deliberation, and his persistency, and that he never stopped his investigation
through being satisfied with appearances which first present themselves; and that his disposition was to keep his friends, and not to be
soon tired of them, nor yet to be extravagant in his affection; and to be
satisfied on all occasions, and cheerful; and to foresee things a long way
off, and to provide for the smallest without display; and to check immediately popular applause and all flattery; and to be ever watchful
over the things which were necessary for the administration of the
empire, and to be a good manager of the expenditure, and patiently to
endure the blame which he got for such conduct; and he was neither
superstitious with respect to the gods, nor did he court men by gifts
or by trying to please them, or by flattering the populace; but he showed
sobriety in all things and firmness, and never any mean thoughts or
action, nor love of novelty. . . . There was in him nothing harsh, nor
implacable, nor violent, nor, as one may say, anything carried to the
sweating point; but he examined all things severally, as if he had abundance of time, and without confusion, in an orderly way, vigorously
and consistently.   And that might be applied to him which is recorded
of Socrates, that he was able both to abstain from, and to enjoy, those
things which many are too weak to abstain from, and cannot enjoy
without excess.   But to be strong enough both to bear the one and to
be sober in the other is the mark of a man who has a perfect and in-
vincible soul, such as he showed in the illness of Maximus.

17. To the gods I am indebted for having good grandfathers, good
parents, a good sister, good teachers, good associates, good kinsmen
and friends, nearly everything good. . . .

19. The Old and New Education contrasted

(Tacitus, *Dialogue concerning Oratory*, chaps. 28, 29, 34, and 35)

This dialogue, the scene of which is laid in the year 75 A.D.,
contrasts well the old Roman training with that which took its
place.   It will of course be evident that Tacitus was not particularly favorable to the newer education.

28. . . . Before I enter on the subject, let me premise a few words on
the strict discipline of our ancestors, in educating and training up their
children.   In the first place the son of every family was the legitimate
offspring of a virtuous mother.   The infant, as soon as born, was not
consigned to the mean dwelling of a hireling nurse, but was reared and
cherished in the bosom of its mother, whose highest praise it was to
take care of her household affairs, and attend to her children.   It was
customary likewise for each family to choose some elderly relation of

approved conduct, to whose charge the children were committed. In her presence not one indecent word was uttered; nothing was done against propriety and good manners. The hours of study and serious employment were settled by her direction; and not only so, but even the diversions of the children were conducted with modest reserve and sanctity of manners. Thus it was that Cornelia, the mother of the Gracchi, superintended the education of her illustrious issue. It was thus that Aurelia trained up Julius Cæsar; and thus Atia formed the mind of Augustus. The consequence of this regular discipline was, that the young mind, whole and sound, and unwarped by irregular passions, received the elements of the liberal arts with hearty avidity. Whatever was the peculiar bias, whether to the military art, the study of the laws, or the profession of eloquence, that engrossed the whole attention, that was imbibed thoroughly and totally.

29. In the present age what is our practice? The infant is committed to a Greek chambermaid, and a slave or two, chosen for the purpose, generally the worst of the whole household train, and unfit for any office of trust. From the idle tales and gross absurdities of these people, the tender and uninstructed mind is suffered to receive its earliest impressions. Throughout the house not one servant cares what he says or does in the presence of his young master; and, indeed, how should it be otherwise? since the parents themselves are so far from training their young families to virtue and modesty, that they set them the first examples of luxury and licentiousness. Thus our youth gradually acquire a confirmed habit of impudence, and a total disregard of that reverence they owe both to themselves and to others. To say truth, it seems as if a fondness for horses, actors, and gladiators, the peculiar and distinguishing folly of this our city, was impressed upon them even in the womb: and when once a passion of this contemptible sort has seized and engaged the mind, what opening is there left for the noble arts? Who talks of anything else in our houses? If we enter the schools, what other subjects of conversation do we hear among the boys? The preceptors themselves choose no other topic more frequently to entertain their hearers; for it is not by establishing a strict discipline, or by giving proofs of their genius, that this order of men gain pupils, but by fawning and flattery. Not to mention how ill instructed our youth are in the very elements of literature, sufficient pains are by no means taken in bringing them acquainted with the best authors, or in giving them a proper notion of history, together with a knowledge of men and things. The whole that seems to be considered in their education is, to find out a person for them called a rhetorician. I will presently give you some account of the introduction of this profession at Rome, and show you with what contempt it was received by our ancestors. . . .

34. The practice of our ancestors was agreeable to this theory. The

youth who was intended for public declamation, was introduced by his father, or some near relation, with all the advantages of home discipline and a mind furnished with useful knowledge, to the most

eminent orator of the time, whom thenceforth he attended upon all occasions; he listened with attention to his patron's pleadings in the tribunals of justice, and his public harangues before the people; he heard him in the warmth of argument; he noted his sudden replies; and thus, in the field of battle, if I may so express myself, he learned the first rudiments of rhetorical warfare. The advantages of this method are obvious: the young candidate gained courage, and improved his judgment; he studied in open day, amidst the heat of the conflict, where nothing weak or idle could be said with impunity; where everything absurd was instantly rebuked by the judge, exposed to ridicule by the adversary, and condemned by the whole body of advocates. In this way they imbibed at once the pure and uncorrupted streams of genuine eloquence. But though they chiefly attached themselves to one particular orator, they heard likewise all the rest of their contemporary pleaders, in many of their respective debates; and they had an opportunity of acquainting themselves with the various sentiments of the people, and of observing what pleased or disgusted them most in the several orators of the forum. Thus they were supplied with an instructor of the best and most improving kind, exhibiting, not the feigned semblance of Eloquence, but her real and lively manifestation: not a pretended, but a genuine adversary, armed in earnest for the combat; an audience, ever full and ever new, composed of foes as well as friends, and where not a single expression could fall uncensured, or unapplauded. . . .

FIG. 4. READING A MANUSCRIPT

35. On the other hand, our modern youth are sent to the mountebank schools of certain declaimers called rhetoricians: a set of men who made their first appearance in Rome a little before the time of Cicero. And that they were by no means approved by our ancestors plainly appears from their being enjoined, under the censorship [1] of Crassus and Domitius, to shut up their *schools of impudence*, as Cicero expresses it. But I was going to say, our youths are sent to certain academies, where it is hard to determine whether the place, the company, or the method of instruction is most likely to infect the minds of young people, and produce a wrong turn of thought. There can be nothing to inspire

[1] 92 A.D.; 662 A.U.C.

respect in a place where all who enter it are of the same low degree of understanding; nor any advantage to be received from their fellow-students, where a parcel of boys and raw youths of unripe judgments harangue before each other, without the least fear or danger of criticism. And as for their exercises, they are ridiculous in their very nature. They consist of two kinds, and are either persuasive or controversial. The first, as being easier and requiring less skill, is assigned to the younger lads; the other is the task of more mature years. But, good gods! with what incredible absurdity are they composed! And this as a matter of course, for the style of the declamations must needs accord with the preposterous nature of the subjects. Thus being taught to harangue in a most pompous diction, on the rewards due to tyrannicides, on the election to be made by deflowered virgins, on the licentiousness of married women, on the ceremonies to be observed in time of pestilence, with other topics,[1] which are daily debated in the schools, and scarce ever in the forum; when they come before the real judges . . .

20. Attempts to prohibit the Introduction of the Greek Higher Learning at Rome

(Suetonius, *Lives of Eminent Rhetoricians*, chap. 1)

The dread of Greek higher learning found frequent expression at Rome during the second century B.C. Cato the Elder, who died in 148 B.C., labored hard to prevent changes which were under way. Suetonius gives us two decrees which were aimed to prevent the introduction of rhetorical schools, but which were without effect. These are:

(a) Decree of the Roman Senate, 161 B.C.

In the consulship of Caius Fannius Strabo, and Marcus Valerius Messala: the Prætor Marcus Pomponius moved the Senate, that an act be passed respecting Philosophers and Rhetoricians. In this matter, they have decreed as follows: 'IT SHALL BE LAWFUL for M. Pomponius, the Prætor, to take such measures, and make such provisions, as the good of the Republic, and the duty of his office, require, that no Philosophers or Rhetoricians be suffered at Rome.'

(b) Decree of the Censor, 92 B.C.

IT IS REPORTED to us that certain persons have instituted a new kind of discipline; that our youth resort to their schools; that they have assumed the title of Latin Rhetoricians; and that young men waste their time there for whole days together. Our ancestors have ordained what

[1] These are specimen topics of themes debated in the rhetorical schools.

instruction is fitting their children should receive, and what schools they should attend. These novelties, contrary to the customs and instructions of our ancestors, we neither approve, nor do they appear to us good. Wherefore it appears to be our duty that we should notify our judgment both to those who keep such schools, and those who are in the practice of frequenting them, that they meet our disapprobation.

21. Difficulty in Learning to Read illustrated by a Page from Vergil

The facsimile on the opposite page is from a very perfect copy of the Latin text, preserved in the Vatican Library, at Rome. It probably dates from about 200 A.D., and is a fine specimen of the copyist's art.

The writing is in capital letters, and only the phrases are punctuated. The period only is used. If placed at the top of the line it means our period; if in the middle, our comma; and if at the bottom, our semicolon.

The difficulty experienced in learning to read even such a perfect copy as this can be seen by comparing it with the same Latin words below, but properly spaced, punctuated, and capitalized.

ÆNEIDOS, LIBER SEXTUS

Minotaurus inest, Veneris monumenta nefandæ; 26
Hic labor ille domus et inextricabilis error;
Magnum reginæ sed enim miseratus amorem
Dædalus; ipse dolus tecti ambagesque resolvit,
Cæco regens filo vestigia. Tu quoque magnam
Partem opero in tanto, sineret dolor, Icare, haberes, 31
Bis conatus erat casus effingere in auro;
Bis patriæ cecidere manus. Quin protinus omnia
Perlegerent oculis, ni jam præmissus Achates
Afforet, atque, una Phœbi, Triviæque sacerdos,
Deiphobe Glauci, fatur quæ talia regis: 36
"Non hoc ista sibi tempus spectacula poscit;
Nunc grege de intacto septem mactare juvencos
Præstiterit, totidem lectas de more bidentes."

MINOTAVRVSINESTVENERISMONVMENTANEFANDAE
HICLABORILLEDOMVSETINEXTRICABILISERROR
MAGNVMREGINAESEDENIMMISERATVSAMOREM
DAEDALVSIPSEDOLOSTECTIAMBAGESQVERESOLVIT
CAECARIGENSFILIOVESTIGIANTVQVOQVEMAGNAM
PARIEMOPEREINTANTOSINEREIDOLORICAETHABERES
BISCONATVSERATICASVSEFFINGEREINAVRO
BISPATRIAECECIDEREMANVSQVINPROTINVSOMNIA
TERLIGERENTOCVLISNILAMIRAEMISSVSACHATES
ADFOREADQVNAPHOEBEIRVILAEQVESACERDOS
DELPHOBEGLAVCHATVRQVAEFALIAREGI
NONHOCISIASSIBILIMPVSSPECTACVLAPOSCIT
NVNCGRICEDEINIACTOSEPTEMMACTAREIVVENCOS
PRAESIITERITOTIDEMLECTASEXMOREBIDENTIS

FIG. 5. A PAGE OF THE "ÆNEID" OF VERGIL
Difficulty experienced in learning to read illustrated by a page from Vergil
(From a very perfect copy, in the Vatican Library at Rome)

22. The Education given by a Father

(Horace, *Satires*, book 1, 6, lines 65–80)

The Roman poet Horace, who lived from 65 to 8 B.C., and whose father gave him a good education somewhat after the old type, and afterwards educated him at Rome and at Athens, leaves us this description of the education which he received.

And yet, if the faults and defects of my nature are moderate ones, and with their exception my life is upright (just as if one were to censure blemishes found here and there on a handsome body), if no one can truly lay to my charge avarice, meanness, or frequenting vicious haunts, if (that I may praise myself) my life is pure and innocent, and my friends love me, I owe it all to my father; he, though not rich, for his farm was a poor one, would not send me to the school of Flavius, to which the first youths of the town, the sons of the centurions, the great men there, used to go, with their bags and slates on their left arm, taking the teacher's fee on the Ides of eight months in the year; but he had the spirit to carry me, when a boy, to Rome, there to learn the liberal arts which any knight or senator would have his own sons taught. Had any one seen my dress, and the attendant servants, so far as would be observed in a populous city, he would have thought that such expense was defrayed from an old hereditary estate. He himself was ever present, a guardian incorruptible, at all my studies.

23. The *Ludi Magister*

Martial, a Spaniard, who lived from 43 to 104 A.D., and who spent many years in Rome, has left us some fifteen hundred *Epigrams* on Roman life and society. Two of these, which relate to the teacher in the primary school, are reproduced below.

(a) *To the Master of a Noisy School*

(*Epigrams*, book IX, no. 68)

What right have you to disturb me, abominable schoolmaster, object abhorred alike by boys and girls? Before the crested cocks have broken silence, you begin to roar out your savage scoldings and blows. Not with louder noise does the metal resound on the struck anvil, when the workman is fitting a lawyer on his horse;[1] nor is the noise so great in the large amphitheater, when the conquering gladiator is applauded by his partisans. We, your neighbors, do not ask you to allow us to sleep for the whole night, for it is but a small matter to be occasionally awakened; but to be kept awake all night is a heavy affliction. Dismiss your scholars, brawler, and take as much for keeping quiet as you receive for making a noise.

---

[1] A sneer at the equestrian statues of lawyers.

(b) *To a Schoolmaster*

(*Epigrams*, book x, no. 62)

Schoolmaster, be indulgent to your simple scholars; if you would have many a long-haired youth resort to your lectures, and the class seated round your critical table love you. So may no teacher of arithmetic, or of swift writing, be surrounded by a greater ring of pupils. The days are bright, and glow under the flaming constellation of the Lion, and fervid July is ripening the teeming harvest. Let the Scythian scourge with its formidable thongs, such as flogged Marsyas of Celænæ, and the terrible cane, the schoolmaster's sceptre, be laid aside, and sleep until the Ides of October.[1] In summer, if boys preserve their health, they do enough.

24. Oratory the Aim of Education

(Cicero, *De Oratore*, book i)

Cicero, whose *De Oratore* was published in 55 B.C., presents a good description of the orator as the then ideal of Roman higher education, and describes the training necessary as viewed by the most successful orator of the time. The following selections illustrate this ideal.

IV. . . . For when our empire over all nations was established, and after a period of peace had secured tranquillity, there was scarcely a youth ambitious of praise who did not think that he must strive, with all his endeavors, to attain the art of speaking. For a time, indeed, as being ignorant of all method, and as thinking there was no course of exercise for them, or any precepts of art, they attained what they could by the single force of genius and thought. But afterwards, having heard the Greek orators, and gained an acquaintance with Greek literature, and pro-

FIG. 6. M. TULLIUS CICERO (106–43 B.C.)

cured instructors, our countrymen were inflamed with an incredible passion for eloquence. The magnitude, the variety, the multitude of all kinds of causes, excited them to such a degree, that to that learning which each had acquired by his individual study, frequent practice, which was superior to the precepts of all masters, was at once added. There were then, as there are also now, the highest inducements offered for the cultivation of this study, in regard to public

---

[1] The usual time for the opening of the school term.

favor, wealth, and dignity. The abilities of our countrymen (as we may judge from many particulars) far excelled those of the men of every other nation. For which reasons, who would not justly wonder that in the records of all ages, times, and states, so small a number of orators should be found?

But the art of eloquence is something greater, and collected from more sciences and studies, than people imagine. V. For who can suppose that, amid the greatest multitude of students, the utmost abundance of masters, the most eminent geniuses among men, the infinite variety of causes, the most ample rewards offered to eloquence, there is any other reason to be found for the small number of orators than the incredible magnitude and difficulty of the art? A knowledge of a vast number of things is necessary, without which volubility of words is empty and ridiculous; speech itself is to be formed, not merely by choice, but by careful construction of words; and all the emotions of the mind, which nature has given to man, must be intimately known; for all the force and art of speaking must be employed in allaying or exciting the feelings of those who listen. To this must be added a certain portion of grace and wit, learning worthy of a well-bred man, and quickness and brevity in replying as well as attacking, accompanied with a refined decorum and urbanity. Besides, the whole of antiquity and a multitude of examples is to be kept in the memory; nor is the knowledge of laws in general, or of the civil law in particular, to be neglected.

25. On Oratory

(Quintilian, *Institutes of Oratory*, Preface, and book II, chaps. XVI and XVII)

The following extract gives Quintilian's estimate of the importance of oratory in the life of a Roman.

Preface: 9. We are to form, then, the perfect orator, who cannot exist unless as a good man; and we require in him, therefore, not only consummate ability in speaking, but every excellence of mind. 10. For I cannot admit that the principles of moral and honourable conduct are, as some have thought, to be left to the philosophers; since the man who can duly sustain his character as a citizen, who is qualified for the management of public and private affairs, and who can govern communities by his counsels, se them by means of laws, and improve them by judicial enactments n certainly be nothing else but an orator. 11. Although I ackno dge, therefore, that I shall adopt some precepts which are contained the writings of the philosophers, yet I shall maintain, with justice and truth, that they belong to my subject, and have a peculiar relation to the art of oratory. 12. If we have constantly occasion to discourse of justice, fortitude, temperance, and other similar topics, so that a cause can scarce be found in which some such discussion does not occur, and if all such subjects are to be illustrated by invention and elocution, can it be doubted that, wherever power of intellect and copiousness of language are required, the art of the orator is to be there preëminently exerted? . . .

Book II. Chap. XVI: 17. Even to men, to whom speech has been denied, of how little avail is divine reason! If, therefore, we have received from the gods nothing more valuable than speech, what can we consider more deserving of cultivation and exercise? or in what can we more strongly desire to be superior to other men, than in that by which man himself is superior to other animals, especially as in no kind of exertion does labour more plentifully bring its reward? 18. This will be so much the more evident, if we reflect from what origin, and to what extent, the art of eloquence has advanced, and how far it may still be improved.   19. For, not to mention how beneficial it is, and how becoming in a man of virtue, to defend his friends, to direct a senate or people by his counsels, or to lead an army to whatever enterprise he may desire, is it not extremely honourable to attain, by the common understanding and words which all men use, so high a degree of esteem and glory as to appear not to speak or plead, but, as was the case with Pericles, to hurl forth lightning and thunder?

26. Privileges granted to Physicians and Teachers by Constantine

(*Code*, book 10, 53, 6; trans. by Norton)

The following grant of immunities and privileges to physicians and teachers in the higher schools of the time was made by Constantine, in 333 A.D.   The grant is very interesting as forming a precedent and a type for the many grants of immunity and privilege made later on to priests and monks and university scholars. (See especially Readings **38** and **51**.)

THE EMPEROR CONSTANTINE, AUGUSTUS, TO THE PEOPLE:

We direct that physicians, and chiefly imperial physicians, and eximperial physicians, grammarians and other professors of letters, together with their wives and sons, and whatever property they possess in their own cities, be immune from all payment of taxes and from all civil or public duties, and that in the provinces they shall not have strangers quartered on them or perform any official duties, or be brought into court, or be subject to legal process, or suffer injustice; and if any one harass them shall be punished at the discretion of the Judge.   We also command that their salaries and fees be paid, so that they may more readily instruct many in liberal studies and the above mentioned Arts.   Proclaimed on the fifth day before the Kalends of October (September 27) at Constantinople, in the Consulship of Dalmatius and Zenophilas.

CHAPTER IV

THE RISE AND CONTRIBUTION OF CHRISTIANITY

THE Readings in this chapter deal with the rise and victory of Christianity, its challenge to all that for which Rome had stood, the ensuing persecutions of the Christians, the final triumph, the rejection of pagan learning by the Fathers of the Western branch of the new Church, the meager educational system developed for those assuming membership and for those desiring solitude, and the perfection of the administrative organization of the early Church.

The educational maxims selected from The Talmud (27) reveal the importance given to the position of teacher among the Hebrew people after their return from captivity. Saint Paul, in his Epistle (28), states the message he carried to the Romans while the picture he gives of life in intellectual Athens (29) is an interesting one. The extracts from Minucius Felix and Tertullian (30 a-b), Pliny and Trajan (31 a-b), Tertullian (32), Eusebius (33), Workman (34), and Kingsley (35) show well Christianity and paganism in conflict — a conflict which could not end in compromise. Unwilling to be absorbed by Roman society on any other than exclusive terms, the Christians freely gave up their lives rather than perform the simplest rite of the old pagan worship. The extracts from Pliny (31 a) and Workman (34) are interesting as showing the tests used to determine loyalty to the State. The final victory of the Christian faith is seen in the Edict of Toleration of Galerius (36), and the two extracts from the Theodosian Code decreeing the Christian faith (37) and granting privileges and immunities to the clergy (38). The analogy of the latter to the similar grant to Roman physicians and teachers (26) is interesting.

To train the new Christian members in the essentials of their faith some form of instruction was early found necessary, and a growing need for some unity of faith also manifested itself. The first was met by the establishment of catechumenal instruction in the churches, which is well described by the extracts from the Apostolic Constitutions (39) and Leach (40), while the second was answered by the first formulation of belief, in 325 A.D., in the

Nicene Creed (42). The extract from the Apostolic Constitutions, ordering Christians to confine their readings to the sacred writings and to abstain from heathen books (41), is interesting as illustrating the reaction of the Western Church Fathers against all pagan learning which they gradually came to regard as a robbery from God. The Eastern branch of the Church, fortunately, was much more tolerant.

To those who wished to withdraw still further from pagan society and worldly life, and to live a life of holy seclusion in small groups and in out-of-the-way places, the Church developed monasticism, with monasteries for men and nunneries for women. The most famous of the monasteries were those whose members followed the rule of life instituted by Saint Benedict, and who were known as Benedictines. Three extracts from Benedict's Rule are given (43) to show the debt of posterity to this order. The selection from Archbishop Lanfranc (44), enforcing the Benedictine rule requiring reading and study, is typical of many similar orders issued during the Dark Ages by the Church or monastic authorities. The letter of Saint Jerome on the education of girls (45) reveals well the extreme reaction of Christianity to all pagan life.

The three great contributions of ancient society to modern civilization — those of Greece, Rome, and Christianity — had now been made, and had been more or less fused together into a great religious organization. This faced a stormy future. During the dark period of the Middle Ages the onslaughts of barbarians from the north tested all its strength to keep civilization from extinction. That it was able to do so was in part the result of the peculiar character of its faith, and in part due to the strong administrative organization which it evolved based on that of the Roman State.

27. Educational Maxims from the Talmud

The Talmud is a collection of writings of the Rabbins or scribes of the people, written between 70 B.C. and 500 A.D., and consists of interpretations of "the Law and the Prophets" for the guidance and instruction of the people. Most Jews regard the Talmud as second in importance only to the Old Testament. The following extracts reveal the great emphasis placed by the Rabbins on the proper training of children.

1 He who studies and teaches others possesses treasures and riches.

2 He who has learned and does not impart his knowledge unto others disregards the Word of God.

3 It is not permitted to live in a place where there is neither master nor school.

4 Jerusalem was destroyed because her instructors were not respected.

5 If both the father and the teacher are threatened with any material loss, the latter should be protected first.

6 As soon as the child begins to speak the father should teach him to say in Hebrew, "The law which Moses commanded us is the heritage of the congregation of Jacob," and, "Hear, O Israel, the Eternal our God is one God."

7 The teacher should strive to make the lesson agreeable to the pupils by clear reasons, as well as by frequent repetitions, until they thoroughly understand the matter and are able to recite it with great fluency.

8 No man can acquire a proper knowledge of the Law unless he endeavors to fix the same in his memory by certain marks and signs.

9 Let the honor of the pupil be as dear to thee as thine own.

10 He who gives instruction to an unworthy pupil will suffer for the consequences thereof.

11 The study of the Law is very important because it leads to good actions. He whose good actions exceed his wisdom, his wisdom shall endure.

12 Just as a man is bound to have his son instructed in the Law, so also should he have his son taught some handicraft or profession. Whosoever does not teach his son a handicraft teaches him to be a thief.

13 One learns much from his teachers, more from his school-fellows, but most of all from his pupils.

14 The instruction of children should not be interrupted, even for the purpose of building a Holy Temple.

15 Only those pupils should be punished in whom the master sees that there are good capacities for learning, and who are inattentive; but if they are dull and cannot learn they should not be punished. Punish with one hand and caress with two.

28. Saint Paul to the Romans

(Romans, I, 1–17)

In this extract from the Epistle of Paul the Apostle to the Romans, Paul states his mission to the Roman people and what it is he brings to them.

Paul, a servant of Jesus Christ, called to be an apostle, separated unto the gospel of God,

2. (Which he had promised afore by his prophets in the holy scriptures,)

3. Concerning his Son Jesus Christ our Lord, which was made of the seed of David according to the flesh;

4. And declared to be the Son of God with power, according to the spirit of holiness, by the resurrection from the dead:

5. By whom we have received grace and apostleship, for obedience to the faith among all nations, for his name:

6. Among whom are ye also the called of Jesus Christ:

7. To all that be in Rome, beloved of God, called to be saints: Grace to you, and peace, from God our Father, and the Lord Jesus Christ.

8. First, I thank my God through Jesus Christ for you all, that your faith is spoken of throughout the whole world.

9. For God is my witness, whom I serve with my spirit in the gospel of his Son, that without ceasing I make mention of you always in my prayers;

10. Making request, if by any means now at length I might have a prosperous journey by the will of God to come unto you.

11. For I long to see you, that I may impart unto you some spiritual gift, to the end ye may be established;

12. That is, that I may be comforted together with you by the mutual faith both of you and me.

13. Now I would not have you ignorant, brethren, that oftentimes I purposed to come unto you, (but was let hitherto,) that I might have some fruit among you also, even as among other Gentiles.

14. I am debtor both to the Greeks, and to the Barbarians; both to the wise, and to the unwise.

15. So, as much as in me is, I am ready to preach the gospel to you that are at Rome also.

16. For I am not ashamed of the gospel of Christ: for it is the power of God unto salvation to every one that believeth; to the Jew first, and also to the Greek.

17. For therein is the righteousness of God revealed from faith to faith: as it is written, The just shall live by faith.

29. Saint Paul to the Athenians

(Acts XVII, 16–23)

The following quotation from The Acts shows Saint Paul in Athens, and gives somewhat of a picture of the kind of intellectual life found there in the first century, A.D.

16. Now while Paul waited for them at Athens, his spirit was stirred in him, when he saw the city wholly given to idolatry.

17. Therefore disputed he in the synagogue with the Jews, and with the devout persons, and in the market daily with them that met with him.

18. Then certain philosophers of the Epicureans, and of the Stoics, encountered him.   And some said, What will this babbler say? other some, He seemeth to be a setter forth of strange gods: because he preached unto them Jesus, and the resurrection.

19. And they took him, and brought him unto Areopagus, saying, May we know what this new doctrine, whereof thou speakest, is?

20. For thou bringest certain strange things to our ears: we would know therefore what these things mean.

21. (For all the Athenians, and strangers which were there, spent their time in nothing else, but either to tell or to hear some new thing.)

22. Then Paul stood in the midst of Mars' hill, and said, Ye men of Athens, I perceive that in all things ye are too superstitious.

23. For as I passed by, and beheld your devotions, I found an altar with this inscription, TO THE UNKNOWN GOD.   Whom therefore ye ignorantly worship, him declare I unto you.

30. The Crimes of the Christians

The Roman and Christian points of view as to the nature of the Christian worship and loyalty to the emperor are well set forth in the two following extracts; the first from the Roman writer Minucius Felix's *Octavius*, and the second from Tertullian's *Apology*.

(a) The Roman Point of View

I purposely pass over many things, for those that I have mentioned are already too many; and that all these, or the greater part of them, are true, the obscurity of their vile religion declares.   For why do they endeavor with such pains to conceal and to cloak whatever they worship, since honorable things always rejoice in publicity, while crimes are kept secret?   Why have they no altars, no temples, no acknowledged images?   Why do they never speak openly, never congregate freely, unless for the reason that what they adore and conceal is either worthy of punishment, or something to be ashamed of? . . .

(b) The Christian Point of View

10. "You do not worship the gods," you say; "and you do not offer sacrifice to the Emperors."   Well, we do not offer sacrifice for others, for the same reason that we do not for ourselves, namely, that your gods are not at all the objects of our worship.   So we are accused of sacrilege and treason. . . .

32. There is also another and a greater necessity for our offering prayer in behalf of the Emperors, nay, for the complete stability of the Empire, and for Roman interests in general. For we know that a mighty shock is impending over the whole earth — in fact, the very end of all things threatening dreadful woes is only retarded by the continued existence of the Roman Empire. We have no desire, then, to be overtaken by these dire events; and in praying that their coming may be delayed, we are lending our aid to Rome's duration. . . .

33. But why dwell longer on the reverence and sacred respect of Christians to the Emperor, whom we cannot but look up to as called by our Lord in his office? so that on valid grounds I might say Cæsar is more ours than yours, for our God has appointed him. Therefore, as having this property in him, I do more than you for his welfare, not merely because I ask it of Him who can give it, nor because I ask it as one who deserves to get it, but also because, in keeping the majesty of Cæsar within due limits, and putting it under the Most High, and making it less than divine, I commend him the more to the favor of the Deity, to whom alone I make him inferior. But I place him in subjection to one I regard as more glorious than himself. Never will I call the Emperor God. . . .

35. This is the reason, then, why Christians are counted public enemies: that they pay no vain, nor false, nor foolish honors to the Emperor; that, as men believing in the true religion, they prefer to celebrate their festal days with a good conscience, instead of with common wantonness. . . .

31. The Persecution of the Christians as Disloyal Citizens of the Roman Empire

(Pliny, *Letters*, book x, letters 96 and 97)

Pliny the Younger (62–113 A.D.), a distinguished Roman Senator and man of letters, was appointed governor of Bithynia, a province lying along the central southern coast of the Black Sea, in Asia Minor, by the Emperor Trajan, about 112 A.D. The following letter from Pliny to the Emperor asking for instructions as to how to deal with the disloyal Christians, and Trajan's reply, are of special value as displaying both the tolerant attitude of the Roman government toward their religion as such, and the peculiar difficulties met in dealing with them.

(a) Pliny to Trajan

It is my custom, my Lord, to refer to you all things concerning which I am in doubt. For who can better guide my indecision or enlighten my ignorance?

I have never taken part in the trials of Christians: hence I do not know for what crime nor to what extent it is customary to punish or investigate.   I have been in no little doubt as to whether any discrimination is made for age, or whether the treatment of the weakest does not differ from that of the stronger; whether pardon is granted in case of repentance, or whether he who has ever been a Christian gains nothing by having ceased to be one; whether the *name* itself without the proof of crimes, or the crimes, inseparably connected with the *name*, are punished.   Meanwhile, I have followed this procedure in the case of those who have been brought before me as Christians.   I asked them whether they were Christians a second and a third time and with threats of punishment; I questioned those who confessed; I ordered those who were obstinate to be executed.   For I did not doubt that, whatever it was that they confessed, their stubbornness and inflexible obstinacy ought certainly to be punished.

There were others of similar madness, whom, because they were Roman citizens, I have noted for sending to the City.   Soon, the crime spreading, as is usual when attention is called to it, more cases arose. An anonymous accusation containing many names was presented. Those who denied that they were or had been Christians, ought, I thought, to be dismissed, since they repeated after me a prayer to the gods and made supplication with incense and wine to your image, which I had ordered to be brought for the purpose together with the statues of the gods, and since besides they cursed Christ, not one of which things, they say, those who are really Christians can be compelled to do.

Others, accused by the informer, said that they were Christians and afterwards denied it; in fact they had been but had ceased to be, some many years ago, some even twenty years before.   All both worshipped your image, and cursed Christ.   They continued to maintain that this was the amount of their fault or error, that on a fixed day they were accustomed to come together before daylight and to sing by turns a hymn to Christ as a god, and that they bound themselves by oath, not for some crime, but that they would not commit robbery, theft, or adultery, that they would not betray a trust nor deny a deposit when called upon.   After this it was their custom to disperse and to come together again to partake of food, of an ordinary and harmless kind, however; even this they had ceased to do after the publication of my edict in which according to your command I had forbidden associations.

Hence I believed it the more necessary to examine two female slaves, who were called deaconesses, in order to find out what was true, and to do it by torture.   I found nothing but a vicious, extravagant suspicion.   Consequently I have postponed the examination and make haste to consult you.   For it seemed to me that the subject would justify consultation, especially on account of the number of those in peril. For many of all ages, of every rank, and even of both sexes are and will be called into danger.

The infection of this superstition has not only spread to the cities, but even to the villages and country districts. It seems possible to stay it and bring about a reform. It is plain enough that the temples, which had been almost deserted, have begun to be frequented again, that the sacred rights, which had been neglected for a long time, have begun to be restored, and that fodder for victims, for which till now there was scarcely a purchaser, is sold. From which one may readily judge what a number of men can be reclaimed if repentance is permitted.

(b) Trajan's Reply

You have followed the correct procedure, my Secundus, in conducting the cases of those who were accused before you as Christians, for no general rule can be laid down as a set form. They ought not to be sought out; if they are brought before you and convicted, they ought to be punished, provided that he who denies that he is a Christian, and proves this by making supplication to our gods, however much he may have been under suspicion in the past, shall secure pardon on repentance. In the case of no crime should attention be paid to anonymous charges, for they afford a bad precedent and are not worthy of our age.

32. Effect of the Persecutions

(Tertullian, *Apology*, chap. 50)

The early Christian spirit is shown in the following extract from Tertullian (c. 150–230 A.D.), one of the Fathers of the Western Church. His *Apology* is an important work on the relations of the Christians and the imperial government.

Nor does your cruelty, however exquisite, avail you; it is rather a temptation to us. The oftener we are mown down by you, the more in number we grow; *the blood of Christians is seed*. Many of your writers exhort to the courageous bearing of pain and death, as Cicero in *Tusculans*, as Seneca in his *Chances*, as Diogenes, Pyrrhus, Callinicus; and yet their words do not find as many disciples as Christians do, teachers not by words, but by their deeds. That very obstinacy you rail against is the preceptress. For who that contemplates it, is not excited to inquire what is at the bottom of it? who, after inquiry, does not embrace our doctrines? and when he has embraced them, desires not to suffer that he may become partaker of the fulness of God's grace, that he may obtain from God complete forgiveness, by giving in exchange his blood? For that secures the remission of all offences.

33. Edicts of Diocletian against the Christians

(Eusebius, P., *Church History*, book VIII, chaps. 2, 6)

The following descriptions of the edicts of Diocletian, 303 A.D.,
are from the early Church historian, Eusebius Pamphili, who was
Bishop of Cæsarea from 314 to his death, about 340 A.D.

2. This was the nineteenth year of the reign of Diocletian, in Dys-
trus (which the Romans call March), when the feast of the Saviour's
passion was near at hand, and royal edicts were published everywhere,
commanding that the churches should be razed to the ground, the
Scriptures destroyed by fire, those who held positions of honor degraded, and the household servants, if they persisted in the Christian
profession, be deprived of their liberty.

And such was the first decree against us.   But issuing other decrees
not long after, the Emperor commanded that all the rulers of the
churches in every place should be first put in prison and afterwards
compelled by every device to offer sacrifice.

6. Then as the first decrees were followed by others commanding
that those in prison should be set free, if they would offer sacrifice, but
that those who refused should be tormented with countless tortures;
who could again at that time count the multitude of martyrs throughout each province, and especially throughout Africa and among the
race of the Moors, in Thebais and throughout Egypt, from which having already gone into other cities and provinces, they became illustrious in their martyrdoms!

34. Certificate of having sacrificed to the Pagan Gods

(Quoted from Workman, H. B., *Persecutions in the Early Church*, p. 340.
London, 1906)

The following certificate, issued in Egypt during the persecutions of Decius, in 250 A.D., comes from an old papyrus, found in
1893.   It was issued in a small village in Egypt, and shows how
suspected Christians were forced to clear themselves of suspicion
by sacrificing publicly to the old gods.

*To the Commissioners of Sacrifice in the Village of Alexander's Island:
from Aurelius Diogenes, the son of Satabus, of the Village of Alexander's
Island, aged 72 years: — scar on his right eyebrow.*

I have always sacrificed regularly to the gods, and now, in your
presence, in accordance with the edict, I have done sacrifice, and
poured the drink offering, and tasted of the sacrifices, and I request
you to certify the same.   Farewell.

Handed in by me, Aurelius Diogenes.

I certify that I saw him sacrificing . . . [Signature obliterated,] Magistrate.

Done in the first year of the Emperor, Cæsar Gaius Messius Quintus Trajanus Decius, Pius, Felix, Augustus: the second of the month Epith.   (June 26, 250 A.D.)

35. The Empire and Christianity in Conflict

(Kingsley, Chas., Introduction to *Hypatia;* selected)

The Reverend Charles Kingsley (1819–75), an English writer, in the Introduction to his historical novel *Hypatia*, gives a good picture of the conflict between the Empire and the Christian Church, and the final victory of the latter, from which the following selection has been taken.

For somewhat more than four hundred years the Roman Empire and the Christian Church, born into the world almost at the same moment, had been developing themselves side by side as two great rival powers, in deadly struggle for the possession of the human race. The weapons of the Empire had been not merely an overwhelming physical force, and a ruthless lust of aggressive conquest: but, even more powerful still, an unequalled genius for organization, and an uniform system of external law and order.   This was generally a real boon to conquered nations, because it substituted a fixed and regular spoliation for the fortuitous and arbitrary miseries of savage warfare: but it arrayed, meanwhile, on the side of the Empire the wealthier citizens of every province, by allowing them their share in the plunder of the laboring classes beneath them.   These, in the country districts, were utterly enslaved; while in the cities, nominal freedom was of little use to masses kept from starvation by the alms of the government, and drugged into brutish good-humor by a vast system of public spectacles, in which the realms of nature and of art were ransacked to glut the wonder, lust, and ferocity of a degraded population.

Against this vast organization the Church had been fighting for now four hundred years, armed only with its own mighty and all-embracing message, and with the manifestation of a spirit of purity and virtue, of love and self-sacrifice, which had proved itself mightier to melt and weld together the hearts of men than all the force and terror, all the mechanical organization, all the sensual baits with which the Empire had been contending against that Gospel in which it had recognized instinctively, and at first sight, its internecine foe.

And now the Church had conquered.   The weak things of this world had confounded the strong.   In spite of the devilish cruelties of persecutors; in spite of the contaminating atmosphere of sin which surrounded her; in spite of having to form herself, not out of a race of pure and separate creatures, but by a most literal "new birth" out of those very fallen masses who insulted and persecuted her; in spite of having to endure within herself continual outbursts of the evil passions in which her members had once indulged without check; in spite of a thousand counterfeits which sprung up around her and within her, claiming to be parts of her, and alluring men to themselves by that very exclusiveness and party arrogance which disproved their claim; in spite of all she had conquered. The very emperors had arrayed themselves on her side. Julian's last attempt to restore paganism by imperial influences had only proved that the old faith had lost all hold upon the hearts of the masses; at his death the great tide wave of new opinion rolled on unchecked, and the rulers of the earth were fain to swim with the stream; to accept, in words at least, the Church's law as theirs; to acknowledge a King of kings to whom even they owed homage and obedience; and to call their own slaves their "poorer brethren," and often, too, their "spiritual superiors."

But if the emperors had become Christian, the Empire had not. Here and there an abuse was lopped off; or an edict was passed for the visitation of prisons and for the welfare of prisoners; or a Theodosius was recalled to justice and humanity for a while by the stern rebukes of an Ambrose. But the Empire was still the same: still a great tyranny, enslaving the masses; crushing national life; fattening itself and its officials on a system of world-wide robbery; and, while it was paramount, there could be no hope for the human race.

36. The Edict of Toleration by Galerius

(Lactantius, *On the Death of the Persecutors*, chaps. 34, 35)

Lactantius was a teacher of rhetoric at Nicomedia, and later was appointed tutor to one of Constantine's sons. He wrote a history of Christianity from Nero to Galerius, from which this edict is taken.

34. Among other arrangements which we are always accustomed to make for the prosperity and welfare of the Republic, we had desired formerly to bring all things into harmony with the ancient laws and public order of the Romans, and to provide that even the Christians who had left the religion of their fathers should come back to reason; since, indeed, the Christians themselves, for some reason, had followed such a caprice and had fallen into such a folly that they would not obey the institutes of antiquity, which perchance their own ancestors had first established; but at their own will and pleasure, they would thus make laws unto themselves which they should observe, and would collect various peoples in divers places in congregations. Finally, when our law had been promulgated to the effect that they should con-

form to the institutes of antiquity, many were subdued by the fear of danger, many even suffered death.   And yet since most of them perse-vered in their determination, and we saw that they neither paid the reverence and awe due to the gods nor worshipped the God of the Christians, in view of our most mild clemency and the constant habit by which we are accustomed to grant indulgence to all, we thought that we ought to grant our most prompt indulgence also to these, so that they may again be Christians and may hold their conventicles, provided that they do nothing contrary to good order.   But we shall tell the magistrates in another letter what they ought to do.

Wherefore, for this our indulgence, they ought to pray to their God for our safety, for that of the Republic, and for their own, that the Republic may continue uninjured on every side, and that they may be able to live securely in their homes.

35. This edict is published at Nicomedia on the day before the Ka-lends of May, in our eighth consulship and the second of Maximus.

37. The Faith of Catholic Christians

(Theodosian Code)

In 438 a collection of Roman laws was issued under the title of *Codex Theodosianus*.   One of these laws, dated 380, shows how completely the Christian belief had come to dominate the Roman State.

We desire that all those who are under the sway of our clemency shall adhere to that religion which, according to his own testimony, coming down even to our own day, the blessed apostle Peter delivered to the Romans, namely, the doctrine which the pontiff Damasus (Bishop of Rome) and Peter, Bishop of Alexandria, a man of apostolic sanctity, accept.   According to the teachings of the apostles and of the Gospel we believe in one Godhead of the Father, Son, and Holy Ghost, the blessed Trinity, alike in majesty.

We ordain that the name of Catholic Christians shall apply to all those who obey this present law.   All others we judge to be mad and demented; we declare them guilty of the infamy of holding heretical doc-trine; their assemblies shall not receive the name of churches.   They shall first suffer the wrath of God, then the punishment in accordance with divine judgment we shall inflict.

38. Privileges and Immunities granted the Clergy

(Theodosian Code)

Another selection from the *Codex Theodosianus*, a collection of Roman laws made in 438 A.D.   The following grants of privileges and immunities made to the clergy show still further the hold of

the Church organization on the Roman State.   Compare these
privileges with those previously granted (R. 26) to physicians and
surgeons.

319 A.D.   Those who exercise the functions of divine worship, that
is to say those who are called clerics (*clerici*), shall be exempt from all
public burdens, lest otherwise they might be called away from their
sacred duties through some one's malicious interference.

349 A.D.   From public burdens and from every disquietude of civil
office all clerics shall be free, and their sons shall continue in the Church
if they are not subject to public responsibilities.

377 A.D.   We decree that all priests, deacons, subdeacons, exorcists,
lectors, and doorkeepers, likewise all who are in higher orders, shall
be free from personal taxes.

361 A.D.   In every city, in every town, hamlet, and burg, whoever,
according to the spirit of the Christian law, shall have sincerely striven
to bring home to all its supreme and peculiar merits shall enjoy permanent protection.   We should rejoice and be exceeding glad in the
faith, knowing that our empire is maintained more by religion than by
officials or by the labor and sweat of the body.

412 A.D.   It is right that clerics, whether they be bishops, priests,
deacons, or those of lower rank, ministers of the Christian law, should
be accused only before a bishop — unless there is some reason why the
case should be considered elsewhere.

39. How the Catechumens are to be instructed

(From the *Apostolic Constitutions*)

This extract gives a good idea of the early Catechumenal instruction.

Let him, therefore, who is to be taught the truth in regard to piety
be instructed before his baptism in the knowledge of the unbegotten
God, in the understanding his only begotten Son, in the assured acknowledgement of the Holy Ghost.   Let him learn the order of the
several parts of the creation, the series of providence, the different
dispensations of the laws.   Let him be instructed how the world was
made, and why man was appointed to be a citizen therein; let him also
know his own nature, of what sort it is; let him be taught how God
punished the wicked with water and fire, and did glorify the saints in
every generation — I mean Seth, and Enos, and Enoch, and Noah,
and Abraham and his posterity, and Melchizedek, and Job, and Moses,
and Joshua, and Caleb, and Phineas the priest, and those that were
holy in every generation; and how God still took care of and did not
reject mankind, but called them from their error and vanity to the
acknowledgement of the truth at various seasons, reducing them from

bondage and impiety unto liberty and piety, from injustice to righteousness, from death eternal to everlasting life. Let him that offers himself to baptism learn these and the like things during the time that he is a catechumen; and let him who lays his hands upon him adore God, the Lord of the whole world, and thank him for his creation, for his sending Christ his only begotten Son, that he might save man by blotting out his transgressions, and that he might remit ungodliness and sins, and might "purify him from all filthiness of flesh and spirit," and sanctify man according to the good pleasure of his kindness, that he might inspire him with the knowledge of his will, and enlighten the eyes of his heart to consider of his wonderful works, and make known to him the judgments of righteousness, that so he might hate every way of iniquity, and walk in the way of truth, that he might be thought worthy of the laver of regeneration, to the adoption of sons, which is in Christ, that "being planted together in the likeness of the death of Christ," in hopes of a glorious communication, he may be mortified to sin, and may live to God, as to his mind, and word, and deed, and may be numbered together in the book of the living. And after this thanksgiving, let him instruct him in the doctrines concerning our Lord's incarnation, and in those concerning his passion, and resurrection from the dead, and assumption.

40. Catechumenal Schools of the Early Church

(Leach, A. F., *The Schools of Mediæval England*, p. 8. London, 1915)

The following description of catechumenal instruction, by one of the foremost authorities on early education, gives a good picture of the nature and the work of these schools.

Catechetical schools, so called, were nothing more than courses of lectures to catechumens, who, whether they were new converts or long-standing Christians, were grown-up people being prepared for baptism by catechesis, that is oral instruction, in the principles of the Christian faith. In the first three centuries of the Christian Church no one dreamt of baptizing infants. To do so would have seemed not so much profane, though it would have been that, as preposterous. Baptism was the supreme rite, the admission to the highest grade in the Christian gild, not as now the first initiation into it. Tertullian, writing in the third century on Baptism, exhorts the faithful to get over the business of marriage and founding families before they incur the awful responsibilities of baptism, a regeneration, a new birth of the soul, which was freed from all sin thereby, a "baptism of repentance." He asks, referring to the proposal made by some that children of three or four years old — no one had suggested new-born babies — should be baptized, why should the age of innocence be in a hurry to get its sins remitted? A century and a half later, when Augustine, at the age of fourteen, clamoured to be baptized, his mother told him to wait until he was older and had a deeper sense of responsibility.   To be baptized was to be illuminated, and a passage in the Epistle to the Hebrews had given rise to, or perhaps rather expressed, the current belief that mortal sin committed after baptism could not be forgiven.   "For as touching those who once have been illuminated . . . but then have fallen away it is impossible to renew them again unto repentance."   The age of thirty, the traditional age at which Christ was baptized, was regarded as the normal age for baptism, but many put it off to their death-beds, and then risked being unable to receive it because through physical or mental weakness they were unable to repeat or understand the formulas.

Catechumens therefore were grown persons being informed or instructed in the mysteries of Christianity, translated by the Latin *audientes*, hearing or audience.

There are two sets of early catechetical lectures extant.   The famous Didache or Teaching of the Apostles, now recognized as being a guide to catechists, is simply an exposition of the doctrines and services of the Church, a theological treatise.   The Catechetical Lectures of Cyril of Alexandria, Bishop of Jerusalem, delivered in 347, are eighteen homilies or expository sermons, addressed to grown-up congregations. The title of the first is "To those to be enlightened," the *illuminandi*. The second is on the necessity for "Repentance and remission of sins," and the third expounds that "Baptism gives remission."   The last thirteen go steadily through the Creed, expounding and explaining the meaning and importance of its articles.   There is not a word in them to suggest that this catechist is educating the young.   Chiefly he is arguing against the heathen as a missionary nowadays might in preaching to Hindoos, Brahmins, or Chinese sages.

41. Christians should abstain from all Heathen Books

(From the *Apostolic Constitutions*)

The *Apostolic Constitutions*, compiled at various times before the early part of the fourth century, was intended as a manual of instruction in conduct and worship for the use of the clergy and the educated laity, and gives a good idea of ecclesiastical usages and of the attitude of the Church as it had developed up to the time of its final victory in the reign of Constantine.

VI. Abstain from all the heathen books.   For what hast thou to do with such foreign discourses, or laws, or false prophets, which subvert the faith of the unstable?   For what defect dost thou find in the law of God, that thou shouldst have recourse to those heathenish fables?   For if thou hast a mind to read history, thou hast the books of the Kings; if books of wisdom or poetry, thou hast those of the prophets, of Job, and the Proverbs, in which thou wilt find greater depth of sagacity than in all the heathen poets and sophisters, because these are the words of the Lord, the only wise God. If thou desirest something to sing, thou hast the Psalms; if the origin of things, thou hast Genesis; if laws and statutes, thou hast the glorious law of the Lord God. Do thou, therefore, utterly abstain from all strange and diabolical books. Nay, when thou readest the law, think not thyself bound to observe the additional precepts; though not all of them, yet some of them. Read those barely for the sake of history, in order to the knowledge of them, and to glorify God that he has delivered thee from such great and so many bonds. Propose to thyself to distinguish what rules were from the law of nature, and what were added afterwards, or were such additional rules as were introduced and given in the wilderness to the Israelites, after the making of the calf; for the law contains those precepts which were spoken by the Lord God before the people fell into idolatry, and made a calf like the Egyptian Apis — that is, the ten commandments. But as to those bonds which were further laid upon them after they had sinned, do not thou draw them upon thyself; for our Saviour came for no other reason but that he might deliver those that were obnoxious thereto from the wrath which was reserved for them, that he might fulfil the Law and the Prophets, and that he might abrogate or change those secondary bonds which were superadded to the rest of the law. For therefore did he call to us, and say, "Come unto me, all ye that labor and are heavy laden, and I will give you rest." When, therefore, thou hast read the Law, which is agreeable to the Gospel and the Prophets, read also the books of the Kings, that thou mayst thereby learn which of the kings were righteous, and how they were prospered by God, and how the promise of eternal life continued with them from him; but those kings which went a-whoring from God did soon perish in their apostasy by the righteous judgment of God, and were deprived of his life, inheriting, instead of rest, eternal punishment. Wherefore by reading these books thou wilt be mightily strengthened in the faith, and edified in Christ, whose body and member thou art.

42. The Nicene Creed as framed in 325 A.D.

(From Mitchell, E. K., *Canons and Creeds of the First Four Councils*, p. 3)

The Council of Nicæa, in Asia Minor, was called by the Emperor Constantine, in the summer of 325 A.D. Some three hundred bishops, mostly of the Eastern branch of the Church, were present at this first general Council of the Church. The following creed was the first authoritative formulation of the articles of faith of the Church.

We believe in one God, the FATHER Almighty, Maker of all things visible and invisible.   And in one Lord JESUS CHRIST, the Son of God, begotten of the Father, the only-begotten; that is, of the essence of the Father, God of God, Light of Light, very God of very God, begotten, not made, being of one essence with the Father; by whom all things were made, both in heaven and on earth; who for us men, and for our salvation, came down and was incarnate and was made man; he suffered, and the third day he rose again, ascended into heaven; and he shall come to judge the living and the dead.   And in the Holy Ghost. But those who say: "There was a time when he was not"; and, "He was not before he was made"; and, "He was made out of nothing," or, "He is of another substance or essence," or, "alterable" — they are condemned by the holy catholic and apostolic church.

43. The Rule of Saint Benedict

(Extracts from the translation in Henderson, E. F., *Historical Documents of the Middle Ages*, p. 274 *et seq.*   London, 1896)

Though monasticism in the West had begun as early as 340, and became established by the beginning of the fifth century, the really great impulse to monastic life was given by Saint Benedict, a native Italian with large genius for organization.   In 529 he founded the monastery of Monte Casino, between Rome and Naples, on the site of an ancient temple of Apollo, and later others in the vicinity.   For all these he established his "Rule," a document of some length, divided into seventy-three different commands or rules.   It was generally adopted by the monasteries of western Europe, those following the rule being known as Benedictines.   The most important rules, from the standpoint of education and civilization, were numbers 38, 42, and 48, the important parts of which are reproduced below.   To rule 48, in particular, we are in large part indebted for the copying of manuscripts and the preservation of learning throughout the Middle Ages.

Prologue. . . . we are about to found, therefore, a school for the Lord's service; in the organization of which we trust that we shall ordain nothing severe and nothing burdensome.   But even if, the demands of justice dictating it, something a little irksome shall be the result, for the purpose of amending vices or preserving charity; — thou shalt not therefore, struck by fear, flee the way of salvation, which can not be entered upon except through a narrow entrance.

38. *Concerning the weekly reader.*   At the tables of the brothers when they eat the reading should not fail; nor may any one at random dare

to take up the book and begin to read there; but he who is about to read for the whole week shall begin his duties on Sunday. And, entering upon his office after mass and communion, he shall ask all to pray for him, that God may avert from him the spirit of elation. And this verse shall be said in the oratory three times by all, he, however, beginning it: "O Lord, open thou my lips and my mouth shall show forth thy praise." And thus, having received the benediction, he shall enter upon his duties as reader. And there shall be the greatest silence at table, so that the muttering or the voice of no one shall be heard there, except that of the reader alone. But whatever things are necessary to those eating and drinking, the brothers shall so furnish them to each other in turn, that no one shall need to ask for anything. But if, nevertheless, something is wanted, it shall rather be sought by the employment of some sign than by the voice. Nor shall any one presume there to ask questions concerning the reading or anything else; nor shall an opportunity be given: unless perhaps the prior wishes to say something, briefly, for the purpose of edifying. Moreover, the brother who reads for the week shall receive bread and wine before he begins to read, on account of the holy communion, and lest, perchance, it might be injurious for him to sustain a fast. Afterwards, moreover, he shall eat with the weekly cooks and servitors. The brothers, moreover, shall read or sing not in rotation; but the ones shall do so who will edify *their* hearers. . . .

42. *That after "completorium" no one shall speak.* At all times the monks ought to practice silence, but most of all in the nocturnal hours. And thus at all times, whether of fasting or of eating: if it be mealtime, as soon as they have risen from the table, all shall sit together and one shall read selections or lives of the Fathers, or indeed anything that will edify the hearers. But not the Pentateuch or Kings; for, to weak intellects, it will be of no use at that hour to hear this part of Scripture; but they shall be read at other times. But if the days are fast days, when Vespers have been said, after a short interval they shall come to the reading of the selections as we have said; and four or five pages, or as much as the hour permits having been read, they shall all congregate, upon the cessation of the reading. If, by chance, any one is occupied in a task assigned to him, he shall nevertheless approach. All therefore being gathered together, they shall say the completing prayer; and, going out from the "completorium," there shall be no further opportunity for any one to say anything. . . .

48. *Concerning the daily manual labour.* Idleness is the enemy of the soul. And therefore, at fixed times, the brothers ought to be occupied in manual labour; and again, at fixed times, in sacred reading. Therefore we believe that, according to this disposition, both seasons ought to be arranged; so that, from Easter until the Calends of Octo-

ber, going out early, from the first until the fourth hour they shall do what labour may be necessary. Moreover, from the fourth hour until about the sixth, they shall be free for reading. After the meal of the sixth hour, moreover, rising from table, they shall rest in their beds

with all silence; or, perchance, he that wishes to read may so read to himself that he do not disturb another. And the nona (the second meal) shall be gone through with more moderately about the middle of the eighth hour; and again they shall work at what is to be done until Vespers. But, if the exigency or poverty of the place demands that they be occupied by themselves in picking fruits, they shall not be dismayed: for then they are truly monks if they live by the labours of their hands, as did also our fathers and the apostles. Let all things be done, with moderation, however, on account of the faint-hearted. From the Calends of October, moreover, until the beginning of Lent they shall be free for reading until the second full hour. At the second hour the tertia (morning service) shall be held, and all shall labour at the task which is enjoined upon them until the ninth. The first signal, moreover, of the ninth hour having been given, they shall each one leave off his work; and be ready when the second signal strikes. Moreover, after the refection they shall be free for their readings or for psalms. But in the days of Lent, from dawn until the third full hour, they shall be free for their readings; and, until the tenth full hour, they shall do the labour that is enjoined on them. In which days of Lent they shall all receive separate books from the library; which they shall read entirely through in order. These books are to be given out on the first day of Lent. Above all there shall certainly be appointed one or two elders, who shall go round the monastery at the hours in which the brothers are engaged in reading, and see to it that no troublesome brother chance to be found who is open to idleness and trifling, and is not intent on his reading; being not only of no use to himself, but also stirring up others. If such a one — may it not happen — be found, he shall be admonished once and a second time. If he do not

FIG. 7. A MONK IN A SCRIPTORIUM

(From an old manuscript in the library of the city of Soissons, France)

The monk is reading. Before him is a writing-table. Cupboards about the room are for manuscripts

amend, he shall be subject under the Rule to such punishment that the others may have fear. Nor shall brother join brother at unsuitable hours. Moreover, on Sunday all shall engage in reading: excepting those who are deputed to various duties. But if any one be so negligent and lazy that he will not or can not read, some task shall be imposed upon him that he can do; so that he be not idle. On feeble or delicate brothers such a labour or art is to be imposed, that they shall neither be idle, nor shall they be so oppressed by the violence of labour as to be driven to take flight. Their weakness is to be taken into consideration by the abbot.

44. Enforcing Lenten Reading in the Monasteries

(An English Benedictine Rule; Archbishop Lanfranc, 1070; trans. by J. W. Clark, *Care of Books*, pp. 67–68. London, 1901)

The better to enforce the rule for Lenten reading, supplementary rules were made after the rise of the reform movement among the monasteries. The following rule, issued to the English Benedictines in 1070 A.D., is illustrative of many others.

On the Monday after the first Sunday in Lent . . . before the brethren go in to Chapter, the librarian ought to have all the books brought together into the Chapter-House and laid out on a carpet, except those which had been given out for reading during the past year: these the brethren ought to bring with them as they come into Chapter, each carrying his book in his hand. Of this they ought to have had notice given to them by the aforesaid librarian on the preceding day in Chapter. Then let the passage in the Rule of S. Benedict about the observance of Lent be read, and a discourse be preached upon it. Next let the librarian read a document setting forth the names of the brethren who have had books during the past year; and let each brother, when he hears his own name pronounced, return the book which had been entrusted to him for reading; and let him who is conscious of not having read the book through which he had received, fall down on his face, confess his fault, and pray for forgiveness.

Then let the aforesaid librarian hand to each brother another book for reading; and when the books have been distributed in order, let the aforesaid librarian in the same Chapter put on record the names of the books, and of those who receive them.

45. Saint Jerome on the Education of Girls

(Letter to Læta)

The following letter from Saint Jerome (c. 340–420) was written to the Roman matron Læta, regarding the education of her little daughter Paula. Sent from his retirement at Bethlehem, in 403, it is an important document in the history of early Christian education for girls. He gave similar advice in his *Letter to Gaudentius*, regarding the education of her daughter Pacatula. Both letters are pervaded by the ascetic spirit of the age and of the monastic East. Læta later followed Saint Jerome's advice, sending Paula to a nunnery near Bethlehem, where she finally became abbess of a nunnery founded there by her grandmother.

Thus must a soul be educated which is to be a temple of God. It must learn to hear nothing and to say nothing but what belongs to the fear of God. It must have no understanding of unclean words, and no knowledge of the world's songs. Its tongue must be steeped while still tender in the sweetness of the Psalms. Boys with their wanton thoughts must be kept from Paula: even her maids and female attendants must be separated from worldly associates. For if they have learned some mischief they may teach more.

Get for her a set of letters made of boxwood or of ivory and called each by its proper name. Let her play with these, so that even her play may teach her something. And not only make her grasp the right order of the letters and see that she forms their names into a rhyme, but constantly disarrange their order and put the last letters in the middle and the middle ones at the beginning that she may know them all by sight as well as by sound.

Moreover, so soon as she begins to use the style upon the wax, and her hand is still faltering, either guide her soft fingers by laying your hand upon hers, or else have simple copies cut upon a tablet; so that her efforts confined within these limits may keep to the lines traced out for her and not stray outside of these. Offer prizes for good spelling and draw her onwards with little gifts such as children of her age delight in.

And let her have companions in her lessons to excite emulation in her, that she may be stimulated when she sees them praised. You must not scold her if she is slow to learn, but must employ praise to excite her mind, so that she may be glad when she excels others and sorry when she is excelled by them. Above all you must take care not to make her lessons distasteful to her, lest a dislike for them conceived in childhood may continue into her maturer years. The very words which she tries bit by bit to put together and pronounce ought not to be chance ones, but names specially fixed upon and heaped together for the purpose, those for example of the prophets or the apostles or the list of patriarchs from Adam downwards, as it is given by Matthew and Luke. In this way while her tongue will be well trained, her memory will be likewise developed.

Again, you must choose for her a master of approved years, life, and learning. A man of culture will not, I think, blush to do for a kinswoman or a high-born virgin what Aristotle did for Philip's son when, descending to the level of an usher,[1] he consented to teach him his letters. Things must not be despised as of small account in the absence of which great results can not be achieved. The very rudiments and first beginnings of knowledge sound differently in the mouth of an educated man and of an uneducated. Accordingly you must see that the child is not led away by the silly coaxing of women to form a habit of shortening long words or of decking herself with gold and purple. Of these habits one will spoil her conversation and the other her character. She must not therefore learn as a child what afterwards she will have to unlearn.

The eloquence of the Gracchi is said to have been largely due to the way in which from their earliest years their mother spoke to them. Hortensius became an orator while still on his father's lap. Early impressions are hard to eradicate from the mind. When once wool has been dyed purple, who can restore it to its previous whiteness? An unused jar long retains the taste and smell of that with which it was first filled. Grecian history tells us that the imperious Alexander, who was lord of the whole world, could not rid himself of the tricks of manner and gait which in his childhood he had caught from his governor Leonidas. We are always ready to imitate what is evil; and faults are quickly copied where virtues appear unattainable. Paula's nurse must not be intemperate, or loose, or given to gossip. Her bearer must be respectable, and her foster-father of grave demeanor. . . .

Let her very dress and garb remind her to Whom she is promised. Do not pierce her ears or paint her face, consecrated to Christ, with white lead or rouge. Do not hang gold or pearls about her neck or load her head with jewels, or by reddening her hair make it suggest the fires of Gehenna. . . .

When Paula comes to be a little older and to increase like her Spouse in wisdom and stature and in favor with God and man, let her go with her parents to the temple of her true Father, but let her not come out of the temple with them. Let them seek her upon the world's highway amid the crowds and the throng of their kinsfolk, and let them find her nowhere but in the shrine of the Scriptures, questioning the prophets and apostles on the meaning of that spiritual marriage to which she is vowed. Let her imitate the retirement of Mary whom Gabriel found alone in her chamber. . . .

And let it be her daily task to bring you the flowers which she has culled from Scripture. Let her learn by heart so many verses from the Greek, and let her be instructed in the Latin also. For, if the tender lips are not from the first shaped to this, the tongue is spoiled by a foreign accent and its native speech debased by alien elements. You must yourself be her mistress, a model on which she may form her

---

[1] A term much used in England for an assistant teacher.

childish conduct.   Never either in you or in her father let her see what she can not imitate without sin.   Remember both of you that you are the parents of a consecrated virgin, and that your example will teach her more than your precepts.

Flowers are quick to fade, and a baleful wind soon withers the violet, the lily, and the crocus.   Let her never appear in public unless accompanied by you.   Let her never visit a church or a martyr's shrine unless with her mother.   Let no young man greet her with smiles, no dandy with curled hair pay compliments to her.   If our little virgin goes to keep solemn eves and all-night vigils, let her not stir a hair's breadth from her mother's side.

She must not single out one of her maids to make her a special favorite or a confidante.   What she says to one all ought to know.   Let her choose for a companion not a handsome well-dressed girl, able to warble a song with liquid notes, but one pale and serious, sombrely attired and with the hue of melancholy.   Let her take as her model some aged virgin of approved faith, character, and chastity, apt to instruct her by word and by example.

She ought to rise at night to recite prayers and psalms; to sing hymns in the morning; at the third, sixth, and ninth hours to take her place in the line to do battle for Christ; and, lastly, to kindle her lamp and to offer her evening sacrifice.   In these occupations let her pass the day, and when night comes let it find her still engaged in them.   Let reading follow prayer with her, and prayer again succeed to reading.   Time will seem short when employed on tasks so many and so varied.

Let her learn, too, how to spin wool, to hold the distaff, to put the basket in her lap, to turn the spinning wheel and to shape the yarn with her thumb.   Let her put away with disdain silken fabrics, Chinese fleeces, and gold brocades; the clothing which she makes for herself should keep out the cold and not expose the body which it professes to cover.   Let her food be herbs and wheaten bread, with now and then one or two small fishes.   And that I may not waste more time in giving precepts for the regulation of her appetite, let her meals always leave her hungry and able on the moment to begin reading or chanting.   I strongly disapprove — especially for those of tender years — of long and immoderate fasts in which week is added to week, and even oil and apples are forbidden as food.   I have learned by experience that the ass toiling along the highway makes for an inn when it is weary. . . .

Let her treasures be not silks or gems, but manuscripts of the Holy Scriptures; and in these let her think less of gilding, and Babylonian parchment, and arabesque patterns, than of correctness and accurate punctuation.   Let her begin by learning the Psalter, and then let her gather rules of life out of the proverbs of Solomon.   From the Preacher let her gain the habit of despising the world and its vanities.   Let her follow the example set in Job of virtue and patience. Then let her pass on to the Gospels, never to be laid aside when once they have been taken in hand. Let her also drink in with a willing heart the Acts of the Apostles and the Epistles. As soon as she has enriched the storehouse of her mind with these treasures, let her commit to memory the prophets, the heptateuch, the books of Kings and of Chronicles, the rolls also of Ezra and Esther. When she has done all these she may safely read the Song of Songs, but not before: for, were she to read it at the beginning, she would fail to perceive that, though it is written in fleshly words, it is a marriage song of a spiritual bridal. And not understanding this she would suffer hurt from it. Cyprian's writings let her have always in her hands. The letters of Athanasius and the treatises of Hilary she may go through without fear of stumbling. Let her take pleasure in the works and wits of all in whose books a due regard for the faith is not neglected. But if she reads the works of others, let it be rather to judge them than to follow them.

You will answer, "How shall I, a woman of the world, living at Rome, surrounded by a crowd, be able to observe all these injunctions?" In that case do not undertake a burthen to which you are not equal. When you have weaned Paula as Isaac was weaned, and when you have clothed her as Samuel was clothed, send her to her grandmother and aunt; give up this most precious of gems, to be placed in Mary's chamber and to rest in the cradle where the infant Jesus cried. Let her be brought up in a monastery, let her be one amid companies of virgins, let her learn to avoid swearing, let her regard lying as sacrilege, let her be ignorant of the world, let her live the angelic life, while in the flesh let her be without the flesh, and let her suppose that all human beings are like herself.

CHAPTER V
NEW PEOPLES IN THE EMPIRE

The Readings in this chapter deal with the period of the breakdown of the Roman authority in the provinces, and the barbarian deluge. From being on the defensive the Empire, after two centuries of resistance, finally fell before the repeated onslaughts of peoples who had gradually come to realize Roman weakness and barbarian strength. It was a period of great tribal movements, and when the movements were over and the different tribes had finally settled down within the boundaries of the old Empire, the old civilization had in large part vanished. To the Christian Church was left the task of preserving what remained and of building up a new civilization in western Europe. This required nearly a thousand years. The task confronting the Church was that of transforming the sixth-century barbarian into the civilized man of the fifteenth century, ready to begin anew the upward march of civilization. This long, weary thousand years covered the period known as the Middle Ages. Up to the eleventh century was a particularly difficult period; after that the tide began to turn.

The Readings given here, and in succeeding chapters, serve to illustrate the enormous problem facing the few constructive forces in this ancient society. Cæsar (46) and Tacitus (47) briefly describe the manners and the degree of civilization of the invading Germans. Dill (48) gives an interesting description of how the ancient world was shocked by the news that Rome had been taken and sacked by the barbarian Alaric, in 410 A.D., while the extract from Giry and Réville (49) pictures the passing of Roman towns as the barbarians came into control. Kingsley (50) writes with sympathetic pen of the invaders and what they brought into the ancient world. Reading 51 is a general form, much used in the Middle Ages, by which to grant privileges and immunities to churches, monasteries, and church officers, so that they might pursue their civilizing work unhampered by the barbarian chieftains. Number 52 is a specific grant to a monastery, by Charlemagne, of much the same privileges and immunities.

46. The Hunting Germans and their Fighting Ways

(Cæsar, *Commentaries*, book VI, chaps. 21–23)

Caius Julius Cæsar (c. 100–44 B.C.), in his *Commentaries on the Gallic Wars*, published at Rome in 51 B.C., gives us a good picture of the life and manners of the German tribes east of the Rhine, as he learned them during his period of dealing with them. The *Commentaries* are noted for their accuracy and excellent literary style.

Chap. 21. The Germans differ much from these usages [of the Gauls to the west, previously described], for they have neither Druids to preside over sacred offices, nor do they pay great regard to sacrifices. They rank in the number of gods those alone whom they behold, and by whose instrumentality they are obviously benefited, namely, the sun, fire, and the moon; they have not heard of the other deities even by report. Their whole life is occupied in hunting and in the pursuits of the military art; from childhood they devote themselves to fatigue and hardships. . . .

Chap. 22. They do not pay much attention to agriculture, and a large portion of their food consists in milk, cheese, and flesh; nor has any one a fixed quantity of land or his own individual limits; but the magistrates and the leading men each year apportion to the tribes and families, who have united together, as much land as, and in the place in which, they think proper, and the year after compel them to remove elsewhere. For this enactment they advance many reasons — lest, seduced by long-continued custom, they may exchange their ardor in the waging of war for agriculture; lest they may be anxious to acquire extensive estates, and the more powerful drive the weaker from their possessions; lest they construct their houses with too great a desire to avoid heat and cold; lest the desire of wealth spring up, from which cause divisions and discords arise; and that they may keep the common people in a contented state of mind, when each sees his own means placed on an equality with [those of] the most powerful.

Chap. 23. It is the greatest glory to the several states to have as wide deserts as possible around them, their frontiers having been laid waste. They consider this the real evidence of their prowess, that their neighbors shall be driven out of their lands and abandon them, and that no one dare settle near them; at the same time they think that they shall be on that account the more secure, because they have removed the apprehension of a sudden incursion. When a state either repels war waged against it, or wages it against another, magistrates are chosen to preside over that war with such authority, that they have the power of life and death. In peace there is no common magistrate, but the chiefs of provinces and cantons administer justice and determine controversies among their own people. Robberies which are committed beyond the boundaries of each state bear no infamy, and they avow that these are committed for the purpose of disciplining their youth and of preventing sloth.   And when any of their chiefs has said in an assembly "that he will be their leader, let those who are willing to follow, give in their names"; they who approve of both the enterprise and the man arise and promise their assistance and are applauded by the people; such of them as have not followed him are accounted in the number of deserters and traitors, and confidence in all matters is afterward refused them.   To injure guests they regard as impious; they defend from wrong those who have come to them for any purpose whatever, and esteem them inviolable; to them the houses of all are open and maintenance is freely supplied.

47. The Germans and their Domestic Habits

(Tacitus, *Germania*, chaps. 4 ff. to 20)

The Latin historian, Cornelius Tacitus (c. 54–117), about the year 100 wrote and published a book called *Germania*, describing the character, habits, and political institutions of the Germans.   He had never visited Germany and probably obtained his information from Roman traders and soldiers.   While regarded as an accurate historical writer, he nevertheless has been suspected of attempting to point a moral for the Romans by his descriptions of the better side of German life.   The following extract gives a very favorable picture of their domestic ways.

I agree in the opinion that the Germans have never inter-married with other nations; but to be a race pure, unmixed, and stamped with a distinct character.   Hence a family likeness pervades the whole, though they are so numerous: — eyes stern and blue; ruddy hair; large bodies, powerful in sudden exertions, but impatient of toil and labor, least of all capable of sustaining thirst and heat.   Cold and hunger they are accustomed by their climate and soil to endure.

The land, though varied to a considerable extent in its aspect, is yet universally shagged with forests, or deformed by marshes; moister on the side of Gaul, more bleak on the side of Noricum and Pannonia.   It is productive of grain, but unkindly to fruit trees.   It abounds in flocks and herds, but generally of a small breed. . . .

It is well known that the Germans do not inhabit cities.   They dwell scattered and separate, as a spring, meadow, or grove may chance to invite them.   [In their villages] they are not acquainted with the use of mortar and tiles; and for every purpose use rude unshapen timber, fashioned with no view to beauty; but they take great pains to coat parts of their buildings with a kind of earth, so pure and shining that it gives them the appearance of painting.   They also dig underground caves, and cover them over with a great quantity of manure. These they use as winter retreats and granaries. . . .

The marriage bond is strict and severe among them; nor are any of their manners more praiseworthy than this. Almost singly among the Barbarians they content themselves with one wife (though a very few great chiefs are polygamists). When a woman is married she is admonished by the ceremonial that she comes to her husband as a partner of his toils and dangers, to suffer and to dare equally with him in peace and in war. The women live therefore fenced around with chastity, corrupted by no seductive spectacles, no convivial excitements. Adultery is extremely rare among so numerous a people (and profligate women are outcasts from society). Every mother suckles her own children and does not deliver them into the hands of servants and nurses (as at Rome). The young people are equally matched in their marriage, and the children inherit the vigor of their parents.

48. Effect on the Roman World of the News of the Sacking of Rome by Alaric

(Dill, S., *Roman Society in the Last Century of the Western Empire*, p. 305. 2d ed., London, 1899)

The following selection from the important book by Professor Dill states the profound impression created throughout the civilized world by the news of the fall and sacking of the Eternal City. The picture drawn by Saint Jerome may be a little over-colored; still the effect produced by the news was staggering.

In 410, when after the failure of all negotiations, the city [of Rome] had at last fallen a prey to the army of Alaric, everything was changed. Eight hundred years had passed since Rome had been violated by the Gauls of Brennus. In spite of all the troubles on the frontiers, in spite of the alarms of the great invasions of the second, third, and fourth centuries, the sacred centre of government had never realized the possibility that her own stately security would ever be disturbed. Not only had all true sons of Rome a religious faith in her mission and destiny, but they had good reason to rely on the awe which she inspired in the barbarous races who ranged around her frontiers.

But now the spell was broken; the mystery and awe which surrounded the great city had been pierced and set at naught. The moral force, so much more important in government than the material, had been weakened and desecrated. The shock given by this catastrophe to old Roman confidence and pride must, for the time, have been overwhelming. We can conjecture the feelings [of men of the time . . .] from the words Saint Jerome penned in his cell in Bethlehem in the year 411. Although he had fled from the world, he was still a Roman at heart, steeped in her literary culture, and proud of her great history. When the rumor of the fall of Rome reached him, he broke off his commentary on Ezekiel; his voice was choked with sobs as he thought of the capture of the great city, "which had taken captive all the world."

In an earlier letter, referring to the invasion of the eastern provinces, he says that his soul shudders at the ruin of his time.   For twenty years all the lands from Constantinople to the Julian Alps are drenched with Roman blood.   The provinces are a prey to Alans, Huns, Vandals, and Marcomanni.   Matrons and virgins devoted to God, the noble and the priest, are made a sport of these monsters.   The churches are demolished; the bones of the martyrs are dug up; horses are stabled at the altars of Christ.   "The Roman world is sinking in ruin, . . . and yet we wish to live, and think that those who have been taken from such a scene are to be mourned rather than deemed happy in their fate.   It is through our sins that the barbarians are strong."

[In another letter] he speaks of the countless hordes that have swept from the Rhine to the Pyrenees.   Great cities like Mainz, Rheims, and Nantes have been wiped out; the provinces of Aquitaine, Lyons, and Narbonne have been desolated, thousands have been butchered even in the churches, and famine has completed the work of the sword.

49. Fate of the Old Roman Towns

(By Giry and Réville, in Lavisse et Rambaud's *Histoire Générale;* trans. by Bates and Titsworth, in their *Emancipation of Medieval Towns*.   Henry Holt & Co., New York, 1907.   Reproduced by permission)

The following selection describes briefly the decline and obliteration of the Roman towns which took place with the decline in power of Rome and the coming of the barbarians into the Empire.

The history of the towns and of urban civilization during the first centuries of the Middle Ages is little known; indeed it would be truer to say that it is almost entirely unknown..   The meager documents which these times have left us touch only the greater political events, the history of kings and of the more prominent characters; as to the fate of the people, the anonymous masses, they give us but rare and vague ideas.   Nevertheless, though explicit statements are lacking, we may see in part what was the lot of the urban groups and of the individuals who composed them.

The Roman Empire bequeathed to the Middle Ages a goodly number of towns.   Of these the most important, by reason of population, wealth, and rank, were the cities.   There were about one hundred and twelve such towns in ancient Gaul.   Other towns, called *castra*, were simply fortified places.   The cities, which for a long time had enjoyed a considerable degree of freedom, possessed municipal institutions; but this régime, under the oppressive action of the fisc and of an overwhelming centralization, was in full disintegration as early as the fourth century, even before the invasions had precipitated the fall of the Empire. In the anarchy which followed the arrival of the Barbarians, nothing remained standing of all this structure, for no one was interested in preserving it. The Roman municipal régime expired.

What, then, became of the cities? In most of them a certain personage soon distinguished himself among the inhabitants and gained over them an undisputed preëminence: this was the bishop. He was no longer simply the first priest of his town, he was its lord. As early as the end of the seventh century, perhaps before, Tours was under the rule of its bishop. Thus it was that most of the old Roman cities became, in the Middle Ages, episcopal seigniories. This was the case with Amiens, Laon, Beauvais, and many others.

All, however, did not have the same fate. Some, in consequence of wars, or of partitions, passed into the hands of lay princes. Angers belonged to the count of Anjou, Bordeaux to the duke of Aquitaine; Orleans and Paris were directly under the king. Elsewhere, beside the old city where the bishop ruled, there sprang up a new town, the bourg, which was under another lord, lay or ecclesiastical: thus at Marseilles the city was under the bishop, and the town under the viscount. In the same way the bourg was distinguished from the city at Arles, Narbonne, Toulouse, and Tours. Other places again, pillaged, ruined, and depopulated, lost their rank as towns and were reduced to simple villages, or were even blotted out. London, after the English invasions, was a heap of ruins, and the courses of the old Roman roads which intersected it were so completely obscured that the new streets, marked out in the same directions when the town was reviving in the Middle Ages, no longer coincided with them. Viriconium, one of the richest of the British cities, was reduced to nothing, and it is only in our times (1857) that its exact situation has been discovered. In the same way the destruction of the Portus Itius, which stood upon the shores of the Strait of Dover, and that of Tauroentum, upon the coast of Provence, were so complete that to this day scholars do not agree as to where they were located.

Such are the vague ideas which we possess concerning the political changes in the Roman towns at the beginning of the Middle Ages: with so much the more reason do we know nothing of the history of the small towns, of the simple fortified bourgs, which were built in great numbers at the end of the Empire. All must have come to constitute seigniories, but we do not know how this transformation took place.

50. The Invaders, and what they brought

(Kingsley, Chas., Introduction to *Hypatia;* selected)

The Reverend Charles Kingsley (1819–75), an English writer, in the Introduction to his historical novel *Hypatia* gives a good pen picture of the invasions and their effect on the western world, though perhaps rather idealizing the barbarian and underestimating the Roman. The following selection is taken from this work.

The health of a Church depends not merely on the creed which it professes, not even on the wisdom and holiness of a few great ecclesiastics, but on the faith and virtue of its individual members. The

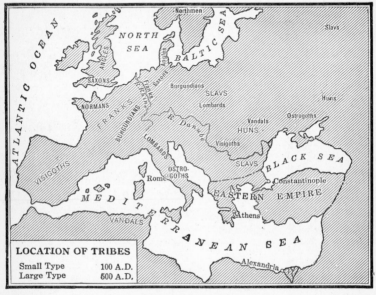

FIG. 8. THE GERMAN MIGRATIONS

mens sana must have a *corpus sanum* to inhabit. And even for the Western Church, the lofty future which was in store for it would have been impossible, without some infusion of new and healthier blood into the veins of a world drained and tainted by the influence of Rome.

And the new blood . . . was at hand. The great tide of those Gothic nations, of which the Norwegian and the German are the purest remaining types, though every nation of Europe, from Gibraltar to St. Petersburg, owes to them the most precious elements of strength, was sweeping onward, wave over wave, in a steady southwestern current across the whole Roman territory, and only stopping and recoiling when it reached the shores of the Mediterranean. Those wild tribes were bringing with them into the magic circle of the Western Church's influence the very materials which she required for the building up of a future Christendom, and which she could find as little in the Western Empire, as in the Eastern; comparative purity of morals; sacred respect for woman, for family life, law, equal justice, individual freedom, and, above all, for honesty in word and deed; bodies untainted by hereditary effeminacy, hearts earnest though genial, and blest with a strange willingness to learn, even from those whom they despised; a brain equal to that of the Roman in practical power, and not too far behind that of the Eastern in imaginative and speculative acuteness.

And their strength was felt at once. Their vanguard, confined with difficulty for three centuries beyond the Eastern Alps, at the expense of sanguinary wars had been adopted, wherever it was practicable, into the service of the Empire; and the heart's core of the Roman legion was composed of Gothic officers and soldiers. But now the main body had arrived. Tribe after tribe was crowding down to the Alps, and trampling upon each other on the frontiers of the Empire. The Huns, singly their inferiors, pressed them from behind with the irresistible weight of numbers; Italy, with her rich cities and fertile lowlands, beckoned them on to plunder; as auxiliaries, they had learned their own strength and Roman weakness; a *casus belli* was soon found. How iniquitous was the conduct of the sons of Theodosius, in refusing the usual bounty, by which the Goths were bribed not to attack the Empire! — The whole pent-up deluge burst over the plains of Italy, and the Western Empire became from that day forth a dying idiot, while the new invaders divided Europe among themselves. . . . The countless treasures which five centuries of rapine had accumulated around the Capitol, had become the prey of men clothed in sheepskin and horsehide; and the sister of an emperor had found her beauty, virtue, and pride of race, worthily matched by those of the hard-handed Northern hero who led her away from Italy as his captive and his bride,[1] to found new kingdoms in South France and Spain, and to drive the newly arrived Vandals across the Straits of Gibraltar into the then blooming coast-land of Northern Africa. Everywhere the mangled limbs of the Old World were seething in the Medea's caldron, to come forth whole, and young, and strong. The Longbeards, noblest of their race, had found a temporary resting-place upon the Austrian frontier, after long southward wanderings from the Swedish mountains, soon to be dispossessed again by the advancing Huns, and, crossing the Alps, to give their name forever to the plains of Lombardy. A few more tumultuous years, and the Franks would find themselves lords of the Lower Rhineland; and before the hairs of Hypatia's scholars had grown gray, the mythic Hengist and Horsa would have landed on the shores of Kent and an English nation have begun its world-wide life.

[1] Adolf, the Visigoth, carried captive from Rome the sister of the Emperor Honorius, the beautiful and learned Placidia, who became his wife.

51. General Form for a Grant of Immunity to a Bishop

(Trans. by Cheyney, E. P., *Documents Illustrative of Feudalism*, p. 11)

The following general form, used commonly during the Middle Ages to extend large powers and immunities to the bishops of the Church, illustrates both the form of grant and the extensive nature of the powers and immunities granted.

A. *Grants of Immunity from the Visits of the King's Officials*

We believe that it increases the great strength of our realm, if with benevolent deliberation we concede opportune benefits to certain churches, — or to certain other specified parties, — and under God's protection write them down to endure permanently. Therefore, may your Zeal know that we have seen fit upon petition to grant such a benefit, for our eternal reward, to that apostolic man, Lord ——, bishop of the city of ——; that in the vills belonging to the church of that lord, which he is seen to have at the present time, either by our gift or that of any one else, or which in the future godly piety shall wish to add to the possessions of that holy place, no public judge shall at any time presume to enter, for the hearing of causes or for the exaction of payments, but the prelate himself, or his successors in God's name shall be able to rule over these possessions as enjoying complete immunity.

We decree, therefore, that neither you, nor your subordinates, nor your successors, nor any public judicial power shall presume at any time to enter upon the vills of the same church anywhere in our kingdom, either those granted by royal bounty, or by that of private persons, or those which shall in future be granted; either for the purpose of settling disputes, or to exact fines for any cause, or to obtain lodgment, entertainment, or sureties. But whatever the treasury might expect from fines or otherwise, either from freemen, serfs, or others within the fields or boundaries of the aforesaid church, or dwelling upon its lands, — this revenue we surrender, for our future welfare, in order that it may be applied to the expenses of the same church by the hand of those ruling it, forever.

And what we, in the name of God and for the remedy of our soul and that of our children after us, have granted from full devotion, let not the royal sublimity itself, nor the reckless cupidity of any of the magistrates be tempted to violate.

And in order that the present decree may, by the aid of God, remain inviolate now and hereafter, we have ordained that this be certified by the subscription of our hand.

SEAL

52. Powers and Immunities granted to the Monastery of Saint Marcellus

The following powers and immunities were granted by Charlemagne to the monastery of Saint Marcellus, at Châlons-sur-Sâone, France, in 776 A.D. The document is a specific case, of which the preceding document (**R. 51**) is a general form, and shows what large legal powers and exemptions from authority were granted by the kings to monasteries and monks, as well as to churches and clergy.

Charles, by the grace of God King of the Franks and Lombards and Patrician of the Romans, to all having charge of our affairs, both present and to come:

By the help of the Lord, who has raised us to the throne of this kingdom, it is the chief duty of our clemency to lend a gracious ear to the needs of all, and especially ought we devoutly to regard that which we are persuaded has been granted by preceding kings to Church foundations for the saving of souls, and not to deny fitting benefits, in order that we may deserve to be partakers of the reward, but to confirm them in still greater security.

Now the illustrious Hubert, bishop and ruler of the church of St. Marcellus, which lies below the citadel of Châlons, where the precious martyr of the Lord himself rests in the body, has brought it to the attention of our Highness that the kings who preceded us, or our lord and father of blessed memory, Pippin, the preceding king, had by their charters granted complete immunities to that Monastery, so that in the towns or on the lands belonging to it no public judge, nor any one with power of hearing cases or exacting fines, or raising sureties, or obtaining lodging or entertainment, or making requisitions of any kind, should enter.

Moreover, the aforesaid bishop, Hubert, has presented the original charters of former kings, together with the confirmations of them, to be read by us, and declares the same favors to be preserved into modern times; but desiring the confirmation of our clemency, he prays that our authority may confirm this grant anew to the Monastery.

Wherefore, having inspected the said charters of former kings, we command that neither you, nor your subordinates, nor your successors, nor any person having judicial powers shall presume to enter into the villages which may at the present time be in possession of that Monastery, or which hereafter may have been so bestowed by God-fearing men, or (may be about to be so bestowed) (?). Let no public officer enter for the hearing of causes, or for exacting fines, or procuring sureties, or obtaining lodging or entertainment, or making any requisitions, but in full immunity, even as the favor of former kings has been continued down to the present day, so in the future also shall it, through our authority, remain undiminished.　And if in past times through any negligence of Abbots, or lukewarmness of rulers, or the presumption of public officers anything has been changed or torn away, removed or withdrawn from these immunities, let it be by our authority and favor restored.　And, further, let neither you nor your subordinates presume to infringe or violate what we have granted.

But if there be any one, Dominus, Comes, Domesticus, Vicarius, or one girded with any judicial power whatsoever, by the indulgence of the good or by the favor of pious Christians or kings, who shall have presumed to infringe or violate these immunities, let him be punished with a fine of six hundred solidi, two parts to go to the library of this Monastery, and the third part to be paid into our treasury, so that impious men may not rejoice in violating that which our ancestors or good Christians may have conceded or granted.　And whatever our treasury may have had a right to expect from this source, shall go to the profit of the men of this church of St. Marcellus the martyr, to the better establishment of our kingdom and the good of those who shall succeed us.

And that this decree may firmly endure, we have ordered it to be confirmed with our own hand under our seal.

SEAL　　　Seal of Charles, the most glorious king.　Given on the thirtieth of April in the eleventh and fifth year of our reigns.　Done at Heristal.

CHAPTER VI
EDUCATION DURING THE EARLY MIDDLE AGES

I. CONDITION AND PRESERVATION OF LEARNING

THE Readings in this chapter deal with the condition of learning after the downfall of the Roman Empire, the work of the monasteries in preserving the old pagan learning and the arts of reading and writing, and the efforts of Kings Charlemagne and Alfred to revive the study of letters in their domains.

To such a low ebb had all learning declined, after the barbarian invasions, that but few schools remained in Gaul and northern Italy, and these were needed only for the purposes of the Church. All through the early Middle Ages the monasteries or the Church offered the only means to an education, and the only type of career for which learning was needed. Parents wishing their children to follow careers usually gave them to a monastery, for which gift fixed forms of dedication (53 a) were used. Beside agriculture, various forms of manual labor, and acts of devotion, life in a monastery also called for some form of literary labor. For most of the monks this meant reading, though a few specialized and became copyists, and some monasteries specialized on book copying and thus became the publishers of the Middle Ages. The work of copying books is well described in Numbers 54 and 55, both being chronicles from old monastic writers. Some nunneries also became noted for their book work, the work of one nun being described in Reading 56. The preparation and binding of books was a long and important process, and the work of the monks is well described in the extract from Symonds (57). When the manufacture of a book had been completed it was customary to inscribe in it an anathema, to protect it from theft. Samples of these anathemas are reproduced from Clark (58 a-f).

During the early part of the Middle Ages learning was better preserved in England than on the Continent, and the extracts from Bede (59 a-c) and Alcuin (60) give good pictures of the teaching of Theodore at Canterbury and Ælbert at York. Alcuin also describes the more important books in the celebrated cathedral library at York (61).

In 768 A.D., there came to the throne as king of the great Frankish nation one of the greatest rulers of all time — Charlemagne.   Finding learning in a most deplorable condition in his kingdom, and realizing the need for training for his clergy, he began a series of efforts to bring scholars and teachers into Frankland.   The most important man brought in was Alcuin, from York, who arrived in 782, and spent the remainder of his life in educational labors there.   Organizing first a Palace School, he began the instruction of Charlemagne's immediate household.   A good sample of the instruction prepared for Charlemagne's son, Pepin, is reproduced in Number **62**.   Under Alcuin's inspiration a number of proclamations on education were issued (**64 a-c**), and a collection of edited sermons (**63**) was issued to the churches.   After fourteen years as Charlemagne's teacher and minister of education, Alcuin retired to the monastery at Tours, where, as Abbot, he spent the remainder of his life in directing the copying of books and in training scholars.   In a letter to Charlemagne, asking for books from England to copy (**65**), we get a good picture of the deplorable educational conditions of the time, as well as of the old man's thirst for learning.

England, too, was later ravaged by the Danes, as was northern France by the Northmen, and learning fell into decay in both places.   England especially suffered, and King Alfred, in his Introduction to Pope Gregory's *Pastoral Care* (**66**), gives us a good picture of the sad conditions which had come about in his kingdom. As Charlemagne, before him, he too was forced to seek scholars from abroad (**67**) to restore learning at home.   The education he gave his son (**68**) is indicative of the best training of the time.

Many of the mediæval monasteries grew into large and important institutions, one of the most notable of which was that of Saint Gall, in Switzerland.   The ground plan of this monastery in the ninth century (**69**) shows what a large institution it had become, and the description appended reveals the varied activities carried on within the walls of one of the larger institutions.

53. Form for offering a Child to a Monastery; the Monastic Vow; and a Letter of Honorable Dismissal

(From Migne, *Patrologia*, 66, col. 842, 821, 859)

The forms which follow represent examples used in offering a child to a monastery, the monastic vows which were taken, and the letter of honorable dismissal which a monk carried with him when he transferred from one monastery to another. It is interesting, as illustrating the continuity of our intellectual life and legal procedure, to compare these three forms with the modern forms for releasing parentage of a child for adoption by another, any form of modern vow, and the letter of honorable dismissal given a college student leaving one college to enter another.

(a) Form of offering a Child to a Monastery

The dedication of children to the service of God is sanctioned by the example of Abraham and of many other holy men, as related in the Old and the New Testaments. Therefore, I, (name) now offer in the presence of abbot (name), this my son, (name), to omnipotent God and to the Virgin Mary, mother of God, for the salvation of my soul and of the soul of my parents. I promise for him that he shall follow the monastic life in this monastery of (name), according to the rule of St. Benedict, and that from this day forth he shall not withdraw his neck from the yoke of this service. I promise also that he shall never be tempted to leave by me or by anyone with my consent.

(b) The Monastic Vow

I hereby renounce my parents, my brothers and relatives, my friends, my possessions and my property, and the vain and empty glory and pleasure of this world. I also renounce my own will, for the will of God. I accept all the hardships of the monastic life, and take the vows of purity, chastity, and poverty, in the hope of heaven; and I promise to remain a monk in this monastery all the days of my life.

(c) Letter of Honorable Dismissal from a Monastery

This our brother (name), has desired to dwell in another monastery where it seems to him that he can best serve the Lord and save his own soul. Know ye, therefore, that we have given him permission by this letter of dismissal to betake himself thither.

54. The Copying of Books at a Monastery

(From Abbot Heriman's account of the restoration of the monastery of Saint Martin, at Tournay, in Flanders; trans. in Maitland, S. R., *The Dark Ages*, pp. 413-14. London, 1844)

The writer here relates how the first Abbot, who was installed in 1093, not being much of a manager, turned the organization and direction of the work of the monastery over to the Prior, with good results.

... The abbot greatly rejoiced, and used to thank God, who had given him a man that had relieved him from the anxiety and bustle of worldly affairs. For, committing to him the whole charge of the external affairs of our monastery, he gave himself up so entirely to the duties of a monk, and to silence, that frequently he did not go out of the monastery for a month together, but, being devoted to reading, he took the utmost pains to promote the writing of books. He used, in fact, to exult in the number of writers which the Lord had given him; for if you had gone into the cloister, you might in general have seen a dozen young monks sitting on chairs in perfect silence, writing at tables carefully and artificially constructed. All Jerome's *Commentaries on the Prophets*, all the works of Saint Gregory, and everything that he could find of Saint Augustine, Ambrose, Isidore, Bede, and the Lord Anselm, then Abbot of Bec, and afterwards Archbishop of Canterbury, he caused to be diligently transcribed. So that you would scarcely have found such a library at any monastery in that part of the country, and everybody was begging for our copies to correct their own. Our monastery was at that time in great reputation, and in a high state of discipline; for in the whole province of Rheims there were at that period only three monasteries which followed the customs of Clugni — namely, Anchin, Afflighem, and our own. The monastery of Clugni at that time excelled all others belonging to the kingdom of the Francs in monastic order; for the rigor of the Cistercians had not then sprung up, and the Lord Norbert had not as yet been heard of.

55. Work of a Monk in writing and copying Books

(From Othlonus' *De ipsius tentationibus, varia fortuna, et scriptis;* trans. in Maitland, S. R., *The Dark Ages*, pp. 417–19. London, 1844)

Othlonus, a monk of Saint Emmeram's, at Ratisbon, born about 1013 A.D., has left us an interesting picture of his work as author and copyist, which shows how he disposed of the books produced. Just what books he copied he does not say, and we do not know.

For the same reason I think it proper to add an account of the great knowledge and capacity for writing which was given me by the Lord in my childhood. When as yet a little child, I was sent to school, and quickly learned my letters; and I began, long before the usual time of learning, and without any orders from the master, to learn the art of writing. But in a furtive and unusual manner, and without any teacher, I attempted to learn that art. From this circumstance I got a habit of holding my pen in a wrong manner; nor were any of my teachers afterwards able to correct me in that point; for I had become too much accustomed to it to be capable of altering. Many who saw this unanimously decided that I should never write well; but, by the grace of God, it turned out otherwise, as is known to many persons. For, even in my childhood, and at the time when, together with the other boys, the tablet was put into my hands, that I might learn to write, it appeared that I had some notion of writing, to the no small surprise of those who saw it. Then, after a short time, I began to write so well, and was so fond of it, that in the place where I learned, that is, in the monastery of Tegernsee, (in Bavaria, almost in a line between Munich and Innsbruck,) I wrote many books. And being sent into Franconia while I was yet a boy, I worked so hard at writing while I was there, that before I returned I had nearly lost my sight. This I resolved to mention, in the hope that I may excite some others to a similar love of labour; and that, by recounting to others the grace of God which had granted to me such benefits, I may lead them to magnify that grace of God with me. And the better to do this, I think it proper to relate how I laboured in writing afterwards, when I had returned from Franconia, for I was there when the Emperor Henry died, and Conrad came to the throne (in the year 1024).

Then, after I came to be a monk in the monastery of St. Emmeram, I, was soon induced, by the request of some of them, again to occupy myself so much in writing that I seldom got any interval of rest, except on festivals, and at such times as work could not be performed. In the meantime, there came more work upon me; for, as they saw that I was generally reading, or writing, or composing, they made me the schoolmaster. By all which things I was, through God's grace, so fully occupied, that I frequently could not allow my body the necessary rest. And when I had a mind to compose anything, I very commonly could not find time for it, except on holydays, or by night, being tied down to the business of teaching the boys, and the transcribing which I had been persuaded to undertake. Therefore, beside the books which I composed myself, which I wrote to give away for the edification of those who asked for them, and of others to whom I gave them unasked, I wrote nineteen missals — ten for the abbots and monks in our own monastery, four for the brethren at Fulda, five for those in other places; three books of the Gospels, and two with the Epistles and Gospels, which are called Lectionaries; beside which I wrote four service books for matins. Afterwards, old age and infirmity of various kinds hindered me; especially the tedious interruption which lasted for a very long time through various anxieties, and the grief which was caused by the destruction of our monastery; but to Him who is the Author of all good, and who alone governs all things, and who has vouchsafed to give many things to me unworthy, be praise eternal, be honour everlasting.

I think it right also to relate, as far as I am able to recollect, how many books I have given to different monasteries and friends; and first I would mention the monks at Fulda, because, as I worked a great deal in their monastery, writing many books which I sent to our monastery, so in ours I wrote out some books which they had not; and, if I remember right, I sent them seven. To the monks of Hirschfeld, two books; and when I returned from those parts and came to Amarbach, I gave one to the abbot of that place. Afterwards, being under obligation to brother William, I gave him four books, among which there was a very valuable missal. To the abbot of Lorsch, one book; to certain friends dwelling in Bohemia, four books; to a friend at Passau, one book; to the monastery of Tegernsee, two books; to the monastery of Pryel, near us, one volume, in which were three books. And also I gave one book, and various epistles, to my sister's son, who was living there. To the monastery of Obermunster I gave three books; and to that of Nidermunster, one book. Moreover, to many others I gave or sent, at different times, sermons, proverbs, and edifying writings.

56. Work of a Nun in copying Books

(An account by a monk of Wessobrunn, in Bavaria, written in 1513; trans. in Maitland, S. R., *The Dark Ages*, pp. 419–21. London, 1844)

The following selection describes the rather extraordinary labors of a nun in copying books, and the type of books she copied.

Diemudis was formerly a most devout nun of this our monastery of Wessobrunn. For our monastery was formerly double, or divided into two parts, — that is to say, of monks and nuns. The place of the monks was where it now is; but that of the nuns where the parish church now stands. This virgin was most skilful in the art of writing. For though she is not known to have composed any work, yet she wrote with her own hand many volumes in a most beautiful and legible character, both for divine service and for the public library of the monastery, which are enumerated in a list written by herself in a certain plenarius (missal). For in that list the following books pertaining to divine service are enumerated:

A Missal, with the Gradual and Sequences.

Another Missal, with Gradual and Sequences, which was given to the Bishop of Treves.

Another Missal, with the Epistles, Gospels, Gradual and Sequences.

Another Missal, with the Epistles and Gospels for the whole year; and the Gradual and Sequences, and the entire service for Baptism.

A Missal, with Epistles and Gospels.

A Book of Offices.

Another Book of Offices, with the Baptismal Service, which was given to the Bishop of Augsburgh.

A Book with the Gospels and Lessons.

A Book with the Gospels.

A Book with the Epistles.

These books she wrote, as I have said, for the use and ornament of divine service. With the following she adorned our library, of which only those which are marked thus § still remain there.[1]   For the others, either through the burning of the monastery, (which is said to have happened twice,) or by the negligence and sloth of subsequent monks, have perished and are lost; for the list already mentioned specifies the following books belonging to the library:

A Bible, in two volumes, which was given for the estate in Pisinberch.

A Bible, in three volumes.

The Morals of Saint Gregory, (that is, his Commentary on Job,) in six volumes, the first and third of which are lost.

Saint Gregory ad Regaredum.

Saint Gregory on Ezechiel, and some other things, in one volume.

Sermons and Homilies of Ancient Doctors, three volumes.

Origen on the Old Testament.

—— on the Canticles.

Augustine on the Psalms, iii volumes.

—— on the Gospel, and the First Epistle of Saint John, ii volumes; the first missing.

—— Epistles, to the number of lxxv.

—— Treatises, 'De verbis Domini,' 'De Sermone Domini in Monte,' 'De Opere Monachorum,' and 'De Agone Christiano,' 'De Adorando,' 'De Professione Viduitatis,' 'De Bono Conjugali,' 'De Virginitate.'

Saint Jerome's Epistles, to the number of clxiv.

The Tripartite History of Cassiodorus, (that is, the compendium of ecclesiastical history which he made, in the sixth century, from Epiphanius's Latin Version of Socrates, Sozomen, and Theodoret.)

Eusebius's Ecclesiastical History.

Saint Augustine, Fifty Sermons; The Life of Saint Sylvester; Jerome against Vigilantius, and 'De Consolatione Mortuorum'; The Life of Saint Blaise; The Life of Saint John the Almoner (Patriarch of Alexandria early in the seventh century.   I presume, from the way in which they are put together, that these formed only one volume, as also the following:)

Paschasius on the Body and Blood of Christ; The Conflict of Lanfranc with Berengarius; the Martyrdom of Saint Dionysius; The Life of Saint Adrian, pope, &c.

Saint Jerome 'De Hebraicis Quæstionibus,' and many other works by him and other writers.

Saint Augustine's Confessions.

Canons.

The Gloss, alphabetically arranged.   (I suppose this is meant by 'Glossa per A.B.C. composita.')

These are the volumes written with her own hand by the aforesaid

[1] I translate as it stands; but I do not see that any books in the list are so marked, or in any way distinguished from the others. (Maitland.)

handmaid of God, Diemudis, to the praise of God and of the holy apostles, Peter and Paul, the patrons of this monastery. But at what period she lived I could never discover, since, in all the books, (we charitably hope from humility,) she omitted to mention her name and the time when she finished.

57. Scarcity and Cost of Books

(Symonds, J. A., *The Renaissance in Italy*, vol. II, pp. 127-29. London, 1888)

The following short extract from Symonds gives the contents of two libraries in northern Italy, and the cost of books before the days of printing.

Scarcity of books was at first a chief impediment to the study of antiquity. Popes and princes and even great religious institutions possessed far fewer books than many farmers of the present age. The library belonging to the Cathedral Church of S. Martino at Lucca in the ninth century contained only nineteen volumes of abridgments from ecclesiastical commentaries. The Cathedral of Novara in 1212 could boast copies of Boethius, Priscian, the *Code of Justinian*, the *Decretals*, and the *Etymology* of Isidorus, besides a Bible and some devotional treatises. This slender stock passed for great riches. Each of the precious volumes in such a collection was an epitome of mediæval art. Its pages were composed of fine vellum adorned with pictures. The initial letters displayed elaborate flourishes and exquisitely illuminated groups of figures. The scribe took pains to render his caligraphy perfect, and to ornament the margins with crimson, gold, and blue. Then he handed the parchment

FIG. 9. A MEDIÆVAL WRITER

(From a manuscript in the National Library, at Paris)

The scribe is seated in a chair, with a writing desk attached. He holds a pen in one hand, and a knife for erasing in the other. The table before him is covered with bound books

sheets to the binder, who encased them in rich settings of velvet or carved ivory and wood, embossed with gold and precious stones. The edges were gilt and stamped with patterns. The clasps were wrought silver, chased with niello. The price of such masterpieces was enormous. Borso d'Este, in 1464, gave eight gold ducats to Gherardo

Ghislieri of Bologna for an illuminated Lancellotto, and in 1469 he bought a Josephus and Quintus Curtius for forty ducats. His great Bible in two volumes is said to have cost 1,375 sequins. Rinaldo degli Albizzi notes in his Memoirs that he paid eleven golden florins for a Bible at Arezzo in 1406. Of these MSS. the greater part were manufactured in the cloisters.

58. Anathemas to Protect Books from Theft

(From Clark, J. W., *The Care of Books*, pp. 77–78. London, 1901)

In addition to chaining books with heavy rod and chains to their case, it was customary to inscribe an anathema in the volume, further to protect them against removal. The following are examples of such inscriptions.

(a) This book belongs to S. Maximin at his monastery of Micy, which abbat Peter caused to be written, and with his own labour corrected and punctuated, and on Holy Thursday dedicated to God and S. Maximin on the altar of S. Stephen, with this imprecation that he who should take it away from thence by what device soever, with the intention of not restoring it, should incur damnation with the traitor Judas, with Annas, Caiaphas, and Pilate. Amen.

(b) Should any one by craft or any device whatever abstract this book from this place (Jumièges) may his soul suffer, in retribution for what he has done, and may his name be erased from the book of the living and not be recorded among the Blessed.

(c) This book belongs to S. Alban. May whoever steals it from him or destroys its title be anathema. Amen.

(d) May whoever steals or alienates this manuscript, or scratches out its title, be anathema. Amen.

(e) May whoever destroys this title, or by gift or sale or loan or exchange or theft or by any other device knowingly alienates this book from the aforesaid Christ Church, incur in this life the malediction of Jesus Christ and of the most glorious Virgin His Mother, and of the Blessed Thomas, Martyr. Should however it please Christ, who is patron of Christ Church, may his soul be saved in the Day of Judgment.

(f) Wher so ever y be come over all
    I belonge to the Chapell of gunvylle hall;
    He shal be cursed by the grate sentens
    That felonsly faryth and berith me thens.
    And whether he bere me in pooke or sekke,
    For me he shall be hanged by the nekke,
    (I am so well beknown of dyverse men)
    But I be restored theder agen.

59. The Venerable Bede on Education in Early England

(Bede, *Ecclesiastical History of England;* edited by C. Plummer, book IV, 1, 2, 20)

The Venerable Bede (673–735), a famous scholar and historian and the author of many books, was a lifelong student at the twin monasteries of Wearmouth and Yarrow, in North Britain.   In his *Ecclesiastical History of England* he has left us our chief picture of education in England in his time.   The following selections are illustrative.

(a) The Learning of Theodore

Now there was in the monastery of Niridanum, which is not far from Naples in Campania, abbot Hadrian, an African by birth, well learned in sacred literature, and versed in both monastic and ecclesiastical discipline, and highly skilled in the Greek equally with the Latin tongue. . . .

There was at the same time (668 A.D.) in Rome a monk known to Hadrian, whose name was Theodore, born at Tarsus in Cilicia, a man instructed in secular and divine literature both Greek and Latin; of approved character and venerable age, that is, about 66 years old. Hadrian suggested him to the Pope to be ordained bishop, and the suggestion was adopted.

(b) Theodore's Work for the English Churches

Theodore then arrived at his church in the second year after his consecration, on Sunday, 27 May (670 A.D.), and lived in it 21 years, 3 months and 26 days.   He soon travelled through the whole island, wherever it was inhabited by the English race.   For he was willingly received and listened to by every one, and everywhere in the company and with the assistance of Hadrian he sowed the right rule of life, the canonical rite for the celebration of Easter.   And he was the first of the archbishops to whom the whole English church consented to do fealty. And because, as we have said, both were abundantly learned both in sacred and profane literature, rivers of saving knowledge daily flowed from them to irrigate the hearts of the band of pupils whom they brought together, insomuch that they passed on to their hearers the knowledge even of the art of metre, of astronomy and of ecclesiastical arithmetic, together with volumes of the sacred text.   A proof of this is that even to-day (c. A.D. 731) some of their pupils are still living, who know the Latin and Greek languages as well as their native tongue. Never since the English came to Britain were there happier times than these, in which, under brave and Christian kings, they were a terror to all barbarian tribes, when the aspirations of all hung on the lately revealed joys of the kingdom of heaven, and every one who wished to become learned in holy Writ, had masters at hand to teach him.

Besides, they thenceforth began to learn in all the churches of the English the notes of ecclesiastical chants, which hitherto they had only known in Kent. The first singing master (except James whom we mentioned above) in the Northumbrian churches was Stephen Æddi, who was invited from Kent by the venerable Wilfred, who was the first among the bishops of English birth to teach the catholic method of life to the churches of the English.

(c) How Albinus succeeded Abbot Hadrian

In the fifth year of King Osred, the most reverend father abbot Hadrian, fellow-worker in the word of God with bishop Theodore of blessed memory, died. Among other proofs of his learning and that of Theodore is this, that his pupil Albinus, who succeeded him in the rule of the monastery, was so advanced in the study of literature, that he had no small knowledge of the Greek language and knew the Latin tongue as well as that of the English, which was his native tongue.

60. Alcuin's Description of the School at York

(On the Saints of the Church at York; trans. by James Rai)

The cathedral school at York, England, was one of the oldest of the English schools. In 732 Egbert became archbishop of York, and the *scholasticus* of the school under him was Ælbert or Ethelbert. He raised the school to a place of first importance. Alcuin, born about 735, entered the cathedral school as a child, was taught by Ælbert, and later became master of the school himself. In one of his poems he has described the instruction under Ælbert. The whole mediæval curriculum will be noted in this description.

Bide with me for a while, I pray ye, youth of York, while I proceed with poetic steps to treat of him, because here he often drenched your senses with nectar, pouring forth sweet juices from his honey-flowing bosom. Fairest Philosophy took him from his very cradle and bore him to the topmost towers of learning, opening to him the hidden things of wisdom. He was born of ancestors of sufficient note, by whose care he was soon sent to kindly school, and entered at the Minster in his early years, that his tender age might grow up with holy understanding. Nor was his parents' hope in vain; even as a boy as he grew in body so he became proficient in the understanding of books.

Then pious and wise, teacher at once and priest, he was made a colleague of Bishop Egbert, to whom he was nearly allied by right of blood. By him he is made advocate of the clergy, and at the same time is preferred as master in the city of York.

There he moistened thirsty hearts with diverse streams of teaching and the varied dews of learning, giving to these the art of the science of grammar, pouring on those the rivers of rhetoric.   Some he polished on the whetstone of law, some he taught to sing together in Æonian chant, making others play on the flute of Castaly, and run with the feet of lyric poets over the hills of Parnassus.   Others the said master made to know the harmony of heaven, the labours of sun and moon, the five belts of the sky, the seven planets, the laws of the fixed stars, their rising and setting, the movements of the air, the quaking of sea and earth, the nature of men, cattle, birds and beasts, the divers kinds of numbers and various shapes.   He gave certainty to the solemnity of Easter's return; above all, opening the mysteries of holy writ and disclosing the abysses of the rude and ancient law.   Whatever youths he saw of conspicuous intelligence, those he joined to himself, he taught, he fed, he loved; and so the teacher had many disciples in the sacred volumes, advanced in various arts.   Soon he went in triumph abroad, led by the love of wisdom, to see if he could in find other lands anything novel in books or schools, which he could bring home with him.   He went also devoutly to the city of Romulus, rich in God's love, wandering far and wide through the holy places.   Then returning home, he was received everywhere by kings and princes as a prince of doctors, whom great kings tried to keep that he might irrigate their lands with learning.   But the master hurrying to his appointed work, returned home to his fatherland by God's ordinance.   For no sooner had he been borne to his own shores, than he was compelled to take on him the pastoral care, and made high priest at the people's demand. . . .

61. Alcuin's Catalogue of the Cathedral Library at York

(On the Saints of the Church of York; trans. by West)

On the death of Egbert, Archbishop of York, in 766, Alcuin was given charge of the cathedral library, then a famous one for its time.   In a continuation of the preceding poem, Alcuin has left a sort of metrical catalogue of its more important volumes, which has been rendered into English verse by Professor West.

> There shalt thou find the volumes that contain
> All of the ancient fathers who remain;
> There all the Latin writers make their home
> With those that glorious Greece transferred to Rome, —
> The Hebrews draw from their celestial stream,
> And Africa is bright with learning's beam.
>
> Here shines what Jerome, Ambrose, Hilary thought,
> Or Athanasius and Augustine wrought.
> Orosius, Leo, Gregory the Great,
> Near Basil and Fulgentius coruscate.

Grave Cassiodorus and John Chrysostom
Next Master Bede and learned Aldhelm come,
While Victorinus and Boethius stand
With Pliny and Pompeius close at hand.

Wise Aristotle looks on Tully near.
Sedulius and Juvencus next appear.
Then come Albinus, Clement, Prosper too,
Paulinus and Arator. Next we view
Lactantius, Fortunatus. Ranged in line
Virgilius Maro, Statius, Lucan, shine.
Donatus, Priscian, Probus, Phocas, start
The roll of masters in grammatic art.
Eutychius, Servius, Pompey, each extend
The list. Comminian brings it to an end.

There shalt thou find, O reader, many more
Famed for their style, the masters of old lore,
Whose many volumes singly to rehearse
Were far too tedious for our present verse.

62. Specimen of Alcuin's Palace-School Instruction

(From Alcuin's *Disputation of Pepin, the Most Noble and Royal Youth, with Albinus the Scholastic*)

This most interesting example of catechetical instruction was prepared by Alcuin for the use of Pepin, son of Charlemagne, then a youth of sixteen years. Albinus was a nickname for Alcuin. The following extracts are illustrative.

1. General questions and answers.

P. What is writing?	A. The custodian of history.
P. What is speech?	A. The interpreter of the soul.
P. What produces speech?	A. The tongue.
P. What is the tongue?	A. The whip of the air.
P. What is air?	A. The guardian of life.
P. What is life?	A. The joy of the good, the sorrow of the evil, the expectation of death.
P. What is death?	A. An inevitable event, an uncertain journey, a subject of weeping to the living, the fulfilment of wills, the thief of men.

P. What is man?

A. The slave of death, a transient traveller, a host in his dwelling.

P. What is man like?

A. Like a fruit-tree.

P. How is man placed?

A. Like a lantern exposed to the wind.

P. Where is he placed?

A. Between six walls.

P. Which are they?

A. Above, below; before, behind; right, left.

P. To how many changes is he liable?

A. To six.

P. Which are they?

A. Hunger and satiety; rest and work; waking and sleeping.

P. What is sleep?

A. The image of death.

P. What is the liberty of man?

A. Innocence.

P. What is the head?

A. The top of the body.

P. What is the body?

A. The domicile of the soul.

2. *Questions of a scientific nature.*

P. What is the sun?

A. The splendor of the universe, the beauty of the sky, the glory of day, the distributor of the hours.

P. What is the moon?

A. The eye of night, the dispenser of dew, the prophet of storms.

P. What are the stars?

A. The pictures of the roof of the heavens, the guides of sailors, the ornament of night.

P. What is rain?

A. The reservoir of the earth, the mother of the fruits.

P. What is fog?

A. Night in day, a labor of the eyes.

P. What is wind?

A. The disturbance of the air, the commotion of the waters, the dryness of the earth.

P. What is frost?

A. A persecutor of plants, a destroyer of leaves, a fetter of the earth.

P. What is autumn?

A. The barn of the year.

63. Charlemagne sends out an Edited Collection of Sermons for Use throughout the Year

To enable the churches to conduct their services better, Charlemagne had prepared a number of copies of sermons and lesson-readings, "in two volumes, suitable for the whole year," which he sent out in 786, accompanied by the following letter.

Charles, confiding in the aid of God, King of the Franks and Lombards, and Patrician of the Romans, to the religious lectors subject to our power.

Since the divine clemency always guards us at home and abroad, in the issues of war or in the tranquillity of peace, though human insignificance is in no way able to pay back his benefits, nevertheless, because our God is inestimable in his mercy, He approves benignly the goodwill of those devoted to His service. Therefore, because we take care constantly to improve the condition of our churches, we have striven with watchful zeal to advance the cause of learning, which has been almost forgotten by the negligence of our ancestors; and, by our example, also we invite those whom we can to master the study of the liberal arts. Accordingly, God aiding us in all things, we have already corrected carefully all the books of the Old and New Testaments, corrupted by the ignorance of the copyists.

Incited, moreover, by the example of our father Pippin, of venerated memory, who by his zeal decorated all the churches of the Gauls with the songs of the Roman church, we are careful by our skill to make these churches illustrious by a series of excellent lectionaries. Finally because we have found the lectionaries for the nocturnal offices, compiled by the fruitless labor of certain ones, in spite of their correct intention, unsuitable because they were written without the words of their authors and were full of an infinite number of errors, we cannot suffer in our days discordant solecisms to glide into the sacred lessons among the holy offices, and we purpose to improve these lessons. And we have entrusted this work to Paul the deacon, our friend and client. We have directed him to peruse carefully the sayings of the catholic fathers and to choose, so to speak, from the most broad meadows of their writings certain flowers, and from the most useful to form, as it were, a single garland. He, desiring to obey devoutly our highness, has read through the treatises and sermons of the different catholic fathers, has chosen from each the best, and has presented to us in two volumes lessons suitable for the whole year and for each separate festival, and free from error. We have examined the text of all these with our wisdom, we have established these volumes by our authority, and we deliver them to your religion to be read in the churches of Christ.

64. Charlemagne's General Proclamations as to Education

(Trans. by Munro, D. C., in his *Laws of Charles the Great*)

Issued by Charlemagne, in 787, to the abbots of the different monasteries, reproving their illiteracy and exhorting them to the study of letters. This has been called "the first general charter of education for the Middle Ages." Only the copy of the Proclamation addressed to the Abbot Baugulf of Fulda has escaped destruction. This reads as follows:

(a) The Proclamation of 787 A.D.

Charles, by the grace of God, King of the Franks and Lombards and Patrician of the Romans, to Abbot Baugulf and to all the congregation, also the faithful committed to you, we have directed a loving greeting by our ambassadors in the name of omnipotent God.

Be it known, therefore, to your devotion pleasing to God, that we, together with our faithful, have considered it to be useful that the bishoprics and monasteries entrusted by the favor of Christ to our control, in addition to the order of monastic life and the intercourse of holy religion, in the culture of letters also ought to be zealous in teaching those who by the gift of God are able to learn, according to the capacity of each individual, so that just as the observance of the rule imparts order and grace to honesty of morals, so also zeal in teaching and learning may do the same for sentences, so that those who desire to please God by living rightly should not neglect to please him also by speaking correctly. For it is written: "Either from thy words thou shalt be justified or from thy words thou shalt be condemned." (Matthew, xii, 37.) For although correct conduct may be better than knowledge, nevertheless knowledge precedes conduct. Therefore, each one ought to study what he desires to accomplish, so that so much the more fully the mind may know what ought to be done, as the tongue hastens in the praises of omnipotent God without the hindrances of errors. For since errors should be shunned by all men, so much the more ought they to be avoided as far as possible by those who are chosen for this very purpose alone, so that they ought to be the especial servants of truth.

For when in the years just passed letters were often written to us from several monasteries in which it was stated that the brethren who dwelt there offered up in our behalf sacred and pious prayers, we have recognized in most of these letters correct thoughts and uncouth expressions; because what pious devotion dictated faithfully to the mind, the tongue, uneducated on account of the neglect of study, was not able to express in the letter without error. Whence it happened that we began to fear lest perchance, as the skill in writing was less, so also the wisdom for understanding the Holy Scriptures might be much less than it rightly ought to be. And we all know well that, though errors of speech are dangerous, far more dangerous are errors of the understanding.

Therefore, we exhort you not only not to neglect the study of letters, but also with most humble mind, pleasing to God, to study earnestly in order that you may be able more easily and more correctly to penetrate the mysteries of the divine Scriptures. Since, moreover, images, trophes and similar figures are found in the sacred pages, no one doubts that each one in reading these will understand the spiritual sense more quickly if previously he shall have been fully instructed in the mastery of letters. Such men truly are to be chosen for this work as have both the will and the ability to learn and a desire to instruct others. And may this be done with a zeal as great as the earnestness with which we commend it. For we desire you to be, as it is fitting that soldiers of the church should be, devout in mind, learned in discourse, chaste in conduct and eloquent in speech, so that whosoever shall seek to see you out of reverence for God, or on account of your reputation for holy conduct, just as he is edified by your appearance, may also be instructed by your wisdom, which he has learned from your reading or singing, and may go away joyfully giving thanks to omnipotent God. Do not neglect, therefore, if you wish to have our favor, to send copies of this letter to all your suffragans and fellow-bishops and to all the monasteries. (And let no monk hold courts outside of his monastery or go to the judicial and other public assemblies. Farewell. (*Legens valeat.*))

In 789 Charlemagne supplemented the above with the following general admonition:

(b) The Proclamation of 789 A.D.

And we also demand of your holiness that the ministers of the altar of God shall adorn their ministry by good manners, and likewise the other orders who observe a rule and the congregations of monks. We implore them to lead a just and fitting life, just as God Himself commanded in the Gospel. "Let your light so shine before men that they may see your good works and glorify your Father which is in heaven," so that by their example many may be led to serve God; and let them join and associate to themselves not only children of servile condition, but also sons of free men. And let schools be established in which boys may learn to read. Correct carefully the Psalms, the signs in writing (*notas*), the songs, the calendar, the grammar, in each monastery or bishopric, and the catholic books; because often some desire to pray to God properly, but they pray badly because of the incorrect books. And do not permit your boys to corrupt them in reading or writing. If there is need of writing the Gospel, Psalter and Missal, let men of mature age do the writing with all diligence.

(c) In 802 he ordered further:

(We will and command) that laymen shall learn thoroughly the creed and the Lord's prayer.

These three documents reveal a deep interest in the improvement of the learning of the clergy, and a large vision as to needs in that uncouth and illiterate age. The hand that prepared them was doubtless Alcuin's, though they appear in the name of Charlemagne.

65. Letter from Alcuin to Charlemagne

(Alcuin's *Letters;* trans. by C. W. Colby)

In 796, Charlemagne appointed Alcuin Abbot of the monastery of Saint Martin's at Tours, after fourteen years' service as head of the palace school at the Frankish court. Alcuin was now sixty-one years old, and he spent the remaining eight years of his life here as Abbot, largely engaged in supervising the work of copying books. This letter, written to Charlemagne in 796, shortly after taking up his work at Tours, is interesting as describing his work in Frankland. In it he contrasts the learning with that of his homeland, and appeals for books to copy. His praise of wisdom and frequent quotations from Scripture are characteristic of the man.

But I, your Flaccus,[1] am doing as you have urged and wished. To some who are beneath the roof of Saint Martin I am striving to dispense the honey of Holy Scripture; others I am eager to intoxicate with the old wine of ancient learning; others again I am beginning to feed with the apples of grammatical refinement; and there are some whom I long to adorn with the knowledge of astronomy, as a stately house is adorned with a painted roof. I am made all things to all men that I may instruct many to the profit of God's Holy Church and to the lustre of your imperial reign. So shall the grace of Almighty God toward me be not in vain and the largess of your bounty be of no avail. But I your servant lack in part the rarer books of scholastic lore which in my native land I had, thanks to the unsparing labour of my master and a little also to my own toil. This I tell your excellency on the chance that in your boundless and beloved wisdom you may be pleased to have me send some of our youths to take thence what we need, and return to France with the flowers of Britain; that the garden may not be confined to York alone but may bear fruit in Tours, and that the south wind blowing over the gardens of the Loire may be charged with perfume. Then shall it be once more as is said in Solomon's Song from which I quote: "Let my beloved come into his garden and eat his pleasant fruits." And he shall say to his young men: "Eat, O friends;

---

[1] The members of that literary circle which formed itself about Charlemagne and Alcuin assumed among themselves Hebrew or Greek or Latin names. Charlemagne himself was David; Alcuin, Horatius Flaccus; Angilbert, Homer; Enginhard, Calliopeus, etc.

drink, yea drink abundantly, O beloved. I sleep, but my heart waketh." Or that sentence of the prophet Isaiah which encourages us to learn wisdom: "Ho, every one that thirsteth, come ye to the waters, and he that hath no money; come ye, buy and eat; yea, come, buy wine and milk without money and without price."

This is a matter which has not escaped your most noble notice, how through all the pages of Holy Scripture we are urged to learn wisdom. In toiling toward the happy life nothing is more lofty, nothing more pleasant, nothing bolder against vices, nothing more praiseworthy in every place of dignity; and moreover, according to the words of philosophers, nothing is more essential to government, nothing more helpful in leading a moral life, than the beauty of wisdom, the praise of learning and the advantages of scholarship. Whence also wisest Solomon exclaims in its praise. "For wisdom is better than all things of price and no object of desire is to be compared with her. She exalts the meek, she brings honours to the great. Kings reign by her aid, and lawgivers decree justice. Happy are they who keep her ways, and happy are they who watch at her gates daily." O Lord King, exhort the youths who are in your excellency's palace to learn wisdom with all their might, and to gain it by daily toil while they are yet in the flush of youth, so that they may be deemed worthy to grow grey in honour, and by the help of wisdom may reach everlasting happiness. But I, according to the measure of my little talent, shall not be slothful to sow the seeds of wisdom among your servants in this region, mindful of the saying, "In the morning sow thy seed and in the evening withhold not thy hand: for thou knowest not whether shall prosper, either this or that, or whether they both alike shall be good."

In the morning I sowed in Britain studies which have flourished for a generation. Now as it were towards even I do not cease with blood grown cold to sow in Francia. And in both places I hope that by the Grace of God the seed may spring. The solace of my broken strength is this saying of Saint Jerome who in his letter to Nepotian has it: "Almost all the strength of an old man's body is changed and wisdom alone grows as the rest dwindles." And a little later: "The old age of those who have trained their youth in honest arts and have meditated in the law of the Lord day and night, becomes more learned with age, more polished by use, wiser by the lapse of time, and reaps the sweetest fruits of studies long grown old." In which letter whoever wishes may read much in praise of wisdom and the studies of the ancients, and may learn how the ancient sought to flourish in the beauty of wisdom. Ever advance toward this wisdom, beloved of God and praiseworthy on earth, and delight to recognize zeal; and adorn a nobility of worldly lineage with the greater nobility of the mind. In which may our Lord Jesus Christ, who is the virtue and wisdom of God, guard thee, exalt thee, and make thee enter the glory of his blessed and everlasting vision.

66. State of Learning in England in Alfred's Time

(From King Alfred's Introduction to the Anglo-Saxon translation of *Pastoral Care*,
by Pope Gregory the Great. English Text Society version, p. 2. Sweet, 1871)

This shows how learning in England had decayed since the days
when Alcuin was at York, due to the plundering and pillaging by
the Danes. England had once supplied scholars to Frankland,
but must now seek them abroad. King Alfred (king from 871 to
901) gives here a remarkable picture of the conditions of his time.

FIG. 10. ALFRED THE GREAT

In 1901, on the thousandth anniversary of
his death, a lofty bronze statue was set up
to his memory at Winchester, on which is
inscribed:

"Alfred found learning dead,
    And he restored it;
Education neglected,
    And he revived it;
The laws powerless,
    And he gave them force;
The Church debased,
    And he raised it;
The land ravaged by a fearful enemy,
    From which he delivered it."

King Alfred bids greet Bishop
Waerferth with loving words
and with friendship; and I let
it be known to thee that it has
very often come into my mind
what wise men there formerly
were throughout England, both
of sacred and secular orders;
and what happy times there
were then; and how the kings
who had power over the nation
in those days obeyed God and
his ministers; how they preserved peace, morality, and order at home, and at the same
time enlarged their territory
abroad; and how they prospered both in war and in wisdom; and also the sacred orders, how zealous they were
both in teaching and learning,
and in all the services they
owed to God; and how foreigners came to this land in search
of wisdom and instruction, the
which we should now have to
get from abroad if we were to
have them.

So general became the decay
of learning in England that
there were very few on this side of the Humber who could understand
the rituals in English, or translate a letter from Latin into English; and
I believe that there were not many beyond the Humber. There were so
few, in fact, that I cannot remember a single person south of the Thames
when I came to the throne. Thanks be to God Almighty that we now

have some teachers among us. And therefore I command thee to disengage thyself, as I believe thou art willing, from worldly matters as often as thou art able, that thou mayst apply the wisdom which God has given thee wherever thou canst. Consider what punishments would come upon us if we neither loved wisdom ourselves nor suffered other men to obtain it: we should love the name only of Christian, and very few of the Christian virtues.

When I thought of all this I remembered also how I saw the country before it had been ravaged and burned; how the churches throughout the whole of England stood filled with treasures and books. There was also a great multitude of God's servants, but they had very little knowledge of the books, for they could not understand anything of them because they were not written in their own language. As if they had said: "Our forefathers, who formerly held these places, loved wisdom, and through it they obtained wealth and bequeathed it to us. In this we can still see their traces, but we cannot follow them, and therefore we have lost both the wealth and the wisdom, because we would not incline our hearts after their example."

When I remembered all this, I wondered extremely that the good and wise men who were formerly all over England, and had learned perfectly all the books, did not wish to translate them into their own language. But again I soon answered myself and said, "Their own desire for learning was so great that they did not suppose that men would ever be so careless, and that learning would so decay; and they wished, moreover, that the wisdom in this land might increase with our knowledge of languages." Then I remembered how the law was first known in Hebrew, and when the Greeks had learned it how they translated the whole of it into their own language, and all other books besides. And again the Romans, when they had learned it, translated the whole of it, through learned interpreters, into their own language. And also all other Christian nations translated a part of it into their own language.

Therefore it seems better to me, if you agree, for us also to translate some of the books into the language which we can all understand; and for you to see to it, as can easily be done if we have tranquillity enough, that all the free-born youth now in England, who are rich enough to be able to devote themselves to it, be set to learn as long as they are not fit for any other occupation, until that they are well able to read English writing; and let those afterwards be taught more in the Latin language who are to continue learning, and be promoted to a higher rank.

When I remembered how the knowledge of Latin had decayed throughout England, and yet that many could read English writing, I began, among other various and manifold troubles of this kingdom, to translate into English the book which is called in Latin *Pastoralis*, and in English *Shepherd's Book*, sometimes word by word, and sometimes according to the sense, as I had learned it from Plegmund, my arch-bishop, and Asser, my bishop, and Grimbold, my mass-priest, and John, my mass-priest. And when I had learned it, as I could best understand it and most clearly interpret it, I translated it into English.

I will send a copy of this to every bishopric in my kingdom; and on each copy there shall be a clasp worth fifty mancuses. And I command, in God's name, that no man take the clasp from the book, or the book from the minster. It is uncertain how long there may be such learned bishops, as thanks be to God there now are nearly everywhere; therefore I wish these copies always to remain in their places, unless the bishop wishes to take them with him, or they be lent out anywhere, or any one wish to make a copy of them.

67. Alfred obtains Scholars from abroad

(Asser's *Life of Alfred the Great;* trans. by J. A. Giles, p. 70. London, 1885)

Asser, the companion and friend of the king, here describes his efforts to obtain scholars from Mercia (west central England, which had been overrun by the Danes) and from Frankland.

But God at that time, as some consolation to the king's benevolence, yielding to his complaint, sent certain lights to illuminate him, namely, Werefrith, bishop of the church of Worcester, a man well versed in divine scripture, who, by the king's command, first turned the books of the Dialogues of Pope Gregory and Peter, his disciple, from Latin into Saxon, and sometimes putting sense for sense, interpreted them with clearness and elegance. After him was Plegmund, a Mercian by birth, archbishop of the church of Canterbury, a venerable man, and endowed with wisdom; Ethelstan also, and Werewulf, his priests and chaplains, Mercians by birth and erudite. These four had been invited out of Mercia by King Alfred, who exalted them with many honours and powers in the kingdom of the West-Saxons, besides the privileges which archbishop Plegmund and bishop Werefrith enjoyed in Mercia. By their teaching and wisdom the king's desires increased unceasingly, and were gratified. Night and day, whenever he had leisure, he commanded such men as these to read books to him; for he never suffered himself to be without one of them, wherefore he possessed a knowledge of every book. . . .

But the king's commendable avarice could not be gratified even in this; wherefore he sent messengers beyond the sea to Gaul, to procure teachers, and he invited from thence Grimbald, priest and monk, a venerable man and good singer, adorned with every kind of ecclesiastical discipline and good morals, and most learned in holy scripture. He also obtained from thence John, also priest and monk, a man of most energetic talents, and learned in all kinds of literary science, and skilled in many other arts. By the teaching of these men the king's mind was much enlarged, and he enriched and honoured them with much influence.

68. The Education of the Son of King Alfred

(Asser's *Life of Alfred the Great;* trans. by J. A. Giles, p. 68. London, 1885)

Asser was Bishop of Sherborne and a familiar friend of the king. He died about 909. The following extract gives a picture of the kind of education given Alfred's son, Ethelwerd, and doubtless represents the best of the possible training at that time.

Ethelwerd, the youngest (of Alfred's children), by the divine counsels and the admirable prudence of the king, was consigned to the schools of learning where, with the children of almost all the nobility of the country, and many also who were not noble, he prospered under the diligent care of his teachers. Books in both languages, namely Latin and Saxon, were read in the school. They also learned to write, so that before they were of an age to practice manly arts, namely, hunting and such pursuits as befit noblemen, they became studious and clever in the liberal arts. Edward and Ethelswitha were bred up in the king's court and received great attention from their attendants and nurses; nay, they continue to this day, with the love of all about them, and showing affability, and even gentleness, towards all, both natives and foreigners, and in complete subjection to their father; nor, among their other studies which appertain to this life and are fit for noble youths, are they suffered to pass their time idly and unprofitably without learning the liberal arts; for they have carefully learned the Psalms and Saxon books, especially the Saxon poems, and are continually in the habit of making use of books.

69. Ninth-Century Plan of the Monastery at Saint Gall

(After an old plan, reconstructed by Professor Robert Willis, *Arch. Jour.*, v, 86)

This monastery was located at Saint Gall, in the canton of that name, in Switzerland. In 614 A.D. an Irish hermit, Saint Gall, built his cell in the thick forest there, and lived there until his death, in 640. It then became a shrine for pilgrims, and about 750 was transformed into a Benedictine monastery. This monastery grew rapidly, and for the next three centuries was one of the chief seats of learning and education in Europe. The plan of the monastery, at the height of its development, is reproduced on the following page, and the explanation given below the plan will make it intelligible.

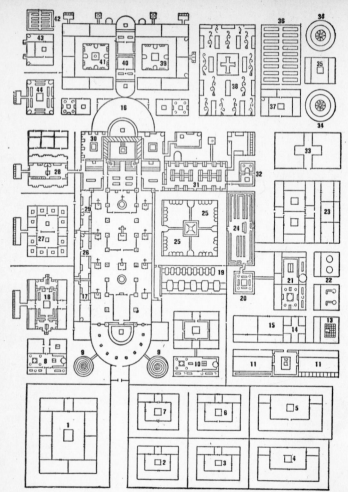

FIG. 11. NINTH-CENTURY PLAN OF THE MONASTERY OF SAINT GALL
SWITZERLAND

1. Large building unmarked on the original plan. 2. Servants' quarters. 3. Pig-
sty. 4. Stable. 5. Cattle-shed. 6. Goat-house. 7. Sheep-shed. 8. Brew-house
and bake-house for guests. 9. Towers with spiral staircases. 10. Guest-house
for the poor, with brew-house and bake-house attached. 11. Another stable.
12. Quarters for servants. 13. House for drying fruits. 14. Storehouse for
grain for brewing. 15. Cooper shop and wood-turning shop. 16. Church. 17.
Porter's lodge. 18. House for greater guests. 19. Cellar with storehouses above.
20. Kitchen for monks. 21. Brew-house and bake-house for monks. 22. Buildings with mills. 23. Shops of shoemakers, saddlers, carvers, tanners, goldsmiths,
blacksmiths, fullers, shield-makers, and sword-makers. 24. 1st floor, refectory; 2d
floor, wardrobe. 25. Garth with cloisters. 26. Schoolmaster's lodging. 27. School.
28. Abbot's house. 29. Home of visiting monks. 30. 1st floor, scriptorium; 2d
floor, library. 31. Dormitory, heating apparatus on 1st floor. 32. Baths. 33.
Granary and threshing-floor. 34. Hen-houses and duck-houses. 35. Poultry-keeper's
house. 36. Kitchen garden. 37. Gardener's house. 38. Cemetery and orchard.
39. House for novices. 40. Chapel for novices and invalids. 41. Infirmary. 42.
Garden of medicinal plants. 43. Physician's house. 44. House for blood-letting.

CHAPTER VII

EDUCATION DURING THE EARLY MIDDLE AGES

II. SCHOOLS ESTABLISHED AND INSTRUCTION PROVIDED

THE Readings of this chapter deal with the same period following the downfall of Roman authority as did the preceding chapter, but with the different types of schools established and the kind of education provided by the Church to enable it to meet the needs of the age, and help it in its struggle against barbarism.

The first selection, from Leach (70), clearly distinguishes between two types of schools — the song and the grammar schools; while the one from Mullinger (71) does the same for the monastic and the episcopal (or cathedral) schools. The latter also mentions the more famous schools of each type during the early Middle Ages. Selection 72 outlines the duties of the different cathedral officers, particularly those of the Precentor and the Schoolmaster. Another type of later Middle-Age educational foundation is described in the selection (73), relating to the grants for founding a chantry school. These chantry grants began about the close of the period under consideration, were later extended to include grammar schools (142), and became quite common during the later Middle Ages.

The subject-matter of instruction was naturally a survival from the old Roman schools, and was known as the *Seven Liberal Arts*. The selection from Rhabanus Maurus, describing each of these Seven Liberal Arts (74 a-g), gives a good outline of the uses and subject-matter of each of these great mediæval disciplines, and reveals the meager scope of the learning of the time. The Colloquy of Abbot Ælfric (75) is a good sample of the simple Latin reading matter in common use, as a sort of reading primer, before taking up classical or sacred writings following the study of grammar.

During the early Middle Ages the great subject of study was Grammar, and the importance of a study of this fundamental art is well set forth in the extract from Quintilian (76). That but little could have been done, during this time, in the arts having a scientific basis, due to the very meager general knowledge of the day even among the so-called learned classes, is well evidenced by the two extracts from the thirteenth-century Encyclopædia of Bartholomew Anglius (77 a-b), relating to the chemical elements and the movements of the planets. That this book continued to be translated into the vernaculars, and to be reissued for three centuries after its first compilation, tells much as to the need it met and filled. The selection from Cott, listing a tenth-century schoolmaster's books (78), is also interesting as showing the meager library, both in number of volumes and scope of subject-matter, of a scholar of the time.

The struggle of the Church to enforce law and order during this period was a long and a difficult one. One of the means tried was that of the proclamation of a Truce of God. One of the earliest of these, declaring three bloodless days a week, is reproduced (79). Another means was the adoption and sanctification of chivalry, which was used to refine and civilize the barbarian nobility. A good description of such utilization of chivalry by the Church is given in the selection reproduced from Gautier (80). For the peasant and serf the educational influence of the Church was exercised largely through its services, a good description of which is given by Draper (81).

Toward the latter part of the darkest period of the Middle Ages the Church, having established itself as the master, and seeing that the tide was turning, began to exercise a mild pressure for some form of education for certain of the sons of freemen. A good example of this is reproduced from the Statutes of Winchester Diocese, in England (82). The Church also evolved a supervisory system for the schools it had created, under a supervising principal (*Scholasticus; Precentor*), and with teachers' licenses (83), legal forms for appointment (84 a), and oaths of office (84 b) to be subscribed to before entering upon the duties of a position. These forms are the precursors of the teacher's certificate, notice of appointment, and contract of to-day.

70. Song and Grammar Schools in England

(Leach, A. F., *The Schools of Mediæval England*, p. 6. London, 1915)

The writer from whom the following selection is taken is a foremost English authority on the history of early education in England. Of the song and grammar schools he writes:

These Song Schools became even more general than the Grammar Schools. The Song School at Rochester is expressly mentioned by Bede in Theodore's time as being derived from Canterbury. Putta, whom Archbishop Theodore found at Rochester, and made bishop

FIG. 12. INTERIOR OF A NORMAN SCHOOL, TWELFTH CENTURY
(After Wright, *Homes of Other Days*, p. 130)
In the original cut the bench on which the scholars are seated forms a complete circle. To the left are two writers, while to the right is the teacher, who seems to be lecturing. In the center is the teacher's desk

there, is described "as well instructed in ecclesiastical learning, . . . and especially skilled in the art of chanting in church after the Roman fashion, which he had learnt from the pupils of the blessed Pope Gregory himself." This Putta, when Rochester was ravaged by the King of Mercia in 675, settled down as a simple parish priest in Mercia and went about "teaching church singing (*ecclesiæ carmina*) wherever he was asked."

The twin schools of Grammar and Song, which have often been confounded as if they were one school, are found side by side in connexion with all the great churches, that is in all the great centers of population, from the age of Augustine and Ethelbert to the age of Cranmer and Edward VI, as distinct foundations, completely differentiated in function as they were in their teaching, and generally in their government. In small places they were sometimes united under one master. Though as late as 1519 a school-author, who had been Headmaster first of Eton and then of Winchester, William Horman, asserted in echo of Quintilian, himself copying the Greeks, that, without a knowledge of music, grammar cannot be perfect, yet the teaching of singing and music, so often rashly asserted to be the main work of the pre-Reformation school, and the Song Schools which gave it, were always subordinate and secondary to the teaching of Grammar and the Grammar School. To a large extent the Song Schools performed the function of Elementary Schools, while the Grammar Schools were the Secondary Schools, and, before the days of Universities, gave university or higher education as well.

71. The Episcopal and Monastic Schools

(Mullinger, J. B., *The Schools of Charles the Great*, pp. 130–33. London, 1877)

The first study of any importance in English of the work of Charlemagne and Alcuin was the one from which the following selection is taken, a book now difficult to obtain. Mr. Mullinger here contrasts the work of the episcopal and monastic schools, and throws much light on educational conditions during the early mediæval period.

From this time (817), we are accordingly able to distinguish, with somewhat more precision, the different training of the monastic and episcopal schools. Of the latter, indeed, throughout the ninth century, it is impossible to give much more than a conjectural account, as there existed no systematic organization. Léon Maître, in his endeavor to supply the want, presents us with a series of confused gleanings, the greater part of which apply evidently to the schools of the monasteries. Close to the cathedral precincts, and under the immediate supervision of the bishop, a school for boys, all destined to become priests, was confided to the care of one of the canons, known from his office as the *scholasticus*. . . .

The education provided in these schools may be described as a kind of minor to the Benedictine major. In the range of subjects it probably went little beyond the teaching of the schools of Cassian, but its method was more careful and efficient. We may picture to ourselves a group of lads seated on the floor, which was strewn with clean straw, their waxen tablets in their hands, and busily engaged in noting down the words read by the *scholasticus* from his manuscript volume. So rarely did the pupil, in those days, gain access to a book, that to *read* (*legere*) became synonymous with to *teach*. The scholars traced the words on their tablets, and afterwards, when their notes had been corrected by the master, transferred them to a little parchment volume, the treasured depository, with many, of nearly all the learning they managed to acquire in life. We have already investigated the probable extent and character of that learning, and it may safely be assumed that in the cathedral school the customary limits were seldom passed. In the ninth century, at least, only two examples of Church education in

Frankland stand forth as examples of a higher culture — the one, that at Orleans, under Theodulfus; the other, that at Rheims.

The lively interest taken by Theodulfus in everything that related to the education of his day is attested by numerous facts, . . . Ably seconded by the poet Wulfin, Theodulfus raised the school at Orleans to considerable eminence. It became especially famous for the number, beauty, and accuracy of its manuscripts.

Yet more renowned was the episcopal school at Rheims, which, under the protection of Hincmar, the oracle and arbiter of the state in the days of Charles the Bald, and under the teaching of archbishop Fulk, of Remy of Auxerre, and of Hucbald, claims the proud distinction of having preserved, in this century, that tradition of learning which links the episcopal schools with the University of Paris.

But throughout the ninth century, and indeed for the greater part of the period known as "the Benedictine era" — the four centuries preceding the reign of Philip Augustus — the work of the episcopal schools was completely eclipsed by that of the monasteries. At Corbey, near Amiens, under Adelhard and Wala, who both retired thither, and under Paschasius Radbertus, was gathered a society eminent for its learn-

FIG. 13. A SCHOOL OF MENDICANT MONKS
(After a miniature of manuscript No. 21,252 in the Burgundy Library, Brussels. The miniature dates from the early fifteenth century)

ing and illustrious as a parent foundation. It disappears beneath the waves of the Norman invasion; but its namesake, New Corbey, in Saxony, sustained with equal reputation, and more auspicious fortunes, the scholarly traditions of the age. The great abbey of Saint Riquier, under the rule of Angilbert, rivalled the school at Rheims in literary activity; and an inventory of its possessions, made in the year 831 by the direction of Lewis the Pious, included a library of no less than 231 volumes. The abbey of Saint Martin at Metz, under the rule of Aldricus, was scarcely less celebrated; a Bible presented by its monks to Charles the Bald and the missal of Bishop Drogo are still preserved, and rank among the most valued specimens of ninth-century art. The society of Saint Mihiel-sur-Meuse enjoyed the instruction of Smaragdus, whose compend from Donatus frequently appears in the catalogues of the libraries of the period. Saint Bertin, in the diocese of Cambrai, laid claim to the distinguished honour of having educated Grimbald, King Alfred's able seconder in his efforts toward a restoration of learning in England. At Ferrières, in the Gâtinais, the genius of Lupus Servatus shone forth in the troublous and disheartening period which immediately preceded and followed upon the division of the empire.

The South and South-West present fewer evidences of culture; and in the ninth century no foundation, either in Normandy or Brittany, can be said to have reached celebrity; while in Aquitaine, if we except the labours of Benedict of Aniane in the diocese of Montpellier, the efforts of Lewis the Pious on behalf of his patrimonial kingdom seem to have been baffled by the frequent recurrence of war.

72. The School at Salisbury Cathedral

(As provided for in the *Foundation Statutes* of the Cathedral, of 1091 A.D.; trans. by A. F. Leach)

This extract from the Cathedral Statutes outlines the duties of the different church officers, and particularly sets forth the authority of the Precentor and Schoolmaster connected therewith.

The Institution of Osmund

These are the dignities and customs of the church of Salisbury, which I, Osmund, bishop of that church, in the name of the Holy Trinity, in the year of our Lord 1091, established and granted to the persons and canons of the same church, with the advice of the lords, the archbishop and other my co-bishops whose names are subscribed, and with the assent of the lord King William; namely, that Dean and Chanter, Chancellor and Treasurer shall be continually resident in the church at Salisbury, without any kind of excuse. . . . Nothing can excuse the canons from being personally resident in the church of Salisbury, except attendance at the schools and the service of the lord King, who can have one in his chapel, and the archbishop one, and the bishop three.

The dean presided over all canons and vicars as regards the cure of souls and correction of conduct.

The precentor ought to rule the choir as to chanting and can raise or lower the chant.

The treasurer is pre-eminent in keeping the treasures and ornaments and managing the lights. In like manner the chancellor in ruling the school and correcting the books.

The archdeacons excel in the superintendence of parishes and the cure of souls.

Dean and precentor, treasurer and chancellor, receive double, the rest of the canons single commons.

The sub-dean holds from the dean the archdeaconry of the city and suburbs, the succentor from the precentor all that pertains to the singing. If the dean is away from the church the sub-dean fills his place, and the succentor in like manner the precentor's.

The schoolmaster ought to hear and determine the lessons, and carry the church seal, compose letters and deeds and mark the readers on the table, and the precentor in like manner the singers. . . .

73. Foundation Grant for a Chantry School

(Foundation Grant of Aldwincle Chantry; trans. by A. F. Leach)

A very common form of later mediæval school foundation was what was known as the Chantry, a priest being provided for in an endowment to say prayers for the repose of some soul, and being required to do some teaching besides to occupy his time. This selection illustrates such a foundation. The priest here provided for was also to give instruction in spelling and reading to six poor boys of the town. The grant is dated November 8, 1489, but in substance is like many much earlier documents.

To all sons of holy mother church . . . William Chamber, of Aldwincle, in the county of Northampton, health. . . .

. . . I make known to you all by these presents that I . . . have given . . . to Sir John Seliman, chaplain, for his maintenance and that of his successors . . . celebrating divine service every day at the altar of Saint Mary the Virgin, in the parish church of All Saints . . . for all the souls aforesaid for ever my manor of Armeston [and other property].

That this ordinance may endure for ever I will and ordain that the chantry aforesaid shall be for ever called "The chantry of William Chamber, William Aldwincle and Elizabeth their wife," and that the chaplain for the time being shall every day . . . celebrate mass at the altar aforesaid. . . .

Moreover I will and ordain that the said chaplain for the time being shall teach and instruct, in spelling and reading, six of the poorest boys of the town of Aldwincle aforesaid, to be named by me and my wife Elizabeth while we are alive, and after our death three named by the rector of Saint Peter's church in Aldwincle aforesaid, and the other three by the chaplain for the time being, freely, without demanding or taking any remuneration from their parents or friends; and the boys, when they have been so instructed and taught, shall say every night in All Saints' church in Aldwincle aforesaid, at the direction of the chaplain aforesaid, for our souls and the souls of all the faithful departed, the psalm "Out of the deep," with the prayers "Incline thine ear" and "God of the faithful."

74. The Seven Liberal Arts

(Rhabanus Maurus, *Education of the Clergy;* trans. by F. V. N. Painter, from the German text of Schulz, Gansen, and Keller, in his *Great Pedagogical Essays.* American Book Co., New York, 1905. Reproduced by permission.)

Rhabanus Maurus (784?–856) was a pupil of Alcuin at Tours, and afterwards became *Scholasticus* of the monastery at Fulda (818); was Abbot there from 822 to 842; and in 847 was made Archbishop of Mainz. He was a devoted student of the Seven Liberal Arts and of classical and Biblical literatures. The work from which the following extract is taken was written in 819.

The first of the liberal arts is Grammar, the second Rhetoric, the third Dialectic, the fourth Arithmetic, the fifth Geometry, the sixth Music, the seventh Astronomy.

(*a*) *Grammar.* Grammar takes its name from the written character, as the derivation of the word indicates. The definition of grammar is this: Grammar is the science which teaches us to explain the poets and historians; it is the art which qualifies us to write and speak correctly. Grammar is the source and foundation of the liberal arts. It should be taught in every Christian school, since the art of writing and speaking correctly is attained through it. How could one understand the sense of the spoken word or the meaning of letters and syllables, if one had not learned this before from grammar? How could one know about metrical feet, accent, and verses, if grammar had not given one knowledge of them? How should one learn to know the articulation of discourse, the advantages of figurative language, the laws of word formation, and the correct forms of words, if one had not familiarized himself with the art of grammar?

All the forms of speech, of which secular science makes use in its writings, are found repeatedly employed in the Holy Scriptures. Every one, who reads the sacred Scriptures with care, will discover that our (biblical) authors have used derivative forms of speech in greater and more manifold abundance than would have been supposed and believed. There are in the Scriptures not only examples of all kinds of figurative expressions, but the designations of some of them by name; as allegory, riddle, parable. A knowledge of these things is proved to be necessary in relation to the interpretation of those passages of Holy Scripture which admit of a two-fold sense; an interpretation strictly literal would lead to absurdities. Everywhere we are to consider whether that, which we do not at once understand, is to be apprehended as a figurative expression in some sense. A knowledge of prosody, which is offered in grammar, is not dishonorable, since among the Jews, as Saint Jerome testifies, the Psalter resounds sometimes with iambics, sometimes with Alcaics, sometimes chooses sonorous Sapphics, and sometimes even does not disdain catalectic feet. But in Deuteronomy and Isaiah, as in Solomon and Job, as Josephus and Origen have pointed out, there are hexameters and pentameters. Hence this art, though it may be secular, has nothing unworthy in itself; it should rather be learned as thoroughly as possible.

(b) *Rhetoric.* According to the statements of teachers, rhetoric is the art of using secular discourse effectively in the circumstances of daily life. From this definition rhetoric seems indeed to have reference merely to secular wisdom. Yet it is not foreign to ecclesiastical instruction. Whatever the preacher and herald of the divine law, in his instruction, brings forth in an eloquent and becoming manner; whatever in his written exposition he knows how to clothe in adequate and impressive language, he owes to his acquaintance with this art. Whoever at the proper time makes himself familiar with this art, and faithfully follows its rules in speaking and writing, needs not count it as something blameworthy. On the contrary, whoever thoroughly learns it so that he acquires the ability to proclaim God's word, performs a true work. Through rhetoric anything is proved true or false. Who would have the courage to maintain that the defenders of truth should stand weaponless in the presence of falsehood, so that those, who dare to represent false, should know how by their discourse to win the favor and sympathy of the hearers, and that, on the other hand, the friends of truth should not be able to do this; that those should know how to present falsehood briefly, clearly, and with the semblance of truth, and that the latter, on the contrary, should clothe the truth in such an exposition, that listening would become a burden, apprehension of the truth a weariness, and faith in the truth an impossibility?

(c) *Dialectic.* Dialectic is the science of the understanding, which fits us for investigations and definitions, for explanations, and for distinguishing the true from the false. It is the science of sciences. It teaches how to teach others; it teaches learning itself; in it the reason marks and manifests itself according to its nature, efforts, and activities; it alone is capable of knowing; it not only will, but can lead others to knowledge; its conclusions lead us to an apprehension of our being and of our origin; through it we apprehend the origin and activity of the good, of Creator and creature; it teaches us to discover the truth and to unmask falsehood; it teaches us to draw conclusions; it shows us what is valid in argument and what is not; it teaches us to recognize what is contrary to the nature of things; it teaches us to distinguish in controversy the true, the probable, and the wholly false; by means of this science we are able to investigate everything with penetration, to determine its nature with certainty, and to discuss it with circumspection.

Therefore the clergy must understand this excellent art and constantly reflect upon its laws, in order that they may be able keenly to pierce the craftiness of errorists, and to refute their fatal fallacies.

(d) *Arithmetic.* Arithmetic is the science of pure extension determinable by number; it is the science of numbers. Writers on secular

FIG. 14. A SCHOOL: A LESSON IN LOGIC

(After a woodcut at the end of a copy of the third edition of *Parvus et Magnus Chato*, now in the library of Saint John's College, Oxford, and which was printed by Caxton in 1481)

science assign it, under the head of mathematics, to the first place, because it does not presuppose any of the other departments. Music, geometry, and astronomy, on the contrary, need the help of arithmetic; without it they cannot arise or exist. We should know, however, that the learned Hebrew Josephus, in his work on Antiquities, Chapter VIII of Book I, makes the statement that Abraham brought arithmetic and astronomy to the Egyptians; but that they as a people of penetrating mind, extensively developed from these germs the other sciences. The holy Fathers were right in advising those eager for knowledge to cultivate arithmetic, because in large measure it turns the mind from fleshly desires, and furthermore awakens the wish to comprehend what with God's help we can merely receive with the heart. Therefore the significance of number is not to be underestimated. Its very great

value for an interpretation of many passages of Holy Scripture is manifest to all who exhibit zeal in their investigations. Not without good
reason is it said in praise of God, "Thou hast ordained all things by
measure, number, and weight." (Book of Wisdom XI, 21.)

But every number, through its peculiar qualities, is so definite that
none of the others can be like it. They are all unequal and different.
The single numbers are different; the single numbers are limited; but
all are infinite.

Those with whom Plato stands in especial honor will not make bold
to esteem numbers lightly, as if they were of no consequence for the
knowledge of God. He teaches that God made the world out of numbers. And among us the prophet says of God, "He forms the world by
number." And in the Gospel the Savior says, "The very hairs of your
head are all numbered.". . . Ignorance of numbers leaves many things
unintelligible that are expressed in the Holy Scripture in a derivative
sense or with a mystical meaning.

(e) *Geometry.* We now come to the discussion of geometry. It is an
exposition of form proceeding from observation; it is also a very common means of demonstration among philosophers, who, to adduce at
once the most full-toned evidence, declare that their Jupiter made use
of astronomy in his works. I do not know indeed whether I should
find praise or censure in this declaration of the philosophers, that Jupiter engraved upon the vault of the skies precisely what they themselves draw in the sand of the earth.

When this in a proper manner is transferred to God, the Almighty
Creator, this assumption may perhaps come near the truth. If this
statement seems admissible, the Holy Trinity makes use of geometry
in so far as it bestows manifold forms and images upon the creatures
which up to the present day it has called into being, as in its adorable
omnipotence it further determines the course of the stars, as it pre-
scribes their courses to the planets, and as it assigns to the fixed stars
their unalterable position. For every excellent and well-ordered arrangement can be reduced to the special requirements of this science. . . .

This science found realization also at the building of the tabernacle
and the temple; the same measuring rod, circles, spheres, hemispheres,
quadrangles, and other figures were employed. The knowledge of all
this brings to him, who is occupied with it, no small gain for his spiritual culture.

(f) *Music.* Music is the science of time intervals as they are perceived in tones. This science is as eminent as it is useful. He who is a
stranger to it is not able to fulfil the duties of an ecclesiastical officer in
a suitable manner. A proper delivery in reading and a lovely rendering
of the Psalms in the church are regulated by a knowledge of this science. Yet it is not only good reading and beautiful psalmody that we

owe to music; through it alone do we become capable of celebrating in the most solemn manner every divine service.   Music penetrates all the activities of our life, in this sense namely, that we above all carry out the commands of the Creator and bow with a pure heart to his commands; all that we speak, all that makes our hearts beat faster, is shown through the rhythm of music united with the excellence of harmony; for music is the science which teaches us agreeably to change tones in duration and pitch.   When we employ ourselves with good pursuits in life, we show ourselves thereby disciples of this art; so long as we do what is wrong, we do not feel ourselves drawn to music.   Even heaven and earth, as everything that happens here through the arrangement of the Most High, is nothing but music, as Pythagoras testifies that this world was created by music and can be ruled by it.   Even with the Christian religion music is most intimately united; thus it is possible that to him, who does not know even a little music, many things remain closed and hidden.

(g) *Astronomy*.   There remains yet astronomy which, as some one has said, is a weighty means of demonstration to the pious, and to the curious a grievous torment.   If we seek to investigate it with a pure heart and an ample mind, then it fills us, as the ancients said, with great love for it.   For what will it not signify, that we soar in spirit to the sky, that with penetration of mind we analyze that sublime structure, that we, in part at least, fathom with the keenness of our logical faculties what mighty space has enveloped in mystery!   The world itself, according to the assumption of some, is said to have the shape of a sphere, in order that in its circumference it may be able to contain the different forms of things.   Thus Seneca, in agreement with the philosophers of ancient times, composed a work under the title, "The Shape of the Earth."

Astronomy, of which we now speak, teaches the laws of the stellar world.   The stars can take their place or carry out their motion only in the manner established by the Creator, unless by the will of the Creator a miraculous change takes place.   Thus we read that Joshua commanded the sun to stand still in Gibeon, that in the days of King Josiah the sun went backward ten degrees, and that at the death of the Lord the sun was darkened for three hours.   We call such occurrences miracles, because they contradict the usual course of things, and therefore excite wonder.

That part of astronomy, which is built up on the investigation of natural phenomena in order to determine the course of the sun, of the moon, and stars, and to effect a proper reckoning of time, the Christian clergy should seek to learn with the utmost diligence, in order through the knowledge of laws brought to light and through the valid and convincing proof of the given means of evidence, to place themselves in a position, not only to determine the course of past years according to truth and reality, but also for further times to draw confident conclusions, and to fix the time of Easter and all other festivals and holy days and to announce to the congregation the proper celebration of them.

The seven liberal arts of the philosophers, which Christians should learn for their utility and advantage, we have, as I think, sufficiently discussed. We have this yet to add. When those, who are called philosophers, have in their expositions or in their writings, uttered perchance some truth, which agrees with our faith, we should not handle it timidly, but rather take it as from its unlawful possessors and apply it to our own use.

75. A Mediæval Latin Colloquy

(Leach, A. F., *Educational Charters*, pp. 37–47. London, 1911)

After boys had learned to read Latin words and had begun to study the grammar, often a simple Latin colloquy was read before taking up sacred or classical writers. The following, composed by the English Abbot Ælfric, in 1005, is illustrative of the type and interesting for the instruction as to proper living which it contains.

Boys. Master, we children ask you to teach us to speak correctly for we are unlearned and speak corruptly.

Master. What do you want to say?

FIG. 15. A MEDIÆVAL SCHOOL

(From the *Manuale scholarium*. Reproduced from Fick's *Auf Deutschland's hohen Schulen*)

B. What do we care what we say so long as we speak correctly and say what is useful, not old-womanish or improper.

M. Will you be flogged while learning?

B. We would rather be flogged while learning than remain ignorant; but we know that you will be kind to us and not flog us unless you are obliged.

M. I ask you what you are saying to me. What work have you?

1st Boy. I am a professed monk and I sing seven times a day with the brethren and I am busy with reading and singing; and meanwhile I want to learn to speak Latin.

M. What do these companions of yours know?

1st Boy. Some are ploughmen, others shepherds, some are cowherds, some too are hunters, some are fishermen, some hawkers, some merchants, some shoemakers, some salters, some bakers of the place.

M. What do you say, ploughboy, how do you do your work?

P. Oh, sir, I work very hard. I go out at dawn to drive the oxen to the field, and yoke them to the plough; however hard the winter I dare not stay at home for fear of my master; and having yoked the oxen and made the plough-share and coulter fast to the plough, every day I have to plough a whole acre or more.

M. Have you any one with you?

P. I have a boy to drive the oxen with the goad, and he is now hoarse with cold and shouting.

M. What more do you do in the day?

P. A great deal more. I have to fill the oxen's bins with hay, and give them water, and carry the dung outside.

M. Oh, it is hard work.

P. Yes, it is hard work, because I am not free.

(So they go on through all the other occupations. At the end there is a discussion as to who does the best work and which is the most useful, and a counsellor is called in to decide the question. He decides that divine service comes first, but among secular crafts agriculture, because it feeds all. Then the smith and the wheelwright point out that the ploughman is no use without the plough which they make.)

The counsellor says: Oh, all you good fellows and good workers, let us end this dispute and have peace and harmony among us, and let each help the other by his craft, and let us all meet at the ploughman's, where we find food for ourselves and fodder for our horses. And this is the advice I give all workmen, that each of them should do his work as well as he can, as the man who neglects his work is dismissed from his work. Whether you are a priest or a monk, a layman or a soldier, apply yourself to that, and be what you are, as it is a great loss and shame for a man not to be what he is and what he ought to be.

M. Now, children, how do you like this speech?

B. We like it very much, but what you say is too deep for us, and is beyond our age. But talk to us in a way we can follow so that we may understand what you are talking about.

M. Well, I ask you why you are learning so diligently?

B. Because we do not want to be like beasts, who know nothing but grass and water.

(The master then goes off into a disquisition whether they want to be worldly wise, full of craft, or otherwise. They complain again that he is too deep for them.)

But talk to us so that we may understand, not so profoundly.

M. Well, I will do what you ask. You, boy, what did you do to-day?

B. I did many things. At night when I heard the bell, I got out of bed and went to church and sang the nocturne with the brethren. Then we sang the martyrology and lauds; after that, prime and the seven psalms with litanies and first mass; next tierce, and did the mass of the day; after that we sang sext, and ate and drank and slept; and then we got up again and sang nones, and now here we are before you ready to listen to what you tell us.

M. When will you sing vespers or compline?

B. When it's time.

M. Were you flogged to-day?

B. I was not, because I was very careful.

M. And how about the others?

B. Why do you ask me that? I daren't tell you our secrets. Each one knows whether he was flogged or not.

M. Where do you sleep?

B. In the dormitory with the brethren.

M. Who calls you to nocturnes?

B. Sometimes I hear the bell, and get up; sometimes my master wakes me with a ground-ash.

M. All you good children and clever scholars, your teacher exhorts you to keep the commandments of God, and behave properly everywhere. Walk quietly when you hear the church bells and go into church, and bow to the holy altars, and stand quietly and sing in unison, and ask pardon for your sins, and go out again without playing, to the cloister or to school.

76. Quintilian on the Importance of Grammar

(Quintilian, *Institutes of Oratory*, book I, chap. IV; trans. by J. S. Watson. London, 1892)

Though Quintilian's treatise existed only in fragmentary form until 1416, when a copy was found at the monastery of Saint Gall, in Switzerland (**R. 127**), Quintilian's ideas, which represented the best Roman practice, were followed in the teaching of Grammar in the schools of the Middle Ages. The following selection from his *Institutes* outlines the many different aspects of this important subject.

1. In regard to the boy who has attained facility in reading and writing, the next object is instruction from the grammarians (language masters; teachers of languages and literature). Nor is it of importance whether I speak of the Greek or Latin grammarian, though I am inclined to think that the Greek should take the precedence.

2. Both have the same method. This profession, then, distinguished as it is, most compendiously, into two parts, the art *of speaking correctly*, and the *illustration of the poets*, carries more beneath the surface than it shows on its front.

3. For not only is the *art of writing* combined with that of speaking, but *correct reading* also precedes illustration, and with all these is joined the exercise of *judgment*, which the old grammarians (of Alexandria), indeed, used with such severity, that they not only allowed themselves to distinguish certain verses with a particular mark of censure, and to remove, as spurious, certain books which had been inscribed with false titles, from their sets, but even brought some authors within their canon, and excluded others altogether from classification.

4. Nor is it sufficient to have read the poets only; every class of writers must be studied, not simply for matter, but for words, which often receive their authority from writers. Nor can grammar be complete without a knowledge of music, since the grammarian has to speak of metre and rhythm; nor if he is ignorant of astronomy, can he understand the poets, who, to say nothing of other matters, so often allude to the rising and setting of the stars in marking the seasons; nor must he be unacquainted with philosophy, both on account of numbers of passages, in almost all poems, drawn from the most abstruse subtleties of physical investigation, and also on account of Empedocles among the Greeks, and Varro and Lucretius among the Latins, who have committed the precepts of philosophy to verse.

5. The grammarian has also need of no small portion of eloquence, that he may speak aptly and fluently on each of those subjects which are here mentioned. Those therefore are by no means to be regarded who deride this science as trifling and empty, for unless it lays a sure foundation for the future orator, whatever superstructure you raise will fall; it is a science which is necessary to the young, pleasing to the old, and an agreeable companion in retirement, and which alone, of all departments of learning, has in it more service than show.

6. Let no man, therefore, look down on the elements of grammar as small matters; not because it requires great labour to distinguish consonants from vowels, and to divide them into the proper number of semivowels and mutes, but because, to those entering the recesses, as it were, of this temple, there will appear much subtlety on points, which may not only sharpen the wits of boys, but may exercise even the deepest erudition and knowledge.

77. The Elements, and the Movements of the Planets

(Translated from the Encyclopædia of Bartholomew Anglius, entitled *On the Properties of Things*, written about the middle of the thirteenth century. Edited by Robt. Steele, *Mediæval Lore*. London, 1893)

The Encyclopædia of scientific matters from which the following is taken was a small one-volume work, written in Latin, probably before 1260, and was intended to explain to the priest and preaching friars, as well as to the small educated class then beginning to form, the properties of natural things, and the allusions to natural objects met with in the Scriptures. In time it became very popular in France, Holland, and Spain as well, being translated into French in 1372, and into Spanish, Dutch, and English in 1397. After the invention of printing, and before the rise of the newer scientific ideas, it was repeatedly reissued in both the Latin and the native languages.

The two extracts which follow illustrate physical and astronomical conceptions toward the close of the Middle Ages.

(a) Of the Elements

Elements are simple, and the least particles of a body that is compound. And it is called least touching us, for it is not perceived by wits of feeling. For it is the least part and last in undoing of the body, as it is first in composition. And is called simple, not for an element is simple without any composition, but for it hath no parts that compound it, that be diverse in kind and in number as some medlied bodies have: as it fareth in metals of the which some parts be diverse; for some part is air, and some is earth. But each part of fire is fire, and so of others. Elements are four, and so there are four qualities of elements, of the which every body is composed and made as of matter. The four elements are Earth, Water, Fire, and Air, of the which each hath his proper qualities. Four be called the first and principal qualities, that is hot, cold, dry, and moist: they are called the first qualities because they slide first from the elements into the things that be made of elements. Two of these qualities are called Active, heat and coldness. The other are dry and wetness and are called Passive.

(b) Of Double Moving of the Planets

All the planets move by double moving; by their own kind moving out of the west into the east, against the moving of the firmament; and by the other moving out of the east into the west, and that by ravishing of the firmament. By violence of the firmament they are ravished every day out of the east into the west. And by their kindly moving, by the which they labour to move against the firmament, some of them fulfil their course in shorter time, and some in longer time. And that is for their courses are some more and some less. For Saturn abideth in every sign xxx months, and full endeth its course in xxx years. Jupiter dwelleth in every sign one year, and full endeth its course in xij years. Mars abideth in every sign xlv days, and full endeth its course in two years. The sun abideth in every sign xxx days and ten hours and a half, and full endeth its course in ccclxv days and vj hours. Mercury abideth in every sign xxviij days and vj hours, and full endeth its course in cccxxxviij days. Venus abideth in every sign 29 days, and full endeth its course in 348 days. The moon abideth in every sign two days and a half, and six hours and one bisse less, and full endeth its course from point to point in 27 days and 8 hours. And by entering and out passing of these 7 stars into the 12 signs and out thereof every thing that is bred and corrupt in this nether world is varied and disposed, and therefore in the philosopher's book Mesalath it is read in this manner: 'The Highest made the world to the likeness of a sphere, and made the highest circle above it movable in the earth, pight and stedfast in the middle thereof; not withdrawing toward the left side, nor toward the right side, and set the other elements moveable, and made them move by the moving of 7 planets, and all other stars help the planets in their working and kind.' Every creature upon Earth hath a manner inclination by the moving of the planets, and destruction cometh by moving and working of planets. The working of them varieth and is diverse by diversity of climates and countries. For they work one manner of thing about the land of blue men, and another about the land and country of Slavens. . . . In the signs the planets move and abate with double moving, and move by accidental ravishing of the firmament out of the East into the West; and by kindly moving, the which is double, the first and the second. The first moving is the round moving that a planet maketh in its own circle, and passeth never the marks and bounds of the circle. The second moving is that he maketh under the Zodiac, and passeth alway like great space in a like space of time. And the first moving of a planet is made in its own circle that is called Eccentric, and it is called so, for the earth is not the middle thereof, as it is the middle of the circle that is called Zodiac. Epicycle is a little circle that a planet describeth, and goeth about therin by the moving of its body, and the body of the planet goeth about the roundness thereof. And therefore it sheweth, that the sun and other planets move in their own circles; and first alike swift, though they move diversely in divers circles. Also in these circles the manner moving of planets is full wisely found of astronomers, that are called Direct, Stationary, and Retrograde Motion. Forthwight moving is in the over part of the circle that is called Epicycle, backward is in the nether part, and stinting and abiding or hoving is in the middle.

78. A Tenth-Century Schoolmaster's Books

(Cott. Dom., I. f., 55 b. Leach, A. F., *The Schools of Mediæval England*, p. 95. Aberdeen, 1915)

An interesting bit of evidence as to what was actually taught in the schools of England in the tenth century may be seen from the following entry on the fly-leaf of a book, the same being the master's list of his own books. The book in which the entry was made was a copy of the *De natura rerum* (On the Nature of Things) of

Isidore of Seville (570–636), the author of one of the great mediæval Encyclopædias. The book is now in the British Museum. The entry is:

þis syndon ða bec þe æþestaney papan. ðen æcupa. repuin.
psius. ðe apter metrica. Donatum. Excepptiones ðemetrica
apte. Apocalipsin. Donatum maiorem. Alchuinum. Glossa
supcatonem. libellu ðe gramaticam que papis.
Sedulium. 7 i. se juni. pæs alf poldey preostes.
Glossa supdonatu. Dialozopum.

A translation of this shows that the schoolmaster possessed the following books:

These are the things that were Athestane's:
  Of the nature of things (Isidore);
  Persius;
  On the art of meters;
  The small Donatus;
  Extracts on the art of meter;
  The Apocalypse;
  The large Donatus;
  Alcuin;
  A Gloss (notes) on Cato;
  A little book on the art of grammar, which begins
    "The earth which part";
  Sedulius;
  One arithmetic, which was Alfwold the priest's.
  A Gloss on Donatus.
  Dialogues.

79. The Truce of God

(*Monumenta Germaniæ Historica, Leges,* II, 55; trans. by Munro, in *Translations and Reprints from Sources of European History,* vol. I, no. 2)

The Truce of God, first established by the Church at the Council of Clermont, France, in 1095, though having been proposed in Southern France as early as 990, was an effort on the part of the Church, aided by some of the rulers of the time, to mitigate the horrors and extent of private warfare by commanding the cessation of hostilities on four days a week, and on all holy days of the Church, under pain of severe penalties.

The following proclamation of the Archbishop of Cologne to the Bishop of Münster, in 1083, gives the form of the truce he established, twelve years before the definite church decree, and also throws much light on the conditions of society among the Germans in the valley of the Rhine at that time.

Inasmuch as in our own times the Church, through its members, has been extraordinarily afflicted by tribulations and difficulties, so that tranquillity and peace were wholly despaired of, we have endeavored with God's help to come to its aid, in the midst of its sufferings and perils. And by the advice of our faithful subjects we have at length provided this remedy, so that we might to some extent reëstablish, on certain days at least, the peace which, because of our sins, we could not make enduring. Accordingly we have enacted and set forth the following:

Having called together those under us to a legally summoned council, which was held at Cologne, the chief city of our province, in the church of Saint Peter, in the 1083d year of our Lord's Incarnation, in the sixth indiction, on the twelfth day before the Kalends of May, after arranging other business, we have caused to be read in public what we proposed to do in this matter. After this had been fully discussed by all, both clergy and people with God's aid reached an agreement, and we set forth in what manner and during what parts of the year the peace should be observed, namely:

That from the first day of the Advent of our Lord through Epiphany, and from the beginning of Septuagesima to the eighth day after Pentecost and through that whole day, and throughout the year on every Sunday, Friday, and Saturday, and on the fast days of the four seasons, and on the eve and the day of all the apostles, and on all days canonically set apart — or which shall in future be set apart — for fasts or feasts, this decree of peace shall be observed; so that both those who travel and those who remain at home may enjoy security and the most entire peace, so that no one may commit murder, arson, robbery, or assault, no one may injure another with a sword, club or any kind of weapon. Let no one, however irritated by wrong, presume to carry arms, shield, sword, or lance, or any kind of armor, from the Advent of our Lord to the eighth day after Epiphany, and from Septuagesima to the eighth day after Pentecost. On the remaining days, indeed, namely, on Sundays, Fridays, apostles' days, and the vigils of the apostles, and on every day set aside, or to be set aside, for feasts or feasts, arms may be carried, but on this condition, that no injury shall be done in any way to any one.

If it shall be necessary for any one, during the period of the peace — i.e. from the Advent of our Lord to the eighth day after Epiphany, and from Septuagesima to the eighth day after Pentecost — to go from one bishopric into another in which the peace is not observed, he may bear arms, but on the condition that he shall not injure any one, except in self-defense if he is attacked; and when he returns into our diocese he shall immediately lay aside his arms. If it shall happen that any castle is besieged during the days which are included within the peace, the besiegers shall cease from attack unless they are set upon by the besieged and compelled to beat the latter back.

And in order that this statute of peace should not be violated by any one rashly or with impunity, a penalty was fixed by the common consent of all, namely: If a free man or noble violates it, i.e. commits homicide, or wounds any one, or is at fault in any manner whatever, he shall be expelled from his lands, without any indulgence on account of the payment of money or the intercession of friends, and his heirs shall take all his property. If he holds a fief, the lord to whom it belongs shall receive it again. Moreover, if it appear that his heirs after his expulsion have furnished him any support or aid, and if they are convicted of it, the estate shall be taken from them and revert to the king. But if they wish to clear themselves of the charge against them, they shall take oath, with twelve who are equally free or equally noble.

If a slave kills a man, he shall be beheaded; if he wounds a man, he shall lose a hand; if he does an injury any other way with his fist or a club, or by striking with a stone, he shall be shorn and flogged. If, however, he is accused and wishes to prove his innocence, he shall clear himself by the ordeal of cold water, but he must himself be put into the water and no one in his place. If, however, fearing the sentence decreed against him, he flees, he shall be under a perpetual excommunication; and if he is known to be in any place, letters shall be sent thither, in which it shall be announced to all that he is excommunicate, and that it is unlawful for any one to associate with him. In the case of boys who have not yet completed their twelfth year, the hand ought not to be cut off; but only in the case of those who are twelve years or more of age. Nevertheless, if boys fight, they shall be whipped and prevented from fighting.

It is not an infringement of the peace if any one orders his delinquent slave, pupil, or any one in any way under his charge, to be chastised with rods or sticks. It is also an exception to this constitution of peace if the lord king publicly orders an expedition to attack the enemies of the kingdom, or is pleased to hold a council to judge the enemies of justice. The peace is not violated if, during the times specified, a duke, or other counts, magistrates, or their substitutes, hold courts and inflict punishment legally on thieves, robbers, and other criminals.

The statute of this noble peace is especially enacted for the safety of those engaged in feuds; but after the end of the peace they are not to dare to rob and plunder in the villages and houses, since the laws and penalties enacted before the institution of the peace are still legally valid to restrain them from crime, and, moreover, because robbers and highwaymen are excluded from this divine peace, and indeed from any peace.

If any one attempts to oppose this pious institution and is unwilling to promise peace to God with the others, or to observe it, no priest in our diocese shall presume to say a mass for him, or shall take any care for his salvation; if he is sick, no Christian shall dare to visit him; on his deathbed he shall not receive the eucharist, unless he repents. The supreme authority of the peace pledged to God and generally extolled by all will be so great that it will be observed not only in our times, but forever among our posterity, because if any one shall presume to infringe or violate it, either now or ages hence, he is irrevocably excommunicated by us.

The responsibility for carrying out the above-mentioned penalties against the violaters of the peace rests no more with the counts, local judges, or officials than with the whole people in general. They are to be especially careful not to show friendship or hatred, nor to do anything contrary to justice in punishing, nor to conceal crimes, which may be hidden, but to bring them to light. No one is to receive money for the release of those taken in fault, or to attempt to aid the guilty by any favor of any kind, because whoever does this incurs the intolerable damnation of his soul; and all the faithful ought to remember that this peace has not been promised to men, but to God, and therefore must be observed so much the more rigidly and firmly. Wherefore we exhort all in Christ to guard inviolably this necessary contract of peace, and if any one hereafter presumes to violate it, let him be damned by the ban of irrevocable excommunication and by the anathema of eternal perdition. . . .

In 1095, at the Council of Clermont, France, the Truce of God was officially proclaimed. The original decree has been lost, but the Canon adopted by the Council was as follows:

Be it enacted, that monks, clergymen, women, and those who may be with them, shall remain in peace every day; farther, on three days, viz., the second, third, and fourth days of the week, an injury done to any one shall not be considered an infraction of the Peace; but on the remaining four days, if any one injures another, he shall be considered a violater of the sacred Peace, and shall be punished in the manner decreed.

80. How the Church used Chivalry

(Selected from Gautier, Léon, *La Chevalerie;* trans. by H. Frith. London, 1891)

The following selections, chosen from chapter 1 of Gautier's work, show how useful the Church made the institution of chivalry in regulating the life of the half-civilized warrior of the feudal age.

Chivalry is not one of those official institutions which make their appearance suddenly in history, promulgated by a pope and decreed by a sovereign.

Religious as it might have been, it had nothing in its origin that reminded one of the foundations of a religious order. One may in fact declare, that every single monastic order has been conceived in the mind of an individual. The grand Benedictine order arose out of the intelligence of Saint Benedict, and the Franciscan order from the heart of Saint Francis. There is no parallel to this in the case of chivalry, and it would be useless to search for the place of its birth or for the name of its founder. What a great archæologist of our day has said of the Romance architecture is scientifically applicable to the birth of chivalry. It was born everywhere at once, and has been everywhere at the same time the natural effect of the same aspirations and the same needs. There was a moment when the Christians in the East experienced the necessity of sheltering themselves at prayers in churches built of stone which could not be burned; and then, to use the graceful terms of Raoul Glaber, the Christian soil was everywhere covered with the white robes of new churches.

Hence the Romance architecture. There was another moment when people everywhere felt the necessity of tempering the ardour of the old German blood, and of giving to their ill-regulated passions an ideal. Hence chivalry!

Chivalry, as we shall presently show, arose from a German custom which has been idealized by the Church.

It is less an institution than an ideal.

Many volumes have been written upon this noble subject, and a few words will be sufficient to define clearly chivalry and the knight. "Chivalry is the Christian form of the military profession: the knight is the Christian soldier.". . .

There is a sentence of Tacitus which here comes to the front and which illustrious scholars have brought out before us; this is the celebrated passage from the *Germania* which refers to a German rite in which we really find all the military elements of our future chivalry. The scene took place beneath the shade of an old forest. The barbarous tribe is assembled, and one feels that a solemn ceremony is in preparation. Into the midst of the assembly advances a very young man, whom you can picture to yourself with sea-green eyes and long fair hair and perhaps some tattooing. A chief of the tribe is present, who without delay places gravely in the hands of the young man a *framea* and a buckler. Failing a sovereign ruler, it is the father of the youth — who presently will be a man — it is his father or some relative who undertakes this delivery of weapons. "Such is the 'virile robe' of these people," as Tacitus well puts it: "Such is the first honour of their youth. Till then the young man was only one in a family; he becomes by this rite a member of the Republic. . . . This sword and buckler he will never abandon, for the Germans in all their acts, whether public or private, are always armed. So, the ceremony finished, the assembly separates, and the tribe reckons a *miles* — a warrior — the more. That is all!"

The solemn handing of arms to the young German — such is the first germ of chivalry which Christianity was one day to animate into life. . . . In time the Church came to intervene positively in the education of the German *miles*. The time was rough, and it is not easy to picture a more distracted period than that in the ninth and tenth centuries. . . . Countries were on the way to be formed, and people were asking to which country they could best belong. Independent kingdoms were founded which had no precedents, and were not destined to have a long life. . . . People were fighting everywhere more or less — family against family — man to man. No road was safe, the churches were burned, there was universal terror, and every one sought protection. The king had no longer strength to resist any one, and the counts made themselves kings. The sun of the realm was set, and one had to look to the stars for light. As soon as the people perceived a strong man-at-arms, resolute, defiant, well established in his wooden keep, well fortified within the lines of his hedge, behind his palisade of dead branches, or within his barriers of planks; well posted on his hill, against his rock, or on his hillock, and dominating all the surrounding country, as soon as they saw this each said to him, "I am your man"; and all these weak ones grouped themselves around the strong one, who next day proceeded to wage war with his neighbors. Thence supervened a terrible series of private wars. Every one was fighting, or thinking of fighting. . . .

It was then, it was in that terrible hour — the decisive epoch in our history — that the Church undertook the education of the Christian soldier; and it was at that time by a resolute step she found the feudal baron in his rude wooden citadel, and proposed to him an ideal.

This ideal was chivalry! . . .

That chivalry may be considered a great military confraternity as well as an eighth sacrament will be conceded after a careful perusal of the text. But, before familiarising themselves with these ideas, the rough spirits of the ninth, tenth, and eleventh centuries had to learn the principles of them. The chivalrous ideal was not conceived "all of a piece," and certainly it did not triumph without sustained effort; so it was by degrees, and very slowly, that the Church succeeded in inoculating the almost animal intelligence and the untrained minds of our ancestors with so many virtues. Nothing is improvised — such is the law of history. Whoever cannot see it is blind. This same Church which we have to thank for the best elements of our chivalry has scarcely put down slavery in eight or nine hundred years. It cannot, as a matter of fact, march with a more rapid step. . . .

In the hands of the Church which wished to mould him into a Christian knight, the feudal baron was a very intractable individual. No one could be more brutal or more barbarous than he. . . .

. . . The Church said "Moderate your courage." They did moderate it, and their savagery by degrees became their prowess. . . . First loyalty, then *largesse*, then moderation, and finally that perfection of civilized chivalry which we call courtesy. Honour crowns them all. "Death rather than dishonour": the whole code of chivalry is contained in these four words, which, by the grace of God, have become a commonplace term with us. It is the grand saying of Hue le Maine, brother of the King of France, before Antioch: "Who does not prefer death to dishonour has no right in *seignorie*." And throughout the Middle Ages this motto was preserved.

No matter in what sequence the Church bestowed these virtues upon the warrior, she gave him a definite aim and object — a precise law.

The law was the Decalogue, the Ten Commandments of chivalry, which we propose to illustrate.

The object was to enlarge the Kingdom of God on earth.

When our knights attended mass one might have seen them, before the reading of the second lesson, draw their swords and hold them unsheathed in their hands until the reading of the lesson was finished. This defiant attitude seemed to imply their readiness to defend the Gospel. "If the Word is to be defended, we are ready."

This is the whole spirit of chivalry.

81. Educational Influences of the Church Services

(Draper, J. W., *History of the Intellectual Development of Europe*, vol. II, p. 202. New York, 1876)

For the great mass of the people of western Europe there was no other education during the long Middle Ages than that given by daily toil, training to do what others had done before, and the religious services of the Church. Draper describes very well the influence of the last in the following selection.

And yet we must not undervalue the power once exercised on a non-reading community by oral and scenic teachings. What could better instruct it than a formal congregating of neighborhoods together each Sabbath-day to listen in silence and without questioning? In those great churches, the architectural grandeur of which is still the admiration of our material age, nothing was wanting to impress the worshipper. The vast pile, with its turrets or spire pointing to heaven; its steep inclining roof; its walls, with niches and statues; its echoing belfry; its windows of exquisite hues and of every form, lancet, or wheel, or rose, through which stole in the many-colored light; its chapels, with their pictured walls; its rows of slender, clustering columns, and arches tier upon tier; its many tapering pendants; the priest emerging from his scenic retreat; his chalice and forbidden wine; the covering paten, the cibory, and the pix. Amid clouds of incense from smoking censers, the blaze of lamps, and tapers, and branching candlesticks, the tinkling of silver bells, the play of jewelled vessels and gorgeous dresses of violet, green, and gold, banners and crosses were borne aloft through lines of kneeling worshippers in processional services along the aisles. The chanting of litanies and psalms gave a foretaste of the melodies of heaven, and the voices of the choristers and sounds of the organ now thundered forth glory to God in the highest, now whispered to the broken in spirit, peace.

82. How the Church Urged that the Elements of Religious Education be Given

(Statutes Diocesan Council, Winchester Diocese, England. Leach, A. F., *History of Winchester College*, p. 40)

The following statutes, dating from 1295, are interesting as showing the mild pressure exerted by the Church in one English diocese to secure a little learning for the members and their children.

In the churches near the school of the city of Winchester or in other walled cities of our diocese, let scholars only be appointed to carry the holy water.

Moreover, let the rectors, vicars, and parish priests take care that the boys in their parishes know the Lord's Prayer, the Creed, and the Salutation of the Blessed Virgin, and how to cross themselves rightly.

Let inquiry also be made of the grown-up laymen when they come to confession whether they know this exactly, that if by any chance they do not know it, as is very often the case, they may be taught it by the same priests.

Let boys' parents also be induced to let their boys, when they have learnt to read the psalter, learn singing also, so that after they have learnt higher subjects they may not be compelled to return to learn this, nor as being ignorant of this be always less fit for divine service.

83. Licenses to be Required to Teach Song

(From the Chapter Acts of Lincoln Cathedral, England, 1305; trans. by A. F. Leach)

This document shows how carefully the Precentor, or others acting for him, guarded the right to license elementary or song schools in the bishopric of Lincoln, England.

Be it remembered that on Saturday next after the feast of the Con-

version of Saint Paul all the parish clerks of the churches of the city of
Lincoln were teaching boys in the churches singing or music; and being
present in chapter before Masters Robert de Lacy and William of
Thornton, who charged them that they had held adulterine schools to
the prejudice of the liberty of the mother church, they firmly denied
that they were keeping any schools in the churches, or teaching boys
singing; but as they could not deny that they had at some time done so,
the said Masters Robert and William made them swear, holding the
most holy Gospels, that they will not henceforward keep any adulterine
schools in the churches, nor teach boys song or music, without license
from the (Song) Master.

84. Form of Appointment and Oath of a Grammar-School Master

The following notice of appointment as a schoolmaster at
Northallerton, in 1385, shows a form of notification of election
to a position as teacher used at that time in England.

*(a) Appointment of Master of Song and Grammar School, Northallerton,
15 December, 1385*

(Leach, A. F., *Early Yorkshire Schools*, vol. ii, p. 61)

Robert, Prior of the Cathedral Church of Durham, Ordinary of the
Spiritualities of Saint Cuthbert in York diocese, to our beloved in Christ,
Sir William of Leeds, chaplain, health in the embraces of the Saviour.

Considering you on the praiseworthy evidence of trustworthy persons sufficient and fit to teach boys as well song as grammar, We confer on you by these presents our school of Allerton, as well of song as of
grammar, as they have been heretofore accustomed to be conferred, by
way of charity.   To have and to rule from the date of these presents for
the term of three years next following as long as you behave yourself
well and uprightly, and personally show effective diligence in teaching
boys.

In witness whereof our seal is appended to these presents.

Dated at Durham 15 December, A.D. 1385.

The following oath of office of a grammar-school master at
Cambridge, England, dating from c. 1276, to the Archdeacon of
the diocese at Ely, shows the ecclesiastical control exercised over
grammar schools in the diocese.

(b) Oath of a Grammar-School Master

(The Archdeacon of Ely's book; trans. by C. H. Cooper, in his
Annals of Cambridge.)

You shall swear obedience to the archdeacon of the church of Ely
and his officers, and will never attempt anything, by yourself or

through another, nor after your power permit any attempt against his archidiaconal jurisdiction.

You will swear further that you will, during your time, bear faithfully all the charges falling on the Cambridge Grammar School according to the hitherto approved custom, without any extortion from the scholars of the aforesaid school; and if anything shall be otherwise attempted by you or by another in your name, you grant that you are, in virtue of the oath you have taken, *ipso facto* deprived of the same school until you shall have been able to obtain redress from him whose business it is. All this you promise that you will observe faithfully. So help you God etc.

CHAPTER VIII

INFLUENCES TENDING TOWARD A REVIVAL OF LEARNING

The Readings of this chapter are illustrative of a number of the more important movements which took place in the eleventh and twelfth centuries, and which did much to prepare the way for the rise of the universities in the thirteenth century and the revival of learning in the fourteenth. The development of a new and, for the time, wonderful Mohammedan civilization in Spain; the rise of Scholasticism within the Western Church; the recovery of the Roman legal code, the revival of the study of Roman law; the restoration of the old city life and commerce; and the rise of merchant and trade guilds in the cities — these were the most important of the new influences and movements which indicated that a revival of learning in the western world was about to begin.

The first of these new influences was the rapid development of Mohammedan civilization and learning in Spain. The influence exerted by this on western Europe, chiefly through the introduction of the lost texts of Aristotle and some new mathematical knowledge, is indicated in the Readings. The first selection (85) pictures the Mohammedan civilization at its best, and the second (86) reveals their remarkable scientific work. The next selection, which is a list of Aristotle's works known to western Europe by 1300 (87), shows the extent to which Christian Europe drew upon Mohammedan translations. The greatness of Aristotle's mind is testified to by the Mohammedan Averroës (88), while the reception given to his writings in the rising universities at Oxford and Paris is indicated by the testimony of Roger Bacon (89) and the four extracts from the Paris Statutes (90 a-d). The latter extend over a period of forty-four years, and cover the time from the earlier prohibition of his works to their later full acceptance by the Western Church authorities.

The new questioning attitude of a few thinkers within the Church, another of the new movements of the time, is well shown by the extracts from Abelard's new textbook on Theology, *Sic et Non* (91 a-b), while the great reconciling and harmonizing work of the Scholastics, all within lines which the Church fully approved, is well set forth in the brief extract from Rashdall (92).

The revival of legal study was another of the important new influences of the period under consideration. The extract from the *Institutes of Justinian* (93), which was an important and introductory part of the famous *Justinian Code*, sets forth well the nature of this introductory textbook on Roman law, the recovery of which formed the basis for the new study of Roman law in western Europe.

The rise of the mediæval town, and of the merchant and trade guilds within the town, were other important new movements which indicated a change in thinking and in human endeavor. The two extracts from Giry and Réville (94 a-b) describe the evolution of these towns over a period of centuries. The charter of rights and privileges granted by Henry II to the town of Wallingford, England (95), is an important document as showing not only what rights and privileges a town could beg, buy, or wring from a king, but also as indicating the important position held, at that early date, by the rising guild merchant in such a town. It reveals clearly the evolution of a merchant class as a new Estate. Closely following the rise of these merchant guilds came the trade guilds, and the selections giving the oath of a freeman (96), and the ordinances of the guild of white-tawyers (97), reveal the nature and scope of these new organizations, and the control these mediæval guilds exercised over their members and their trade. These guilds not only developed apprentice education for the sons of their members, but also, in time, schools of their own (98) as well. The old indenture of apprenticeship reproduced (99) is typical of such documents, not only at the time, but also for centuries to come.

These new influences and movements indicate that the long period of the Dark Ages was approaching an end. They point unmistakably to the rise of new classes in society and to an approaching intellectual awakening, as well as to a revival of the old long-lost Greek and Roman learning. The eleventh and twelfth centuries were turning-points of great significance in the history of our western civilization, and with the opening of the wonderful thirteenth century the western world was at last headed toward a new life and modern ways of thinking.

85. The Moslem Civilization in Spain

(Draper, J. W., *History of the Intellectual Development of Europe*, vol. II, pp. 30, 33–34; 42–45. New York, 1876)

The following selection gives an interesting picture of life in Mohammedan Spain in the time of its Golden Age.

Scarcely had the Arabs become firmly settled in Spain when they commenced a brilliant career. Adopting what had now become the established policy of the Commanders of the Faithful in Asia, the Emirs of Cordova distinguished themselves as patrons of learning, and set an example of refinement strongly contrasting with the condition of the native European princes. Cordova, under their administration, at its highest point of prosperity, boasted of more than two hundred thousand houses, and more than a million of inhabitants. After sunset, a man might walk through it in a straight line for ten miles by the light of the public lamps. Seven hundred years after this time there was not so much as one public lamp in London. Its streets were solidly paved. In Paris, centuries subsequently, whoever stepped over his threshold on a rainy day stepped up to his ankles in mud. Other cities, as Granada, Seville, Toledo, considered themselves as rivals of Cordova. The palaces of the khalifs were magnificently decorated. Those sovereigns might well look down with supercilious contempt on the dwellings of the rulers of Germany, France, and England, which were scarcely better than stables — chimneyless, windowless, and with a hole in the roof for the smoke to escape, like the wigwams of certain Indians. The Spanish Mohammedans had brought with them all the luxuries and prodigalities of Asia. . . . The representation of the human form was religiously forbidden . . . For this reason, the Arabs never produced artists; religion turned them from the beautiful, and made them soldiers, philosophers, and men of affairs. . . . There were, for the master himself, grand libraries. The Khalif Alhakem's was so large that the catalogue alone filled forty volumes. He had also apartments for the transcribing, binding, and ornamenting of books. A taste for caligraphy and the possession of splendidly-illustrated manuscripts seems to have anticipated in the khalifs, both of Asia and Spain, the taste for statuary and paintings among the later popes of Rome. . . .

In the midst of all this luxury, which cannot be regarded by the historian with disdain, since in the end it produced a most important result in the south of France, the Spanish khalifs, emulating the example of their Asiatic compeers, and in this strongly contrasting with the popes of Rome, were not only the patrons, but the personal cultivators of all the branches of human learning. One of them was himself the author of a work on polite literature in not less than fifty volumes; another wrote a treatise on algebra. When Zaryab the musician came from the East to Spain, the Khalif Abderrahman rode forth to meet him in honour. The College of Music in Cordova was sustained by ample government patronage, and produced many illustrious professors.

Our obligations to the Spanish Moors in the arts of life are even more marked than in the higher branches of science, perhaps only because our ancestors were better prepared to take advantage of things connected with daily affairs. They set an example of skilful agriculture, the practice of which was regulated by a code of laws. Not only did they attend to the cultivation of plants, introducing very many new ones, they likewise paid great attention to the breeding of cattle, especially the sheep and horse. To them we owe the introduction of the great products, rice, sugar, cotton, and also, as we have previously observed, nearly all the fine garden and orchard fruits, together with many less important plants, as spinach and saffron. To them Spain owes the culture of silk; they gave the Xeres and Malaga their celebrity for wine. They introduced the Egyptian system of irrigation by floodgates, wheels, and pumps. They also promoted many important branches of industry; improved the manufacture of textile fabrics, earthenware, iron, steel; the Toledo sword-blades were everywhere prized for their temper. The Arabs, on their expulsion from Spain, carried the manufacture of a kind of leather, in which they were acknowledged to excel, to Morocco, from which country the leather itself has now taken its name. They also introduced inventions of a more ominous kind — gunpowder and artillery. The cannon they used appeared to have been made of wrought iron. But perhaps they more than compensated for these evil contrivances by the introduction of the mariner's compass.

The mention of the mariner's compass might lead us correctly to infer that the Spanish Arabs were interested in commercial pursuits, a conclusion to which we should also come when we consider the revenues of some of their khalifs. That of Abderrahman III. is stated at five and a half million sterling — a vast sum if considered by its modern equivalent, and far more than could possibly be raised by taxes on the produce of the soil. It probably exceeded the entire revenue of all the sovereigns of Christendom taken together. From Barcelona and other ports an immense trade with the Levant was maintained, but it was mainly in the hands of the Jews, who, from the first invasion of Spain by Musa, had ever been the firm allies and collaborators of the Arabs. Together they had participated in the dangers of the invasion; together they had shared its boundless success; together they had held in irreverent derision, nay, even in contempt, the woman-worshippers and polytheistic savages beyond the Pyrenees — as they mirthfully called those whose long-delayed vengeance they were in the end to feel; together they were expelled. Against such Jews as lingered behind the hideous persecutions of the Inquisition were directed. But in the days of their prosperity they maintained a merchant marine of more than a thousand ships.   They had factories and consuls on the Tanaïs.   With Constantinople alone they maintained a great trade; it ramified from the Black Sea and East Mediterranean into the interior of Asia; it reached the ports of India and China, and extended along the African coast as far as Madagascar.   Even in these commercial affairs the singular genius of the Jew and Arab shines forth.   In the midst of the tenth century, when Europe was about in the same condition that Caffraria is now, enlightened Moors, like Abul Cassem, were writing treatises on the principles of trade and commerce.   As on so many other occasions, on these affairs they have left their traces.   The smallest weight they used in trade was the grain of barley, four of which were equal to one sweet pea, called in Arabic carat.   We still use the grain as our unit of weight, and still speak of gold as being so many carats fine.

Such were the Khalifs of the West; such their splendour, their luxury, their knowledge; such some of the obligations we are under to them — obligations which Christian Europe, with singular insincerity, has ever been fain to hide.   The cry against the misbeliever has long outlived the Crusades.   Considering the enchanting country over which they ruled, it was not without reason that they caused to be engraven on the public seal, "The servant of the Merciful rests contented in the decrees of God."   What more, indeed, could Paradise give them? But, considering also the evil end of all this happiness and pomp, this learning, liberality, and wealth, we may well appreciate the solemn truth which these monarchs, in their day of pride and power, grandly wrote in the beautiful mosaics on their palace walls, an ever-recurring warning to him who owes dominion to the sword, "There is no conqueror but God."

86. Learning among the Moslems of Spain

(Draper, J. W., *History of the Intellectual Development of Europe*, vol. II, pp. 36–42. New York, 1876)

The following is a continuation of the preceding selection.

The khalifs of the West carried out the precepts of Ali, the fourth successor of Mohammed, in the patronage of literature.   They established libraries in all their chief towns; it is said that not fewer than seventy were in existence.   To every mosque was attached a public school, in which the children of the poor were taught to read and write, and instructed in the precepts of the Koran.   For those in easier circumstances there were academies, usually arranged in twenty-five or thirty apartments, each calculated for accommodating four students; the academy being presided over by a rector.   In Cordova, Granada, and other great cities, there were universities, frequently under the superintendence of Jews; the Mohammedan maxim being that the real learning of a man is of more public importance than any particular religious opinions he may entertain. In this they followed the example of the Asiatic khalif, Haroun Alraschid, who actually conferred the superintendence of his schools on John Masué, a Nestorian Christian. The Mohammedan liberality was in striking contrast with the intolerance of Europe. Indeed, it may be doubted whether at this time any European nation is sufficiently advanced to follow such an example. In the universities some of the professors of polite literature gave lectures on Arabic classical works; others taught rhetoric or composition, or mathematics, or astronomy. From these institutions many of the practices observed in our colleges were derived. They held Commencements, at which poems were read and orations delivered in the presence of the public. They had also, in addition to these schools of general learning, professional ones, particularly for medicine.

With a pride perhaps not altogether inexcusable, the Arabians boasted of their language as being the most perfect spoken by man. . . . It is not then surprising that, in the Arabian schools, great attention was paid to the study of language, and that so many celebrated grammarians were produced. By these scholars, dictionaries, similar to those now in use, were composed; their copiousness is indicated by the circumstance that one of them consisted of sixty volumes, the definition of each word being illustrated or sustained by quotations from Arab authors of acknowledged repute. They had also lexicons of Greek, Latin, Hebrew; and cyclopædias such as the "Historical Dictionary of Sciences" of Mohammed Ibn Abdallah, of Granada. . . . Their poetical productions embraced all the modern minor forms — satires, odes, elegies, etc.; but they never produced any work in the higher walks of poesy, no epic, no tragedy. Perhaps this was due to their false fashion of valuing the mechanical execution of a work. They were the authors and introducers of rhyme; . . . this is the more interesting to us, since it was from the Provençal poetry, the direct descendant of these efforts, that European literature arose. Sonnets and romances at last displaced the grimly-orthodox productions of the wearisome and ignorant fathers of the Church.

. . . Many of their learned men were travellers and voyagers, constantly moving about for the acquisition or diffusion of knowledge, their acquirements being a passport to them wherever they went, and a sufficient introduction to any of the African or Asiatic courts. They were thus continually brought into contact with men of affairs, soldiers of fortune, statesmen, and became imbued with much of their practical spirit; and hence the singularly romantic character which the biographies of many of these men display, wonderful turns of prosperity, violent deaths. The scope of their literary labours offers a subject well worthy of meditation; it contrasts with the contemporary ignorance of Europe. Some wrote on chronology; some on numismatics; some, now that military eloquence had become objectless, wrote on pulpit oratory; some on agriculture and its allied branches, as the art of irrigation. Not one of the purely mathematical, or mixed, or practical sciences was omitted.

Out of a list too long for detailed quotation, I may recall a few names. Assamh, who wrote on topography and statistics, a brave soldier, who was killed in the invasion of France, A.D. 720; Avicenna, the great physician and philosopher, who died A.D. 1037; Averroës, of Cordova, the chief commentator on Aristotle, A.D. 1198. It was his intention to unite the doctrines of Aristotle with those of the Koran. To him is imputed the discovery of spots upon the sun. . . . Abu Othman wrote on zoölogy; Alberuni, on gems — he had travelled to India to procure information; Rhazes, Al Abbas, and Al Beithar, on botany — the latter had been in all parts of the world for the purpose of obtaining specimens. Ebn Zoar, better known as Avenzoar, may be looked upon as the authority in Moorish pharmacy. Pharmacopœias were published by the schools, improvements on the old ones of the Nestorians: to them may be traced the introduction of many Arabic words, such as syrup, julep, elixir, still used among apothecaries. A competent scholar might furnish not only an interesting, but valuable book, founded on the remaining relics of the Arab vocabulary; for, in whatever direction we may look, we meet, in the various pursuits of peace and war, of letters and of science, Saracenic vestiges. Our dictionaries tell us that such is the origin of admiral, alchemy, alcohol, algebra, chemise, cotton, and hundreds of other words. The Saracens commenced the application of chemistry, both to the theory and practice of medicine, in the explanation of the functions of the human body and in the cure of its diseases. Nor was their surgery behind their medicine. Albucasis, of Cordova, shrinks not from the performance of the most formidable operations in his own and in the obstetrical art; the actual cautery and knife are used without hesitation. He has left us ample descriptions of the surgical instruments then employed; and from him we learn that, in operations on females in which considerations of delicacy intervened, the services of properly instructed women were secured. How different was all this from the state of things in Europe: The Christian peasant, fever-stricken or overtaken by accident, hied to the nearest saint-shrine and expected a miracle; the Spanish Moor relied on the prescription or lancet of his physician, or the bandage and knife of his surgeon.

In Mathematics the Arabians acknowledged their indebtedness to two sources, Greek and Indian, but they greatly improved upon both. The Asiatic khalifs had made exertions to procure translations of Euclid, Apollonius, Archimedes, and other Greek geometers. Almainon, in a letter to the Emperor Theophilus, expressed his desire to visit Constantinople if his public duties would have permitted. He requests of him to allow Leo the mathematician to come to Bagdad to impart to him a portion of his learning, pledging his word that he would restore him quickly and safely again. "Do not," says the high-minded khalif, "let diversity of religion or of country cause you to refuse my request. Do what friendship would concede to a friend. In return, I offer you a hundred weight of gold, a perpetual alliance, and peace." True to the instincts of his race and the traditions of his city, the Byzantine sourly and insolently refused the request, saying that "the learning which had illustrated the Roman name should néver be imparted to a barbarian."

From the Hindus the Arabs learned arithmetic, especially that valuable invention termed by us the Arabic numerals, but honourably ascribed by them to its proper source, under the designation of "Indian numerals." They also entitled their treatises on the subject "Systems of Indian Arithmetic." This admirable notation by nine digits and cipher occasioned a complete revolution in arithmetical computations. As in the case of so many other things, the Arab impress is upon it; our word cipher, and its derivatives, ciphering, etc., recall the Arabic word tsaphara or ciphra, the name for the o, and meaning that which is blank or void. Mohammed Ben Musa, said to be the earliest of the Saracen authors on algebra, and who made the great improvement of substituting sines for chords in trigonometry, wrote also on this Indian system. He lived at the end of the ninth century; before the end of the tenth it was in common use among the African and Spanish mathematicians. Ebn Junis, A.D. 1008, used it in his astronomical works. From Spain it passed into Italy, its singular advantage in commercial computation causing it to be eagerly adopted in the great trading cities. We still use the word algorithm in reference to calculations. The study of algebra was intently cultivated among the Arabs, who gave it the name it bears. Ben Musa, just referred to, was the inventor of the common method of solving quadratic equations. In the application of mathematics to astronomy and physics they had long been distinguished. Almaimon had determined with considerable accuracy the obliquity of the ecliptic. He had also ascertained the size of the earth from the measurement of a degree on the shore of the Red Sea — an operation implying true ideas of its form, and in singular contrast with the doctrine of Constantinople and Rome. While the latter was asserting, in all its absurdity, the flatness of the earth, the Spanish Moors were teaching geography in their common schools from globes. In Africa, there is still preserved, with almost religious reverence, in the library at Cairo, one of brass, reputed to have belonged to the great astronomer Ptolemy. Al Idrisi made one of silver for Roger II, of Sicily; and Gerbert used one which he had brought from Cordova in the school he established at Rheims. It cost a struggle of several centuries, illustrated by some martyrdoms, before the dictum of Lactantius and

Augustine could be overthrown. Among problems of interest that were solved may be mentioned the determination of the length of the year by Albategnius and Thebit Ben Corrah; and increased accuracy was given to the correction of astronomical observations by Alhazen's great discovery of atmospheric refraction. Among the astronomers, some composed tables; some wrote on the measure of time; some on the improvement of clocks, for which purpose they were the first to apply the pendulum; some on instruments, as the astrolabe. The introduction of astronomy into Christian Europe has been attributed to the translation of the works of Mohammed Fargani. In Europe, also, the Arabs were the first to build observatories; the Giralda, or tower of Seville, was erected under the superintendence of Geber, the mathematician, A.D. 1196, for that purpose. Its fate was not a little characteristic. After the expulsion of the Moors it was turned into a belfry, the Spaniards not knowing what else to do with it.

87. Works of Aristotle known by 1300

(List adapted from Norton, *Readings in the History of Education; Mediæval Universities.* Cambridge, 1909)

This Greek scientist and philosopher lived from 384 to 322 B.C., and wrote his organization of human knowledge in Athens between 335 B.C. and his death. His was the greatest organizing mind of antiquity, and it is no wonder that he came eventually to dominate mediæval thinking. The following list of his works shows what had been recovered by 1300. Abélard, the great mediæval scholar of France, who died in 1142, knew certainly only 1 and 2, though it is possible he had knowledge of 3 and 4. By 1150 all the *Organon* was known; between 1200 and 1270 most of the other works were translated; and by 1300 the twenty-one listed were known. For the next three centuries these were the great textbooks in the Faculty of Arts in the European universities.

Many of these came in from Mohammedan sources in Spain, having experienced translation from the Greek into Syriac, then into Arabic, and then into Latin and Castilian, and were quite imperfect. After the capture of Constantinople by the Crusaders and the Venetians, in 1203, the original Greek texts began to find their way westward, and were translated directly into the Latin. By 1500 all had been retranslated from the original Greek, and the newer Latin editions were in use.

The following list was known by 1300:

I. Logical treatises commonly referred to as the *Organon*, or Methodology.
    *1. Categories.
    *2. On Interpretation.
    *3. Prior Analytics.
    *4. Posterior Analytics.
    *5. Topics.
    *6. Sophistical Refutations.

II. Moral and Practical Philosophy.
    7. Politics.
    *8. Ethics.
    9. Rhetoric.
    10. Poetics.

III. Natural Philosophy.
    11. A Physical Discourse (Physics).
    *12. On the Heavens.
    13. On Generation and Destruction.
    *14. Meteorologics.
    *15. Researches about Animals.
    *16. On Parts of Animals.
    17. On Locomotion of Animals.
    18. On Generation of Animals.
    *19. On the Soul.
    20. Appendices to the work "On the Soul."
        *(a) On Sense and Sensible Things.
        *(b) On Memory and Recollection.
        *(c) On Sleep and Waking.
        (d) On Dreams and Prophesying in Sleep.
        (e) On Longevity and Shortlivedness.
        (f) On Youth and Old Age.
        *(g) On Life and Death.
        (h) On Respiration.

IV. Rational Philosophy.
    *21. Metaphysics.

---

* Prescribed as regular texts at the University of Paris, in the *Statutes* of 1254. All others were optional.

88. Averroës, on Aristotle's Greatness

(Averroës; Introduction to his Commentary on Aristotle's *Physics*)

Abu'l Walid Mohammed Averroës, born at Cordova in 1126, of distinguished parents, became the greatest of all commentators on Aristotle, and exerted, through the translation of his works into Latin, a profound influence on the thinking of western

Europe.   His translations were the medium whereby much of the lost Aristotle was restored to western civilization.   He expresses himself as to Aristotle's greatness as follows.

Aristotle was the wisest of the Greeks and constituted and completed logic, physics, and metaphysics.   I say that he constituted these sciences, because all the works on these subjects previous to him do not deserve to be mentioned and were completely eclipsed by his writings I say that he put the finishing touches on these sciences, because none of those who have succeeded him up to our time, to wit, during nearly fifteen hundred years, have been able to add anything to his writings or to find in them any error of any importance.   Now that all this should be found in one man is a strange and miraculous thing, and this privileged being deserves to be called divine rather than human.

89. How Aristotle was Received at Oxford

(A description by Roger Bacon; trans. by Rashdall)

The following description by Roger Bacon, an English monk, who died in 1294, indicates a rather more tardy reception of Aristotle at Oxford than at Paris.

But a part of the philosophy of Aristotle has come slowly into the use of the Latins.   For his *Natural Philosophy* and *Metaphysics*, and the *Commentaries* of Averroës and of others, were translated in our times, and were excommunicated at Paris before the year of our Lord 1237 on account of (their heretical views on) the eternity of matter and of time, and on account of the (heresies contained in the) book on *Interpretation of Dreams* (which is the third book on *Sleep and Wakefulness*), and on account of the many errors in the translation.   The *Logicalia* were also slowly received and read, for the blessed Edmund, Archbishop of Canterbury, was the first at Oxford, in my time, to lecture on the book of *Elenchi* (*Sophistical Refutations*), and I saw Master Hugo who at first read the book of *Posterior Analytics*, and I saw his opinion.   So there were few (books) which were considered worth (reading) in the aforesaid philosophy of Aristotle, considering the multitudes of Latins; nay, exceedingly few and almost none, up to this year of our Lord 1292.   So, too, the *Ethics* of Aristotle has been tardily tried and has lately been read by Masters, though only here and there.   And the entire remain-

FIG. 16.   ARISTOTLE
(384–322 B.C.)

ing philosophy of Aristotle in a thousand volumes, in which he treated all the knowledges, has never yet been translated and made known to the Latins.

90. How Aristotle was Received at Paris
(From Chartularium Universitatis Parisiensis, vol. 1; trans. by Norton)

The hesitant attitude of the ecclesiastical authorities toward the study of Aristotle, and later his adoption as the great supporter and bulwark of theology, is well shown in the following regulations adopted at Paris, between 1210 and 1254 A.D.

(a) Church Council, Paris, 1210

Nor shall the books of Aristotle on Natural Philosophy, and the Commentaries (of Averroës on Aristotle) be read in Paris in public or in secret; and this we enjoin under pain of excommunication.

(b) Statutes of the Papal Legate for the University, 1215

The treatises of Aristotle on Logic, both the Old and the New, are to be read in the schools in the regular and not in the extraordinary courses. On feast-days (holidays) nothing is to be read except . . . the Ethics, if one so chooses, and the fourth book of the Topics. The books of Aristotle on Metaphysics or Natural Philosophy, or the abridgments of these works, are not to be read.

(c) Statutes of Pope Gregory for the University, 1231

Furthermore, we command that the Masters of Arts . . . shall not use in Paris those books on Natural Philosophy which for a definite reason were prohibited in the provincial council (of 1210), until they have been examined and purged from every suspicion of error.

(d) Statutes of the Masters of Arts for the University, 1254

None of Aristotle's works is now forbidden. Of the twenty-one in the list given in Reading **87**, the ones marked with a * are now prescribed as regular texts.

91. Abelard's *Sic et Non*
(Cousin, V., Ouvrages Inédits d'Abélard)

As a teacher of theology at Paris, early in the twelfth century, Abélard (1079–1142) prepared a little textbook for the use of his pupils, entitled *Sic et Non* (Yea and Nay). It was in the form of a large number of questions as to Church dogma and practices, in which, after stating the question, he presented the arguments on both sides as gleaned from Scriptures and advanced by the Christian Fathers, but drew no conclusions.   In the introduction he stated his method, it being his desire to stimulate thinking. The following extracts indicate the nature of the work.

(a) *From the Introduction to Sic et Non*

In truth, constant or frequent questioning is the first key to wisdom; and it is, indeed, to the acquiring of this (habit of) questioning with absorbing eagerness that the famous philosopher, Aristotle, the most clear-sighted of all, urges the studious when he says: "It is perhaps difficult to speak confidently in matters of this sort unless they have often been investigated.   Indeed, to doubt in special cases will not be without advantage."   For through doubting we come to inquiry, and through inquiry we perceive the truth.   As the Truth Himself says: "Seek and ye shall find, knock and it shall be opened unto you."   And He also, instructing us by His own example, about the twelfth year of His life wished to be found sitting in the midst of the doctors, asking them questions, exhibiting to us by His asking of questions the appearance of a pupil, rather than, by preaching, that of a teacher, although there is in him, nevertheless, the full and perfect wisdom of God.

Now when a number of quotations from (various) writings are introduced they spur on the reader, and allure him into seeking the truth in proportion as the authority of the writing itself is commended. . . .

In accordance, then, with these forecasts it is our pleasure to collect different sayings of the holy Fathers as we planned, just as they have come to mind, suggesting (as they do) some questioning from their apparent disagreement, in order that they may stimulate tender readers to the utmost effort in seeking the truth and may make them keener as the result of their seeking.

(b) *Types of Questions he raised for Debate*

Of the 158 questions he raised and gave evidence on, the following are illustrative.

Should human faith be based on reason, or no?
Is God one, or no?
Is God a substance, or no?
Does the first Psalm refer to Christ, or no?
Is sin pleasing to God, or no?
Is God the author of evil, or no?
Is God all-powerful, or no?
Can God be resisted, or no?
Has God free will, or no?
Was the first man persuaded to sin by the devil, or no?
Was Adam saved, or no?

Did all the apostles have wives except John, or no?

Are the flesh and blood of Christ in very truth and essence present in the sacrament of the altar, or no?

Do we sometimes sin unwillingly, or no?

Does God punish the same sin both here and in the future, or no?

Is it worse to sin openly than secretly, or no?

92. The Great Work of the Schoolmen

(Rashdall, H., *Universities of Europe in the Middle Ages*, vol. 1, p. 365. Oxford, 1895

The following statement gives a good summary of the organizing and reconciling work of the Schoolmen, as well as of their services in satisfying the intellectual hunger of the age.

The Dominican Theologians made peace between the contending factions by placing Aristotle and the Fathers side by side, and deferring as reverentially to one as to the other, except on the few fundamental points upon which the former could not be interpreted into harmony with the latter. The Scholastic form of argument, which attained its full development in Aquinas — a chain of authorities and syllogisms in defence of one thesis, another series for the opposite view, a conclusion in harmony with Augustine or Aristotle as the case might be, and a reply to the opposing arguments by means of ingenious distinction or reconciliation — afforded exceptional facilities for the harmonious combination of orthodoxy and intellectuality.

The Dominicans showed the Latin Churchmen how to be ingenious, startling, brilliant, even destructive, without suspicion of heresy. (Saint) Bernard would have been shocked at the idea of inventing or even of fairly stating objections to the Catholic Faith. By the time of Aquinas it was felt that the better the imaginary opponent's case could be stated, the more credit there was in refuting it. The scholar's intellectual enjoyment of thirty ingenious arguments against the Immortality of the Soul was not diminished by the thirty-six equally ingenious arguments with which the attack would immediately be met. In scholastic disputation . . . restless intellectual activity found an innocent outlet, love of controversy and speculation an innocent gratification; and into the love of controversy and speculation the real ardour for truth and knowledge, which distinguished the age of Berengar and the age of Abélard, had for the most part degenerated.

93. The Justinian Code

(Justinian, Preface to the *Institutes;* trans. by Sandars)

The great compilation of Roman law known as the *Corpus Juris Civilis* was perfected at Constantinople by a staff of eminent jurists, under the direction of the Emperor Justinian, in 529-33 A.D.   It consisted of the *Code*, in twelve books; the *Digest*, in fifty books; and the *Institutes*, in four books.   The first contained the Statutes of the Emperors; the second extracts from legal opinions by Roman lawyers; and the third was an elementary textbook for students, somewhat like the English Blackstone.   In the introduction to the *Institutes* Justinian explains the nature of the entire compilation.

When we had arranged and brought into perfect harmony the hitherto confused mass of imperial constitutions (i.e. the Code), we then extended our care to the vast volumes of ancient law; and, sailing as it were across the mid ocean, have now completed, through the favour of heaven, a work that once seemed beyond hope (i.e. the Digest).

When by the blessing of God this task was accomplished, we summoned the most eminent Tribonian, master and ex-quæstor of our palace, together with the illustrious Theophilus and Dorotheus, professors of law, all of whom have on many occasions proved to us their ability, legal knowledge, and obedience to our orders; and we have specially charged them to compose, under our authority and advice, *Institutes*, so that you may no more learn the first elements of law from old and erroneous sources, but apprehend them by the clear light of imperial wisdom; and that your minds and ears may receive nothing that is useless or misplaced, but only what obtains in actual practice. So that, whereas, formerly, the junior students could scarcely, after three years' study, read the imperial constitutions, you may now commence your studies by reading them, you who have been thought worthy of an honour and a happiness so great that the first and last lessons in the knowledge of the law should issue for you from the mouth of the emperor.

When, therefore, by the assistance of the same eminent person Tribonian and that of other illustrious and learned men, we have compiled the fifty books, called *Digests* or *Pandects*, in which is collected the whole ancient law, we directed that these *Institutes* should be divided into four books, which might serve as the first elements of the whole science of law.

In these books a brief exposition is given of the ancient laws, and of those also, which, overshadowed by disuse, have been again brought to light by our imperial authority.

These four books of *Institutes* thus compiled, from all the Institutes left us by the ancients, and chiefly from the commentaries of our Gaius, both in his Institutes and in his work on daily affairs, and also from many other commentaries, were presented to us by the three learned men we have above named.   We have read and examined them and have accorded to them all the force of our constitutions.

Receive, therefore, with eagerness, and study with cheerful diligence, these our laws, and show yourselves persons of such learning that you may conceive the flattering hope of yourselves being able, when your course of legal study is completed, to govern our empire in the different portions that may be entrusted to your care.

Given at Constantinople, on the eleventh day of the calends of December, in the third consulate of the Emperor Justinian, ever August (533).

94. The Early Mediæval Town

(By Giry and Réville, in Lavisse et Rambaud's *Histoire Générale;* trans. by Bates and Titsworth, in their *The Emancipation of the Medieval Towns.* Henry Holt, New York, 1907. Reproduced by permission)

The following extract is a continuation of Reading 49, and describes briefly the formation of new towns and the condition of towns-people down to the thirteenth century.

(a) To the Eleventh Century

Care should be taken not to overestimate the importance of the urban communities during the first centuries of the Middle Ages. They were more numerous than important, and it is probable that they were neither very populous nor very rich. In a backward state of civilization it is impossible for towns to develop. A large city can live only by the exchange of its products for those things which it does not produce but which are brought to it. Without commerce there can be no large cities. Now, in that obscure age which extends from the fifth to the tenth century, all commerce was reduced to an indispensable minimum, except during an ephemeral renaissance in the time of Charlemagne. Only the shores of the Mediterranean continued to be frequented by merchants, and the relations between Provence, Italy, Greece, and the Orient were never entirely broken. In consequence, the cities of that privileged region preserved, it seems, a commercial class and a certain degree of prosperity. Everywhere else commerce was nearly annihilated, because there was neither the security nor the centers of exchange which it needed. Each domain lived upon itself, was almost self-sufficient; made the iron, wood, and woolen articles it needed, as well as produced its own wheat. The towns probably did the same; they were rural bourgs, and the inhabitants were peasants who worked on the surrounding land. Besides, custom did not aid in their development. Kings, nobles, Gallo-Roman and Germanic proprietors preferred to live in the country; the towns were no longer the theater of great events.

It is difficult to form a clear picture of the urban groups at that time and of the people that composed them. The new small towns huddled around the castles, abbeys, and churches. The old cities, once spacious, razed their former suburbs and restricted their limits so as to have less area to defend, as at Paris, Bordeaux, Evreux, Poitiers, and Sens. Roman monuments are discovered to-day outside the enclosures which these towns made for themselves at the time of the inva-

FIG. 17. A TYPICAL MEDIÆVAL TOWN

A Prussian town, containing walls, castle, cathedral, watch-towers, and closely-huddled buildings

sions. All towns, whenever possible, encircled themselves with ramparts, with embattled walls surrounded by moats, and armed their counterscarps with traps, abatis, and palisades. Inside the city the population, although not numerous, must have lived crowded together, as the architecture of the houses shows. The Roman dwelling was spread out in a comfortable way, with a large inner court, the atrium, and was generally low. Now the atrium was given up, filled in, and the roof rose high over a series of stories, which perhaps already were built so as to overhang, to gain still more room. As for monuments, the only ones which adorned the towns were those which the Romans had left. And sometimes even these were appropriated to strange uses, like the temple of Vesuna at Périgueux, which was changed into a tower for purposes of defense, or like the circus of Nîmes, which sheltered a part of the inhabitants and formed a veritable "quarter." Sometimes, too, these monuments were destroyed that the materials might be used for other constructions, especially for fortifications.

Between the church and the seigniorial dwelling, which was usually built to one side upon a precipitous hill or upon an artificial mound, the townsman passed his monotonous life, happy when a private war or an incursion for pillage did not bring upon his house or upon him the horrors of assault. Of political rights, he had none. The lord or his officers ruled the inhabitants as masters, imposed dues upon them, arrested, and judged them. The civil condition of the inhabitants must also have grown harder. It seems, indeed, that the number of freemen had noticeably diminished in the towns as well as in the country. Perhaps the cities of the south, thanks to their privileged situation, may have escaped in part this social decline; but this decline was general in the north, where only those preserved their independence who made it their business to bear arms in the following of a seignior and to live at the expense of others.

Thus from the sixth to the tenth century, townsmen did not count in society. Bishop Adalberon, in a famous poem to King Robert, considered around him only two classes; churchmen and nobles, beneath whom, but very far beneath, were the commons who worked.

(b) By the Thirteenth Century

On the whole, nothing could be more variable, or diverse, than the condition of the towns in the middle of the thirteenth century. Diverse in their origin, some dated back to antiquity; others, born of the wretchedness of the times, during the ninth and tenth centuries, were slowly formed by continuous agglomeration about a monastery or castle; a goodly number were of recent and artificial formation and owed their existence to the intelligent initiative of a few barons. Diverse in their history, some sustained struggles that were prolonged and hard, and sometimes savage; many bought more privileges than they gained by conquest; certain ones neither had to fight nor spend money, and saw themselves granted privileges which they did not ask for. Diverse in their prerogatives, some became independent republics, others consular municipalities or sworn communes, free like the lords, and involved like them in the feudal hierarchy; some, finally, possessed liberties so strictly limited to the civil and administrative order that historians have made of them a separate class, under the name of towns of burgessy. These innumerable differences should not surprise us; it is the law of life and of progress. Societies, like species, become diversified as they develop.

Development, in fact, is the common characteristic of the history of urban populations of the Middle Ages; the variety of their development is infinite. Let us note the profound transformation they underwent. In place of small bourgs, continually narrowing their boundaries in order to have less to defend, and becoming depopulated through wars, pillage, and famines that commerce no longer mitigated, were substituted more numerous and larger towns, which outgrew their walls and had powerful suburbs, and in which, thanks to the impulse of industry and trade, inhabitants abounded. In place of miserable and servile populations succeeded new generations, which attained competence, sometimes wealth, and through competence liberty: personal and civil liberty always and everywhere; often also collective and political liberty, although in infinitely varied degrees and very unequally distributed.   The towns from the seventh to the tenth century seemed mute; a sepulchral atmosphere pervaded them.   In the thirteenth century the cities hummed like hives.   The streets were still narrow, irregular, and unsanitary, but they were teeming with life.   Encumbering them were bales, baskets, venders crying their wares, and enormous signs swinging in the wind, which sometimes imperiled the safety of passers-by.   It was a new civilization bursting into bloom.   Splendid monuments arose, attesting the public prosperity and the genius of modest, unknown builders; romanesque and gothic churches lifted toward heaven their domes, campaniles, or spires; glorious belfries, which dominated and threatened their surroundings, awaiting the approaching time when the inimitable town halls, with their brilliant ornamentations of stone, should cause them to be forgotten.   The town bell was the public voice of the city, as the church bell was the voice of souls.   The city in the thirteenth century lived, spoke, and acted.   It was a new factor in society.   A heretofore unknown order, which grand and distant destinies awaited, was slowly growing.   This order was the Third Estate.

95. An English Town Charter

(Gross, Charles, *The Gild Merchant*, vol. ii, p. 244.   Oxford, 1890)

The following town charter, granted by Henry II (1154–89), to the town of Wallingford, England, is illustrative of these mediæval documents.   Note the importance of the guild merchant in the government of the town and in freedom of travel.

Henry, by the grace of God, King of England, Duke of Normandy and Aquitaine, and Count of Anjou, . . . I command you that my burgesses of Wallingford shall have my secure peace through my whole land of England and Normandy, wherever they may be.   And know that I have given and conceded to them forever all their liberties and laws and customs well and honorably, just as they had them best and most honorably in the time of King Edward, and in the time of my great grandfather King William, and of his son, the second King William, and in the time of King Henry, my grandfather; that is to say, that they should have freely the guild merchant with all its customs and laws, so that neither my bailiff nor any justice of mine should meddle with their guild; but only their own alderman and officer.   And if my officers or any justice shall have brought suit against them in any plea or for any occasion or shall have wished to lead them into a suit, I forbid it, and require that they should not make defense in any manner, except in their own proper portmote.   And if the reeve himself shall implead them on any occasion without an accuser, they shall not respond, and if on account of any transgression, or by a right judgment any one of them shall have made forfeiture by a right consideration of the burgesses, to the reeve shall he pay it. I forbid, moreover, and require that there shall be no market in Crowmarsh, nor any merchant, unless he is in the guild of merchants; and if any one goes out from the borough of Wallingford and lives from the merchandise of the same Wallingford, I command that he should make the right guild of the merchants with the same burgesses, wherever he may be, within the borough or without. Know moreover, that I have given and conceded forever to all the men of Wallingford full quittance from my yearly rent, which they were accustomed to pay from the borough of Wallingford, that is to say, from that which pertains to me in the borough. All these laws and customs and liberties and quittances I give to them and concede forever, and all others which they are able to show that their ancestors had, freely, quietly, and honorably, just as my citizens of Winchester ever had them at the best; and this on account of the great service and labor which they sustained for me in the acquisition of my hereditary right in England. I concede to them, moreover, that wherever they shall go in their journeys as merchants, through my whole land of England and Normandy, Aquitaine and Anjou, "by water and by strand, by wood and by land," they shall be free from toll and passage fees, and from all customs and exactions; nor are they to be troubled in this respect by any one, under a penalty of £10. I forbid, moreover, and require under the same penalty, that the reeve of Wallingford shall not make any fine of scotale or New Year's gift from any one, and that he shall not establish any custom in Wallingford which shall injure the burgesses of the town. Of this grant and concession, the witnesses are Theobald, archbishop of Canterbury and others. Given at Oxford, the first day before the Ides of January.

96. Oath of a New Freeman in a Mediæval Town

(Sharpe, R.R., *Calendar of Letter Books Preserved among the Archives of the Corporation of the City of London at the Guildhall*, Letter Book D, p. 195. London, 1899–1912)

Apprenticeship in England goes back to the thirteenth century. The regulations as to freemen, their oaths, and the number and conditions of apprenticeship were early prescribed. The following oath of a Freeman has been preserved at the Guildhall, in London, and dates from 1275.

Ye shall swear that ye shall be faithful and loyal unto our Lord the King, King of England . . . and the franchises and customs of the City ye shall maintain according to your power. . . . Ye shall take no apprentice for less than seven years, and ye shall cause him to be enrolled as such within the first year of your covenant, and at the end of his term, if he has well and loyally served you, you shall cause his egress to be enrolled. . . . And ye shall take no apprentice unless he be a free man and not a bondsman. All of which points aforesaid ye shall well and truly keep, so God you help and all his saints.

97. Ordinances of the White-Tawyer's Guild

(Riley, Henry T., *Memorials of London*, p. 232)

The following ordinances of the guild of white-tawyers, that is those who dressed leather with salt, alum, and other substances, to give it a white surface, is typical of guild regulations and guild activities of the time. The date of the document is uncertain, but probably about the middle of the fourteenth century.

In honor of God, of our Lady, and of all Saints, and for the nurture of tranquillity and peace among the good folks the megucers, called white-tawyers, the folks of the same trade have, by assent of Richard Lacer, mayor, and of the aldermen, ordained the points under-written.

In the first place, they have ordained that they will find a wax candle, to burn before our Lady in the church of Allhallows, near London wall.

Also, that each person of the said trade shall put in the box such sum as he shall think fit, in aid of maintaining the said candle.

Also, if by chance any one of the said trade shall fall into poverty, whether through old age or because he cannot labor or work, and have nothing with which to keep himself, he shall have every week from the said box 7d. for his support, if he be a man of good repute. And after his decease, if he have a wife, a woman of good repute, she shall have weekly for her support 7d. from the said box, so long as she shall behave herself well and keep single.

And that no stranger shall work in the said trade, or keep house for the same in the city, if he be not an apprentice, or a man admitted to the franchise of the said city.

And that no one shall take the serving-man of another to work with him, during his term, unless it be with the permission of his master.

And if any one of the said trade shall have work in his house that he cannot complete, or if for want of assistance such work shall be in danger of being lost, those of the said trade shall aid him, that so the said work be not lost.

And if any one of the said trade shall depart this life, and have not wherewithal to be buried, he shall be buried at the expense of their common box. And when any one of the said trade shall die, all those of the said trade shall go to the vigil, and make offering on the morrow.

And if any serving-man shall conduct himself in any other manner than properly toward his master, and act rebelliously toward him, no one of the said trade shall set him to work, until he shall have made amends before the mayor and aldermen; and before them such misprision shall be redressed.

And that no one of the said trade shall behave himself the more thoughtlessly, in the way of speaking or acting amiss, by reason of the points aforesaid; and if any one shall do to the contrary thereof, he shall not follow the said trade until he shall have reasonably made amends.

And if any one of the said trade shall do to the contrary of any point of the ordinances aforesaid, and be convicted thereof by good men of the same trade, he shall pay to the Chamber of the Gildhall of London, the first time 2s., the second time 40d., the third time half a mark, and the fourth time 10s., and shall forswear the trade.

Also, — that the good folks of the same trade shall once in the year be assembled in a certain place, convenient thereto, there to choose two men of the most loyal and befitting of the said trade, to be overseers of work and all other things touching the trade for that year; which persons shall be presented to the mayor and aldermen for the time being, and sworn before them diligently to inquire and make search, and loyally to present to the said mayor and aldermen such defaults as they shall find touching the said trade without sparing any one for friendship or for hatred, or in any other manner. And if any one of the said trade shall be found rebellious against the said overseers, so as not to let them properly make their search and assay, as they ought to do; or if he shall absent himself from the meeting aforesaid, without reasonable cause, after due warning by the said overseers, he shall pay to the Chamber, upon the first default, 40d.; and on the second like default, half a mark; and on the third one mark; and on the fourth, 20s., and shall forswear the trade forever.

Also, that if the overseers shall be found lax and negligent about their duty, or partial to any person for gift or for friendship, maintaining him or voluntarily permitting him to continue in his default, and shall not present him to the mayor and aldermen, as before stated, they are to incur the penalty aforesaid.

Also, that each year, at such assemblies of the good folks of the said trade, there shall be chosen overseers, as before stated. And if it be found that through laxity or negligence of the said governors such assemblies are not held, each of the said overseers is to incur the said penalty.

Also, that all skins falsely and deceitfully wrought in their trade which the said overseers shall find in the hands of any person, citizen or foreigner, within the franchise shall be forfeited to the said chamber, and the worker thereof amerced in manner aforesaid.

Also, that no one who has not been an apprentice, and has not finished his term of apprenticeship in the said trade, shall be made free of the same trade; unless it be attested by the overseers for the time being, or by four persons of the said trade, that such person is able and sufficiently skilled to be made free of the same.

Also, that no one of the said trade shall induce the servant of another to work with him in the said trade, until he has made a proper fine with his first master, at the discretion of the said overseers, or of four reputable men of the said trade. And if any one shall do to the contrary thereof, or receive the serving workman of another to work with him during his term, without leave of the trade, he is to incur the said penalty.

Also, that no one shall take for working in the said trade more than they were wont heretofore, on the pain aforesaid; that is to say, for the dyker (package of ten) of Scotch stags, half a mark; the dyker of Irish stags, half a mark; the dyker of Spanish stags, 10s., for the hundred of goat skins, 20s., the hundred of roe leather, 16s., for the hundred skins of young deer, 8s.; and for the hundred of kid skins, 8s.

98. School of the Guild of Saint Nicholas

(Report of the Commissioner of Edward VI, Toulmin Smith, *Ordinances of English Guilds*, p. 105. In Old English Text Society Pubs.)

Many of the guilds, after the twelfth century, began to maintain schools for the education of the children of their members. During the reign of Edward VI (1547–53) an investigation as to schools was made, and in the Report of the King's Commissioner the following item appears regarding the School of the Guild of Saint Nicholas, in Worcester, England.

"There hath byn tyme owt of mynde, a ffree scole kept within the said citie, in a grete halle belongyng to the said Guylde, called Trynite Halle; the scolemaster whereof for the tyme beyng hath hade yerely, for his stypend, ten pounds; whereof was paid, owt of the revenues of the

FIG. 18. A MEDIÆVAL SCHOOLMASTER

said landes, by the Master and Stewards of the said Guylde for the tyme beyng, vj, li, xii j. s. iii j. d.; And the resydewe of the said stypend was collected and gathered of the denocioun and benyvolence of the brothers and systers of the said Guylde. . . . They prowyded and have founde an honest and lernyed scolemaster, within the said halle, in lyke manner as they before tyme dyd; that is to say, one John Obyner, bachelor of arts; who hath there, at this present tyme, a boue the number of a hundred scolers."

99. Indenture of Apprenticeship, 1396

(From the *Archæological Journal*, London, 1872, vol. XXIX, 184. Trans. by H. C.)

The following Indenture of Apprenticeship was executed in Northampton, England, in 1396, and is typical of apprenticeship documents for hundreds of years thereafter.

This Indenture testifies that thus it is agreed between John Hyndlee of Northampton, Brazier, on the one part, and Thomas Edward, son of Gilbert Edward of Windsor, on the other part, that the aforesaid Thomas shall place himself and serve as apprentice to the said John Hyndlee, to be subject to this John Hyndlee and his assigns well and faithfully after the custom of apprentices, from the feast of All Saints next following after the present date up to the end of the seven years next succeeding shall have been fulfilled and completed, to the art called brazier's craft, practiced by the said John, during this time learning humbly.

Subject to him during the term of seven years aforesaid, the above-mentioned Thomas Edward shall keep secret all concerns of his said master John Hyndlee which ought to be concealed. He shall not do any injury to John, his master, nor see any done, but shall quickly prevent anything of the kind and shall protect his said master steadfastly from this time forth. He shall not absent himself from his aforesaid service. He shall not employ the goods and cattle of the said John, his master, without his permission. Booths, prostitutes, dies, dice, and similar games he shall not frequent, at the expense of his aforesaid master. He shall by no means commit fornication or adultery with any woman of the house and family of the said John, his master, nor shall he marry a wife, without the consent of his said master. The precepts, legal mandates, and reasonable requirements of the said John, his master, are to be faithfully observed by said Thomas; he shall diligently fulfill them, and obey the commands fully, during the whole period of his term above noted. And if the said Thomas should default from any of his agreements or from the prescribed articles, then said Thomas, according to the manner and the amount of his defection, shall make reparation to his master, John aforesaid, and shall double the term of his apprenticeship before mentioned, repeating his said service.

And the aforesaid John Hyndlee and his assigns shall direct said Thomas, his apprentice, in the above-mentioned arts in the best way said John knows and is able to do, they shall teach and instruct him. Or, if they can make him learn in no other way, let them do it by punishment.   Moreover, said John shall give to the teaching and informing of said Thomas in the art called the Pewterer's craft as much as he knows how and is able to do beyond the limits of his first duties.   And said John shall conceal (a hole in the deed) from said Thomas, his apprentice, none of the aforesaid arts, during the above-mentioned term.

Finally, said John and his assigns shall furnish to said Thomas everything necessary to him, his food and clothing, linen, bedding, housing, shoes, et cetera, enough to suffice him each year according as the age and stature of the said Thomas increase during the term aforesaid.

In testimony of this matter the above-mentioned parties have affixed to these Indentures their seals alternately.

Dated at Northampton, the Sunday next after the feast of Saint Luke, the apostle and evangelist, in the nineteenth year of the reign of King Richard the Second, following the Conquest.

Witnesses: — Henry Caysho, then mayor of the city of Northampton, William Wale and John Wodeward, bailiffs of the same.   Richard Gosselyn, John Esex Smyth, and others.

CHAPTER IX
THE RISE OF THE UNIVERSITIES

THE Readings contained in this chapter relate to the rise of the mediæval university, the organization of its instruction, and the influence of these institutions on the intellectual life of the later mediæval period. Slowly evolving out of some cathedral or monastery school, which had for long been noted for the high character of its instruction, the universities of mediæval Europe finally arose, were chartered as a mediæval guild, and in time became important not only intellectually, but socially and politically as well. For centuries they were almost the only homes of free thought. The value of their work is well set forth in the final selection of the chapter (124), by the great historian of these mediæval institutions.

The table giving country and date of foundation of these great mediæval institutions (100) shows the slow progress of new ideas in the Europe of that day, and the direction and rate of that progress. As both teachers and students were regarded as *clerici* they naturally possessed the privileges and immunities of the clergy (51), but, these not being regarded as sufficient for the new traveling scholars, new privileges and exemptions and protections were extended to both masters and students. Of these new privileges the grants of Frederick Barbarossa in Italy (101), King Philip Augustus at Paris (102), Count Rupert at Heidelberg (103) and Philip IV of France (104) have been selected as typical. The charter granted to the new university of Heidelberg (103) is also typical of these early documents, and is noteworthy for the detailed provision it made for the future university.

As these universities in time brought many strangers to the cities in which they were located, and as these persons needed eating and sleeping accommodations and thus helped local business, as well as adding to the intellectual prestige of the city, the different cities interested began to vie with one another in making special concessions to secure a university, and some even were willing to spend much money in maintaining such an institution. The privileges granted by Vercelli, to induce a migrating body of professors and students from Padua to locate there (**105**), is a good example of the first; and the selection from Villani, as to the cost for maintaining a university (**106**), is a good example of the second.   The efforts made by the English king to secure scholars from Paris (**109**) is another example of the first type.   As the early universities were in no way held to place by buildings and equipment, as is a modern university, it was easy for them to move to some other city whenever conditions did not please them. This right of *cessatio* was formally recognized by Papal Bull (**107**), and was frequently exercised (**108, 109**) for reasons that to-day seem trivial.

As the early universities were essentially guilds, with the stages of apprentice, journeyman, and master represented, the right to create and license masters was recognized almost from the first. The Bulls of Popes Gregory IX (**107**) and Nicholas IV (**111**), giving such right to Paris, are typical and illustrative.   The form of this license to teach is well shown in the document reproduced from Rashdall (**112**).

The courses of reading or lectures required for the different degrees are shown in the documents giving the requirements for the Arts degree at Paris (**113**), Leipzig (**114 a–b**), and Oxford (**115**); while the requirements for the still higher professional degrees in theology, civil and canon law, and medicine are well illustrated in the statement of Oxford requirements for each (**116 a–b**), and the Paris requirements for the degree in medicine (**117**).   The scholastic character of the theological instruction may be inferred from the criticisms made by Roger Bacon (**118**), a keen Oxford scholar and monk of the latter part of the thirteenth century.

The scarcity of books before the invention of printing did much to keep the character of the instruction on a low level, the master being compelled to "read" from the one text available and comment from his "gloss."   This lack of books is shown by the list of twenty-seven volumes contained in a scholar's library, left by will to the University of Paris (**119**); by Roger Bacon's lament (**120**); and by the Paris statute prescribing the character of the classroom instruction to be given (**121**).   The latter also throws some light on the classroom conduct of the time.   Selections **122** and **123** reproduce two of the earliest schedules of lectures known, the one at Toulouse (**122**) dating from 1309, and the one from Leipzig (**123**) from 1519.

100. University Foundations before 1600, by Countries

(After Rashdall and Minerva)

The table given below shows the progress, rate, and direction

		Italy	France	Great Britain
Studia Generalia before or without Bulls	12th century	? Salerno. 1158? Bologna. 1188 Reggio.*	? Paris. 1181? Montpellier.	1167–8 (?) Oxford.
	13th century	1204 Vicenza.* 1215 Arezzo.* 1222 Padua.* 1228 Vercelli.* 1246 Siena;* I in 1357.	Bef. 1231 Orleans.* ? Angers.*	1209 Cambridge;* P. in 1318.
Studia Generalia founded by Papal or Imperial Bull (or in Spain by Royal Charter)	13th century	1224 Naples, I. 1244–5 Curia Romana, P. 1248 Piacenza, P.	1230 Toulouse; P. in 1233.	
	14th century	1303 Rome, P. 1308 Perugia, P. 1318 Treviso, I. 1343 Pisa, P. 1349 Florence, P. 1361 Pavia, I. 1391 Ferrara, P.	1303 Avignon, P. 1332 Cohors, P. 1339 Grenoble, P. 1365 Orange, I.	
	15th century	1405 Turin, P. 1444 Catania, P.	1409 Aix, P. 1422 Dole, P. 1431 Poitiers,* P. 1437 Caen, P. 1441 Bordeaux, P. 1459 Valence, P. 1460 Nantes, P. 1464 Bourges, P. 1485 Besançon, P.	1413 St. Andrews, P. 1451 Glasgow, P. 1494 Aberdeen P.
	16th century	1540 Macerata. 1548 Messina (Sicily). 1556 Sassari. 1596 Cagliari.	1572 Nancy.	1583 Edinburgh. 1591 Dublin.

* Founded by a migration from some other university.   P. Founded by Papal Bull.   I. Founded by Imperial Edict.   R. Founded by Royal Charter (Spain).

100. University Foundations before 1600, by Countries (*cont.*)

(After Rashdall and Minerva)

of progress in founding the universities of mediæval Europe.

Spain and Portugal	Germania, Bohemia and the Low Countries	Other Countries
c. 1250 Valladolid; P. in 1346.		
1212–14 Palencia, R. Bef. 1230 Salamanca, R. 1254 Seville, R; P. in 1260. 1290 Lisbon-Coimbra, P.		
1300 Lerida, R. 1349 Perpignan, P. 1359 Huesca, R.	1347–8 Prague, P., I. 1365 Vienna, P. 1379 Erfurt; P. in 1392. 1385 Heidelberg, P. 1388 Cologne, P.	1364 Cracow (Poland); P. in 1397. 1367 Fünfkirchen (Hungary), P. 1389 Buda (Hungary), P.
1450 Barcelona, P. 1474 Saragossa, P. 1483 Palma, R. 1482 Avila, R. 1489 Siguenza, P. 1499 Alcalá, P. 1500 Valencia, P.	1402 Würzburg [1554]. 1409 Leipzig,* P. 1419 Rostock, P. 1425 Louvain, P. 1454 Trèves; P. in 1473. 1428 Griefswald;*P.* in 1455. 1455–6 Freiburg-im-Breisgau, P. 1459 Bâle, P. 1459 Ingolstadt; P. in 1472. Transferred in 1802 to Landshut and in 1826 to Munich. 1476 Mainz. 1476–7 Tübingen.	1465–7 Poszony or Pressburg (Hungary), P. 1477 Upsala (Sweden), P. 1477 Copenhagen(Denmark), P.
1502 Seville. 1504 Santiago. 1508 Madrid. 1531 Grenada. 1580 Oviedo.	1502 Halle-Wittenberg (Pr.); 1817 to Halle. 1506 Frankfurt (Pr.); removed to Breslau in 1811. 1527 Marburg (Pr.). 1544 Königsburg (Pr.). 1558 Jena. 1566 Olmütz (Moravia). 1567 Strassburg (Alsace). 1568 Braunsberg (Pr.). 1575 Leyden (Holland). 1576 Helmstädt; dissolved in 1809. 1578 Altorf; afterward dissolved. 1586 Gräz (Aust.).	1531 Sarospatak (Hungary). 1537 Lausanne (Switz.). 1559 Geneva (Switz.). 1588 Kiev (Russia).

* Founded by a migration from some other university. P. Founded by Papal Bull. I. Founded by Imperial Edict. R. Founded by Royal Charter (Spain).

101. Privileges for Students who Travel for Study

(*Monumenta Germaniæ Historica; Leges*, II, p. 114; trans. by Munro, in *Translations and Reprints from Sources of European History*, vol. II, no. 3, p. 2)

With the increase in the number of students who journeyed some distance to study, under famous cathedral-school teachers, the need for their better protection began to be evident.   Many of these came from afar, and at a time when international courtesies and public safety were little known.   As the presence of many strangers, attracted to a city or a little state to hear some noted teacher read and comment on the famous text-books of the time, added much to its prestige and wealth, it came to be worth while to offer them inducements to come, in the form of special favors and additional safety.

By way of giving students better protection, however, the Emperor Frederick Barbaross, in 1158, issued the following document, the first of its kind of which we have record.   This was said to have been obtained for the benefit of students going to Bologna to study civil and canon law, but it was made general, and applied to students and professors anywhere.   Freedom from arrest for certain causes, and trial before the professors or bishop instead of the city authorities, were valuable privileges, and once granted were tenaciously retained by the universities.   One still finds survivals of these ancient privileges in the jails and courts of the German universities, and in the English universities.

After a careful consideration of this subject by the bishops, abbots, dukes, counts, judges, and other nobles of our sacred palace, we, from our piety, have granted this privilege to all scholars who travel for the sake of study, and especially, to the professors of divine and sacred laws, namely, that they may go in safety to the places in which the studies are carried on, both they themselves and their messengers, and may dwell there in security.   For we think it fitting that, during good behavior, those should enjoy our praise and protection, by whose learning the world is enlightened to the obedience of God and of us, his ministers and the life of the subjects is moulded; and by a certain special love we defend them from all injuries.

For who does not pity those who exile themselves through love of learning, who wear themselves out in poverty in place of riches, who expose their lives to all perils and often suffer bodily injury from the vilest men — this must be endured with vexation.   Therefore, we declare by this general and ever to be valid law, that in the future no one shall be so rash as to venture to inflict any injury on scholars, or to occasion any loss to them on account of a debt owed to them by an inhabitant of their province — a thing which we have learned is sometimes done by an evil custom. And let it be known to the violaters of this constitution, and also to those who shall at the time be the rulers of the places, that a four-fold restitution of property shall be exacted from all and that, the mark of infamy being affixed to them by the law itself, they shall lose their office forever.

Moreover, if any one shall presume to bring a suit against them on account of any business, the choice in this matter shall be given to the scholars, who may summon the accusers to appear before their professors or the bishop of the city, to whom we have given jurisdiction in this matter. But if, in sooth, the accuser shall attempt to drag the scholar before another judge, even if his cause is a very just one, he shall lose his suit for such an attempt.

We also order this law to be inserted among the imperial constitutions under the title, *ne filius pro patre*, etc.

Given at Roncaglia, in the year of our Lord 1158, in the month of November.

102. Privileges granted the Students at Paris by Philip Augustus

(*Chartularium Universitatis Parisiensis*, vol. i, no. i, p. 59; trans. by Munro, *Translations and Reprints from Sources of European History*, vol. ii, no. 3, pp. 4–7)

This is the first royal privilege granted at Paris which has been preserved to us. It dates from 1200. Since students and teachers could leave the city so easily, and thus seriously interfere with its prosperity, it was desirable to make many concessions to them to make them satisfied to remain. Later, in the interests of law and order, many of these privileges had to be withdrawn. Here the king makes very liberal grants.

In the Name of the sacred and indivisible Trinity, amen. Philip, by the grace of God, King of the French. Let all men know, now and in the future, that for the terrible crime owing to which five of the clergy and laity at Paris were killed by certain malefactors, we shall do justice as follows: that Thomas, then provost, concerning whom more than all others the students have complained, because he denies the deed, we shall consign to perpetual imprisonment, in close confinement, with meagre fare, as long as he shall live; unless, perchance, he shall choose to undergo publicly at Paris the ordeal by water. If he succeeds, never henceforth at Paris nor anywhere else in our own land shall he be our provost or bailiff; nor elsewhere, if we are able to prevent it; nor shall he in the future enter Paris.

. . . concerning the safety of the students at Paris in the future, by the advice of our subjects we have ordained as follows: we will cause all the citizens of Paris to swear that if any one sees an injury done to any student by any layman, he will testify truthfully to this, nor will any one withdraw in order not to see (the act). And if it shall happen that any one strikes a student, except on self-defense, especially if he strikes the student with a weapon, a club or a stone, all laymen who see (the act) shall in good faith seize the malefactor or malefactors and deliver them to our judge; nor shall they withdraw in order not to see the act, or seize the malefactor, or testify to the truth. Also, whether the malefactor is seized in open crime or not, we will make a legal and full examination through clerks or laymen or certain lawful persons; and our count and our judges shall do the same. And if by a full examination we or our judges are able to learn that he who is accused, is guilty of the crime, then we or our judges shall immediately inflict a penalty, according to the quality and nature of the crime; notwithstanding the fact that the criminal may deny the deed and say that he is ready to defend himself in single combat, or to purge himself by the ordeal by water.

Also, neither our provost nor our judges shall lay hands on a student for any offense whatever; nor shall they place him in our prison, unless such a crime has been committed by the student, that he ought to be arrested. And in that case, our judge shall arrest him on the spot, without striking him at all, unless he resists, and shall hand him over to the ecclesiastical judge, who ought to guard him in order to satisfy us and the one suffering the injury. And if a serious crime has been committed, our judge shall go or shall send to see what is done with the student. If, indeed, the student does not resist arrest and yet suffers any injury, we will exact satisfaction for it, according to the aforesaid examination and the aforesaid oath. Also our judges shall not lay hands on the chattels of the students at Paris for any crime whatever. But if it shall seem that these ought to be sequestrated, they shall be sequestrated and guarded after sequestration by the ecclesiastical judge, in order that whatever is judged legal by the church, may be done with the chattels. But if students are arrested by our count at such an hour that the ecclesiastical judge can not be found and be present at once, our provost shall cause the culprits to be guarded in some student's house without any ill-treatment, as is said above, until they are delivered to the ecclesiastical judge. . . .

In order, moreover, that these (decrees) may be kept more carefully and may be established forever by a fixed law, we have decided that our present provost and the people of Paris shall affirm by an oath, in the presence of the scholars, that they will carry out in good faith all the above-mentioned. And always in the future, whosoever receives from us the office of provost in Paris, among the other initiatory acts of his office, namely, on the first or second Sunday, in one of the churches of Paris, — after he has been summoned for the purpose, —

shall affirm by an oath, publicly in the presence of the scholars, that he will keep in good faith all the above-mentioned. And that these decrees may be valid forever, we have ordered this document to be confirmed by the authority of our seal and by the characters of the royal name, signed below.

Done near Betisi in the 1200th year of the Incarnation of our Lord, in the 21st year of our reign, those being present in our palace whose names and signs are placed below.

The office of Seneschal vacant. Seal of Guy, the Cup-bearer.

Seal of Matthew, the Chamberlain. Seal of Drogo, the Constable.

Done during a vacancy (monogram) in the Chancellorship.

103. Charter of the University of Heidelberg

(Emminghaus, *Corpus Juris Germanici;* trans. by Henderson)

The following complete university charter, dating from 1386, is interesting in showing how much Paris formed a model, and also the extent of the grant of privileges to the master and scholars.

a. We, Rupert the elder, by the grace of God Count Palatine of the Rhine, elector of the Holy Empire and duke of Bavaria — lest we seem to abuse the privilege conceded to us by the apostolic see of founding a place of study at Heidelberg like to that at Paris, and lest, for this reason, being subjected to the divine judgment, we should merit to be deprived of the privilege granted, — do decree with provident counsel, which decree is to be observed there unto all time, that the university of Heidelberg shall be ruled, disposed and regulated according to the modes and matters accustomed to be observed in the university of Paris. Also that, as a handmaid of the Parisian institution — a worthy one, let us hope, — the latter's steps shall be imitated in every way possible; so that, namely, there shall be four faculties in it: the first, of sacred theology or divinity; the second, of canon and civil law, which, by reason of their similarity, we think best to comprise under one faculty; the third, of medicine; the fourth, of liberal arts — of the threefold philosophy, namely, primal, natural, and moral, three mutually subservient daughters. We wish this institution to be divided and marked out into four nations, as it is at Paris; and that all these faculties shall make one university, and that to it the individual students, in whichever of the said faculties they are, shall indivisibly belong like lawful sons of one mother. Likewise that that university shall be governed by one rector, and that the different masters and teachers, before they are admitted to the common pursuits of our institution, shall swear to observe the statutes, laws, privileges, liberties and franchises of the same, and not reveal its secrets, to whatever grade they may rise.   Also that they will uphold the honour of the rector and the rectorship of our university, and will obey the rector in all things lawful and honest, whatever be the grade to which they may afterwards happen to be promoted.   Moreover that the different masters and bachelors shall read their lectures and exercise their scholastic functions and go about in caps and gowns of a uniform and similar nature, according as that has been observed at Paris up to this time in the different faculties.   And we will say that if any faculty, nation or person shall oppose the aforesaid regulations, or pertinaciously refuse to obey them or any one of them — which God forbid, — from that time forward that same faculty, nation or person, if it do not desist upon being warned, shall be deprived of all connection with our aforesaid institution, and shall not have the benefit of our defence or protection.   Moreover we will and ordain that as the university as a whole may do for those assembled here and subject to it, so each faculty, nation or province of it may found lawful statutes and ones suitable to its needs, provided that through them or any one of them no prejudice is done to the above regulations and to our institution, and that no kind of impediment arise from them.   And we will that when the separate bodies shall have passed the statutes for their own observance, they may make them perpetually binding on those subject to them and on their successors.   And as in the university of Paris the different servants of the institutions have the benefit of the different privileges which its masters and scholars enjoy, so in starting our institution in Heidelberg, we grant, with even greater liberality, through these presents, that all the servants, viz.: its Pedells, librarians, lower officials, preparers of parchment, scribes, illuminators and others who serve it, may each and all, without fraud, enjoy in it the same privileges, franchises, immunities and liberties with which its masters or scholars are now or shall hereafter be endowed.

b. Lest in the new community of the city of Heidelberg, their faults being unpunished, there be an incentive to the scholars of doing wrong, we ordain with provident counsel by these presents, that the bishop of Worms, as judge ordinary of the clerks of our institution, shall have and possess, now and hereafter while our institution shall last, prisons, and an office in our town of Heidelberg for the detection of criminal clerks.   These things we have seen fit to grant to him and his successors, adding these conditions: that he shall permit no clerk to be arrested unless for a misdemeanour; that he shall restore any one detained for such fault or for any light offence to his master or to the rector if he asks for him, a promise having been given that the culprit will appear in court and that the rector or master will answer for him if the injured parties should go to law about the matter.   Furthermore that, on being requested, he will restore a clerk arrested for a crime on slight evidence, upon receiving a sufficient pledge — sponsers if the prisoner can obtain them, otherwise an oath if he can not obtain sponsors — to the effect that he will answer in court the charges against him; and in all these things there shall be no pecuniary exactions, except that the clerk shall give satisfaction, reasonably and according to the rule of the aforementioned town, for the expenses which he incurred while in prison. And that he will detain honestly and without serious injury a criminal clerk thus arrested for a crime where the suspicion is grave and strong, until the truth can be found out concerning the deed of which he is suspected. And he shall not for any cause, moreover, take away any clerk from our aforesaid town, or permit him to be taken away, unless the proper observances have been followed, and he has been condemned by judicial sentence to perpetual imprisonment for a crime. We command our advocate and bailiff and their servants in our aforesaid town, under pain of losing their office and our favour, not to put a detaining hand on any master or scholar of our said institution, nor to arrest him nor allow him to be arrested, unless the deed be such a one that that master or scholar ought rightly to be detained. He shall be restored to his rector or master, if he is held for a slight cause, provided he will swear and promise to appear in court concerning the matter; and we decree that a slight fault is one for which a layman, if he had committed it, ought to have been condemned to a light pecuniary fine. Likewise, if the master or scholar detained be found gravely or strongly suspected of the crime, we command that he be handed over by our officials to the bishop or to his representative in our said town, to be kept in custody.

c. By the tenor of these presents we grant to each and all the masters and scholars that, when they come to said institution, while they remain there, and also when they return from it to their homes, they may freely carry with them both coming and going, throughout all the lands subject to us, all their things which they need while pursuing their studies, and all the goods necessary for their support, without any duty, levy, imposts, tailles, gabelles, or other exactions whatever. And we wish them and each one of them, to be free from all the aforesaid imposts when purchasing corn, wines, meat, fish, clothes and all things necessary for their living and for their rank. And we decree that the scholars from their stock in hand of provisions, if there remain over one or two waggonloads of wine without their having practiced deception, may after the feast of Easter of that year sell it *en gros* without paying impost. We grant to them, moreover, that each day the scholars, of themselves or through their servants, may be allowed to buy in the town of Heidelberg, at the accustomed hour, freely and without impediment or hurtful delay, any eatables or other necessaries of life.

d. Lest the masters and scholars of our institution of Heidelberg may be oppressed by the citizens, avarice inducing them, through the extortionate price of lodgings, we have seen fit to decree that henceforth each year, after Christmas, one expert from the university on the part of the scholars, and one prudent, pious and circumspect citizen on the part of the citizens, shall be deputed to fix on the price for the students' lodgings. Moreover we will and decree that the different masters and scholars shall, through our bailiff, our judge and the officials subject to us, be defended and maintained in the quiet possession of the lodgings given to them free or of those for which they pay rent. Moreover, by the tenor of these presents, we grant to the rector and the university, or to those deputed by them, entire and total jurisdiction concerning the paying of rents for the lodgings occupied by the students, concerning the making and buying of codices, and the borrowing of money for other purposes by the scholars of our institution; also concerning the payment of assessments, together with everything that arises from, depends on and is connected with these.

e. In addition we command our officials that, when the rector requires their and our aid and assistance for carrying out his sentences against scholars who try to rebel, they shall assist our clients and servants in this matter; first, however, obtaining lawful permission to proceed against clerks from the lord bishop of Worms, or from one deputed by him for his purpose.

104. Exemption of Masters and Students from Taxation

(Charter of Philip IV, 1340–41, to the University of Paris; trans. by Norton)

It became customary to confer many privileges on both masters and students of the mediæval universities, such as freedom from military service, exemption from arrest and deportation for trial, the right to be tried by the university authorities instead of the civil or ecclesiastical, the right to be confined in the university jail in punishment, exemption from taxation, etc. The following grant of exemption from taxation is an example of these privileges, and is noteworthy for the large exemptions allowed.

To the aforesaid Masters and Scholars [of Paris], now in attendance at the University, and to those who are hereafter to come to the same University, or who are actually preparing in sincerity so to come, also while [they are] staying at the University, or returning to their own homes, *we grant* . . . that no layman, of whatever condition or prominence he may be, whether he be a private person, prefect, or bailiff, shall disturb, molest, or presume otherwise in any way whatsoever to seek to extort anything from the aforesaid Masters and Scholars, in person, family or property, under pretext of toll, *tallia* [special form of feudal tax], tax, customs, or other such personal taxes, or other personal exaction of any kind, while they are either coming to the University itself, or actually preparing in sincerity to come, or returning to their own homes; and whose status as scholars shall be established by the proper oath.

105. Privileges granted the University of Vercelli

(From a document printed in Rashdall, H., *The Universities of Europe in the Middle Ages*, vol. II, p. 746. Oxford, 1895)

In 1228 a body of masters and students, dissatisfied with their treatment at Padua, migrated to Vercelli, another Italian city. In establishing a university there they entered into an elaborate contract with the city, which was incorporated into the city charter and was to hold for eight years, by which the city, in consideration of a university being established in Vercelli, agreed, among other things, to loan money to students at lower than the regular rates, and to see that the markets were properly supplied with food without increase in price. The following provisions in the contract throw much light on early university practices.

. . . Likewise the town of Vercelli shall provide salaries (for professors) which shall be deemed competent by two scholars and two townsmen, and if they disagree the Bishop shall decide the matter . . . and said salaries shall be for one Theologian, three Masters of Laws, two Decretalists, two teachers of Natural Philosophy, two Logicians, and two Grammarians. (These professors shall be chosen by the rectors of the university. The town will send out at its own expense) trustworthy messengers under oath, who shall in good faith, and in the interests of the university of Vercelli, seek out the chosen Masters and Teachers, and shall use their best endeavors to bind them to lecture in the city of Vercelli. (The town will preserve peace within its borders, will consider scholars and their messengers neutral in time of war, will grant them the rights of citizens, and will respect the legal jurisdiction of the rectors, except in criminal and other specially mentioned cases.)

Likewise, the town of Vercelli will provide two copyists, through whom it will undertake to furnish men able to supply to the scholars copies in both kinds of Law (Civil and Canon) and in Theology, which shall be satisfactory and accurate both in text and in glosses, and the students shall pay for their copies (no extortionate prices but) a rate based on the estimate of the rectors (of the university).

. . . Likewise, the scholars or their representatives shall not pay the tributes in the district of Vercelli which belong and accrue to the town of Vercelli. . . . The Podesta (Chief Magistrate) and the town itself shall be bound to send, throughout the cities of Italy and elsewhere (as shall seem expedient to them) notice that a university has been established at Vercelli, and to invite scholars to come to the University of Vercelli.

106. Cost to a City of maintaining a University

(Matteo Villani's *Chronicle*, book I, cap. 8; trans. by J. A. Symonds, in his *Revival of Learning*, vol. II, pp. 119–20. London, 1888)

This selection gives some estimate as to the commercial importance of a university to a city.

The importance attached by great cities to their universities as a source of strength, may be gathered from the chapter in Matteo Villani's Chronicle describing the foundation of the *studio pubblico* in Florence. He expressly mentions that the Signory were induced to take this step in consequence of the depopulation inflicted by the Black Death of 1348. By drawing residents to Florence from other States, they hoped to increase the number of the inhabitants, and to restore the decayed fame and splendor of the commonwealth. At the same time they thought that serious studies might put an end to the demoralization produced in all classes by the plague. With this object in view, they engaged the best teachers, and did not hesitate to devote a yearly sum of 2500 gold florins to the maintenance of their school. Bologna, which owed even more than Florence to its university, is said to have lavished as much as half its revenue, about 20,000 ducats,[1] on the pay of professors and other incidental expenses. The actual cost incurred by the cities through their schools cannot, however, be accurately estimated, since it varied from year to year according to the engagements made with special teachers. At Pavia, for example, in 1400, the university supported in Canon Law several eminent doctors, in Civil Law thirteen, in Medicine five, in Philosophy three, in Astrology one, in Greek one, and in Eloquence one. Whether this staff was maintained after the lapse of another twenty years we do not know for certain.

107. Right to suspend Lectures (*Cessatio*)

(Bull of Pope Gregory IX for Paris, 1231; trans. by D. C. Munro)

One of the most effective rights of the mediæval university was the right of *cessatio*, that is, to suspend lectures and go on a strike as a means of enforcing a redress of grievances against either town or church authorities. This right was frequently exercised and often for trivial offenses, usually bringing the offending party to terms rather promptly. The following Papal Bull of 1231, conferring this right on the University of Paris, is typical of rights elsewhere conferred or assumed. This continued in force at Paris until 1499, when the last attempt at a *cessatio* took place.

[1] A ducat was worth approximately $2.30 in terms of our money and the prices of a quarter of a century ago.

And if, perchance, the assessment [right to fix the prices] of lodgings is taken from you, or anything else is lacking, or an injury or outrageous damage, such as death or the mutilation of a limb, is inflicted on one of you, unless through a suitable admonition satisfaction is rendered within fifteen days, you may suspend your lectures until you have received full satisfaction. And if it happens that any one of you is unlawfully imprisoned, unless the injury ceases on a remonstrance from you, you may, if you judge it expedient, suspend your lectures immediately.

108. A *Cessatio* at Oxford (1209)

(Chron. *Roger of Wendover* (Rolls Series), 84, II, p. 51; trans. by Leach)

This is an early example of the *cessatio*, and illustrates how vigorously the early universities contended with both Church and civil authorities for the right of freedom of internal government.

About the same time a clerk, who was studying the liberal arts at Oxford, by accident killed a woman, and when he found she was dead, sought safety in flight. But the bailiff of the town and others who came up and found the woman dead, began to try to find the murderer in his hostel, which he had hired with three other clerks, and not finding the criminal, took his three friends, who knew almost nothing about the murder, and threw them into prison. A few days afterwards, on the orders of the king of the English, in contempt of the liberty of the church, they were taken outside the town and hung. On this nearly 3000 clerks, masters and scholars alike, left Oxford, not a single one of the whole University remaining. Some of them went to study the liberal arts at Cambridge, some to Reading, but the town of Oxford was left empty.

109. England invites Scholars to leave Paris

(*Chartularium Universitatis Parisiensis*, vol. I, p. 119; trans. by Norton)

In 1229 there were serious student riots at Paris, during a carnival, and several persons were wounded. The city authorities made reprisals, putting two students to death. For this a *cessatio* was declared, and the masters and students left the city, going to Angers, Orleans, Rheims, and other *studia*, at the first two of which rival universities were established. The bishop launched excommunications against the deserters in vain, and the university remained closed for two years. As a bid to obtain some of the striking masters and students, King Henry III of England issued the following urgent invitation. As the result of this many came and settled at Cambridge, virtually reviving the institution after a period of quiescence covering fifteen years (1214–29).

The King; Greeting to the Masters and the whole body of scholars at Paris. Humbly sympathizing with the exceeding tribulations and distresses which you have suffered at Paris under an unjust law, we wish by our pious aid, with reverence to God and His holy church, to restore your status to its proper condition of liberty. Wherefore we have concluded to make known to your entire body that if it shall be your pleasure to transfer yourselves to our kingdom of England and to remain there to study, we will for this purpose assign to you cities, boroughs, towns, whatsoever you may wish to select, and in every fitting way will cause you to rejoice in a state of liberty and tranquillity which should please God and fully meet your needs.

In testimony of which &c. Witnessed by the King at Reading, July 16. (1229)

110. Early Licensing of Professors to teach

(Bull of Pope Gregory IX, *Chartularium Universitatis Parisiensis*, vol. I, p. 237; trans. by Compayre)

The universities being an evolution from the cathedral schools, the licensing to teach in them naturally came from the bishop, or his representative. In the cathedral schools this was the *Scholasticus;* in the universities this official evolved into a *Chancellor*, a term still used by a few of our universities instead of the modern designation of *President*. The Chancellor at Paris received the following charge, in 1231, in a Bull from Pope Gregory IX.

Future chancellors shall swear not to receive as professors of theology and canon law any but worthy men, able to do honor to their precepts, and they shall reject all who are unworthy, without respect either to persons or to nations. Before conferring the license, the chancellor shall allow three months to elapse, dating from the day the license was asked for, and during these three months he shall make inquiries of the professors of theology and other serious and instructed persons, in order to become acquainted with the life and manners, the knowledge, capacity, love of study, perfectibility, and other qualities needful in those who aspire to teach; and, these inquiries finished, he shall grant or refuse the license according to his conscience.

111. The Right to grant Licenses to teach

(Bull of Pope Nicholas IV, 1292; trans. by Norton)

Masters and Doctors of Paris, Bologna, and Oxford were early recognized as qualified to teach anywhere, without further examination. Other universities gradually accepted the custom established at these university mothers. The right to grant such license, the *jus ubique docendi*, came to be regarded as the essence of a *Studium Generale*. The following Papal Bull, of 1292, formally grants this right to Paris.

Desiring, therefore, that the students in the field of knowledge in the city of Paris, may be stimulated to strive for the reward of a Mastership, and may be able to instruct, in the Faculties in which they have deserved to be adorned with a Master's chair, all those who come from all sides, — we decree, by this present letter, that whoever of our University in the aforesaid city shall have been examined and approved by those through whom, under apostolic authority, the right to lecture is customarily bestowed on licentiates in said faculties, according to the custom heretofore observed there, — and who shall have from them license in the Faculty of Theology, or Canon Law, or Medicine, or the Liberal Arts, — shall thenceforward have authority to teach everywhere outside of the aforesaid city, free from examination or test, either public or private, or any other new regulation as to lecturing or teaching. Nor shall he be prohibited by any one, all other customs and statutes to the contrary notwithstanding; and whether he wishes to lecture or not in the Faculties referred to, he shall nevertheless be regarded as a Doctor.

112. A University License to teach

(Document printed in Rashdall; *The Universities of Europe in the Middle Ages*, vol. II, part II, p. 734. Oxford, 1895)

The following form, reproduced by Rashdall, is dated 1710, but is considered by him as probably similar to the mediæval forms used. A comparison of this form with a modern Ph.D. diploma reveals an interesting similarity between the two.

Inasmuch as you have been presented to me for examination in both (Civil and Canon) Laws and for the customary approval, by the Most Illustrious and the Most Excellent D.D. (naming the Promoters), golden Knights, Counts Palatine, Most Celebrated Doctors, and inasmuch as you have since undergone an arduous and rigorous examination, in which you bore yourself with so much learning and distinction that that body of Most Illustrious and Excellent Promoters without one dissenting voice, — I repeat, without one dissenting voice, — have judged you worthy of the laurel, therefore by the authority which I have as Archdeacon and senior Chancellor, I create, publish, and name you, N. N., Doctor in the aforesaid Faculties, giving to you every privilege of lecturing, of ascending the Master's chair, of writing glosses, of interpreting, of acting as Advocate, and of exercising also the functions of a Doctor here and everywhere throughout the world; furthermore, of enjoying all those privileges which those happy individuals, who have been so deserving in these fostering colleges, are accustomed to use and enjoy.

And I trust that all these things will forever result in the increase of your fame and the honor of our Colleges, to the praise and glory of Almighty God and of the ever blessed Virgin Mary.

113. Books required at Paris for the Arts Degree

(Chartularium Universitatis Parisiensis, vol. I, p. 119)

The following books were prescribed for the A.B. and A.M. degrees at Paris by the Statutes of 1254. The list does not distinguish the books required for the baccalaureate degree only, but gives for both degrees together. It will be noted that books on some of the Seven Liberal Arts are missing.

The great preponderance of Aristotle in the list is noticeable, showing how completely Aristotle had been adopted by this time as the great authority of mediæval Europe. In addition to having heard lectures on these subjects, the candidate must also have taken part in a number of disputations.

I. The "Old" Logic.
    1. Introduction to the Categories of Aristotle (Isagoge), Porphyry.
    2. Categories, and On Interpretation, Aristotle.
    3. Divisions, and Topics except Bk. IV, Boethius.

II. The "New" Logic.
    1. Prior and Posterior Analytics, Aristotle.
    2. Sophistical Refutations,   "
    3. Topics,   "

III. Moral Philosophy.
    1. Ethics, 4 Bks.,   "

IV. Natural Philosophy.
    1. Physics,   "
    2. On the Heavens and the Earth,   "
    3. Meteorics,   "
    4. On Animals,   "
    5. " the Soul,   "
    6. " Generation,   "
    7. " Sense and Sensible Things,   "
    8. Sleep and Waking,   "
    9. Memory and Recollection,   "

10. On Life and Death,   Aristotle.
11. " Plants,   " (?)
V. Metaphysics.
     1. Metaphysics,   "
VI. Other Books.
     1. On the Six Principles, Gilbert de la Porrée.
     2. Barbarismus (Bk. 3, Larger Grammar), Donatus.
     3. Grammar (Major and Minor), Priscian.
     4. On Causes, Costa ben Luca.
     5. On the Differences of Spirit and Soul (another translation of On Causes).

114. Books required at Leipzig for the Arts Degree

(Zarncke, *Statutenbücher der Universität Leipzig*, pp. 311–12)

The following books were prescribed for the A.B. and the A.M. degrees at Leipzig, in 1410. Contrasted with Paris, a little earlier (**R. 113**), it will be seen that Aristotle is less prominent, that the Seven Liberal Arts are better represented, and that the whole shows a much better balanced course. The time requirements for each subject are also given here, showing a course requiring from twenty-two and one half to twenty-eight and one half months for the A.B. degree, and from forty-two to sixty-six and one half months additional for the A.M. degree.

(*a*) *Books required at Leipzig for the Degree of A.B. in 1410*

I. Grammar.
     1. Last two books of Priscian.   (2 months.)
II. Logic.
     1. Tractatus (Summulæ), Petrus Hispanus.   ($2\frac{1}{2}$ to 3 months.)
     2. The "Old" Logic.   (3 to 4 months.)
     3. The "New" Logic, except Topics.   ($6\frac{1}{2}$ to 7 months.)
III. Natural Philosophy.
     1. Physics.   (6 to 9 months.)
     2. On the Soul.   (2 months.)
IV. Mathematics.
     1. On the Material Sphere (Sacrobosco).   (5 to 6 weeks.)

(*b*) *Books required at Leipzig for the Degree of A.M. in 1410*

I. Logic.
     1. Logic of Heytisbury.
     2. Topics, Aristotle.   (3 to 4 months.)
II. Moral and Practical Philosophy.
     1. Ethics.   (6 to 9 months.)
     2. Politics.   (4 to 9 months.)
     3. Economics.   (3 weeks.)

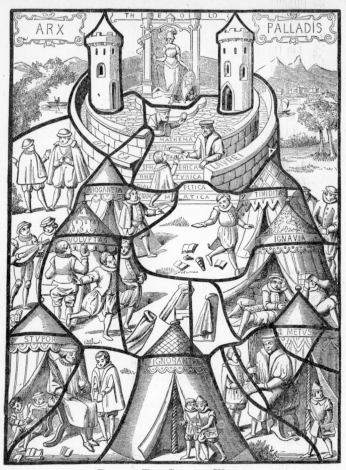

FIG. 19. THE CAMP OF WISDOM

(From *Les Arts et Métiers au Moyen Age*, p. 252)

An allegorical stained-glass window, the work of Lorraine artists of the sixteenth century, and now in the Library of Strassburg. This shows the wise youth passing up the steps of the Trivium and Quadrivium and the three Philosophies to the inner court of the Temple of Wisdom, with Theology still ahead and over all. Other youths are seen wasting their time.

III. Natural Philosophy.

      1. On the Heavens and the Earth.   ($3\frac{1}{2}$ to 4 months.)

      2. On Generation and Destruction.   (7 weeks to 2 months.)

      3. Meteorics.   ($3\frac{1}{2}$ to 4 months.)

      4. Parva Naturalia.   ($2\frac{1}{2}$ to 3 months.)   The books on: —

          a. Sense and Sensible Things.

          b. Sleep and Waking.

        c. Memory and Recollection.
        d. Longevity and Shortlivedness.
IV. Metaphysics.
     1. Metaphysics. (5 to 9 months.)
V. Mathematics.
     1. Astronomy: Theory of the Planets (Gerard of Cremona). (5 to 6 weeks.)
     2. Geometry: Euclid. (5 to 9 months.)
     3. Arithmetic: Common Arithmetic (Sacrobosco). (3 weeks to 1 month.)
     4. Music: Music (John de Muris). (3 weeks to 1 month.)
     5. Optics: Common Perspective (John of Pisa). (3 to $3\frac{1}{2}$ months.)

115. Books required at Oxford for the Arts Degree

(Rashdall, H., *The Universities of Europe in the Middle Ages*, vol. II, part II, pp. 455–58. Oxford, 1895)

The following list of books shows those required for the A.B. and the A.M. degrees at Oxford in the period 1408–31. It is a more elastic course of study than the one at Paris, and Aristotle is less prominent. More alternatives or elections were offered the student than at either Paris or Leipzig. A clear attempt is seen to keep up the traditions that an Arts course should include the *Trivium* and *Quadrivium* of the earlier Middle Ages, as well as the "three philosophies" introduced by the rediscovery of Aristotle early in the thirteenth century.

For B.A. (*Admissio ad lecturam alicuius libri Facultatis Artium*):
    Four years' study.

For Determination.
    To have been admitted as above, and "read" some book of Aristotle.
    To have disputed for a year as "General Sophister" *in Parviso.*
    To have responded *de questione.*
    To have heard: Donatus, *Barbarismus;* Arithmetic (*Algorismus integrorum*); the method of finding Easter (Computus ecclesiasticus); (Joannes de Sacra Bosco), *Tractatus de Sphæra;* Porphyry, *Isagoge;* Gilbert de la Porrée, *Sex Principia;* Aristotle, *Sophistici Elenchi-lectionatim* in College or Hall.
    The Old and New Logic, except the Boethius, *Topics*, bk. IV, *cursorie* from Bachelors in the Public Schools.

For License and Inception:
    Three years' additional study.

To have been admitted *ad lecturam alicujus libri Aristotelis*, and to have lectured thereon.

To have been admitted to determine.

To have responded *apud Augustinenses*, and taken part in a certain number of other disputations.

To have heard (in addition to the books already read for B.A.). (Stat. of 1431.)

In the Seven Arts:

Grammar.......Priscian "in majore vel minore." (One term.)

Rhetoric........The *Rhetoric* of Aristotle. (Three terms.)
(Or the *Topics* of Boethius, bk. IV; or Cicero, *Nova Rhetorica;* or Ovid's *Metamorphoses;* or "*Poetria Virgilii.*")

Logic...........Aristotle, *De Interpretatione.* (Three terms.)
(Or Boethius, *Topics* (first three books); or Aristotle, *Prior Analytics,* or *Topics.*)

Arithmetic......Boethius. (One term.)

Music..........Boethius. (One term.)

Geometry.......Euclid (? six books.)
(Or Alhazen. [Two terms]; or Vitellio, *Perspectiva.*)

Astronomy......(Ptolemy?) *Theorica Planetarum.* (Two terms.)
(Or Ptolemy, *Almagesta.*)

In the Three Philosophies:

Natural..........Aristotle, *Physica* or *De cœlo et mundo.* (Two terms.)
(Or *De proprietatibus elementorum,* or *Meteorica,* or *De vegetabilibus et plantis,* or *De Anima,* or *De Animalibus,* or "any of the smaller books.")

Moral...........Aristotle, *Ethica,* or *Economica,* or *Politica.* (Three terms.)

Metaphysical....Aristotle, *Metaphysica.* (Two terms.)

116. Requirements for the Professional Degrees at Oxford

(Rashdall, H., *The Universities of Europe in the Middle Ages*, vol. II, part II, pp. 452–55. Oxford, 1895)

Rashdall gives the following requirements for the professional degrees for mediæval Oxford, though without any particular dates. They cover the requirements in the early fourteenth century.

(a) Theology

For Opponency:

For M.A. candidates, four or five years' study (i.e. apparently to be *in the fifth year*), presumably divided between the *Bible* and *Sentences*, since three years' *auditio* of the Bible are required for Inception.

For others, eight years in the study of Arts; six or seven years in Theology.

For B.D. (*Admissio ad lecturam libri Sententiarum*):

For M.A. candidates, two years more, i. e. seven years in all.

For others, two years more, i.e. eight years in all.

Certain Opponencies, number not specified.

For License:

Two years' further study.

To have lectured on one book of the Bible and on the Sentences.

An examinatory Sermon at Saint Mary's.

Eight Responsions to non-graduate Opponents.

To dispute (as Opponent) with every Regent D.D.

Vespers.

In the fifteenth century an additional Sermon was added by Statute.

(b) Canon Law

For Bachelor of Decrees: (*Admissio ad lecturam extraordinariam alicuius libri Decretalium*):

Five years' study of Civil Law.

To have heard the *Decretals* twice, and the *Decretum* for two years.

For Inception as Doctor of Decrees:

To have read extraordinarie two or three "causes" or the tractate *De Simonia,* or *De Consecratione,* or *De Pœnitentia* (parts of the *Decretum*).

To have opposed and responded to the questions of every Regent.

To have given one lecture for each Regent.

(After Inception, two years, afterwards one year of Necessary Regency.)

(c) Civil Law

For B.C.L. (*Admissio ad lecturam libelli Institutionum*):

For M.A. candidates, four years' study.

For others, six years' study.

For License ad legendum aliquod volumen Juris Civilis (e.g. *the Digestum Novum* or *Infortiatum*):

To have heard the *libri apparitati* of the Civil Law.

For Inception:

(No additional *time* specified.)

To have lectured on the *Institutes,* the *Digestum Novum,* and the *Infortiatum.*

To have given an ordinary lecture for each Regent Doctor.

To have opposed and responded in the School of each Decretist.

(d) Medicine

For M.B. (*Admissio ad legendum librum Aphorismorum*).
    (No time specified.)

For admission "*ad practicandum*" in Oxford:
    For M.A. candidates, four years' study.
    To pass an examination conducted by the Regent Doctors.
    For others, eight years' study and examination.

For License and Inception:
    For M.A. candidates, six years' study (in all).
    To have "read" one book of *Theorica* (i.e. the *Liber Tegni* of
        Galen, or *Aphorismi* of Hippocrates), "pro majori parte."
    To have "read" one book of *Practica* (i.e. *Regimenta Acutorum* of
        Hippocrates, *Liber Febrium* of Isaac, or the *Antidotarium* of
        Nicholas).
    To have responded to and opposed in the Schools of the Regents
        for two years.
    For others, to have been admitted to practice, as above: eight
        years' study (in all): to have given the above lectures.

117. The Course in Medicine at Paris

(*Chartularium Universitatis Parisiensis*, vol. I, no. 453, p. 517; trans. by Munro)

The following required course in Medicine at Paris, 1270–74,
gives the books used, and will prove of special interest to students
interested in the study of medicine. It also shows the influence
of Arabic writers on European learning in this subject. It is a
poorer course of study than that provided at Montpellier, though
Montpellier probably had the foremost medical faculty in Europe
at that time.

This is the form for licensing bachelors of medicine. First, the master under whom the bachelor is, ought to testify to the chancellor, in
the presence of the masters called together for this purpose, concerning
the suitability of licensing the bachelor. He ought to prove his time
of study by at least two examinations; and the time which he ought to
have studied is five and one half years, if he has ruled in arts or has been
a licentiate; or six, if he has not.

The course of study is as follows:

I. He ought to have heard:

    1. The Ars Medica (probably *Liber Tegni*, of Galen) twice in
    the regular courses and once in an extraordinary course,
    with the exception of Theophilus. (Theophilus was a
    Byzantine physician, said to have lived in the seventh
    century, A.D.)

2. On Urines, which is sufficient to have heard once in either a regular or an extraordinary course.

3. The Viaticum (composed by Abu Djàrfar Ahmad, disciple of Isaac) twice in regular courses.

4. The other books of Isaac (a Jewish physician who wrote several books on medicine which were translated from the Arabic by Constantine the African) once in a regular course, twice in extraordinary courses, except the Particular Diets, which it is sufficient to have heard in an extraordinary or regular course.

5. The Book of Antidotes (Book of Antidotes was then used in about the same sense as Book of Mendicaments. This one was by Nicholas of Salerno) of Nicholas, once.

6. The Verses of Ægidius are not required. (Ægidius of Corbeil taught at Paris under Philip Augustus. He wrote his works in verse.)

II. Also, he ought to have read:

1. The books on Theory and Practice. (By this Denifle thinks the Opus Pantegni, by Ali ben Abbâs, is meant. This was divided into Theory and Practice. It was sometimes attributed to Constantine the African.)

And he ought to swear this. Moreover, if any one is convicted of perjury or lying he, although licensed, may be degraded.

118. Roger Bacon on the Teaching of Theology

(Roger Bacon, *Opera Inedita*, p. lvi; trans. by J. S. Brewer. London, 1859)

The following comment by the English monk, Roger Bacon, written in 1292, shows how the great mediæval textbooks on theology gradually superseded the study of the Bible. This tendency increased with time. Luther tells us that he was twenty years old when, by accident, he saw a Bible for the first time in the library of the University of Erfurt.

FIG. 20. ROGER BACON (1214?–94)

Although the principal study of the theologian ought to be in the text of Scripture, as I have proved in the former part of this work, yet in the last fifty years theologians have been principally occupied with questions (for debate) as all know, in tractates and summæ, — horseloads, composed by many,— and not at all with the most holy text of God. And accordingly, theologians give a readier reception to a treatise of scholastic questions than they will do to one about the text of

Scripture. . . . The greater part of these questions introduced into theology, with all the modes of disputation and solution, are in the terms of philosophy, as is known to all theologians, who have been well exercised in philosophy before proceeding to theology. Again, other questions which are in use among theologians, though in terms of theology, viz., of the Trinity, of the fall, of the incarnation, of sin, of virtue, of the sacraments, etc., are mainly ventilated by authorities, arguments, and solutions drawn from philosophy. And therefore the entire occupation of theologians now-a-days is philosophical, both in substance and method.

119. List of Books left by Will to the University of Paris

(*Chartularium Universitatis Parisiensis*, vol. 1, no. 437, p. 493; trans. by Munro)

The following document, reproducing a clause from a will and the list of twenty-seven books contained in the private library of Master Stephen, presented to Paris, in 1271, as a loan collection for poor and deserving theological students, is interesting as showing what a prominent churchman and scholar of that day had accumulated.

To all the officers of the court at Paris who shall read this document, greeting in the Lord. We make known that John of Orleans, constituted master in our presence, canon and chancellor of Paris, acknowledges and admits that he has received and had from the venerable man master Nicholas, arch-deacon of the church at Paris, formerly chancellor of the aforesaid church at Paris, the books named below — to be lent to the poor students studying theology, — according to a certain clause contained in the will of master Stephen of blessed memory, formerly arch-deacon of Canterbury, which is inserted in the present document, as follows:

I will and command that my books on theology shall be delivered to the chancellor of Paris who, for the sake of piety, shall lend them to poor students studying theology at Paris who are without books; in such a manner, however, that each chancellor, each year, shall receive back the aforesaid books and after receiving them shall deliver and lend them, each year, to the poor students, as shall seem expedient.

The names of the books are as follows:

1. The Bible complete, with a glossary.
2. Genesis and Exodus, glossed, in one volume.
3. The books of Solomon, glossed, in one volume.
4. Exodus, glossed by itself.
5. Job, glossed by itself.
6. Ezekiel, glossed by itself.
7. The Gospels, glossed by themselves, in one volume.

8. The Psalter, with a complete glossary.
9. The four books of Sentences. (Peter Lombard's work.)
10. The books of Numbers.
11. Joshua, Judith, Ruth, Deuteronomy, glossed, in one volume.
12. The four books of Kings, Chronicles, first and second.
13. Esdras, first and second of Maccabees, Amos, glossed, in one volume.
14. The Twelve Prophets, glossed, in one volume.
15. The Psalter, glossed and complete.
16. The Epistles of Paul, glossed.
17. The Psalter, glossed and complete.
18. The Historia Scolastica of Pierre le Mangeur.
19. The four Gospels, glossed.
20. The Epistles of Paul, glossed, with a smaller glossary.
21. The Psalter, glossed and complete.
22. The first and second books of Maccabees, glossed as far as the tenth chapter.
23. The Gospel of Mark.
24. The Gospels, glossed.
25 and 26. The Bible in two volumes, with marginal notes, which Bishop Stephen presented.
27. The original of the Sentences of master Peter Lombard, in a certain volume, bound in calf, now somewhat worn, with round copper nails in the covers.

We, the above-mentioned official, have thought indeed that, in testimony and witness of all the above-mentioned, we ought to place on the present writing the seal of the court at Paris, together with the seal of the aforesaid chancellor; hoping and asking that his successors, who shall be chancellors, shall order and do with the aforesaid books, for the sake of the divine piety, according to the contents of the aforesaid clause.

Done in the year of our Lord, 1271, Wednesday, the feast of the Apostles Simon and Jude.

120. The Scarcity of Books on Morals

(Roger Bacon; trans. by J. S. Brewer. London, 1859)

Roger Bacon (1214?–94), writing as to the scarcity of books on morals, especially in the works of four classic writers, says:

The scientific books of Aristotle, of Avicenna, of Seneca, of Cicero, and other ancients cannot be had except at a great cost; their principal works have not been translated into Latin, and copies of others are not to be found in ordinary libraries or elsewhere. The admirable books of Cicero *De Republica* are not to be found anywhere, as far as I can hear, although I have made anxious inquiry for them in different parts of the world and by various messengers. And so of many other books of which I send extracts to your beatitude. I could never find the works of Seneca, until after the time when I received your commands, although I made diligent search for them during twenty years and more. And so it is with many more most useful books connected with the sciences of morals.

121. Methods of Instruction in the Arts Faculty at Paris

(Bulæus, *Historia Universitatis Parisiensis*, vol. IV, p. 332; trans. by Norton)

The following Statute of the Masters of Arts at Paris, enacted in 1355, compares the two methods of lecturing, and also throws an interesting side-light on university classroom manners of the time.

Two methods of reading the books of the Liberal Arts have been tried:

By the first, the Masters of Philosophy from their chairs rapidly set forth their own words, so that the mind of the listener can take them in, but his hand is not able to write them down; by the second, they pronounce them slowly so that the listeners are able to write them down in their presence with the pen. By diligent examination and mutual comparison of these ways the first method is found to be the better, because the conceptual power of the ordinary mind warns us to imitate it in our lectures. Therefore, we, one and all, Masters of Arts, both lecturing and not lecturing, being especially convoked for this purpose . . . have made a statute to this effect:

All lecturers, Masters as well as Scholars, of the same Faculty, whenever and wherever they happen to be reading any book in regular order or course in the same Faculty, or to be discussing a question according to this or any other method of exposition, shall follow the former method of reading to the best of their ability, to wit: presenting it as though no one were writing it in their presence. It is in accordance with this method that discourses and recommendations are made in the University, and it is followed by Lecturers in the rest of the Faculties.

Transgressors of this Statute, whether Masters or Scholars, we deprive thenceforth of their positions as lecturers, or honors, offices, and the rest of their means of support under our Faculty, for one year. But if any one repeats the offense, we double the penalty for the first repetition; for the second we quadruple it, and so on. And auditors who interfere with the execution of this our Statute by shouting or whistling or raising a din, or by throwing stones, either personally or through their attendants or accomplices, or in any other way, we deprive of and cut off from our company for one year, and for each repetition we increase the penalty to twice and four times the length as above.

122. Time-Table of Lectures in the Arts Faculty at the University of Toulouse, 1309

(Constructed from the Latin Statute of that date by Paetow, S. J., in his *The Arts Course at Mediæval Universities*.   Univ. Ill. Studies, vol. III, no. 7, p. 96.   1910)

The time-table given on page 180 was sanctioned in 1309 (the University was founded in 1230), to avoid conflicts and disputes between masters and students, and is one of the earliest known. Norton gives a somewhat similar though less well-arranged time-table for the Arts Faculty at Leipzig, under date of 1519 (**R. 123**).   Both schedules show the great hold of Aristotle.

The statute does not name the exact hour when lectures began in the morning, but it was probably about six o'clock, the usual opening hour at most mediæval universities.   The various periods must have been something like an hour and a half long, including the intermission between, as period six is stated as beginning at three in the afternoon.   Period seven had no definite length, being all the time left after the close of period six.

Books used as a basis for the lectures are given in *italics*.   Unless otherwise indicated on the schedule, all books are those of Aristotle.

123. Schedule of Lectures, Faculty of Arts, University of Leipzig

(Compiled by Norton from Zarncke's *Statutenbücher der Universität Leipzig*.   Reproduced in his *Readings in the History of Education; Mediæval Universities*, p. 134. Cambridge, 1909)

The earliest orderly arrangement of lectures which Norton discovered was the one framed for Leipzig, in 1519, which the Statutes of that date announce as "an accurate arrangement of the Lectures of the Faculties of Fine Arts, hour by hour, adapted to a variety of intellects and to diverse interests."   It is reproduced on page 181.   A comparison of this schedule with that of the Arts portion of a modern university, or even with the program of studies in a normal school, will be interesting.

Time-Table of Lectures — Arts Faculty — University of Toulouse — 1309

Periods		1st Year	2d Year	3d Year	4th Year
1st Period	Winter Term	Prior and Posterior Analytics	Topics Sophistical Refutations	Same as first year	Same as second year
	Summer Term	Ethics (First five books)	Ethics (Last five books)	On the Soul	Ethics (Again begun)
2d Period	Winter Term	Isagoge of Porphyry Categories On Interpretation Priscian Minor	Same	Same	Same
	Summer Term	Six Principles of Gilbert de la Porrée Divisions of Boethius, or first three books of his Topics Priscian to be finished	Same	Same	Same
3d Period		Just after the lectures of the Masters certain Bachelors, appointed for the purpose, reviewed the work given by the Masters in the morning. Two groups of Bachelors were appointed to do the work, one from the beginning of the Winter Term to Easter, and the other from Easter to the end of the Summer Term.			
4th Period		No scheduled work. Possibly extraordinary lectures by Bachelors were given on Priscian and the "Old Logic" at this time.			

MID-DAY MEAL

Period				1st Year	2d Year	3d Year	4th Year
5th Period				Time set apart for conferences of the Bachelors, or for doing other things which the Masters might designate.			
6th Period	Extraordinary lectures by Bachelors		Topics Sophistical Refutations	Prior and Posterior Analytics		Same as first year	Same as second year
	Extraordinary lectures by Bachelors and Masters		Physics	On Generation and Destruction		On the Heavens and the Earth Meteorites	Metaphysics
		Parva Naturalia		1. Sense and Sensible Things 2. Memory and Recollection 3. Sleep and Waking 4. Longevity and Shortlivedness 5. Life and Death 6. Respiration and Expiration 7. Youth and Old Age			
				On the Causes of Motion of Animals On the Locomotion of Animals			

Time-Table of Lectures — Arts Faculty — University of Leipzig — 1519

Summer	Winter	Summer	Winter
6 A. M.		**1 P. M.**	
Metaphysics. Introduction (Porphyry). Categories.	Metaphysics. On Interpretation. Logic (Aquinas).	Posterior Analytics. Sense and Sensation. Memory and Recollection. Sleep and Waking. Longevity and Shortlivedness.	Topics (4 Bks.) Generation and Destruction. Being and Essence (Aquinas).
On Six Principles (Gilbert de la Porrée). Physics (Digest of Aristotle by Albertus Magnus).			
		Institutes of Oratory (Quintilian).	
8 A. M.			
Physical Hearing (sic). Physics? Reading and Disputation by candidates for A.B. and A.M. Grammar (Priscian).		**2 P. M.**	
		On the Soul (3 Bks). Common Arithmetic, and On the Sphere (Sacrobosco).	On the Heavens and the Earth. On the Substance of the World (Averroes). Common Perspective, i.e., Optics (John of Pisa).
11 A.M.			
Logic: Summulae (Petrus Hispanus).		Theory of the Planets (Gerard of Cremona). Ethics. Politics. Economics. Magna Moralia, *i. e.*, Ethics, abbreviated from Aristotle and Eudemus.	
Rhetoric, (Cicero to Herennius). Physical Auscultation (Themistius).	On the Orator (Cicero). On the Vital Principle (Themistius).		
		4 P. M.	
		Theocritus. Herodotus. Virgil. Aristotle, Problems.	

124. Value and Influence of the Mediæval University

(Rashdall, H., *The Universities of Europe in the Middle Ages*, vol. II, part II, pp. 703-12. Oxford 1895)

The standard history of the origin, development, customs, practices, work, and influence of the mediæval universities is the three-volume one by Rashdall. It has been rated as " the best history of the subject in any language." From the concluding chapter of this work the following extracts are taken.

What was the real value of the education which the mediæval university imparted? . . .

To the modern student, no doubt, the defects of a mediæval education lie upon the surface. The external defects of the University organization have already been incidentally noticed. In the older Uni-

FIG. 21. A LECTURE AT A MEDIÆVAL UNIVERSITY

(After an illustration printed at Paris, in 1487)

The students are seated in rows, while beneath the professor is seated the mace bearer of the institution, holding upright his symbol of authority and prepared if necessary to preserve order

versity system of northern Europe there is the want of selection and consequent incompetency of the teachers, and the excessive youth of the students in Arts. In the higher Faculties too we have encountered the constant effort on the part of the Doctors to evade the obligation of teaching without surrendering its emoluments, while the real teaching devolved upon half-trained Bachelors. It is, indeed, in the Student-Universities that the chairs would appear to have been most competently filled and their duties most efficiently discharged; in mediaeval times students were more anxious to learn than teachers were to teach. In the earlier period again there was an utter want of discipline among students who ought to have been treated as mere schoolboys. The want was partially corrected (in England) by the growth of the College system, but the improvement in this respect was balanced by the decay and degradation in the higher intellectual life of the Universities. . . . There is considerable reason to believe that in the Middle Ages a larger proportion than at the present day of the nominal students derived exceedingly little benefit from their University education. . . . In the earlier part of our period this must have been peculiarly the case, when so little exertion on the part of the student himself was required. A man was allowed year after year to sit through lectures of which he might not understand one word; later on this defect was partly remedied by the multiplication of "exercises" in College and Hall.

For the fairly competent student the main defects of a mediaeval education may be summed up by saying that it was at once too dogmatic and too disputatious. Of the superstitious adherence to Aristotle or other prescribed authority sufficient illustrations have already been given. It is, of course, a direct outcome of the intellectual vice of the age — a vice of which the human mind was by no means cured by the Renaissance or the Reformation. It lasted longest where it was most out of place. In the middle of the seventeenth century a Doctor of Medicine was compelled by the English College of Physicians to retract a proposition which he had advanced in opposition to the authority of Aristotle, under threat of imprisonment. It may seem a contradiction to allege that this education by authority

FIG. 22. A UNIVERSITY DISPUTATION

was at the same time too controversial. Yet the readiness with which the student was encouraged to dispute the thesis of a prescribed opponent, and the readiness with which he would swear to teach only the system of a prescribed authority, were but opposite sides of the same fundamental defect — the same fatal indifference to facts, the facts of external nature, the facts of history, and the facts of life. Books were put in the place of things. This is a defect which was certainly not removed by the mere substitution of Classics for Philosophy. . . .

But, because it is easy enough to pick holes in the education of the past, it must not for one moment be supposed that the education either of the scholastic or of the ultra-classical period was of little value. Up to a certain point — and this is the one consolation to the educational historian — the value of education is independent either of the intrinsic value or of the practical usefulness of what is taught. . . . It was emphatically so in the Middle Ages. Kings and princes found their statesmen and men of business in the Universities — most often, no doubt, among those trained in the practical science of Law, but not invariably so. Talleyrand is said to have asserted that Theologians made the best diplomatists. It was not the wont of the practical men of the Middle Ages to disparage academic training. The rapid multiplication of Universities during the fourteenth and fifteenth centuries was largely due to a direct demand for highly educated lawyers and administrators. In a sense the academic discipline of the Middle Ages was too practical. It trained pure intellect, encouraged habits of laborious subtlety, heroic industry, and intense application, while it left uncultivated the imagination, the taste, the sense of beauty, — in a word, all the amenities and refinements of the civilized intellect. It taught men to think and to work rather than to enjoy. Most of what we understand by "culture," much of what Aristotle understood by the "noble use of leisure," was unappreciated by the mediæval intellect. On the speculative side the Universities were (as has been said) "the school of the modern spirit": they taught men to reason and to speculate, to doubt and to inquire, to find a pleasure in the things of the intellect both for their own sake and for the sake of their applications to life. They dispelled forever the obscurantism of the Dark Ages. From a more practical point of view their greatest service to mankind was simply this, that they placed the administration of human affairs — in short the government of the world — in the hands of educated men. The actual rulers — the Kings or the aristocrats — might often be as uneducated or more uneducated than modern democracies, but they had to rule through the instrumentality of a highly educated class.

In criticizing mediæval culture and education, attention is sometimes too much confined to the Scholastic Philosophy and Theology.

The Scholastic Philosophy and Theology do, indeed, represent the highest intellectual development of the period. But they do not represent the most widely diffused or the most practically influential of mediæval studies. Law was the leading Faculty in by far the greater number of mediæval Universities: for a very large proportion of University students the study of Arts, in so far as they pursued it at all, took the place of a modern school rather than of a modern University. From a broad political and social point of view one of the most important results of the Universities was the creation, or at least the enormously increased power and importance, of the lawyer-class. Great as are the evils which society still owes to lawyers, the lawyer-class has always been a civilizing agency. Their power represents at least the triumph of reason and education over caprice and brute force. Lawyers have moderated or regulated despotism even when they have proved its most willing tools: just as in modern democratic communities their prominence must be looked upon as an important conservative check upon democracy.

Over the greater part of Europe the influence of the Universities meant more than this. It brought with it the increasing modification of legal and political institutions by the Roman Law, whether directly or through the Canon Law, whether by avowed adoption or by gradual and unconscious infiltration and imitation. This too was a civilizing agency, though here again an increase of civilization had often to be bought by a decline of rude, barbaric liberty. . . .

It is more directly relative to our subject to examine what have been the effects of the mediæval Universities upon our modern educational system. The genius of the Middle Age showed itself above all in the creation of institutions. The institutions of the Middle Age are greater — they may prove more imperishable — even than its Cathedrals. The University is a distinctly mediæval institution. By this is implied not merely that in the most altered and the most modern of the Schools so called there are customs, offices, titles, for the explanation of which we must go back to the history of the thirteenth century with its Guild movement, its Cathedral Schools, and especially its great struggle between the Chancellor of Paris and the Society of Masters. The very idea of the institution is essentially mediæval, and it is curious to observe how largely that idea still dominates our modern schemes of education.

CHAPTER X

THE REVIVAL OF LEARNING

THE Readings contained in this chapter illustrate the great Revival of Learning or Renaissance of the fourteenth and fifteenth centuries. This revival began in Italy, and for a century absorbed the energies of a small but very devoted body of scholars, inspired by a patriotic ardor for the recovery of their lost intellectual inheritance, and actuated by a modern spirit of investigation and criticism. In that century they ransacked Europe for lost books, brought to light the old monastic treasures, reconstructed and edited them, and, in the process, reconstructed Roman life and literature and history. In searching for, copying, comparing, questioning, inferring, criticizing, and editing, they awakened that modern scientific spirit which, applied later to problems of religion, nature, and government, has been productive of such great results. In awakening this modern scientific spirit, in developing an historical appreciation, and in creating a craving for truth for its own sake, they ushered in the modern, as contrasted with the mediæval, age.

The first selection (125), a letter of Petrarch to a friend, returning a volume of Cicero he had borrowed to copy, breathes a spirit of literary appreciation new in the ancient world. The second (126), recording Boccaccio's visit to the famous monastery at Monte Cassino and his finding its great library in ruins, also reveals the new feeling for the ancient learning. Even more is this shown in the letter of Poggio Bracciolini to his friend in Italy (127 a), describing his visit to the monastery at Saint Gall, in Switzerland, and his finding there a copy of the long-lost Quintilian's *Institutes of Oratory*. His friend's reply (127 b) is equally interesting as breathing the same new spirit. The difficulties involved in restoring and copying these old manuscripts, before the days of printing, may be inferred from the page from one of the copied manuscripts, reproduced as selection 128.

After the pioneers had done their work, and the revival of ancient learning, both Greek and Latin, was well under way all over central and northern Italy, a number of societies, usually called

Academies, were formed in different Italian cities, much as societies might be formed to-day to study or exploit any new subject
of study. The brief description of these by Symonds (**129**) gives
a good idea as to their nature and work.

This new learning awakened deep patriotic feeling in Italy,
and was tremendously aided by the wealthy men then ruling the
northern Italian cities. They not only aided the scholars finan-
cially, but in particular they built up many for-the-time large collections of books. Vespasiano, a famous book-collector of Florence, seems to have been called upon to assist in most of these
undertakings, and in his *Lives of Illustrious Men of the Fifteenth
Century* he has left us a number of very interesting pen-pictures
of these men and of his part in the work they carried through.
Three selections from this volume are reproduced here, describing
the collecting and copying done for the Medicean Library at
Florence (**130**), the library for Duke Frederic of Urbino (**131**), and
the beginnings of the famous Vatican Library at Rome (**132**).
These selections not only describe the methods of book-collecting before the days of printing, but also give a good idea as
to the nature and number of the books which the libraries contained.

Of the two remaining selections of this chapter, from Green's
celebrated history, the first (**133**) describes the introduction of
the new learning at Oxford and the religious effects produced
there by it; and the second (**134**) reveals the rapidly developing
taste for books which came as a result of the revival, and shows
how this led naturally to the invention of printing.

125. Petrarch on copying a Work of Cicero's

(From one of his letters. Robinson and Rolfe, *Petrarch*, p. 275. Putnams, New York,
1898; reproduced by permission)

The following letter of Petrarch, returning a copy of Cicero
after he had copied it, clearly reveals his great passion for the
classical authors, and especially for the master stylist, Cicero.
Petrarch was of Florentine parentage, but the family was in
exile, and he was born at Arezzo, in 1304. The family removed
to Avignon, in southern France, when Petrarch was nine years
old. He studied law at the universities of Montpellier and Bologna. In 1341 he was crowned poet laureate at Rome. He
traveled extensively, and died in 1374, near Padua.

Your copy of Cicero has been in my possession four years and more. There is good reason, though, for so long a delay; namely, the great scarcity of copyists who understand such work. It is a state of affairs that has resulted in an incredible loss of scholarship. Books that by their nature are a little hard to understand are no longer multiplied,

and have ceased to be generally intelligible, and so have sunk into utter neglect, and in the end have perished. This age of ours consequently has let fall, bit by bit, some of the richest and sweetest fruits that the tree of knowledge has yielded; has thrown away the results of the vigils and labors of the most illustrious men of genius, — things of more value, I am almost tempted to say, than anything else in the whole world. . . .

But I must return to your Cicero. I could not do without it, and the incompetence of the copyists would not let me possess it. What was left for me but to rely upon my own resources, and press these weary fingers and this worn and ragged pen into the service? The plan that I followed was this. I want you to know it, in case you should ever have to grapple with a similar task. Not a single word did I read except as I wrote. But how is that, I hear some one say; did you write without knowing what it was that you were writing? Ah! but from the very first it was enough for me to know that it was a work of Tullius, and an extremely rare one too. And then as soon as I was fairly started, I found at every step so much sweetness and charm, and felt so strong a desire to advance, that the only difficulty which I experienced in reading and writing at the same time came from the fact that my pen could not cover the ground so rapidly as I wanted it to, whereas my expectation had been rather that it would outstrip my eyes, and that my ardor for writing would be chilled by the slowness of my reading.

So the pen held back the eye, and the eye drove on the pen, and I covered page after page, delighting in my task, and committing many and many a passage to memory as I wrote. For just in proportion as the writing is slower than the reading does the passage make a deep impression and cling to the mind.

FIG. 23. PETRARCH
(1304–74)

126. Boccaccio's Visit to the Library at Monte Cassino

(Note by Benvenuto da Imola, in explaining a passage in Dante; trans. by Symonds, J. A., in his *Renaissance in Italy*, vol. ii, p. 133. London, 1888)

Benvenuto, a pupil of Boccaccio, has here left us a melancholy picture of the library of this great Benedictine monastery, which had evidently fallen into decay at the time of Boccaccio's visit.

He said that when he was in Apulia, attracted by the celebrity of the convent, he paid a visit to Monte Cassino, whereof Dante speaks. Desirous of seeing the collection of books, which he understood to be a very choice one, he modestly asked a monk — for he was always most courteous in manners — to open the library, as a favor, for him. The monk answered stiffly, pointing to a steep staircase, "Go up; it is open." Boccaccio went up gladly; but he found that the place which held so great a treasure, was without a door or key. He entered, and saw grass sprouting on the windows, and all the books and benches thick with dust. In his astonishment he began to open and turn the leaves of first one tome and then another, and found many and divers volumes of ancient and foreign works. Some of them had lost several sheets; others were snipped and pared all round the text and mutilated in various ways. At length, lamenting that the toil and study of so many illustrious men should have passed into the hands of most abandoned wretches, he departed with tears and sighs. Coming to the cloister, he asked a monk whom he met, why those valuable books had been so disgracefully mangled. He answered that the monks, seeking to gain a few *soldi*, were in the habit of cutting off sheets and making psalters, which they sold to boys. The margins too they manufactured into charms, and sold to

FIG. 24. BOCCACCIO
(1313–75)

women. So then, O man of study, go to and rack your brains; make books that you may come to this!

127. The Finding of Quintilian's *Institutes of Oratory* at Saint Gall

(Letter of Poggio Bracciolini to a friend, and his reply; trans. by Symonds, J. A., in his *Renaissance in Italy*, vol. II, pp. 135–37. London, 1888)

The famous Council of Constance met at Constance, Switzerland, from 1414 to 1418, in an attempt to settle a controversy over the Papacy and to secure a reformation in church government. It succeeded in the first, but not in the second.

One of the delegates to the Council was Manual Chrysoloras, the first Greek teacher in the West, who died and was buried at Constance, in 1415. Another of those in attendance was **Poggio Bracciolini** (1380–1459), a pupil of Chrysoloras and a devoted Renaissance scholar. He was then Apostolic Secretary, attending the Council by virtue of his office. During the intervals of the Council, Poggio searched the neighboring monasteries of Switzerland and southern Germany for lost books. The following selection from one of his letters describes his visit (1416) to the famous Swiss monastery of Saint Gall, and his finding the Quintilian manuscript and other treasures there.

(a) Letter of Poggio Bracciolini

I verily believe that, if we had not come to the rescue, he [Quintilian] must speedily have perished; for it cannot be imagined that a man magnificent, polished, elegant, urbane, and witty could much longer have endured the squalor of the prison-house in which I found him, the savagery of his jailers, the forlorn filth of the place. He was indeed right sad to look upon, and ragged, like a condemned criminal, with rough beard and matted hair, protesting by his countenance and garb against the injustice of his sentence. He seemed to be stretching out his hands, calling upon the Romans, demanding to be saved from so unmerited a doom. Hard indeed it was for him to bear, that he who had preserved the lives of many by his eloquence and aid, should now find no redresser of his wrongs, no saviour from the unjust punishment awaiting him. But as it often happens, to quote Terence, that what you dare not wish for comes to you by chance, so a good fortune for him, but far more for ourselves, led us, while wasting our time in idleness at Constance, to take a fancy for visiting the place where he was held in prison. The Monastery of Saint Gallen lies at the distance of some twenty miles from that city. Thither, then, partly for the sake of amusement and partly of finding books, whereof we heard there was a large collection in the convent, we directed our steps. In the middle of a well-stocked library, too large to catalogue at present, we discovered Quintilian, safe as yet and sound, though covered with dust and filthy with neglect and age. The books, you must know, were not housed according to their worth, but were lying in a most foul and obscure dungeon at the very bottom of a tower, a place into which condemned criminals would hardly have been thrust; and I am firmly persuaded that if any one would but explore those *ergastula* of the barbarians wherein they incarcerate such men, we should meet with like good fortune in the case of many whose funeral orations have long ago been pronounced. Besides Quintilian, we exhumed the three first books, and a half of the fourth book of the *Argonautica* of (Valerius) Flaccus, and the *Commentaries* of Asconius Pedianus upon eight orations of Cicero.

When the manuscript was being copied, his friend, Lionardo Bruni, wrote to him as follows:

(b) Reply of Lionardo Bruni

The republic of letters has reason to rejoice not only in the works you have discovered, but also in those you have still to find. What a glory for you it is to have brought to light by your exertions the writings of the most distinguished authors! Posterity will not forget that manuscripts which were bewailed as lost beyond the possibility of restoration, have been recovered, thanks to you. As Camillus was called the second founder of Rome, so may you receive the title of the second author of the works you have restored to the world. Through you we now possess Quintilian entire; before we only boasted the half of him, and that defective and corrupt in text. O precious acquisition! O unexpected joy! And shall I, then, in truth be able to read the whole of that Quintilian which, mutilated and deformed as it has hitherto appeared, has formed my solace? I conjure you send it me at once, that at least I may set eyes on it before I die.

These two letters reveal something of the spirit and emotions of those engaged in the revival and reconstruction of Latin literature and history.

128. Reproducing Books before the Days of Printing

(Sandys, J. E., *History of Classical Scholarship*, vol. II, p. 24. Cambridge, 1903)

Among the volumes found at Saint Gall, and copied by the enthusiasts for the recovery of the ancient manuscripts, was a copy of the *Argonautica* of the Roman writer, Valerius Flaccus, who died about 90 A.D. The last page and signature of his manuscript (see p. 192) illustrates well the slow method of reproducing books before the days of printing.

129. Italian Societies for studying the Classics

(Symonds, J. A., *The Renaissance in Italy*, vol. II, pp. 359–61. London, 1888)

In the fifteenth century there was founded, in almost every important Italian city, one or more Academies to promote the new learning. Those at Venice, Florence, Rome, and Naples were the most famous. They took their name from the Academy of Plato, at Athens. The one at Florence was called the Platonic Academy of Florence. The following description of the Academy at Rome, founded in 1425 by an Italian who assumed the old Roman name of Pomponius Lætus, shows the effect of the revival of classical studies on its devotees. In 1500 a "New Academy of Hellenists" was founded at Venice, after the same plan, the mem-

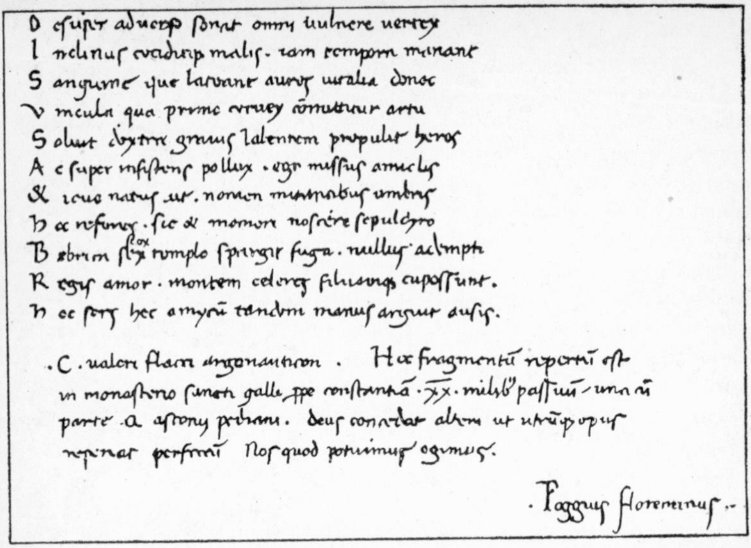

FIG. 25. A COPIED MANUSCRIPT

Last page, colophon, and signature of Valerius Flaccus' *Argonautica*, copied at Saint Gall, in 1416, by the Florentine Poggio, a pupil of the Greek teacher, Chrysoloras

bers assuming Greek names, the meetings being conducted in Greek, and one of the purposes being to edit some Greek author every month.

Under these Popes [unfriendly to the new learning] humanism had to flourish, as it best could, in the society of private individuals. Accordingly, we find the Roman scholars forming among themselves academies and learned circles. Of these the most eminent took its name from its founder, Julius Pomponius Lætus. . . . Pomponius derived his scholarship from Valla, and devoted all his energies to Latin literature, refusing, it is even said, to learn Greek, lest it should distract him from his favorite studies. He made it the object of his most serious endeavors not only to restore a knowledge of the ancients, but also to assimilate his life and manners to their standard. Men praised in him a second Cato for sobriety of conduct, frugal diet, and rural industry. He tilled his own ground after the methods of Varro and Columella, went a-fishing and a-fowling on holidays, and ate his sparing meal like a Roman Stoic under the spreading branches of an oak on the Campagna. The grand mansions of the prelates had no attractions for him. He preferred his own modest house upon the Esquiline, his garden on the Quirinal. It was here that his favorite scholars conversed with him at leisure; and to these retreats of the philosopher came strangers of importance, eager to behold a Roman

living in all points like an antique sage.   The high school (university)
owed much to his indefatigable industry.   Through a long series of
years he lectured upon the chief Latin authors, examining their text
with critical accuracy, and preparing new editions of their works.   Before daybreak he would light his lantern, take his staff, and wend his
way from the Esquiline to the lecture-room, where, however early the
hour and however inclement the season, he was sure to find an overflowing audience.   Yet it was not as a professor that Pomponius
Lætus acquired his great celebrity, and left a lasting impress on the
society of Rome.   This he did by forming an academy for the avowed
purpose of prosecuting the study of Latin antiquities and promoting
the adoption of antique customs into modern life.   The members assumed classical names, exchanging their Italian patronymics for fancy
titles like Callimachus Experiens, Asclepiades, Glaucus, Volscus, and
Petrejus.   They yearly kept the birthday feast of Rome, celebrating
the Palilia with Pagan solemnities, playing comedies of Plautus, and
striving to revive the humors of the old Atellan farces.

130. Founding of the Medicean Library at Florence

(Vespasiano, *Lives of Illustrious Men of the Fifteenth Century;* from the *Life of Cosimo
de' Medici;* trans. by Whitcomb, in his *Literary Source Book of the Italian Renaissance,* p. 77.   Univ. Pa., 1898; by permission)

Vespasiano was a book-collector of Florence, which during his
day was the leading literary and artistic center of the western
world.   In his *Lives of Illustrious Men of the Fifteenth Century* he
has left us good pictures of men and events of his time.   He died
in 1498.   The following selection from his book describes the
founding of one of the great Italian libraries, that of Cosimo de'
Medici (1389–1446), and illustrates the difficulty of book-collecting before the days of printing.   A picture of one of the stalls in
this library is to be found in the accompanying Text Book (Fig.
71, p. 251).

When he had finished the residence and a good part of the church,
he fell to thinking how he should have the place peopled with honest
men of letters; and in this way it occurred to him to found a fine library; and one day when I happened to be present in his chamber, he
said to me: "In what way would you furnish this library?"   I replied
that as for buying the books it would be impossible, for they were not
to be had.   Then he said: "How is it possible then to furnish it?"   I
told him that it would be necessary to have the books copied.   He
asked in reply if I would be willing to undertake the task.   I answered
him, that I was willing.   He told me to commence my work and he
would leave everything to me; and as for the money that would be

necessary he would refer the matter to Don Archangel, then prior of the monastery, who would draw bills upon the bank, which should be paid. The library was commenced at once, for it was his pleasure that it should be done with the utmost possible celerity; and as I did not lack for money I collected in a short time forty-five writers, and finished 200 volumes in twenty-two months; in which work we made use of an excellent arrangement, that of the library of Pope Nicholas, which he had given to Cosimo, in the form of a catalogue made out with his own hands. . . .

And since there were not copies of all these works in Florence, we sent to Milan, to Bologna and to other places, wherever they might be found. Cosimo lived to see the library wholly completed, and the cataloguing and arranging of the books; in all of which he took great pleasure, and the work went forward, as was his custom, with great promptness.

131. Founding of the Ducal Library at Urbino

(Vespasiano, *Lives of Illustrious Men of the Fifteenth Century;* from the *Life of Frederic of Urbino,* trans. by Whitcomb, in his *Literary Source Book of the Italian Renaissance,* pp. 73-77. Univ. of Pa., 1898; by permission)

Another selection from the Florentine bookseller, Vespasiano (d. 1498). This description of the founding of the ducal library at Urbino, and of the books obtained for it, shows the scope, the time, and the cost required for making one of the largest book collections of the time.

XXVIII. Coming to the holy doctors, who are in Latin, he wished to have all the books of the four doctors; and what letters! what books! and how excellent! having no regard for expense. The four doctors having been finished, he then desired all the works of Saint Bernard, and all the holy doctors of antiquity; he desired that none should be wanting: Tertullian, Hilary, Remi, Hugh of Saint Victor, Isidore, Anselm, Rabanus Maurus, and all the holy doctors of antiquity that have ever written. Coming from the Latins to the sacred writings of the writers, which are converted into Latin, he desired in Latin the works of Dionysius the Areopagite, of Saint Basil, Cyril, Gregory of Nyssa, Eusebius, all his works, Ephraem the Monk, the most excellent writer Origen. Coming to the Latin doctors, as well in philosophy as in theology, all the works of Saint Thomas Aquinas, all the works of Albertus Magnus, all the works of Alexander of Hales, all the works of Scotus, all the works of Bonaventura, the works of Richard of Mediavilla; all the works of the Archbishop Antoninus, and all the modern doctors who are of authority, he wished to have, down to the Conformities of Saint Francis; all the works upon civil law, most beautiful texts; all the lectures of Bartolo, in kid-skin, and many writers in civil law. The

Bible, most excellent book, he had done in two pictured volumes, as rich and fine as might be made, covered with gold brocade, enriched with silver; and he had this done so elegantly, as the first of all writings. And all the commentaries, those of the Master of the Sentences, of Nicholas de Lyra, and all the doctors of antiquity who have written commentaries, as well the Latins as the Greeks, and all the glossary of Nicholas de Lyra; this is a book like to which in this age no other has been made. All the writers of astronomy and their commentaries; all the works on geometry with commentaries; all the works on arithmetic; all the works on architecture, all the works *De re militari*, all books treating of the machines of the ancients for conquering a country, and those of the moderns, which was a very remarkable volume. Books of painting, of sculpture, of music, of canon law, and all the texts and lectures and the *Summa* of the bishop of Ostia, and more works in this department. *Speculum innocentiæ*. In medicine all the works of Avicenna, all the works of Hippocrates, of Galen, the *Continente* of Almansor *plus quam commentum*, all the works of Averroës, both on logic and on natural and moral philosophy. A book of all the ancient councils; all the works of Boetius, as well on logic as on philosophy and on music.

XXIX. All the works of the modern writers, commencing with Pope Pius. He has all the works of Petrarch, both Latin and vulgar; all the works of Dante, Latin and vulgar; all the works of Boccaccio in Latin; all the works of Messer Coluccio; all the works of Messer Lionardo d'Arezzo, both original and translations; all the works of Brother Ambrogio original and translations; all the works of Messer Gianozzo Manetti, as well originals as translations; all the works of Guerrino, original and translations; all the works of Panormita, as well in verse as in prose; all the works of Messer Francisco Filelfo, both in prose and in verse, original and translations; all the works of Perotti, translations and original; all the works of Campano, in prose and in verse; all the original works of Maffeo Vegio; all the works of Nicolò Secondino, translations and original, he who was interpreter for the Greeks and Latins at the council of the Greeks in Florence; all the works of Pontanus, original and translations; all the works of Bartolomeo Fazi, translations and original; all the works of Gasparino; all the works of Pietro Paulo Vergerio, original and translations; all the works of Messer John Argyropolus, translated, that is; the whole of the Philosophy and Logic of Aristotle, as well moral as natural, except the *Politics;* all the works of Messer Francisco Barbaro, translations and original; all the works of Messer Lionardo Giustiniano, both original and translations; all the works of Donato Acciaiuoli, original and translations; all the original works of Alamanno Renuccini; all the original works of Messer Cristofano da Prato Vecchio; all the works of Messer Poggio, both translations and original; all the works of Messer Giovanni Tortella, both original and translations; all the translations of Messer Francesco d' Arezzo, who lived at the court of King Ferrando; all the works of Lorenzo Valla, translations and original.

XXX.   Having acquired all the books of every department which were to be found, written both by ancient and modern doctors, and translations as well in every branch, he desired to have all the Greek books that were to be found; all the works of Aristotle in Greek; all the works of Plato, each volume bound in the finest kid-skin; all the works of Homer in one volume, the *Iliad*, the *Odyssey* and the *Batracomiomachia;* all the works of Sophocles; all the works of Pindar; all the works of Menander; and as well all the poets that were to be found in the Greek tongue; all the Lives of Plutarch, in one most excellent volume; the Cosmography of Ptolemy, with illustrations, in Greek, a most excellent book; all the moral works of Plutarch, a most worthy book; all the works of Herodotus, of Pausanias, of Thucydides, of Polybius; all the works of Demosthenes and of Æschines; Plotinus the philosopher, all his works; all the commentaries that are found among the Greeks, as for example the commentaries upon Aristotle; all the works of Theophrastus, the *Physica de plantis;* all the Greek lexicographers, the Greek with the Latin explanation; all the works of Hippocrates and of Galen; all the works of Xenophon; part of the Bible in Greek; all the works of Saint Basil; all the works of Saint John Chrysostom; all the works of Saint Athanasius, of Saint John of Damascus; all the works of Saint Gregory of Nazianzus, of Gregory of Nyssa, of Origen, of Dionysius the Areopagite, of John Climacus, of Saint Ephraem the Monk, of Æneas the Sophist; the Collations of John Cassianus, the Book of Paradise, *Vitæ sanctorum patrum ex Ægypto;* the Lives of Barlaam and Jesaphat; a Psalter in three tongues, a wonderful thing, in Hebrew, Greek and Latin, verse for verse, a most excellent book; all the books on geometry, on arithmetic, and on astronomy that are found in any language.   There are numerous Greek books, by various authors, which when he was not able to get them otherwise, he sent for them, desiring that nothing should be wanting in any tongue which it was possible to acquire.   There were to be seen Hebrew books, all that could be found in that language, beginning with the Bible, and all those who have commented upon it, Rabbi Moses, and other commentators.   Not only are these Hebrew books the Holy Scriptures, but also on medicine, on philosophy and in all branches, all that could be acquired in that tongue.

XXXI.   His Lordship having completed this worthy task at the great expense of more than 30,000 ducats, among the other excellent and praiseworthy arrangements which he made was this, that he undertook to give to each writer a title, and this he desired should be covered with crimson embellished with silver.   He began, as has been noted above, with the Bible, as the foremost of all, and had it covered, as was said, with gold brocade. Then beginning with all the doctors of the Church, he had each one covered with crimson and embellished with silver; and so with the Greek doctors as well as with the Latins. As well philosophy, history, and books on medicine and all the modern doctors; in such a manner that there are innumerable volumes of this kind, a thing gorgeous to behold. In this library all the books are beautiful in the highest degree, all written with the pen, not one printed, that it might not be disgraced thereby; all elegantly illuminated, and there is not one that is not written on kid-skin. There is a singular thing about this library, which is not true of any other; and this is, that of all the writers, sacred as well as profane, original works as well as translations, not a single page is wanting from their works, in so far as they are in themselves complete; which cannot be said of any other library, all of which have portions of the work of a writer, but not all; and it is a great distinction to possess such perfection. Some time before I went to Ferrara, being at Urbino at his Lordship's court, and having catalogues of all the libraries of Italy, commencing with that of the pope, of Saint Mark at Florence, of Pavia — and I had even sent to England to obtain a catalogue of the library of the university of Oxford, — I compared these with that of the duke, and I saw that all were faulty in one particular; that they had numerous copies of the same work, but they had not all the works of one writer complete as this had; nor were there writers of every branch as in this.

132. Founding of the Vatican Library at Rome

(Vespasiano, *Lives of Illustrious Men of the Fifteenth Century;* selected from the *Life of Nicholas V;* trans. by Whitcomb, in his *Literary Source Book of the Italian Renaissance*, pp. 70–73. Univ. Pa., 1898; by permission)

Another selection from Vespasiano describing the beginnings of the famous Vatican Library at Rome, by Pope Nicholas V, in 1450. It also not only illustrates well the difficulties of book-collecting before the days of printing, but the enormous work done and cost required in making available old and important books.

Owing to the jubilee of 1450 a great quantity of money came in by this means to the apostolic see, and with this the pope commenced building in many places, and sent for Greek and Latin books, wherever he was able to find them, without regard to price. He gathered together a large band of writers, the best that he could find, and kept them in constant employment. He also summoned a number of learned men, both for the purpose of composing new works and of translating such existing works as were not already translated, giving them most abundant provision for their needs meanwhile; and when the works were translated and brought to him, he gave them large sums of money, in order that they should do more willingly that which they undertook to do.

He made great provision for the needs of learned men. He gathered together great numbers of books upon every subject, both Greek and Latin, to the number of five thousand volumes. So at his death it was found by inventory that never since the time of Ptolemy had half that number of books of every kind been brought together. All books he caused to be copied, without regard to what it cost him, and there were few places where his Holiness had not copiers at work. When he could not procure a book for himself in any way, he had it copied.

After he had assembled at Rome, as I said above, many learned men at large salaries, he wrote to Florence to Messer Giannozzo Manetti, that he should come to Rome to translate and compose for him. And when Manetti left Florence and came to Rome, the pope, as was his custom, received him with honor, and assigned to him, in addition to his income as secretary, six hundred ducats, urging him to attempt the translation of the books of the Bible and of Aristotle, and to complete the book already commenced by him, *Contra Judæos et gentes;* a wonderful book, if it had been completed, but he carried it only to the tenth book. Moreover he translated the New Testament, and the Psalter, . . . with five apologetical books in defense of this Psalter, showing that in the Holy Scriptures there is not one syllable that does not contain the greatest of mysteries.

It was Pope Nicholas' intention to found a library in Saint Peter's, for the general use of the whole Roman curia, which would have been an admirable thing indeed, if he had been able to carry it out, but death prevented his bringing it to completion. He illumined the Holy Scriptures through innumerable books, which he caused to be translated; and in the same way with the works of the pagans, including certain works upon grammar, of use in learning Latin, — the *Orthography* of Messer Giovanni Tortelle, who was of his Holiness' household and worked upon the library, a worthy book and useful to grammarians; the *Iliad* of Homer; Strabo's *De situ orbis* he caused to be translated by Guerrino, and gave him five hundred florins for each part, — that is to say, Asia, Africa, and Europe; that was in all fifteen hundred florins. Herodotus and Thucydides he had translated by Lorenzo Valla, and rewarded him liberally for his trouble; Xenophon and Diodorus, by Messer Poggio; Polybius, by Nicolo Perotto, whom, when he handed it to him, he gave five hundred brand-new papal ducats in a purse, and said to him that it was not what he deserved, but that in time he would take care to satisfy him.

133. The New Learning at Oxford

(Green, J. R., *Short History of the English People*, pp. 303–05. London, 1888)

The following selection gives a good picture of the effect of the introduction of the New Learning into England, and particularly the thorough-going character of the religious reform produced by the revival of the ancient learning in such men as Colet, Erasmus, and More.

. . . The capture of Constantinople by the Turks, and the flight of its Greek scholars to the shores of Italy, opened anew the science and literature of the older world at the very hour when the intellectual energy of the Middle Ages had sunk into exhaustion. The exiled Greek scholars were welcomed in Italy, and Florence, so long the home of freedom and of art, became the home of an intellectual revival. The poetry of Homer, the drama of Sophocles, the philosophy of Aristotle and of Plato woke again to life beneath the shadow of the mighty dome with which Brunelleschi had just crowned the City by the Arno. All the restless energy which Florence had so long thrown into the cause of liberty she flung, now that her liberty was reft from her, into the cause of letters. The galleys of her merchants brought back manuscripts from the East as the most precious portion of their freight. In the palaces of her nobles fragments of classic sculpture ranged themselves beneath the frescoes of Ghirlandajo. The recovery of a treatise of Cicero's or a tract of Sallust's from the dust of a monastic library was welcomed by a group of statesmen and artists who gathered in the Rucellai gardens with a thrill of enthusiasm. Foreign scholars soon flocked over the Alps to learn Greek, the key of the new knowledge, from the Florentine teachers. Grocyn, a fellow of New College, was perhaps the first Englishman who studied under the Greek exile, Chalcondyles; and the Greek lectures which he delivered in Oxford on his return mark the opening of a new period in our history. Physical as well as literary activity awoke with the re-discovery of the teachers of Greece, and the continuous progress of English science may be dated from the day when Linacre, another Oxford student, returned from the lectures of the Florentine Politian to revive the older tradition of medicine by his translation of Galen.   .

But from the first it was manifest that the revival of letters would take a tone in England very different from the tone it had taken in Italy, a tone less literary, less largely human, but more moral, more religious, more practical in its bearings both upon society and politics. The awakening of a rational Christianity, whether in England or in the Teutonic world at large, began with the Italian studies of John Colet; and the vigour and earnestness of Colet were the best proof of the strength with which the new movement was to affect English religion. He came back to Oxford utterly untouched by the Platonic mysticism or the semi-serious infidelity which characterized the group of scholars round Lorenzo the Magnificent. He was hardly more influenced by their literary enthusiasm. The knowledge of Greek seems to have had one almost exclusive end for him, and this was a religious end. Greek was the key by which he could unlock the Gospels and the New Testament, and in these he thought he could find a new religious standing-ground. It was this resolve of Colet to fling aside the traditional dogmas of his day and to discover a rational and practical religion in the Gospels themselves, which gave its peculiar stamp to the theology of the Renascence. His faith stood simply on a vivid realization of the person of Christ. In the prominence which such a view gave to the moral life, in his free criticism of the earlier Scriptures, in his tendency to simple forms of doctrine and confessions of faith, Colet struck the key-note of a mode of religious thought as strongly in contrast with that of the later Reformation as with that of Catholicism itself. The allegorical and mystical theology on which the Middle Ages had spent their intellectual vigour to such little purpose fell at one blow before his rejection of all but the historical and grammatical sense of the Biblical text. The great fabric of belief built up by the mediæval doctors seemed to him simply "the corruptions of the Schoolmen." In the life and sayings of its Founder he found a simple and rational Christianity, whose fittest expression was the Apostle's creed. "About the rest," he said with characteristic impatience, "let divines dispute as they will." Of his attitude toward the coarser aspects of the current religion his behaviour at a later time before the famous shrine of Saint Thomas at Canterbury gives us a rough indication. As the blaze of its jewels, its costly sculptures, its elaborate metal-work burst on Colet's view, he suggested with bitter irony that a saint so lavish to the poor in his lifetime would certainly prefer that they should possess the wealth heaped round him since his death. With petulant disgust he rejected the rags of the martyr which were offered for his adoration, and the shoe which was offered for his kiss. The earnestness, the religious zeal, the very impatience and want of sympathy with the past which we see in every word and act of the man, burst out in the lectures on Saint Paul's Epistles which he delivered at Oxford. Even to the most critical among his hearers he seemed "like one inspired, raised in voice, eye, his whole countenance and mien, out of himself." Severe as was the outer life of the new teacher, a severity marked by his plain black robe and the frugal table which he preserved amidst his later dignities, his lively conversation, his frank simplicity, the purity and nobleness of his life, even the keen outbursts of his troublesome temper, endeared him to a group of scholars among whom Erasmus and Thomas More stood in the foremost rank.

134. The New Taste for Books

(Green, J. R., *Short History of the English People*, pp. 294–95. London, 1888)

The following interesting selection pictures the decay of the mediæval learning, the rising curiosity for secular knowledge, the increased use of books, and finally the invention of the great art of printing.

. . . The literature of the Middle Ages was dying out with the Middle Ages themselves; in letters as in life their thirst for knowledge had spent itself in the barren mazes of the scholastic philosophy, their ideal of warlike nobleness faded away before the gaudy travestie of a spurious chivalry, and the mystic enthusiasm of their devotion shrank at the touch of persecution into a narrow orthodoxy and a flat morality. The clergy, who had concentrated in themselves the intellectual effort of the older time, were ceasing to be an intellectual class at all. The monasteries were no longer seats of learning. "I found in them," said Poggio, an Italian traveller twenty years after Chaucer's death, "men given up to sensuality in abundance, but very few lovers of learning, and those of a barbarous sort, skilled more in quibbles and sophisms than in literature." The erection of colleges, which was beginning, failed to arrest the quick decline of the universities both in the numbers and learning of their students. Those at Oxford amounted to only a fifth of the scholars who had attended its lectures a century before, and "Oxford Latin" became proverbial for a jargon in which the very tradition of grammar had been lost. All literary production was nearly at an end. Historical composition lingered on indeed in compilations of extracts from past writers, such as make up the so-called works of Walsingham, in jejune monastic annals, or worthless popular compendiums. But the only trace of mental activity is to be found in the numerous treatises on alchemy and magic, on the elixir of life or the philosopher's stone, a fungous growth which most unequivocally witnesses to the progress of intellectual decay. On the other hand, while the older literary class was dying out, a glance beneath the surface shows us the stir of a new interest in knowledge among the masses of the people itself. The correspondence of the Paston family, which has been happily preserved, not only displays a fluency and vivacity as well as a grammatical correctness which would have been impossible in familiar letters a few years before, but shews country squires discussing about books and gathering libraries. The very character of the authorship of the time, its love of compendiums and abridgements of the scientific and historical knowledge of its day, its dramatic performances or mysteries, the commonplace morality of its poets, the popularity of its rimed chronicles, are additional proofs that literature was ceasing to be the possession of a purely intellectual class and was beginning to appeal to the people at large. The increased use of linen paper in place of the costlier parchment helped in the popularization of letters. In no former age had finer copies of books been produced; in none had so many been transcribed. This increased demand for their production caused the processes of copying and illuminating manuscripts to be transferred from the scriptoria of the religious houses into the hands of trade-guilds, like the Guild of Saint John at Bruges, or the Brothers of the Pen at Brussels. It was, in fact, this increase of demand for books, pamphlets, or fly-sheets, especially of a grammatical or religious character, in the middle of the fifteenth century that brought about the introduction of printing. We meet with it first in rude sheets simply struck off from wooden blocks, "block-books" as they are now called, and later on in works printed from separate and moveable types. Originating at Maintz with the three famous printers, Gutenberg, Fust, and Schoeffer, the new process travelled southward to Strasburg, crossed the Alps to Venice, where it lent itself through the Aldi to the spread of Greek literature in Europe, and then floated down the Rhine to the towns of Flanders. It was probably at the press of Colard Mansion, in a little room over the porch of Saint Donat's at Bruges, that Caxton learnt the art which he was the first to introduce into England.

CHAPTER XI
EDUCATIONAL RESULTS OF THE REVIVAL OF LEARNING

THE Readings contained in this chapter illustrate the educational results of the Italian Revival of Learning, as shown in the changes in the schools in Italy, France, Germany, and England. Beginning with the court schools of Italy, the resulting reform of education gradually extended to northern lands. The largest amount of space is given to the results in England and to the work and character of the English grammar school, because we in America drew our early educational ideas and practices direct from England. The Boston Latin School, founded in 1635, was a direct descendant of the English grammar schools and English educational traditions.

The first selection (135) is from the tractate by Guarino da Verona on the teaching of the new literatures, and in this he describes the method employed so successfully by his father in his Italian court school. He also lays down his new dictum as to the fundamental importance of a knowledge of Greek and Latin for the educated man. The second selection (136) describes the course of study at the French college of Guyenne, at Bordeaux, one of the leading exponents of the new humanism in France. The third selection (137) outlines the course of instruction which Sturm, employing the new humanism, finally evolved for his famous classical *gymnasium* at Strassburg. These two furnish an interesting comparison.

The introduction of humanistic studies into the English secondary schools was largely due to Colet, through the re-founding of Saint Paul's School in London, in 1510. This school, though at first bitterly opposed, soon established the type for nearly all the English grammar schools founded or reorganized thereafter. The extracts from Colet's Statutes for the school (138 a-c) are given to show the character of the provisions he made for the new school. The introduction of the new learning into England was also greatly aided by the English court, and the selection from Ascham (139) is given to show Queen Elizabeth's deep in-

terest in the new studies. For Colet's school Lily wrote a new
type of Latin Grammar. This became a famous textbook and
continued in use for centuries, and the Introduction contributed
thereto by Colet is reproduced (**140**) to show his kindly interest
in good learning.

Even before the new humanistic type of school had been introduced into England some efforts at securing schools directed by
university-trained teachers, instead of clerics, had been made, of
which the school established by William Sevenoaks is a good
example. His will is reproduced (**141**) to show the type of school
he wanted to establish. The chantry grammar school founded
by John Percival (**142**), and the efforts of the city authorities of
Sandwich to provide a grammar school (**143**), both illustrate the
interest such new-type schools had awakened in England.

The course of study for Eton College, one of the largest and
best-endowed of the English grammar schools, as reproduced
(**144**), shows how thoroughly the new humanistic studies had
made a home for themselves in the larger grammar schools within
half a century after Colet's re-foundation of Saint Paul's; while
the description by Adam Martindale (**145**) of the instruction he
received in a small country grammar school, about 1635, is interesting as showing how thoroughly the new learning had by that
time penetrated to even the small and remote grammar schools
of England. It was in 1635 that the Boston Latin School, the
first Latin grammar school in America, was founded by English
settlers, most of whom had been educated in these English grammar schools. Our educational traditions for secondary education
thus go back, through the English-type Latin grammar school,
directly to the Italian Renaissance.

After a time the new humanistic studies began to lose their
earlier importance as cultural studies, due in part to a change in
teaching methods. The emphasis now came to be placed upon
drill and intellectual discipline instead of the humanistic spirit,
and in consequence the schools in time became formal and lifeless. This came to be particularly true of such instruction in the
hands of the Jesuits, though it extended to secondary education
in all lands and among all creeds. The description of such formal
instruction by the Jesuit Campion (**146**) illustrates well how formal drill and minute analysis of the old authors had replaced the
earlier humanistic culture. .

135. Guarino on Teaching the Classical Authors

(A letter; trans. by Woodward, W. H., in his *Vittorino da Feltre*, pp. 161–72.
Cambridge, 1897)

Battisto Guarino was the son of Guarino da Verona (1374–
1460), and in a lengthy letter, under date of 1459, he describes
*The Order and the Method to be Ob-
served in Teaching and in Reading
the Classical Authors*, as then being
carried out by his father in his famous school at Ferrara.   By way
of preface he says:

In offering this short Treatise for
your acceptance, I am fully aware that
you need no incentive to regard the
pursuit of Letters as the most worthy
object of your ambition. But you may
find what I have written a not un-
welcome reminder of our past intercourse, whilst it may prove of use
to other readers into whose hands it
may fall.   For I have had in view not
only students anxious for guidance in
their private reading, but masters
in search of some definite principles
of method in teaching the Classics.

FIG. 26. GUARINO DA VERONA
(1374–1460)

Hence I have treated both of Greek and of Latin Letters, and I have
confidence that the course I have laid down will prove a thoroughly
satisfactory training in literature and scholarship.

Guarino begins the letter with a discussion as to the nature of
the schoolmaster, and then passes to a consideration of methods
of teaching Latin, which study he says "is so important that no
one who is ignorant of it can claim to be thought an educated
man."   Vergil, he says, should be learned by heart.   He then
proceeds:

§3. I have said that ability to write Latin verse is one of the essential
marks of an educated person.   I wish now to indicate a second, which is
of at least equal importance, namely, familiarity with the language and
literature of Greece.   The time has come when we must speak with no
uncertain voice upon this vital requirement of scholarship.   I am well
aware that those who are ignorant of the Greek tongue decry its necessity, for reasons which are sufficiently evident.   But I can allow no

doubt to remain as to my own conviction that without a knowledge of Greek, Latin Scholarship itself is, in any real sense, impossible. I might point to the vast number of words derived or borrowed from the Greek, and the questions which arise in connection with them; such as the quantity of the vowel sounds, the use of the diphthongs, obscure orthographies and etymologies. . . . The Greek grammar, again, can alone explain the unusual case-endings which are met with in the declension of certain nouns, mostly proper names, which retain their foreign shape; such as "Dido" and "Mantus." Nor are these exceptional forms confined to the poetic use. But I turn to the authority of the great Latins themselves, to Cicero, Quintilian, Cato and Horace: they are unanimous in proclaiming the close dependence of the Roman speech and Roman literature upon the Greek, and in urging by example as well as by precept the constant study of the older language. To quote Horace alone:

> "Do you, my friends, from Greece your models draw,
> And day and night to con them be your law."

And again,

> "To Greece, that cared for naught but fame, the Muse
> Gave genius, and a tongue the gods might use."

In such company I do not fear to urge the same contention.

Were we, indeed, to follow Quintilian, we should even begin with Greek in preference to Latin. But this is practically impossible, when we consider that Greek must be for us, almost of necessity, a learned and not a colloquial language; and that Latin itself needs much more elaborate and careful teaching than was requisite to a Roman of the imperial epoch. On the other hand, I have myself known not a few pupils of my father — he was, as you know, a scholar of equal distinction in either language — who, after gaining a thorough mastery of Latin, could then in a single year make such progress with Greek that they translated accurately entire works of ordinary difficulty from that language into good readable Latin *at sight*. Now proficiency of this degree can only be attained by careful and systematic teaching of the rudiments of the Grammar, as they are laid down in such a manual as the well-known one of Manuel Chrysoloras, or in the abridgement which my father drew up of the original work of his beloved master. . . .

Our scholar should make his first acquaintance with the Poets through Homer, the sovereign master of them all. For from Homer our own poets, notably Vergil, drew their inspiration; and in reading the *Iliad* or the *Odyssey* no small part of our pleasure is derived from the constant parallels we meet with. Indeed we see in them as in a mirror the form and manner of the Æneid figured roughly before us, the incidents, not less than the simile or epithet which describes them, are, one might say, all there. In the same way, in his minor works

Vergil has borrowed from Theocritus or Hesiod. After Homer has been attempted the way lies open to the other Homeric poets and to the Dramatists.

He next discusses the use and importance of the historical writers, and the different Latin texts, and then says:

The course of study which I have thus far sketched out will prove an admirable preparation for that further branch of scholarship which constitutes Rhetoric, including the thorough examination of the great monuments of eloquence, and skill in the oratorical art itself. The first work to claim our attention in this subject is the *Rhetoric* of Cicero, in which we find all the points of Oratory concisely but comprehensively set forth. The other rhetorical writings of Cicero will follow, and the principles therein laid down must be examined in the light of his own speeches. Indeed the student of eloquence must have his Cicero constantly in his hand; the simplicity, the lofty moral standard, the practical temper of his writings render them a peculiarly noble training for a public speaker. Nor should the admirable Quintilian be neglected in this same connection.

It will be desirable also to include the elements of Logic in our course of studies, and with that the *Ethics* of Aristotle, and the Dialogues of Plato; for these are necessary aids to the proper understanding of Cicero. The Ciceronian Dialogue, in form and in matter, seems often to be modelled directly upon Plato. None of his works however are so attractive to myself personally as the *De Officiis* and the *Tusculans*. The former reviews all the main duties of life; the latter exhibits a wealth of knowledge most valuable — both as to material and expression — to every modern writer. I would add that some knowledge of the principles of Roman Law will be helpful to the full understanding of Latin authors.

A master who should carry his scholars through the curriculum which I have now laid down may have confidence that he has given them a training which will enable them, not only to carry forward their own reading without assistance, but also to act efficiently as teachers in their turn. . . .

At Verona. xv Kal. Mar. MCCCCLVIIII.

136. The Collège de Guyenne

(Digest by W. H. Woodward, of Vinet's *Disciplina et ratio docendi* (c. 1570). In *Studies in Education during the Age of the Renaissance*, chap. VIII. Cambridge, 1906)

In 1534 the governing corporation of the city of Bordeaux, in southwestern France, decided to reorganize the boys' school there along the new humanistic lines. Under a series of able principals

the school was raised to first rank.   The school was reorganized
as a reformed grammar school of ten classes, with a two-year
course in the Faculty of Arts in the university there added.   The
greatest period of prosperity of the school was during the prin-
cipalship of Élie Vinet (1556–70), and he has left us a descriptive
outline of its course of instruction, *disciplina et ratio docendi*, as
he knew it.   It represents the flowering period of the French Renaissance, and is comparable to the school plan of Sturm (**R. 137**),
Melancthon (**R. 161**), or of Eton (**R. 144**) at the same period.

By classes the organization was as follows:

Tenth, or Lowest Class.   Entered at six or seven.   Boys known as
    "Alphabetarii" or "Abecedarii."

  Textbooks: the *Alphabetum;* the Pater Noster, the Seven Peniten-
    tial Psalms, and the Ave Maria; and the *Libellus Puerulorum.*

  Tests for promotion: ability to read the above, to decline and to
    conjugate, and to write legibly.

Ninth Class.   This was the largest in the school, indicating that
    many boys learned the above privately and entered the school
    at seven or eight.

  Textbooks: Reading and writing in both French and Latin, for
    both fluency and speed.

  Latin accidence of both noun and verb.

  The *disticha de moribus* of Cato, with French parallel transla-
    tion; and

  Cordier's *Exempla partium orationis*, a small handbook of
    grammar.

Eighth Class.   Age eight or nine.

  Textbooks: Selection of Cicero's *Letters*, selected scenes from
    Terence, and the *Colloquia* of Cordier.

Seventh Class.   Age nine or ten.

  Textbooks: Selections from *Letters* of Cicero continued; the Latin
    Grammar of Despantère, written in Latin hexameters.

  Much emphasis on style and composition.   French the language
    of instruction for the Latin.

Sixth Class.   Age ten or eleven.

  Cicero's *Letters* the standard prose text.   Much memorization for
    form, and much explanation of construction.

Fifth Class.   Age eleven or twelve.

  Cicero's *Letters* still the standard prose text, with emphasis as
    above.   Also one play of Terence, and one book of the *Epistolæ*
    of Ovid.   Rules of prosody now learned.

Fourth Class.   Age twelve or thirteen.

  Pupils now study for first time an oration of Cicero, and study with it a manual of rhetoric, such as the *De Copia* of Erasmus. Chief poetical work read in this class the *Tristia* of Ovid.

Much grammatical questioning; frequent exercises in composition; dictation of simple materials for writing Latin verse.

Greek begun in this class. Grammar begun.

Third Class. Age thirteen or fourteen.

The *Epistolæ Familiares* or *Ad Atticum* of Cicero, and one other oration; the *Metamorphoses* of Ovid.

Much emphasis on rhetoric, syntax, verse composition, and Latin composition in prose and verse.

Greek continued. Grammar of Theodore Gaza.

Second Class. Age fourteen or fifteen.

Cicero's orations, selected; or readings from Vergil, Ovid, or Lucan.

Roman history now studied.

Much learning by heart; prose and verse composition; and emphasis on rhetoric.

Latin declamation now first undertaken.

Greek continued. Grammar and reading.

Arithmetic begun.

First Class. Age fifteen or sixteen.

The art of oratory, from Cicero or Quintilian.

Speeches of Cicero, in illustration.

History from Livy, Seneca, Justin, Eubropius, and P. Mela.

Poetry read from Vergil, Lucan, Persius, Juvenal, Horace, and Ovid.

Composition in prose and verse, and declamation.

Greek continued. Readings in Demosthenes and Homer.

Arithmetic extended to simple proportion, and square and cube root.

Faculté des Arts. First year. Age sixteen or seventeen.

Aristotelian Logic, from Latin version.

The *Isagoge* of Porphyry.

Greek continued.

The *Mathematicorum Breviarium* of Psellus, a dry compendium of arithmetic, music, geometry, and astronomy.

Faculté des Arts. Second year. Age seventeen or eighteen.

Aristotle's *Physica*, the *De Cælo*, and other commonly read scientific works. A study of natural philosophy, though based on ancient learning. No observation or independent thought.

Greek and mathematics continued, as above, with Proclus *de Sphæra* added.

To the above digest of the curriculum, more minutely detailed by Woodward, he adds:

We have interesting light upon general methods of class instruction as pursued in the school. The retention of the mediæval disputation, in the rational form of mutual questioning under the control of the form (class) master, was a safeguard against the prevalent fault of lecturing or dictating to the class which Erasmus so frequently ridiculed as the practice of the unskilled teacher or of the pedant parading his erudition. The construing lesson lasted as a rule for one hour, and was followed by such disputation: the pupils asked questions of each other, propounded difficulties, discussed the matter of the text and the notes given by the master. This exercise occupied half an hour. On Saturdays, in place of a set lesson at midday, disputations were arranged in which form was pitted against form. Six pupils from each brought up as many compositions in prose or in verse which had been worked in advance. These were written out in large text hand, and pinned to a screen or on the wall of the class-room: Below each line of the script was left a clear space for interlinear correction and criticism. Thus the opposers could make careful examination of each exercise, detect errors and propound improvements. This disputation lasts an hour.

Although French, as has been shown, was regularly employed for an instrument of Latin construing and composition, it was not allowed to be used in school or play-ground except by the juniors: . . . Elder boys were required to use Latin in addressing little boys, and only when not understood were they to repeat their words in French. The words of the statute of the University of Paris as revised in 1599 show that to the very end of the century the same principle was upheld in the authoritative seat of French learning. . . .

The school hours were from 8–10, 12–1, 3–5, with an extra hour twice weekly in the case of pupils reading Greek and mathematics. Sunday was, apart from one exercise for the upper forms, a whole holiday, as were certain Saints' days. On some important vigils, about fifty during the year, a half holiday was allowed. Mass was attended daily by the entire school. The school year began in September, and continued till the beginning of August.

137. Sturm's Course of Study at Strassburg

(Reconstructed from Sturm's *Plan* (1538), his *Classical Letters* (1565), and the *Examinations* (1578)

In 1537 Johann Sturm (1507–89) was placed at the head of the municipal Latin school, founded some years earlier by the city of Strassburg. The school had not been successful, and Sturm was given a free hand. He reorganized the school as a humanistic Latin school, omitting, however, the sports and contests of the Italian Court Schools and the English Grammar Schools; divided it into ten classes, with a teacher in charge of each; and soon made it the most famous Latin school of its day in Europe. For forty-five years he directed this school, which he called a *Gymnasium*. The following was the course of study:

1. *Tenth Class — Entered at the age of 7.*

Purpose to lay a good foundation.

Form and correct pronunciation of alphabet.

Beginnings of Latin reading, writing, and spelling.

Learn declensions and conjugations in Latin.

German Catechism to be committed to memory.

2. *Ninth Class — Age 8 to 9.*

More thorough grounding in Latin declensions and conjugations.

FIG. 27. JOHANN STURM (1507–89)

Many Latin words to be learned, especially names of common objects, as much like Roman children did as possible.

Much reading of simple Latin and memorizing of words and phrases. Inflection of all nouns and verbs.

3. *Eighth Class — Age 9 to 10.*

Special care that the boys do not forget what has been learned in earlier classes.

Thorough grounding in each of the eight parts of speech.

Each declension and conjugation to be fully mastered.

To read Sturm's *Letters of Cicero*, with constant reference to grammatical construction, and certain Latin dialogues.

Written exercises in style to replace oral drill.

4. *Seventh Class — Age 10 to 11.*

Rules of Latin syntax, based on Cicero, to be well ground in.

Subjects to be assigned for exercises in style.

German Catechism to be translated into Classical Latin.

Learn the scale and intervals in music.

Read two dialogues in Sturm's printed collection, the second book of *Letters of Cicero*, the precepts of Cato, the Catechism in Latin, and the "Sunday Sermons."

Written exercises in style.

5. *Sixth Class — Age 11 to 12.*

Read Cicero's longer *Letters;* also the *Andria* of Terence, and selections from Æsop, Bishop Ambrose, Martial, and Horace.

Written exercises to secure greater elegance in style.

Saturday and Sunday to be given to the shorter Latin cate-chism of Luther, and the reading of some letters of the Hieronymians.

Greek to be commenced in this class.

In music emphasis on time.

Boys now to be proficient in grammar, and to have a store of Latin words for every-day objects.

6. *Fifth Class — Age 12 to 13.*

Enlarge Latin vocabulary to words for unknown objects.

Meter in Latin poetry to be studied, with scanning.

Mythology to be learned.

Read Cicero's *Cato* and *Lælis*, and the *Eclogues* of Vergil.

Boys to complete their encyclopedias of Latin words.

Style to be still more thoroughly cultivated. Verse writing to be begun.

Examples of eloquence for translation, and then re-translated into Latin.

Greek to be continued; vocabulary to be enlarged; simple reading.

Pauline epistles to be read.

Now to be well grounded in Greek and Latin grammar.

7. *Fourth Class — Age 13 to 14.*

Much drill on what has been so far learned.

"Diligent practice" to be continued on style.

Read sixth oration against Verres, second book of Cicero's *Letters to Friends*, part of *Adelphi* of Terence, and the epis-tles and satires of Horace in Latin; in Greek, the "Book of Examples."

Much drill on Greek grammar.

Pauline epistles to be read.

8. *Third Class — Age 14 to 15.*

Range of previous studies to be enlarged.

Rhetoric to be begun.

Read third book of Cicero's *Letters to Friends*, the *Menippus* of Lucian, and the sixth book of Vergil's *Æneid* in Latin; in Greek, the first book of the *Iliad* or the *Odyssey*, and the best efforts of Demosthenes to be carefully studied.

Select orations in Greek to be translated into Latin, and vice versa.

Change *Odes* of Pindar and Horace into different meter.

Comedies of Terence and Plautus to be acted.

9. *Second Class — Age 15 to 16.*

> Literal interpretation of Greek poets and orators.
>
> Connection between oratorical and poetic usage.
>
> Striking passages to be copied into books for learning.
>
> Similar work with Latin authors, with comparisons.
>
> Daily exercises in style very important.
>
> Rhetoric to be studied now from a text, and applied to orations of Demosthenes and Cicero.
>
> Logic to be introduced in this class.
>
> On Sundays, the Epistles of Saint Paul to the Romans to be learned by heart.
>
> Acting of plays to continue, being extended to include those of Aristophanes, Euripides, or Sophocles.
>
> Read the second *Philippic* of Demosthenes, Cicero's pleas in behalf of Roscius Amerinus and Caius Rabirius, and the first book of the *Iliad*.
>
> Elementary work in mathematics.

10. *First Class — Age 16 to 17.*

> Logic and rhetoric to be extended, and applied to Cicero and Demosthenes.
>
> Readings from Vergil, Homer, Thucydides, and Sallust.
>
> Much translation and re-translation, writing in prose and poetry, and declamation. Dramatic representations every week.
>
> Epistles of Saint Paul to be expounded, after the manner of the old rhetoricians.
>
> In geometry, first book of Euclid studied.
>
> Some very elementary instruction in astronomy.

138. Colet's Statutes for Saint Paul's School, London

(*Statutes* of 1518, the original *Statutes* of 1510 being permanently lost. Lupton, J. H., *Life of Colet*. London, 1887)

John Colet (1465–1519), an enthusiastic humanist, was made Dean of Saint Paul's Cathedral in London, in 1500, and in 1510 he re-founded the school of Saint Paul's Churchyard as a New-Learning school. In a series of *Statutes*, first in 1510 and again in 1518, he made detailed provision for its government and the instruction in it. The *Statutes* begin with the words:

John Colett, the sonne of henry Colett Dean of paules desiring nothing more thanne Educacion and bringing vpp chyldren in good Maners and litterature in the yere of our Lorde a mli fyve hundreth and twelff bylded a Scole in the Estende of paulis Church for cliij to be taught fre in the same.

From the *Statutes* of 1518 we quote three selections which show the care he exercised to put around the pupils the proper religious atmosphere, to prevent the instruction being wasted on poorly prepared or inattentive children, and to insure that pure Latin and Greek, and not monastic Latin, be taught. Many of his expressions are very interesting and quaint. The *Statutes* are also interesting as having been written in English instead of in Latin.

(a) Religious Observances

The Chapelyn —

There shalbe also in the Scole a preist that dayly as he can be disposed shall sing masse in the chapell of the Scole and pray for the children to prosper in good lyff and in good litterature to the honor

FIG. 28. JOHN COLET (1465–1519)

of God and oure Crist Jesu. At this masse whenever the bell in the scole shall knyll to sacryng thenne all the children in the scole knelyng in theyr Settes shall with lift upp handis pray in the tyme of sacrying. After the sacryng whenne the bell knilleth agayn, they shall sit downe ageyn to theyr lernyng.

This preist sum good honest and vertuouse manne shalbe chosyn fro tyme to tyme by the wardens and assistence of the Mercery, he shall also lerne or yf he be lerned helpp to teche in the scole yf it shall seme conuenient to the hye Maister or ellis not.

He shall haue no benefice with cure nor service nor no other office nor occupacion but attend allonly vpon the scole he shall teche the children the catechyzon and Instruction of the articles of the faith and the X commaundmentis in Inglish.

His wages shal be viii^{li} by the yere and lyvery gowne of xxj^{s} vii^{d} delyured in cloth.

(b) Admission of Children

The Mayster shal reherse these artycles to them that offer theyr children, on this wyse here followynge.

If your chylde can rede & wryte latyn & englisshe sufficiently, soo that he be able to rede & wryte his owne lessons, then he shal be admytted into the scole for a scholer.

If your childe after reasonable season proued be founde here vnapte and vnable to lernynge, than ye warned therof shal take hym awaye, that he occupye not here rowme in vayne.

If he be apte to lerne, ye shal be content that he contynue here tyl he haue some competent literature.

If he be absent vi dayes & in that mean season ye shewe not cause reasonable (reasonable cause is al onely sekenes) than his rowme to be voyde, without he be admytted agayne & paye iiij.d.

Also after cause shewed yf he contynue so absent tyl the weke of admyssyon in the nexte quarter, & than ye shewe not the contynuaunce of his sekenes, than his rowme to be voyde and he none of the scole, tyl he be admytted agayne and paye iiii.d. for wrytinge of his name.

Also yf he fall thryse in to absence, he shall be admytted no more.

Your chylde shal on childermasse daie wayte upon the bysshop at Poules and offer there.

Also ye shal fynde hym waxe in wynter.

Also ye shal fynde hym convenient bokes to his lernynge.

If the offerer be content with these artycles, than let his chylde be admytted.

(c) *The Course of Study*

As towchyng in this scole what shalby taught of the maisters and lernyd of the scolers, it passith my wit to devyse and determyn in particuler but in generall to speke and sum what to saye my mynde, I wolde they were taught all way in good litterature both laten and greke, and goode auctours suych as haue the veray Romayne eliquence joyned withe wisdome specially Cristyn auctours that wrote theyre wysdome with clene and chast laten other in verse or in prose, for my entent is by thys scole specially to incresse knowledge and worshipping of god and oure lorde Crist Jesu and good Cristen lyffe and maners in the Children.

And for that entent I will the Chyldren lerne ffirst aboue all the Cathechyzon in Englysh and after the accidence that I made or sum other yf eny be better to the purpose to induce chyldren more spedely to laten spech And thanne Institutum Christiani homines which that leryned Erasmus made at my request and the boke called Copia of the same Erasmus And thenne other auctours Christian as lactancius prudentius and proba and sedulius and Juuencus and Baptista Mantuanus and suche other as shalby tought convenyent and moste to purpose vnto the true laten spech all barbary all corrupcion all laten adulterate which ignorant blynde folis brought into this worlde and with the same hath distayned and poysenyd the plde laten spech and the varay Romayne tong which in the tyme of Tully and Salust and Virgill and Terence was vsid, whiche also seint Jerome and seint ambrose and seint Austin and many hooly doctors lernyed in theyr tymes. I say that ffylthynesse and all such abusyon which the later blynde worlde brought in which more ratheyr may be callid blotterature thenne litterature. I vtterly abbanysh and Exclude oute of this scole and charge the Maisters that they teche all way that is the best and instruct the chyldren in greke and Redyng vnto them suych auctours that hathe with wisdome joyned the pure chaste eloquence.

139. Ascham on Queen Elizabeth's Learning

(Ascham, Roger, *The Scholemaster*. Arber ed., book II, p. 194. London, 1570)

One of the enthusiastic teachers of the New Learning in England was Roger Ascham (1516–68), who had studied at Saint John's College, Cambridge — a center of the new learning — under Sir John Cheke, one of the greatest teachers of teachers. His years there Ascham often referred to as "my swete tyme at Cambridge." Ascham in turn became a great teacher of reformed Latin and Greek, the tutor of Queen Elizabeth, and wrote *The Scholemaster* to show the advantages of a mild discipline and his method of double translation in teaching languages. Of Queen Elizabeth he wrote:

. . . And by theis authorities and reasons am I moued to thinke, this waie of double translating, either onelie or chieflie, to be fittest, for the spedy and perfit atteyning of any tong. And for spedy atteyning, I durst venture a good wager, if a scholer, in whom is aptnes, loue, diligence, and constancie, would but translate, after this sorte, one litle booke in *Tullie*, as *de senectute*, . . . that scholer, I say, should cum to a better knowledge in the Latin tong, than the most part do, that spend four or fiue yeares, in tossing all the rules of Grammer in common scholes. . . . And a better, and nerer example herein, may be, our most noble Queene *Elizabeth*, who neuer toke yet, Greeke nor Latin Grammer in her hand, after the first declining of a nowne and a verbe, but onely by this double translating of *Demosthenes* and *Isocrates* dailie without missing euerie forenone, for the space of a yeare or two, hath atteyned to soch a perfite vnderstanding in both the tonges, and to soch a readie vtterance of the latin, and that wyth soch a judgement, as they be fewe in nomber in both the vniuersities, or els where in England, that be, in both tonges, comparable with her Maiestie.

140. Colet's Introduction of Lily's Latin Grammar

William Lily (1468–1522), one of the early English humanists, was appointed headmaster of the newly founded Saint Paul's School, in London, in 1512, shortly after his return from Italy. For this school he wrote *Lily's Latin Grammar*, a book which entirely eclipsed his fame as a schoolmaster, and which was to the sixteenth and seventeenth centuries what Donatus had been to the Middle Ages. For this book Colet wrote the following Introduction:

I haue . . . made this lytel boke, not thynkynge that I coude say ony thynge beter than hath be sayd before, but I toke this besynes, hauynge grete pleasure to shewe the testymony of my good mynde vnto the schole. In whiche lytel warke yf ony newe thynges be of me, it is alonely that I haue put tese partes in a more clere ordre, and haue made them a lytel more easy to yonge wyttes than (methynketh) they were before. . . . Wherfore I praye you, all lytel babys, all lytel chyldren, lerne gladly this lytel treatyse, and commende it dylygently vnto your memoryes. Trustynge of this begynnynge that ye shal procede and growe to parfyt lyterature, and come at the last to be gret clarkes. And lyfte vp your lytel whyte handes for me, whiche prayeth for you to god. To whom be al honour and imperyal maieste and glory. Amen.

141. Foundation Bequest for Sevenoaks Grammar School

(Will of William Sevenoaks; trans. by A. F. Leach, *Educational Charters*, p. 399. Cambridge, 1911)

The following bequest, under date of July 4, 1432, to provide for a grammar-school master who should be "by no means in holy orders," but be in connection with a parish church, is a type of a number of similar foundations for grammar schools made in England between 1200 and 1500. This foundation is particularly interesting as showing an effort to provide a school that should be taught by a university-trained teacher, instead of by a cleric.

In God's name, Amen.

Whereas among other works of piety which flow from the fountain of charity to think upon the needy and poor is before all called blessed: led by this consideration, I, William Sevenoaks, citizen and grocer of London, being of good understanding and perfect memory, on the fourth day of the month of July A.D. 1432, and in the year of the reign of King Henry the Sixth after the Conquest, the tenth, concerning all my lands and tenements with a wharf adjoining, and the buildings built thereon and all other the appurtances which I lately have had by the demise and feoffment of Margaret, who was the wife of Robert Walton, in Petty Wales street in the parish of All Saints Barking church, near the tower of London, do frame make and ordain my present testament in this manner.

First, I bequeath and commend my soul to God Almighty, my Creator and saviour, to the Blessed Virgin Mary his mother and all saints, and my body to be buried where God has arranged.

Also, I give and bequeath all my aforesaid lands and tenements with a wharf adjoining and with the buildings thereon built, and all other the appurtances, unto Mr John Charlton, Rector of Sevenoaks church in the county of Kent, to Master Vicar of the same church, and to the church-wardens of the same church and to other parishioners of that church, To Have and to Hold to them and their successors the Parsons, Vicars, Church-wardens, and Parishioners of the said Church hereafter for the time being all the said lands, tenements (etc.) of the chief Lord of the fees thereof by the services thereof due and of right accustomed, for ever; after the manner and form and under the conditions hereafter expressed, that is to say:

First, (to pay an annuity of 20 marks to Margaret Walton for life, and after her death) do find and maintain forever one Master, an honest man, sufficiently advanced and expert in the science of grammar, B.A., by no means in holy orders, to keep a Grammar School in some convenient house within the said town of Sevenoaks with my goods, having obtained the license of the King or by other lawful means according to the discretion of my executors, and to teach and instruct all poor boys whatsoever coming there for the sake of learning, taking nothing of them or their parents or friends for the teaching and instructing them. For I will that the said rector (etc.) and their successors for the time being out of the issues and revenues of all the lands and tenements aforesaid with their appurtances, do pay yearly to the aforesaid Master of Grammer by way of salary or stipend for his service and labour to be done and exercised as aforesaid, 10 marks sterling at the four principal terms of the year by equal portions. Moreover I will and order that if any, and as often as it happens that any such master or teacher in grammar decease, depart or for the least time voluntarily cease from such determination, that then within at least the next quarter following another such master, if any such can conveniently be found, be newly elected and chosen by the said rector or vicar, wardens and parishioners and their successors to inhabit and keep school and determine in the same house in ways, manner and form aforesaid.

142. Foundation Bequest for a Chantry Grammar School

(Document executed by John Percyvall, January 25, 1503. Reproduced by A. F. Leach, *Educational Charters*, p. 436. Cambridge, 1911)

This document established a combined chantry and grammar school, instead of the usual elementary song-chantry, and is typical of many earlier as well as later mediæval foundations for the founding of an advanced type of school.

Foundation of Free Grammar School by ex-Lord Mayor
25 Jan. 1503

To all people to whome this present writyng indented shall come, John Percyvall, Knyght and late Maire of the city of London, sendith Gretyng in our Lord God euerlastyng.

Where afore this tyme I, consideryng that in the countie of Chester, and specially aboute the towne of Maxfeld, fast by the which Towne I was borne, God of his habundant grace hath sent and daily sendeth to the Inhabitaunts there copyous plentie of children, to whose lernyng and bryngyng forth in conyng and vertue right fewe Techers and Scole-maisters ben in that contre, wherebye many children for lake of such techyng and draught in conyng fall to Idleness, and so consequently live disolutely all their dayes, whiche cause with the graciouse mocion of the most Reverende ffader in God and my singler good Lord Thomas, Archebyshop of Yorke, hath moch stered me of such litle good as God of his grace hath me sent to purvay a preist to syng and pray for me and my freends at Maxfeld aforesaid And there to kepe a Free Gramer Scole for children for euermore. . . .

Wherefore and whereupon I, the said John Percyvall, by this present

FIG. 29. AN ENGLISH SCHOOL
(After a woodcut printed in *De Heteroclytis Nominibus.* London, 1521)

wrytyng indented, make and declare my wille, as to the disposicion of all the said londs and tenements, as well as x marcs by yere redy pur-veied as of the said other yerely v marcs, that is to wete of the said hole x li by yere in the maner and fourme hereafter ensuyng, that is to say . . . the same londs and tenements by good and adequate conveyaunce shall be put in ffeoffement to [17 persons named].

To th' entent that they and their heirs of the issues and profects of all the said londes and tenements shall fynde and susteyne a vertues Preest conyng in Gramer and graduate. The same preest to synge and saye his deuyne seruice dayly, as his disposicion shall be, in the parisshe churche of Maxfeld aforesaid, praying for my soule and for the soule of Dame Thomasyn my wyf, the soulles also of our Faders Moders benefactors and the soule of Richard Sutton, gentilman, for the good and holsome counsell which he hath given me to the perfourmance of this my will, and for all Cristen soules.

And I woll that the said Preest shall alwey kepe and contynew in the said Town of Maxfeld a Fre Gramer Scole techyng there Gentilmens Sonnes and other godemennes children of the Towne and contre theareabouts, wherby they shall more grow in conyng and vertue to the laude and praise of Almyghtie God and to their owne confort and profett.

And I woll that the said Preest and his scolers with him every evynyng upon feryall or wurchyng dayes shall synge afore some Image of Our Lady in the said Chirch an antempne of our Blessed Lady, and after antempne doon to say the psalm of De profundis with the colletts for my soule and other souls aforesaid. And I woll that the said Preest daily in his Masse after his first lavatory at the South ende of the awter shall turn him aboute to the people and there say the psalm of the De profundis with the Colletts for my soule and other souls aforesaid.

And that the same preest with his scolers euery yere aboute such tyme of the yere as it shall hap me to decease shall holde and kepe in the circh of Maxfeld aforsaid myn obyte or annyuersary by note, that is to say, Placebo and Dirige on nyght and Masse of Requyem on the morow folowyng praiyng for my soule and other souls above reherced.

Also I woll that the said Preest shall well ouersee the said scolers and cause theym euery hold day to be at the said chirche there at the tyme of Mateyns, Masse and Evensong, there helpyng to syng and to say their seruices wele and vertuously without jangling or talking or other idell occupacion.

And I woll that the said Preest shall alway be chosen elect and admitted to the same seruice by my feoffees [etc.] and the so chosen and admytted to contynue in the same seruice as long as he shall be of good and vertuous disposicion and duely kepe his seruice and Gramer Scole as is aforesaid.

[Power to remove him at a quarter's notice, except 'my kynnesman Maister William Bridgys,' who is to hold 'without any expulsion or ammovyng from the same.']

And I woll that all the residue and surplusage of the said yerely £10 above the reparacions of the same londs and tenements and other ordinary and casuall charges of the same And ouer the said yerely 6s. 8d. for the wages of the rent-gaderer shall alwey goo and remayne to the said preest for his yerely salary and wages. . . .

In witnesse of which premyssis to either parte of this my Will endented I have put my seale, Writen the xxv day of January, the yere of Our Lord God m^l fyve hundreth and two, and the xviijth yere of the reigne of King Henry the vijth.

143. English City Grammar-School Foundations

(Boys, William, *History of Sandwich*, p. 199. Canterbury, 1892)

After the reformed grammar-school idea had taken root in England, and the humanistic type of secondary school, with its emphasis on pure Latin grammar and speech, religion, manners,

FIG. 30. GRANTHAM FREE GRAMMAR SCHOOL
The school attended by Isaac Newton as a boy. A good type
of grammar-school interior of the time

and play, with some Greek, had become the established type, a few such schools were founded or aided by the cities. The following selection from the Records of the Corporation of Sandwich, England, describes the foundation of such a school, in 1579, and forms an interesting precedent for the later New England town action in founding town grammar schools.

21st may 5th. Elizabeth.

It was moved by the maior what a godly acte and worthie of memorye yt shuld be to make and fownd a free schoole within the towne for the godly educacion of children in the knowledge and feare of God, and

that God therefor wold blesse the towen the better; and required therefore, that euery inhabitant within this towen wold consyder so good an
acte and to knowe what euery man wold willengly give thereto; and
that he and his brethern as they did judge that a very godly work so
thei wold lardgely give of their porcions that the same might be stab-
lished; which said mocion liked well all men.   And so with one consent
they offeryd to giue euery man for the same worke according to their
abillytye as followythe, viz.

Here follows the list of subscribers and the amount given by
each Jurat, Councilman, and others, a total of £286, 7s. 2d. being
subscribed, which was a very considerable sum for that time.

144. Course of Study at Eton, in 1560

(Maxwell-Lyte, H. C., *History of Eton College*, p. 149.   London, 1899)

The following brief outline of the authors read at Eton, in 1560,
which is typical of other English grammar schools of the period,
shows how completely the new humanistic learning had by this
time been introduced into the grammar schools of England.   An
entirely new type of secondary school had been created since
about 1200, and this had now been reformed and redirected along
new lines.   In addition to the subjects of study, religion, sports,
and good manners received special emphasis.

CURRICULUM OF ETON IN 1560

LOWER OR USHER'S SCHOOL

First Form

The *Disticha de Moribus* of Dionysius Cato.
The *Exercitation Linguæ Latinæ* of John Lewis Vives.

Second Form

Terence.
Lucian's *Dialogues* (in Latin).
Æsop's *Fables* (in Latin).

Third Form

Terence.
Æsop's *Fables* (in Latin).
Selections by Sturmius from Cicero's *Epistles*.

UPPER OR MASTER'S SCHOOL

Fourth Form

Terence.
Ovid's *Tristia*.
Epigrams of Martial, Catullus, and Sir Thomas More.

Fifth Form

Ovid's *Metamorphoses*.
Horace.
Cicero's *Epistles*.
Valerius Maximus.
Lucius Florus.
Justin.
Epitome Troporum of Susenbrotus.

Sixth and Seventh Forms

Cæsar's *Commentaries*.
Cicero *de Officiis* and *de Amicitia*.
Vergil.
Lucan.
Greek Grammar.

The lower boys had to decline and conjugate words, and their seniors had to repeat rules of grammar, for the illustration of which short phrases, called 'Vulgaria' were composed and committed to memory. Some sort of Latin composition, however brief, was a necessary portion of the daily work of every Eton scholar.   In the lower forms it was confined to the literal translation of an English sentence or passage, while in the Fifth Form it consisted of a theme on a subject set by the schoolmaster.   The boys in the Sixth and Seventh Forms wrote verses.

145. Course of Study in a Country Grammar School

(Free School of Saint Helens, England, as related by Adam Martindale.   Watson, F., *English Grammar Schools to 1660*, p. 486.   Cambridge, 1908)

This description of an English country grammar school of about 1635 is by a former pupil of the school.

As for the proficience I made under my master 'twas this: He received me when I was learning in *As in præsenti* and Cato, and instructed me for prose in Corderius, Æsop's Fables, Tullie's Offices, epistles, and orations, together with Aphthonius for Latin in prose, and the Greek Grammars of Camden first, and Clenard afterwards, together with a Greek Catechism, and lastly the Greek Testament (for I proceeded no further with him); and for poetry in Mantuan, Terence, Ovid's Epistles and Metamorphoses, Virgil, and Horace.   The rhetorics he read to us were Susenbrotus first and Talæus afterwards. Mine exercises were usually A piece of Latin (of which he himself dictated the English) every day of the week, save Thursdays and Saturdays; and besides somewhat weekly as I rose in ability, first a dialogue in imitation of Corderius, or Pueriles Confabulatiunculæ, then an epistle wherein I was to follow Cicero, though (alas!) at a great distance.

Then themes (as we called them) in the way of Aphthonius, consisting of many parts and taking up one side of half a sheet pretty thick written, and (towards the latter end) good store of verses on the back side, most hexameters and pentameters, but some sapphics and adonics. All that were presumed by their standing able to discourse in Latin were under a penalty if they either spoke English or broke Priscian's head; but barbarous language, if not incongruous for grammar, had no punishing but derision. These were the orders we were subject to at teaching hours; yea, though we had liberty by twos to go forth of the school upon our necessary occasions, real or pretended, and sometimes (when the humour took him) he would tie us to them at our times for play.

Fig. 31.   A South-European Fifteenth-Century School

(After an illuminated engraving in Brulefer's *Bonaventure sententiar*, printed at Venice, in 1504)

146. The Degeneracy of Classical Instruction

(Simpson, Richard, *Life of Campion*, p. 105.   London, 1896)

The following selection describes the teaching of Edward Campion, a Jesuit teacher of rhetoric at Prague, and relates to the year 1574.   It illustrates well how the early humanistic spirit, under the Ciceronian-style impulse, had given place to a narrow formalism and a minute dissection of the classical authors.

In class, he first made his scholars repeat a passage they had learned out of school-hours; then the monitors collected the written exercises, which he looked over and corrected.   While he was thus occupied, the boys were trying to imitate a passage of a poet or an orator, which he had set them, or to write a brief account of a garden, a church, a storm, or any other visible object; to vary a sentence in all possible ways; to translate it from one language into another; to write Greek or Latin verses; to convert verses from one metre into another; to write epigrams, inscriptions, epitaphs; to collect phrases from good authors; to apply the figures of rhetoric to a given subject; or to collect all the topics or commonplaces that are applicable to it.   After this came a summary of the former day's lesson, and then the lecture of the day, on one of Cicero's speeches, was read, and the boys were examined upon it. The composition was to be on a given pattern.   First, he was to explain his text, and to discriminate the various interpretations of it.   Next, he was to elucidate the writer's art, and to display his tricks of composition, invention, disposition and style; the reasons of his dignity, his persuasiveness, or his power, and the rules of verisimilitude and illustration which he followed.   Thirdly, the professor had to produce parallel or illustrative passages from other authors.   Fourthly, he was to confirm the author's facts or sentiments by other testimony, or by the saws of the wise.   Fifthly, he was to illustrate the passage in any other way he could think of.   Each lecture did not necessarily include all these points; but such was the range and the order prescribed for the points that were adopted.

CHAPTER XII
THE REVOLT AGAINST AUTHORITY

THE few Readings contained in this chapter have been selected to illustrate first, the demands for church reform and the necessity for evolution to avoid revolution, and second, in case the reforms were refused, the natural consequences both to the reformer and to the Church.

One marked effect of the Revival of Learning in northern lands was the deepening of an impulse, already under way, for moral and religious reform. In France, England, and in German lands there had been many before Luther who objected to the practices of the Church. One of the earliest and most influential of these was John Wycliffe, in England. A hundred and fifty years before the Protestant Revolt broke in Germany he had attacked the methods of the Church in no uncertain terms. For this Pope Gregory XI had addressed Bulls to the King of England and to the Archbishop of Canterbury, and in 1377 had ordered the Chancellor of the University of Oxford to arrest Wycliffe and deliver him for trial. Selection **147** is illustrative of Wycliffe's attacks, attacks which found much sympathy among the English people. That the Pope was aware of this is evident from the closing injunction of his Bull to the Chancellor, where he says:

Besides, if there should be, which God forbid, in your university, subject to your jurisdiction, opponents stained with these [Wycliffe's] errors, and if they should obstinately persist in them, proceed vigorously and earnestly to a similar arrest and removal of them, and otherwise as shall seem good to you. Be vigilant to repair your negligence which you have hitherto shown in the premises, and so obtain our gratitude and favor.

Gregory's successor, Pope Urban VI, continued unsuccessfully to try to stop Wycliffe. Shortly after Wycliffe's death (1384) his followers replied to the charges against him, stating that they regarded Pope Urban as Antichrist and as bearing no resemblance to "Seint Petur in erthe," and attacked his life and doctrines. In particular they condemned the church theory of "indulgences," as may be seen from selection **148**. Wycliffe's work was deeply influential in England, and through court influences was carried to Bohemia, where it led to the martyrdom of John Huss, in 1415.

By the beginning of the fifteenth century the demand for church reform had become general. From 1378 to 1417 there were two Popes, one at Rome and one at Avignon, in France, each claiming to be the rightful successor, and the contest which took place between the two injured the Papacy greatly throughout Christendom. In 1414 a Council of the Church met at Constance, in Switzerland, to heal the breach, and, among other things, drew up a list of eighteen important reforms in church practices and procedure which it demanded, but unsuccessfully. These are enumerated in selection **149**. Princes, legislative assemblies, citizens, priests, and sometimes even bishops protested in vain. Extracts from the protests of the Cathedral preacher at Strassburg, and his prediction of a religious revolt if matters were not remedied, are contained in selection **150,** as typical of many of the time. Selection **151** reproduces fourteen of the ninety-five theses of Luther, as illustrating his point of view and the nature of the academic protests he at first made.

Gradually led from protest to open revolt, Luther was finally excommunicated from the Church, in 1520, and the Diet of Worms, in 1521, ordered him arrested and confined, his writings burned, and his sympathizers treated as he was to be. We can understand this attitude better if we remember that the heretic was the anarchist of the Middle Ages, and was virtually guilty of treason to the State. The selection from Saint Thomas Aquinas's *Summa Theologica* (**152**) will serve to make clearer the dangerous position of Luther and his followers, as viewed by the Church. The final selection (**153**) reproduces the English Act of Supremacy, which severed England from the Church of Rome and erected the King as head of the English Church and the defender of the faith in England.

147. Wycliffe on the Enemies of Christ

(Arnold, Thomas, *Select English Works of John Wycliffe*, vol. I, p. 208. Oxford, 1869)

John Wycliffe (1320?–84), a popular English preacher and Oxford divinity graduate, was led by a study of the Bible to attack many of the claims and practices of the Church. His revolt against authority was as direct and vigorous as the later revolt of Luther, but he lacked the printing-press which Luther had to

give effectiveness to his challenge.   His attacks, however, deep-
ened the English feeling of unrest.   The following selection is a sample of his at-
tacks, this being against the head of the Church in England
for his opposition to the trans-
lation of the Bible into Eng-
lish, and naming the Pope and cardinals, bad bishops and rulers, and the mendicant friars as the three chief enemies of
Christ.   Wycliffe was only one of many who attacked the
practices of the Church and the lives of its representatives
in the days before Luther.

FIG. 32. JOHN WYCLIFFE (1320-84)

And herfore to greet Bishop
Engelond, as men seien, is yvel
paied (pleased) that Goddis lawe is writun in Englis, to lewide men
(laymen); and he pursueth a preest, for that he writith to men this
Englishe, and somonith him and traveilith him, that it is hard to him
to rowte.   And thus he pursueth another preest by the helpe of Phari-
seis, for he prechide Cristis gospel freeli withouten fadlis.

O men that ben on Cristis half, helpe ye now agens Anticrist! for
the perilous tyme is comen that Crist and Poul telden bifore.   Butt
oo confort is of knygttis, that thei savoren myche the gospel and han
wille to rede in Englishe the gospel of Cristis liif.   For aftirward, if God
wole, this lordship shal be taken from preestis; and so the staaff that
makith hem hardi agens Crist and his lawe.   The firste is the pope and
cardinals, bi fals lawe that thei han made; the secounde is emperours
(and) bishopis, whiche dispisen Cristis lawe; the thridde is thes Phari-
sees possessioners and beggeris.   Alle thes three, Goddis enemyes, trav-
eilen in ypocrisie, and in worldi coveitise, and idilnesse in Goddis lawe.
Crist helpe his Chirche from these fendis, for thei figten perilously.

148. Wycliffe's Followers attack the Pope and the Practice of Indulgences

(Arnold, Thomas, *Select English Works of John Wycliffe*, vol. II, pp. 457-58.
Oxford, 1870)

Wycliffe died in 1384, and shortly after his death his followers
issued a defense, in which they charged the then Pope, Urban VI,

as being the Antichrist, and attacked, one hundred and thirty-three years before Luther's theses, the church theory as to indulgences.   They said, in part:

Furste, that this pope Urban tho sixte beres not strength of Seint Petur in erthe, but thai affermen hym to be the son of Anticriste, and that no verrey pope was sith tho tyme of Silvester (I) pope.

Here Cristen men seyne pleynly, that whatever pope or other preste, in maner of lyvynge or techynge or lawis-makynge, contrarius Crist, is verrey Anticrist, adversary of Jesus Crist, and of his apostlis, ande of alle Cristen pepul. . . .

Tho secunde tyme, See ye Cristen pepl, tho willeful poverte of Jesus Crist, how he hade nougt by worldly lordschipe one howse where he mygt reste his heved, but lyved by temporale almes of Mary Mawdeleyne ande other holy wymmen, as tho gospel sais.   Ande see ye wisely, whether oure popis, makyng stronge palayces with pore mennes lyvelodis, with al ther glorie of richesses and jewelis, acordem with this poreness of Crist.

Tho thrid tyme, See, yee Cristen pepul, tho charitabul lyif of Crist, ande like whether oure popis contrarien hym.   Where he was moste bisye in spirituale occupacione, these popis bene moste bisy in delynge of beneficis to him that moste muck brynggen or worldly favour. . . .

Where Criste mekely travelid with grete penaunce upon his fete to preche tho gospel, these popes, more then emperoures, resten in palaycis chargid with pretious in ther feete and in al ther stynkynge carione, ande prechen not tho gospel to Cristen men, but crien ever aftur glorye and riches, and make newe lawes for to magnify ther worldly state, that Crist and his apostlis durste never do.

Where Crist gafe his precious blode and lyif for to make pes and charite, these popis maken ande mayntenys werre thoroweout Cristendame, for to hold ther worldly state, moste contrarie ageyne Crist and his apostlis, ande herto spenden tho almes of kyngis, and appressen Cristen rewenes by newe subsidies.

And, that is werst, thai senden indulgencis, foundid as thai faynen on Cristis charite and his dethe, to sle alle men contrarie to theire lustis.   Certis this semes contrarious to Crist and his lovers.   Seynt Robert Grosthede (Bishop of Lincoln) sais that this court is cause, welle, and begynnynge of destruccione of Cristendame, and loser of al tho worlde.   Ande trewly, if thai be thus contrary to Crist in lyvynge and techyng, as ther open dedis and tho world crien, thai ben cursid heretikis, manquellars bodily and gostly, Anticrist, and Sathanas transfigurid into aungelis (of) ligt.   Ande, as this worthi clerk Grosthede proves, ande certis no man is verrey pope but in als myche as he sewis Crist; and in so myche Cristen men wole do aftur hym, ande no more, for alle bulles and censuris, for no creature of God.

149. List of Church Abuses demanding Reform

(Von der Hardt, *Magnum Constantiense Concilium*, vol. IV. 1452)

A dominant note, running through later mediæval writings and sermons, is a constant criticism of the Church and a demand for reform. In 1414–18 a Council of the Church, meeting at Constance, in Switzerland, made a serious attempt in this direction by drawing up a list of the abuses within the Church which it felt should be remedied. The attempt at reform failed, but the list of abuses, in view of the Protestant Revolt which broke a century later, is interesting.

The holy Council of Constance decrees and ordains that the Supreme Pontiff who shall next, by the grace of God, assume office, shall, in conjunction with this holy council, or with the deputies of the several *nations*, reform the Church, before the council dissolves, in head and members, as well as the Roman curia, in accordance with justice and the proper organization of the Church, in all the respects enumerated below, which are presented by the *nations* as requiring reform:

The number, character and nationality of the Lords Cardinals.

The Reservations made by the Apostolic See.

The Annates both the *servitia communia* and *servitia minuta*.

The Collation to Benefices and Expectative Favors.

Appeals to the Roman Curia.

The functions of the (papal) Chancery and Plenitentiary.

Exemptions and Incorporations made during the Schism.

Benefices *in Commendam*.

Confirmation of Elections.

Income during Vacancies.

The non-alienation of the possessions of the Roman Church or other churches.

For what reasons and in what manner shall a Pope be corrected or deposed?

The Extirpation of Heresy.

Dispensations.

The means of support of Pope and Cardinals.

Indulgences.

Tenths.

150. A German Priest's Views as to Coming Reform

(L. Dacheux, *Jean Geiler*. Paris, 1876. Trans. by Coulton)

Johann Geiler (1445–1510) took his doctorate in Theology at Freiburg, and became Cathedral Preacher at Strassburg, in 1478. This position he held until his death. He hated the abuses of the

Church of his time and thundered against them.   He died believing that a catastrophe was impending.   Two extracts from his sermons will illustrate his feeling as to the need for reforms.

Preaching before the Emperor Maximilian, a few years before his death, he cried out:

Since neither Pope nor Emperor, kings nor bishops, will reform our life, God will send a man for the purpose.   I hope to see that day, but I am too old.   Many of you will see it; think then, I pray you, of these last words.

In another sermon on existing conditions, he said:

O Lord my God, how falsely now do even those live who seem most spiritual — Parsons and Monks, Beguines and Penitents.   Their study is not to work God's works but to conceal the devil's works.   Among these all is outward show, and there is no truth, nought else but dung besnowed or buried under snow; without is the glistering whiteness of righteousness and honesty, but within a conscience reeking with vermin and with the stench of sin.   The day shall come when the Sun of Righteousness shall melt the snow, and then shall the secrets of your hearts be revealed.   And would that the filth of our sins were at least covered with the appearance of snow, that our sin, like Sodom, were not published abroad without shame!

151. Luther's Theses illustrated

(Ranke, *Deutsche Geschichte in Zeitalter der Reformation*, vol. IV, p. 83; trans. by Wace and Buchheim)

The ninety-five theses which Martin Luther made out and nailed to the church door in Wittenberg in October, 1517, were after the university form of challenge to debate, and were in Latin.   Of them Luther himself said that they were not his mature conclusions, and that they contained nothing he would stubbornly adhere to, but that they were "somewhat obscurely expressed, as was the custom in such cases," so that his opponent in debate might not be too easily driven to the wall.   In a letter to Pope Leo, six months afterward, Luther expressed surprise and regret that they should

FIG. 33. MARTIN LUTHER (1483–1546)

have been given such wide circulation.   The reproduction of a few of the theses will illustrate their nature.

In the desire and with the purpose of elucidating the truth, a disputation will be held on the underwritten propositions at Wittenberg, under the presidency of the Reverend Martin Luther, Monk of the Order of Saint Augustine, Master of Arts and Sacred Theology, and ordinary Reader of the same in that place.   He therefore asks those who cannot be present and discuss the subject with us orally, to do so by letter in their absence, In the name of our Lord Jesus Christ. Amen. . . .

5. The Pope has neither the will nor the power to remit any penalties, except those which he has imposed by his own authority, or by that of the canons.

6. The Pope has no power to remit any guilt, except by declaring and warranting it to have been remitted by God; or at most by remitting cases reserved for himself; in which cases, if his power were despised, guilt would certainly remain.

13. The dying pay all penalties by death, and are already dead to the canon laws, and are by right relieved from them.

20. Therefore the Pope, when he speaks of the plenary remission of all penalties, does not mean really of all, but only of those imposed by himself.

21. Thus those preachers of indulgences are in error who say that, by the indulgences of the Pope, a man is loosed and saved from all punishment.

22. For in fact he remits to souls in purgatory no penalty which they would have had to pay in this life according to the canons.

23. If any entire remission of all penalties can be granted to any one, it is certain that it is granted to none but the most perfect, that is to very few.

24. Hence, the greater part of the people must needs be deceived by this indiscriminate and high-sounding promise of release from penalties.

25. Such power as the Pope has over purgatory in general, such has every bishop in his own diocese, and every curate in his own parish, in particular.

88. Again; what greater good could the Church receive than if the Pope, instead of once, as he does now, were to bestow these remissions and participations a hundred times a day on any one of the faithful?

89. Since it is the salvation of souls, rather than money, that the Pope seeks by his pardons, why does he suspend the letters and pardons granted long ago, since they are equally efficacious?

91. If then pardons were preached according to the spirit and mind of the Pope, all these questions would be resolved with ease; nay, would not exist.

94. Christians should be exhorted to strive to follow Christ, their head, through pains, deaths, and hells.

95. And thus trust to enter heaven through many tribulations, rather than in the security of peace.

152. Saint Thomas Aquinas on the Treatment of Heresy

(*Summa Theologica*, Sec. Secundæ, Quæst. xi, Art. iii; trans. by J. H. Robinson, in *Pennsylvania Reprints*, vol. iii, no. 6)

Thomas Aquinas (1225?–74) was a famous Italian Dominican scholar, generally regarded as one of the three great scholastics of the Middle Ages. He brought scholasticism to its highest development by harmonizing Aristotle with the doctrines of the Church. His *Summa Theologica*, written during the last three years of his life, has ever since been accepted as an authoritative statement of the doctrines of the Church.

The selection here given deals with heresy, the great crime of the Middle Ages and early modern times, a crime worthy of the most severe punishment. The heretic was the anarchist of that time, one who was virtually guilty of treason to an institution necessary for salvation and the upholder of order and government. Not only was the heretic excommunicated and placed under political disabilities, but even torture and death were regarded as justified to stamp out the dangerous contagion. Considering the age, the mildness and fairness of the reasoning in the selection here given will be apparent.

The selection also affords a good example of the plan of organization and treatment of this famous textbook.

Proceeding to the third question. First. It would appear that heretics are to be tolerated, for the Apostle says (2 Timothy, ii, 24), "*The Lord's servant must be gentle, in meekness, correcting them that oppose themselves to the truth; if peradventure God may give them repentance unto the knowledge of the truth, and they may recover themselves out of the snare of the devil.*" But if heretics are not tolerated but delivered over unto death, they are deprived of the opportunity of repentance. Hence, this would seem contrary to the precept of the Apostle.

Second. Moreover, that which is necessary in the church must be tolerated. But heresies are necessary in the church. For the Apostle says (1 Corinthians, xi, 19), "*For there must be also heresies among you that they which are approved may be made manifest among you.*" Therefore, it would seem that heresies are to be tolerated.

Third. Moreover, the Lord commands his servants (Matthew, xiii), that they should let the tares grow until the harvest, which is the end of the world, as is explained in the Interlinear Glossa. But the tares signify the heretics according to the interpretation of the saints. Therefore heretics are to be tolerated.

But against this is to be urged the saying of the Apostle (Titus, iii,

10), "A man that is heretical after a first and second admonition, refuse, knowing that such a one is perverted."

I reply that heretics must be considered from two points of view, namely, as regards the heretic himself, and secondly, as regards the church. As for the heretics themselves, there is their sin for which they deserve not only to be separated from the church by excommunication, but to be sent out of the world by death. It is, indeed, a much more serious offence to corrupt the faith, upon which depends the life of the soul, than to falsify coin, by means of which the temporal life is sustained. Hence, if counterfeiters and other malefactors are justly hurried to death by secular rulers, much the more may those who are convicted of heresy not only be excommunicated but justly put to a speedy death. But on the side of the church, there is mercy looking for the conversion of the erring. She does not therefore condemn immediately, but only after a first and second admonition, as the Apostle teaches. Should the heretic still prove stubborn, the church, no longer hoping for his conversion, shall provide for the safety of others by separating him from herself by a sentence of excommunication. She further relinquishes him to the secular judgment to be put out of the world by death. Jerome also says (on the passage in Galatians, v), "a little leaven"; and as provided in 24. qu. 3, cap. 16 (Canon Law). *"Foul flesh must be cut away, and mangy sheep must be kept from the fold lest the whole house be burned, the whole mass corrupted, the whole body be destroyed. Arius was but a spark in Alexandria but since this spark was not promptly quenched, the whole world has been devastated by the flames."*

As to the first argument, namely that which relates to the meekness in which a heretic should be admonished a first and a second time; if, after that, he refuses to return he is to be looked upon as perverted, as appears from the authority of the Apostle above cited (in the argument beginning, *But against*).

As to the second argument, any advantage which may proceed from heretics, is in no way intentional on their part, as for example, the proof they furnish according to the Apostle, of the constancy of the faithful, or as Augustine says — *Lib. I de gen., cont. Mänich.* (cap. 1, about the middle) — *"Let us put away all slothfulness, carefully searching the Holy Scriptures."* Their intention is, on the contrary, to corrupt the faith, and this is most harmful. We should, therefore, give more weight to those conscious aims which would cut them off, rather than the unintentional good, which would seem to countenance their toleration.

To the third argument we may reply, as it is written in the Decretals 24, qu. 3, cap. Beginning, *It is to be observed that excommunication is one thing and extirpation another*. One is excommunicated with a view, as the Apostle says (1 Cor. v, 5), *"that the spirit may be saved in the day of the Lord."* That heretics shall be totally extirpated by death, is not however, contrary to the command of God, for that command is to be understood as applying only in the case when the tares cannot be destroyed, without destroying the wheat at the same time, as has been said in the preceding question, art. 8, argument 1, when we treated of heretics in common with infidels.

153. The English "Act of Supremacy"

(26 Henry VIII, c. 1, 1534, *Statutes of the Realm*, III, p. 492)

The following act passed by the English Parliament, in 1534, definitely severed England from Rome, and established the King as the head of the English Church. It illustrates the parliamentary side of the Reformation.

An Act concernynge the Kynges Highnes to be supreme heed of the Churche of Englande and to have auctoryte to reforme and redresse all errours, heresyes and abuses yn the same.

Albeit the Kynges Majestie justely and rightfully is and oweth to be the supreme heed of the Churche of Englande, and so is recognysed by the clergy of this Realme in theyr convocacions; yet neverthelesse for corroboracion and confirmacion thereof, and for increase of vertue in Cristis Religion within this Realme of England, and to represse and extirpe all errours, heresies and other enormyties and abuses heretofore used in the same. Be it enacted by auctority of this present Parliament that the Kyng our Soveraign Lorde, his heires and successours Kynges of this Realme shall be takyn, acceptyed, and reputed the onely supreme heed in erthe of the Churche of England callyd Anglicana Ecclesia, and shall have and enjoye annexed and unyted to the Ymperyall Crowne of this Realme as well the title and style thereof, as all Honours Dignyties prehemynences jurisdiccions privileges auctorities ymunyties profitis and commodities to the said dignyties of supreme heed of the same Churche belongyng and apperteyning: And that our said Soveraigne Lorde his heires and successours Kynges of this Realme shall have full power and auctorite from tyme to tyme to visite represse redresse reforme order correct restrayne and amende all suche errours heresies abuses offences contempts and enormyties whatsoever they be whiche by any maner spirituall auctoryte or juristiccion ought or maie lawfullye be reformyd repressyd ordred redressyd correctyd restrayned or amendyd, most to the pleasure of almyghtie God the increase of vertue yn Chrystis Religion and for the conservacy of the peace unyte and tranquylyte of this Realme: Any usage custome foreyne laws foreyne auctoryte prescripcion or anye other thinge or thinges to the contrarie hereof notwithstandinge.

CHAPTER XIII

EDUCATIONAL RESULTS OF THE PROTESTANT REVOLTS

I. LUTHERANS AND ANGLICANS

THE Readings in this chapter illustrate the development of Protestant education among the Lutherans and Anglicans. The first selection, from Rashdall (**154**), deals with the diffusion of education in later mediæval times, from which we may infer something as to the effect of the Reformation on educational institutions. The selection on the literary style of the different translations of the Bible (**155**), contrasting these with the Ciceronian, is an interesting explanation of the hold which these vernacular translations obtained from the first.

The extract from Luther's long address (**156**) is quite typical of the whole, and reveals his belief in the importance of the higher classical schools, when properly reformed, as a means for training learned ministers for the churches. Luther saw very clearly the need for teachers and preachers, and sets forth plainly the importance of the teacher's work (**157**). He even advances very modern arguments for the compulsory attendance of children at school (**158**).

Having abolished the old Church of Rome régime, it was necessary that the Lutherans reorganize the churches under the new form of worship, and for this some outline or form was necessary. These were supplied by the so-called *Kirchenordnungen*, worked out for the churches by Luther, Melanchthon, and Bugenhagen. An example of these is given in **159,** from which their comprehensive nature may be discerned.

The schools also needed reorganization to fit them into the new Protestant state régime, and for this *Schuleordnungen* also were needed. Three of these are reproduced, the one prepared for Brieg (**160**), the Saxony Plan of Melanchthon (**161**), and the state school system adopted for Würtemberg (**162**). An outline of the *Schulemethode* adopted for the principality of Gotha, and a brief sketch of the important work of Duke Ernest, are given in **163**.

In England the Reformation zeal for education was far less

marked than in German lands, and took more the form of regulations to insure conformity to the new faith. Selections illustrating the careful church supervision of a teacher's acts and beliefs
are given in **164**; the type of penalties imposed on non-conforming
schoolmasters by law in **165**; a type of oath of fealty required of
a grammar-school master is given in **167**; an elementary-school
teacher's license is reproduced in **168**; and typical grammar-school
statutes regarding prayers are given in **169**. Reading **166** gives
the essential features of the English Act of Conformity of 1662,
an act which did much to drive good teachers from the work.
One of the important results of the Reformation, in all Protestant
lands, was that the people obtained the Bible in the vernacular,
and selection **170** sets forth the great importance of this in educating the people in England, and in influencing English literary art.

It is often said that the Reformation was destructive of schools,
and this certainly was the case in England. The general results
afterward were worse, in so far as numbers and opportunities
were concerned, than before. That many of the schools abolished
or re-founded needed reform may be seen from the extracts relating to the cathedral school at Canterbury (**171, 172**), the chief
cathedral church in England. The details of the re-foundation
by Henry VIII (**172**) give a clear idea of the type of reformed
humanistic cathedral grammar school established there.

Elementary education in England remained for the nineteenth
century to establish, as the nation soon settled down to the no-
business-of-the-State attitude which persisted up to modern times.
The State was, however, early forced to give attention to the
needs of the children of paupers. Due to the change of England
from an agricultural to a manufacturing nation, numbers of
poor from the rural districts flocked into the growing cities,
and a long series of Poor-Law legislation ensued. This cul-
minated in the famous Poor-Relief and Apprenticeship Law
of 1601 (**174**), toward which England had for some time been
tending (**173**).

154. Diffusion of Education in Mediæval Times

(Rashdall, H., *Universities of Europe in the Middle Ages*, vol. II, part 2,
pp. 600–04. Oxford, 1895)

The following extract from Rashdall, an unusually careful
scholar, dealing with the preparatoiy education of a mediæval

university student, throws an interesting side light on mediæval education in general.

There is no reason to believe that boys came to attend these inferior Grammar Schools in the University towns except from the immediate neighborhood. The majority of scholars must have learned reading, writing, and the rudiments of Grammar nearer home. As to where and how this knowledge was acquired, we have little detailed information. An investigation into the Grammar Schools of the Middle Ages would be a subject for a separate treatise. Suffice it to say that the old ecclesiastical Schools, in connexion with Cathedrals or other important Churches, were not destroyed by the growth of the Universities, and other Schools of the same kind were founded from time to time. Where the Universities were within easy reach, they were probably restricted for the most part to the study of Grammar, and sometimes the rudiments of Logic. In districts remote from Universities there were ecclesiastical Schools of a higher type, which certainly taught a full course of Logic as well as Grammar, and in some cases perhaps the whole range of a University Arts Course. In some countries the bulk of the inferior clergy must have received their education in such Schools. At Vienna, Erfurt, and elsewhere, Schools of this character became a nucleus for the later Universities.

Where there was no Cathedral, Grammar Schools were attached to some Collegiate Church, or to ordinary Parish Churches. Sometimes there was an endowment for such schools: elsewhere they were supported by the Municipality, or, in places like Canterbury or Bury, taught by the Monastery. In other cases, no doubt, they were taught by some poor 'parochial chaplain' in return for the scholars' fees alone. Even in country parishes the Canon Law required that the parish clerk should be able to teach the boys to read as well as to sing their Psalter. How far such regulations were actually carried out, it is of course impossible to determine with pre-

FIG. 34. A GERMAN FIFTEENTH-CENTURY SCHOOL

(Reproduced from a woodcut on the title-page of an edition of Boethius' *De disciplina scholarium cum notabile commento*, printed by Henricus Quentell, at Cologne, in 1498, and now in the Library of Stanford University)

cision. But it may be stated with some confidence that at least in the later Middle Ages the smallest towns and even the larger villages possessed Schools where a boy might learn to read and acquire the first rudiments of ecclesiastical Latin: while, except in very remote and thinly populated regions, he would never have had to go very far from home to find a regular Grammar School. That the means of education in reading, writing, and the elements of Latin were far more widely diffused in medieval times than has sometimes been supposed is coming to be generally recognized by students of medieval life. The knowledge of reading and writing and of the elements of Latin was by no means confined to the clergy: 'the bailiff of every manor kept his accounts in Latin.' A Grammar Master often formed part of the establishment of a great noble or prelate, who had pages of gentle family residing in his house for education. In other cases a boy of a well-to-do family no doubt received his earliest education from a chaplain or 'clerk' of his father, or from a private tutor or neighboring Priest engaged for the purpose.

In the Grammar School the rudiments of a classical education were imparted in much the same way as at the present day. Donatus and Alexander de Villa Dei were the Grammars. After the Psalms had been learned (this much was taught in the most elementary Schools of all), Cato served for Delectus, after which the boy might be put into Ovid and possibly Vergil. In the absence of dictionaries the Master no doubt literally 'read' the book to the pupils, i.e. construed it to them and afterwards required them to do the same. In England books were construed into French as well as English. Questions were asked in parsing and exercises set in prose and verse. Disputations in Grammar . . . were also a favorite institution. After the boy had once entered the University all this ceased. No more classical books were construed, and we hear comparatively little of composition, though verse-making sometimes entered into University Examinations. Lectures in Grammar meant formal lectures on the elaborate grammatical treatises of Priscian and Donatus, or the more popular Alexander de Villa Dei.

155. The Vernacular Style of the Translations of the Bible

(From an article in the Literary Supplement of the London *Times*, 1911)

The following short extract from a very interesting article on the English Bible applies with almost equal force to Luther's German translation, in that each was couched in simple, homely phrases so unlike the language of the scholar of the day. This gave to each a strong appeal to the masses of the people, fixed the style of the vernacular, popularized religion, and greatly strengthened the Reformation cause.

It was genuine enthusiasm for a high moral ideal which made the beauty. If Wyclif and his associates provided the seed, it was Tindale and Cloverdale who raised the plant; the revisers of 1611 only pruned and trained it. . . . While Tindale was working alone in exile there was no promise in English literature. Chaucer's light had set in darkness; tho he had died less than one hundred and fifty years before, he was not so easily read as he is to-day; and Wyclif's Bible, tho more vernacular in style than Chaucer, was suffering the same obsolescence. Shakspere, without whom we can reckon nothing, was unborn. It was unforeseen and unimaginable that at that time a book should arise unmatched in the world for its beauties and mastery of style.

The style of prose eludes differentiation and description; it is one of the most complex and intangible of all phenomena that invite distinction, but its history in western Europe offers a simple classification into two main divisions, the Ciceronian and the non-Ciceronian or Romantic. These terms are not satisfactory, but they do indicate a real distinction. Cicero, founding himself on the Greek orators, perfected a manner of writing which, wherever it was known, affected European literature. Since he wrote in the language which was for centuries written and spoken by the learned all over Europe, we can not suppose that any one could wholly escape from some relics of his tradition; but his art was so elaborate that without familiarity and practice it could not be approached or attempted; and it is so far removed from colloquial speech and untrained expression as to be almost unintelligible and repulsive to the natural man. . . .

Our Bible, then, is in the Romantic style of prose; and, comparing our literature with the one literature in the world with which we can feel pride in comparing it, we may say that to the Greeks Herodotus' history held something like the same literary position as our Bible holds with us — an early and inimitable masterpiece of abounding natural grace, whose simple charm set it above the reach of the conscious rules of grammarians, a model which no one who had sufficient taste to admire would attempt to rival. . . .

What England would have been if the Bible had never become a household book is a hypothetical problem for the moral philosopher; and if we ask how much we owe to the literary excellence of our translation, that question is not a wholly literary one, but it has a very important literary aspect, of which we may venture to speak without intruding upon morals or theology or the field of esoteric scholarship. For three hundred years, and we may almost say from the date of the first dissemination of Tindale's New Testament, the average Englishman has been subjected to an influence of incalculable magnitude, the greater because he has been unaware of its unusual character; for the Bible that he has read and revered has not only more beauty than any other vernacular rendering that any other nation has possessed, but it is in its vital parts more beautiful and intimate than its originals.

156. Luther to the Mayors and Magistrates of Germany

(Martin Luther, *Letter to the Mayors and Aldermen of all Cities of Germany in behalf of Christian Schools*, 1524; trans. in Barnard's *American Journal of Education*, vol. IV, pp. 429–30, 437–38)

Luther issued this address to the rulers of the German cities. The following extracts from it show his reasoning, and reveal the spirit of the Address. His great belief in the study of the languages for the sake of understanding the Bible is also clearly demonstrated.

To the Mayors and Councilmen of all the Towns of Germany:

Grace and peace from God the Father, and our Lord Jesus Christ. Beloved rulers, wise and sagacious men, . . . I would have you freely, cheerfully and in a spirit of love, give me your attention; since, doubtless, if ye obey me herein, ye obey not me, but Christ, and whoever does not follow my precepts, despises Christ, and not me.   Wherefore I beseech you all, beloved rulers and friends, for the sake of God and of poor neglected youth, do not count this a small matter, as some do, who, in their blindness, overlook the wiles of the adversary.   For it is a great and solemn duty that is laid upon us, a duty of immense moment to Christ and to the world, to give aid and council to the young. And in so doing we likewise promote our own best interests.   And remember, that the silent, hidden and malicious assaults of the devil can be withstood only by manly Christian effort.   Beloved rulers, if we find it necessary to expend such large sums, as we do yearly, upon artillery, roads, bridges, dykes, and a thousand other things of the sort, in order that a city may be assured of continued order, peace, and tranquillity, ought we not to expend on the poor suffering youth therein, at least enough to provide them with a schoolmaster or two?   God, the Almighty, has, in very deed, visited us Germans with the small rain of his grace, and vouchsafed to us a right golden harvest.   For we have now among us many excellent and learned young men, richly furnished with knowledge, both of the languages and of the arts, who could do great good, if we would only set them to the task of teaching our little folks.   Do we not see before our very eyes, that a boy may now be so thoroughly drilled in three years, that, at fifteen or eighteen, he shall know more than hitherto all the high schools and cloisters put together have ever been able to impart?   Yea, what other thing have the high schools and cloisters ever achieved, but to make asses and blockheads? Twenty, forty years would they teach you, and after all you would know nothing of Latin, or of German either; and then, too, there is their shameful profligacy, by which how many ingenuous youths have been led astray!   But, now that God has so richly favored us, in giving us such a number of persons competent to teach these young folks, and to mould their powers in the best manner, truly it behooves us not to throw his grace to the wind, and not to suffer him to knock at our door in vain. . . .

"This may be so," you reply; "but, though we ought to have schools, and must have them, still what will it profit us to have Latin, Greek, Hebrew, and your other liberal arts taught in them? Will not German suffice to teach us all of the Bible and the Word of God that is essential to salvation?" Alas, I fear me, that we Germans must ever be and continue to be mere brutes and wild beasts, as our neighbors with such good reason style us. . . . Surely, were there no other good to be got from the languages, the bare thought that they are a noble and a glorious gift from God, wherewith he has visited and enriched us, almost beyond all other nations, this thought, I say, ought to be a powerful motive, yea, an allurement to cultivate them. . . . For the prince of darkness is shrewd enough to know that, where the languages flourish, there his power will soon be so rent and torn that he cannot readily repair it. But now, since he cannot keep them from expanding into a vigorous growth, and from bearing fruit, he is at work, devising how he may render them dwarfed and sickly, if so be that they may decay and die of themselves. . . .

. . . For, as the light of the sun dispels the shadows of the night, so do the languages render useless all the glosses of the Fathers. Since now, it becomes Christians to regard the Scriptures as the one only book, which is all their own, and since it is a sin and a shame for us not to be familiar with our own book, nor with the language and the word of our God; — so it is a still greater sin and shame, for us not to learn the languages, especially now that God is bringing to us and freely offering us learned men, and suitable books, and everything which we need for this purpose, and is, so to speak, urging us to the task, so desirous is he to have his book open to us. O, how joyful would those beloved Fathers have been, if they could have come to the knowledge of the Scriptures, and have learned the languages so easily as we now may do it. . . .

But, you say, "we can not bring all our children up to be students; we can not spare them; we need them at home to work for us." I answer, "I do not ask for the establishment of such schools, as we have had hitherto, where our young men have spent twenty or thirty years over Donatus or Alexander, and yet have not learned anything at all. We have now another world, and things are done after a different pattern. And I ask no more than this, namely, that boys shall attend upon such schools as I have in view, an hour or two a day, and none the less; spend the rest of their time at home, or in learning some trade, or doing whatever else you will; thus both these matters will be cared for together, while they are young and opportunities are favorable. For else, they would haply spend tenfold this time in gunning and ball-playing. So, too, your little girls may easily find time enough to go to school an hour a day, and yet do all their household duties; for they now devote more than that to overmuch play, dancing, and sleep.

It is very plain that all we need, is a cordial and earnest determination to train up our youth aright, and by this means furnish the world with wise and efficient men. For the devil is better pleased with coarse blockheads and with folks who are useful to nobody; because where such characters abound, then things do not go on prosperously here on the earth.

Hence, there is great need, not for the sake of the young alone, but also for the welfare and stability of all our institutions, temporal and spiritual alike, that we should begin at once, and in good earnest, to attend to this matter. . . .

Wherefore, dearly beloved rulers, bend yourselves to the work which God so strictly enjoins upon you, which your office involves, which our youth stand so much in need of, and which neither the world nor the spirit can afford to do without. We have lain, alas, too long in the darkness of corruption and death; too long have we been German beasts. Let us now act as becomes reasonable beings, so that God may mark our gratitude for the good things he has given us, and that other lands may see that we, too, are men; nay, more, that we are men who can either learn somewhat from them, or impart somewhat to them: so, through us, the world shall be made better. I have done my part; and with longing have I desired to bring aid and counsel to this German land. . . .

157. Luther's Conception of the Dignity and Importance of the Teacher's Work

(Martin Luther, *Sermon on the Duty of Sending Children to School;* trans. in Barnard's *American Journal of Education,* vol. IV, p. 441)

Another extract from the same source as the preceding.

Where were your supply of preachers, jurists, and physicians, if the arts of grammar and rhetoric had no existence? These are the fountain, out of which they all flow. I tell you, in a word, that a diligent, devoted school-teacher, preceptor, or any person, no matter what his title, who faithfully trains and teaches boys, can never receive an adequate reward, and no money is sufficient to pay the debt you owe him; so, too, said the pagan, Aristotle. Yet we treat them with contempt, as if they were of no account whatever; and, all the time, we profess to be Christians. For my part, if I were, or were compelled to leave off preaching and to enter some other vocation, I know not an office that would please me better than that of schoolmaster, or teacher of boys. For I am convinced that, next to preaching, this is the most useful, and greatly the best labor in all the world, and, in fact, I am sometimes in doubt which of the positions is the more honorable. For you can not teach an old dog new tricks, and it is hard to reform old sinners, but this is what by preaching we undertake to do, and our labour is often spent in vain; but it is easy to bend and train young trees, though haply in the process some may be broken. My friend, nowhere on earth can you find a higher virtue than is displayed by the stranger, who takes your children and gives them a faithful training, — a labor which parents very seldom perform, even for their own offspring.

158. Luther on the Duty of compelling School Attendance

(Martin Luther, *Sermon on the Duty of Sending Children to School;* trans. in Barnard's *American Journal of Education*, vol. IV, pp. 440–41)

In a long sermon, written in 1530, to be preached in Lutheran churches throughout Germany, Luther admonishes the people to send their children to school. In the extract from this sermon given below Luther urges compulsion to attend, basing the right to compel attendance on the general right of the State to protect itself and advance its welfare.

I hold it to be incumbent on those in authority to command their subjects to keep their children at school; for it is, beyond doubt, their duty to insure the permanence of the above-named offices and positions, so that preachers, jurists, curates, scribes, physicians, schoolmasters, and the like, may not fail from among us; for we cannot do without them. If they have the right to command their subjects, the able-bodied among them, in time of war, to handle musket and pike, to mount the walls, or to do whatever else the exigency may require; with how much the more reason ought they to compel the people to keep their children at school, inasmuch as here upon earth the most terrible of contests, wherein there is never a truce, is ever going on, and that with the devil himself, who is lying in wait, by stealth and unawares, if so be that he may drain city and kingdom, and empty quite out of them all the brave and good, even until he has removed the kernel utterly, and naught shall be left but a mere shell, full of idle mischief-makers, to be mere puppets in his hands to do his pleasure. Then will your city or your country suffer a true famine, and, without the smoke of conflict, will be silently destroyed from within, and that without warning. Even the Turk manages in another way; for he takes every third child throughout his empire, and trains him to some calling perforce. How much more, then, ought our rulers to put at least some children to school; not that I would have a boy taken away from his parents, only that he should be educated, for his own good and the general welfare, to some calling that shall yield him abundant fruits of his industry. Wherefore, let magistrates lay these things to heart, and let them keep a vigilant look-out; and, wherever they see a promising lad, have him pledged at school.

159. An Example of a Lutheran *Kirchenordnung*

(Hamburg *Kirchenordnung* of 1529; trans. by Robbins)

After the Reformation in Germany it was necessary to reorganize the churches and schools in the cities and towns as Lutheran churches and schools, and to provide a basis for such reorganizations a series of church and school ordinances were drawn up. These followed old established lines, but required changes to adapt themselves to the new faith. Several hundred of these *Ordnungen* are in existence, some being quite simple and others very comprehensive. An example of the latter is the one adopted for the city of Hamburg, in 1529. Its contents were as follows:

1. Of schools. 2. On the sifting of pupils by the teacher. 3. On the permanence of schools. 4. Public lectures. 5. The library. 6. German writing schools. 7. Girls' schools. 8. Students. 9. Pastors, chaplains, and other clergymen. 10. The superintendent and his assistant. 11. Selection of teachers and predicants. 12. The reception of such persons into the work of the church. 13. The work of predicants. 14. Sermons on Sundays and feast days. 15. Preaching on Saturdays and Mondays. 16. Preaching on other week days. 17. Special times for instruction in the catechism. 18. The paschal season. 19. Sacred stories at other seasons. 20. On preaching in Lent. 21. Confession and sacrament. 22. Visitation of sick and poor. 23. Matrimony. 24. The bans. 25. Consecration. 26. Visitation of criminals. 27. Children baptized at home. 28. Baptism of children according to our "use." 29. Support of predicants. 30. Sextons. 31. Organists. 32. Midwives. 33. Pictures and images. 34. Ringing the call to prayer for peace. 35. Festivals. 36. Business to be avoided on the afternoon of the holy day. 37. Singing and reading by pupils in the parish churches. 38. The Mass. 39. Administration of the Mass. 40. The "Common Chest" and the deacon in charge of it. 41. Administration of funds for the poor. 42. Administration of funds. 43. The deacon in charge of the funds. 44. The four councillors. 45. General accounting of the stewards. 46. Stewards. 47. Of stewards in general. 48. Miscellaneous. 49. Conclusion.

160. An Example of a Lutheran *Schuleordnung*

(Brieg, *Schuleordnung* of 1581; trans. by Robbins)

The following selection is an example of the more comprehensive *Schuleordnung* of the Lutheran sixteenth-century period. Its contents are as follows:

Part I

1. Introductory. General need and purpose of education.
2. Class division and basis of division. Each class is treated separately and work is prescribed for each day of the week. Thus, for the Fourth Class the following is prescribed for Mondays, Tuesdays, Thursdays, and Fridays:

   At six o'clock: Catechism.

   At seven o'clock: Reading.

   At eight o'clock: Presentation of dialogues by boys in pairs. After that follow exercises in Latin forms.

   At twelve o'clock: Writing and correction of exercises (Latin and German).

   At one o'clock: Declensions, conjugations, etc.

   At two o'clock: Exercises for increasing vocabulary, — with short statement of method.
3. Disputations and declamations.
4. Holidays.
5. Examinations and promotions.

Part II

1. The rector: Duties and jurisdiction.
2. Duties of professors and associates.
3. Duties of pupils in general.
4. Piety.
5. Duties of pupils to teachers.
6. Duties of pupils in school.
7. Instruction in regard to study, style, and memory work. (11 rules.)
8. Dismissal. (Four rules in regard to leaving school and going home.)
9. Conduct on the street. (10 rules.)
10. Conduct and service at home. (10 rules.)
11. Duties to strangers. (11 rules.)
12. Duties of *pædagogi* and assistants. (13 rules governing the conduct of those, who, while students, are private instructors.)
13. Duties of those who live in the halls. (12 rules.)
14. School employees. (10 rules.)
15. Funerals. (10 rules.)
16. Punishments. (10 rules.)
17. Duties of decurions and monitors. (10 rules.)
18. Disputation and declamation. (10 rules.)
19. The poor and the holders of stipends. (10 rules.)
20. Recreation and refreshment. (21 rules.)

    Conclusion. Admonition to teachers and pupils to keep the rules.

161. Melanchthon's Saxony Plan

(From Melanchthon's *Book of Visitation;* trans. in Barnard's *American Journal of Education*, vol. IV, pp. 749–51)

In 1527 Melanchthon was requested by the Elector of Saxony to head a commission of three to travel over the kingdom and report on its needs as to schools. It was probably the earliest of the school surveys. In 1528 the *Report*, or *Book of Visitation*, was published. This contained the following plan for the organization of schools throughout the kingdom. The great importance attached by Melanchthon to the Latin grammar school, and especially to the study of Latin grammar, will be evident to the reader.

School Plan

Preachers also should exhort the people of their charge to send their children to school, so that they may be trained up to teach sound doctrine in the church, and to serve the state in a wise and able manner. Some imagine that it is enough for a teacher to understand German. But this is a misguided fancy. For he, who is to teach others, must have great practice and special aptitude; to gain this, he must have studied much, and from his youth up. . . .

. . . In our day there are many abuses in children's schools. And it is that these abuses may be corrected, and that the young may have good instruction, that we have prepared this plan. In the first place, the teachers must be careful to teach the children Latin only, not German, nor Greek, nor Hebrew, as some have heretofore done, burdening the poor children with such a multiplicity of pursuits, that are not only unproductive, but positively injurious. Such schoolmasters, we plainly see, do not think of the improvement of the children at all, but undertake so many languages solely to increase their own reputation. In the second place, teachers should not burden the children with too many books, but should rather avoid a needless variety. Thirdly, it is indispensable that the children be classified into distinct groups.

FIG. 35.
PHILIPP MELANCHTHON
(1497–1560)

The First Group. The first group shall consist of those children who are learning to read. With these the following method is to be adopted: They are first to be taught the child's-manual, containing the alphabet, the creed, the Lord's prayer, and other prayers. When they have learned this, Donatus and Cato may both be given them; Donatus for a reading-book, and Cato they may explain after the following manner: the schoolmaster must give them the explanation of a verse or two, and then in a few hours call upon them to repeat what he has thus said; and in this way they will learn a great number of Latin words, and lay up a full store of phrases to use in speech. In this they should be exercised until they can read well. Neither do we consider it time lost, if the feebler children, who are not especially quick-witted, should read Cato and Donatus not once only, but a second time. With this they should be taught to write, and be required to show their writing to the school-master every day. Another mode of enlarging their knowledge of Latin words is to give them every afternoon some words to commit to memory, as has been the custom in schools hitherto. These children must likewise be kept at music, and be made to sing with the others, as we shall show, God willing, further on.

The Second Group. The second group consists of children who have learned to read, and are now ready to go into grammar. With these the following regulations should be observed: The first hour after noon every day all the children, large and small, should be practiced in music. Then the schoolmaster must interpret to the second group the fables of Æsop. After vespers, he should explain to them the Pædology of Mosellanus; and, when this is finished, he should select from the Colloquies of Erasmus some that may conduce to their improvement and discipline. This should be repeated on the next evening also. When the children are about to go home for the night, some short sentence may be given them, taken perhaps from a poet, which they are to repeat the next morning, such as, "*Amicus certus in re incerta cernitur.*" — A true friend becomes manifest in adversity. Or "*Fortuna, quem nimium foret, stultum facit.*" — Fortune, if she fondles a man too much, makes him a fool. Or this from Ovid: "*Vulgus amicitias utilitate probat.*" — The rabble value friendships by the profit they yield.

In the morning the children are again to explain Æsop's fables. With this the teacher should decline some nouns or verbs, many or few, easy or difficult, according to the progress of the children, and then ask them the rules and the reasons for such inflection. And at the same time when they shall have learned the rules of construction, they should be required to *construe*, (parse,) as it is called; this is a very useful exercise, and yet there are not many who employ it. After the children have thus learned Æsop, Terence is to be given to them; and this they must commit to memory, for they will now be older, and able to work harder. Still the master must be cautious, lest he overtask them. Next after Terence, the children may take hold of such of the comedies of Plautus as are harmless in their tendency, as the *Aulularia*, the *Trinummus*, the *Pseudolus*, etc.

The hour before mid-day must be invariably and exclusively devoted to instruction in grammar: first etymology, then syntax, and lastly prosody. And when the teacher has gone thus far through with the grammar, he should begin it again, and so on continually, that the children may understand it to perfection. For if there is negligence here, there is neither certainty nor stability in whatever is learned beside. And the children should learn by heart and repeat all the rules, so that they may be driven and forced, as it were, to learn the grammar well.

If such labor is irksome to the schoolmaster, as we often see, then we should dismiss him, and get another in his place, — one who will not shrink from the duty of keeping his pupils constantly in the grammar. For no greater injury can befall learning and the arts, than for youth to grow up in ignorance of grammar. . . .

The Third Group. Now, when these children have been well trained in grammar, those among them who have made the greatest proficiency should be taken out, and formed into a third group. The hour after mid-day they, together with the rest, are to devote to music. After this the teacher is to give an explanation of Vergil. When he has finished this, he may take up Ovid's Metamorphoses, and the latter part of the afternoon Cicero's "Offices," or "Letters to Friends." In the morning, Vergil may be reviewed, and the teacher, to keep up practice in the grammar, may call for constructions and inflections, and point out the prominent figures of speech.

The hour before mid-day, grammar should still be kept up, that the scholars may be thoroughly versed therein. And when they are perfectly familiar with etymology and syntax, then prosody (*metrica*) should be opened to them, so that they can thereby become accustomed to make verses. For this exercise is a very great help toward understanding the writings of others; and it likewise gives the boys a rich fund of words, and renders them accomplished in many ways. In course of time, after they have been sufficiently practiced in the grammar, this same hour is to be given to logic and rhetoric. The boys in the second and third groups are to be required every week to write compositions, either in the form of letters or of verses. They should also be rigidly confined to Latin conversation, and to this end the teachers themselves must, as far as possible, speak nothing but Latin with the boys; thus they will acquire the practice by use, and the more rapidly for the incentives held out to them.

162. The School System established in Würtemberg

(Digest of an article by Karl von Raumer; trans. by Barnard, in his *American Journal of Education*, vol. VI, pp. 426–34)

The first German State to organize a complete system of schools was Würtemberg, in southwestern Germany. This marked the real beginning of the German system, and the example of Würtemberg was copied throughout Germany. The School Code, first issued in 1559 by the reigning Duke, and approved by the Diet of the State in 1565, provided for a state school system designed "to carry youth from the elements through the successive grades to the degree of culture demanded for offices in the Church and in the State." The Code, in outline, provided for the following schools:

1. Teutsch (German) Schools

Beginning school. Boys and girls separate. Instruction in reading and writing German, religion, and music. Such schools to be set up in every little village and hamlet. Teachers in such schools to be relieved from beadle and mass services in the churches. These schools free, and for the masses.

2. Latin Schools

A fully equipped school to have six classes, but many had less. These known as private schools. They were divided into six classes, as follows:

First or Lowest Class. (9 to 11 years of age.) Pupils in this class learned to pronounce and read Latin and began building up a vocabulary. Readings from Cato.

Second Class. (10 to 12 years of age.) Cato continued. Declensions and conjugations. Grammar studied. Vocabulary enlarged. Translation from the Latin catechism. Much drill on phrases. Music taught.

Third Class. (11 to 13 years of age.) Much drill on phrases. Reading of fables and dialogues. Letters of Cicero begun. Readings from Terence for elegance and purity. Syntax begun. Music continued.

At close of this year might be transferred to the Cloister Schools (3).

Fourth Class. (12 to 14 years of age.) Cicero's "Letters to his Friends"; his treatises on "Friendship" and "Old Age"; and Terence to be read. Syntax finished; prosody begun.

Music continued.

Greek grammar begun, with readings from the smaller Greek catechism of Brentius.

Fifth Class. (13 to 15 years of age.) All previous work to be perfected. In this class read Cicero's "Familiar Letters" and his "Offices." Also Ovid's *de Tristibus*, and the Gospels in Greek and Latin. Much attention to prosody and to exercises in style. Music continued.

Sixth Class. (14 to 16 years of age.) Cicero's "Speeches," Sallust, and the Æneid of Vergil to be read. Much attention to the elegancies of the Latin tongue, and to pure poetical diction. Successful imitation of the idiom and phraseology of Cicero the aim.

In Greek to complete the grammar, and to read Xenophon's *Cyropædia* and the larger catechism of Brentius.

Music, especially sacred, to be practiced, and the recitations of the day to be begun by singing either the *Veni sancte Spiritus* or the *Veni Creator Spiritus*.

Conversation, both in and out of school, to be in Latin.

Logic and Rhetoric to be read in this class.

3. The Lower Cloister or Grammar Schools

Could be entered after completing the Third Class, at 12 to 14 years of age. Designed for selected boys, who were to be trained for the service of the Church.

Course of study paralleled the three upper classes of the Latin Schools, but with much more emphasis on theological doctrine.

4. The Higher Cloister Schools

Entered at 15 to 16 years of age, to prepare for the University, which was usually entered at about 16 or 17.

Read Cicero and Vergil. Continued emphasis on style and purity and elegance of diction. Phrase book constructed.

Continue Greek grammar, and read Demosthenes.

Continue music, and study musical theory.

Continue Logic and Rhetoric.

Begin Arithmetic and Astronomy.

Disputations fortnightly on questions of grammar, logic, rhetoric, or the sphere.

Strict discipline, and emphasis on theology.

5. The State University at Tübingen

Studies: Greek, Hebrew, Latin, Logic, Rhetoric, Mathematics, and Theology.

This Code laid the foundation for the school system which continued to the present century. For example, Barnard reports that, in 1832, there was in the State a complete system of vernacular elementary schools, eighty-three Latin schools, four cloister schools, and the University at Tübingen.

163. The *Schulemethode* of Duke Ernest of Saxe-Coburg-Gotha

(Digest of a description by Barnard, in *Am. Jour. of Educ.*, vol. xx, pp. 576–84)

One of the most wonderful pieces of educational work carried out in any German State in the seventeenth century was that of Ernest the Pious, who was the ruling prince of the little state of Saxe-Coburg-Gotha, in Thuringia, from 1640 to 1675. The Thirty

Years' War (1618–48) had practically destroyed the schools. In 1641 he ordered a "school-visitation" to ascertain the condition of the schools and churches. Inviting to his little kingdom a schoolmaster by the name of Andreas Reyher, who was familiar with the work of Ratich (Ratke) and Comenius, the two drew up a School Code (*Schulemethode*) which was alike the making of the schools of Gotha and a matter of derision and astonishment to his people. First published in 1642, it was revised and republished in 1648, 1653, 1662, 1672, and 1685. It contained minute regulations about everything that concerned schools and teachers, school government and superintendence, and the relations of parents and children to the schools.

Duke Ernest obtained teachers, built schoolhouses, prepared school books, and sent the children to school, and in time transformed his kingdom into one of the most prosperous spots in all Europe. His became the best type of school system organized in German lands before the late eighteenth century.

A digest of his *Schulemethode* shows the following organization:

Chapter I. The Nature of Schools in General. The obligation to attend.

Attendance after five. Attendance in summer and winter. Vacations. School books. Methods of beginning instruction. Special attention to be given to poor and backward children.

Chapter II. Of the Instruction in the Lowest Class.

Beginners to learn Bible verses, the Lord's Prayer, the articles of faith, the Ten Commandments, and morning and evening prayers. Class to advance from spelling to reading in the year.

Chapter III. Of the Instruction in the Intermediate Class.

Luther's Catechism to be committed to memory. Much instruction in religion. Psalms, and prayers in rhyme. Penmanship to be begun. Addition, subtraction, and the multiplication table. Hymns and singing.

Chapter IV. Of the Instruction in the Upper Class.

Subjects of study: religion, reading, writing, arithmetic, music, composition, and spelling. The Bible the authority for spelling.

Church doctrine as it relates to dying, certain prayers, family life, and regulations as to baptism, marriage, burial, and dress. Hard drinking to be interdicted.

Chapter V. Lessons in School Hours.

Outlines the class programs, by days and hours.

Chapter VI. The Method to Teach the Catechism Understandingly.
Every word to be learned by heart, as Luther advised; in the upper classes to be explained. Minister to assist teacher weekly.

FIG. 36. A GERMAN SCHOOLROOM IN THE SIXTEENTH CENTURY
(After a woodcut by Hans Burgkmair [1472–1559]. From Rhyn's *Kulturgeschichte des deutschen Volkes*, vol. II, p. 46)

Chapter VII. The Manner in which the Sermon is to be Remembered and Examined.
Sunday morning assembly of children, and march to the church.
Outline of the sermon to be written down.

Chapter VIII. The Natural and Useful Sciences, and how to Teach them.
This closely follows the outline of Comenius.

(*a*) Natural Science. Teacher to explain hour glass, sun dial, points of compass, signs of zodiac, rising and setting of sun and moon, shooting stars, thunder and lightning, observation of wind and weather, herbs and trees, plants and animals, observation of anatomy of a pig when butchered.

(*b*) Ecclesiastical and secular. Cities, towns, ditches, streams, courts, laws, taxes, merchants, the blessings of schools, and good rules for domestic life.

(*c*) Other sciences. Surveying, measures, carpenter's rule, angles, circles, plummet, weights, balance, lever, rollers, ropes, etc. to be explained.

Chapter IX. Of Christian Discipline and Godliness.
Good discipline necessary, and punishments.

Chapter X.   Of the Duties and Conduct of Children.

Moral conduct.   Attendance at school.   Prayers.   Manners.   Clean-liness.   Courtesies.   Bad Language.   Stealing.   Lies.

Chapter XI.   Duties of the Teacher and his Assistants.

Attention to.   Kindness.   Punishment; types of.   Diligence before God, and wise use of gifts.   To attend sermon, and live by its precepts. To lead a godly, quiet, retired life, and to be respectful and obedient to his superiors.

Chapter XII.   Duties of Parents and Guardians.

Obligations of parents to educate and care for and guide their chil-dren.   Parents to be fined if children fail to attend school.   Good discipline at home.

Chapter XIII.   The Annual Examination.

Of the school, the teacher, and the children by the ministers and superintendents of the school.

Of this work Barnard says:

These are the contents of the school manual (*methodus*), the grandest work of the many grand creations of Ernes the Pious, and that in a time when life and property were trodden into the dust, and when licentious mobs stubbornly resisted the establishment of schools — a work which was destined to be the foundation of a new edifice in Ger-many, because A. H. Franké, (whose father was counselor to the duke,) carried into effect subsequently the principles of the school-methodus in Halle, and rendered it thus available for all schools.   The new regulations were received with laughter and derision in the prin-cipality of Gotha itself; yet the duke was not disconcerted.   He first obtained better teachers, built twenty new school-houses as models, established a new school-inspection, and charged rector Reyher to get the necessary school-books for teachers and pupils.   *The German Horn-book and Speller for children of the principality of Gotha* was published, 1641; *The German Reader*, 1642; and both were given gratis to each child, an instruction which is still in force.   Reyher published later the *Arithmetica*, and (1656) the *Short Instruction* in natural objects, in some useful sciences, in ecclesiastic and secular institutions of the country, and in some " domestic prescripts "; and in 1655 he published some patterns of catechising on penitence, the virtues and vices spoken of in the Ten Commandments, on the value of the holy communion, &c.   When it was reported to the duke that some teachers did not study satisfactorily for their self-improvement, he issued an order that they should study arithmetic and writing more earnestly, either by themselves or with their pastors, or the inspectors of schools.   To im-prove the domestic education of the children, a "short instruction" was published (1654) "on the behavior, &c., of children," when going to school, at dinner, at home, in church, at play, at supper, when going to bed, when in company of strangers, on rising early, &c. This instruction was not only posted in every village, but the duke decreed, May 1, 1654, that it should be read in every school on examination day, in presence of the mayor, citizens, and elders of every township.

164. The Careful Supervision of the Teacher's Acts and Religious Beliefs in England

(Strype, John. (a) *The History of the Life and Acts of the Most Reverend Father in God, Edmund Grindal, Archbishop of Canterbury*, p. 378. Oxford, 1821. (b) Ibid., *The Life and Acts of Matthew Parker*, vol. II, p. 335. Oxford, 1821. Summarized by Stowe, in his *Elizabethan Grammar Schools*, p. 68)

After the English Church had been separated from Rome and separately established by the Act of Supremacy (**R. 153**), and after the coming of Elizabeth to the throne (r. 1558–1603), the English Church authorities began a very strict supervision of the manners, morals, and religious teachings and beliefs of the teachers in the schools. Two extracts will show the extent to which this was carried.

(a) Letter of Queen's Council to Archbishop Grindle, June 18, 1580

. . . for as much as a great deal of the corruption in religion grown throughout the realm, proceedeth of lewd schoolmasters, that teach and instruct children as well publicly as privately in men's houses; infecting each where the youth without regard had unto (a matter . . . chiefly to be looked into by every Bishop within his diocese) it is thought meet for redress thereof, that you cause all such schoolmasters as have charge of children, to be by the Bishop of the diocese, or such as he shall appoint, examined touching their religion: and if they shall be found corrupt and unworthy, to be displaced, and proceeded withal as other recusants; and fit and sound persons placed in their rooms.

(b) Dismissal of a teacher for non-conformity

In 1573 the mastership of the free school at Aylesham became vacant. Of the three men who applied for the position, Mr. Harrison, M.A., Cambridge, appeared to be best qualified, and was highly recommended by the Mayor and Aldermen of Norwich. Rumor's of Harrison's lack of complete conformity, however, had reached Archbishop Parker, who wrote and urged the Bishop of Norwich not to admit Harrison, who was finally admitted upon condition that he would keep and execute the statutes of the school, in reading the authors there appointed (it had been asserted that he had condemned the reading of profane authors to children), that he would quarrel neither with his Pastor nor with his neighbors, that he would hold no "strange opinions" nor defend them obstinately in prophesying, or any other conference, and that "he should use no unlawful games, neither vain nor disordered company." Harrison's term of office was not long. While acting as godfather to an infant about to be baptized he requested the Deacon "to change the word of the bok, viz. *thou* into *you;* and to leave out the sign of the cross: as for *Dost thou forsake*, he would have had him say, *Do you forsake;* for *Dost thou believe, Do you believe;* and when it was asked, *Wilt thou be baptized in this faith ?* it was answered, *We do bring this child to be baptized into the faith of Christ.*" Such signs of non-conformity could not be tolerated in a schoolmaster and the Bishop declared his position forfeited, and appointed or admitted a Mr. Sutton whose candidacy had been supported by Archbishop Parker.

165. Penalties on Non-Conforming Schoolmasters

(23 Elizabeth, 1580; c. I. *Statutes of the Realm*, 1819 ed., vol. IV, p. 656, s. 5)

The following statute of 1580 carried the matter of penalizing non-conforming schoolmasters still further, and shows the type of penalty inflicted on those employing teachers not sound in the faith, and the emphasis placed on the proper form of religious teaching by the State Church in England after the Reformation.

An Acte to reteine the Queenes Majestie's subjectes in their due obedience

V. Penalty on Corporations employing Schoolmasters not resorting to Church £10; on Schoolmaster, Disability and Imprisonment.

And be yt further enacted, that yf any person or persons, Bodye Pollitike or Corporate, after the Feaste of Pentecost next cominge, shall kepe or mainteyne any Scholemaster, which shall not repayre to Churche as ys aforesaid, or be alowed by the Bisshopp or Ordinarye of the Diocesse where such Scholemaster shal be so kept, shall forfaite and lose for everye moneth so keeping him £10; Provided that no suche Ordinarye or their ministers shall take any thinge for the said Allowaunce; and suche Scholemaster or Teacher presuminge to teache contrarie to this Acte, and beinge therof Lawfullye (convicted) shall be disabled to be a Teacher of youth, and shall suffer ymprisonment without Baile or Maineprise for one yeare.

166. The English Act of Conformity of 1662

(14 Charles II, cap. 4; Transcript, *Statutes of the Realm*, vol. v, p. 364)

This, the last and most exacting Act of Uniformity in religion in England, received the royal assent May 19, 1662. For two centuries it crushed the secondary schools of England.

The Act begins by reciting that in the first year of the reign of Elizabeth (1558) there was compiled a uniform order of service and prayer for the realm, and that this was enjoined by Parliament, and that "divers persons abstain from conforming to it" and ministers (Dissenters) neglect to use it, to rectify which situation the present Act of Uniformity is proclaimed, and the appended Book of Common Prayer is ordered used uniformly throughout the realm. All clergymen must take oath, on a prescribed form, that they assent to it and will use it in their services, and those that neglect to do so within one month are to be deprived of all religious offices and functions and thereafter forbidden to officiate at any form of service. This was intended to drive out all non-conforming ministers, and to prohibit service by such.

To make the Act still more onerous and effective, it was further provided:

And be it further enacted by the authority aforesaid, that every dean, canon, and prebendary of every cathedral or collegiate church, and all masters and other heads, fellows, chaplains, and tutors of or in any college, hall, house of learning or hospital, and every public professor and reader in either of the Universities and in every college elsewhere, and every parson, vicar, curate, lecturer, and every other person in Holy Orders, and every schoolmaster keeping any public or private school, and every person instructing or teaching any youth in any house or private family as a tutor or schoolmaster, who upon the first day of May, which shall be in the year of our Lord God 1662, or at any time thereafter, shall be incumbent or have possession of any deanery, canonry, prebend, mastership, headship, fellowship, professor's place or reader's place, parsonage, vicarage, or any other ecclesiastical dignity or promotion, or of any curate's place, lecture, or school, or shall instruct or teach any youth as tutor or schoolmaster, shall before the feast-day of St. Bartholomew which shall be in the year of our Lord 1662, or at or before his or their respective admission to be incumbent or have possession aforesaid, subscribe the declaration or acknowledgment following, *scilicet:*

"I, *A.B.* do declare that it is not lawful, upon any pretence whatsoever, to take arms against the king; and that I do abhor that traitorous position of taking arms by his authority against his person or against those that are commissionated by him; and that I will conform to the liturgy of the Church of England, as it is now by law established: and I do declare that I do hold there lies no obligation upon me, or on any other person, from the oath commonly called the Solemn League and Covenant, to endeavour any change or alteration of government either in Church or State; and that the same was in itself an unlawful oath, and imposed upon the subjects of this realm against the known laws and liberties of this kingdom." . . .

And if any schoolmaster, or other person, instructing or teaching youth in any private house or family, as a tutor or schoolmaster, shall instruct or teach any youth as a tutor or schoolmaster, before license obtained from his respective archbishop, bishop, or ordinary of the diocese, according to the laws and statutes of this realm (for which he shall pay twelve pence only), and before such subscription and acknowledgment made as aforesaid; then every such schoolmaster and other, instructing and teaching as aforesaid, shall for the first offence suffer three months' imprisonment without bail or mainprize; and for every second, and other such offence, shall suffer three months' imprisonment without bail or mainprize, and also forfeit to his majesty the sum of five pounds: and after such subscription made, every such parson, vicar, curate, and lecturer shall procure a certificate under the hand and seal of the respective archbishop, bishop, or ordinary of the diocese (who are hereby enjoined and required upon demand to make and deliver the same), and shall publicly and openly read the same, together with the declaration or acknowledgment aforesaid, upon some Lord's day within three months then next following, in his parish church where he is to officiate, in the presence of the congregation there assembled, in the time of divine service; upon pain that every person failing therin shall lose such parsonage, vicarage or benefice, curate's place, or lecturer's place respectively, and shall be utterly disabled and (*ipso facto*) deprived of the same; and that the said parsonage, vicarage or benefice, curate's place, or lecturer's place shall be void, as if he was naturally dead.

This Act was followed, in 1665 (17 Charles II, cap. 2), by what was known as "The Five Mile Act," which forbade any minister to preach or teacher to teach "within five miles of any city or town corporate, or borough that sends burgesses to Parliament, within his majesty's kingdom of England," or "to teach any public or private school, or take boarders or tablers that are taught or instructed by him or her self, or any other," under penalty of £40 and six months in prison.

These Acts were modified, in 1670, by the English Courts, so as not to apply to teachers in endowed elementary schools where the teacher was the appointee of the founder or the lay patron of the school, and the result was that between 1660 and 1730 approximately 1100 endowed elementary schools were created, largely to escape the stringent provisions of the above Acts. For secondary education they remained unmodified until the second half of the nineteenth century, with the result that the secondary schools declined in influence, and for two centuries were virtually withdrawn from the national life. "Men would not become schoolmasters," says Montmorency, "when only political or religious hypocrites were allowed to teach."

167. Oath of a Grammar-School Master

(Carlisle, N., *A Concise Description of the Endowed Grammar Schools in England and Wales*, vol. ii, p. 714. London, 1818)

Each grammar-school master was required to take an oath of fealty. This was an old institution in the Church (**R. 84 b**), and probably goes back to Roman civic requirements. The following oath, as required by the foundation statutes of Kirby Stephen School (1566), is illustrative and typical. In the parish church, and in the presence of at least two Governors of the school, the Churchwardens, twelve men of the parish, and any surviving heirs of the founder, this oath had to be taken by each new Master. It likewise illustrates the close connection of the Church and education in England, the English National Church merely taking the place of the Romanish Church which it had displaced.

I do swear by the contents of this book, that I will freely without exacting any money, diligently instruct and teach the children of this parish, and all others that shall resort to me, in Grammar and other humane doctrine, according to the statutes thereof made, — and I shall not read to them any corrupt or reprobate books or works set forth at any time contrary to the determination of the universal catholique church, whereby they may be infected in their youth in any kind of heresie or corrupt doctrine, or else to be indured to insolent manner of living: And further shall observe all the statutes and ordinances of this schoole now made, or hereafter to be made which concern me, and shall doe nothing in the prejudice thereof, but help to maintain the same from time to time during my aboad herein to the best of my power — so help my God, and the contents of this book.

168. An English Elementary-School Teacher's License

(Strype, John, *Life and Acts of John Whitgift, D.D.*, vol. iii, Appendix, p. 384. London, 1822)

The following is a license granted by Archbishop Whitgift, of Canterbury, to one William Swetnam, of London, in 1599, licensing him to teach the beginnings of learning to children. (Compare with **Rs. 83, 84**.)

John by divine providence Archbishop of Canterbury, of all England Primate and Metropolitan; to all Christian people to whom these presents shall come, sendeth greetings in our Lord God everlasting. These are to let you understand, that upon receipt of sufficient testimony of the good life and conversation of William Swetnam, of the parish of Saint Margaret Patens in London, fishmonger; and upon further examination of him, being first sworn in due form to the supremacy of the Queen's most excellent Majesty, and subscribing to the Articles agreed upon by the Clergy in anno 1562, we have licensed, and by these presents do license the said William Swetnam, to teach and instruct children in the principles of reading, and introduction into the *accidence;* and also to write, and to cast accounts, in any parish within the city of London, or our peculiar Churches of Canterbury, within the said city. Enjoyning him, that every week he do instruct his children and scholars in the Catechism made and set forth by Mr. Alexander Nowel, now Dean of the cathedral church of Saint Paul in London: and that he with his scholars, so many as shall be of the parish where he shall teach, do usually and commonly resort and repair, on all *sabbaths* and *festival* days, to the church of the parish where he shall so teach· and he with his scholars do reverently hear Divine service and sermons, and dutifully and diligently attend ther unto, And also we will, this our license to endure, during his good behavior, and our pleasure; and no otherways. In witness whereof, we have caused this our seal of our office of principal registry to be put hereunto. Dated this 20th day of July, in the year of our Lord 1599, and of our translation the 16th.

In 1603 a new Statute made all schoolmasters in the realm subject to license by the Bishop, as a condition precedent to teaching.

169. Grammar-School Statutes regarding Prayers

(Cowper, H. S., *Hawkshead*, p. 475. London, 1899)

Much emphasis has been laid upon religion in the English grammar schools. The boys have been required to attend both the services of the English Church and the devotional exercises of the school itself. Morning and evening prayers have been and still are an established feature of English grammar-school life. These prayers were usually prescribed by some church official, though they were sometimes appointed by the master, and sometimes even placed in the Statutes of the school by the founder. The following extracts from the Statutes for the grammar school at Hawkshead, as laid down by the founder, are typical and illustrate the character of the prayers required.

Also I ordayne and Constytute, that certayne godlye prayers hereafter set downe and ymediatelie followinge in these Constytucons, be
made in the said schole by the scholemaster for the tyme beinge, the
usher and the schollers of the same schole, eu^rie mornynge before the
said scholemaster, and usher begin to teache the said schollers and
everie eveninge ymediatelie before the breakinge up of the said schole,
And eu^rie day before they goe to dynner to singe a Psalme in Meter in
the said schole.

A Praier for the Morninge

Most mightie go, and m^rcyfull ffather, we sinners by nature, yett
thy Children by grace, here pstrate before thy devyne Matie, doe
acknowledge our Corrupcon in nature, by reason of our synnes to be
suche, that we ar not able as of our selues to thinke one good thought
much lesse able to pffytte in good learninge and lyterature, and to
come to the knowledge of thy sonne Chryste o^r sauiour, except yt shall
please the of thie great grace and goodnes to illumynate o^r understand-
inge, to streghten o^r feable memories, to instructe us by thy holie
spyritt, and soe power upon us thy good guifts of grace, that we may
learne to knowe to practyse those thyngs in these o^r studies, as may
most tende to the glorye of thy name, to the profitt of thy Churche,
and to the pformaunce of our Chrystyan dewtie, Heare us O god,
graunt this ou^r Peticon, and blysse o^r studies O heavenlye ffather, for
thy sonne Jesus Chrystes sake, in whose name we call upon the, and
saye O our father, &c.

The Statutes also included prayers to be offered for "the
Queenes Majestie," evening prayers, and prayers to be offered
"at breakings up of the Schole."

170. Effect of the Translation of the Bible into English

(Green, J. R., *Short History of the English People*, pp. 460–62. London, 1888)

The wonderful moral and educational influence of the translation and setting up of the English Bible in the churches of England is described by Green, as follows:

No greater moral change ever passed over a nation than passed over
England during the years which parted the middle of the reign of
Elizabeth from the meeting of the Long Parliament. England became
the people of a book, and that book was the Bible. It was as yet the
one English book which was familiar to every Englishman; it was read
at churches and read at home, and everywhere its words, as they fell
on ears which custom had not deadened, kindled a startling enthusiasm. . . . The popularity of the Bible was due to other causes beside
that of religion. The whole prose literature of England, save the

lorgotten tracts of Wyclif, has grown up since the translation of the Scriptures by Tyndale and Coverdale. So far as the nation at large was concerned, no history, no romance, hardly any poetry, save the little-known verse of Chaucer, existed in the English tongue when the Bible was ordered to be set up in churches. Sunday after Sunday, day after day, the crowds that gathered round Bonner's Bibles in the nave of Saint Paul's, or the family group that hung on the words of the Geneva Bible in the devotional exercises at home, were leavened with a new literature. Legend and annal, war-song and psalm, State-roll and biography, the mighty voices of prophets, the parables of Evangelists, stories of mission journeys, of perils by the sea and among the heathen, philosophic arguments, apocalyptic visions, all were flung broadcast over minds unoccupied for the most part by any rival learning. The disclosure of the stores of Greek literature had wrought the revolution of the Renascence. The disclosure of the older mass of Hebrew literature wrought the revolution of the Reformation. But the one revolution was far deeper and wider in its effects than the other. No version could transfer to another tongue the peculiar charm of language which gave their value to the authors of Greece and Rome. . . . But the tongue of the Hebrew, the idiom of the Hellenistic Greek, lent themselves with a curious felicity to the purposes of translation. As a mere literary monument, the English version of the Bible remains the noblest example of the English tongue, while its perpetual use made it from the instant of its appearance the standard of our language. For the moment however its literary effect was less than its social. The power of the book over the mass of Englishmen showed itself in a thousand superficial ways, and in none more conspicuously than in the influence it exerted on ordinary speech. It formed, we must repeat, the whole literature which was practically accessible to ordinary Englishmen. . . .

But far greater than its effect on literature or social phrase was the effect of the Bible on the character of the people at large. Elizabeth might silence or tune the pulpits; but it was impossible for her to silence or tune the great preachers of justice, and mercy, and truth, who spoke from the book which she had again opened for her people. The whole moral effect which is produced now-a-days by the religious newspaper, the tract, the essay, the lecture, the missionary report, the sermon, was then produced by the Bible alone; and its effect in this way, however dispassionately we examine it, was simply amazing. . . . The whole temper of the nation felt the change. A new conception of life and of man superseded the old. A new moral and religious impulse spread through every class.

171. Ignorance of the Monks at Canterbury and Messenden

(British Museum MSS., Arundel 68, f. 69; trans. by A. F. Leach)

At the visitation of the monastery at Canterbury, made on September 9, 1511, by the Archbishop, the Most Reverend Father William Warham, a number of defects were noted in the monastery and ordered reformed. Two of these relate to the condition of learning among the monks, and were set down as follows:

(5) Also a skilled teacher of grammar shall be provided to teach the novices and other youths grammar. For in default of such instruction it happens that most of the monks celebrating mass and performing other divine service are wholly ignorant of what they read, to the great scandal and disgrace both of religion in general and the monastery in particular.

(6) Also provision shall be made that the novices and other monks may not henceforth be without books.

Again, in 1531, we find another extract which shows that the monks of one of the northern monasteries had practically lost the use of the language of the Church. In that year the Bishop of Lincoln, in northern England, addressing the monks at the monastery of Messenden, wrote:

And for that ye be ignorant and have small understanding of Laten, we have drawen our said Injunctions in our vulgare Englishe tong to the intent that ye shuld the better undyrstand and knowe them, and soo see them more surely observed and kepte in every parte.

172. The Re-Foundation of the Cathedral School at Canterbury

(Parker MS., Corpus Christi College, Cambridge, 120, f. 15; trans. by A. F. Leach)

In 1541 Henry VIII re-founded the old Canterbury Cathedral School as a reformed-church grammar and song school, and for its government drew up and promulgated a long Statute, from which the following selections have been made. The course of study outlined shows the Renaissance influence in full force, and the influence of Colet's school in London.

Henry VIII by the grace of God, King of England, France and Ireland, Defender of the Faith, and on earth supreme head of the Church of England and Ireland, to all the sons of holy mother church to whose notice this present writing shall come, greeting. . . .

1. The whole number of those who shall be maintained in the cathedral and metropolitical church of Christ at Canterbury

First we decree and ordain that there shall be for ever in the said church a Dean, 12 Canons, 6 Preachers, 12 Minor Canons, a deacon, a sub-deacon, 12 lay-clerks, a master of the choristers, 10 choristers, two Informators of boys in grammar, of whom one shall be the teacher and the other the under-teacher, 50 boys to be taught grammar, 12 poor to be maintained at the expense of the church, 2 vergers (wand-bearers), 2 sextons (sub-sacrists), 4 servants in the church to ring the bells and arrange other things, two door-keepers who shall be also bara-bers, a maniciple, a butler and an under-butler, a cook and an under-cook; who shall to the number aforesaid each in his rank sedulously serve in the same church according to our statutes and ordinances.

26. The Choristers and their [Master] number

We decree and ordain that in our church aforesaid there shall be at the election or nomination of the Dean, or in his absence the Sub-dean, and Chapter, ten choristers, boys of tender age with clear voices and fit for singing, to serve the choir, minister and sing. For their instruction and education, as well in good behaviour as in skill in singing, we will that besides the twelve clerks before-named one shall be elected by the Dean [etc.] and Chapter, of good character, upright life and skilled in singing and playing the organ, to diligently employ himself in teaching the boys, playing the organ at the proper time, and singing divine service. And if he shall be found negligent or idle in teaching he shall after three warnings be deposed from office. And he shall be bound by oath faithfully to discharge his office.

27. The Grammar Boys and their Teachers

That piety and good letters may in our church aforesaid for ever blossom, grow and flower and in their time bear fruit for the glory of God and the advantage and adornment of the commonwealth, we decree and ordain that there shall always be in our cathedral church of Canterbury, elected and nominated by the Dean or in his absence the Sub-dean and Chapter, 50 boys, poor and destitute of the help of their friends, to be maintained out of the possessions of the church, and of native genius as far as may be and apt to learn: whom however we will shall not be admitted as poor boys of our church before they have learnt to read and write and are moderately learned in the first rudiments of grammar, in the judgment of the Dean or in his absence the Sub-dean and the Head Master;

And we will that these boys shall be maintained at the expense of our church until they have obtained a moderate knowledge of Latin grammar and have learnt to speak and to write Latin. The period of four years shall be given to this, or if it shall so seem good to the Dean or in his absence the Sub-dean, and the Head Master, at most five years and not more.

. . . .

33. The celebration of Divine Service

. . . We will further that both teachers of grammar shall be present in choir on feast-days clothed in garments befitting the choir; one of them having the seat in choir next above the minor canons, the other next after the minor canons.

Moreover we will that the grammar boys who are maintained at the expense of the church shall be present in choir on feast-days, in a proper habit, and diligently do whatever duty is imposed on them by the Precentor; unless they have been otherwise directed by the Head Master. And these boys too we will shall on every day in the year when the sacred mysteries are performed at High Mass be present at the elevation of the body of the Lord, and stay there till the singing of the Agnus Dei is done; and meanwhile, two and two, meditate and say the Psalms "Have mercy on me, O Lord," and "God, have mercy upon us," and "O Lord Jesu Christ," "Out of the deep I cried," with the prayer "Absolve, we beseech thee."

38. Alms and students

The usual qualities which are found in an architect and other overseers of works in pressing on their work, namely, industry and diligence, ought also to be found in pedagogues and teachers of the tender youth, that they may as it were enter into a friendly conspiracy and contention between themselves to imbue thoroughly the scholars committed to their trust with piety and good letters; and not to study their own advantage or indulge their own love of ease so much as to look to their proficiency and the public benefit, so that they may be seen to do their duty fairly in everything. And this they will be able to do much more successfully if they endeavor sedulously to follow the order we have prescribed.

The whole number of the scholars shall be divided into five or six ranks or classes. The Under Master shall teach the three lower, and the Head Master the three upper classes.

The Course of Study

No one shall be admitted into the school who cannot read readily, or who does not know by heart in the vernacular the Lord's Prayer, the Angelic Salutation, the Apostles' Creed and the Ten Commandments. Those who are wholly ignorant of grammar shall learn the accidents of nouns and verbs, as it were out of class. When they have learnt these they shall be taken into the First Class.

In the First Class they shall learn thoroughly by heart the rudiments in English; they shall learn to put together the parts of speech; and to turn a short phrase of English into Latin; and gradually to approach other easy constructions.

In the Second Class they shall learn a little higher; they shall know the genders of nouns and the inflections of verbs written in Latin; they shall run through Cato's verses, Æsop's Fables, and some familiar Colloquies.

In the Third Class they shall endeavor to make right varyings on the nouns and anomalous verbs, so that no noun or verb may be found anywhere which they do not know how to inflect in every detail. In this form too they shall make Terence's Comedies, Mantuanus' Eclogues, and other things of that sort thoroughly familiar to them.

These classes the Under Master shall take diligent care of, instilling and inculcating the lesser rudiments into his pupils so as to make them fit and prepared to receive higher instruction.

The Under Master shall come into school at 6 A.M., and immediately after saying the prayers to God which we have prescribed, shall make his scholars daily say by heart one of the eight parts of speech until they are ready in each. Nor shall he omit on any other day to dictate to his pupils an English sentence, and that a short one, which he shall teach them to turn exactly into Latin, and to write it carefully in their parchment note-books.

In short, in anything to be done in the school the Under Master shall be subject to and shall obey the Head Master; and shall consult him on the method and plan of teaching; so that they may both agree in their great zeal for the profit of the scholars. Both too shall endeavour to teach their pupils to speak openly, finely and distinctly, keeping due decorum both with their body and their mouth.

In the Fourth Form the boys shall be taught to know the Latin syntax readily; and shall be practiced in the stories of poets, and familiar letters of learned men and the like.

In the Fifth Form they shall commit to memory the Figures of Latin Oratory and the rules for making verses; and at the same time shall be practiced in making verses and polishing themes; then they shall be versed in translating the chastest Poets and the best Historians.

Lastly, in the Sixth Form they shall be instructed in the formulas of "Copiousness of Words and Things" written by Erasmus; and learn to make varyings of speech in every mood, so that they may acquire the faculty of speaking Latin, as far as is possible for boys. Meanwhile they shall taste Horace, Cicero, and other authors of that class. Meanwhile they shall compete with one another in declamations so that they may leave well learned in the school of argument.

These classes principally the Head Master shall try to polish in Latin.

He shall come into school by 7 o'clock to perform his duty of teaching thoroughly. He too every other day shall make some English sentence into Latin and teach the flock committed to him to change it into many forms. Moreover let him understand that he has charge of the whole school.

So every week he ought to visit the whole flock, once, twice, or three times, and diligently test the abilities of the scholars and ascertain their progress in learning. If he shall prove any of them, after testing them in every way, to be slow and wholly strangers to the Muses, he shall faithfully warn their friends not to let them, being wholly unfit for letters, waste their time in vain and fill the places of others. But those he shall find to be fit and industrious he shall, at least three times a year, call up to the higher forms, namely from the first to the second, from the second to the third, and so on as each shall be thought fit. This shall be done in the presence of and after consultation with the Under Master in the case of those who are entrusted to his care.

Moreover at 6 P.M. the scholars shall return to school, and until 7 P.M. shall do their repetition and render to their fellow-pupils who have become ripe in learning, several masters also being present, whatever they have learnt through the day.

When leave to play is given they shall play and sport together, lest, wandering about here and there, they incur some loss of character, and wanting to do other things their minds gradually become estranged from learning. And they shall not practice any games which are not of a gentlemanly appearance and free of all lowness.

Lastly, whatever they are doing in earnest or in play they shall never use any language but Latin or Greek.

173. Origin of the English Poor Law of 1601

(Nicholls, Sir George, *History of the English Poor Law*, vol. 1, pp. 192–93. London, 1860)

The following selection, by the author of the standard history of English Poor-Law legislation, is of interest as revealing the gradual development of the idea of compulsory taxation for the care and education of the poor. On this precedent our early American educational legislation was based.

The 43 Elizabeth was not, we have seen, the result of a sudden thought or a single effort, but was gradually framed upon the sure ground of experience; and it is curious to trace the successive steps by which its chief enactment, that of a compulsory assessment for the relief of the poor, came at length to be established. First, the poor were restricted from begging, except within certain specified limits. Next, the several towns, parishes, and hamlets were required to support their poor by charitable alms, so that none of necessity might be compelled "to go openly in begging," and collections were to be made for them on Sundays, and the parson was to stir up the people to be bountiful in giving. Then houses and materials for setting the poor on work were to be provided by the charitable devotion of good people, and the minister was every Sunday specially to exhort the parishioners to contribute liberally. Next the collectors for the poor, on a certain Sunday after divine service, were to set down in writing what each householder was willing to give weekly for the ensuing year; and if any should be obstinate and refuse to give, the minister was gently to exhort him, and, if he still refused, then to report him to the bishop, who was to send for and again gently exhort him; and if still refractory, the bishop was to certify the same to the justices in sessions, and bind him over to appear there, when the justices were once more gently to move and persuade him; and if he would not be persuaded, they were then to assess him in such sum as they thought reasonable. This prepared the way for the more general assessment authorized by 14 and 39 Elizabeth, which again led to the complete and universal assessment of property established by the present Act (**R. 174**).

174. The English Poor-Relief and Apprenticeship Law of 1601

(43 Elizabeth, cap. II. *Statutes at Large of England and Great Britain*, vol. II, pp. 603–04)

This law marks the great turning point of English Poor-Law legislation, and is still the foundation of the English Poor-Law. It also contains the essential features embodied in subsequent taxation for schools. Without the usual preamble, setting forth the evils to be corrected and the good expected from it, as in the case of most other Statutes, this one plunges at once into the matter at hand. The important sections of the Act create a Board of Overseers of the Poor, give them the power of forcible taxation, empower them to apprentice certain children, and they may compel rich parishes to aid poor ones. The Act read as follows:

AN ACT FOR THE RELIEF OF THE POOR

1. Board of Overseers of the Poor created. Be it enacted by the Authority of this present Parliament, That the Churchwardens of every Parish, and Four, Three or Two substantial Householders there, as shall be thought meet, having respect to the Proportion and Greatness of the same Parish and Parishes, to be nominated yearly in the *Easter* Week, or within One Month after *Easter*, under the Hand and Seal of Two or more Justices of the Peace in the same County, whereof one to be of the *Quorum*, dwelling in or near the same Parish or Division where the same Parish doth lie, shall be called Overseers of the Poor of the same Parish; And they, or the greater Part of them, shall take Order from Time to Time, by and with the Consent of Two or more such Justices of Peace as is aforesaid, for setting to work the Children of all such whose Parents shall not by the said Churchwardens and Overseers, or the greater Part of them, be thought able to keep and maintain their Children; and also for setting to work all such Persons, married or unmarried, having no Means to maintain them, and use no ordinary and daily Trade of Life to get their Living by: And also to raise weekly or otherwise (by Taxation of every Inhabitant, Parson, Vicar and other, and of every Occupier of Lands, Houses, Tithes impropriate, Propriations of Tithes, Coal Mines or salable Underwoods in the said Parish, in such competent Sum and Sums of Money, as they shall think fit) a convenient Stock of Flax, Hemp, Wool, Thread, Iron and other necessary Ware and Stuff, to set the Poor on work, and also competent Sums of Money for and towards the necessary Relief of the Lame, Impotent, Old, Blind, and such other among them, being poor and not able to work, and also for the putting out of such Children to be Apprentices, to be gathered out of the same Parish, according to the Ability of the same Parish, and to do and execute all other Things, as well for the disposing of the said Stock as otherwise concerning the premises, as to them shall seem convenient.

II. Meetings and powers of Board. Which said Churchwardens and Overseers so to be nominated, or such of them as shall not be let by Sickness or other just Excuse, to be allowed by Two such Justices of Peace or more as is aforesaid, shall meet together at the least once every Month in the Church of the said Parish, upon the *Sunday* in the Afternoon after Divine Service, there to consider of some good Course to be taken, and of some meet Order to be set down in the Premises; and shall within Four Days after the End of their Year, and after other Overseers nominated as aforesaid, make and yield up to such Two Justices of Peace as is aforesaid, a true and perfect Account of all Sums of Money by them received, or rated and sessed and not received, and also of such Stock as shall be in their Hands, or in the Hands of any of the Poor to work, and of all other Things concerning their said Office; and such Sum or Sums of Money as shall be in their Hands shall pay and deliver over to the said Churchwardens and Overseers newly nominated and appointed as aforesaid; upon Pain that every one of them absenting themselves, without lawful Cause as aforesaid, from such Monthly Meeting for the Purpose aforesaid, or being negligent in their Office, or in the Execution of the Orders aforesaid, being made by and with the Assent of the said Justices of Peace, or any Two of them before mentioned, to forfeit for every such Default or Absence or Negligence Twenty Shillings.

III. Equalizing tax-levy among parishes. And be it also enacted,

That if the said Justices of Peace do perceive that the Inhabitants of any Parish are not able to levy among themselves sufficient Sums of Money for the Purposes aforesaid, that then the said Two Justices shall and may tax, rate and assess as aforesaid any other of other Parishes, or out of any Parish, within the Hundred where the said Parish is, to pay such Sum or Sums of Money to the Churchwardens and Overseers of the said poor Parish for the said purposes, as the said Justices shall think fit, according to the Intent of this Law: And if the said Hundred shall not be thought to the said Justices able and fit to relieve the said several Parishes not able to provide for themselves as aforesaid, then the Justices of Peace at their General Quarter-Sessions, or the greater Number of them, shall rate and assess as aforesaid, any other of other Parishes, or out of any Parish, within the said County, for the Purposes aforesaid, as in their Discretion shall seem fit.

IV. Enforcing the tax-levy. And that it shall be lawful, as well for the present as subsequent Churchwardens and Overseers, or any of them, by Warrant from any Two such Justices of Peace, as is aforesaid, to levy as well the said Sums of Money, and all Arrearages, of every one that shall refuse to contribute according as they shall be assessed, by Distress and Sale of the Offender's Goods, as the Sums of Money or Stock which shall be behind upon any Account to be made as aforesaid, rendering to the Parties the Overplus; and in Defect of such Distress, it shall be lawful for any such Two Justices of the Peace to commit him or them to the Common Gaol of the County, there to remain without Bail or Mainprize until Payment of the said Sum, Arrearages and Stock; and the said Justices of Peace, or any one of them, to send to the House of Correction or Common Gaol such as shall not employ themselves to Work, being appointed thereunto as aforesaid; and also any such Two Justices of Peace to commit to the said Prison every one of the said Churchwardens and Overseers which shall refuse to account, there to remain, without Bail or Mainprize, until he have made a true account, and satisfied and paid so much as upon the said Account shall be remaining in his Hands.

V. Apprenticing of children and erecting workhouses. And be it further enacted, That it shall be lawful for the said Churchwardens and Overseers, or the greater Part of them, by the Assent of any Two Justices of the Peace aforesaid, to bind any such Children, as aforesaid, to be Apprentices, where they shall see convenient, till such Man Child shall come to the Age of Four and twenty Years, and such Woman Child to the Age of One and twenty Years, or the time of her Marriage; the same to be as effectual to all purposes, as if such Child were of full Age, and by Indenture of Covenant bound him or herself. And to the Intent that necessary Places of Habitation may more conveniently be provided for such poor impotent People; Be it enacted by the Authority aforesaid, That it shall and may be lawful for the said Churchwardens and Overseers, or the greater Part of them, by the Leave of the Lord or Lords of the Manor, whereof any Waste or Common within their Parish is or shall be parcel, and upon Agreement before with him or them made in Writing, under the Hands and Seals of the said Lord or Lords, or otherwise, according to any Order to be set down by the Justices of Peace of the said County at their General Quarter-Sessions, or the greater Part of them, by like leave and Agreement of the said Lord or Lords in Writing under his or their Hands and Seals, to erect, build and set up in fit and convenient Places of Habitation in such Waste or Common, at the general Charges of the Parish, or otherwise of the Hundred or County, as aforesaid, to be taxed, rated and gathered in manner before expressed, convenient Houses of Dwelling for the said impotent Poor; and also to place Inmates, or more Families than one in one Cottage or House; one Act made in the one and thirtieth of her Majesty's Reign, intituled, *An Act against the erecting and maintaining of Cottages*, or any Thing therein contained to the contrary notwithstanding: Which Cottages and Places for Inmates shall not at any Time after be used or employed to or for any other Habitation, but only for Impotent and Poor of the same Parish, that shall be there placed from Time to Time by the Churchwardens and Overseers of the Poor of the same Parish, or the most Part of them, upon the Pains and Forfeitures contained in the said former Act made in the said One and thirtieth Year of her Majesty's Reign.

VI. Appeal from decisions. Provided always, That if any Person or Persons shall find themselves grieved with any Sess or Tax, or other Act done by the said Churchwardens and other Persons, or by the said Justices of Peace, that then it shall be lawful for the Justices of Peace, at their General Quarter-Sessions, or the greater Number of them, to take such Order therein, as to them shall be thought convenient; and the same to conclude and bind all the said Parties.

CHAPTER XIV
EDUCATIONAL RESULTS OF THE PROTESTANT REVOLTS
II. CALVINISTS AND CATHOLICS

THE Readings in this chapter illustrate the development of education, following the Protestant Revolt, among the Calvinists and the Catholics.

Geneva, in Switzerland, from 1541 to 1565, during the control of Calvin, was the Rome of Protestantism. Calvin established there a typical Calvinistic college, of which there were many others in France, leading to the Huguenot universities there maintained. Selection **175** gives an outline of the course of study provided at Geneva, and shows how closely humanism and a reformed religion were associated in northern lands.

The interest of the Calvinistic Dutch in education is well set forth in the scheme of education adopted, in 1618, at the Synod of Dort (**176**), and the work of the Dutch in developing schools (**177**) and the character of the schools developed (**178**) are well set forth by the selections reproduced. The great educational law among the followers of John Knox, the Scotch Presbyterians, is reproduced in the next selection (**179**).

The documents for the Catholics are long, and usually enter into minute detail as to the purpose and nature of the school organization to be provided. The two most important were the *Ratio Studiorum* of the Jesuits, concerning which a brief historical statement is inserted (**180**), the document itself being too long to reproduce; and the Rules framed by La Salle for his teaching organization, the Brothers of the Christian Schools. The more important educational regulations from the latter are reproduced in **182**. Reading **181** is descriptive of the seventeenth-century religious purpose which dominated the education of girls in Catholic lands.

175. Course of Study at the College of Geneva

(Digest from Woodward, W. H., *Studies in Education during the Renaissance*, pp. 159–60. Cambridge, 1906)

The following abstract of the course of study in the Collège de la Rive, at Geneva, as set forth in the Constitution of 1559, is that of the famous public school there which was inspired and governed by Calvin himself. Like other Protestant foundations in northern lands, this shows clearly the influence of the Italian revival and the introduction of the humanistic learning. The school had seven classes, the seventh being the lowest. The work of each class was as follows:

Class VII. In this class the pupils will learn the letters, and write them to form syllables, using a Latin-French reading book. Reading French, and afterwards Latin from a French-Latin Catechism. Drawing, and writing letters of the alphabet.

Class VI. Declensions and conjugations are begun; these occupy the first half year. Parts of speech learnt in French and Latin; more practice in hand-writing. Easy Latin sentences learnt orally, and repeated as practice in conversation.

Class V. Parts of speech finished: elements of syntax: the *Eclogues* of Vergil read: first steps in written Latin composition: Latin and French employed side by side.

Class IV. Latin syntax continued. Cicero's *Letters* begun; composition exercises are based on these. Prosody, with reading of Ovid in illustration. Greek begun; declension and conjugation; elementary construing.

Class III. Greek Grammar systematically learnt, with comparison of the two languages. Cicero, — *Letters, De Amicitia, De Senectute,* — these treatises to be turned into Greek. The *Æneid,* Cæsar, and Isocrates read.

Class II. Chief stress laid upon reading: — Livy, Xenophon, Polybius, Herodian and Homer. Logic begun: — propositions, syllogism; to be illustrated from Cicero's orations. Once a week the Gospel narrative in Greek.

Class I. Logic systematically taught from approved compendium (such as Melanchthon's); the elements of rhetoric in connection with it, and elocution. The whole doctrine of rhetoric illustrated from Cicero's speeches, and from Demosthenes (the Olynthiacs and Philippics). Homer and Vergil also analysed for rhetorical purposes. Two original "declamationes" are prepared monthly. Once a week an Epistle of Saint Paul or other apostle is read in Greek.

The choice of authors and the place of logic deserve attention, not less than the acceptance of the vernacular in junior classes.

176. Scheme of Christian Education adopted at the Synod of Dort

(Scheme as adopted, November 30, 1618; trans. by Barnard, in *American Journal of Education*, vol. v, pp. 77–78)

The Dutch Synod of Dort (1618–19) on November 30, 1618, adopted a regulation for the Christian education of children and youth, jointly in the family, the school, and the church, as follows:

In order that the Christian youth may be diligently instructed in the principles of religion, and be trained in piety, three modes of catechising should be employed. I. In the House, by Parents. II. In the Schools, by Schoolmasters. III. In the Churches, by Ministers, Elders, and Catechists, especially appointed for the purpose. That these may diligently employ their trust, the Christian magistrates shall be requested to promote, by their authority, so sacred and necessary a work; and all who have the oversight of churches and schools shall be required to pay special attention to this matter.

I. Parents. The office of Parents is diligently to instruct their children and their whole household in the principles of the Christian religion, in a manner adapted to their respective capacities; earnestly

Fig. 37. Family Instruction in the Bible
(Drawn from a painting by the French artist Jean Greuze [1725–1805])

and carefully to admonish them to the cultivation of true piety; to engage their punctual attendance on family worship, and take them with them to the hearing of the Word of God. They should require their children to give an account of the sermons they hear, especially those on the Catechism; assign them some chapters of Scripture to read, and certain passages to commit to memory; and then impress and illustrate the truths contained in them in a familiar manner, adapted to the tenderness of youth. Thus they are to prepare them for being catechised in the schools, and by attendance on these to encourage them and promote their edification. Parents are to be exhorted to the faithful discharge of this duty, by the public preaching of the Word; but specially at the ordinary period of family visitation, previous to the administration of the Lord's Supper; and also at other times by the minister, elders, etc. Parents who profess religion, and are negligent in this work, shall be faithfully admonished by the ministers; and, if the case requires it, they shall be censured by the Consistory, that they may be brought to the discharge of their duty.

II. SCHOOLS. Schools, in which the young shall be properly instructed in the principles of Christian doctrine, shall be instituted, not only in cities but also in towns and country places where heretofore none have existed. The Christian magistracy shall be requested that well-qualified persons may be employed and enabled to devote themselves to the service; and especially that the children of the poor may be gratuitously instructed, and not be excluded from the benefit of the schools. In this office none shall be employed but such as are members of the Reformed Church, having certificates of an upright faith and pious life, and of being well versed in the truths of the Catechism. They are to sign a document, professing their belief in the Confession of Faith and the Heidelberg Catechism, and promising that they will give catechetical instruction to the youth in the principles of Christian truth according to the same. The schoolmasters shall instruct their scholars according to their age and capacity, at least two days in the week, not only causing them to commit to memory, but also by instilling into their minds an acquaintance with the truths of the Catechism. (An elementary small Catechism, the Compendium, and the Heidelberg Catechism, are those specified to be used by the different grades of children and youth.) The schoolmasters shall take care not only that the scholars commit these Catechisms to memory, but that they shall suitably understand the doctrines contained in them. For this purpose, they shall suitably explain to every one, in a manner adapted to his capacity, and frequently inquire if they understand them. The schoolmasters shall bring every one of the pupils committed to their charge to the hearing of the preached Word, and particularly the preaching on the Catechism, and require from them an account of the same.

III. MINISTERIAL SUPERVISION. In order that due knowledge may be obtained of the diligence of the schoolmasters, and the improvement of the youth, it shall be the duty of the MASTERS, WITH AN ELDER, and, if necessary, with a magistrate, to visit all the schools, private as well as public, frequently, in order to excite the teachers to earnest diligence, to encourage and counsel them in the duty of catechising, and to furnish an example by questioning them, addressing them in a friendly and affectionate manner, and exciting them to early piety and diligence. If any of the schoolmasters should be found neglectful or perverse, they shall be earnestly admonished by the ministers, and, if necessary, by the Consistory, in relation to their office. The ministers, in the discharge of their public duty in the Church, shall preach on the Catechism. These sermons shall be comparatively short, and accommodated, as far as practicable, to the comprehension of children as well as adults. The labors of those ministers will be praiseworthy who diligently search out country places, and see that catechetical instruction be supplied and faithfully preserved. Experience teaches that the ordinary instruction of the Church, catechetical and other, is not sufficient for many, to instill that knowledge of the Christian religion which should, among the people of God, be well grounded; and also testifies that the living voice has very great influence; that familiar and suitable questions and answers, adapted to the apprehension of each individual, is the best mode of catechising, in order to impress the principles of religion upon the heart. It shall be the duty of a minister to go, with an elder, to all capable of instruction, and collect them in their houses, the Consistory chamber, or some other suitable place, (a number particularly of those more advanced in years,) and explain familiarly to them, the articles of the Christian faith, and catechise them according to the circumstances of their different capacities, progress, and knowledge. They shall question them on the matter of the public sermons on the Catechism. Those who desire to unite with the Church shall, three or four weeks before the administration of the Lord's Supper, be more carefully and frequently instructed, that they may be better qualified, and be more free to give a satisfactory account of their faith. The ministers shall employ diligent care to ascertain those who give any hopeful evidence of serious concern for the salvation of their soul, and invite them to them; assembling those together who have like impressions, and encouraging to friendly intercourse and free conversation with each other. These meetings shall commence with appropriate prayer and exhortation. If all this shall be done by the ministers with that cordiality, faithfulness, zeal, and discretion that become those that must give an account of the flock committed to their charge, it is not to be doubted that in a short time abundant fruit of their labors shall be found in growth in religious knowledge, and holiness of life, to the glory of God, and the prosperity of the Church of Christ.

177. Work of the Dutch in developing Schools

(Kilpatrick, Wm. H., *The Dutch Schools of New Netherland and Colonial New York*, pp. 19–21. Washington, 1912)

The following extract from Dr. Kilpatrick's excellent study of the work of the Dutch in developing schools gives a good picture of what was done in the Netherlands, during the time that country was at the zenith of its prosperity and greatness as a nation.

Among the institutions carried to the New World, few, if any, had deeper roots in the life of the Dutch than church and school. Devotion to the principles of the reformed religion had been, in great degree, the secret of the long and stubborn opposition to Spanish oppression. That same devotion had been the greatest single force in creating the new commonwealth. As a most important means of fixing and preserving the reformed faith, the parochial school had become an indispensable part of the organization of the new church. Interwoven thus with the very life of the church was a school system in which the schoolmaster was an officer in the church, and the curriculum of the school included conscious preparation for participation in the service of the public worship.

How the school came to occupy this unique relationship to the church can here be told only in barest outline, since the account of it would be the story of the growth of the church itself. Even before the reformers could assemble openly in the Netherlands, the first national synod of the Dutch Church, held "in exile" at Wezel, in 1568, had seen the strategic value of the parochial school. Music, it declared, must be introduced into the church schools, of which some were already in existence. Schoolmasters as well as parents must train the children in the catechism. Deacons were specifically charged with "the care and founding of schools"; and schoolmasters were reckoned along with the ministers, elders, and deacons as "public persons" of the church. The second national synod at Emden, in 1571, likewise "in exile," to the same end, required all classes in their regular meetings, to ask of each church "whether the care of the poor and of schools is maintained." The provincial Synod of Dort (1574), the first on Netherland soil, treated schools in yet greater detail, emphasizing, among other things, the careful selection by the church of proper places for schools, adequate salaries for schoolmasters to be furnished by the secular authorities, and subscription to the creed by all schoolmasters. Limitations of space forbid the presentation of all the acts relating to schools of the successive national synods. The Synods of Dort (1578), Middelburg (1581), and The Hague (1586), all treated of schools and of the duty of the church to support them. The great Synod of Dort (1618–19), as the last of the national synods, gave final form to the creed and practice of the Dutch Reformed Church. In the matter of schools, it substantially summed up the preceding synodal enactments. Schools must be instituted in country places, towns, and cities. Religious instruction must be given. The Christian magistracy should see to it that well-qualified persons taught, with suitable compensation. The children of the poor should be instructed free. In all schools only orthodox Chris-

tians might teach.   To secure these ends suitable means of church inspection of schools were devised.   By the time of this synod the church
had not only thoroughly organized its system of parochial schools, but

FIG. 38. A DUTCH SCHOOL OF THE SIXTEENTH CENTURY

through the requirement of creed subscription had reached out its hand
to all educational institutions of whatever grade.

But it must not be supposed that the Church alone was interested in
education.   From an early date the Dutch had taken an increasing interest in the public control and support of education.   In Haarlem the
"city school" existed certainly as early as 1461.   In the same city, in
1522, we find the burgomasters guaranteeing a salary of 200 carolus
guilders to the rector of the school.   The Hague in 1536 had a "great
school" with a rector and three masters, supported in part by a per
capita levy of 2 carolus guilders upon all the pupils in the private
schools of the city.   To this income the city added for the rector "a
yearly pension of four or five great pounds."   Utrecht, both city and
Province, may be taken as typical of public secular interest in schools.
As early as 1522 is found a payment by the municipal authorities to the
"rector scolarium" on account of a chorus.   In 1567 the city paid an
item of 4 pounds for "the benches for the school children in Jesus
School."   Some years later a similar appropriation was made for the
free instruction of poor young children.   In 1576 it was resolved by the
city thenceforth to maintain the Saint Jerome School "with adequate
salaries."   Numerous records of instructions issued in the seventeenth

century to rectors and masters of this school give a very good account of the inner working of the Latin school among the Dutch of that period. A church order for the whole Province of Utrecht was issued in 1590, and another in 1612. In the latter were included directions for schools, schoolmasters, and sextons. Schools of four kinds were recognized, public or trivial, parochial, private, and schools for the country districts. The selection of instructors, the fixing of curricula, and the general supervision were given to the municipal authorities, with varying degrees of participation in control granted to the church. In 1644 the city of Utrecht adopted a detailed plan for the free instruction of the poor by apportioning them among its four parochial schools. The country schools of the Province were regulated separately in an order of 18 sections, issued in 1654, one of the best available accounts of Dutch school management of the seventeenth century. In matters of education, there is no reason to suppose that Utrecht was in advance of other Provinces of the United Netherlands. Before the Reformation public schools were found in individual cities. Beginning about 1580 the Provinces took up the work, making general regulations for the control of schools everywhere. By the middle of the seventeenth century the whole country — rural districts as well as cities and towns — appears to have been well provided with schools of various grades, controlled and often also supported by the public secular authorities.

178. Character of the Dutch Schools of 1650, as shown by the Textbooks used

(Kilpatrick, Wm. H., *The Dutch Schools of New Netherland and Colonial New York*, p. 34. Washington, 1912)

The great purpose of all vernacular schooling, following the Reformation, was the teaching of religion. The ordinary subjects of the elementary school were taught from books the content of which was almost entirely religious. This may be illustrated by the following list and description of the texts adopted for the Dutch province of Utrecht, in 1650.

The textbooks used in the better elementary schools are probably pretty well represented by the list officially promulgated at Utrecht, in 1650.

Het groot en kleyn A.B.C. boeck;
De Heydelberchse Catechismus;
De Evangelien ende Epistelen;
De Trap der Jeugt;
De Historien van David;
Proverbia Salomonis;
De spiegel der Jeugt van de Nederlandse oorlogen;

De sendbrieven van de nieuwe editie met eenige stichtelyke dichten daar achter.

The first three of these are sufficiently indicated by their translated titles: The Great and Small A B C Book, the Heidelberg Catechism, and the Gospels and Epistles. The alphabet books were generally called "cock books," from the picture of a crowing cock found thereon. On the title page of one of these appeared:

> "We must know the alphabet very well
> Before we can readily read any book."

In addition to the alphabet, these books contained the Lord's Prayer, the commandments, and the prayers. The Heidelberg Catechism was the authoritative catechism of the Reformed Dutch Church. The Gospels and the Epistles served as a reading book. "De Trap der Jeugt" means literally "The Stairway of Youth," but the writer has not been able to find any indication of its contents. The Proverbs of Solomon is again a reading book. "De Spiegel der Jeugt," literally "The Mirror of Youth," treated of the wars of the Dutch people. "De Sendbrieven," etc., are the Epistles of the New Testament.

179. The Scotch School Law of 1646

(*Acts of Parliaments of Scotland*, II Februarii, 1646. *Report of Record Commission*, vol. VI, p. 216)

The Reformation in Scotland dates from 1560. In 1616 the Privy Council ordered each church parish to assume the obligation of supporting a school. This was ratified by an Act of the Scotch Parliament in 1633, and in 1646 more definite legislation was approved, the important portions of which read:

The Estates of Parliament now conveened, in the fifth session of this first Triennall Parliament, Considering how prejudiciall the want of Schools in many congregations hath been, and how beneficiall the founding thereof in every congregation will be to this Kirk and Kingdom; Do therefore Statute and Ordain, That there be a Schoole founded, and a Schoole master appointed in every Parish (not already provided) by advice of the Presbyterie: And to this purpose, that the Heritors in every congregation meet among themselves, and provide a commodious house for a Schoole, and modifie a stipend to the Schoole master, which shall not be under Ane hundred Merks, nor above Tua hundred Merks, to be paid yeerly at two Terms: And to this effect that they set down a stent upon every ones rent of stock and teind in the Parish, proportionally to the worth thereof, for maintenance of the Schoole, and payment of the Schoole masters stipend; Which stipend is declared to be due to the Schoole masters by and attour the casualities which formerly belonged to Readers and Clerks of Kirk Sessions. And if the Heritors shall not conveene, or being conveened shall not agree amongst themselves, Then, and in that case the Presbyterie shall nominate twelve honest men within the bounds of the Presbyterie, who shall have power to establish a Schoole, modifie a stipend for the Schoole master, with the latitude before expressed, and set down a stent for payment thereof upon the Heritors, which shall be as valide and effectuall as if the same had been done by the Heritors themselves.

180. The *Ratio Studiorum* of the Jesuits

(Pachtler, G. M., *Ratio Studiorum;* in *Monumenta Germania Pædagogica*, 4 vols. Berlin, 1886–1900)

Great care was exercised by the Jesuits in working out their outlines of instruction, known as the *Ratio Studiorum*. The Society was sanctioned in 1540, and the first Constitution of the Order was issued that year. The first edition of the *Ratio*, however, was not issued until 1586, and this was subject to experiment and trial until 1599, when the final *Ratio* was issued. This then remained unchanged until 1832, when some modern studies were added.

Their schools were divided into two courses, the *studia inferiora*, covering six years, beginning at about the age of ten; and the *studia superiora*, or philosophical course, covering two to three years. A theological course of four to six years completed the program. For all these years the *Ratio* made detailed provision; allowed for the adjustment of the instruction to meet local needs; enjoined the use of Latin as the language of the classroom and the school; regulated the daily, weekly, monthly, and yearly programs of work; provided for the careful regulation of the lives of the students; declared Saint Thomas Aquinas the true teacher to be followed; and instructed the teachers to draw their history from unadulterated sources, to defend the Vulgate Bible, and to refute the errors of all other translations.

A brief digest of the 1686 edition may be found in Barnard's *American Journal of Education*, vol. xxvii, pp. 165–75; and a digest of the more important educational regulations of the 1699 edition in F. V. N. Painter's *Great Pedagogical Essays* (American Book Company, New York, 1905), pp. 188–202. Both are too long to quote here.

181. The Dominant Religious Purpose in the Education of French Girls

(Gréard, V. C. O., *Mémoire sur l'enseignement secondaire des filles*, p. 55; trans. by Compayré)

The following description of the oversight of the education of girls at Port Royal (1643–60), which bears on the training of girls generally in the seventeenth century, reveals something of the intense religious nature of school and conventual education of that time. The chief education of girls in Catholic lands was given in the convents, where the emphasis was laid on preparation for another world than this.

A strange emotion, even at the distance of centuries, is caused by the sight of those children keeping silent or speaking in a whisper from rising till retiring, never walking except between two nuns, one in front and the other behind, in order to make it impossible, by slackening their pace on the pretext of some indisposition, for them to hold any communication; working in such a way as never to be in companies of two or three; passing from meditation to prayer, and from prayer to instruction; learning, beside the catechism, nothing but reading and writing; and, on Sunday, "a little arithmetic, the older from one to two o'clock, and the younger from two to half past two"; the hands always busy to prevent the mind from wandering; but without being able to become attached to their work, which would please God as much the more as it pleased themselves the less; opposing all their natural inclinations, and despising the attentions due the body "destined to serve as food for worms"; doing nothing, in a word, except in the spirit of mortification. Imagine those days of fourteen and sixteen hours, slowly succeeding one another, and weighing down on the heads of those poor little sisters, for six or eight years in that dreary solitude, where there was nothing to bring in the stir of life, save the sound of the bell announcing a change of exercise or of penance, and you will comprehend Fénelon's feeling of sadness when he speaks of the shadows of that deep cavern in which was imprisoned and, as it were, buried the youth of girls.

182. Rules of the Order "Brothers of the Christian Schools"

(From *The Conduct of Schools*, 1811 edition; trans. by Barnard, in *American Journal of Education*, vol. xxx, pp. 930–31)

The Conduct of Schools, based on rules originally drawn up by La Salle in 1681, and originally issued in 1720, was to this Order what the *Ratio Studiorum* was to the Jesuits. The details were so wisely drawn that but little change is noted between the 1720 and the 1811 editions. Perhaps the most important occurs in regulation 20, in which Latin, for the more advanced pupils, is added to the original instruction in French alone. The more important regulations relating to the school work are as follows:

1. The Institution des Frères des Écoles Chrétiennes is a society which professes to conduct schools gratuitously. The design of this institution is to give a Christian education to children. With this object in view, the Frères conduct schools where children may be placed under the management of masters from morning until evening, so that the masters may be able to teach them to live honestly and uprightly, by instructing them in the principles of our holy religion, by teaching them Christian precepts, and by giving them suitable and sufficient instruction.

FIG. 39. J. B. DE LA SALLE
(1651–1719)

2. The spirit of the institution is a spirit of faith which ought to encourage its members to attribute all to God, to act as continually in the sight of God, and in perfect conformity, to His orders and His will. The members of this association should be filled with an ardent zeal for the instruction of children, for their preservation in innocence and the fear of God, and for their entire separation from sin.

.   .   .   .

19. The Frères shall instruct their pupils after the method prescribed to them by the institution.

20. They shall teach their scholars to read French and Latin, and to write.

21. They shall teach them also orthography, and arithmetic, the matins and vespers, le Pater, l'Ave Maria, le Credo et le Confiteor, and the French translations of these prayers, the Commandments of God and of the Church, the responses of the holy mass, the Catechism, the duties of a Christian, and the maxims and precepts that our Lord has left us in the holy Testament.

22. They shall teach the Catechism half an hour daily.

27. The Frères shall not receive from the scholars, or their parents, either money or any other present, at any time.

30. They shall exhibit an equal affection for all their poor scholars, and more for the poor than for the rich; because the object of the institution is the instruction of the poor.

31. They shall endeavor to give their pupils, by their conduct and manners, a continual example of modesty, and of all the other virtues which they ought to be taught, and which they ought to practice.

37. The Frères shall take the greatest care that they very rarely punish their children, as they ought to be persuaded that, by refraining as much as possible from punishment, they will best succeed in properly conducting a school, and in establishing order in it.

38. When punishment shall have become absolutely necessary, they shall take the greatest care to punish with the greatest moderation and presence of mind, and never to do it under the influence of a hasty movement, or when they feel irritated.

39. They shall watch over themselves that they never exhibit the least anger or impatience, either in their corrections, or in any of their words or actions; as they ought to be convinced, that if they do not take these precautions the scholars will not profit from their correction, (and the Frères ought never to correct except with the object of benefiting their children) and God will not give the correction His blessing.

40. They shall not at any time give to their scholars any injurious epithet or insulting name.

41. They shall also take the greatest care not to strike their scholars with hand, foot, or stick, nor to push them rudely.

42. They shall take great care not to pull their ears, their hair, or their noses, nor to fling any thing at them; these kinds of corrections ought not to be practiced by the Frères, as they are very indecent and opposed to charity and Christian kindness.

43. They shall not correct their scholars during prayers, or at the time of catechising, except when they cannot defer the correction.

44. They shall not use corporal punishment, except when every other means of correction has failed to produce the right effect.

58. The Frère-director shall be inspector over all the schools in his town; and when more than one inspector is necessary for one house of Frères, the other inspector shall report to the Frère-director twice a week on the conduct of each Frère, on the condition of his class, and on the progress of his scholars.

CHAPTER XV

EDUCATIONAL RESULTS OF THE PROTESTANT REVOLT

III. THE REFORMATION AND AMERICAN EDUCATION

THE Readings contained in this chapter illustrate the period of transplanting the characteristic European institutions, forms of government, and religious attitudes to American shores. The settlement of America was in large part a phase of the movement of Protestant sects to the new world to establish there homes and churches where they might enjoy a degree of religious freedom not possible in the old home-lands. Each sect or nationality so migrating to America took with it the characteristic forms of church and school observances known in the old home-lands, and these were faithfully reproduced in the new colonies. As a result we find established in America, in the seventeenth century, the main types of schools existing at the time of the migration in the mother-land from which the settlers came. They were also dominated by the same deep religious purpose as the home-land schools.

The first selection (**183**) reveals the Puritan attitude, and shows one reason why they desired to go somewhere where they could rear their children amid better surroundings. The second (**184**) describes their leaving England for Holland, and exhibits the motives which eventually led them to emigrate to America. Once on American soil their deep solicitude for education showed itself in the founding of an English-type college (**185**), for which rules and requirements, typical of the time, were drawn up (**186 a-d**), and to which the customary European privileges (**187**) were granted. They also showed their interest in education in the creation of typical English-type Latin grammar schools in the new towns they founded, as is shown by the agreement (**188**) for the founding of the grammar school at Roxbury, Massachusetts, and the rules for the government of the grammar school at New Haven (**189**).

Still more, finding that some parents and masters of apprentices were negligent, the Massachusetts Bay Puritans enacted the two famous laws of 1642 (**190**) and 1647 (**191**), laws which laid the foundations upon which state school systems in the United States have since been created.   Selection **192** shows how the courts compelled the towns to enforce these laws for schools. Topsfield, Massachusetts, here being cited for violating the Law of 1642.   These laws deeply influenced legislation in the other Puritan colonies of New England, the Connecticut Law of 1650 (**193**) being clearly inspired by the two Massachusetts laws, and the Plymouth Colony legislation (**194 a-d**) also showing clear evidence of similar inspiration.

The Calvinistic Dutch, who settled New Amsterdam and surrounding places, also brought to the new world the practices of their home-land, setting up here Dutch parochial schools which were clearly copies of those at home.   The character of the home schools is shown by selections **176-78,** given in the preceding chapter, and in this chapter are reproduced selections (**195, 196**) which indicate the nature of the instruction given and the combined church-and-school duties of the teacher.   We here see the elementary teacher in the process of being evolved from the church precentor and sexton fo the Middle Ages.

In the central colonies the different sects established church schools of the types known at home, and assumed the regular home attitude toward schools and learning.   The selection from the rules of discipline of the Quakers (**199**) reveals their attitude, and the minutes from the proceedings of the governing council (**198**) reproduce the order creating the first school in Philadelphia, the year the colony was settled.   Selection **197** gives the law regarding the establishment of schools proposed by the Quaker governors for the colony, but which was so contrary to all English precedents that it was vetoed by William and Mary.

In all the colonies another typical English educational idea was set up — that of the apprenticing of orphans and poor children to learn a trade, and to be taught to read and write and to be instructed in religion.   In the Puritan colonies this was purely supplemental to the creation of schools, but in Virginia and the southern colonies it for long formed almost the only type of education provided.   The chief Virginia laws relating to the apprenticing of the children of the poor and vagrant and dissolute young people are given in selection **200 a,** and three extracts from North

Carolina court records are given in selection **200 b.** Selection **201** reproduces a Massachusetts apprenticeship agreement of 1727.

Selection **202** gives a digest of the most celebrated school text-book used in the colonies, *The New England Primer.* For a century and a half this was the important introductory school reading book in all the non-Anglican American colonies.

183. The Puritan Attitude

(Josiah Nichols, "The Plea for the Innocent"; a pamphlet of 1602. From Hanbury's *Historical Memorials*, vol. 1, p. 3)

The following selection gives a good idea as to the Puritan attitude toward the character of the Reformation which had taken place in England, and the Puritan demand for further improvements in Christian life and in church oversight of the morals of the people.

In the beginning of her Majesty's most happy reign, the gospel being published and preachers ordained to teach the people, many people, within a while feeling some taste of the heavenly comfort, began to delight in hearing of sermons, singing of psalms, in reading, and godly talk of Holy Scriptures which they were taught; and therewithal did somewhat refrain profane and unprofitable customs; and sometimes they admonished their neighbors if they did swear, and pray them to go with them to the sermon; the greater sort of the people, being old barrels which could hold no new wine, addicted partly to popery and partly to licentiousness, having many of them no other God but their bellies, would deride and scoff at them, and called them "holy brethren" and "holy sisters"; saying, "He is one of the pure and unspotted brethren!"

184. The Puritans leave England

(William Bradford, *History of Plymouth Plantation*. Reprint, Boston, 1856)

The following extracts from the History by Governor Bradford (1590–1657) cover the period from the beginnings of the persecutions of the Separatists, as those who did not conform to the practices of the Church of England were termed, through the period of their exile in Holland, and show the motives which finally induced them to emigrate to America.

But, after these things, they could not long continue in any peaceable condition; but were hunted and persecuted on every side; so as their former afflictions were but as flea-bitings in comparison of these which now came upon them. For some were taken and clapt up in prison.

Others had their houses beset and watched, night and day; and hardly escaped their hands: and the most were fain to fly and leave their houses and habitations, and the means of their livelihood. Yet these and many other sharper things which afterwards befell them were no other than they looked for; and therefore were they the better prepared to bear them by the assistance of God's grace and spirit.

Yet seeing themselves molested; and that there was no hope of their continuance there as a church; by a joint consent, they resolved to go into the Low Countries, where they heard was freedom of religion for all men; as also how sundry, from London and other parts of the land of England, had been exiled and persecuted for the same cause, and were gone thither, and lived at Amsterdam and in other places of the land of Holland.

So, after they had continued together about a year; and kept their meetings every Sabbath in one place or another, exercising the worship of God amongst themselves, notwithstanding all the diligence and malice of their adversaries; they, seeing they could no longer continue in that condition, resolved to get over in Holland as they could. Which was in the years 1607 and 1608. . . .

Being now come into the Low Countries, they saw many goodly and fortified cities strongly walled and guarded with troops of armed men. Also they heard a strange and uncouth language; and beheld the different manners and customs of the people, with their strange fashions and attires; all so far differing from their plain country villages, wherein they were bred and had lived so long, as it seemed they had come into a new world. . . .

And when they had lived at Amsterdam about a year, Master Robinson, their pastor, and some others of best discerning, seeing how Master John Smith and his company were already falling into contention with the church that was there before them; and no means they could use, would do any good to cure the same: and also that the flames of contention were likely to break out in the ancient church itself, as afterwards lamentable came to pass.

For these, and some other reasons, they removed to Leyden, a fair and beautiful city, and of a sweet situation: but made more famous by the university wherewith it is adorned: in which, of late, has been so many learned men. But wanting that traffic by sea which Amsterdam enjoys, it was not so beneficial for their outward means of living and estates. But being now here pitched, they fell to such trades and imployments as they best could; valuing peace and their spiritual comfort above any other riches whatsoever; and at length they came to raise a competent and comfortable living; but with hard and continual labor.

Being thus settled, after many difficulties; they continued many years in a comfortable condition, injoying much sweet and delightful society and spiritual comfort together in the ways of God, under the able ministry and prudent government of Master John Robinson and Master William Brewster, who was an assistant unto him, in the place of an elder, unto which he was now called and chosen by the church. So as they grew in knowledge and other gifts and graces of the spirit of God, and lived together in peace and love and holiness.

And many came unto them, from divers parts of England; so as they grew to a great congregation. . . .

Our reverend pastor, Master John Robinson of late memory; and our grave elder, Master William Brewster, now both at rest with the Lord; considering, amongst many other inconveniences; how hard the country was where we lived; how many spent their whole estate in it, and were forced to return for England; how grievous it was to live from under the protection of the state of England; how likely we were to lose our language and our name of English; how little good we did, or were likely to do, to the Dutch, in reforming the sabbath; how unable there to give such education to our children as we ourselves had received; in their grave wisdoms they thought we might more glorify God, do more good to our country, better provide for our posterity, and live to be more refreshed by our labours than ever we could do in Holland where we were. . . .

Now these their private thoughts, upon mature deliberation they imparted to the brethren of the congregation which, after much private discussion, came to public agitation, till at length the Lord was solemnly sought in the congregation by fasting and prayer to direct us.

Who moving our hearts more and more to the work, we sent some of good abilities over into England, to see what favour or acceptance such a thing might find with the king.

These also found God going along with them, and got Sir Edwin Sandys, a religious gentleman then living, to stir in it. Who procured Sir Robert Naunton, then principal secretary of state to King James of famous memory, to move his Majesty, by a private motion, to give way to such a people, who could not so comfortably live under the government of another state, to

FIG. 40. THE MAYFLOWER
(From the National Museum model)

"Thanks be to God for winter time!
That bore the Mayflower up,
To pour amid New England snows
The treasures of its cup."

enjoy their liberty of conscience under his gracious protection in America; where they would endeavour the advancement of his

Majesty's dominions and the enlargement of the gospel by all due means.

This, his Majesty said, was a good and honest motion: and asking what profits might arise in the part we intended (for our eye was on the most northern parts of Virginia) it was answered "fishing." To which he replied with his ordinary asserveration, "So God have my soul! 't is an honest trade! It was the apostles' own calling!"

But afterwards he told Sir Robert Naunton, who took all occasions to further it, that we should confer with the bishops of Canterbury and London. . . .

After this, they who stayed accompanied us to Delfshaven, (about twenty-four miles from Leyden) where we were to embark; and there feasted us again. And after prayer performed by our pastor, where a flood of tears was poured out, they accompanied us to the ship, but were not able to speak one to another for the abundance of sorrow to part. But we only going aboard the ship lying to the quay and ready to set sail, the wind being fair, we gave them a volley of small shot and three pieces of ordnance; and so lifting up our hands to each other, and our hearts for each other to the Lord our God, we departed and found his presence with us in the midst of our manifold straits that he carried us through. . . .

185. The Founding of Harvard College

(*New England's First Fruits*. London, 1643. *Mass. Hist. Col.*, 1792, vol. 1, pp. 242–46)

The following extract from a pamphlet published in London in 1643, records the founding (in 1636) of the "new colledge" for the colony. It was originally a letter dated "Boston, Sept. 26, 1642."

After God had carried us safe to *New England*, and wee had builded our houses, provided necessaries for our liveli-hood, rear'd convenient places for Gods worship, and setled the Civill Government: One of the next things we longed for, and looked after was to advance *Learning*, and perpetuate it to Posterity, dreading to leave an illiterate Ministery to the Churches, when our present Ministers shall lie in the Dust. And as wee were thinking and consulting how to effect this great Work; it pleased God to stir up the heart of one Mr. *Harvard* (a godly Gentleman and a lover of Learning, there living amongst us) to give the one halfe of his Estate (it being in all about 1700. l.) towards the erecting of a Colledge, and all his Library: after him another gave 300. l. others after them cast in more, and the publique hand of the State added the rest: the Colledge was, by common consent, appointed to be at *Cambridge*, a place very pleasant and accommodate and is called (according to the name of the first founder) *Harvard Colledge*.

The Edifice is very faire and comely within and without, having in it a spacious Hall; (where they daily meet at Commons, Lectures, Exercises) and a large Library with some Bookes to it, the gifts of diverse of our friends, their Chambers and studies also fitted for, and possessed by the Students, and all other roomes of Office necessary and convenient, with all needfull Offices thereto belonging: And by the side of the Colledge a faire *Grammar* Schoole, for the training up of young Schollars, and fitting of them for *Academicall Learning*, that still as they are judged ripe, they may be received into the Colledge of this Schoole. Master *Corlet* is the Mr., who hath very well approved himselfe for his abilities, dexterity and painfulnesse in teaching and education of the youth under him.

Over the Colledge is master *Dunster* placed, as President, a learned conscionable and industrious man, who has so trained up his Pupills in the tongues and Arts, and so seasoned them with the principles of Divinity and Christianity that we have to our great comfort, (and in truth) beyond our hopes, beheld their progresse in Learning and godlinesse also; the former of these hath appeared in their publique declamations in *Latine* and *Greeke*, and Disputations Logicall and Philosophicall, which they have beene wonted (besides their ordinary Exercises in the Colledge-Hall) in the audience of the Magistrates, Ministers, and other Schollars, for the probation of their growth in Learning, upon set dayes, constantly once every moneth to make and uphold: The latter hath been manifested in sundry of them by the savoury breathings of their Spirits in their godly conversation. Insomuch that we are confident, if these early blossomes may be cherished and warmed with the influence of the friends of Learning, and lovers of this pious worke, they will by the help of God, come to happy maturity in a short time.

FIG. 41. JOHN HARVARD
(1607–38)
(From French's statue in Cambridge)

Over the Colledge are twelve Overseers chosen by the generall Court, six of them are of the Magistrates, the other six of the Ministers, who are to promote the best good of it, and (having a power of influence into all persons in it) are to see that every one be diligent and proficient in his proper place.

186. The First Rules for the Government of Harvard College

(*New England's First Fruits.* London, 1643. *Mass. Hist. Col.*, 1792, vol. I, pp.242–46.

The following rules governing admission to, studies in, and graduation from Harvard College, under date of 1642, are very interesting as revealing the great religious purpose of the institution, the limited and European-Renaissance character of the instruction, and the mediæval university type of requirements for degrees.

(a) Entrance Requirements

1. When any Schollar is able to understand *Tully*, or such like classicall Latine Author *extempore*, and make and speake true Latine in Verse and Prose, *suo ut aiunt Marte;* And decline perfectly the Paradigim's of *Nounes* and *Verbes* in the *Greek* tongue: Let him then and not before be capable of admission into the Colledge.

(b) Rules and Precepts

2. Let every Student be plainly instructed, and earnestly pressed to consider well, the maine end of his life and studies is, *to know God and Jesus Christ which is eternall life*, Joh. 17. 3. and therefore to lay *Christ* in the bottome, as the only foundation of all sound knowledge and Learning.

And seeing the Lord only giveth wisedome, Let every one seriously set himselfe by prayer in secret to seeke it of him, *Prov.* 2, 3.

3. Every one shall so exercise himselfe in reading the Scriptures twice a day, that he shall be ready to give such an account of his proficiency therein, both in *Theoretticall* observations of the Language, and *Logick*, and in *Practicall* and spirituall truths, as his Tutor shall require, according to his ability; seeing *the entrance of the word giveth light, it giveth understanding to the simple*, Psalm 119. 130.

4. That they eschewing all profanation of Gods Name, Attributes, Word, Ordinances, and times of Worship, doe studie with good conscience, carefully to retaine God, and the love of his truth in their mindes else let them know, that (notwithstanding their Learning) God may give them up *to strong delusions*, and in the end *to a reprobate minde*, 2. Thes. 2. 11, 12. Rom. 1. 28.

5. That they studiously redeeme the time; observe the generall houres appointed for all the Students, and the special houres for their owne *Classis:* and then dilligently attend the Lectures without any disturbance by word or gesture. And if in any thing they doubt, they shall enquire as of their fellowes, so, (in case of *Non satisfaction*) modestly of their Tutors.

6. None shall under any pretence whatsoever, frequent the company and society of such men as lead an unfit, and dissolute life.

Nor shall any without his Tutors leave, or (in his absence) the call of Parents or Guardians, goe abroad to other Townes.

7. Every Schollar shall be present in his Tutors chamber at the 7th. houre in the morning, immediately after the sound of the Bell, at his opening the Scripture and prayer, so also at the 5th. houre at night, and

then give account of his owne private reading, as aforesaid in Particular the third, and constantly attend Lectures in the Hall at the houres appointed?   But if any (without necessary impediment) shall absent himself from prayer or Lectures, he shall bee lyable to Admonition, if he offend above once a weeke.

8. If any Schollar shall be found to transgresse any of the Lawes of God, or the Schoole, after twice Admonition, he shall be lyable, if not *adultus*, to correction, if *adultus*, his name shall be given up to the Overseers of the Colledge, that he may bee admonished at the publick monethly Act.

(c) The times and order of their Studies, unlesse experience shall show cause to alter

The second and third day of the weeke, read Lectures, as followeth.

To the first yeare at 8th. of the clock in the morning *Logick*, the first three quarters, *Physicks* the last quarter.

To the second yeare at the 9th. houre, *Ethicks* and *Politicks*, at convenient distances of time.

To the third yeare at the 10th. *Arithmetick* and *Geometry*, the three first quarters, *Astronomy* the last.

Afternoone

The first yeare disputes at the second houre.
The 2d. yeare at the 3d. houre.
The 3d. yeare at the 4th. every one in his Art.

The 4th. day reads Greeke

To the first yeare the *Etymologie* and *Syntax* at the eighth houre.
To the 2d. at the 9th. houre, *Prosodia* and *Dialects*.

Afternoone

The first yeare at 2d. houre practice the precepts of *Grammar* in such Authors as have variety of words.

The 2d. yeare at 3d. houre practice in *Poësy, Nonnus, Duport,* or the like.

The 3d. yeare perfect their *Theory* before noone, and exercise *Style, Composition, Imitation, Epitome*, both in Prose and Verse, afternoone.

The fift day reads Hebrew, and the Easterne Tongues

Grammar to the first yeare houre the 8th.
To the 2d. *Chaldee* at the 9th. houre.
To the 3d. *Syriack* at the 10th. houre.

Afternoone

The first yeare practice in the Bible at the 2d. houre.
The 2d. in *Ezra* and *Danel* at the 3d. houre.
The 3d. at the 4th. houre in *Trestius* New Testament.

The 6th. day reads Rhetorick to all at the 8th. houre

Declamations at the 9th. So ordered that every Scholler may declaime once a moneth. The rest of the day *vacat Rhetoricis studiis.*

The 7th. day reads Divinity Catecheticall at the 8th. houre
Common places at the 9th. houre
Afternoone

The first houre reads history in the Winter,
The nature of plants in the Summer.
The summe of every Lecture shall be examined before the new Lecture be read.

(d) Requirements for Degrees

Every Schollar that on proofe is found able to read the Originalls of the *Old* and *New Testament* into the Latine tongue, and to resolve them *Logically;* withall being of godly life and conversation; And at any publick Act hath the Approbation of the Overseers and Master of the Colledge, is fit to be dignified with his first Degree.

Every Schollar that giveth up in writing a *System,* or *Synopsis,* or summe of *Logick,* Naturall and Morall *Phylosophy, Arithmetick, Geometry* and *Astronomy:* and is ready to defend his *Theses* or positions: withall skilled in the Originalls as abovesaid: and of godly life & conversation: and so approved by the Overseers and Master of the Colledge at any publique *Act,* is fit to be dignified with his 2d. Degree.

187. Extracts from the Charters of Harvard and Brown Colleges

(Charter of Harvard College, 1650; Brown College, 1764)

The two extracts which follow show the influence of earlier European university foundations on the beginnings of American colleges, in the matter of privileges and exemptions. Compare with Readings **103-105.**

(a) The Harvard College Charter of 1650

(Act of the Massachusetts General Court, creating the College a Corporation, 1650)

And, further, be it ordered by this Court and the authority thereof, that all the lands, tenements, or hereditaments, houses, or revenues, within this jurisdiction, to the aforesaid President or College appertaining, not exceeding the value of five hundred pounds per annum, shall from henceforth be freed from all civil impositions, taxes, and rates; all goods to the said corporation, or to any scholars thereof, appertaining, shall be exempted from all manner of toll, customs, and excise whatsoever; and that the said President, Fellows, and scholars, together with the servants, and other necessary officers to the said President or College appertaining, not exceeding ten, — viz. three to the President and seven to the College belonging, — shall be exempted from all personal civil offices, military exercises or services, watchings and wardings; and such of their estates, not exceeding one hundred pounds a man, shall be free from all country taxes or rates whatsoever, and none others.

(b) The Brown College Charter of 1764
(Act of the General Assembly of the English Colony of Rhode Island in Providence Plantation in America, 1764)

And furthermore, for the greater encouragement of the Seminary of learning, and that the same may be amply endowed and enfranchised with the same privileges, dignities, and immunities enjoyed by the American colleges, and European universities, We do grant, enact, ordain, and declare, and it is hereby granted, enacted, ordained, and declared, That the College estate, the estates, persons, and families of the President and Professors, for the time being, lying, and being within the Colony, with the persons of the Tutors and students, during their residence at the College, shall be freed and exempted from all taxes, serving on juries, and menial services: And that the persons aforesaid shall be exempted from bearing arms, impresses, and military services, except in case of an invasion.

188. Founding of the Free School of Roxburie (Massachusetts)
(Dillaway, C. K., *A History of the Grammar School in Roxburie*, pp. 7–8. Roxbury, 1860)

In 1645 a large number of the inhabitants of Roxbury signed an agreement to provide for the maintenance of a school for the town, which read as follows:

Whereas, the Inhabitantes of Roxburie, in consideration of their relligeous care of posteritie, have taken into consideration how necessarie the education of theire children in Literature will be to fitt them for public service, both in Churche and Commonwealthe, in succeeding ages. They therefore unanimously have consented and agreed to erect a free schoole in the said Towne of Roxburie, and to allow Twenty pounds per annum to the Schoolemaster, to bee raised out of the Messuages and part of the Lands of the severall donors (Inhabitantes of the said Towne) in severall proportions as hereafter followeth under their handes. And for the well ordering thereof they have chosen and elected some Feoffees who shall have power to putt in or remove the Schoolemaster, to see to the well ordering of the schoole and schoolars, to receive and pay the said twenty pounds per annum to the Schoolemaster, and to dispose of any other gifte or giftes which hereafter may or shall be given for the advancement of learning and education of children. . . .

In consideration of the premises, the Donors hereafter expressed for the severall proportions or annuities by them voluntarily undertaken and underwritten, Have given and granted and by these presents doe for themselves their heires and Asignees respectively hereby give and grant unto the present Feoffees . . . the severall rents and summes hereafter expressed under their handes. . . . To have and to hould receive and enjoy the said annual rents or summes to the only use of the Free Schoole in Roxburie.

In 1666 it was proposed that the whole town, as a town, unite in maintaining the school, but a meeting called to consider the matter resulted in no positive action. In 1671 a citizen of the town, dying in London, willed to the board of trustees of the school nearly two hundred acres of land in Roxbury, and this was used to endow the school.

In 1770 the enumeration of pupils in the Roxbury school showed an attendance of 85, distributed as follows:

Latin scholars	9	Testament	10
Cypherers	20	Psalter	10
Writers	17	Spellers	85

189. Rules and Regulations for the Government of the New Haven Hopkins Grammar School

(Transcribed from the Records of the School, by Mr. Lyman Baird. In Barnard's *American Journal of Education*, vol. IV, p. 710)

The following rules and regulations for this early Connecticut grammar school are very interesting as showing the religious purpose of the instruction, the dependence upon town and dame schools for preliminary training for admission, and the plan of government and instruction in the school.

Orders of ye Committee of Trustees for the Grammar Schoole at New Haven to be observed and attended in ye said Schoole, made, agreed upon and published in ye sd Schoole in ye Yeare 1684

1. The Erection of ye sd Schoole being principally for ye Institucion of hopeful youth in ye Latin tongue, and other learned Languages soe far as to prepare such youths for ye Colledge and publique service of ye Country in Church, & Commonwealth. The Chiefe work of ye Schoole-Mr. is to Instruct all such youth as are or may be by theire parents or Friends sent, or Committed unto him to yt end with all diligence faithfulness and Constancy out of any of ye townes of this County of New haven upon his sallary accompt only, otherwise Gratis. And if any Boyes are sent to ye Mr of ye said Schoole from any other part of ye

Colony, or Country, Each such boy or youth to pay ten shillings to ye
Mastr at or upon his entrance into ye said Schoole.

2. That noe Boyes be admitted into ye sd Schoole for ye learning of
English Books, but such as have been before taught to spell ye letters
well & begin to Read, thereby to perfect theire right Spelling, & Reading, or to learne to write, & Cypher for numeracion, & addicion, & noe
further, & yt all others either too young & not instructed in letters &
spelling, & all Girles be excluded as Improper & inconsistent wth such
a Grammar Schoole as ye law injoines, as is ye Designe of this Settlemt,
And yt noe Boyes be admitted from other townes for ye learning of
English, without liberty & specially licence from ye Comitte.

3. That the Master & Schollars duly attend the Schoole Houres viz.
from 6 in ye morning to 11 o Clock in ye forenoone, And from 1 a Clock
in the afternoone to 5 a Clock in the afternoone in Summer & 4 in Winter.

4. That the Mr shall make a list or Catalogue of his Schollars names
And appoint a Monitor in his turne fore one week or longer tyme as the
Mr shall see Cause, who shall every morning & noone et at least once a
day at ye set tyme Call over ye names of ye Schollars and Note down
the Late Commers, or Absent, And in fit season Call such to an accompt That the faulty, & truants may be Corrected or reproved, as
their fault shall desearve.

5. That the Schollars being called together the Mr shall every morning begin his work with a short Prayer for a blessing on his Laboures &
theire Learning.

6. That the prayer being ended the Master shall Assigne to every of
his Schollars theire places of Sitting according to theire degrees of
learning.   And that (having theire Parts, or Lessons appointed them)
they keep theire Seates, & stir not out of Doors, with [out] Leave of the
Master, and not above two at one tyme, & soe successively: unless in
Cases of necessity.

7. That ye Schollars behave themselves at all tymes, especially in
Schoole tyme with due Reverence to theire Master, & with Sobriety &
quietnes among themselves, without fighting, Quarrelling or calling
one anothr or any others, bad names, or useing bad words in Cursing,
taking the name of God in vaine, or other prophane, obscene, or Corrupt speeches which if any doe, That ye Mr Forthwith give them due
Correcion.   And if any prove incorrigible in such bad manners & wicked
Corrupting language & speeches, notwithstanding formr warnings,
admonishions & Correcion that such be expelled ye Schoole as pernicious
& dangerous examples to ye Rest.

8. That if any of ye Schoole Boyes be observed to play, sleep, or behave themselves rudely, or irreverently, or be any way disorderly at
meeting on ye Saboath Daye or any other tyme of ye Publiqe worships
of God That upon informacion or Complaint thereof to ye due Con-

viccion of the offender or offenders, The Master shall give them due Correccions to ye degree of ye Offence. And yt all Correccions be wth Moderacion.

9. That noe Lattine Boyes be allowed upon any pretence (sickness, and disability excepted) to withdraw, or absent themselvs from the Schoole, without liberty graunted by the Master, and yt noe such liberty be granted but upon ticket from ye Parents or frends, & on grounds sufficient as in Cases extraordinary or absolute necessity.

10. That all the Lattin Schollars, & all other of ye Boyes of Competent age and Capacity give the Mr an accompt of one passage or sentence at least of ye sermons the foregoing Saboth on ye 2d day morning. And that from 1 to 3 in ye afternoone of every last day of ye week be Improved by ye Mr in Catechizing of his Schollars yt are Capeable.

190. The Massachusetts Law of 1642

(*Records of the Governor and Company of the Massachusetts Bay in New England*, vol. II, pp. 6–7. Boston, 1853)

This earliest colonial law regarding education, under date of April 14, 1642, reads as follows:

This Co^{r}t, taking into consideration the great neglect of many parents & masters in training up their children in learning, & labo^r, & other implyments which may be proffitable to the common wealth, do hereupon order and decree, that in euery towne ye chosen men appointed for managing the prudentiall affajres of the same shall henceforth stand charged with the care of the redresse of this evill, so as they shalbee sufficiently punished by fines for the neglect thereof, upon presentment of the grand iury, or other information or complaint in any Court within this iurisdiction; and for this end they, or the greater numbe^r of them, shall have power to take account from time to time of all parents and masters, and of their children, concerning their calling and implyment of their children, especially of their ability to read & understand the principles of religion & the capitall lawes of this country, and to impose fines upon such as shall refuse to render such accounts to them when they shall be required; and they shall have power, with consent of any Court or the magistrate, to put forth apprentices the children of such as they shall [find] not to be able & fitt to imploy and bring them up. They shall take . . . that boyes and girles be not suffered to converse together, so as may occasion any wanton, dishonest, or immodest behavio^r; & for their better performance of this trust committed to them, they may divide the towne amongst them, appointing to every of the said townesmen a certaine number of families to have special oversight of. They are also to provide that a sufficient quantity of materialls, as hemp, flaxe, ec^{ra}, may be raised in their severall townes, & tooles & implements provided for working out the same; & for their assistance in this so needfull and beneficiall imploym^t, if they meete wth any difficulty or opposition wch they cannot well master by their own power, they may have reco^{r}se to some of the ma^{trats}, who shall take such course for their help & incuragm^t as the occasion shall require according to iustice; & the said townesmen, at the next Co^{r}t in those limits, after the end of their year, shall give a breife account in writing of their proceedings herein, provided that they have bene so required by some Co^{r}t or magistrate a month at least before; & this order to continew for two yeares, & till the Co^{r}t shall take further order./

191. The Massachusetts Law of 1647

(Records of the Governor and Company of the Massachusetts Bay in New England, vol. II, p. 203. Boston, 1853)

This famous Act, often spoken of as "the old deluder, Satan, Act," was enacted under date of November 11, 1647, and reads as follows:

It being one cheife proiect of ye ould deluder, Satan, to keepe men from the knowledge of ye Scriptures, as in form^r times by keeping y^m in an unknowne tongue, so in these latt^r times by perswading from ye use of tongues, y^t so at least ye true sence & meaning of ye originall might be clouded by false glosses of saint seeming deceivers, y^t learning may not be buried in ye grave of o^r fath^{rs} in ye church and commonwealth, the Lord assisting o^r endeavo^{r}s, —

It is therefore ord^{r}ed, y^t ev^{r}y towneship in this iurisdiction, aft^r ye Lord hath increased y^m number to 50 houshold^{rs}, shall then forthwth appoint one wthin their towne to teach all such children as shall resort to him to write & reade, whose wages shall be paid eith^r by ye parents or mast^{rs} of such children, or by ye inhabitants in gen^{r}all, by way of supply, as ye maior part of those y^t ord^r ye prudentials of ye towne shall appoint; provided, those y^t send their children be not oppressed by paying much more y^n they can have y^m taught for in oth^r townes; & it is furth^r ordered, y^t where any towne shall increase to ye numb^r of 100 families or househould^{rs}, they shall set up a grammer schoole, ye m^r thereof being able to instruct youth so farr as they shall be fited for ye university, provided, y^t if any towne neglect ye performance hereof above one yeare, y^t every such towne shall pay 5 £ to ye next schoole till they shall performe this order.

192. Presentment of the Town of Topsfield, for Violating the Law of 1642

(Records and Files of Quarterly Courts of Essex County, Massachusetts, 1636–1671, vol. IV, p. 212. Salem, 1911–14)

That the courts were insistent that the Law of 1642 be enforced may be seen from the following court order, issued to be served on the Selectmen of Topsfield, Massachusetts, for not properly enforcing the law.

Warrant to the constable of Topsfield, dated Mar. 2, 1668:

Whereas the law published by the Honered Generall Court lib. I, pag 76, doe require all Townes from time to time to dispose of all single persons and inmates within their Towns to service or otherwise and in pag. 16, tit. children & youth, It is required of the selectmen that they see that all youth under family Government be taught to read perfectly the english tongue, have knowledge in the capital laws, and be taught some orthodox catechism, and that they be brought up to some honest employment, profitable to themselves and to the commonwealth, and in case of neglect, on the part of famaly Governours, after admonition given them, the sayd selectmen are required, with the helpe of two magistrates, or next court of that shire, to take such children or apprentices from them, and place them forth with such as will looke more straitly to them. The neglect wherof, as by sad experience from court to court abundantly appears, doth occasion much sin and prophanes to increase among us, to the dishonor of God, and the ensueing of many children and servants, by the dissolute lives and practices of such as doe live from under family Government and is a great discouragement to most family governours, who consciently indeavour to bring up their youth in all christian nurture, as the laws of God and this commonwealth doth require; [said constable was ordered to acquaint selectmen of the town that] the court doth expect and will require that the sayd laws be accordingly attended, the prevalency of the former neglect notwithstanding, and you are also required to take a list of the names of those young persons within the bounds of your Town, and all adjacent farmes, though out of all Towne bounds, who do live from under family government viz. doe not serve their parents or masters, as children apprentices, hired servants, or journeymen ought to do, and usually did in our native country, being subject to there commands & discipline and the same you are to returne to the next court to be held at Ipswich the 30 day of this month, etc.; signed by Robert Lord, cleric; and served by Thomas Dorman, constable of Topsfield, who returned that he had made the selectmen acquainted with Mathew Hooker, who was all that he found in the town.

193. The Connecticut Law of 1650

(Codification of 1650; in Barnard's *American Journal of Education*, vol. IV, p. 660)

Connecticut here follows the Massachusetts legislation. After the law reproduced below, Connecticut also added and enacted, under the heading of SCHOOLS, the Massachusetts "old deluder, Satan, law" of 1647 in full. This legislation remained unchanged in Connecticut until 1792.

Children

Forasmuch as the good Education of Children is of singular behoofe and benefitt to any Commonwealth; and whereas many parents and masters are too indulgent and negligent of theire duty in that kind;

It is therefore ordered by this Courte and Authority thereof, that the Select men of euery Towne in the several precincts and quarters where they dwell, shall have a vigilant eye over their brethern and neighbors, to see, first, that none of them shall suffer so much barbarism in any of their families, as not to endeavor to teach by themselves or others, their children and apprentices so much learning as may enable them perfectly to read the English tongue, and knowledge of the capital laws, upon penalty of twenty shillings for each neglect therein; also, that all masters of families, do, once a week, at least catechise their children and servants, in the grounds and principles of religion; and if any be unable to do so much, that then, at the least, they procure such children or apprentices to learn some short orthodox catechism, without book, that they may be able to answer to the questions that shall be propounded to them out of such catechisms by their parents or masters, or any selectmen, when they shall call them to a·trial of what they have learned in this kind; and further, that all parents and masters do breed and bring up their children and apprentices in some honest lawful [calling,] labor, or employment, either in husbandry or some other trade profitable for themselves and the commonwealth, if they will not nor can not train them up in learning, to fit them for higher employments, and if any of the selectmen, after admonition by them given to such masters of families, shall find them still negligent of their duty, in the particulars aforementioned, whereby children and servants become rude, stubborn and unruly, the said selectmen, with the help of two magistrates, shall take such children or apprentices from them, and place them with some masters for years, boys until they come to twenty-one, and girls to eighteen years of age complete, which will more strictly look unto and force them to submit unto government, according to the rules of this order, if by fair means and former instructions they will not be drawn unto it.

Here follows the Massachusetts Law of 1647, as given in the preceding selection.

194. Plymouth Colony Legislation

(*Plymouth Colony Records*, vol. XI, *Laws*)

Plymouth Colony was not joined to that of Massachusetts Bay to form Massachusetts until 1692, and previous to that date Plymouth Colony enacted the following legislation regarding education and schools.

Schools

(a) Elementary schools recommended

1658, 1663.   It is proposed by the Court vnto the seurall Townshipes of this Jurisdiction as a thinge they ought to take into theire serious consideration That some course may be taken that in euery Towne there may be a schoolmaster sett vp to traine vp children to reading and writing (p. 142).

(b) Aid asked for Harvard College

1672.   Wee being Informed that it is vpon the harts of our Naighbours of the Massachusetts Collonie to support and Incurrage that Nursary of Learning att harveard Colledge in Cambridge in New England from whence haue through the blessing of God Issued many worthy and vseful persons for Publique seruice in Church and Commonwealth; being alsoe Informed that diuers Godly and well affected in England are redy to Assist therein by way of contributing considerable sumes prouided the Countrey heer are forward to promote the same; and that the seuerall Townes in the Massachusetts haue bine very free in theire offerings thervnto; wee alsoe being by letters from them Invited and Insighted to Joyne with them in soe good a worke; and that wee may haue an Interest with others In the blessing that the Lord may please fron thence to convey vnto the Countrey; this Court doth therefore earnestly comend it to the Minnesters and Elders in each Towne, that they takeing such with them as they shall thinks meet; would particularly and earnestly moue and stirr vp all such in theire seuerall townes as are able to contribute vnto this worthy worke be it in mony or other good pay; and that they make a returne of what they shall effect heerin vnto the Court that shall sit in october next whoe will then appoint meet psons to receiue the contributions and faithfully to dispose of the same for the ends proposed (pp. 232, 233).

(c) Income from Fishing for Schools

1673.   It is ordered by the Court that the charge of the free Scoole, which is three and thirty pounds a yeare shalbe defrayed by the Treasurer out of the proffitts ariseing by the ffishing att the Cape vntil such Time as that the minds of the ffreemen be knowne conserning it which wilbe returned to the next Court of election (p. 233).

1674.   This Court haueing receiued by the deputies of the seuerall townes the signification of the minds of the Major pte of the freemen of this Collonie that all the proffits of the ffishing att Cape Code graunted by the Court for the erecting and Maintaining of a Scoole be still continewed for that end if a competent Number of Scollars shall appeer to be devoated thervnto, which this Court Judges not to be lesse then eight or ten Doe therfore heerby confeirme the Graunt of the aforsaid proffitts of the ffishing att the Cape to the Maintainance of the Scoole; and that there be noe further demaunds, besides the said proffitts of the Cape demaunded of the Country for the Maintainance of the said Scoole (p. 237).

(d) Grammar schools to be maintained

1677. fforasmuch as the Maintainance of good litterature doth much tend to the advancement of the weale and flourishing estate of societies and Republiques.

This Court doth therfore order; That in whatsoeuer Townshipp in this Gourment consisting of fifty familier or vpwards; any meet man shalbe obtained to teach a Gramer scoole such townshipp shall allow att least twelue pounds in currant marchantable pay to be raised by rat on all the Inhabitants of such Towne and those that haue the more emediate benifitt therof by theire childrens going to scoole with what others may voulentarily giue to promote soe good a work and generall good, shall make vp the resedue Nessesarie to maintaine the same and that the proffitts ariseing of the Cape ffishing; heertofore ordered to maintaine a Gramer scoole in this Collonie, be distributed to such Townes as haue such Gramer scholes for the maintainance therof; not exceeding fiue pounds p annum to any such Towne vnlesse the Court Treasurer or other appointed to manage that affaire see good cause to adde thervnto to any respectiue Towne not exceeding fiue pounds more p annum; and further this Court orders that euery such Towne as consists of seauenty families or vpwards and hath not a Gramer scoole therin shall allow and pay vnto the next Towne which hath such Gramer scoole kept vp amongst them, the sume of fiue pounds p annum in currant Marchantable pay, to be leuied on the Inhabitants of such defectiue Townes by rate and gathered and deliuered by the Constables of such Townes as by warrant from any Majestrate of this Jurisdiction shalbe required (pp. 246, 247).

195. Contract with a Dutch Schoolmaster, Flatbush, New York

(Trans. by Platt, D. J., *Annals of Public Education in the State of New York, 1626–1746*, pp. 65–67. Albany, 1872)

Specific and very particular agreements were made by the Dutch with their early schoolmasters, as the following document of 1682 shows. It also reveals the multiple nature of the schoolmaster's duties, — teacher, chorister, janitor, and sexton, and is of importance as showing the elementary schoolmaster in the process of evolution out of the church sexton.

SCHOOL SERVICE. I. The School shall begin at eight o'clock, and go out at eleven; and in the afternoon shall begin at one o'clock and end at four. The bell shall be rung when the school commences.

II. When the school begins, one of the children shall read the morning prayer, as it stands in the catechism, and close with the prayer before dinner; in the afternoon it shall begin with the prayer after dinner, and end with the evening prayer. The evening school shall begin with the Lord's prayer, and close by singing a psalm.

III. He shall instruct the children on every Wednesday and Saturday, in the common prayers, and the questions and answers in the catechism, to enable them to repeat them the better on Sunday before the afternoon service, or on Monday, when they shall be catechised before the congregation. Upon all such occasions, the schoolmaster shall be present, and shall require the children to be friendly in their appearance and encourage them to answer freely and distinctly.

IV. He shall be required to keep his school nine months in succession, from September to June, in each year, in case it should be concluded upon to retain his services for a year or more, or without limitation; and he shall then be required to be regulated by these articles, and to perform the same duties which his predecessor, Jan Thibaud, above named, was required to perform. In every particular therefore, he shall be required to keep school, according to this seven months agreement, and shall always be present himself.

CHURCH SERVICE. I. He shall keep the church clean, and ring the bell three times before the people assemble to attend the preaching and catechism. Also before the sermon is commenced, he shall read a chapter out of the Holy Scriptures, and that, between the second and third ringing of the bell. After the third ringing he shall read the ten commandments, and the twelve articles of our faith, and then take the lead in singing. In the afternoon after the third ringing of the bell, he shall read a short chapter, or one of the Psalms of David, as the congregation are assembling; and before divine service commences, shall introduce it, by the singing of a Psalm or Hymn.

II. When the minister shall preach at Brooklyn, or New-Utrecht, he shall be required to read twice before the congregation, from the book commonly used for that purpose. In the afternoon he shall also read a sermon on the explanation of the catechism, according to the usage and practice approved of by the minister. The children as usual, shall recite their questions and answers out of the catechism, on Sunday, and he shall instruct them therein. He, as chorister, shall not be required to perform these duties, whenever divine service shall be performed in Flatlands, as it would be unsuitable, and prevent many from attending there.

III. For the administration of Holy Baptism, he shall provide a basin with water, for which he shall be entitled to receive from the parents, or witnesses, twelve styvers.[1] He shall, at the expense of the church, provide bread and wine, for the celebration of the Holy Supper;

---

[1] A styver was equal to about two cents.

He shall be in duty bound promptly to furnish the minister with the name of the child to be baptized, and with the names of the parents and witnesses. And he shall also serve as messenger for the consistory.

IV. He shall give the funeral invitations, dig the grave, and toll the bell, for which service he shall receive for a person of fifteen years and upwards, twelve guilders, and for one under that age, eight guilders. If he should be required to give invitations beyond the limits of the town, he shall be entitled to three additional guilders, for the invitation of every other town, and if he should be required to cross the river, and go to New York, he shall receive four guilders.

SCHOOL MONEY. He shall receive from those who attend the day school, for a speller or reader, three guilders a quarter, and for a writer four guilders. From those who attend evening school, for a speller or reader, four guilders, and for a writer, six guilders shall be given.

SALARY. In addition to the above, his salary shall consist of four hundred guilders, in grain, valued in Seewant, to be delivered at Brooklyn Ferry, and for his services from October to May, as above stated, a sum of two hundred and thirty-four guilders, in the same kind, with the dwelling-house, barn, pasture lot and meadows, to the school appertaining. The same to take effect from the first day of October, instant.

Done and agreed upon in Consistory, under the inspection of the Honorable Constable and Overseers, the 8th, of October, 1682.

Constable and Overseers	*The Consistory*
CORNELIUS BARRIAN,	CASPARUS VAN ZUREN, Minister,
RYNIER AERTSEN,	ADRIAEN REYERSE,
JAN REMSEN,	CORNELIS BARENT VANDWYCK.

I agree to the above articles, and promise to perform them according to the best of my ability.

JOHANNES VAN ECKKELEN.

196. Rules regulating a Schoolmaster in New Amsterdam

(Minutes of the Orphan Masters of New Amsterdam, vol. II, p. 115; trans. by B. Fernow. New York, 1907)

The following instructions given Evert Pietersen, a schoolmaster employed in New Amsterdam in 1661, by the public authorities, are probably typical of those given other schoolmasters. They are reproduced as showing the nature and the fee basis of the Dutch elementary schools.

Instructions and Rules for Schoolmaster Evert Pietersen, drawn up by the Burgomasters of this city with advice of the Director General and Council.

1. He shall take good care, that the children, coming to his school, do so at the usual hour, namely at eight in the morning and one in the afternoon.

2. He must keep good discipline among his pupils.

3. He shall teach the children and pupils the Christian Prayers, commandments, baptism, Lord's supper, and the questions with answers of the catechism, which are taught here every Sunday afternoon in the church.

4. Before school closes he shall let the pupils sing some verses and a psalm.

5. Besides his yearly salary he shall be allowed to demand and receive from every pupil quarterly as follows: For each child, whom he teaches the a b c, spelling and reading, 30 st.; for teaching to read and write, 50 st.; for teaching to read, write, and cipher, 60 st.; from those who come in the evening and between times pro rata a fair sum. The poor and needy, who ask to be taught for God's sake he shall teach for nothing.

6. He shall be allowed to demand and receive from everybody, who makes arrangements to come to his school and comes before the first half of the quarter preceding the first of December next, the school dues for the quarter, but nothing from those, who come after the first half of the quarter.

7. He shall not take from anybody, more than is herein stated. Thus done and decided by the Burgomasters of the City of Amsterdam in N.N., November 4, 1661.

197. The Pennsylvania Law of 1683

(Laws of the 2d General Assembly of Pennsylvania Colony, chap. CXII. From Wickersham, J. P., *History of Education in Pennsylvania*, p. 39. Lancaster, 1886)

William Penn received his charter from the King, in 1681, and arrived in 1682. The first Colonial Assembly met that year, and the second a year later. This second Assembly enacted a law which for the time marked a very progressive attitude for this colony. It was enforced here and there, as the court records show, but was later vetoed by William and Mary as being opposed to English traditions and practices. It was reënacted in 1693, but soon became a dead letter, and Pennsylvania's opportunity to follow in the footsteps of Massachusetts was lost. The law reads:

And to the end that poor as well as rich may be instructed in good and commendable learning, which is to be preferred before wealth, *Be it enacted*, etc., That all persons in this Province and Territories thereof, having children, and all guardians and trustees of orphans, shall cause such to be instructed in reading and writing, so that they may be able to read the Scriptures and to write by the time they attain to twelve years of age; and that then they be taught some useful trade or skill, that the poor may work to live, and the rich if they become poor may not want: of which every County Court shall take care. And in case such parents, guardians, or overseers shall be found deficient in this respect, every such parent, guardian, or overseer shall pay for every such child, five pounds, except there should appear an incapacity in body or understanding to hinder it.

198. The First School in Philadelphia

(*Minutes of the Pennsylvania Colonial Council*, 1683. From Wickersham, J. P., *History of Education in Pennsylvania*, p. 41. Lancaster, 1886)

The first attempt to carry out the Pennsylvania law of 1683 was made in Philadelphia, that same year, as is shown by the following minutes of the Colonial Council. Flower opened a school there in October, 1683.

At a Council held at Philadelphia, ye 26th of ye 10th month, 1683. Present: Wm. Penn, Propor & Govr., Theo. Holmes, Wm. Haigue, Lasse Cock, Wm. Clayton.

The Govr and Provll Councill having taken into their Serious Consideration the great Necessity there is of a School Master for ye instruction & Sober Education of youth in the towne of Philadelphia, Sent for Enock flower, an Inhabitant of the said Towne, who for twenty Year past hath been exercised in that care and imployment in England, to whom haveing Communicated their Minds, he Embraced it upon the following Terms: to Learne to read English 4s by the Quarter, to Learne to read and write 6s by ye Quarter, to learne to read, Write and Cast accot 8s by ye Quarter; for Boarding a Scholler, that is to say, dyet, Washing, Lodging, & Scooling, Tenn pounds for one whole year.

199. Early Quaker Injunctions regarding Schools

(*Rules of Discipline of the Yearly Meeting of Friends*. Quoted by Murray, David; *History of Education in New Jersey*, p. 23)

The following extracts, quoted by Murray, relate to the period between 1746 and 1787 (the colony of Pennsylvania was founded in 1683), and illustrate the interest of the Quakers in the establishment of parochial schools.

Schools. The education of our youth in piety and virtue, and giving them useful learning under the tuition of religious, prudent persons, having for a great number of years enjoyed the solid attention of this meeting, advices thereon have from time to time been issued to the several subordinate meetings. It is renewedly desired that quarterly, monthly, and preparative meetings may be excited to proper exertions for the institution and support of schools, there being but little doubt that as Friends are united and cherish a disposition of liberality for the assistance of each other in this important work, they will be enabled to make such provision for the accommodation and residence of a teacher with a family as would be an encouragement to well-qualified persons to engage in this arduous employment. . . .

It is therefore proposed: (1) That a lot of ground be provided in each monthly or preparative meeting, sufficient for a garden, orchard, grass for a cow, etc., and a suitable house erected thereon. (2) That funds be raised by contribution, bequests, etc., in each meeting; the interest of which to be applied either in aid of the tutor's salary or lessening the expenses of Friends in straitened circumstances, in the education of their children. (3) That a committee be appointed in each monthly or preparative meeting to have the care of schools and the funds for their support, and that no tutor be employed but with their consent.

200. Apprenticeship Laws in the Southern Colonies

A. IN VIRGINIA

(Hening's *Statutes of Virginia*, vol. I, pp. 260, 336–37, and vol. II, p. 298)

All of the early Virginia legislation relating to education refers either to William and Mary College, founded in 1693, or to the education of orphans and the children of the poor. The three laws relating to the apprenticeship of the latter, under date of 1643, 1646, and 1672, provide:

(1) *Law of 1643*

The guardians and overseers of all orphants shall carefully keep and preserve such estates as shall be committed to their trusts either by order of court or otherwise. And shall likewise render an exact accompt once everie year to the commissioners of the several county courts, respectively, of the said estates and of the increase and improvement, who are hereby to keep an exact register thereof. And all overseers and guardians of such orphants are enjoyned by authority aforesaid to educate and instruct them according to their best endeavors in Christian religion and in the rudiments of learning and to provide for their necessaries according to the competents of their estate.

(2) *Law of 1646*

Commissioners of the several counties shall make choice of two children, male or female, eight or seven years at least, to be sent to James City (Jamestown) to be employed in the public flax factory work under such master and masters as shall thus be appointed, in carding, knitting, spinning, and so on, and that said children shall be furnished from the counties with six barrels of corn, two coverlids, one rugg, one blanket, one bed, one wooden bowl or tray, two pewter spoons, a sow shote of six months, and two laying hens, convenient apparel, both linen and woolen, with hose and shoes. That there be two houses built by the first of April next, forty feet long apeace with good substantial timber. The houses to be twenty feet broad apeace, eight foot high in the pitche, and a stack of brick chimney standing in the midst of each house, and that they be lofted with sawne boards and made with convenient partitions, commissioners have caution not to take up children from such parents who by reason of their poverty are disable to maintain and educate them. That the governor hath agreed with the Assembly for the sum of ten thousand pounds of to-bo to be paid him the next crop to build such houses.

(3) Law of 1672

That the justices of the peace in every county doe put the laws of England against vagrants, idlers, and dissolute persons, in strict execution, and the respective county courts shall and are hereby empowered and authorized to place out all the children whose parents are not able to bring them up apprentices to tradesmen, the males till one and twenty years of age and the females to other necessary employment till eighteen years of age and no longer, and the church wardens of every parish shall [be] strictly enjoyned by the courts to give them an account at their Orphans Courts of all such children within their parish.

B. IN NORTH CAROLINA

(*Colonial Records of North Carolina*, vol. I, pp. 448, 577, and vol. II, p. 266)

The English practice of apprenticing orphans and poor children, best exemplified by Virginia, extended into the other southern colonies, as the following selected North Carolina court records, dated 1695, 1703, and 1716, clearly show.

(1) Upon ye Peticon of Hon^{ell} Thomas Harvey esq^r Ordered y^t W^m ye son of Timothy Pead late of the County of Albemarle Dec^d being left destitute be bound unto ye s^d Thomas Harvey esq^r and Sarah his wife untill he be at ye age of twenty one years and the said Thomas Harvey to teach him to read. (February, 1695.)

(2) Upon a petition of Gabriell Newby for two orphants left him by Mary Hancock the late wife of Thom^s Hancocke and proveing the same by the oathes of Eliz. Steward and her daughter the Court doe agree to bind them unto him he Ingagen & promising before the Court to doe his endeavours to learne the boy the trade of a wheelwright and likewise give him at the expiration of his time one year old heifer and to ye girle at her freedome one Cow and Calfe besides the Custome of the

Country and has promised to ye next orphans Court to Sign Indentures for that effect.   (March, 1703.)

(3) Upon the Peticon of John Swain praying that Elizabeth Swain his sister an Orphane Girle bound by the Precinct Court of Chowan to John Worley Esqr May in time of her service be taught to read by her said Master Ordered, that she be taught to read.   (November, 1716.)

201. A New England Indenture of Apprenticeship

(Stiles, H. R., *The History of Ancient Windsor, Connecticut*, vol. i, p. 442. New York, 1859.)

Such agreements as the following were very common in all the colonies in colonial days.   This shows well the relations which existed between master and apprentices in Connecticut.

This Indenture witnesseth that Jonathan Stoughton, son of Thomas Stoughton of Windsor in the county of hartford and Coloney of Connecticut in new england, with his father's consent hath put him selfe an apprentice to Nathan day of the aboue sd windsor county and coloney: blacksmith and white smith to Learn his art, trade or mystery after the manner of an Apprentice to serue him until the sd Jonathan Stoughton attaines the age of twenty-one years, during all which time the sd apprentice his master faithfully shall serue, his secrets keep, his Lawfull commands gladly obaye he shall not do any damage to his sd master nor see it don by others without giueing notice thereof to his sd master. he shall not waste his sd master's goods or Lend them unLawfully to aney, he shall not commit fornication nor contract matrimony within the sd terme. at cards, dice or any other unlawfull game he shall not play whereby his sd master may suffer damage.   he shall not absent himself day nor night from his master's service without his leave. nor haunt ale houses, Taverns or playhouses butt in all things behave himselfe as a faithfull apprentice ought to do during ye sd terme, and the sd master shall do his utmost to teach and Instruct ye sd apprentice In the boue mentioned blacksmith and white smiths trade and mistery and to teach or caus the sd apprentice to be Taught the art of Arithmatick to such a degree that he may be able to keep a book well, and provide for him meat, drink, apparel, washing and lodging and phisick in sickness and health suitable for such an apprentice during the sd terme, and att the end of sd terme the sd master shall furnish the sd apprentice with two good new suits of apparel boath wooling and lining for all parts of his body suitable for such an apprentice besids that apparel he carrieth with him and for the performance of all and every the sd covenants and agreement either of the sd parties bind themselves unto the other by these presents in witness whereof they have interchangeably put their hands and seals this first day of September in the year of our Lord god, 1727.

202. The New England Primer

(Abstract of a reprint of an edition of about 1785–90 reproduced recently by Ginn & Co., Boston. Original in the library of Mr. G. A. Plimpton, of New York)

This famous little schoolbook first appeared about 1690, and for the next century and a quarter it was the chief school and reading book in use among the Dissenters and Lutherans in America. It went through many editions, and was altered somewhat from time to time to suit the peculiar religious views of the publisher's patrons. A little book of but eighty-eight pages, three and a quarter by four and a half inches in size, it expressed so well the gloomy religious atmosphere of Calvinistic New England that it was retained in use long after better reading matter had appeared.

Unlike the early *Protestant Primer* of Melanchthon (Wittenberg, 1524), or the *Orbis Pictus* of Comenius (1654), both of which had contained some secular reading matter, *The New England Primer* was religious throughout. Even the illustrated alphabet, which in early editions was secular in tone, was later revised so as better to express the prevailing religious conceptions of the period. A brief analysis of the contents of this famous *Primer* will prove interesting, as showing the nature of the instruction in reading and religion given in the colonial schools.

Each copy contained on its first leaf a rude woodcut of the ruling monarch, and later of some Revolutionary hero, and a page of Proverbs relating to filial duty and serving God. Sometimes a religious poem was printed for the latter. Then followed the title-page. In the edition at hand this was followed by a poem on "Good Boys at their Books" (1 page); the letters, vowels and consonants (1 page); two pages of easy syllables (ab, abs); words of one syllable (1 page); words of two to six syllables (2 pages); the Lord's Prayer and the Creed (1 page); an illustrated alphabet (2 pages); the rhymed alphabet (4 pages, of which the first is given in the illustrated page printed here); ten half-page pictures of animals, with a rhyme under each, of which the following is an example:

> "The Butterfly in gaudy dress,
> The worthless Coxcomb doth express."

Next comes a two-page poem of "Praise for Learning" to read, the first page of which is reproduced here. Then follows an alphabet of "Lessons for Youth," of three pages, the first of which is also reproduced. The next two and a half pages contain Watt's beautiful "Cradle Hymn," beginning:

> "Hush, my dear, lie still and slumber,
> Holy angels guard thy bed."

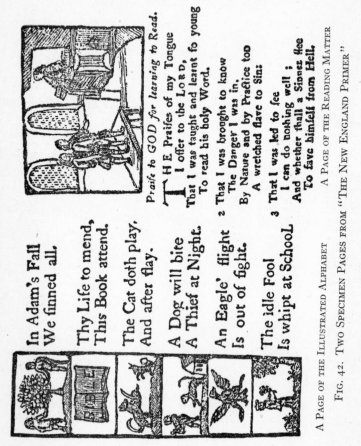

A PAGE OF THE ILLUSTRATED ALPHABET   A PAGE OF THE READING MATTER

FIG. 42. TWO SPECIMEN PAGES FROM "THE NEW ENGLAND PRIMER"

This is followed by three and a half pages of Verses for Children, and four pages of rhymed prayers and admonitions, among which one finds the old familiar

> "Now I lay me down to sleep."

Next comes a seven-page rhymed "Advice to Children," written by John Rogers, a London minister, who was burned at the stake at Smithfield, in 1554, and which was bequeathed by him to the wife and nine children he was about to leave. After a page picture, showing the event, the poem begins:

> "Give Ear my Children to my Words,
>   whom God hath dearly bought,
> Lay up his Laws within your Heart,
>   and point them in your thought.
> I leave you here a little book,
>   for you to look upon,
> That you may see your father's face,
>   when he is dead and gone."

This was evidently a much-prized poem.

Next comes a page of "Instructive Questions and Answers," of which the following are illustrative:

Who was the first Man?	*Adam.*
Who was the first Woman?	*Eve.*
Who was the first Murderer?	*Cain.*
Who was the first Martyr?	*Abel.*
Who was the first Translated?	*Enoch.*
Who was the oldest Man?	*Methuselah.*
Who built the Ark?	*Noah.*

This was followed by the *pièce de résistance* of the whole book, "The Shorter Westminster Catechism," the first page of which is reproduced as Figure 131 in the accompanying History. This required twenty-four pages of the book. Next comes a famous native production of nine and a half pages, by John Cotton, the first page of which is reproduced on page 315. The volume is now concluded with a nine and a half page rhymed dialogue between Christ, a Youth, and the Devil, which also was a great favorite in New England. The Youth declares:

> "Those days which God to me doth send,
>   In pleasure I'm resolved to spend."

The Devil expresses great pleasure at the decision, while Christ entreats the Youth not to obey the Devil's voice. The Youth, though, will not listen until too late. After a long argument, Christ finally, out of patience, calls Death to come and take the Youth "before he has half lived out his days." The Youth, terrified, now begs to be spared, but Christ is obdurate; Death takes him; and the poem ends with the following words:

DEATH

"Youth, I am come to fetch thy breath,
And carry thee to th' shades of death,
No pity on thee can I show,
Thou hast thy God offended so.
Thy soul and body I'll divide,
Thy body in the grave I'll hide,
And thy dear soul in hell must lie
With Devils to eternity.

THE CONCLUSION

"Thus ends the days of woful youth,
Who won't obey nor mind the truth;
Nor hearken to what preachers say,
But do their parents disobey.
They in their youth go down to hell,
Under eternal wrath to dwell.
Many don't live out half their days
For cleaving unto sinful ways."

This *Primer* exercised a great influence on the New England character. It was used by both church and school, the school-master drilling on the Catechism in the school, and the people reciting it yearly in the churches. Every home possessed copies of the book, and it was for sale at all bookstores, even in the smaller places, for a century and a half. It was also used extensively outside of New England, it being essentially the book of the Dissenters in the American colonies. Sometimes it was printed under the title of *The Columbian Primer*, *The American Primer*, or, *The New York Primer*, but the public preferred *The New England Primer* to any other title. Its total sales have been estimated to have been at least three million copies.[1] It was used in the Boston Dame Schools as late as 1806, and in the country districts still later. The cities abandoned it first, and gradually it was replaced everywhere by a new type of secular reading book which developed in America, after the rise of a na-

[1] "For one hundred years this Primer was *the* schoolbook of the dissenters of America, and for another hundred, it was frequently reprinted. In the unfavorable locality (in a sectarian sense) of Philadelphia, the accounts of Benjamin Franklin and David Hall show that, between 1749 and 1766, that firm sold 37,100 copies of it. Livermore stated, in 1849, that within the last dozen years ' 100,000 copies of modern editions have been circulated.' An over-conservative claim for it is to estimate an annual average sale of 20,000 copies during a period of one hundred and fifty years, or a total sale of 3,000,000 copies." (Ford, *The New England Primer*, p. 45.)

tional consciousness and the beginning of the national life. Compared with the primers and first readers we have to-day it seems crude and extremely poor, but probably no modern textbook will ever exercise the influence which this early religious text exer-

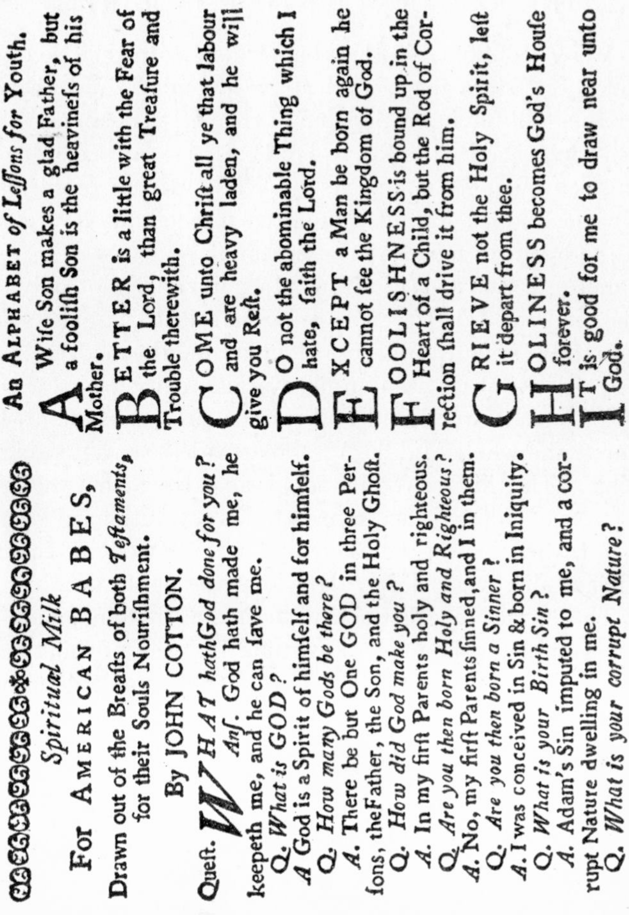

An **ALPHABET** of *Lessons for Youth.*

A Wise Son makes a glad Father, but a foolish Son is the heaviness of his Mother.

B ETTER is a little with the Fear of the Lord, than great Treasure and Trouble therewith.

C OME unto Christ all ye that labour and are heavy laden, and he will give you Rest.

D O not the abominable Thing which I hate, faith the Lord.

E XCEPT a Man be born again he cannot see the Kingdom of God.

F OOLISHNESS is bound up in the Heart of a Child, but the Rod of Correction shall drive it from him.

G RIEVE not the Holy Spirit, left it depart from thee.

H OLINESS becomes God's House forever.

I T is good for me to draw near unto God.

AN ALPHABET OF LESSONS FOR YOUTH.

Spiritual Milk

For AMERICAN BABES,

Drawn out of the Breasts of both *Testaments*, for their Souls Nourishment.

By JOHN COTTON.

Queft. W HAT hath God done for you?

A Anf. God hath made me, he keepeth me, and he can fave me.

Q. *What is GOD?*

A God is a Spirit of himfelf and for himfelf.

Q. *How many Gods be there?*

A. There be but One GOD in three Perfons, theFather, the Son, and the Holy Ghoft.

Q. *How did God make you?*

A. In my firft Parents holy and righteous.

Q. *Are you then born Holy and Righteous?*

A. No, my firft Parents finned, and I in them.

Q. *Are you then born a Sinner?*

A. I was conceived in Sin & born in Iniquity.

Q. *What's your Birth Sin?*

A. Adam's Sin imputed to me, and a corrupt Nature dwelling in me.

Q. *What is your corrupt Nature?*

FIRST PAGE OF JOHN COTTON'S "SPIRITUAL MILK"

FIG. 43. TWO OTHER PAGES FROM THE "NEW ENGLAND PRIMER"

---

cised over both children and adults during our colonial period. It has been said of it that "it taught millions to read, and not one to sin." The Psalter, the Testament, and the Bible were its natural continuation, and constituted the main further reading books in the schools of the colonies.

An inexpensive photographic reprint of an edition of 1727, with an historical introduction, is Paul Leicester Ford's *The New England Primer* (Dodd, Mead & Co., New York, 1899).

CHAPTER XVI
THE RISE OF SCIENTIFIC INQUIRY

THE Readings contained in this chapter deal with the rise of the study of the modern mathematical, astronomical, and physical sciences as a still further expression of the new critical, questioning spirit awakened by the Revival of Learning; the beginnings of modern scientific method, and its application to the problems of the universe; and the formulation of this method and its fruitfulness in the hands of modern investigators.

The first selection (**203**) is from Macaulay, and not only sets forth the fundamental defects of all ancient science, but also shows how the ancient scientific purpose differed from the modern. The seconds election (**204**), from an old German chronicle, is a good illustration of the wonderful and miraculous, which flourished throughout the whole Middle Ages and made scientific progress impossible. The third selection (**205**) is an extract from the dedicatory letter of Copernicus, prefixed to his revolutionary volume (1543) on the motions of the heavenly bodies. Modern scientific methods and discovery clearly date from the publication of this book. The extract reveals the new method of thinking, and is as clear an example of the modern attitude and way of thinking as was the work of Petrarch. The next extract (**206**), describing how Galileo discovered the satellites of Jupiter (1610), also is a wonderfully clear example of modern scientific reasoning.

Modern scientific investigation was unfortunate in its birth, in that it was ushered into the world just as the growing tolerance of the Church, which had marked the latter half of the fifteenth century and the opening years of the sixteenth, was changing to an attitude of suspicion and critical reaction as a result of the Protestant Revolts then sweeping Europe. In lands strongly Protestant this reaction manifested itself but slightly, and in England scarcely at all, but in strong Catholic countries, and especially in Italy, it strove to suppress new thinking as dangerous to orthodoxy. The Spanish Inquisition, a sort of mediæval inquisitorial grand jury, was revived, and became zealous in tracking down and punishing offenders. One of these was Galileo

Galilei, a professor at Pisa, who had made many remarkable scientific discoveries. For defending the Copernican theory he was called to Rome (1615), compelled to recant his "error" (1616) to escape the stake, and for daring later (1632) again to write on the theory was compelled to "abjure his error" (**207**), and was made a virtual prisoner of the Inquisition for the remainder of his life. The selection is introduced to show how far the forces of reaction were stimulated, a century after Magellan's voyage, spurred on by the religious hatreds and warfare then raging in Europe.

The two selections which conclude the chapter deal with the organizing work of Lord Francis Bacon. The first (**208**) is an extract from his famous *Novum Organum*, in which he sets forth some of the difficulties the new scholars of the time had to face. The second (**209**) is Lord Macaulay's estimate as to the importance for modern thought of the organizing work of Bacon.

203. Attitude of the Ancients toward Scientific Study

(T. B. Macaulay, Essay on Lord Bacon; *Edinburgh Review*, July, 1837. Also in his collected *Essays*)

Macaulay, in setting forth how completely Bacon's work was dominated by the desire that philosophy and science should bear fruit, draws the following contrast between the ideas as to scientific study held by the ancients and those aimed at by Bacon.

. . . The ancient philosophy disdained to be useful, and was content to be stationary. It dealt largely in theories of moral perfection, which were so sublime that they never could be more than theories; in attempts to solve insoluable enigmas; in exhortations to the attainment of unattainable frames of mind. It could not condescend to the humble office of ministering to the comfort of human beings. All the schools contemned that office as degrading; some censured it as immoral.

.   .   .   .

The ancient philosophers did not neglect natural science; but they did not cultivate it for the purpose of increasing the power and ameliorating the condition of man. The taint of barrenness had spread from ethical to physical speculations. Seneca wrote largely on natural philosophy, and magnified the importance of that study. But why? Not because it tended to assuage suffering, to multiply the conveniences of life, to extend the empire of man over the material world; but solely because it tended to raise the mind above low cares, to separate it from the body, to exercise its subtility in the solution of very obscure questions. Thus natural philosophy was considered in the light merely of a mental exercise. It was made subsidiary to the art of disputation; and it consequently proved altogether barren of useful discoveries.

. . . .

To sum up the whole, we should say that the aim of the Platonic philosophy was to exalt man into a god. The aim of the Baconian philosophy was to provide man with what he requires while he continues to be man. The aim of the Platonic philosophy was to raise us far above vulgar wants. The aim of the Baconian philosophy was to supply our vulgar wants. The former aim was noble; but the latter was attainable. Plato drew a good bow; but, like Ascestes in Vergil, he aimed at the stars; and therefore, though there was no want of strength or skill, the shot was thrown away. His arrow was indeed followed by a track of dazzling radience, but it struck nothing. . . . Bacon fixed his eye on a mark which was placed on the earth, and within bow shot, and hit it in the white. The philosophy of Plato began in words and ended in words, noble words indeed, words such as were to be expected from the finest of human intellects exercising boundless dominion over the finest of human languages. The philosophy of Bacon began in observations and ended in arts.

The boast of the ancient philosophers was that their doctrine formed the minds of men to a high degree of wisdom and virtue. This was indeed the only practical good which the most celebrated of those teachers even pretended to effect; and undoubtedly, if they had effected this, they would have deserved far higher praise than if they had discovered the most salutary medicines or constructed the most powerful machines. But the truth is that, in those very matters in which alone they professed to do any good to mankind, in those very matters for the sake of which they neglected the vulgar interests of mankind, they did nothing, or worse than nothing. They promised what was impracticable; they despised what was practicable; they filled the world with long words and long beards; and they left it as wicked and as ignorant as they found it.

204. The Credulity of Mediæval People

(Sebastian Franck's *Chronica*, published in 1531; trans. in Bax's *German Society at the Close of the Middle Ages*, pp. 268–71. London, 1894)

The following selection from this important German chronicle gives the reader a good illustration of the ready credulity of mediæval peoples, and their excessive excitability. Dating, as the extract does, from 1516, the year before the outbreak of the Protestant heresy, it presents an interesting picture of the mind of the later Middle Ages.

Anno 1516, Dr. Balthasar Hubmeyer did preach with vehemence against the Jews at Regensburg, showing how great an evil doth arise to the whole German nation, not alone from their faith, but also from their usury, and how unspeakable a tribute their usury doth bear away withal.   Then was there a Council held that they should pray the Emperor to the end that Jews might be driven forth.   Therefore did they (the people) break their synagogue in pieces, also many of their houses, and did build in the place thereof a Temple in honour of Mary, to which they gave the name of The Fair Mary.   This did some visit privily, and told that from that hour was their prayer fulfilled.   So soon, therefore, as the matter became noised abroad, even then was there a running from all parts thither, as though the people were bewitched, of wife, of child, of gentlemen, some spiritual, some worldly, they coming a long way, it might be having eaten nothing.   Certain children who knew not the road did come from afar with a piece of bread, and the people came with so manifold an armoury, even such as it chanced that each had, the while he was at his work, the one with a milking-pail, the other with a hay fork.   Some there were that had scarce aught in the greatest cold, wherewith to cover them in barest need.   Some there were that did run many miles without speaking, as they might be half-possessed or witless; some did come barefoot with rakes, axes and sickles; these had fled from the fields and forsaken their lords; some caméd in a shirt they had by chance laid hands on as they arose from their bed; some did come at midnight; some there were that ran day and night; and there was in all such a running from all lands that, in the space of but one day, many thousands of men had come in.

One there was that saw miracles from so much and so divers silver, gold, wax, pictures and jewels that were brought thither.   There were daily so many masses read that one priest could scarce but meet the other, as he departed from the altar.   When one did read the Communion (Commun), the other did kneel before the altar with his Confiteor.   These things came to pass daily till well-nigh beyond noon, and although many altars were set up both within and without the Temple, yet nevertheless could not one priest but encounter the other.

The learned did sing many Carmina in praise of Fair Mary, and many and divers offices were devised of signs, of pipes and of organs.   Much sick folk did they lead and bear hither, and also, as some do believe, dead men whom they brought home again restored and living.   There befel also many great signs and wonders, the which it would not be fitting to tell of, and whereof an especial cheat was rumoured, in that what any brought thither, did he but vow himself with his offering, straightway he was healed, not alone from his sickness, but the living did also receive also their dead again, the blind saw, the halt ran, did leave their crutches in the Temple, and walked right from thence. Some ran hither from the war; yea, wives from their husbands, children from the obedience and will of their fathers would hither, saying that they might not remain away, and that they had no rest day nor night.

Some as they entered into the Temple and beheld the image straightway fell down as though the thunder had smote them. As the mad rabble beheld how such did fall, they bethought them that it were the power of God, and that each must needs fall in this place. Thus there came to pass such a falling (such as was a foolishness and unrestrained and of the devils likeness) that well-nigh each that came to these places did fall and many from the rabble, who did not fall, believed themselves to be unholy and did enforce themselves straightway to fall, till the Council (Rath) was moved, as they say, to forbid such, and then did the signs and falling cease.

It is wondrous to relate with what strange instruments the people caméd thither; as one was seized in the midst of his labour, he took not the time to lay aside that which he held in his hand but bore it with him, and each ran unshrived away, being driven by his own spirit. But whether the great Holy Spirit did move to such ill-considered tumult against obedience, did drive the mother from the child, the wife from the husband, the servant and the child contrary to the obedience to be rendered to the master and father, I will leave to others to determine. Many do even believe as I do, that it cannot be the work of God inasmuch as it is contrary to His word, work, manner, nature and the interpretation of the Scriptures.

Now this running toward hath held a goodly season, as it may be six or eight years, but hath now ceased, albeit not wholly.

205. How Copernicus arrived at the Theory he set forth

(From the Dedicatory Letter of his *De Revolutionibus Orbium Celestium*, to Pope Paul III, 1543; trans. by Adams, *Yale Review*, vol. i, p. 141)

In a long dedicatory letter, in which he says that he has had the completed manuscript of his book in his study for thirty-six years, but has not published it because he has wished to "avoid theories altogether foreign to orthodoxy," and only does so now at the urgent solicitation of his friends, Copernicus explains to His Holiness how he came to evolve such a theory as he now advances. The steps in his thinking and arriving at his conclusions are well set forth in the following extract from the dedicatory letter, and form an excellent example of a new method of thinking and reasoning, itself thoroughly modern in character.

When I had for a long time thought upon the uncertainty of the traditional mathematical doctrine concerning the paths of the heavenly bodies it seemed to me very lamentable that still no more correct theory had been advanced by philosophers for the movements in that universe which the best and most perfect Architect had made for us, while they have so accurately investigated many relatively unimportant things.

Therefore I took the pains to read through the writings of all the philosophers that I could get together in order to find out if some one of them had not stated the opinion that the movements of the heavenly bodies might be other than the professional mathematicians had asserted. And I did find in reality first in Cicero that Nicetas had thought that the earth moves. Afterwards I read in Plutarch that some others also had been of this opinion. I will quote this passage that all may see it. Plutarch says: *The common opinion is that the earth stands still; but Philolaus the Pythagorean supposes that it moves about the Fire in an oblique circle like the sun and moon. Heraklides of Pontus and Exphantus also teach that the earth moves, not advancing however, but turning like a wheel so that from evening to morning it turns about its own center.*

FIG. 44.
NICHOLAS COPERNICUS
(1473–1543)

When I had received this suggestion I began myself also to meditate upon a motion of the earth. And although this theory might seem nonsensical, yet because I knew that to others before me the liberty had been allowed to suppose all sorts of circles in order to explain the phenomena in the heavens, so it would be permitted me also to try whether on the theory of the motion of the earth more satisfactory explanations than heretofore might not be found for the movements of the heavenly bodies.

After I had then assumed the motions which I assign to the earth in the following work, I found, after careful investigation extending through years, that if the movements of the other planets were referred to the motion of the earth in its orbit and reckoned according to the revolution of each star, not only could their observed phenomena be logically explained, but also the succession of the stars, and their size, and all their orbits, and the heavens themselves would present such a harmonious order that no single part could be changed without disarranging the others and the whole universe. In accordance with this theory I have drawn up the plan of my work.

206. Galileo's Discovery of the Satellites of Jupiter

(Brewster, David, *Martyrs of Science*. London, 1841)

The following selection is illustrative of the work of the early scientists, and shows the new basis for the study of phenomena and the methods of arriving at truth. Galileo was a professor at the University of Pisa, in Italy. Such discoveries were ill received by the followers of Aristotle.

On the 7th of January, 1610, at one o'clock in the morning, when Galileo directed his telescope to Jupiter, he observed three stars near the body of the planet, two being to the east and one to the west of him. They were all in a straight line, and parallel to the ecliptic and appeared brighter than other stars of the same magnitude. Believing them to be fixed stars, he paid no great attention to their distances from Jupiter and from one another. On the 8th of January, however, when, from some cause or other, he had been led to observe the stars again, he found a very different arrangement of them; all the three were on the west side of Jupiter, nearer one another than before and almost at equal distances. Though he had not turned his attention to the extraordinary fact of the mutual approach of the stars, yet he began to consider how

Jupiter could be found to the east of the three stars, when but the day before he had been to the west of two of them. The only explanation which he could give of this fact was that the motion of Jupiter was direct, contrary to the astronomical calculations, and that he had got before these two stars by his own motion.

In this dilemma between the testimony of his senses and the results of calculation, he waited for the following night with the utmost anxiety, but his hopes were disappointed, for the heavens were wholly veiled in clouds. On the 10th, two only of the stars appeared, and both on the east side of the planet. As it was obviously impossible that Jupiter could have advanced from west to east on the 8th of Jan-

FIG. 45
GALILEO GALILEI
(1564–1642)

uary, and from east to west on the 10th, Galileo was forced to conclude that the phenomenon which he had observed arose from the motion of the stars, and he set himself to observe diligently their change of place. On the 11th there were still only two stars, and both to the east of Jupiter, but the more eastern star was now twice as large as the other one, though on the preceding night they had been perfectly equal. This fact threw a new light on Galileo's difficulties, and he immediately drew the conclusion, which he considered to be indubitable, "that there were in the heavens three stars which revolve around Jupiter, in the same manner as Venus and Mercury revolve around the sun." On the 12th of January he again observed them in new positions, and of different magnitudes; and on the 13th he discovered a fourth star, which completed the four secondary planets with which Jupiter is surrounded.

207. The Abjuration of Galileo

(Routledge, R., *History of Science*, p. 123.   London, 1881)

The Copernican theory made a strong appeal to Galileo, and he expounded it with much fervor.   For this he was called to Rome by the Cardinals of the Inquisition, in 1615, who pronounced sentence (Routledge, pp. 119–22) against him; condemned the Copernican theory as "absurd in philosophy" and "expressly contrary to Holy Scripture"; and compelled him to recant (1616).   On the election of a new Pope who had been Galileo's friend he thought that, under the changed conditions, he might now be permitted larger liberty, and in 1632 he published his celebrated *Dialogue on the Two Chief Systems of the World, the Ptolemaic and the Copernican*, in which he took the Ptolemaic side, but upheld it only feebly.   For this he was again called to Rome, and compelled by the Inquisitorial body to recant and abjure, as follows:

I, Galileo Galilei, son of the late Vicenzo Galilei of Florence, aged seventy years, being brought personally to judgment, and kneeling before you, Most Eminent and Most Reverend Lords Cardinals, General Inquisitors of the universal Christian Republic against heretical depravity, having before my eyes the Holy Gospels, which I touch with my own hands, swear, that I have always believed, and now believe, and with the help of God will in future believe, every article which the Holy Catholic and Apostolic Church of Rome holds, teaches, and preaches.   But because I had been enjoined by this Holy Office altogether to abandon the false opinion which maintains that the sun is the center and immovable, and forbidden to hold, defend, or teach the said false doctrine in any manner, and after it had been signified to me that the said doctrine is repugnant with the Holy Scripture, I have written and printed a book, in which I treat of the same doctrine now condemned, and adduce reasons with great force in support of the same, without giving solution, and therefore have been judged grievously suspected of heresy; that is to say, that I held and believed that the sun is the center of the world and immovable, and that the sun is not the center and moveable.

Wishing, therefore, to remove from the minds of your Eminences, and of every Catholic Christian, this vehement suspicion rightfully entertained towards me, with a sincere heart and unfeigned faith, I abjure, curse, and detest the said errors and heresies, and generally every other error and sect contrary to the said Holy Church; and I swear that I will never more in future say or assert anything verbally, or in writing, which may give rise to a similar suspicion of me; but if I shall know any heretic, or any one suspected of heresy, that I will denounce him to this Holy Office, or to the Inquisitor and Ordinary of the place in which I may be.

I swear, moreover, and promise, that I will fulfil, and observe fully, all the penances which have been or shall be laid to me by this Holy Office. But if it shall happen that I violate any of my said promises, oaths, and protestations (which God avert!), I subject myself to all the pains and punishments which have been decreed and promulgated by the sacred canons, and other general and particular constitutions, against delinquents of this description. So may God help me, and His Holy Gospels, which I touch with my own hands.

I, the above-named Galileo Galilei, have abjured, sworn, promised, and bound myself, as above, and in witness thereof with my own hand have subscribed this present writing of my abjuration, which I have recited word for word. At Rome in the Convent of Minerva, 22d June, 1633.

I, Galileo Galilei, have abjured as above with my own hand.

208. Francis Bacon on Scientific Progress

(Francis Bacon, *Novum Organum*, book 1, lxxxviii–xc)

The great service of Francis Bacon to modern science lay in the formulation and statement of the inductive method of work and

thinking, and in pointing out the vast field of usefulness of such a method in discovering truth. This he did in his *Novum Organum*, published in 1620, so named because he regarded it as a great improvement over the deductive *Organon* of Aristotle, which had dominated all thinking during the later Middle Ages. In the following extract from this work Bacon sets forth the difficulties encountered by those who propose the use of new means of arriving at truth.

FIG. 46. FRANCIS BACON
(1561–1626)

We cannot, therefore, wonder that no magnificent Discoveries, worthy of mankind, have been brought to light, whilst men are satisfied and delighted with such scanty and puerile tasks, nay even think that they have pursued or attained some great object in their accomplishment.

lxxxix. Nor should we neglect to observe that Natural Philosophy has, in every age, met with a troublesome and difficult opponent: I mean Superstition, and a blind and immoderate zeal for Religion. For we see that among the *Greeks* those who first disclosed the natural causes of Thunder and Storms to the yet untrained ears of man, were condemned as guilty of impiety towards the Gods. Nor did some of the old Fathers of *Christianity* treat those much better who showed by the most positive proofs (such as no one now disputes) that the Earth is spherical, and thence asserted that there were Antipodes.

Even in the present state of things the condition of discussions on Natural philosophy is rendered more difficult and dangerous by the Summaries and Methods of Divines, who, after reducing Divinity into such order as they could, and bringing it into a Scientific form, have proceeded to mingle an undue proportion of the contentious and thorny Philosophy of *Aristotle* with the Substance of Religion.

.   .   .   .

xc.   Again, in the habits and regulations of Schools, Universities, and the like Assemblies, destined for the abode of learned men, and the improvement of learning, everything is found to be opposed to the progress of the Sciences. For the Lectures and Exercises are so ordered, that any thing out of the common track can scarcely enter the thoughts and contemplations of the mind. If, however, one or two have perhaps dared to use their liberty, they can only impose the labour on themselves, without deriving any advantage from the association of others: and if they put up with this, they will find their industry and spirit of no slight disadvantage to them in making their fortune. For the Pursuits of men in such situations are, as it were, chained down to the writings of particular Authors, and if any one dare to dissent from them, he is immediately attacked as a turbulent and revolutionary spirit. Yet how great is the difference between Civil Matters and the Arts; for there is not the same danger from new activity and new light. In Civil matters even a change for the better is suspected on account of the commotion it occasions; for Civil government is supported by authority, unanimity, fame, and public opinion, and not by demonstration. In the Arts and Sciences, on he contrary, every department should resound, as in mines, with new Works and advances. And this is the Rational, though not the actual, view of the case: for that administration and Government of Science we have spoken of, is wont too rigorously to repress its growth.

209. The Importance of Bacon's Work

(T. B. Macaulay, Essay on Lord Bacon; *Edinburgh Review*, July, 1837)

The following summary states well the importance of the work done by Bacon in formulating the inductive method of study.

. . . Bacon was not, as we have already seen, the inventor of the inductive method. He was not even the person who first analyzed the inductive method correctly, though he undoubtedly analyzed it more minutely than any who preceded him. He was not the person who first showed that by the inductive method alone new truth could be discovered. But he was the person who first turned the minds of speculative men, long occupied in verbal disputes, to the discovery of new and useful truth; and, by doing so, he at once gave to the inductive method an importance and dignity which had never before belonged to it. He was not the maker of that road; he was not the discoverer of that road; he was not the person who first surveyed and mapped that road. But he was the person who first called the public attention to an inexhaustible mine of wealth, which had been utterly neglected, and which was accessible by that road alone. By doing so, he caused that road, which had previously been trodden only by peasants and higglers, to be frequented by a higher class of travellers.

.   .   .   .

By stimulating men to the discovery of new truth, Bacon stimulated them to employ the inductive method, the only method, even the ancient philosophers and the schoolmen themselves being judges, by which new truth can be discovered. By stimulating men to the discovery of useful truth, he furnished them with a motive to perform the inductive process well and carefully. His predecessors had been, in his phrase, not interpreters, but anticipators of nature. They had been content with the first principles at which they had arrived by the most scanty and slovenly induction. And why was this? It was, we conceive, because their philosophy proposed to itself no practical end, because it was merely an exercise of the mind. A man who wants to contrive a new machine or a new medicine has a strong motive to observe accurately and patiently, and to try experiment after experiment. But a man who merely wants a theme for disputation or declamation has no such motive. He is therefore content with premises grounded on assumption, or on the most scanty and hasty induction. Thus, we conceive, the schoolmen acted. On their foolish premises they often argued with great ability; and as their object was "assensum subjugare, non res," to be victorious in controversy, not to be victorious over nature, they were consistent. For just as much logical skill could be shown in reasoning on false as on true premises. But the followers of the new philosophy, proposing to themselves the discovery of useful truth as their object, must have altogether failed of attaining the object if they had been content to build theories on superficial induction.

.   .   .   .

What Bacon did for inductive philosophy may, we think, be fairly stated thus. The objects of preceding speculators were objects which could be attained without careful induction. Those speculators, therefore, did not perform the inductive process carefully. Bacon stirred up men to pursue an object which could be attained only by induction, and by induction carefully performed; and consequently induction was more carefully performed. We do not think that the importance of what Bacon did for inductive philosophy has ever been overrated. But we think that the nature of his services is often mistaken, and was not fully understood even by himself. It was not by furnishing philosophers with rules for performing the inductive process well, but by furnishing them with a motive for performing it well, that he conferred so vast a benefit on society.

CHAPTER XVII

THE NEW SCIENTIFIC METHOD AND THE SCHOOLS

THE Readings contained in this chapter illustrate the application of the new scientific method to the theory and practice of the school, and show the influence exerted by it upon education. Before the eighteenth century this was not large, as the schools remained centers for the preservation of orthodoxy, and conservatively clung to religious instruction as their chief work. Still, some beginnings of importance were made, and these the Readings of this chapter have been selected to illustrate.

The influence of the new thinking manifested itself in three different stages, classified as:

1. *Humanistic realism;* that is, the attempt so to study the classics as to obtain useful knowledge from them.

2. *Social realism,* which largely rejected the learning of the schools as pedantic, and erected an ideal for the education of a gentleman in the affairs of the world by means of the new modern languages, studies, and travel.

3. *Sense realism,* which tried to turn the instruction in the schools to a study of real things, and the teaching of useful information.

Rabelais and Milton stand as examples of the first stage. The selection from Rabelais (210) shows him in sympathy with the best ideas of the age, though prudence compelled him to write as a clown and a fool. The two extracts from Milton give first (211) his statement of the new civic-religious aim of education, and second (212) the program of study he would follow to impart useful knowledge.

Social realism represents the reaction of the nobility and landed gentry against the education of the time. The selection from Adamson (213) states well the reasons for the discontent of these classes with the existing schools. Montaigne and Locke stand as the two most important exemplars of social realism. Both wrote at some length on the education of a gentleman's son, and the three extracts (214, 215, 216) serve well to give the point of view of each. Locke also later wrote an important report on the workhouse education of pauper children. His plan (**217**) was thoroughly typical of English practices, and can be read almost as well in connection with the English attitude as described in chapter XIII or chapter XVIII.

The great exponent of sense realism as applied to education was the Moravian teacher and bishop, Johann Amos Comenius. He was the dominating educational thinker of the seventeenth century, as well as one of the great figures in the history of all education. In a large volume entitled *The Great Didactic* he attempted an organization of the aim, purpose, principles, method, and desirable scope of education, and of this the title-page (**218**) and table of contents (**219**) are reproduced. To show still better the very modern character of his ideas, his plan for the organization of a *gymnasium*, outlined for the authorities at Saros-Patak, in Hungary (1650–54), is reproduced (**220**) in abbreviated form. Compared with the schools of his contemporaries in Europe this was modern in the extreme.

For the schools Comenius wrote a series of textbooks, by means of which the pupil learned not only Latin by a far better method, but also learned about the world of things besides. These textbooks were highly realistic in character. The introductory book, a primer and first reader known as the *Orbis Pictus*, was celebrated for two centuries and was translated into almost all languages. To show the character of this first illustrated schoolbook, a few sample pages, from three different editions of it, are reproduced (**221**). The commanding position of Comenius in the history of education has been well summed up by President Butler, from whose notable address a brief extract (**222**) is taken.

The attempt to introduce the new scientific studies into the schools made but slow headway. In the elementary schools little was done before the nineteenth century, and the same was largely true of the secondary schools, outside of Teutonic lands. In Germany a notable development came in the early establishment of *realschulen*, the need for which is set forth in the extract from Gesner (**223**). In the universities the new scientific learning obtained but little hearing before about the beginning of the eighteenth century. One of the early centers for mathematical and scientific studies was the University of Cambridge, concerning which two selections are introduced. One is a small handbill, under date of 1693 (**225**), in which an instructor offers to give certain scientific and mathematical courses privately; and the other is a scheme of study (224), printed in 1707, in which the mathematical and scientific courses then offered are listed.

210. Rabelais on the Nature of Education

(Rabelais, François, *Heroic Deeds of Pantagruel*, book II, chap. VIII; trans. by Urquhart. London, 1890)

François Rabelais was a French monk, curé, physician, and university scholar who was out of touch with his times, and who keenly satirized the mediæval follies and formalism of his age. In a satirical story of a giant and the education of his son, which he called the *Life of Gargantua* (1535) and the *Heroic Deeds of Pantagruel* (1533), he has given us, under the form of a letter from the giant to his son, his ideas as to the character of the education he thought desirable. This letter classifies Rabelais as a humanistic realist, in sympathy with the best ideas of the scholars of the Italian Renaissance. After a long introduction, the letter concludes as follows:

My dear son: . . . Thou art at Paris, where the laudable examples of many brave men may stir up thy mind to gallant actions, and hast likewise for thy tutor and pedagogue the learned Epistemon, who by his lively and vocal arguments may instruct thee in the arts and sciences.

I intend, and will have it so, that thou learn the languages perfectly; first of all, the Greek, as Quintilian will have it; secondly, the Latin;

FIG. 47
FRANÇOIS RABELAIS
(1483–1553)

and then the Hebrew, for the Holy Scripture-sake; and then the Chaldee and Arabic likewise, and that thou frame thy style in Greek in imitation of Plato; and for the Latin, after Cicero. Let there be no history which thou shalt not have ready in thy memory; — unto the prosecuting of which design, books of cosmography will be very conducible, and help thee much. Of the liberal arts of geometry, arithmetic, and music, I gave thee some taste when thou wert yet little, and not above five or six years old. Proceed further in them, and learn the remainder if thou canst. As for astronomy, study all the rules thereof. Let pass, nevertheless, the divining and judicial astrology, and the arts of Lullius, as being nothing else but plain abuses and vanities. As for the civil law, of that I would have thee to know the fair texts by heart, and then to confer them with philosophy.

Now, in the matter of the knowledge of the works of nature, I would have thee study that exactly; that so there be no sea, river, nor fountain, of which thou dost not know the fishes; all the fowls of the air; all the several kinds of shrubs and trees, whether in forest or orchards; all the sorts of herbs and flowers that grow upon the ground; all the various metals that are hid within the bowels of the earth; together with all the diversity of precious stones, that are to be seen in the orient and south parts of the world. Let nothing of all these be hidden from thee. Then fail not most carefully to peruse the books of the Greek, Arabian, and Latin physicians, not despising the Talmudists and Cabalists; and by frequent anatomies get thee the perfect knowledge of that other world, called the microcosm, which is man. And at some of the hours of the day apply thy mind to the study of the Holy Scriptures; first, in Greek, the New Testament, with the Epistles of the Apostles; and then the Old Testament in Hebrew. In brief, let me see thee an abyss, and bottomless pit of knowledge; for from henceforward, as thou growest great and becomest a man, thou must part from this tranquillity and rest of study, thou must learn chivalry, warfare, and the exercises of the field, the better thereby to defend my house and our friends, and to succor and protect them at all their needs, against the invasion and assaults of evil-doers.

Furthermore I will that very shortly thou try how much thou hast profited, which thou canst not better do, than by maintaining publicly theses and conclusions in all arts, against all persons whatsoever, and by haunting the company of learned men, both at Paris and otherwhere. ... Reverence thy preceptors: shun the conversation of those whom thou desirest not to resemble; and receive not in vain the graces which God hath bestowed upon thee. And, when thou shalt see that thou hast attained to all the knowledge that is to be acquired in that part, return unto me, that I may see thee, and give thee my blessing before I die. My son, the peace and grace of our Lord be with thee, Amen.

Thy Father

GARGANTUA

From Utopia, the 17th day of the month of March

211. Milton's Statement of the Aim and Purpose of Education

(John Milton, Tractate on Education. London, ed. of 1673)

John Milton (1608–74), the English poet and friend of humanity, science, and education, published, in 1644, a little book of twenty-three pages which he called a *Tractate on Education*. In it he defined education, both as to aim and means and scope, as follows:

The end then of Learning is to repair the ruines of our first Parents by regaining to know God aright, and out of that knowledge to love him, to imitate him, to be like him, as we may the neerest by possessing our souls of true vertue, which being united to the heavenly grace of faith makes up the highest perfection.

But because our understanding cannot in this body found it self but on sensible things, nor arrive so clearly to the knowledge of God and things invisible, as by orderly conning over the visible and inferior creature, the same method is necessarily to be followed in all discreet teaching.

And seeing every Nation affords not experience and tradition enough for all kinds of Learning, therefore we are chiefly taught the Languages of those people who have at any time been most industrious after Wisdom; so that Language is but the Instrument conveying to us things usefull to be known.

And though a Linguist should pride himself to have all the Tongues that *Babel* cleft the world into, yet, if he have not studied the solid things in them as well as the Words & Lexicons, he were nothing so much to be esteem'd a learned man, as any Yeoman or Tradesman competently wise in his Mother Dialect only. . . .

I call therefore a compleat and generous Education that which fits a man to perform justly, skilfully and magnanimously all the offices both private and publick of Peace and War.

212. Milton's Program for Study

(John Milton, *Tractate on Education*. London, ed. of 1673)

In the *Tractate* Milton outlines his ideas as to the content of a humanistic-realistic course of instruction for "noble and gentle youth," covering the years from twelve to twenty-one, as follows:

For their Studies, First they should begin with the chief and necessary rules of some good Grammar, either that now us'd (Lily's), or any better. . . . Next to make them expert in the usefullest points of Grammar, . . . some easie and delightful Book of Education would be read to them; whereof the Greeks have store, as *Cebes, Plutarch,* and other Socratic discourses. But in Latin we have none of classic authority extant, except the two or three first Books of *Quintilian,* and some select pieces elsewhere. . . . At the same time, some other hour of the day, might be taught to them the rules of Arithmetick, and soon after the Elements of Geometry even playing, as the old manner was. After evening repast, till bed-time their thoughts will be best taken up in the easie grounds of Religion, and the story of the Scriptures.

The next step (13 to 16) would be to the Authors of *Agriculture, Cato, Varro,* and *Columella,* for the matter is most easie, and if the language be difficult, so much the better, it is not a difficulty above their years. And here will be an occasion of inciting and inabling them hereafter to improve the tillage of their Country, to recover the bad Soil, and to remedy the waste that is made of good; for this was one of *Hercules* praises. Ere half these Authors be read they cannot chuse but be masters of any ordinary prose. So that it will be then seasonable for them to learn in any modern Author, the use of Globes, and all the Maps; first with the old names, and then with the new: or they might be then capable to read any compendious method of natural Philosophy. And at the same time might be entering the Greek tongue, after the same manner as was before prescrib'd in the Latin; whereby the difficulties of Grammar being soon overcome, all the Historical Physiology of *Aristotle* and *Theophrastus* are open before them, and as I may say, under contribution. The like access will be to *Vitruvius*, to *Seneca's* natural questions, to *Mela*, *Celsus*, *Pliny*, or *Solinus*.[1] And having thus past the principles of *Arithmetick*, *Geometry*, *Astronomy* and *Geography* with a general campact of Physicks, they may descend in *Mathematicks* to the instrumental science of *Trigonometry*, and from thence to Fortification, Architecture, Enginry, or Navigation. And in Natural Philosophy they may proceed leisurely from the History of Meteors, Minerals, plants and living Creatures as far as Anatomy (Aristotle).

FIG. 48. JOHN MILTON (1608–76)

Then also in course might be read to them out of some not tedious Writer the Institution of Physic; that they may know the tempers, the humours, the seasons, and how to manage a crudity: which he can wisely and timely do, is not only a great Physitian to himself, and to his friends, but also at some time or other, save an Army by this frugal and expenseless means only; and not let the healthy and stout bodies of young men rot away under him for want of this discipline; which is a great pity, and no less a shame to the Commander. To set forward all these proceedings in Nature and Mathematicks, what hinders, but that they may procure, as oft as shal be needful, the helpful experiences of Hunters, Fowlers, Fishermen, Shepherds, Gardeners, Apothecaries; and in other sciences, Architects, Engineers, Mariners, Anatomists; who doubtless would be ready some for reward, and some to favour such a hopeful Seminary. And this will give them such a real tincture of natural knowledge, as they shall never forget, but daily augment with delight. Then also those poets which are now counted most hard, will be both facil and pleasant, *Orpheus, Hesiod,*

---

[1] Vitruvius wrote on architecture, Seneca on natural philosophy, Mela wrote a geography, Celsus wrote eight books on medicine, Pliny wrote thirty-seven books on natural history, and Solinus wrote an abridged Pliny.

Theocritus, *Aratus*, *Nicander*, *Oppian*, *Dionysius*, and in Latin *Lucretius*, *Manilius*, and the rural part of *Vergil*.

By this time (15 or 16) . . . they may with some judgment contemplate upon moral good and evil. Then will be requir'd a special reinforcement of constant and sound endoctrinating to set them right and firm, instructing them more amply in the knowledge of Vertue and the hatred of Vice; while their young and pliant affections are led through all the moral works of *Plato*, *Xenophon*, *Cicero*, *Plutarch*, *Laertius*, and those *Locrian* remnents; but still to be reduct in their nightward studies wherewith they close the dayes work, under the determinate sentence of *David* or *Solomon*, or the Evange(l)s and Apostolic Scriptures. Being perfect in the knowledge of personal duty, they may then begin the study of Economics. And either now, or before this, they may have easily learnt at any odd hour the *Italian Tongue*. And soon after, but with wariness and good antidote, it wou d be wholesome enough to let them taste some choice Comedies, Greek, Latin, or *Italian:* Those Tragedies also that treat of Household matters, as *Trachiniæ*, *Alcestis*, and the like. The next remove must be to the study of *Politicks;* to know the beginning, end, and reason of Political Societies; that they may not in a dangerous fit of the Common-wealth be such poor, shaken, and uncertain Reeds, of such a tottering Conscience, as many of our great Counsellers have lately shewn themselves, but stedfast pillars of the State.

After this they are to dive into the grounds of Law, and legal Justice; deliver'd first, and with best warrant by *Moses*, and as far as humane prudence can be trusted, in those extoll'd remains of Grecian Lawgivers. *Licurgus*, *Solon*, *Zaleucus*, *Charondas*, and thence to all the Roman *Edicts* and Tables with their *Justinian;* and so down to the *Saxon* and common Laws of *England*, and the Statutes. Sundayes also and every evening may be now understandingly spent in the highest matters of *Theology*, and Church History ancient and modern: and ere this time the Hebrew Tongue at a set hour might have been gain'd, that the Scriptures may be now read in their own original; whereto it would be no impossibility to add the *Chaldey*, and the *Syrian* Dialect. When all these employments are well conquer'd, then will the choice Histories, *Heroic Poems*, and *Attic* Tragedies of stateliest and most regal argument, with all the famous Political Orations offer themselves; which if they were not only read; But some of them got by memory, and solemly pronounc't with right accent, and grace, as might be taught, would endue them even with the spirit and vigor of *Demosthenes* or *Cicero*, *Euripides*, or *Sophocles*.

And now lastly will be the time to read with them those organic arts which inable men to discourse and write perspicuously, elegantly, and according to the fitted stile of lofty, mean, or lowly. Logic therefore so much as is useful, is to be refer'd to this due place with all her well coucht Heads and Topics, untill it be time to open her contracted palm into a gracefull and ornate Rhetorick taught out of the rule of *Plato*, *Aristotle, Phalareus, Cicero, Hermogones, Longinus*. To which Poetry would be made subsequent, or indeed rather precedent, as being suttle and fine, but more simple, sensuous and passionate. I mean not here the prosody of verse, which they could not but have hit on before among the rudiments of Grammar; but that sublime Art which in *Aristitles Poetics*, in *Horace*, and the *Italian* Commentaries of *Castelvetro, Tasso, Mazzoni*, and others, teaches what the laws are of a true Epic Poem, what of a *Dramatic*, what of a *Lyric*, what Decomum is, which is the grand master-piece to observe. This would make them soon perceive what despicable creatures our comm(on) Rimers and Playwriters be, and shew them, what religious, what glorious and magnificent use might be made of Poetry both in divine and humane things. From hence and not till now will be the right season of forming them to be able Writers and Composers in every excellent matter, when they shall be thus fraught with an universal insight into things. Or whether they be to speak in Parliament or Counsel, honour and attention would be waiting on their lips. There would then also appear in Pulpits other Visages, other gestures, and stuff otherwise wrought then what we now sit under, oft times to as great a trial of our patience as any other that they preach to us. These are the Studies wherin our noble and our gentle youth ought to bestow their time in a disciplinary way from twelve to one and twenty; unless they rely more upon their ancestors dead, then upon themselves living.

213. Discontent of the Nobility with the Schools

(Adamson, J. W., *Pioneers of Modern Education*, pp. 177–79. Cambridge, 1905)

The following extract from a recent English writer gives an excellent brief statement as to why the nobility and gentry of the latter part of the sixteenth, and the beginning of the seventeenth, century, turned away from the humanistic schools of their time to the tutor-in-the-home, and to a finishing education in the courtly Academies which characterized the seventeenth and early eighteenth centuries in France, Italy, and German lands.

. . . The discontent with conventional education felt by Montaigne, a recluse when public life was turbulent, was shared by many of his order when more peaceful days arrived and, with them, opportunities to enjoy the elegancies of life.

At a time when travel had become familiar to the leisured class, and the grand tour constituted the crown of a wealthy man's education, the schools did not concern themselves with modern tongues. They exhibited as little interest in those scientific studies, experiments, and inventions, which were so generally in men's thoughts during the six-teen-hundreds, that it became almost "the mode" to dabble in anat-omy, chemistry, or some branch of physics. The schools left the fu-ture soldier ignorant of mathematics as pure science very frequently, and almost always in its practical application to engineering, fortifica-tion, and the like; at school and university the future statesman re-ceived from the *official* round of studies no express training in jurispru-dence, politics, or state-craft generally, regarded as an actual science to be applied, there and then, to life and government. Certain arts, as drawing, painting, music, carving, and other forms of manual skill, were highly esteemed as accomplishments throughout European society in the mid-seventeenth century; the schools did nothing to make their attainment easy. The courtier aimed at a high standard of skill in riding, fencing, and dancing; the ordinary round of instruction gave him no help in these, nor in genealogy and heraldry, nor in the more scholastic studies of history and geography. As for the courtier's all-important study of *conduite*, the art of conversation, compliment, bear-ing, and dress, it was usually supposed that the schools fostered an in-tolerable pedantry quite incompatible with any such elegancies. The collocation of "scholar and gentleman" was a later and an English conception; for the time we are considering Montaigne represents the common opinion in his antithesis of logician (or grammarian) and man of birth.

Courtly education and scholastic education, therefore, fell apart, and the rift grew wider as the seventeenth century advanced and the court of Louis XIV became the model for all courts. The children of the great and noble ceased to attend school, and received their education from private tutors at home, completing the course, in the case of young men, at special establishments called *Academies*, in which the ideals of the courtly education were finally embodied.

The demand for "accomplishments," chiefly of a martial kind, first brought these Academies into being in France, where, during the clos-ing years of the sixteenth century, they began as schools of arms and horsemanship. . . .

214. Montaigne ridicules the Humanistic Pedants

(Michel Seigneur de Montaigne, Essay on the *Education of Children*, 1580; *Essays* book I, chap. XXIV. Florio's translation, 1632)

In 1580 Montaigne published the first volume of his famous *Essays* in French; the first English edition being that of 1603. In the essay on *Pedantry* (chap. XXIV) he ridicules the humanistic type of education which had become common in his time, and the intellectual stupidity which resulted from such training. The following is a typical extract.

If a man passe by, crie out to our people; *Oh what a wise man goeth yonder!* And of another: *Oh what a good man is yonder!* He will not faile to cast his eyes and respect toward the former. A third crier were needful, to say, *Oh what blocke-heads are those!* We are ever readie to aske, *Hath he any skill in the Greeke and Latine tongue? can he write well? doth hee write in prose or verse?* But whether hee be growne better or wiser, which should be the chiefest of his drift, that is never spoken of, we should rather enquire who is better wise, than who is more wise. We labour, and toyle, and plod to fill the memorie, and leave both understanding and conscience emptie. Even as birds flutter and skip from field to field to pecke up corne, or any graine, and without tasting the same, carrie it in their bils, therewith to feed their little ones; so doe our pedants gleane and picke learning from bookes, and never lodge it further than their lips, only to degorge and cast it to the wind.

215. Montaigne's Conception of Education

(Montaigne, Essay on the *Education of Children*, 1580; *Essays*, book I, chap. xxv)

In the next essay, which is in the form of a letter to a lady friend who desired his advice on the *Education of Children,* Montaigne sets forth in some detail his conception of a practical education for a youth of noble birth. In this essay he broke completely with the humanists, and stood clearly for an education of the judgment and understanding — one that would prepare for proper life in the world of things and men. The following extracts from this essay are typical.

FIG. 49
MICHEL DE MONTAIGNE
(1533–92)

A friend of mine then, having read the preceding chapter, the other day told me, that I should a little longer have insisted upon the education of children. . . . But, in truth, all I understand as to that particular is only this, that the greatest and most important difficulty of human science is the education of children. . . .

For a boy of quality, then, who pretends to letters not upon account of profit, nor so much for outward ornament, as for his own proper and peculiar use, and to furnish and enrich himself within, having rather a desire to go out an accomplished cavalier and a fine gentleman, than a mere scholar and a learned man; for such a one, I say, I would also have his friends solicitous to find him out a tutor, who has rather a well-made than a well-filled head; seeking, indeed, both if such a person can be found, but rather to prefer his manners and his judgment before mere learning, and that this man should exercise his charge after a new method.

'T is the custom of schoolmasters to be eternally thundering in their pupils' ears, as they were pouring into a funnel, whilst their business is only to repeat what others have said before: now I would have a tutor to correct this error, and that at the very first, he should, according to the capacity he has to deal with, put it to the test, permitting his pupil to taste and relish things, and of himself to choose and discern them, sometimes opening the way to him, and sometimes leaving him to break the ice himself; that is, I would not have him alone invent and speak, but that he should also hear his pupil speak in turn. Let him make him examine and thoroughly sift every thing he reads, and lodge nothing in his fancy upon simple authority and trust. Aristotle's principles will then be no more principles to him than those of Epicurus and the Stoics: let this diversity of opinions be propounded to and laid before him, he will himself choose, if he is able; if not, he will remain in doubt. For if he embraces the opinions of Xenephon and Plato by his own reason, they will no more be theirs, but become his own. Who follows another follows nothing, finds nothing, nay, is inquisitive after nothing. Let him, at least, know what he knows. It will be necessary that he imbibe their knowledge, not that he be corrupted by their precepts; and no matter if he forget where he had his learning, provided he know how to apply it to his own use. Truth and reason are common to every one, and are no more his who spake them first, than his who speaks them after. . . . To know by rote is no knowledge, and signifies no more but only to retain what one has entrusted to one's memory. That which a man rightly knows and understands, he is free dispenser of at his own full liberty, without any regard to the author from whom he had it, or fumbling over the leaves of his book. A mere bookish learning is both troublesome and ungraceful; and though it may serve for some kind of ornament, there is yet no foundation for any superstructure to be built upon it. . . .

They begin to teach us to live when we have almost done living. The boy we would breed has a great deal less time to spare; he owes but the first fifteen or sixteen years of his life to education; the remainder is due to action: let us therefore employ that short time in necessary instruction. Away with logical subtleties, they are abuses, things by which our lives can never be amended: take the plain philosophical discourses, learn first how rightly to choose, and then rightly to apply them; they are more easy to understand than one of Boccaccio's novels; a child from nurse is much more capable of them than of learning to read and write. Philosophy has discourses equally proper for childhood as for the decrepit age of man. . . .

I would not have this pupil of ours imprisoned and made a slave to his book; nor would I have him given up to the morosity and melancholic humor of a sour, ill-natured pedant.   I would not have his spirit cowed and subdued by applying him to the rack and tormenting him, as some do, fourteen or fifteen hours a day, and so make a pack-horse of him. . . . I would have his outward fashion and mein, and the disposition of his limbs, formed at the same time as his mind. 'T is not a soul, 't is not a body that we are training up, but a man, and we ought not to divide him.   And, as Plato says, we are not to fashion one without the other, but make them draw together like two horses hitched to a coach. . . .

With such a one, after fifteen or sixteen years' study, compare one of our college (secondary school) Latinists, who has thrown away so much time in learning nothing but to speak.   The world is nothing but babble; and I hardly ever yet saw that man who did not rather prate too much, than speak too little; and yet half our age is embezzled this way.   We are kept four or five years to learn words only, and to tack them together into clauses; as many more to form them into long discourse, divided into four or five parts; and other five years at least to learn succinctly to mix and interweave them after a subtle and intricate manner.   Let us leave all this to those who make a profession of it. . . . We do not pretend to breed a grammarian or a logician, but a gentleman; let us leave them to throw away their time at their own fancy: our business lies elsewhere. . . .

No doubt but Greek and Latin are very great ornaments, and of very great use, but we buy them too dear: Not that fine speaking is not a very good and commendable quality; but not so excellent and so necessary as some would make it; and I am scandalized that our whole life should be spent in nothing else.   I would first understand my own language, and that of my neighbors with whom most of my business and conversation lies. . . .

To return to my subject, there is nothing like alluring the appetite and affections; otherwise you make nothing but so many asses laden with books, and by dint of your lash, you give them their pocketful of learning to keep; whereas, to do well, you should not only lodge it with them, but make them espouse it.

216. Locke's Thoughts on Education

(Locke, John, *Some Thoughts Concerning Education*.   London, 1693)

The English philosopher, John Locke, a B.A. from Christ's Church College at Oxford, had for a time (1677–83) served as a tutor to two boys of noble birth.   For his political activity he was exiled (1683–89) during the latter days of the reign of Charles II, and went to Holland to live.   While there he corresponded with his friend, William Clark, an English M.P., on the bringing-up of a boy of good birth and station in life, and after his return to England the letters were edited and published (1693) under the title of *Some Thoughts on Education*. He wrote exclusively on the education of a gentleman by the private-tutor method, and described the practices of English upper-class society rather than the practices of the schools.

The treatise is quite lengthy, and deals with such subjects as

FIG. 50. JOHN LOCKE
(1632–1704)

clothing, diet, habits, punishments, re-wards, manners, good breeding, recrea-tions, requisites of a gentleman, intellec-tual education, the mother tongue, Latin and Greek, recreation, and travel. The following extract is typical and illustrative of Locke's point of view.

As the Father's Example must teach the Child Respect for his Tutor, so the Tutor's Example must lead the Child into those Ac-tions he would have him do. His Practice must by no means cross his Precepts, unless he intend to set him wrong. It will be to no Purpose for the Tutor to talk of the Restraint of the Passions whilst any of his own are let loose; and he will in vain endeavour to reform any Vice or Indecency in his Pupil, which he allows in himself. Ill Patterns are sure to be follow'd more than good Rules; . . .

In all the whole Business of Education, there is nothing like to be less hearken'd to, or harder to be well observ'd, than what I am now going to say; and that is, that Children should, from their first begin-ning to talk, have some *discreet*, *sober*, nay, *wise* Person about them, whose Care it should be to fashion them aright, and keep them from all Ill, especially the infection of bad company. I think this province re-quires great *Sobriety*, *Temperance*, *Tenderness*, *Diligence*, and *Discre-tion;* Qualities hardly to be found united in Persons that are to be had for ordinary Salaries, nor easily to be found any where. . . .

The Consideration of Charge ought not to deter those who are able. The great Difficulty will be where to find a *proper* Person: For those of small Age, Parts, and Vertue, are unfit for this Employment, and those that have greater, will hardly be got to undertake such a Charge. You must therefore look out early, and enquire every where; for the World has People of all Sorts. . . .

. . . one fit to educate and form the Mind of a young Gentleman is not every where to be found, and more than ordinary Care is to be taken in the Choice of him, or else you may fail of your End.

The Character of a sober Man and a Scholar is, as I have above observ'd, what every one expects in a Tutor. This generally is thought enough, and is all that Parents commonly look for: But when such an one has Empty'd out into his Pupil all the Latin and Logick he has brought from the University, will that Furniture make him a fine Gentleman? Or can it be expected, that he should be better bred, better skill'd in the World, better principled in the Grounds and Foundations of true Virtue and Generosity, than his young *Tutor* is?

To form a young Gentleman as he should be, 't is fit his *Governor* should himself be well-bred, understanding the Ways of Carriage and Measures of Civility in all the Variety of Persons, Times, and Places; and keep his Pupil, as much as his Age requires, constantly to the Observation of them. This is an Art not to be learnt nor taught by Books. Nothing can give it but good Company and Observation join'd together. The Taylor may make his Clothes modish, and the Dancing-master give Fashion to his Motions; yet neither of these, tho' they set off well, make a well-bred Gentleman: No, tho' he have Learning, to boot, which, if not well manag'd, makes him more impertinent and intolerable in Conversation. Breeding is that which sets a Gloss upon all his other good Qualities, and renders them useful to him, in procuring him the Esteem and Good-will of all that he comes near. Without good Breeding his other Accomplishments make him pass but for proud, conceited, vain, or foolish.

Courage in an ill-bred Man has the Air and escape not the Opinion of Brutality: Learning becomes Pedantry; Wit, Buffoonry Plainness, Rusticity; good Nature, Fawning. And there cannot be a good Quality in him, which Want of Breeding will not warp and disfigure to his Disadvantage.

. . . .

Besides being well-bred, the *Tutor* should know the World well; the Ways, the Humours, the Follies, the Cheats, the Faults of the Age he is fallen into, and particularly of the Country he lives in. These he should be able to shew to his Pupil, as he finds him capable; teach him skill in Men, and their Manners; pull off the Mask which their several Callings and Pretences cover them with, and make his pupil discern what lies at the Bottom under such Appearances. . . . that when he comes to launch into the Deep himself, he may not be like one at Sea without a Line, Compass, or Sea-Chart; but may have some Notice before-hand of the Rocks and Shoals, the Currents and Quick-sands, and know a little how to steer, that he sink not before he get Experience. . . .

A great Part of the Learning now in Fashion in the Schools of *Europe*, and that goes ordinarily into the Round of Education, a Gentleman may in a good Measure be unfurnish'd with, without any great

Disparagement to himself or Prejudice to his Affairs. But Prudence and good breeding are in all the Stations and Occurrences of Life necessary; and most young Men suffer in want of them, and come rawer and more awkwa d into the World than they should, for this very Reason, because these Qualities, which are of all other the most necessary to be taught, and stand most in need of the Assistance and Help of a Teacher, are generally neglected and thought but a slight or no Part of a *Tutor's* Business. Latin and Learning make all the Noise; and the main Stress is laid upon his Proficiency in Things a great Part whereof belong not to a Gentleman's Calling; which is to have the Knowledge of a Man of Business, a Carriage suitable to his Rank, and be eminent and useful in his Country, according to his Station. . . .

The great Work of a *Governor*, is to fashion the Carriage, and form the Mind; to settle in his Pupil good Habits and the Principles of Virtue and Wisdom; to give him by little and little a View of Mankind, and to work him into a Love and Imitation of what is excellent and praise-worthy; and, in the Prosecution of it, to give him Vigour, Activity, and Industry. The Studies which he sets him upon, are but as it were the Exercises of his Faculties, and Employment of his Time, to keep him from Sauntering and Idleness, to teach him Application, and accustom him to take Pains, and to give him some little Taste of what his own Industry must perfect. For who expects, that under a *Tutor* a young Gentleman should be an accomplish'd Critick, Orator, or Logician? go to the Bottom of Metaphysicks, natural Philosophy, or Mathematicks? or be a Master in History or Chronology? though something of each of these is to be taught him: But it is only to open the Door, that he may look in, and as it were begin an acquaintance, but not to dwell there: And a Governor would be much blam'd that should keep his Pupil too long, and lead him too far in most of them. But of good Breeding, Knowledge of the World, Virtue, Industry, and a Love of Reputation, he cannot have too much: And if he have these, he will not long want what he needs or desires of the other.

. . . We learn not to live, but to dispute; and our Education fits us rather for the University than the World. But 't is no wonder if those who make the Fashion suit it to what they have, and not to what their Pupils want. The Fashion being once establish'd, who can think it strange, that in this, as well as in all other Things, it should prevail? . . . Reason, if consulted with, would advise, that their Children's Time should be spent in acquiring what might be useful to them when they come to be Men, rather than to have their heads stuff'd with a deal of Trash, a great Part whereof they usually never do ('t is certain they never need to) think on again as long as they live; and so much of it as does stick by them they are only the worse for. This is so well known, that I appeal to Parents themselves, who have been at Cost to have their young Heirs taught it, whether it be not ridiculous for their Sons to have any Tincture of that Sort of Learning, when they come abroad into the World? whether any Appearance of it would not lessen and disgrace them in Company? And that certainly must be an admirable Acquisition, and deserves well to make a Part in Education, which Men are asham'd of where they are most concern'd to shew their Parts and Breeding.

217. Locke's Plan for Working-Schools for Poor Children

(Fox Bourne, H. R., *Life of John Locke*, vol. ii, p. 383. London, 1876)

When the English philosopher, John Locke, was sixty-four years old (1696), his high sense of duty induced him to accept an appointment from the King, as Commissioner of Trade and Plantations. In connection with his work in this office he prepared a plan for bringing up the children of paupers. While the plan as proposed was never adopted, it is nevertheless so typical of English attitudes and practices with reference to the education of the children of the poor, and states so clearly the ideas of compulsory education and compulsory taxation, that it is included here as an important document relating to the education of the children of the poor and compulsory taxation therefor.

The children of labouring people are an ordinary burden to the parish, and are usually maintained in idleness, so that their labour is generally lost to the public till they are twelve or fourteen years old.

The most effectual remedy for this that we are able to conceive, and which we therefore humbly propose, is, that, in the fore-mentioned new law to be enacted, it be further provided that working schools be set up in every parish, to which the children of all such as demand relief of the parish, above three and under fourteen years of age, whilst they live at home with their parents, and are not otherwise employed for their livelihood by the allowance of the overseers of the poor, shall be obliged to come.

By this means the mother will be eased of a great part of her trouble in looking after and providing for them at home, and so be at the more liberty to work; the children will be kept in much better order, be better provided for, and from infancy be inured to work, which is of no small consequence to the making of them sober and industrious all their lives after; and the parish will be either eased of this burden or at least of the misuse in the present management of it. For, a great number of children giving a poor man a title to an allowance from the parish, this allowance is given once a week or once a month to the father in money which he not seldom spends on himself at the alehouse, whilst his children, for whose sake he had it, are left to suffer, or perish under the want of necessaries, unless the charity of neighbours relieve them.

We humbly conceive that a man and his wife in health may be able by their ordinary labour to maintain themselves and two children. More than two children at one time under the age of three years will seldom happen in one family. If therefore all the children above three years old be taken off from their hands, those who have never so many, whilst they remain themselves in health, will not need any allowance for them.

We do not suppose that children of three years old will be able at that age to get their livelihoods at the working school, but we are sure that what is necessary for their relief will more effectually have that use if it be distributed to them in bread at that school than if it be given to their fathers in money. What they have at home from their parents is seldom more than bread and water, and that, many of them, very scantily too. If therefore care be taken that they have each of them their belly-full of bread daily at school, they will be in no danger of famishing, but, on the contrary, they will be healthier and stronger than those who are bred otherwise. Nor will this practice cost the overseers any trouble; for a baker may be agreed with to furnish and bring into the school-house every day the allowance of bread necessary for all the scholars that are there. And to this may be also added, without any trouble, in cold weather, if it be thought needful, a little warm water-gruel; for the same fire that warms the room may be made use of to boil a pot of it.

From this method the children will not only reap the fore-mentioned advantages with far less charge to the parish than what is now done for them, but they will be also thereby the more obliged to come to school and apply themselves to work, because otherwise they will have no victuals, and also the benefit thereby both to themselves and the parish will daily increase; for, the earnings of their labour at school every day increasing, it may reasonably be concluded that, computing all the earnings of a child during that whole time will cost the parish nothing; whereas there is no child now which from its birth is maintained by the parish but, before the age of fourteen, costs the parish £50 or £60.

Another advantage also of bringing children thus to a working school is that by this means they may be obliged to come constantly to church every Sunday, along with their schoolmasters or dames, whereby they may be brought into some sense of religion; whereas ordinarily now, in their idle and loose way of breeding up, they are as utter strangers both to religion and morality as they are to industry.

In order therefore to the more effectual carrying on of this work to the advantage of this kingdom, we further humbly propose that these schools be generally for spinning and knitting, or some other part of the woolen manufacture, unless in countries (that is, districts) where the place shall furnish some other materials fitter for the employment of such poor children; in which places the choice of those materials for their employment may be left to the prudence and direction of the guardians of the poor of that hundred. And that the teachers in these schools be paid out of the poor's rate, as can be agreed.

This, though at first setting up may cost the parish a little, yet we humbly conceive (the earnings of the children abating the charge of their maintenance, and as much work being required of each of them as they are reasonably able to perform) it will quickly pay its own charges with an overplus.

That, where the number of the poor children of any parish is greater than for them all to be employed in one school they be there divided into two, and the boys and girls, if thought convenient, taught and kept to work separately.

That the handicraftsmen in each hundred be bound to take every other of their respective apprentices from amongst the boys in some one of the schools in the said hundred without any money; which boys they may so take at what age they please, to be bound to them till the age of twenty-three years, that so the length of time may more than make amends for the usual sums that are given to handicraftsmen with such apprentices.

That those also in the hundred who keep in their hands land of their own to the value of £25 per annum, or upwards, or who rent £50 per annum, or upwards, may choose out of the schools of the said hundred what boy each of them pleases, to be his apprentice in husbandry on the same condition.

That whatever boys are not by this means bound out apprentices before they are full fourteen shall, at the Easter meeting of the guardians of each hundred every year, be bound to such gentlemen, yeomen, or farmers within the said hundred as have the greatest number of acres of land in their hands, who shall be obliged to take them for their apprentices till the age of twenty-three, or bind them out at their own cost to some handicraftsmen; provided always that no such gentlemen, yeomen, or farmer shall be bound to have two such apprentices at one time.

That grown people also (to take away their pretence of want of work) may come to the said working schools to learn, where work shall accordingly be provided for them.

That the materials to be employed in these schools and among other the poor people of the parish be provided by a common stock in each hundred, to be raised out of a certain portion of the poor's rate of each parish as requisite; which stock, we humbly conceive, need be raised but once, for, if rightly managed, it will increase.

218. Title-Page of Comenius's *Great Didactic*

(First English edition, from the original Latin edition. Edited by M. W. Keatinge. London, 1896)

The following title-page indicates well the nature of the treatise.

The Great Didactic

Setting forth

The whole Art of Teaching all Things to all Men

or

A certain Inducement to found such Schools in all the Parishes, Towns, and Villages of every Christian Kingdom, that the entire Youth of both Sexes, none being excepted, shall

Quickly, Pleasantly, & Thoroughly

Become learned in the Sciences, pure in Morals, trained to Piety, and in this manner instructed in all things necessary for the present and for the future life,

in which, with respect to everything that is suggested,

Its FUNDAMENTAL PRINCIPLES are set forth from the essential nature of the matter,

Its TRUTH is proved by examples from the several mechanical arts,

Its ORDER is clearly set forth in years, months, days, and hours, and, finally,

AN EASY AND SURE METHOD is shown, by which it can be pleasantly brought into existence.

219. Table of Contents of Comenius's *Great Didactic*

(First English edition, from the original Latin edition.   Edited by M. W. Keatinge.
London, 1896)

The chapter titles indicate well the plan and scope of this celebrated manual of school organization and instruction.   To show still better the five important divisions into which the treatise is divided, these are stated as division headings, though such do not appear on the Contents page.

Division 1. The aim and purpose of education.

<table>
<tr><td>Chapter</td><td>I.</td><td>Man is the highest, the most absolute, and the most excellent of things created.</td></tr>
<tr><td></td><td>II.</td><td>The ultimate end of man is beyond this life.</td></tr>
<tr><td></td><td>III.</td><td>This life is but a preparation for eternity.</td></tr>
<tr><td></td><td>IV.</td><td>There are three stages in the preparation for eternity: to know oneself (and with oneself all things); to rule oneself; and to direct oneself to God.</td></tr>
<tr><td></td><td>V.</td><td>The seeds of these three (learning, virtue, religion) are naturally implanted in us.</td></tr>
</table>

Division 2. The necessity for the education of all.

<table>
<tr><td>Chapter</td><td>VI.</td><td>If a man is to be produced, it is necessary that he be formed by education.</td></tr>
<tr><td></td><td>VII.</td><td>A man can most easily be formed in early youth, and cannot be formed properly except at this age.</td></tr>
<tr><td></td><td>VIII.</td><td>The young must be educated in common, and for this schools are necessary.</td></tr>
<tr><td></td><td>IX.</td><td>All the young of both sexes should be sent to school.</td></tr>
<tr><td></td><td>X.</td><td>The instruction given in schools should be universal.</td></tr>
</table>

Division 3. The principles underlying school reform.

<table>
<tr><td>Chapter</td><td>XI.</td><td>Hitherto there have been no perfect schools.</td></tr>
<tr><td></td><td>XII.</td><td>It is possible to reform schools.</td></tr>
<tr><td></td><td>XIII.</td><td>The basis of school reform must be exact order in all things.</td></tr>
<tr><td></td><td>XIV.</td><td>The exact order of instruction must be borrowed from nature.</td></tr>
<tr><td></td><td>XV.</td><td>The basis of the prolongation of life.</td></tr>
<tr><td></td><td>XVI.</td><td>The universal requirements of teaching and of learning; that is to say, a method of teaching</td></tr>
</table>

and of learning with such certainty that the desired result must of necessity follow.

XVII. The principles of facility in teaching and in learning.

XVIII. The principles of thoroughness in teaching and in learning.

XIX. The principles of conciseness and rapidity in teaching.

Division 4. The method of instruction.

Chapter   XX. The method of the sciences.

XXI. The method of the arts.

XXII. The method of languages.

XXIII. The method of morals.

XXIV. The method of instilling piety.

XXV. If we wish to reform schools in accordance with the laws of true Christianity, we must remove from them books written by pagans, or, at any rate, must use them with more caution than hitherto.

XXVI. Of school discipline.

Division 5. The organization of instruction.

Chapter   XXVII. Of the four-fold division of schools, based on age and acquirements.

XXVIII. Sketch of the Mother-School.

XXIX. Sketch of the Vernacular-School.

XXX. Sketch of the Latin-School.

XXXI. Of the University, of travelling students, of the College of Light.

XXXII. Of the universal and perfect order of instruction.

XXXIII. Of the things requisite before this universal method can be put into practice.

220. Comenius's Plan for the Gymnasium at Saros-Patak

(Abridged from the outline given in the Introduction to Keatinge's edition of *The Great Didactic*, pp. 140–47)

The following is an abridged outline of Comenius's plan for the *gymnasium* at Saros-Patak, in Hungary, drawn up by him for the authorities during his stay there, covering the years 1650–54. Compared with the celebrated plans of Sturm (**R. 137**) and Calvin (**R. 175**), or the schools of the Jesuits, the modern character of Comenius's proposal is evident. We also find here the new scientific studies receiving due recognition.

Class I. The Vestibular

1. Over the door is to be written:
   "Let no one enter who cannot read."
2. Walls of classroom to have printed on them the Latin alphabet, chief declensions and conjugations, and short maxims relating to conduct.
3. Catechism, hymns, and prayers to be learned.
4. Class book, the *Vestibulum*.
5. Mathematics, elements of arithmetic, point, and line.
6. Music, scales and keys.
7. History, as contained in the *Vestibulum*.
8. Style, construction of sentences.
9. Accessory studies, handwriting and drawing.
10. Games, as suitable to age of pupils.
11. Closing exhibition, and examination.

Class II. The Janual

1. Over the door is to be written:
   "Let no one enter who is ignorant of numbers."
2. On two walls, pictures of objects studied in the *Janua;* on the other two, grammatical rules.
3. Catechism to be thoroughly learned.
4. Class book, the *Janua*, the Latin-Vernacular dictionary, and the Janual Grammar.
5. Mathematics, addition and subtraction, and plane figures in Geometry.
6. Music, more advanced than in Class I.
7. History, as contained in the *Janua*.
8. Style, structure of phrases, sentences, and periods.
9. Games, as chosen by the master.
10. Closing exhibition, pupils to ask one another questions on the *Janua*.

Class III. The Atrial

1. Over the door is to be written:
   "Let no one enter who cannot speak."
2. Walls to be covered with diagrams and maxims of speech.
3. Bible, in an abridged form, to be read and expounded.
4. Class books, the *Atrium*, the *Grammar of Elegance*, and the Latin-Latin dictionary written for the *Atrium*.
5. Mathematics, multiplication and division; the table of Cebes; and solid figures in geometry.
6. Music, harmony. Rudiments of Latin verse.
7. History, famous deeds from the Bible.
8. Style, paraphrasing and transposing.

9. Recreation, at fixed hours.
10. Dramatic selections from the *Schola Ludus*.
11. Boys now to be able to read and speak Latin fluently.

Class IV. *The Philosophical*

1. Over the door is to be written:
   "Let no one ignorant of history enter here."
2. Walls to carry diagrams from arithmetic, geometry, and statics. Adjoining the classroom to be a dissecting room, and a chemical laboratory.
3. New Testament study of the life of Christ and the Apostles; a special collection of hymns and psalms.
4. Class book, the *Palace of Wisdom*, describing natural phenomena.
5. Mathematics, rules of proportion; trigonometry and the elements of statics to be begun.
6. Music, instrumental.
7. History, natural history from Pliny and Ælian.
8. Greek to be begun, and New Testament and selected Greek authors to be read.
9. Recreation not to be neglected, but fewer games.
10. Dramatic performance, using a play dealing with philosophy.

Class V. *The Logical*

1. Over the door is to be written:
   "Let no one enter who is ignorant of natural philosophy."
2. Walls to be covered with rules of logic.
3. Hymns, psalms, and prayers. A Bible manual, *The Gate of the Sanctuary*, to be placed in the pupil's hands. This to contain the whole Scripture history, and to afford reading for the year.
4. Class book, one dealing with the human mind:
   (*a*) Things discovered and to be discovered.
   (*b*) Formal logic.
   (*c*) Mental problems.
5. Mathematics, partnership, alligation, and position in arithmetic; heights, distances, and plane surfaces in geometry.
6. Geography and astronomy, the earth and heavens.
7. Optics.
8. History, of mechanical inventions.
9. Style, exercises from Cornelius Nepos, Cæsar, Curtius, and Justin.
10. Greek, Isocrates and Plutarch.
11. Dramatic performance, illustrating contest between grammar, logic, and metaphysics, and their final reconciliation.

Class VI. *The Political*

1. Over the door is to be written:
   "Let no one enter who cannot reason."

2. Wall pictures to illustrate order and limitation; human body, perfect and imperfect.
3. The whole Bible to be read.
4. Class book, one to deal with human society and the laws of economics.
5. Mathematics, Logistic in arithmetic, and Architectonic in geometry to be learned.
6. Geography and astronomy to be continued, with special attention to theory of planets and laws of eclipses.
7. History, that of the church ritual.
8. Style, readings from Sallust, Cicero, Vergil, and Horace. Compositions in verse permitted, but *not* to be insisted upon.
9. Greek, Thucydides and Hesiod.
10. Play, suitable recreations.
11. Dramatic performance, representing degeneration of Solomon and his moral downfall.

Class VII. The Theological

1. Over the door is to be written:
    "Let no one enter who is irreligious."
2. Walls to be covered with Hebrew and sacred symbols.
3. Devotional psalms and hymns, and a compendium of Christian belief.
4. Class book, to deal with communion of souls with God.
    (*a*) The ascent of the mind to God, following order of *Janua.*
    (*b*) Practical rules for the study of the Scriptures.
    (*c*) A Repertory of Theology, and mysteries of salvation.
5. Mathematics, sacred and mystic numbers in arithmetic, sacred architecture as exemplified in the Ark, Tabernacle, and Temple.
6. History of the church.
7. Oratorical training, for training in preaching.
8. Hebrew to be studied, and Old Testament read.
9. Recreation, as needed.
10. Religious plays, illustrating character of Abraham, David, etc.

221. Comenius's *Orbis Pictus*

In 1658 there appeared, from the presses at Nuremberg, the first school picture-book ever printed. It was an introductory reader for learning Latin, and was entitled *Orbis Sensualium Pictus,* or "The World of Sense Objects Pictured." In it Comenius not only simplified greatly the teaching of Latin, but he shifted the whole emphasis from words to things, and made the teaching of scientific knowledge and useful information a key-note of the book. The success of the book was immediate. It was reprinted in all European lands, and was used as an introductory Latin textbook for nearly two centuries. An American edition was issued in New York as late as 1810.

The following sample pages (Figures 51, 52, 53) illustrate the nature of the book. The page opposite is from a Nuremberg Latin-German edition of 1740; the two pages below reproduce, in reduced form, the title-page and the first page of the alphabet from the English-Latin edition of 1727; and the last page is from the New York edition of 1810.

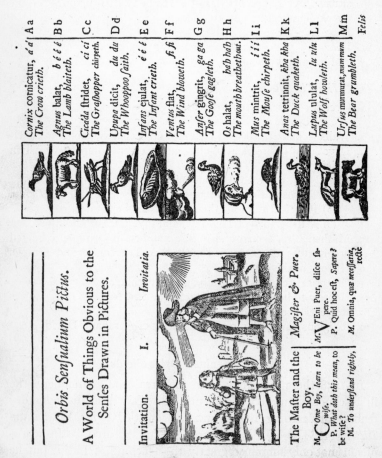

FIG. 51. TWO PAGES FROM THE "ORBIS PICTUS"

The first page, in the edition of 1727. The third page, from the same edition

(199)

Schola 1 f. 1. est officina, f. 1. in qua novelli animi ad *virtutem* formantur; & distinguitur in *classes.*	Die Schul 1 ist eine Werckstatt/ in welcher die jungen Gemüther zur Tugend angewöh (net werden; und wird abgetheilt in Classen.	Novellus, a, um, jung, (neu.) Animus, m. 2. das Gemüt Virtus, f. 3. die Tugend. Classis, f. 3. die Claß.
Præceptor 2 m. 3. sedet in *cathedrâ:* 3 *discipuli* 4 in *subselliis;* 5 ille docet, hi discunt.	Der Schulmeister 2 sitzt auf dem Lehrstul; 3 die Schüler 4 auf Bäncken; 5 jener lehret, diese lernen.	Cathedra. f. 1. der Lehr stul. Discipulus, m. 2. der Schuler. Subsellium, n. 2. die Banck.
Quidam præscribuntur illis cretâ in *tabellâ.* 6	Etliches (den wird ihnen vorgeschrie mit der Kreide an der Tafel. 6	Creta, f. 1. die Kreide. Tabella, f. 1. die Tafel.
Quidam sedent ad *mensam,* & scribunt: 7 Ipse corrigit 8 *menda.*	Etliche sitzen am Tische/ und schreiben: 7. Er verbessert 8 die Fehler.	Mensa, f. 1. der Tisch. Menda, f. 1. & um, n. 2. die Fehler.
Quidam stant, & recitant, memoriæ mandata. 9	Etliche stehen, und sagen her, was sie gelernet. 9	Memória, f. 1. das Ge dächtnis.
Quidam confabu (lantur. 10 ac gerunt se petulantes & negligentes: hi castigantur ferulâ (baculô) 11 & virgâ. 12	Etliche schwätzen, 10 und erzeigen sich muthwillig und unfleißig: die werden gezüchtigt mit dem Backel 11 und der Ruthe/ 12	Pétulans, o. 3 muthwillig Négligens, o. 3. unfleißig. Férula, f. 1. (Báculus, m. 2. & um, n. 2.) der Ba ckel, (Stecken.) Virga, f. 1. die Ruthe.

FIG. 52. A SCHOOL IN COMENIUS'S TIME

Facsimile of a page in the *Orbis Pictus.* Reproduced from a copy of the Nuremberg Latin-German edition of 1740, now in the Hildebrand Library at Stanford University

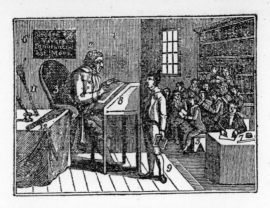

A *School*, 1.
is a Shop in which
Young Wits are fashion'd
to vertue, and it is
distinguished into *Forms*.

The *Master*, 2.
sitteth in a *Chair*, 3.
the *Scholars*, 4.
in *Forms*, 5.
he teacheth, they learn.

Some things
are writ down before them
with *Chalk* on a *Table*, 6.

Some sit
at a Table, and write, 7.
he mendeth their Faults, 8.

Some stand and rehearse
things committed to
memory, 9.

Some talk together, 10.
and behave themselves
wantonly and carelessly;
these are chastised
with a *Ferrula*, 11.
and a *Rod*, 12.

Schola, 1.
est Officina, in quâ
Novelli Animi formantur
ad virtutem, &
distinguitur in *Classes*.

Praeceptor, 2.
sedet in *Cathedrâ*, 3.
Discipuli, 4.
in *Subselliis*, 5.
ille docet, hi discunt.

Quaedam
praescribuntur illis
Cretâ in *Tabellâ*, 6.

Quidam sedent
ad Mensam, & scribunt, 7.
ipse corrigit Mendas, 8.

Quidam stant, & reci-
tant mandata
memoriae, 9.

Quidam confabulantur,
10.   ac gerunt se
petulantes, & negligentes;
hi castigantur
Ferulâ (baculô), 11.
& *Virgâ*, 12.

FIG. 53. AN AMERICAN "ORBIS PICTUS"

Facsimile of a page from the first American edition of the *Orbis Pictus*, printed in New York in 1810. This was an American reprint of the twelfth English edition. The illustrations were redrawn in New York, and in the process of redrawing were very much modernized.

222. The Place of Comenius in the History of Education

(Butler, N. M., An Address; *Proc. N.E.A.*, 1892, pp. 723–28)

The year 1892 marked the three hundredth anniversary of the birth of Comenius, and at the meeting of the National Education Association of that year Dr. Nicholas Murray Butler gave a very able address on his place in history. From this address the following concluding paragraphs have been selected.

The robust and practical character of the proposals of Comenius is most apparent when they are contrasted with the educational doctrines of those who have come after him, particularly Locke, Rousseau, Pestalozzi, and Froebel. Frail as the psychology of Comenius was, it was truer than that of Locke. He knew that the human mind was an organism, an activity, a seed with wonderful potency of growth and development, and not a mere sheet of wax, as the Englishman taught, on whose passive surface the environment merely leaves certain impressions or traces. Locke's thought was of the education of the gentleman; Comenius proclaimed that education was for the race. The single point in which Locke corrected Comenius was in exalting character rather than knowledge as the chief aim in education.

Of Rousseau one may say with Mr. Quick, "His writings and the results produced by them are among the strangest things in history; and especially in matters of education it is more than doubtful if the wise man of the world Montaigne, the Christian philanthropist Comenius, or that 'slave of truth and reason' Locke, had half as much influence as this depraved serving-man." Rousseau's enthusiasm took the form of theory run mad, and the practical impossibility of his educational plans was only exceeded by their philosophical unsoundness. Comenius had been himself a teacher and an organizer of schools. He knew the practical limitations under which any theory is put when reduced to practice. He asked of the school and the pupil nothing that was impossible. He accepted society as he found it and would teach it to reform itself. Rousseau would blow it into a million atoms and deify each.

There is nothing in the history of education so touching as the story of the life of Pestalozzi. His own immortal words, "I lived like a beggar to teach beggars to live like men," only half reveal the story of his unwearied patience, his intense suffering, his self-sacrifices for childhood. His life gave reality to his half-mystical principle that "the essential principle of education is not teaching; it is love." Yet his thought is relatively unimportant. Pestalozzi gave himself to education, but few new principles. His theory of the value of intuition needs to be carefully supplemented, and his insistence on the fact that education is development, a drawing-out and not a putting in, merely repeats the thought on which all the work of Comenius was based. Without that principle, which Comenius had made familiar more than a century before, the work of Pestalozzi would have been of little importance in the history of education. Indeed, it would have been philanthropy merely, not education.

Nor does it detract from the estimate to be put upon Froebel's teachings to say that in almost every important particular they were built upon the foundations laid by the Moravian bishop. Froebel himself was strangely deficient in masculinity and in practical capacity. His exaggerated and absurd symbolism and his unbalanced religiosity, give a certain curious interest and stimulus to his doctrines, but add nothing to their force or their permanent value. His seed-thought is again that of Comenius — Educate by developing the pupil's own activity. Out of it and its corollaries the new education has grown.

The place of Comenius in the history of education, therefore, is one of commanding importance. He introduces and dominates the whole modern movement in the field of elementary and secondary education. His relation to our present teaching is similar to that held by Copernicus and Newton toward modern science, and Bacon and Descartes toward modern philosophy. Yet he was not, in a high sense, an original mind. But his spirit was essentially modern and remarkably receptive. He assimilated the ideas that were inspiring the new civilization and applied them to the school.

223. The Need for *Realschulen* for the New Classes to be educated

(Gesner, J. M., *Minor German Works*, p. 355)

The following extract from a pamphlet entitled *Thoughts on the Organization of a Gymnasium*, published in 1756, by Johann Matthias Gesner (1691–1761), a famous professor of the classics at the new University of Göttingen, is illustrative of the feeling of need which had at that time come to be felt in German lands for a separate type of education for those boys not destined for a scholarly career.

It is a common fault of most of our schools, that in them provision is made only for such as intend to become what are called learned men by profession; and thus a complete acquaintance with Latin is required of all young people, without any distinction. On the contrary, those things are for the most part neglected, which would be indispensable, or at least useful, in common civil life, in the arts and professions, at court and in war. . . . A well-organized gymnasium should, on the contrary, be so arranged that youth, of every extraction, age, character, and distinction, may find their account there, and be taught in them for the common good. Youth may be, with reference to their future life, divided into three classes. 1. Those who are to learn trades, arts, or to be merchants; 2. Those who are to seek their fortune at court or in war; and, 3. Those who are to remain students, and to go to the university.

224. A Cambridge Scheme of Study of 1707

(Wordsworth, Chr., *Scholæ Academicæ*, Appendix IV. Cambridge, 1877)

In 1707, one Robert Green, a fellow of Clare College (B.A., 1699; M.A., 1703), printed *A Scheme of Study*, which contained advice as to what and when and how to study. In addition to the study of Latin, Greek, Ancient History, the Gospels, Sermons, Religious History, and Christian Evidences, with practice in writing and disputing in Latin, he also advised a very liberal program of mathematics and scientific study, which is given below. The program is very interesting as revealing the hold the new scientific learning had obtained at Cambridge by 1707. In few universities at that time could so liberal an offering be found.

The mathematical and scientific studies recommended were as follows:

FIRST YEAR

Second half.
　1. Chronology and Geography, with study of maps.

SECOND YEAR

First half.
　1. Logick — *Burgerdicius, Locke.*
　2. Geometry, Elements of — *Euclid, Sturmius.*
Second half.
　1. Arithmetic.
　2. Algebra.
　3. Corpuscular Philosophy — *Cartes, Varenius, Boyle.*

THIRD YEAR

First half.
　1. Experimental Philosophy, and Chemistry of Minerals, Plants, and Animals — *Philosophical Transactions, Boyle.*
　2. Anatomy of
　　　(*a*) Animals — *Keil, Gibson, Harvey,* etc.
　　　(*b*) Plants and Vegetables — *Grew, Philosophical Transactions.*
　　　(*c*) Minerals — *Hook's Micrograph, Lowenhock.*

Second half.

1. Opticks, Dioptricks, Caloptricks, Colours, Iris — *Newton, Cartes, Kepler,* etc.
2. Conick Sections, and the Nature of Curves — *Newton, Wallis,* etc.

FOURTH YEAR

First half.

1. Mechanical Philosophy, Staticks, Hydrostaticks, Flux and Reflux, Percussion, Gravitation, etc. — *Marriot, Hugens, Boyle, Newton, Wallis,* etc.
2. Fluxions (Calculus), Infinite Series, Arithmetick of Infinites — *Wallis, Newton,* etc.

Second half.

1. Astronomy, Spherical, Hypothetical, Practical, and Physical — *Mercator, Flamstead, Newton, Kepler,* etc.
2. Logarithms and Trigonometry — *Sturmius, Briggs, Newton,* etc.

225. How the New Scientific Studies were begun at Cambridge

(A handbill, reproduced from Chr. Wordsworth's *Scholæ Academicæ*, pp. 254-55. Cambridge, 1877)

The handbill reproduced on the opposite page is illustrative of the way in which the new scientific and mathematical studies first found their way into the universities. Vince was an instructor at the time, and offered the courses as extras. Three years later he was made a professor, and continued to lecture on the same subjects.

Cambridge, Oct. 10, 1793.

On Monday, Nov. 18, at *four* o'Clock in the Afternoon,

The Rev. *S. Vince*, A.M., F.R.S.,

Proposes to begin his *Philosophical Course* of Public Lectures in the *Principles* of the *Four Branches of Natural Philosophy*, with the Application to a great Variety of *Problems*, and on the *Principia* of Sr. I. Newton, with the most useful *deductions*.

To be continued every Monday, Wednesday, and Friday.

That Part of the Course which contains the Lectures on the *Principia*, will for the Conveniency of those who shall then have commenced Sophs, be given at the End of the present and Beginning of the next Term.

And on Tuesday, Nov. 19, at the same Hour, he proposes to begin his *Mathematical Course* of Public Lectures on the Principles of *Arithmetic, Algebra, Fluxions, Trigonometry, plain* and *spherical, Logarithms, Ratios,* &c., &c.

To be continued every Tuesday, Thursday, and Saturday. Each Course to be attended a second Time gratis.

Terms of attendance are 5 Guineas for each Course. They who purpose to attend are requested to send in their names.

CHAPTER XVIII

THEORY AND PRACTICE BY THE MIDDLE OF THE EIGHTEENTH CENTURY

THE Readings of this chapter have been selected first to illustrate the development of educational theory up to the time of Rousseau, and second to illustrate the conditions and practices in the vernacular schools as they had developed up to about 1750.

In the preceding chapters Readings have been given to illustrate ancient and mediæval educational theories; the theories of the Reformation leaders have also been set forth at some length; and in the chapter just before this one the development of educational theory in the sixteenth and seventeenth centuries was illustrated. In this chapter the work of Mulcaster is illustrated by reproducing the table of contents of his *Positions* (226), to show what he attempted to set forth; and the ideas as to education of John Locke are further illustrated by two additional selections, one on the method of teaching Latin (227) and one on the use of the Bible as a reading book (228).

All the remaining Readings of the chapter are given to illustrate the status of elementary education by about the middle of the eighteenth century. The first (229) reproduces the title-pages of two of the earliest spellers, as these show quite well the nature of the volumes and the rather broad purpose they were designed to serve. The next five selections are contemporary pen-pictures of schools and school work, R. 230 describing a common type of American school of about 1760; R. 231 the teachers in the famous Duchy of Gotha (R. 163), as they were in 1741; R. 232 gives a picture of popular education in Sweden during the eighteenth century; R. 233 is an interesting comment on school conditions and the proprietary rights of teachers in the city of Frankfurt-am-Main; R. 234 gives an interesting description of an examination for a teacher's position, in 1793, in Switzerland; and R. 235 reproduces a number of literary descriptions of that famous English institution — the Dame School. Reading 236 is an agreement with a parochial-school teacher, and indicates the nature of his duties and the sources of his emoluments.

The five Readings which follow relate to the establishment of the English religious charity-schools. The first (237) gives the Minutes relating to the establishment of one of the earliest of these schools. The second reproduces first (238 a) the qualifications for a master in such a school and the next (238 b) describes the purpose and nature of the instruction. The third Reading (239) gives a list of the textbooks used in the S.P.C.K. schools, and reproduces the title-pages of two of these books. The fourth (240) is a subscription form for maintaining a charity-school. This subscription form also is illustrative of the means of support for many semi-public schools, in the latter part of the eighteenth century and the early nineteenth as well. The fifth selection (241) is typical of many charity-schools for girls established by the church parishes in England during the eighteenth century.

The Indenture of Apprenticeship (242) is an eighteenth-century document, and shows the form these had taken by 1708. Compare this with Readings 99, 200 a-b, and 201. Reading 243, which follows, shows that the apprenticeship idea was followed even in the training of schoolmasters. The next Reading (244) is an interesting description of the instruction and discipline in the schools of Germany in the eighteenth century, while the one which follows (245) is illustrative of English discipline in the same century, and shows its impartial nature in the careful classification of offenses and punishments. Reading 246, together with 236, describes early methods of school support.

226. Table of Contents of Mulcaster's *Positions*

(Mulcaster, Richard, *Positions*. London, 1581. Reprint, edited by R. H. Quick. London, 1887)

In 1581 there appeared in London a book of more than ordinary importance, "Written by Richard Mulcaster, Master of the Schools erected in London Anno. 1561, in the parish of Sainct Laurence Povvntneie, by the vvorshipfull Companie of the Merchaunt Tailers of the said Citie." It was entitled:

POSITIONS
WHERIN THOSE
PRIMITIVE CIRCUMSTANCES
BE EXAMINED, WHICH ARE
NECESSARIE FOR THE TRAINING
vp of children, either for skill in their
booke, or health in their bodie.

The book was written in a heavy, stilted style, and in rather prolix English, and awakened but little interest. The ideas which Mulcaster advanced, though, were so far in advance of his age that, as Quick well says, educational progress would have been advanced materially had the world listened to this London schoolmaster. The most remarkable ideas of the book are contained in chapters 4–6, 36–38, and 41.

The table of contents of the volume give a rather good idea as to the reforms he proposed. Summarized, these are:

13–19. On talking, silence, laughing, weeping, holding breath, dancing, wrestling, fencing, top, and scourge.

20–27. On walking, running, leaping, swimming, riding, hunting, shooting, and play of ball.

28–34. On nature, quality, time, place, manner, and quantity of exercise.

35. On the master. Importance of good teachers in the beginning years.

36. That both yong boyes, and yong maidens are to be put to learne. Whether all boyes be to be set to schoole. That to many learned be burdenous: to few to bare: wittes well sorted ciuill: missorted seditious. That all may learne to write and reade without daunger. The good of choice, the ill of confusion. The children which are set to learne hauing either rich or poore freindes, what order and choice is to be vsed in admitting either of them to learne. Of the time to chuse.

37. The meanes to restraine the ouerflowing multitude of scholers. The cause why euery one desireth, to haue his childe learned, and yet must yeilde ouer his owne desire to the disposition of his countrie. That necessitie and choice be the best restrainers. That necessitie restraineth by lacke and law. Why it may be admitted that all may learne to writ and reade that can, but no further. What is to be thought of the speaking and vnderstanding of latine, and in what degree of learning that is. That considering our time, and the state of religion in our time law must needes helpe this restraint, with the aunswere to such obiections as are made to the contrarie. That in choice of wittes, which must deale with learning, that wit is fittest for our state which aunswereth best the monarchie, and how such a wit is to be knowne. That choice is to helpe in schooling, in admission into colledges, in proceding to degrees, in preferring to liuings, where the right and wrong of all the foure pointes be handled at full.

38. That yong maidens are to be set to learning, which is proued by the custome of our countrie, by our duetie towardes them, by their naturall abilitie, and by the worthie effectes of such, as haue bene well trained. The ende whereunto their education serueth, which is the cause why and how much they learne. Which of them are to learne. When they are to beginne to learne: What and how much they may learne. Of whom and where they ought to be taught.

39–40. Of the training of young gentlemen; public and private education; travel; types of schools.

41. Of teachers and trainers in generall: and that they be either Elementarie, Grammattical, or Academicall. Of the elemen-

tarie teachers abilitie and entertainement: of the grammar maisters abilitie and his entertainement. A meane to haue both excellent teachers and cunning professours in all kindes of learning: by the diuision of colledges according to professions: by sorting like yeares into the same rowmes: by bettering the studentes allowance and liuing: by prouiding and maintaining notable well learned readers. That for bringing learning forward in her right and best course, there would be seuen ordinarie ascending colledges for tounges, for mathematikes, for philosophie, for teachers, for physicians, for lawyers, for diuines. And that the generall studie of law, would be but onc studie. Euery of these points with his particular proufes sufficient for a position. On the admission of teachers.

42–45. The elementarie years; school management; school faults; parent and teacher coöperation; and peroration.

227. Locke on the Teaching of Latin

(Locke, John, *Some Thoughts concerning Education.* London, 1693)

In the Introduction to Reading 216 we gave a statement as to the origin of Locke's *Thoughts*, which see. The following selection, on the teaching of Latin, gives a good idea as to the reforms Locke proposed in the teaching of the secondary-school subjects of his time.

§ 162. As soon as he can speak *English*, 't is time for him to learn some other Language. This no body doubts of, when *French* is propos'd. And the reason is, because People are accustomed to the right Way of teaching that Language, which is by talking it into Children in constant Conversation, and not by grammatical Rules. The *Latin* Tongue would easily be taught the same Way, if his Tutor, being constantly with him, would talk nothing else to him, and make him answer still in the same Language.

. . . .

§ 164. *Latin* I look upon as absolutely necessary to a Gentleman; and indeed Custom, which prevails over every thing, has made it so much a Part of Education that even those Children are whipp'd to it, and made spend many Hours of their precious Time uneasily in *Latin*, who, after they are once gone from School, are never to have more to do with it as long as they live. Can there be any thing more ridiculous, than that a Father should waste his own Money and his Son's Time in setting him to learn the *Roman Language*, when at the same time he designs him for a Trade, wherein he having no use of *Latin*, fails not to forget that little which he brought from School, and which 't is ten to one he abhors for the ill Usage it procured him? Could it be believed, unless we had every where amongst us Examples of it, that a Child should be forced to learn the Rudiments of a Language which he is never to use in the Course of Life that he is designed to, and neglect all the while the writing of a good Hand and casting Accounts, which are of great Advantage in all Conditions of Life, and to most Trades indispensably necessary? But though these Qualifications, requisite to Trade and Commerce and the Business of the World, are seldom or never to be had at Grammar-Schools, yet thither not only Gentlemen send their younger Sons, intended for Trades, but even Tradesmen and Farmers fail not to send their Children, though they have neither Intention nor Ability to make them Scholars. If you ask them why they do this they think it as strange a Question as if you should ask them, Why they go to Church. Custom serves for Reason, and has, to those who take it for Reason, so consecrated this Method, that it is almost religiously observed by them, and they stick to it, as if their Children had scarce an orthodox Education unless they learned *Lilly's* Grammar.

§ 165. But how necessary soever *Latin* be to some, and is thought to be to others to whom it is of no manner of Use and Service; yet the ordinary Way of learning it in a Grammar-School is that which having had Thoughts about I cannot be forward to encourage. The Reasons against it are so evident and cogent, that they have prevailed with some intelligent Persons to quit the ordinary Road, not without Success, though the Method made use of was not exactly what I imagine the easiest, and in short is this. To trouble the Child with no *Grammar* at all, but to have *Latin*, as *English* has been, without the Perplexity of Rules, talked unto him; for if you will consider it, *Latin* is no more unknown to a Child, when he comes into the World, than *English:* and yet he learns *English* without Master, Rule, or Grammar; and so might he *Latin* too, as Tully did, if he had somebody always to talk to him in this Language.

228. The Bible as a Reading Book

(Locke, John, *Some Thoughts concerning Education.* London, 1693)

In this selection Locke describes the course of study and the textbooks for the elementary education of children in his day, and sets forth some very sensible advice, for the time, regarding the common practice of using the Bible as a school reading-book for children.

§ 157. The Lord's Prayer, the Creeds, and Ten Commandments, 't is necessary he should learn perfectly by heart; but, I think, not be reading them himself in his Primer, but by somebody's repeating them to him, even before he can read. But learning by heart, and *learning to read*, should not I think be mix'd, and so one made to clog the other.

But his *learning to read* should be made as little Trouble or Business to him as might be.

What other Books there are in *English* of the Kind of those above-mentioned, fit to engage the Liking of Children, and tempt them to *read*, I do not know: But am apt to think, that Children being generally delivered over to the Method of Schools, where the Fear of the Rod is to inforce, and not any Pleasure of the Employment to invite them to learn, this Sort of useful Books, amongst the Number of silly ones that are of all Sorts, have yet had the Fate to be neglected; and nothing that I know has been considered of this Kind out of the ordinary Road of the Horn-Book, Primer, Psalter, Testament, and Bible.

§ 158. As for the *Bible*, which Children are usually employ'd in to exercise and improve their Talent *in reading*, I think the promiscuous reading of it through by Chapters as they lie in Order, is so far from being any Advantage to Children, either for the perfecting their *Reading*, or principling their Religion, that perhaps a worse could not be found.   For what Pleasure or Encouragement can it be to a Child to exercise himself in reading those Parts of a Book where he understands nothing?   And how little are the Law of *Moses*, the Song of *Solomon*, the Prophecies in the Old, and the Epistles and *Apocalypse* in the New Testament, suited to a Child's Capacity?   And though the History of the Evangelists and the *Acts* have something easier, yet, taken alto-gether, it is very disproportional to the Understanding of Childhood. I grant that the Principles of Religion are to be drawn from thence, and in the Words of the Scripture; yet none should be propos'd to a Child, but such as are suited to a Child's Capacity and Notions.   But 't is far from this to read through *the whole Bible*, and that for reading's sake. And what an odd jumble of Thoughts must a Child have in his Head, if he have any at all, such as he should have concerning Religion, who in his tender Age reads all the Parts of the *Bible* indifferently as the Word of God without any other Distinction!   I am apt to think, and this in some men has been the very Reason why they never had clear and distinct Thoughts of it all their Lifetime.

229. Two of the Earliest " Spellers "

Under the general name of "Spellers" the first of the school-books which departed from the religious Primer type were classi-fied.   On the opposite page the title-pages of two of these early books are given.   The book by Edmund Coote, first issued in 1596, was a schoolmaster's general manual and guide.   Its very general nature may be seen from the following statement as to its contents.

The alphabet and words to spell	32 pages
Shorter catechism, prayers, and psalms	18 "
Chronology, of various kinds	5 "
Copies for writing	2 "
Arithmetical material	2 "
Alphabetical list of hard words, explained	20 "
Total	79 pages

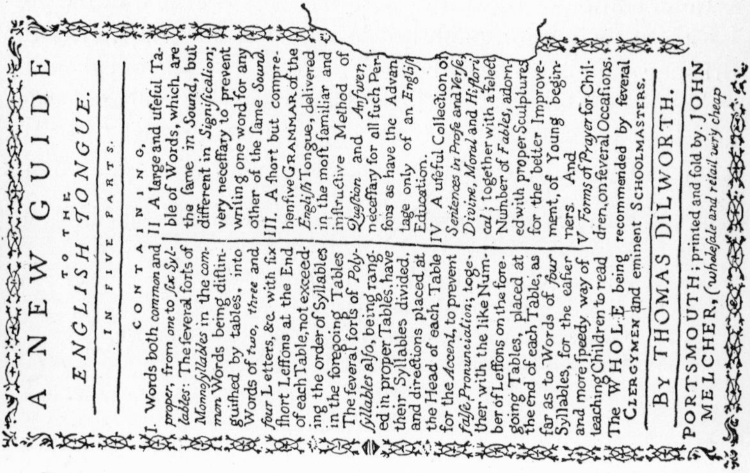

THE
A NEW GUIDE
TO THE
ENGLISH TONGUE.
IN FIVE PARTS.

CONTAINING,

I. Words both common and proper, from one to fix Syllables: The several forts of Monofyllables in the common Words being distinguished by tables. into Words of two, three and four Letters, &c. with fix short Letters at the End of each Table, not exceeding the order of Syllables in the foregoing Tables. The several forts of Polyfyllables also, being ranged in proper Tables, have their Syllables divided, and directions placed at the Head of each Table for the Accent, to prevent false Pronunciation; together with the like Number of Leffons on the foregoing Tables, placed at the End of each Table, as far as to Words of four Syllables, for the easier and more speedy way of teaching Children to read The WHOLE being recommended by several CLERGYMEN and eminent SCHOOLMASTERS.

II. A large and useful Table of Words, which are the fame in Sound, but different in Signification; very neceffary to prevent writing one word for any other of the fame found.

III. A fhort but comprehenfive GRAMMAR of the Englifh Tongue, delivered in the moft familiar and inftructive Method of Queftion and Anfwer, neceffary for all fuch Perfons as have the Advantage only of an Englifh Education.

IV. A ufeful Collection of Sentences in Profe and Verfe, Divine, Moral and Hiftorical; together with a felect Number of Fables, adorned with proper Sculpture for the better Improvement, of Young beginners. And

V. Forms of Prayer for Children, on feveral Occasions.

BY THOMAS DILWORTH.

PORTSMOUTH: printed and fold by JOHN MELCHER, (wholefale and retail very cheap

TITLE-PAGE OF DILWORTH'S "A NEW GUIDE TO THE ENGLISH TONGUE"
(First edition, 1740)

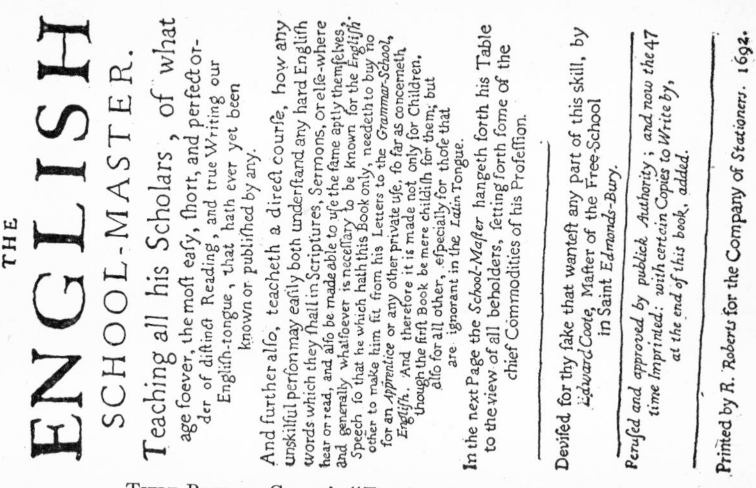

THE
ENGLISH
SCHOOL-MASTER.

Teaching all his Scholars, of what age foever, the moft eafy, fhort, and perfect order of diftinct Reading, and true Writing our English-tongue, that hath ever yet been known or publifhed by any.

And furtheralfo, teacheth a direct courfe, how any unfkilful perfon may eafily both underftand any hard Englifh words which they fhall in Scriptures, Sermons, or elfe-where hear or read, and alfo be made able to ufe the fame aptly themfelves and generally whatfoever is neceffary to be known for the Englifh Speech fo that he which hath this Book only, needeth to buy no other to make him fit from his Letters to the Grammar-School, for an Apprentice or any other private ufe, fo far as concerneth Englifh. And therefore it is made not only for Children, though the firft Book be mere childifh for them; but alfo for all other, efpecially for thofe that are ignorant in the Latin Tongue.

In the next Page the School-Mafter hangeth forth his Table to the view of all beholders, fetting forth fome of the chief Commodities of his Profeffion.

Devifed for thy fake that wanteft any part of this fkill, by Edward Coote, Mafter of the Free-School in Saint Edmonds-Bury.

Perufed and approved by publick Authority; and now the 47 time imprinted: with certain Copies to Write by, at the end of this book, added.

Printed by R. Roberts for the Company of Stationers. 1692.

TITLE-PAGE OF COOTE'S "ENGLISH SCHOOL-MASTER"
(First edition, 1596)

FIG. 54. TITLE-PAGES OF THE EARLIEST ENGLISH SPELLING-BOOKS AND
SCHOOLMASTER'S MANUALS

The book by Thomas Dilworth appeared in 1740, and at once became very popular in both Old and New England. It was more secular in character than any of its predecessors and contained numerous graded lists of words for spelling, a series of graded reading lessons, and some illustrations. The title-page gives the outline of contents of the book.

In an edition of Dilworth's *Schoolmaster's Assistant* in the possession of the author, published in 1797, there appears, after the title-page and two long dedicatory prefaces, two poems eulogizing the author for his great services. One, signed by William Deane, dated at Halifax, October 20, 1765, and addressed "To Mr. Thomas Dilworth, on his Schoolmaster's Assistant," is as follows:

> DILWORTH, the man by gracious Heaven design'd,
> A friend, a father to the human kind;
> Whose active diligence, and warmer zeal
> United, center in the public weal!
> Fain would my muse discharge the debt of praise,
> With fresh addition to thy circling bays.
>
> Learning, the glory of Britannia's isle,
> Within thy fav'rite leaves are taught to smile;
> No more perplexed in error's maze we run,
> And meet the danger which we sought to shun:
> Since, drawn by thee, now shines before our eyes,
> The path where virtue and fair knowledge lies:
> There waits a *Guide* by nicest model plann'd,
> Here stands an Usher with assisting hand;
> A work so clear, delighted we pursue,
> And think the pleasing prospect ever new.
>
> So the kind sun, with all reviving ray,
> Cheers the dark world with an approaching day;
> Before his light the empty shadows fly,
> And nature glows with a serener sky.

230. Noah Webster's Description of Pre-Revolutionary Schools

(Letter, in Barnard's *American Journal of Education*, vol. XXVI, pp. 195–96)

In response to a request, Noah Webster sent Mr. Barnard the following letter. Mr. Webster was born in Connecticut, in 1758, so that the schools he describes are those of the decade preceding the outbreak of the American Revolution.

New Haven, March 10, 1840

Mr. Barnard:

Dear Sir — You desire me to give you some information as to the mode of instruction in common schools when I was young, or before the Revolution. . . .

When I was young, the books used were chiefly or wholly Dilworth's Spelling Books, the Psalter, Testament, and Bible. No geography was studied before the publication of Dr. Morse's small books on that subject, about the year 1786 or 1787. No history was read, as far as my knowledge extends, for there was no abridged history of the United States. Except the books above mentioned, no book for reading was used before the publication of the Third Part of my Institute, in 1785. In some of the early editions of that book I introduced short notices of the geography and history of the United States, and these led to more enlarged descriptions of the country. In 1788, at the request of Dr. Morse, I wrote an account of the transactions in the United States, after the Revolution; which account fills nearly twenty pages in the first volume of his octavo editions.

Before the Revolution, and for some years after, no slates were used in common schools: all writing and operations in arithmetic were on paper. The teacher wrote the copies and gave the sums in arithmetic; few or none of the pupils having any books as a guide. Such was the condition of the schools in which I received my early education.

The introduction of my Spelling Book, first published in 1783, produced a great change in the department of spelling; and, from the information I can gain, spelling was taught with more care and accuracy for twenty years or more after that period, than it has been since the introduction of multiplied books and studies.

No English grammar was generally taught in common schools when I was young, except that in Dilworth, and that to no good purpose. In short, the instruction in schools was very imperfect, in every branch; and if I am not misinformed, it is so to this day, in many branches. Indeed there is danger of running from one extreme to another, and instead of having too few books in our schools, we shall have too many.

I am, sir, with much respect, your friend and obedient servant,

N. Webster

231. Teachers in Gotha in 1741

(From the German of Karl von Raumer; trans. in Barnard's *American Journal of Education*, vol. xx, p. 584)

Though Duke Ernest the Pious (1640–75) had raised little Gotha to a place of first importance by his educational reforms (**R. 163**), the reforms he instituted were not carried forward after his death, and by 1741 we find the school conditions there as indicated by the following "Circular of the Consistory of Gotha" regarding teachers, under date of September 11, 1741.

We have, with great displeasure, perceived that a great many persons make teaching their profession without sufficient cultivation of their faculties. Many of the teachers have employed incapable masters to teach them a little instrumental and vocal music, which is not an important requisite, but they are unable to awaken in the children's heads a true understanding of the Catechism, unable to jot down the sermon, to hear the children recite, much more unable to give instruction about any thing in nature. They know little of penmanship and arithmetic, and yet, in spite of their ignorance, twenty apply for one vacancy in a school, because, as they say, they have learned nothing else by which to make a living. They do so from love of a comfortable life, and from fear of the plough; but this must and shall be stopped, and our most gracious duke has therefore pleased to decree that you (superintendents) are required to select teachers from young men of ability, who will devote themselves for life and with enthusiasm to this work, and to reject bungling boys, &c.

How little such decrees effected, and how little power the consistory possessed to give force to such decrees, is shown by the number of monitory decrees of October 11, 1746; July 7, 1750; October 2, 1750; April 16, 1760. The chairs of the teachers remained occupied by the poorest pupils of the *gymnasium*, discharged corporals, bankrupt tradesmen, and, above all, by servants of the household of a count (patron of a school) who had outlived their usefulness in the family. These brought the once-celebrated Gotha schools into discredit.

232. Description of an Eighteenth-Century Swedish People's School

(From the German of Karl von Raumer; trans. in Barnard's *American Journal of Education*, vol. XXII, p. 701)

The following selection, taken from an article on the history of education in Sweden, describes the elementary vernacular school of that country at the close of the seventeenth century. The description also remained true of such schools well through the eighteenth century. Educational reform in Sweden did not begin until after 1800, and came in part as a result of the introduction of the English monitorial system into the schools of neighboring Denmark.

The leaders of the so-called Period of Freedom manifested much interest in popular enlightenment. In a letter dated February 19, 1768, the governors of the provinces and the consistories were called on to suggest how the instruction of the peasant children could be better organized, how school-houses could be erected, the support of school-teachers obtained, and good school regulations generally could be drawn up. These suggestions, such as they were, were not carried out, for during the whole eighteenth century not more than one hundred and sixty-five stationary schools were established; the instruction outside of their localities being imparted in village schools (*Dorfschulen*) which had no abiding place, the teachers being often very ignorant, and not unfrequently graceless scamps, drunkards, or ruined people, and both subjects and methods being extremely limited and defective. However, the school fees were very small, being two, three, or four *skillings* a week for children learning to read, and six to eight for those who studied writing and ciphering. A Swedish popular school in the seventeenth century presented a peculiar aspect. The discipline was rough, the punishments barbarous. The school was gathered in an ordinary peasant's room, where the occupants carried on their domestic occupations; at the end of the great dining-table sat the teacher, called "master," and near by sat the little children, or "A B C pupils," on stools or benches without any backs, while a little farther away, according to their proficiency, sat the other scholars with their books in their laps; only the few who were learning to cipher and write sat at the master's table. The text-books consisted of the Horn-Book, the Greater and the Lesser Catechisms, together with the Hymn-Book. When the pupil had mastered the art of reading in these three books, and had learned the Catechism by heart — without any test of his understanding it he was ready to graduate, and the teacher was dispensed with. Occasionally children of bright parts or whose parents were in better circumstances, were taught to write and cipher, but copies and manuals, with the proper solutions, were not used, which occasioned great waste of time. This picture is dark, but accurate, even far into the present century.

233. Schools of Frankfurt-am-Main during the Eighteenth Century

(From the German of Karl von Raumer; trans. in Barnard's *American Journal of Education*, vol. XXII, p. 736)

The following extract from a history of education in Frankfurt-am-Main, one of the "Free Hanseatic German Cities," gives an interesting picture of the schools and of the limited educational conditions which must have existed in the eighteenth century in one of the important cities in German lands.

In this form (1591) the Frankfort school system remained, in all essential points unchanged till the re-organization of Frankfort as a free city, in 1815. During this time the number of teachers varied from sixteen to thirty-two, each school being limited to a single assistant and hence restricted to a moderate number of scholars. The schools were sometimes under the charge of female teachers, which is explained by the fact that the school privilege was a real right, transferable by inheritance or sale. The course of study was probably extended so as even sometimes to include French, but there were special charges for instruction in all branches beyond the elementary ones of reading and writing.

That this arrangement, as carried out, was by no means satisfactory, is evident from a reform document by one of the teachers, J. M. Schirmer, in the middle of the 18th century. He proposed that the number of schools should be limited, the teachers paid by the State, a revival of the regulation requiring visitation of the schools, and that all teacherships should be made hereditary. He was especially opposed to the numerous "hedge" schools which had again arisen, kept by "school disturbers" and various kinds of strollers, "lackeys, tailors, shoemakers, stocking weavers, wig makers, journeymen printers, invalid soldiers, and sewing and knitting women," who managed to gain a subsistence by means of instruction in German and the Catechism. But his criticism met with slight response and no attempt at a re-organization was made until within the present century.

234. A Swiss Teacher's Examination, in 1793

(Krüsi, Hermann, *Recollections of my Pedagogical Life*, pp. 2–4. Stuttgart, 1840. Trans. in Barnard's *American Journal of Education*, vol. v, pp. 162–63)

Hermann Krüsi (1775–1844), who became a schoolmaster at eighteen, and at twenty-five joined Pestalozzi and was for sixteen years his main reliance and helper, has left the following account of how he happened to become a teacher, and the nature of the examination he was required to pass to obtain the appointment. It throws much light on the character of popular education in German Switzerland near the close of the eighteenth century.

At the highest point of the pass, where the road turns away from toward Trogen, my life also took another direction. While earning my living as day laborer and errand-man, I was carrying, one warm day in 1793, to the establishment of Zellweger, with which I afterward came into very different relations, a great bundle of yarn from the mountain. As I stopped to rest, all dripping with sweat, at the very summit, a relative met me, who was then treasurer of the town, one Herr Gruber. After the usual greetings, the following conversation ensued, which I yet remember as the turning point of my life.

Gruber. "It is warm."

Myself. "Very warm."

Gruber. "Now that schoolmaster Hörler is going away from Gais, you have a chance to earn your bread a little more easily. Have you no desire to offer yourself for his place!"

Myself. "Wishing will not help me much. A schoolmaster must have knowledge; and I have none."

Gruber. "What a schoolmaster among us needs to know, you at your age can very soon learn."

Myself. "But how, and where? I see no possibility of it."

Gruber. "If you wish it, the means will be easily found. Consider the matter and decide upon it."

He left me. I now had abundance of matter for reflection. But no ray of light came into my mind, although the natural sunlight surrounded my body with brightness and warmth. I scarcely felt my load as I proceeded along the ascents and steeps of the road. Whatever has fallen to my lot since that moment, I look upon as the fruit of this conversation.

Since my leaving the day school, where I had learned and practiced only reading, learning by rote, and mechanical copying, and while I was growing up to adult age, I had so far forgotten to write that I no longer knew how to make all the capital letters; my friend Sonderegger therefore procured me a copy from a teacher in Altstättin, well known as a writing-master. This single copy I wrote over as often as a hundred times, for the sake of improving my handwriting. I had no other special preparation for the profession; but, notwithstanding, I ventured, when the notice was given from the pulpit, to offer myself as a candidate for the place. with but small hopes of obtaining it, but consoling myself with the thought that at least I should come off without shame.

The day of examination came. An elder fellow-candidate was first called before the committee. To read a chapter in the New Testament and to write a few lines, occupied him a full quarter of an hour. My turn now came. The genealogical register, from Adam to Abraham, from the first book of Chronicles, was given me to read. After this, chairman Schläpfer gave me an uncut quill, with the direction to write a few lines. "What shall I write?" I said. "Write the Lord's Prayer, or whatever you like," was the answer. As I had no knowledge of composition or spelling, it may be imagined how my writing looked. However, I was told to retire. After a short consideration, I was, to my wonder and pride, recalled into the room. Here chairman Schläpfer informed me that the whole committee were of the opinion that both candidates knew little; that the other was best in reading, and I in writing.

The other, however, being over forty years old, and I only eighteen, they had come to the conclusion that I should learn what was necessary sooner than he, and as moreover my dwelling-house (the commune had then no school-house of their own) was better adapted for a school-house than his, I should receive the appointment. I was dismissed with friendly advice, and encouraging hopes of increased pay, if my exertions should be satisfactory.

Much attention was excited by the fact that my fellow-candidate, eight days afterward, took a situation as policeman, in which he received three *gulden* a week, while the schoolmaster, who was obliged to furnish his own school-room, had to satisfy himself with two and a half.

235. The English Dame School described

(Poems by the Reverend George Crabbe, 1754–1832; Henry Kirke White, 1785–1806; and William Shenstone, 1714–63)

The English poet Crabbe was essentially a poet of the homely life of the people. In his description of the Borough, in speaking of the "Poor and their Dwellings," he pays a passing tribute of respect and gratitude to his first teacher, in the following lines describing the Dame School he attended:

At her old house, her dress, her air the same,
I see mine ancient letter-loving dame:
"Learning, my child," said she, "shall fame command;
Learning is better than house or land —
For houses perish, lands are gone and spent;
In learning then excel, for that's most excellent."
"And what her learning?" — 'T is with awe to look
In every verse throughout one sacred book
From this her joy, her hope, her peace is sought;
This she has learned, and she is nobly taught.
If aught of mine have gained the public ear;
If RUTLAND deigns these humble Tales to hear,
If critics pardon, what my friends approved;
Can I mine ancient Widow pass unmoved?
Shall I not think what pains the matron took,
When first I trembled o'er the gilded book?
How she, all patient, both at eve and morn,
Her needle pointed at the guarding horn;
And how she soothed me, when with study sad,
I labored on to reach the final zad?
Shall I not grateful still the dame survey,
And ask the Muse the poet's debt to pay?
Nor I alone, who hold a trifler's pen,
But half our bench of wealthy, weighty men,

Who rule our Borough, who enforce our laws;
They own the matron as the leading cause,
And feel the pleasing debt, and pay the just applause:
To her own house is borne the week's supply;
There she in credit lives, there hopes in peace to die.

In another poem, describing "The Schools of the Borough" where he became a curate,[1] he pictures the Dame School in the following words:

To every class we have a school assign'd,
Rules for all ranks and food for every mind:
Yet one there is, that small regard to rule
Or study pays, and still is deem'd a School;
That where a deaf, poor, patient widow sits,
And awes some thirty infants as she knits;
Infants of humble, busy wives, who pay
Some trifling price for freedom through the day.
At this good matron's hut the children meet,
Who thus becomes the mother of the street.
Her room is small, they can not widely stray, —
Her threshold high, they can not run away:
Though deaf, she sees the rebel-heroes shout, —
Though lame, her white rod nimbly walks about;
With band of yarn she keeps offenders in,
And to her gown the sturdiest rogue can pin;
Aided by these, and spells, and tell-tale birds,
Her power they dread and reverence her words.

Another English poet, Henry Kirke White (1758–1806), also describes his school in a somewhat similar vein:

In yonder cot, along whose mouldering walls,
In many a fold the mantling woodbine falls,
The village matron kept her little school —
Gentle of heart, yet knowing well to rule.
Staid was the dame, and modest was the mien,
Her garb was coarse, yet whole and nicely clean;
Her neatly border'd cap, as lily fair,
Beneath her chin was pinn'd with decent care;
And pendent ruffles of the whitest lawn,
Of ancient make her elbows did adorn.
Faint with old age, and dim were grown her eyes;
A pair of spectacles their want supplies.

---

[1] See Barnard's *American Journal of Education*, vol. IV, pp. 582–90, for the poem in full.

These does she guard secure in leather case,
From thoughtless wights in some unweeted place.
Here first I entered, though with toil and pain,
The low vestibule of learning's fane —
Entered with pain, yet soon I found the way,
Though sometimes toilsome, many a sweet display.
Much did I grieve on that ill-fated morn
When I was first to school reluctant borne;
Severe I thought the dame, though oft she tried
To soothe my swelling spirits when I sighed,
And oft, when harshly she reproved, I wept —
To my lone corner broken-hearted crept —
And thought of tender home, where anger never kept;
But, soon inured to alphabetic toils,
Alert I met the dame with jocund smiles —
First at the form, my task for ever true,
A little favorite rapidly I grew;
And oft she strok'd my head, with fond delight
Held me a pattern to the dunce's sight;
And, as she gave my diligence its praise,
Talked of the honors of my future days.

The English poet, William Shenstone, has immortalized, in a poem of three hundred and fifteen lines entitled *The School-mistress*, his early dame-school teacher, and has also given a detailed description of the school. This has been said to rank in poetry with the paintings of Teniers and Wilkie for its truthfulness of portrayal. The poem[1] opens with the following lines:

Ah, me! full sorely is my heart forlorn,
To think how modest worth neglected lies;
While partial fame doth with her blasts adorn
Such deeds alone as pride and pomp disguise;
Deeds of ill-sort and mischievous emprize;
Lend me thy clarion, goddess! let me try
To sound the praise of merit ere it dies;
Such as I oft have chanced to espy,
Lost in the dreary shades of dull obscurity.

In every village mark'd with little spire,
Embowered in trees, and hardly known to fame,
There dwells, in lowly shed and mean attire,
A matron old, whom we schoolmistress name,
Who boasts unruly brats with birch to tame;

---

[1] See Barnard's *American Journal of Education*, vol. iii, pp. 449–55, for the full text of the poem.

They grieven sore, in piteous durance pent,
Awed by the power of this relentless dame,
And oft-times, on vagaries idly bent,
For unkempt hair, or task unconn'd, are sorely shent.

236. A Parochial-School Teacher's Agreement

(Ruttenber, Edw. M., *History of the Town of Newburgh*, p. 245.   Newburgh, 1859)

The following agreement, under date of 1790, between the trustees of this Church-of-England school, located at Newburgh, New York, and the minister and teacher, is interesting as showing the support of the school from the income of old endowment lands and tuition fees, and also as picturing the church-charity type of education provided for the poor of the parish.

(The Trustees) Agreed that the Reverend George H. Sperin shall be entitled to receive the whole of the rents and benefits arising from the Glebe lands, while he continues to officiate as minister, and teaching the inhabitants of the German patent on the following terms, *viz.*: Reading, Writing, Arithmetic, Geography, History and English Grammar at 12 shillings per quarter; Reading, Writing and Arithmetic at 8 shillings per quarter.

Provided always that no children incapable of studying the above branches shall be admitted or received into the school.

And should a poor child come properly recommended as such, he shall be received into the English school gratis.

And if a youth of strong natural ability of the like description offer, he shall be received into the Classical school, also gratis.

Provided also that should the rents and privileges of the Glebe hereafter become more valuable, that then, in such cases, the terms of teaching the children living in the patent shall be reduced in such manner as to be equivalent to said advantages, so far as may relate towards supporting of a school and as the trustees shall deem proper.

237. The Beginnings of an Early English Charity-School

(Minutes of Meetings of Managers.   Reproduced in Cardwell, J. H., *The Story of a Charity School*, Appendix A.   London, 1899)

The school of Saint Anne, Soho, was founded in 1699 by five earnest laymen for the "Poore Boys of the Parish."   This was the sixth such school in England, the first having been founded in Whitechapel, in 1680.   The following extracts from the Minutes give the early history of the school, and the reasons actuating the founders in establishing it.

Certain persons of this Parish understanding the Reasons, that first induc'd the promoters of the late Erected Free School in Westminster to Attempt it, (wch briefly were the pernicious consequences y^t arise from the too great Liberty wch is given to the poorer Sorte of Youth) & observing the great Likelihood of its answering their Design, from the great Change they see already wrought in the Mañers & Carriage of the Said poor Children, & the further happy Results wch may reasonably be hop'd for from them, under their Intended Education, (comparatively with what they woud otherwise have had) & withall considering how greatly this Parish aboundeth with such poor Children, who for want of being better engag'd were seldom out of the Feilds, where from the Company that frequents those places, they generally learn & contract such evil Customs & Acquaintance whereby they become not onely a perpetual Grief & Vexation to their friends, & Annoyance to all about them, but often bring their own lives also, by their wicked Actions, to Shamefull and Untimely Ends. Hereupon Communicating their Minds to some of their Acquaintance, who approving the thing, & Spontaneously offering their Assistance towards the Erecting the like in this Parish, not onely by their Purses, but by their Time, & Recomendation thereof to all those whose Vertuous Conversation they should think would incline them thereto; Dr Hern also upon our Application to him for his Advice therein giving many Wishes to it, we quickly procurd Subscriptions amounting to eighteen Pounds p. An. wch we thought soe hopefull a Beginning, that there was no Ground to Suspect the Design could Sink.   Whereupon at our Assembly Nov^r (10, 16)99 the Persons undernam'd agreed upon a Certain Day of Meeting once a week to Consider and Advise, what ways & Means were most probable to Effect their Design, or bring their Purpose to a perfect Establishment.

(Signatures. . . .)

From the Prospect of Success we have in this Matter from the Subscriptions already made, & our Hopes of their further Enlargem^t through the general Approbation of the thing, 't is Resolv'd, that Mr Edm^d Holmes & Mr Cook do take a Room or Roomes convenient for that Purpose.

That because a Schoolmaster sir for this Business, is not to be had, at every Juncture of time, Enquiry be made after such an One.

. . . .

At a subsequent meeting it was Resolv'd, that the Number Boys first admitted into the School be no more than forty;

That the said forty Boys be Cloath'd by Christmas Eve with Caps, Bands, Coates, Gloves, Shooes & Stockins;

That afterwards, if we find ye Subscriptions rise, so as to answer, the said Number of forty be advanc'd to fifty.   Order'd.

That Mr Cook and Mr Webb desire Mr Mewit (ye Church Warden) to give us his Company at our next Meeting, to ye End, we may Consider how the Boys may be Accomodated wth a Pew in ye Church, wth ye least Inconvenience to the Congregation.

That M^r Ed. Holmes and Mr Cook do make all ye Enquiry they can, what Boys are ye greatest Objects of Charity, & consequently fittest to be reciev'd into this School, & make their Report ye next Meeting.

238. Charity-School Organization and Instruction

(An Account of Charity Schools Lately Erected, etc., p. 4.   London, 1709)

The following regulations as to the master, instruction, and pupils were common in the organization of charity-schools in England. They state well the aim and purpose of the schools maintained, and the nature of the instruction imparted.

In many schools the Orders were to the effects following:

(a) *Qualifications for the Master*

I. The master to be elected for this school, shall be
1. A member of the Church of England of a sober life and conversation, not under the Age of 25 years.
2. One that frequents the Holy Communion.
3. One that hath a good Government of himself and his Passions.
4. One of a Meek Temper and Humble Behaviour.
5. One of a good Genius for Teaching.
6. One who understands well the Ground and Principles of the Christian Religion, and is able to give a good account thereof to the Minister of the Parish or Ordinary on Examination.
7. One who can Write a good Hand, and who understands the Grounds of Arithmetick.
8. One who keeps good order in his Family.
9. One who is approved by the Minister of the Parish (being a Subscriber) before he is presented to be Licensed by the Ordinary.

(b) *Purpose and Nature of the Instruction*

II. The following Orders shall be observed by the Master and Scholars.
1. The Master shall constantly attend his proper Business in the School during the Hours appointed for Teaching, viz., from 7 to 11 in the Morning and from 1 to 5 in the Evening the Summer half year: And from 8 to 11 in the Morning and from 1 to 4 in the Evening the Winter half year; that he may improve the Children in good Learning to the utmost of his Power and prevent the Disorders that frequently happen for want of the Master's Presence and Care.

2. To the End the chief design of this School, which is for the Education of Poor Children in the Rules and Principles of the Christian Religion as professed and taught in the Church of England, may be the better promoted; The Master shall make it his chief Business to instruct the Children in the Principles thereof, as they are laid down in the Church Catechism; which he shall first teach them to pronounce distinctly, and plainly; and then, in order to practice, shall explain it to the meanest capacity, by the help of *The whole Duty of Man*, or some good Exposition approved of by the Minister.

And this shall be done constantly twice a week; that everything in the Catechism may be the more perfectly repeated and understood. And the Master shall take particular care of the Manners and Behaviour of the Poor Children.

And by all proper methods shall discourage and correct the beginnings of Vice, and particularly, Lying, Swearing, Cursing, taking God's name in vain, and the Prophanation of the Lord's Day etc. . . .

FIG. 55
A CHARITY-SCHOOL GIRL IN UNIFORM, SAINT ANNE'S, SOHO

3. The Master shall teach them the true spelling of Words, and Distinction of Syllables, with the Points and Stops, which is necessary to true and good Reading, and serves to make the Children more mindful of what they Read.

4. As soon as the Boys can read competently well, the Master shall teach them to write a fair legible Hand, with the Grounds of Arithmetick, to fit them for Services or Apprentices.

[Note.] The Girls learn to read etc. and generally to knit their Stockings and Gloves, to Mark, Sew, make and mend their Cloaths, several learn to write, and some to spin their Cloaths.

[5, 6. Provides for Church going on Sundays and Saints' days, and Prayers in School twice daily from the Prayer-Book.]

7. [Names-calling at beginning of School] . . . Great Faults as Swearing, Stealing etc., shall be noted down in monthly or

FIG. 56
A CHARITY-SCHOOL BOY IN UNIFORM, SAINT ANNE'S, SOHO

weekly bills to be laid before the Subscribers or Trustees every time they meet, in order to their correction or expulsion.

8. [Holidays.]
9. [Provides that the School is to be free, no charge whatever being made.]
10. [The children are to be sent to school clean.]
11. The Children shall wear their Caps, Bands, Cloaths, and other marks of Distinction every Day, whereby their Trustees and Benefactors may know them, and see what their Behaviour is abroad.

The ordinary charge of a School in London for Fifty Boys Cloath's comes to about £75 per annum, for which a School-Room, Books and Firing is provided, a Master paid, and to each Boy is given yearly Three Bands, one Cap, one Coat, one Pair of Stockings, and one Pair of Shoes.

The cost for a School of 50 Girls is put at £60 a year to include Two Coifs, Two Bands, one Gown and Petticoat, one Pair of knit Gloves, One Pair of Stockings, and Two Pair of Shoes.

239. Textbooks used in an English Charity-School

(Allen, W. O. B., and McClure, E., *History of the S. P. C. K.*, p. 187.   London, 1898)

The following list of books for the use of the pupils in the charity schools of the Society, published by the printer for the Society for the Promotion of Christian Knowledge (S.P.C.K.), and listed in their catalogue of publications for 1719, gives some idea as to the nature of the instruction in the schools of the time.   The list is:

(a) BOOKS Proper to be Used in Charity-Schools

A Bible, Testament, and Common-Prayer Book.
The Church-Catechism.
*The Church-Catechism broke into short Questions.
Lewis's Exposition of the Church-Catechism.
Worthington's Scripture-Catechism.
The first Principles of practical Christianity.
Dr. *Woodward's* Short Catechism, with an Explanation of divers hard Words.
New Method of Catechizing.
Prayers for the Charity-Schools.
The Christian Scholar.
An Exercise for Charity-Schools upon Confirmation.
Pastoral Advice before, and after Confirmation.
The Whole Duty of Man by Way of Question and Answer.

*Abridgment of the History of the Bible, which may be well bound up at the Beginning of the Bible, or at the End.

The Anatomy of Orthography: Or, a practical introduction to the Art of Spelling and Reading *English*.

The Duty of Public Worship proved, &c.

Lessons for Children, Historical and Practical, &c.

Hymns for the Charity-Schools.

* The title-pages of the two above indicated by asterisks are reproduced here, somewhat reduced in size.

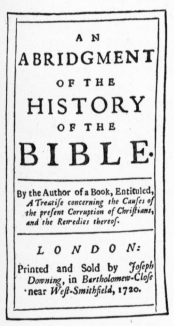

FIG. 57. TWO EARLY CHARITY-SCHOOL TEXTBOOKS

(b) *Digest of Lewis' "Exposition of the Church Catechism"*

W. W. Kemp, in his *Support of Schools in Colonial New York by the Society for the Promotion of the Gospel in Foreign Parts* (New York, 1913, pp. 273–74), gives the contents of the fourth book in the above list, the full title of which was: "The Church Catechism Explained by Way of Question and Answer and confirmed by Scripture Proofs: divided into Five Parts and Twelve Sections; wherein is given a brief and plain Account of: — I. The Christian Covenant. II. The Christian Faith. III. The Christian Obedience. IV. The Christian Prayer. V. The Christian Sacraments." The contents of its ninety-eight pages are as follows, all of the sections given being arranged in the form of question and answer:

240. A Charity-School Subscription Form

(An English form, of the period 1699–1718. After Leach)

The following represents a common English subscription form of the early charity-school period:

Whereas Prophaneness and Debauchery are greatly owing to a gross Ignorance of the Christian Religion, especially among the poorer sort; And whereas nothing is more likely to promote the practice of Christianity and Virtue, than an early and pious Education of Youth; And whereas many poor People are desirous of having their Children Taught, but are not able to afford them a Christian and Useful Education; We, whose Names are underwritten, do agree to pay Yearly, at Four equal Payments, (during Pleasure) the several and respective Sums of Money over against our Names respectively subscribed, for the setting up of a Charity-School in the Parish of .... in the City of .... or in the County of ....for Teaching (Poor Boys, or Poor Girls, or) Poor Children to Read and Instructing them in the Knowledge and Practice of the Christian Religion, as profess'd and taught in the Church of England; and for Learning them such other Things as are suitable to their Condition and Capacity. That is to say

I A. B. do subscribe £ s. d.

241. The Charity-School of Saint John's Parish, Southwark

(From an account of the school printed by the Parish, and reproduced in the *American Journal of Education*, vol. I, pp. 314–15. Boston, 1826)

The following account of a parish-supported charity-school for training girls for domestic service is an interesting and typical example of many English eighteenth-century charitable schools, organized for the education of a limited number of "children of the industrious poor of the parish."

This school was established for the purpose of maintaining, instructing, clothing, qualifying for useful servants, and putting out to service, the female children of the industrious poor of the parish.

The school dates its existence from the year 1735, when, in consequence of the increasing population, this parish was taken out of the adjoining one of Saint Olave: among the first acts of the inhabitants of the newly-established Parish was the formation of a school similar in many respects to that which had, already, for many ages, existed in the mother parish; it provided for the instruction and clothing of a certain number of the female children of the parish, with a view to fit them for service when they arrived at the age for leaving the school; but there was one alteration made in the system of the then infant school, which the experience of now nearly one hundred years proves to the committee to have been most wise and beneficial, viz. the reception of a certain portion of the children so educated into the house, wholly to be maintained, constantly to be under the eye of a vigilant mistress, and the regulations of a domestic family. The obvious tendency of this arrangement is, besides the benefit afforded to the *parents*, by taking their child entirely off their hands, to secure to the *child* the full advantage of the instruction, to rescue her from an exposure to vice and temptation, (by which exposure at home, too frequently, all the good derived at school is lost,) and by the blessing of Providence to train her up in that moral and religious way from which when she is old she may not depart.

The accommodations of the school-house will allow eighteen children to be thus wholly received into it, and maintained; and though this number has for the last few years been necessarily reduced to fifteen, the present committee have now the pleasure to report that the full number will in a few weeks be put into the establishment, and they indulge the hope that long will be the time before that full number is again obliged to be curtailed. The number of children, therefore, now in the school is as follows: — Forty children educated and clothed, of whom eighteen, besides education and clothing, are wholly maintained. This number is certainly small when compared with the size of the parish, and much it is to be wished that more of the female population could derive the benefit of gratuitous instruction; happily, *females* are the only children for whom provision need be made, on account of the royal and munificent foundation of the grammar school of Queen Elizabeth, which not only holds out the advantage of a classical education to those whose parents are desirous that they should avail themselves of it, but extends to some hundreds of the children of a lower class of persons, that measure of useful learning which, were it not for the existence of this institution, the parishioners of Saint John would, undoubtedly, feel the expediency of providing for them.

242. Eighteenth-Century Indenture of Apprenticeship

(Dunlop and Denman, *English Apprenticeship and Child Labor*, p. 352. London, 1912)

The following is a transcript of the record of an Indenture of Apprenticeship preserved at Corsham, England, and dated January 16, 1708. Its similarity to the thirteenth-century document, given in Reading No. **99**, will be evident by comparison of the two, and will reveal how little the regulations of apprenticeship changed during five hundred years.

This Indenture made the sixteenth day of January in the seventh yeare of the Reigne of our Sovraigne Lady Anne of Greate Brittain ffrance and Ireland Queene Defender of the ffaith ex Annoqo Dom 1708 Betweene William Selman of the pish of Corsham in the County of Wiltes Husbandman and Richard Selman son of the sd William Selman of the one pte and Thomas Stokes holder of the pish of Corsham aforesaid Broadweaver of the other pte Witnesseth that the said Richard Selman of his owne voluntaire will and with the consent of his sd ffather William Selman Hath put himselfe an Apprentice unto the said Thomas Stokes and with him hath covenanted to dwell as his Appntice from the day of the date hereof untill the full end and terme of

Seaven Yeares fully to be Compleate and ended during all which tyme the said Richard Selman shall well and faithfully serve him the said Thomas Stokes his master his secrets lawfully to be kept shall keep his Commandmts lawfull and honest shall doe and execute hurt unto his said master hee shall not doe nor consent to be done Tavernes or Ale-houses hee shall not haunt Dice Cardes or any other unlawful games hee shall not use ffornication with any women hee shall not committ during such tyme as he shall stay in his Masters service Matrymony with any woman hee shall not contract or espouse himselfe during the said Terme of Seaven yeares The goods of his said Master inordinately hee shall not wast nor to any man lend without his Masters Lycense from his Masters house or business hee shall not absent himselfe or plong himselfe By Night or by day without his Masters leave, but as a true and faithful servant shall honestly behave himselfe towards his sd Master and all his both in words and deedes And the said Thomas Stokes doth for himselfe his Executors and Administrators promise and Covenant to and with the sd William Selman and Richard Selman his Appntice to teach or cause the said Richard Selman to be taught and instructed in the trade Art science or occupation of a Broadweaver after the best manner that he can or may with moderate Correction finding and allowing unto his sd Servant meate drinke Apparrell Washing Lodging and all other things whatsoever fitting for an appn-tice of that trade during the said term of Seaven yeares And to give unto his sd Appntice at the end of the sd terme double Apparell (to witt) one suite for holy dayes and one for worken days. In witness whereof the said pties to the psent Indentures interchangeably have sett their hands and seales the day and yeare first above written Sealed and Delivered in the psence of Thomas Stokes.

243. Learning the Trade of a Schoolmaster

(*Citty of N. Yorke Indentures*, 1694-1707. MS. folio volume. Copied by Seybolt)

The following New York City indenture of apprenticeship, under registry date of July 18, 1722, indicates that, so general was the apprenticeship plan in use, that at times even the school-master served an apprenticeship to learn his calling.

This Indenture witnesseth that John Campbel Son of Robert Camp-bell of the City of New York with the Consent of his father and mother hath put himself and by these presents doth Voluntarily put and bind himself Apprentice to George Brownell of the Same City Schoolmaster to learn the Art Trade or Mystery . . . for and during the term of ten years. . . . And the said George Brownell Doth hereby Covenent and Promise to teach and Instruct or Cause the said Apprentice to be taught and Instructed in the Art Trade or Calling of a Schoolmaster by the best way or means he or his wife may or can.

244. The Schools of Germany before Pestalozzi

(Diesterweg, Adolph; trans. in Barnard's *Am. Jour. of Educ.*, vol. IV, pp. 343–45)

One of the schoolmen of Prussia most deeply influenced by the reform work of Pestalozzi was Adolph Diesterweg, who has often been called "der deutsche Pestalozzi." In an address in Berlin at the celebration of the centennial of the birth of Pestalozzi, in 1846, Dr. Diesterweg contrasted the schools of Germany before the days of Rousseau and Pestalozzi with the modern schools. That part of his address which described the old schools is given below.

Our present system of common or public schools — that is schools which are open to all children under certain regulations — date from the discovery of printing, in 1436, when books began to be furnished so cheaply that the poor could buy them. Especially after Martin Luther had translated the Bible into German, and the desire to possess and understand that invaluable book became universal, did there also become universal the desire to know how to read. Men sought to learn, not only for the sake of reading the Scriptures, but also to be able to read and sing the Psalms, and to learn the Catechism. For this purpose schools for children were established, which were essentially reading schools. Reading was the first and principal study; next came singing, and then memorizing texts, songs, and the Catechism. At first the ministers taught; but afterward the duty was turned over to the inferior

FIG. 58
ADOLPH DIESTERWEG
(1790–1860)

church officers, — the choristers and sextons. Their duties as choristers and sextons were paramount, and as schoolmasters only secondary. The children paid a small monthly fee; no more being thought necessary, since the schoolmaster derived a salary from the church.

Nobody either made or knew how to make great pretensions to educational skill. If the teacher communicated to his scholars the acquirements above mentioned, and kept them in order, he gave satisfaction; and no one thought any thing about separate institutions for school children. There were no school books distinctively so called; the children learned their lessons in the Bible or the Psalter, and read either in the Old or the New Testament.

Each child read by himself; the simultaneous method was not known,

One after another stepped up to the table where the master sat. He pointed out one letter at a time, and named it; the child named it after him; he drilled him in recognizing and remembering each. Then they took letter by letter of the words, and by getting acquainted with them in this way, the child gradually learned to read. This was a difficult method for him; a very difficult one. Years usually passed before any facility had been acquired; many did not learn in four years. It was imitative and purely mechanical labor on both sides. To understand what was read was seldom thought of. The syllables were pronounced with equal force, and the reading was without grace or expression.

Where it was possible, but unnaturally and mechanically, learning by heart was practiced. The children drawled out texts of Scripture, Psalms, and the contents of the Catechism from the beginning to end; short questions and long answers alike, all in the same monotonous manner. Anybody with delicate ears who heard the sound once, would remember it all his life long. There are people yet living, who were taught in that unintelligent way, who can corroborate these statements. Of the actual contents of the words whose sounds they had thus barely committed to memory by little and little, the children knew absolutely almost nothing. They learned superficially and understood superficially. Nothing really passed into their minds; at least nothing during their school years.

The instruction in singing was no better. The master sang to them the psalm-tunes over and over, until they could sing them, or rather screech them, after him.

Such was the condition of instruction in our schools during the sixteenth, seventeenth, and two-thirds of the eighteenth centuries; confined to one or two studies, and those taught in the most imperfect and mechanical way.

It was natural that youth endowed, when healthy, with an ever increasing capacity for pleasure in living, should feel the utmost reluctance at attending school. To be employed daily, for three or four hours, or more, in this mechanical toil, was no light task; and it therefore became necessary to force the children to sit still, and study their lessons. During all that time, especially in the seventeenth century, during the fearful Thirty Years' War, and subsequently, as the age was sunk in barbarism, the children of course entered the schools ignorant and untrained. "As the old ones sung, so twittered the young." Stern severity and cruel punishments were the order of the day; and by them the children were kept in order. Parents governed children, too young to attend, by threats of the schoolmaster and the school; and when they went, it was with fear and trembling. The rod, the cane, the raw-hide, were necessary apparatus in each school. The punishments of the teacher exceeded those of a prison. Kneeling on peas, sitting on the shame-bench, standing in the pillory, wearing an ass-cap, standing before the school door in the open street with a label on the back or breast, and other similar devices, were the remedies which the rude men of the age devised. To name a single example of a boy whom all have heard of, of high gifts, and of reputable family,—Dr. Martin Luther reckoned up fifteen or sixteen times that he was whipped upon the back in one forenoon. The learning and training corresponds; the one was strictly a mechanical process; the other, only bodily punishment. What wonder that from such schools there came forth a rude generation; that men and women looked back all their lives to the school as to a dungeon, and to the teacher as a taskmaster, and jailer; that the schoolmaster was of a small repute; that understrappers were selected for school duty and school discipline; that dark, cold kennels were used for school-rooms; that the schoolmaster's place, especially in the country, was assigned him amongst the servants and the like.

FIG. 59. AN EIGHTEENTH-CENTURY GERMAN SCHOOL

(Reproduction of an engraving by J. Mettenleiter, now in the Kupferstichkabinet, Munich, and printed in Joh. Ferd. Schlez's *Dorfschulen zu Langenhausen.* Nuremberg, 1795)

This could not last; it has not, thank God! When and by what efforts of admirable men the change took place, I shall relate a little later on.

245. English Free-School Rules, 1734

The following rules and regulations were recently printed in an English periodical, as of the date of 1734, but without stating the school for which they were framed. They may be regarded, though, as authentic, and fairly representative of educational conditions in an age when corporal punishment was the ruling feature of the school. They were evidently framed for some Latin Grammar School of the time.

Imprimis, Whatsoever Boy comes to School past 7 o' th' Clock In the Morning In Summer time, and past 8 o' th' Clock In ye Winter time [without Shewing good reason] Shall receive 3 Lashes.

Item, Whosoever absents himself from School, Either by Truantry, by trying to stay at home, or otherwise; Shall incurr his Master's highest displeasure, Suffer the hissing and Scoffing of ye whole School, Tarry behind the Rest one hour at Night for a week, and besides [as a suitable Reward for his —] shall suffer 12 Lashes.

Item, Whatsoever Boy shall at any time Curse, Swear, or take the Lord's Name in vain, Shall assuredly suffer for such offence, 15 Lashes.

Item, What Boy soever addicts himself to Obscene Talking or foolish Jesting, shall Suffer for each such Transgression.

Item, What Boy soever absents himself from the Service of Almighty God on the Sabbath day, and spends that Day in a wicked man'er In playing & running about, Shall receive 20 Lashes.

Item, Whosoever steals from or defrauds his School-fellow of Ink, Pens, Paper, Quills, or any Other Thing Whatsoever, Shall certainly, when found out and detected, receive 9 Lashes.

246. A New Jersey School Lottery

(Murray, David, *History of Education in New Jersey*, pp. 123–24. Washington, 1899)

The lottery was a very common means, during the latter half of the eighteenth century and the first quarter of the nineteenth, for obtaining money to found or endow churches, colleges, and schools. The following advertisement, under date of July 2, 1753, to establish and maintain a school at Trenton, in New Jersey, is typical of these early means for raising money for a common school.

We, whose names are hereunto subscribed, sons of some of the principal families in and about Trenton, being in some measure sensible of the advantages of learning, and desirous that those who are deprived of it through the poverty of their parents might taste the sweetness of it with ourselves, can think of no better or other method for that purpose than the following scheme of a Delaware-Island lottery[1] for raising 225 pieces of eight (Spanish dollars) toward building a house to accommo-

[1] Lotteries were at that time forbidden in New Jersey, and in order to evade the law they were held on Fish Island, in the river, and were termed Fish-Island, or Delaware-Island lotteries.

date an English and grammar school and paying a master to teach such children whose parents are unable to pay for schooling. It is proposed that the house be 30 feet long, 20 feet wide, and one story high, and built on the southeast corner of the meetinghouse yard in Trenton, under the direction of Messrs. Benjamin Yard, Alexander Chambers, and John Chambers, all of Trenton aforesaid. The managers are: . . .

The drawing was to take place on Fish Island, in the river Delaware, opposite to the town of Trenton, and the money raised by this lottery shall be paid into the hands of Moore Furman, of Trenton, who is under bond for the faithful laying out the money for the uses above. And we, the managers, assure the adventurers, upon our honor, that this scheme in all its parts shall be as punctually observed as if we were under the formalities used in lotteries; and we flatter ourselves the public, considering our laudable design, our age, and our innocence, will give credit to this, our public declaration.

CHAPTER XIX
THE EIGHTEENTH A TRANSITION CENTURY

THE Readings of this chapter deal with the great transition movements which characterized the eighteenth century and made of it a transition century. They cover the political and religious conditions obtaining at the time; the attack on the ancient privileges of both Church and State; the liberalizing movements of the century; the demands for reform in France; the rise of democratic government in England and America; and the sweeping away of the old abuses in France. Only a few of the large number of possible Readings illustrative of eighteenth-century conditions are reproduced in this chapter.

The first (247) gives an interesting picture of the results of ecclesiastical despotism on a nation fast attaining a national consciousness, and contrasts well the outcome of larger religious freedom in England with the lack of it in France. The eighteenth century became one of open rebellion in France. In England reforms were granted, and the evolution in consequence was slower but more peaceful.

The outstanding intellectual genius of the eighteenth century was Voltaire. He attacked privilege in every direction, but particularly the privileges and abuses of the greatest and most powerful institution of his day — the Church. He contributed many articles to the famous *Encyclopédie* edited by Diderot, and one of these, setting forth what he conceived to be the proper relations between Church and State, is here (248) reproduced.

The two extracts from the *Social Contract* of Rousseau (249 a-b) are given to show the nature of the warfare he declared on organized society, and also the fervid character of his reasoning. This book depicted so well the abuses of his age that it became "the Bible of the French Revolutionists."

The writings of Buckle represent extended research, and the selection reproduced (250) from his great history gives an interesting description of the eighteenth-century intellectual progress of the English people.

The Bill of Rights reproduced from the 1776 Pennsylvania

Constitution (251) is one of the shorter of these early documents, but compares fairly well with similar provisions incorporated into present-day constitutions. An interesting comparison may be made between this, the American Declaration of Independence of the same year, and the French Declaration of the Rights of Man of 1791 (253).

The *Cahier* reproduced in part (252) represents one of the more conservative of these famous documents, and is interesting for the conception of education which it gives.

The final selection (253) reproduces the famous French "Declaration of the Rights of Man and of the Citizen," a very influential document clearly modeled after Jefferson's famous Declaration.

247. Ecclesiastical Tyranny in France

(Dabney, R. H., *Causes of the French Revolution*, pp. 190–93. New York, 1888. By permission of the publishers, Henry Holt & Co.)

The following extract from a very interesting volume describes well conditions existing during the eighteenth century in France, and contrasts the situation there and the results with the larger religious freedom of England.

. . . France had been brought by Louis XIV to the brink of ruin. Ecclesiastical tyranny had been exercised in England, it is true, as well as in France, and in every other country. But nothing had taken place in England in the seventeenth century which could at all bear comparison, for instance, with the frightful persecution of the Huguenots by Louis XIV. Of pauperism and misery among the lower classes there was also no lack in England. But the rich were taxed to support the paupers of their parish; they lived among them; and performed duties in return for their power. Bad as was the condition of the English masses, it could bear no comparison whatever with the abject misery of the French. The numerous bread-riots which broke out in various parts of France all during the eighteenth century were ominous signs of the inflammable state of the lower classes. They themselves were too grossly ignorant to organize a revolution; but when the educated and thinking men of the country had been driven by ecclesiastical and governmental tyranny into determined hostility to the existing social system, the Old Régime was doomed. For they found the downtrodden masses eager to be led against their oppressors. In England the condition of the lowest class was far from perfect; but the great body of the middle class was contented enough. The intellectual tyranny of the Established Church was sufficient, in a rationalistic age, to create among thinking men that anti-clerical movement which showed itself in the formation of new sects, and in a literature hostile to the Christian religion. But it was not sufficient to drive the great body of the people into radical opposition.

In France, however, the abuses in the Church were at that time so great as to arouse the opposition of even the conservative classes. Hating the bishops and their privileges, men who, under free institutions, would probably have been on the side of religious conservatism, were eager to read the revolutionary literature that was directed, first, against the priests, and then against Christianity itself. Even the ignorant peasants, the most conservative class in religion, as in all things, were predisposed to hostility to the Church. For although their mental stage of development was far more likely to incline them to fetichism than to philosophic deism or atheism, they nevertheless hated at least the upper clergy on account of the tithes and other ecclesiastical taxes.

. . . Ecclesiastical tyranny in an age of rationalism produced the writings of Bolingbroke and Voltaire, and the eager reception of these writings by the French people was a symptom of the fatal rottenness of the French church. The literature of any age is, indeed, in the first instance, a symptom and a result of the intellectual tendencies of the age, and only secondarily a cause of them, in that it may accelerate and strengthen the movement by which it is itself produced. Probably no writer has ever exercised so great an influence upon his own age as Voltaire did upon his. But even when this has been said, it must be remembered that Voltaire was, after all, but a product of the intellectual tendencies of his day; and the secret of his prodigious success was that he gave utterance, in a style of wonderful clearness and classic simplicity, to the thoughts which, though less distinctly, were already in the minds of his readers. The old edifice of French society had become rotten from top to bottom, and therefore the strokes that were dealt it by the writers of the eighteenth century were sufficient to overturn it. But in England religious radicalism was confined to the intellectual classes; the broad base of society standing firm, because the condition of the middle and lower classes was more favorable than in France.

In France, too, there was political as well as ecclesiastical tyranny; and about the middle of the century the French writers began to attack the State as well as the Church. In England, on the contrary, whatever occasional abuses there may have been, there was more political freedom than in any other country at that time. Since the expulsion of James II, in 1688, the country had ceased to be a monarchy except in name, and had become an aristocratic republic. Representative government in Parliament, local administration of justice in the counties, and other free institutions were safety-valves by which the steam of revolutionary ideas could gradually escape. In France, on the contrary, literature was the only such valve; and literature was ruthlessly persecuted. What wonder, then, that in 1789 the boiler burst, and the long pent-up steam rushed forth with terrific force?

248. Voltaire on the Relations of Church and State

(Voltaire, *Dictionnaire philosophique portatif*; art. *Loi*; trans. by Robinson, in his *Readings in European History*, vol. II, p. 380. Ginn & Co., Boston. Reproduced by permission)

Under the title *Law*, in a dictionary published anonymously in 1764, Voltaire outlined what he conceived to be proper relationships, and indicated the reforms which ought to be made.

No law made by the Church should ever have the least force unless expressly sanctioned by the government. It was owing to this precaution that Athens and Rome escaped all religious quarrels.

Such religious quarrels are the trait of barbarous nations or such as have become barbarians.

The civil magistrate alone may permit or prohibit labor on religious festivals, since it is not the function of the priest to forbid men to cultivate their fields.

Everything relating to marriage should depend entirely upon the civil magistrate. The priests should confine themselves to the august function of blessing the union.

Lending money at interest should be regulated entirely by the civil law, since trade is governed by civil law.

All ecclesiastics should be subject in every case to the government, since they are subjects of the state.

FIG. 60. VOLTAIRE
(1694–1778)

Never should the ridiculous and shameful custom be maintained of paying to a foreign priest the first year's revenue of land given to a priest by his fellow-citizens.

No priest can deprive a citizen of the least of his rights on the ground that the citizen is a sinner, since the priest — himself a sinner — should pray for other sinners, not judge them.

Officials, laborers, and priests should all alike pay the taxes of the state, since they all alike belong to the state.

There should be but one standard of weights and measures and one system of law.

Let the punishment of criminals be useful. A man when hanged is good for nothing: a man condemned to hard labor continues to serve his country and furnish a living lesson.

Every law should be clear, uniform, and precise. To interpret law is almost always to corrupt it.

Nothing should be regarded as infamous except vice.

The taxes should never be otherwise than proportional to the resources of him who pays.

249. The *Social Contract* of Rousseau

(Rousseau, Jean-Jacques, *Contrat social*. Paris, 1762)

Probably no single book did more to undermine the authority of the French Government and make the French Revolution possible than did the *Social Contract* of Rousseau, published in 1762. It has been said that it became the Bible of the French Revolutionists. In it Rousseau declared open warfare upon the Government of his day, though much that he described were but the phantoms of his own brain. Burning with a desire to overthrow society and carry men back to his imaginary state of "Nature," he conjured up in his imagination much of what he wrote. Still, conditions in France in his day were so bad that an element of truth ran through it all and gave the book its great popularity.

FIG. 61.
JEAN-JACQUES ROUSSEAU
(1712–78)

The following extracts, the first dealing with political inequality and the second with ecclesiastical intolerance, are illustrative of the character of the volume.

(a) *Political Inequality*

Are not all the advantages of society for the benefit of the powerful and the rich? Are not all lucrative employments filled by them alone? And is not public authority entirely in their favor? When one of them robs his creditors or commits other rascalities, is he not sure of impunity? Are not the clubbings that he administers, the acts of violence that he commits, the murders and assassinations of which he is guilty, mere matters that are hushed up, and after six months no longer mentioned? — But let this same man *be* robbed, and the entire police force is immediately on the alert; and woe to the innocent man whom he chances to suspect. — A rich man has to pass a dangerous place? See how many escorts he has. — The axle of his carriage breaks? Every one flies to his assistance. — There is a noise at his door? He speaks a word, and silence reigns. — The crowd incommodes him? He makes a sign, and the road is clear. — A waggoner gets in the way of his carriage? His flunkeys are ready to beat the waggoner to death, and fifty honest pedestrians would be crushed under the wheels rather than that the gorgeous equipage of one puppy should be retarded. . . . How different is the picture of him who is poor! The more humanity owes him, the more society refuses him. All doors are closed to him, even when he has the right to have them opened; and if he sometimes obtains justice, he does so with more difficulty than another would have in obtaining pardon for a crime. If there is a *corvée* to be undertaken, or militia to be levied, he is selected to do it. In addition to his own burden, he bears that which is shifted upon him by his richer neighbor. At the least accident that befalls him, every one deserts him. Let *his* poor cart upset, and I hold him lucky if he escapes the outrages of the brisk lackeys of some young duke. In a word, all free assistance flies him in time of need, for the very reason that he has nothing with which to pay for it. But I regard him as a ruined man if he is so unfortunate as to have an honorable spirit, an attractive daughter, and a powerful neighbor. — Let us sum up briefly the relations between the rich man and the poor man: *You have need of me, for I am rich and you are poor. Let us then make a bargain. I will vouchsafe you the honor of being my servant, on condition that you give me what little you have left, to repay me for the trouble I take in lording it over you.*

. . . The whole occupation of kings and their ministers has but two aims, to extend their domination without, and to make it more absolute within. When they allege other aims, they make false pretexts. The expressions *public good, welfare of our subjects, glory of the nation,* so stupidly employed in public edicts, are ever the harbingers of disastrous measures; and the people groan in advance when their masters allude to their paternal solicitude.

(b) Theological and Civil Intolerance

Christianity is a purely spiritual religion, occupied solely with heavenly things; the country of a Christian is not of this world. He does his duty, it is true, but he does it with a profound indifference as to the good or ill success of his efforts. Provided he has nothing to reproach himself with, it matters little to him whether things go well or ill here below. If the state is flourishing, he scarcely dares enjoy the public felicity; he fears to become proud of the glory of his country. If the state degenerates, he blesses the hand of God which lies heavy upon his people. . . .

Should the depository of this [political] power abuse it, he regards this abuse as the rod with which God punishes his children. People would have scruples about driving out the usurper: it would be necessary to disturb the public repose, to use violence, to shed blood; all this accords ill with the gentleness of the Christian, and, after all, what matters it whether one is a slave or free in this vale of misery? The essential thing is to go to paradise, and resignation is but one more means to accomplish it.

. . . .

There is, however, a profession of faith purely civil, of which it is the sovereign's [i.e. the people's] duty to decide upon the articles, not precisely as dogmas of religion, but as sentiments of sociality without which it is impossible to be a good citizen or a faithful subject. Without being able to oblige any one to believe them, the sovereign can banish from the state whoever does not believe them; the sovereign should banish him, not as impious, but as unsocial, as incapable of loving law and justice sincerely, and of sacrificing at need his life to his duty. If any one, having publicly acknowledged these dogmas, conducts himself as if he did not acknowledge them, he should be punished with death; he has committed the greatest of crimes, — he has lied before the law.

The dogmas of civil religion should be simple, few in number, announced with precision, without explanation or commentary. The existence of a powerful, intelligent, benevolent, prescient, and provident Divinity, the life to come, the happiness of the just, the punishment of the wicked, the sacredness of the social contract and the law, — these are the positive dogmas.

As to the negative dogmas, I limit them to one, — intolerance: it enters into the religions which we have excluded. Those who make a distinction between civil intolerance and theological intolerance deceive themselves, to my mind. These two intolerances are inseparable. It is impossible to live in peace with people whom one believes to be damned; to love them is to hate God, who punishes them; they must be redeemed or else tortured. Wherever theological intolerance is admitted, it must have some civil effects; and as soon as it has them the sovereign is no more a sovereign, even in temporal matters. From that time priests are the true masters; kings are but their officers.

250. Changes in English Thinking in the Eighteenth Century

(Buckle, H. T., *History of Civilization in England*, vol. I, pp. 309–15. 2d ed., London, 1858)

The eighteenth century was a period of profound change in English thinking, and many alterations in the life and habits and opportunities of the people took place. The result was enlightening, and paved the way for the emancipation of government from religious control. Buckle traces the more important of these changes, in the following extracts taken from his great work.

In the meantime, an immense change had begun, not only among speculative minds, but also among the people themselves. The increase of scepticism stimulated their curiosity; and the diffusion of education supplied the means of gratifying it. Hence, we find that one of the leading characteristics of the eighteenth century, and which preeminently distinguished it from all that preceded, was a craving after knowledge on the part of those classes from whom knowledge had hitherto been shut out. It was in that great age, that there were first established schools for the lower orders on the only day they had time to attend them, and newspapers on the only day they had time to read them. It was then that there were first seen, in our country, circulating libraries; and it was then, too, that the art of printing, instead of being almost confined to London, began to be generally practiced in country towns. It was also in the eighteenth century, that the earliest systematic efforts were made to popularize the sciences, and facilitate the acquisition of their general principles, by writing treatises on them in an easy and untechnical style; while, at the same time, the invention of Encyclopædias enabled their results to be brought together, and digested in a form more accessible than any hitherto employed. Then, too, we first meet with literary periodical reviews; by means of which large bodies of practical men acquired information, scanty indeed, but every way superior to their former ignorance. The formation of societies for purchasing books now became general; and, before the close of the century, we hear of clubs instituted by reading men among the industrious classes. In every department, the same eager curiosity was shown. In the middle of the eighteenth century, debating societies sprung up among tradesmen; and this was followed by a still bolder innovation, for, in 1769, there was held the first public meeting ever assembled in England, the first in which it was attempted to enlighten Englishmen respecting their political rights. About the same time, the proceedings in our courts of law began to be studied by the people, and communicated to them through the medium of the daily press. Shortly before this, political newspapers arose, and a sharp struggle broke out between them and the two Houses of Parliament touching the right of publishing the debates; the end of which was, that both houses, though aided by the crown, were totally defeated; and, for the first time, the people were able to study the proceedings of the national legislature, and thus gain some acquaintance with the national affairs. . . . Finally, it was reserved for the eighteenth century, to set the first example of calling on the people to adjudicate upon those solemn questions of religion in which hitherto they had never been consulted, though it is now universally admitted that to their growing intelligence these, and all other matters, must ultimately be referred.

The extension of knowledge being thus accompanied by an increased simplicity in the manner of its communication, naturally gave rise to a greater independence in literary men, and a greater boldness in literary inquiries. As long as books, either from the difficulty of their style, or from the general incuriosity of the people, found but few readers, it was evident that authors must rely upon the patronage of public bodies, or of rich and titled individuals. And, as men are always inclined to flatter those upon whom they are dependent, it too often happened that even our greatest writers prostituted their abilities, by fawning upon the prejudices of their patrons. The consequence was, that literature, so far from disturbing ancient superstitions, and stirring up the mind to new inquiries, frequently assumed a timid and subservient air, natural to its subordinate position. But now all this was changed. Those servile and shameful dedications; that mean and crouching spirit; that incessant homage to mere rank and birth; that constant confusion between power and right; that ignorant admiration for every thing which is old, and that still more ignorant contempt for every thing which is new; — all these features gradually became fainter; and authors, relying upon the patronage of the people, began to advocate the claims of their new allies with a boldness upon which they could not have ventured in any previous age.

From all these things there resulted consequences of vast importance. From this simplification, independence, and diffusion of knowledge, it necessarily happened, that the issue of those great disputes to which I have alluded, became, in the eighteenth century, more generally known than would have been possible in any preceding century. It is now known that theological and political questions were being constantly agitated, in which genius and learning were on one side, and orthodoxy and tradition on the other. It became known that the points which were mooted, were not only as to the credibility of certain facts, but also as to the truth of general principles, with which the interests and happiness of Man were intimately concerned. Disputes which had hitherto been confined to a very small part of society, began to spread far and wide, and suggest doubts that served as materials for national thought. The consequence was, that the spirit of inquiry became every year more active, and more general; the desire for reform constantly increased; and if affairs had been allowed to run on in their natural course, the eighteenth century could not have passed away without decisive and salutary changes both in the church and the state.

251. The Bill of Rights of the Constitution of Pennsylvania

(Constitution of Pennsylvania, framed in 1776. Poore, B. P., *Federal and State Constitutions*, vol. II, p. 1541. Washington, 1877)

Practically all the early state constitutions included a long Bill of Rights, and this often contained many of the items and statements of the Declaration of Independence. The following, from the first Pennsylvania constitution, is one of the simplest of these Bills, and is illustrative of what they contained.

A Declaration of the Rights of the Inhabitants of the State of Pennsylvania

I. That all men are born equally free and independent, and have certain natural, inherent, and inalienable rights, amongst which are, the enjoying and defending life and liberty, acquiring, possessing, and protecting property, and pursuing and obtaining happiness and safety.

II. That all men have a natural and inalienable right to worship Almighty God according to the dictates of their own consciences and understanding: And that no man ought or of right can be compelled to attend any religious worship, or to erect or support any place of worship, or maintain any ministry, contrary to, or against, his own free will and consent: Nor can any man, who acknowledges the being of a God, be justly deprived or abridged of any civil right as a citizen, on account of his religious sentiments or peculiar mode of religious worship: And that no authority can or ought to be vested in, or assumed by any power whatever, that shall in any case interfere with, or in any manner controul, the right of conscience in the free exercise of religious worship.

III. That the people of this State have the sole, exclusive and inherent right of governing and regulating the internal police of the same.

IV. That all power being originally inherent in, and consequently derived from, the people; therefore all officers of government, whether legislative or executive, are their trustees and servants, and at all times accountable to them.

V. That government is, or ought to be, instituted for the common benefit, protection, and security of the people, nation, or community; and not for the particular emolument or advantage of any single man, family, or sett of men, who are a part only of that community; And that the community hath an indubitable, unalienable and indefeasible right to reform, alter, or abolish government in such manner as shall be by that community judged most conducive to the public weal.

VI. That those who are employed in the legislative and executive business of the State, may be restrained from oppression, the people have a right, at such periods as they may think proper, to reduce their public officers to a private station, and supply the vacancies by certain and regular elections.

VII. That all elections ought to be free; and that all free men having a sufficient evident common interest with, and attachment to the community, have a right to elect officers, or be elected into office.

VIII. That every member of society hath a right to be protected in the enjoyment of life, liberty and property, and therefore is bound to contribute his proportion towards the expence of that protection, and yield his personal service when necessary, or an equivalent thereto: But no part of a man's property can be justly taken from him, or applied to public uses, without his own consent, or that of his legal representatives: Nor can any man who is conscientiously scrupulous of bearing arms, be justly compelled thereto, if he will pay such equivalent, nor are the people bound by any laws, but such as they have in like manner assented to, for their common good.

IX. That in all prosecutions for criminal offences, a man hath a right to be heard by himself and his council, to demand the cause and nature of his accusation, to be confronted with the witnesses, to call for evidence in his favour, and a speedy public trial, by an impartial jury of the country, without the unanimous consent of which jury he cannot be found guilty; nor can he be compelled to give evidence against himself; nor can any man be justly deprived of his liberty except by the laws of the land, or the judgment of his peers.

X. That the people have a right to hold themselves, their houses, papers, and possessions free from search or seizure, and therefore warrants without oaths or affirmations first made, affording a sufficient foundation for them, and whereby any officer or messenger may be commanded or required to search suspected places, or to seize any person or persons, his or their property, not particularly described, are contrary to that right, and ought not to be granted.

XI. That in controversies respecting property, and in suits between man and man, the parties have a right to trial by jury, which ought to be held sacred.

XII. That the people have a right to freedom of speech, and of writing, and publishing their sentiments; therefore the freedom of the press ought not to be restrained.

XIII. That the people have a right to bear arms for the defence of themselves and the state; and as standing armies in the time of peace are dangerous to liberty, they ought not to be kept up; And that the military should be kept under strict subordination to, and governed by, the civil power.

XIV. That a frequent recurrence to fundamental principles, and a firm adherence to justice, moderation, temperance, industry, and frugality are absolutely necessary to preserve the blessings of liberty, and keep a government free: The people ought therefore to pay particular attention to these points in the choice of officers and representatives, and have a right to exact a due and constant regard to them, from their legislators and magistrates, in the making and executing such laws as are necessary for the good government of the state.

XV. That all men have a natural inherent right to emigrate from one state to another that will receive them, or to form a new state in vacant countries, or in such countries as they can purchase, whenever they think that thereby they may promote their own happiness.

XVI. That the people have a right to assemble together, to consult for their common good, to instruct their representatives, and to apply to the legislature for redress of grievances, by address, petition, or re-monstrance.

In later times, when framing constitutions, it became common to leave out much of the matter contained in the Declaration of Independence, and to make what was retained an introduction to the constitution. The following heading, taken from the present constitution of Ohio, is illustrative of what may to-day be found in nearly all our state constitutions:

THE CONSTITUTION OF THE STATE OF OHIO

We, the people of the State of Ohio, grateful to Almighty God for our freedom, to secure its blessings and promote our common welfare, do establish this constitution.

ARTICLE I
BILL OF RIGHTS
(Here follows a Bill of Rights of twenty Sections)

252. The *Cahiers* of 1789

(Archives Parlementaires, vol. II, pp. 373–78; trans. by Whitcomb)

When the States-General was summoned to meet, in 1789, it was to be composed of representatives of the three orders — Clergy, Nobility, and the Third Estate. Each was to select its representatives, and to guide them se s of instructions, called *cahiers*, were drawn up in each locality. These were often long and detailed, and represented the wishes or grievances of each group. The following extract from the *cahier* of the clergy of Blois, digesting the first five divisions and reproducing the sixth, is interesting as revealing the nature of the clerical conception as to the need for and the character of the education that should be provided for the nation.

CAHIER OF THE CLERGY OF BLOIS

Containing the grievances of the order of the clergy of the bailliage of Blois and of the secondary bailliage of Remorantin.

FIRST DIVISION — RELIGION

This relates to the affairs of the Church, and deplores the extension of religious liberty to non-catholics and the growing freedom of the press.

SECOND DIVISION — CONSTITUTION

Does not see the need for constitutional reform; recognizes the right of the king to rule and to call the States-General; thinks this should meet periodically, that each Order should vote separately, and that no action should be taken except by unanimous consent of all three Orders; that no tax should be laid without the consent of the nation; and that provincial assemblies should be re-created to provide for local government.

THIRD DIVISION — TAXES

The rights of the clergy as to taxation, ancient, but in future willing to bear their proper share; financial ministers should be responsible; and recommends the suppression of some of the most objectionable taxes.

FOURTH DIVISION — JUSTICE

Various recommendations for the reform of the principal abuses and the simplification of legal procedure.

FIFTH DIVISION — THE NOBILITY; THE CHASE

Recommends curtailment of the abuse of the chase over the agricultural lands of peasants, and the establishment of regulations as to the keeping of certain kinds of game.

SIXTH DIVISION — EDUCATION

.   .   .   .

Impressed as we are with the great influence of public education upon the religion, morals and prosperity of the state, we beseech His Majesty to favor it with all his power.   We desire:

1. That public instruction shall be absolutely gratuitous, as well in the universities as in the provincial schools;

2. That the provincial *colleges* shall be entrusted by preference to the corporations of the regular clergy;

3. That many corporations of the regular clergy, which at present are not occupied with the instruction of youth, shall apply themselves to this work, and thereby render themselves more useful to the state;

4. That in towns too small to support a *college* there shall be at least one or more masters, according to the importance of the place, who shall be able to teach the principles of Latinity or the humanities, and that their salaries shall be sufficient to allow of absolutely gratuitous instruction;

5. That this instruction shall be under the supervision of the parish priests and municipal officers;

6. That each candidate seeking permission to teach shall be obliged to produce proofs of correct life and habits, and to give evidence of his capacity in an examination before the principal and professors of the nearest *college*.

7. That masters of schools shall not employ as assistants persons from other localities, unless such persons shall have pursued the same vocation for at least two years in the place where they have studied,

and shall be furnished with references and recognized as competent by means of an examination, as above indicated;

8. That, for the purpose of facilitating the education of girls, communities of religious women, whatever may be their institution, shall be obliged to open free public schools for girls under the supervision of the parish priests.

We beseech His Majesty that after the examination, which shall be made in the States General of the *cahiers* of the various bailliages of the kingdom, this work shall be made public by means of the press, both for the satisfaction of constituents and for the honor of the deputies.

(*This document, recorded in the clerk's office of the bailliage of Blois is signed: Abbé Ponthèves, President. Then follow the signatures of 53 parish priests, 14 priors, 8 canons, 8 priests, 3 deans, 3 abbots, 3 curates, one chaplain, one friar, one deacon, and 27 persons unclassified.*)

253. The French " Declaration of the Rights of Man "

(Buchez et Rouz, *Histoire parlementaire*, vol. XI, p. 404; trans. by Robinson, in his *Readings in European History*, vol. II, p. 409.   Ginn & Co., Boston.   Reproduced by permission)

The "Declaration of the Rights of Man and of the Citizen," which had been demanded as a charter of liberties by many of the *cahiers*, was framed and adopted by the Constituent Assembly and made a part of the first French Constitution of 1791. Almost all the articles in the Declaration seek to remedy some ancient French abuse.   The document is a clear imitation of American precedents, and the comparison of it with the American Declaration of Independence and the Bills of Rights in various American state constitutions is interesting.   This French Declaration exercised great influence in Europe during the nineteenth century, its main ideas being found in many subsequent constitutions.

The representatives of the French people, organized as a National Assembly, believing that the ignorance, neglect, or contempt of the rights of man are the sole cause of public calamities and of the corruption of governments, have determined to set forth in a solemn declaration the natural, inalienable, and sacred rights of man, in order that this declaration, being constantly before all the members of the social body, shall remind them continually of their rights and duties; in order that the acts of the legislative power, as well as those of the executive power, may be compared at any moment with the objects and purposes of all political institutions and may thus be more respected; and, lastly, in order that the grievances of the citizens, based hereafter upon simple and incontestable principles, shall tend to the maintenance of the constitution and redound to the happiness of all. Therefore the National Assembly recognizes and proclaims, in the presence and under the auspices of the Supreme Being, the following rights of man and of the citizen:

ARTICLES

1. Men are born and remain free and equal in rights. Social distinctions may be founded only upon the general good.

2. The aim of all political association is the preservation of the natural and imprescriptible rights of man. These rights are liberty, property, security, and resistance to oppression.

3. The principle of all sovereignty resides essentially in the nation. No body nor individual may exercise any authority which does not proceed directly from the nation.

4. Liberty consists in the freedom to do everything which injures no one else; hence the exercise of the natural rights of each man has no limits except those which assure to the other members of the society the enjoyment of the same rights. These limits can only be determined by law.

5. Law can only prohibit such actions as are hurtful to society. Nothing may be prevented which is not forbidden by law, and no one may be forced to do anything not provided for by law.

6. Law is the expression of the general will. Every citizen has a right to participate personally, or through his representative, in its formation. It must be the same for all, whether it protects or punishes. All citizens, being equal in the eyes of the law, are equally eligible to all dignities and to all public positions and occupations, according to their abilities, and without distinction except that of their virtues and talents.

7. No person shall be accused, arrested, or imprisoned except in the cases and according to the forms prescribed by law. Any one soliciting, transmitting, executing, or causing to be executed, any arbitrary order, shall be punished. But any citizen summoned or arrested in virtue of the law shall submit without delay, as resistance constitutes an offense.

8. The law shall provide for such punishments only as are strictly and obviously necessary, and no one shall suffer punishment except it be legally inflicted in virtue of a law passed and promulgated before the commission of the offense.

9. As all persons are held innocent until they shall have been declared guilty, if arrest shall be deemed indispensable, all harshness not essential to the securing of the prisoner's person shall be severely repressed by law.

10. No one shall be disquieted on account of his opinions, provided their manifestation does not disturb the public order established by law.

11. The free communication of ideas and opinions is one of the most precious of the rights of man. Every citizen may, accordingly, speak, write, and print with freedom, but shall be responsible for such abuses of this freedom as shall be defined by law.

12. The security of the rights of man and of the citizen requires public military forces. These forces are, therefore, established for the good of all and not for the personal advantage of those to whom they shall be entrusted.

13. A common contribution is essential for the maintenance of the public forces and for the cost of administration. This should be equitably distributed among all the citizens in proportion to their means.

14. All the citizens have a right to decide, either personally or by their representatives, as to the necessity of the public contribution; to grant this freely; to know to what uses it is put; and to fix the proportion, the mode of assessment and of collection and the duration of the taxes.

15. Society has the right to require of every public agent an account of his administration.

16. A society in which the observance of law is not assured, nor the separation of powers defined, has no constitution at all.

17. Since property is an inviolable and sacred right, no one shall be deprived thereof except where public necessity, legally determined, shall clearly demand it, and then only on condition that the owner shall have been previously and equitably indemnified.

CHAPTER XX

THE BEGINNINGS OF NATIONAL EDUCATION

THE Readings of this chapter deal with the beginnings of national education in France and the United States, and relate to the work of the French revolutionary theorists and statesmen, and to the beginnings of state education in the new American States.

The first selection (254) is a good brief extract setting forth the great influence in France of the critical writings of Rousseau, itself one of the strange things in history. The second (255) gives an outline of the argument and proposals for national education made in France in 1763, by the parlementarian La Chalotais, and is interesting as revealing the national conception which the philosophers of France had by that time reasoned out. The third selection (256) is a synopsis of the famous bill of Condorcet, in which he proposed (1792) to organize a system of public instruction for France. The next (257) outlines the educational work of the National Convention (1792–95) in France, and shows how far the French statesmen were able to carry out the ideas of the political reformers of the time. The final selection relating to French effort (258) describes the foundation and early work of the Polytechnic School at Paris.

The remaining selections deal with American state beginnings. The first (259) reproduces the important early constitutional provisions of the American States; the next (260) shows the very progressive ideas as to state education which were embodied in the first Ohio Constitution; and the next (261) the broad scope of the system of public instruction proposed for the new State of Indiana. Selection (262) gives a digest of the early state legislation as to public education in those American States which enacted the most significant early school laws, and shows what it was proposed to enforce. The final selection (263) gives a digest of Jefferson's plan of 1799 for the organization of a system of public instruction for Virginia — a plan French in its ideas and scope.

254. The Far-reaching Influence of Rousseau's Writings

(Dabney, R. H., *The Causes of the French Revolution*, pp. 277-79. New York, 1888. Reproduced by permission of the publishers, Henry Holt & Co.)

Among the strangest things in history is the enormous and far-reaching influence exercised by Jean-Jacques Rousseau. Of him Dabney writes:

The plebeian Rousseau, living from hand to mouth, by turns valet, clerk, tramp, tutor, copyist, author, fugitive, was filled with unquenchable hatred of the rich and powerful. This hatred, together with an ardent love of humanity, made him burn with the desire to overthrow society and carry men back to that state of "nature" which he conjured up in his imagination.

Summarizing his work, Dabney writes:

It was, of course, an absurd exaggeration in Napoleon to say that but for Rousseau the Revolution would not have taken place; for Rousseau, like every other individual, was a product of his time, and his writings a result of that revolutionary movement which they merely hastened and strengthened. Still, their influence, in a way, was prodigious. A letter written by Grimm, in 1754, says that the Dijon prize-essay produced a species of revolution at Paris. "It is impossible to express or imagine," says Hume, writing from Paris in 1765, "the enthusiasm of this nation in his favor; . . . no person ever so much engaged their attention as Rousseau. Voltaire and everybody else are quite eclipsed by him." The circulation of his books was enormous. When *La Nouvelle Héloïse* appeared, the booksellers were unable to meet the demand, but lent copies of it at so much a day or so much an hour. At first, as much as twelve *sous* an hour was paid per volume for the privilege of reading it. Painted with all the hues of a fervid imagination, and flaming with the fire of deep conviction, the romances of Rousseau produced upon all sentimental natures, and especially upon women, an indescribable effect. To him, more than to any other individual, it was due that the joys of domestic life were revealed anew to the upper classes in France, and that aristocratic mothers resumed that most beautiful of all maternal duties, the suckling of their own children. The brilliant *salons* no longer exercised such undisputed sway, but the pleasures of country life came into vogue, and even some of the upper nobles began to spend a part of the year upon their country estates. Return to nature and simplicity became the watchword. The style of architecture became simpler, and the old style of landscape gardening, with its long rectilinear avenues of artificially trimmed box-bushes and trees, gave place to the more natural English style with irregular groups of trees growing with their natural ruggedness and strength. Thus the whole aspect of society became tinged with the ideas of Rousseau. For Rousseau gave utterance, with amazing eloquence, to the thoughts that were suited to the radical spirit of the age.

255. La Chalotais's Essay on National Education

(Paris, 1763. Extracts taken from Compayré)

FIG. 62. LA CHALOTAIS (1701–85)

Louis René de Caradeuc de la Chalotais was a French magistrate and statesman, and one of the striking personalities of the pre-revolutionary period. In 1763 appeared La Chalotais's *Essai d'éducation nationale*, a practical and philosophical discussion of the problem of the education of a people. The volume was warmly approved by the political philosophers of the period; was translated into several languages; and was deeply influential later on in France in shaping the attitude of the State toward education. The following brief extracts give some idea as to La Chalotais's reasoning and proposals.

TEACHERS AND PURPOSE

I do not presume to exclude ecclesiastics, but I protest against the exclusion of laymen. I dare claim for the nation an education which depends only on the State, because it belongs essentially to the State; because every State has an inalienable and indefeasible right to instruct its members; because, finally, the children of the State ought to be educated by the members of the State.

It is certain that in the education which was given at Sparta, the prime purpose was to train Spartans. It is thus that in every State the purpose should be to enkindle the spirit of citizenship; and, in our case, to train Frenchmen, and in order to make Frenchmen, to labor to make men of them.

MORAL AND POLITICAL IDEAS

The greatest vice of education, and perhaps the most inevitable, while it shall be entrusted to persons who have renounced the world, is the absolute lack of instruction on the moral and political virtues. Our education does not affect our habits, like that of the ancients. After having endured all the fatigues and irksomeness of the college, the young find themselves in the need of learning in what consist the duties common to all men. They have learned no principle for judging actions, evils, opinions, customs. They have everything to learn on matters that are so important. They are inspired with a devotion which is but an imitation of religion, and with practices which take the place of virtue, and are but the shadow of it.

NATURAL INSTRUCTION

I wish nothing to be taught children except facts which are attested by the eyes, at the age of seven as at the age of thirty.

The principles for instructing children should be those by which nature herself instructs them. Nature is the best of teachers.

Every method which begins with abstract ideas is not made for children.

Let children see many objects; let there be a variety of such, and let them be shown under many aspects and on various occasions. The memory and the imagination of children cannot be overcharged with useful facts and ideas of which they can make use in the course of their lives.

Most young men know neither the world which they inhabit, the earth which nourishes them, the men who supply their needs, the animals which serve them, nor the workmen and citizens whom they employ. They have not even any desire for this kind of knowledge. No advantage is taken of their natural curiosity for the purpose of increasing it. They know how to admire neither the wonders of nature nor the prodigies of the arts.

Education, according to La Chalotais, should be divided into two periods — the first from five to ten years, and the second from ten to seventeen. For these two periods he would have studies, as follows:

STUDIES

First period. The exercises proposed for the first period are as follows: learning to read, write, and draw; dancing and music, which ought to enter into the education of persons above the commonalty; historical narratives and the lives of illustrious men of every country, of every age, and of every profession; geography, mathematical and physical recreations; the fables of La Fontaine, which, whatever may be said of them, ought not to be removed from the hands of children, but all of which they should be made to learn by heart; and besides this, walks, excursions, merriment, and recreations; I do not propose even the studies except as amusements.

Second period. The course of study for the second period should consist of French and Latin literature, or the humanities; a continuation of history, geography, mathematics, and natural history; criticism, logic, and metaphysics; the art of invention; and ethics. He would also add "the English language for science, and the German for war."

TEXTBOOKS

I would have composed for the use of the child histories of every nation, of every century, and particularly of the later centuries, which should be written with greater detail, and which should be read before those of the more remote centuries.   I would have written the lives of illustrious men of all classes, conditions, and professions, of celebrated heroes, scholars, women, and children.

La Chalotais put great dependence on elementary books, which might, he thought, be composed within two years, if the king would encourage the publication of them, and if the Academies would put them up for competition.

These books would be the best instruction which the masters could give, and would take the place of every method.   Whatever course we may take, we cannot dispense with new books.   These books, once made, would make trained teachers unnecessary, and there would then be no longer any occasion for discussion as to their qualities, whether they should be priests, or married, or single.   All would be good, provided they were religious, moral, and knew how to read; they would soon train themselves while training their pupils.

THE STATE AND EDUCATION

It is the State, it is the larger part of the nation, that must be kept principally in view in education; for twenty millions of men ought to be held in greater consideration than one million, and the *peasantry, who are not yet a class* in France, as they are in Sweden, *ought not to be neglected in a system of instruction.*   Education is equally solicitous that letters should be cultivated, and that the fields should be plowed; that all the sciences and the useful arts should be perfected; that justice should be administered and that religion should be taught; that there should be instructed and competent generals, magistrates, and ecclesiastics, and skillful artists and citizens, all in fit proportion.   It is for the government to make each citizen so pleased with his condition that he may not be forced to withdraw from it.

We do not fear to assert, in general, that in the condition in which Europe now is, the people that are the most enlightened will always have the advantage over those who are less so.

256. Outline of Condorcet's Plan for Organizing Public Instruction in France

(Synopsis of the law; trans. from Professor Vallet de Viriville's *Histoire d'Instruction Publique*.   Barnard's *American Journal of Education*, vol. XXII, pp. 652–53)

On April 20–21, 1792, Condorcet submitted to the French Legislative Assembly a Report on behalf of the Committee on Public

Instruction on the need for organizing a complete democratic system of public instruction for France, to insure the perpetuation of liberty and equality, together with a detailed bill (*Projet de Décret*) for carrying out the plan. The bill is long, but the following synopsis of it gives a very good idea as to the nature of the proposals.

The plan instituted five grades of schools, in which the instruction was to be progressive: (1) *Primary Schools;* (2) *Secondary Schools;* (3) *Institutes;* (4) *Lyceums;* (5) a *National Society of Arts and Sciences.*

The *Primary School* receives children at the age of six years. Every village containing over four hundred inhabitants must be provided with one. Tuition will be given in the rules of arithmetic, the first elements of morality, the rudimentary knowledge of natural science and economy, essential either to agriculture, arts, or commerce, according to the rural or manufacturing occupations of the population. Religion will be taught in the churches by the respective ministers of their different creeds. A small collection of books will be furnished to each school for the use of the children.

FIG. 63. CONDORCET
(1743–94)

In *Secondary Schools*, the tuition comprehends grammar; the history and geography of France, and the neighboring countries; drawing; the principles of the mechanical arts; some instruction in moral and social science, with the explanation of the chief laws and regulations of agreements and contracts; the elements of mathematics, natural philosophy, natural history applied to the arts, manufactures, and commerce. Every secondary school will have a library, some models of machinery, and some philosophical instruments. There will be one at least in every district, or a school for every four thousand inhabitants.

Institutes. The studies are divided into four classes, 1. Mathematical and physical sciences. 2. Moral and political science. 3. Application of the sciences to the arts. 4. Literature and the fine arts. Every institute is furnished with a library and a collection of machines and scientific instruments, with a botanic, and agricultural garden; these three collections are public. There will be at least one institute in each department.

Lyceums. The same plan and arrangements as in the Institutes, but on a grander scale, in the extent and profundity of the studies. There should be nine lyceums in France, distributed in different parts of its territory.

National Society of Arts and Sciences. It was actually the Institute enlarged and connected by a close and direct link to instruction and practical science. Its duty was to direct, oversee, simplify, and increase general education. This supervision and directorship was to transmit from the highest to the lowest, from grade to grade, to the inferior ranks of the hierarchy. The law recognized beside these establishments, five societies to encourage the progress of science, letters, and art, but with limited range.

Ways and Means. Instruction in all its degrees outlined was to be gratuitous, and the appropriations necessary for this purpose were estimated at twenty-nine millions of francs. From this sum a periodical allowance of one million three hundred thousand francs was to be devoted to the *Élèves de la patrie.* Condorcet ranks under this term, those penniless children who distinguish themselves, at the beginning, or at any point whatever in their studies, and to whom the state furnished aid in the form of a stipend, in order to permit them to pursue, sheltered from need, the degrees of scientific apprenticeship remaining to be overcome.

257. Founding of the Polytechnic School at Paris

(*Report of English Commissioners on Military Education.* London, 1857. Compiled from a *Report and Appendix*)

Of the more permanent fruits of the educational work of the Convention (1792–95), the founding of a number of higher technical institutions and bureaus, many of which have continued to the present time, stand as memorials. Among these, the Polytechnic School, founded October 22, 1795, was one of the most important creations. The following story of its founding and work gives an interesting picture of this early technical school.

The origin of the *École Polytechnique* dates from a period of disorder and distress in the history of France which might seem alien to all intellectual pursuits, if we did not remember that the general stimulus of a revolutionary period often acts powerfully upon thought and education. It is, perhaps, even more than the Institute, the chief scientific creation of the first French Revolution. . . .

The school and its plan were both owing to an immediate and pressing want. It was to be partly military and partly civil. Military, as well as civil education, had been destroyed by the revolutionists. The committee of public safety had, indeed, formed a provisional school for engineers at Metz, to supply the immediate wants of the army on the frontier, and at this school young men were hastily taught the elements of fortification, and were sent direct to the troops, to learn as they best could, the practice of their art. "But such a method," says the report accompanying the law which founded the school, "does not form engineers *in any true sense of the term* and can only be justified by the emergency of the time. The young men should be recalled to the new school to complete their studies." . . . Such was the immediate motive for the creation of this school. At first, it only included the engineers amongst its pupils. But the artillery were added within a year.

When the school first started there was scarcely another of any description in France. For nearly three years the revolution had destroyed every kind of teaching. The attack upon the old schools, in France as elsewhere, chiefly in the hands of the clergy, had been begun by a famous report of Talleyrand's, presented to the legislative assembly in 1791, which recommended to suppress all the existing academies within Paris and the provinces, and to replace them by an entirely new system of national education through the country. In this plan a considerable number of military schools were proposed, where boys were to be educated from a very early age. When the violent revolutionists were in power, they adopted the destructive part of Talleyrand's suggestions without the other. All schools, from the university downwards, were destroyed; the large exhibitions or *Bourses*, numbering nearly 40,000, were confiscated or plundered by individuals, and even the military schools and those for the public works (which were absolutely necessary for the very roads and the defense of the country) were suppressed or disorganized. The school of engineers at Mézières (an excellent one, where Monge had been a professor) and that of the artillery at La Fère, were both broken up, whilst the murder of Lavoisier, and the well-known saying in respect to it, that "the Republic had no need of chemists," gave currency to a belief, which Fourcroy expressed in proposing the Polytechnic, "that the late conspirators had formed a deliberate plan to destroy the arts and sciences, and to establish their tyranny on the ruins of human reason."

Thus it was on the ruin of all the old teaching, that the new institution was erected; a truly *revolutionary* school, as its founders delighted to call it, using the term as it was then commonly used, as a synonym for all that was excellent. And then for the first time avowing the principle of public competition, its founders, Monge and Fourcroy, began their work with an energy and enthusiasm which they seem to have left as a traditional inheritance to their school. It is curious to see the difficulties the bankruptcy of the country threw in their way, and the vigor with which, assisted by the summary powers of the republican government, they overcame them. They begged the old Palais Bourbon for their building; were supplied with pictures from the Louvre; the fortunate capture of an English ship gave them some uncut diamonds for their first experiments; presents of military instruments were sent from the arsenals of Havre; and even the hospitals contributed some chemical substances. In fine, having set their school in motion, the government and its professors worked at it with such zeal and effect, that within five months after their project was announced, they had held their first entrance examination, open to the competition of all France, and started with three hundred and seventy-nine pupils.

. . . .

During the first years after its foundation the Polytechnic grew and flourished in the general dearth of public teaching, being indeed not merely the only great school, but, until the Institute was founded, the only scientific body in France. Working on its first idea of high professorial lectures, practically applied and explained by *répétiteurs*, its success on its own purely scientific line was, and has continued to be, astonishing. . . . All the great engineers and artillerymen of the Empire belonged to it, and the long pages in its calendar of distinguished men are the measure of its influence on the civil and military services of France. In fact its pupils, at a time of enormous demands, supplied all the scientific offices of the army, and directed all the chief public works, fortresses, arsenals, the improvement of cities, the great lines of roads, shipbuilding, mining, — carried out, in a word, most of the great improvements of Napoleon. He knew the value of his school, "the hen" as he called it, "that laid him golden eggs" — and perhaps its young pupils were not improved by the excessive official patronage bestowed by him upon "the envy of Europe," "the first school in the world." It can not, however, be a matter of surprise, that its vigor and success should have caused Frenchmen, even those who criticise its influence severely, to regard it with pride as an institution unrivaled for scientific purposes.

258. The Work of the National Convention in France

(Barnard's *American Journal of Education*, vol. xx, pp. 227–29)

The National Convention, which was in existence from September 21, 1792, to October 26, 1795, in France, was the third legislative body following the States-General of 1789. It manifested great interest in the organizing of primary education, and many types of projected laws for the organization of a state system of public instruction were discussed by it. The following is a digest of its educational activities in so far as these relate to elementary education, and of the main provisions of the Law of 1795 which it finally enacted.

(a) Various Legislative Proposals

The National Convention, by decrees, dated December 12, 1792, May 30, 1793, and October 21, 1793, ordered and provided for the establishment of primary schools. Every neighborhood, with 400 inhabitants, "must have a public school, in which children of all classes could receive that first education, — physical, moral, and intellectual, — the best adapted to develop in them republican manners, patriotism, and the love of labor, and to render them worthy of liberty and equality." Pupils must be taught to speak, read, and write correctly the French language; the geography of France; the Rights and Duties of Men and Citizens; the first notions of natural and familiar objects; the use of numbers, the compass, the level, the system of weights and measures, the mechanical powers, and measurement of time. They were to be taken often into the fields and the workshops where they might see agricultural and mechanical operations going on, and take part in the same so far as their age would allow.

By a subsequent decree (October 29, 1793,) a local commission of intelligent, public-spirited, and moral persons was to be appointed to locate the school, and hold a public examination of all candidates for the position of teachers, as to their acquirements, aptitude for instruction, and moral character. From a list of the successful candidates, the parents and guardians of the district in which a school was to be opened, if any vacancy existed, might in public meeting choose a teacher. For the teacher thus examined, approved, and selected, the law fixed a minimum salary of 1200 francs, to be paid out of the public treasury. This salary could be increased by the liberality of the district and of the parents. By a decree of December 19th of the same year (1793), "liberty of instruction is proclaimed, — citizens and citizenesses, who can produce a certificate of civism and good morals, can inform the municipal authorities of their intention to teach, and of the subjects which they propose to teach, and open a school where they please." This liberty was abridged by a law passed November 17, 1794, so far as to subject the teacher and his school to the approbation of a "jury of instruction to be chosen by the district administration from among the fathers of families." This law, which was repealed August 31, 1797, provided that the residence of the clergyman, if not already sold for the benefit of the republic under the decree of March 8, 1793, should be assigned to the schoolmaster for a dwelling and a school. The same law added to the penalty (in the law of 1793), of a fine on parents who failed to send their children to school, a requirement "that those young citizens who have not attended school shall be examined, in the presence of the people, at the Feast of the Young, and if they shall be found not to have the requirements necessary for French citizens, shall be excluded from all public functions until they have attained them." To the course of instruction laid down in the decree of 1793, the law of 1794 added "gymnastics, military exercises, and swimming."

There is much that is extravagant in these requirements of a public school to be set up in every neighborhood of 400 inhabitants, poor as the entire rural population of France had been made by exactions of the privileged few, and ignorant as the great majority of parents had been left by all the previous agencies and facilities of education. And yet in these enactments we find expressed the highest aspirations of the most advanced educators of this age, and much that is now realized in the best public schools of Germany and the United States. Just because the law required more than could be performed, or than the existing instrumentalities of administration could educate the public mind to appreciate and sustain, it remained a dead letter, or gave way to enactments less exacting and less salutary.

(b) The Law of 1795 organizing Primary Instruction

The only permanent contribution of this period of French legislation to the system of elementary schools was a chapter of eleven articles in the *Decree concerning the Organization of Public Instruction*, October 25, 1795 (3 Brumaire, year IV), founded on a remarkable report of Daunau, in which the whole subject of public instruction is ably discussed.

This decree was the sole legacy of the conventions of the people which legislated for France in the matter of primary instruction. The following are the provisions respecting primary schools:

Art. 1. There shall be established in every canton of the republic one or more primary schools, whose territorial limits shall be determined by the departmental authorities.

2. There shall be established in every department several juries or committees of instruction, the members not to exceed six, and each to be composed of three members appointed by the departmental authorities.

3. The teachers of the primary schools shall be examined by one of the juries of instruction, and upon the presentation of the municipal authorities, shall be appointed by the departmental administration.

4. They shall be dismissed only on the concurrence of the same authorities, at the proposal of a jury of instruction, and after having had a hearing.

5. In every primary school shall be taught reading, writing, cyphering, and the elements of Republican morals.

6. Every primary teacher shall be furnished by the republic with a residence, (with school-room for his pupils,) and a garden. Instead of a residence and garden, the teacher may be paid an equivalent in money.

7. They, as well as the professors of the central and special schools, may perform other duties, not incompatible with teaching, and receive pay.

8. They shall receive from each pupil an annual fee, to be fixed by the departmental administration.

9. The school fee may be remitted to one-fourth of the pupils of each school, on account of poverty.

10. The regulations of the primary schools shall be decided by the departmental administration, subject to the approbation of the Executive Directory.

11. The municipal authorities shall exercise direct supervision over the primary schools, and shall see to the execution of the laws and decrees of the higher administrations relating to the same.

---

259. Early Constitutional Provisions relating to Education in the United States

(Selected from the early state constitutions, as given in Poore, B. P., *Charters and Constitutions.* 2 vols., Washington, 1877)

Between 1776 and 1800 all the original States, except Connecticut and Rhode Island, framed written state constitutions, and some of the States revised them one or more times before 1800. Of the thirteen original States and Vermont (admitted in 1791), seven of the fourteen had considered education of sufficient importance to warrant the incorporation of a section or article concerning it in their constitutions.

The constitutions of the seven States which had made some constitutional provision regarding education fall into three classes. The first, represented by Delaware and the first Georgia constitution, merely briefly direct the establishment of schools; the second, represented by Massachusetts, New Hampshire, and Vermont, have good sections directing the encouragement of learning and schools; while the third, represented by North Carolina and the first Pennsylvania constitution, direct the establishment of schools wherein tuition shall be cheap. In its second constitution, Pennsylvania went over completely to the maintenance only of a pauper-school system.

The constitutional provisions relating to education in these seven early state constitutions were as follows:

VERMONT, 1. *Constitution of* 1777

Sec. XL. A school or schools shall be established in every town, by the legislature, for the convenient instruction of youth, with such salaries to the masters, paid by each town; making proper use of school lands in each town, thereby to enable them to instruct youth at low prices. One grammar school in each county, and one university in this State, ought to be established by direction of the General Assembly.

Sec. XLI. Laws for the encouragement of virtue and prevention of vice and immorality, shall be made and constantly kept in force; and provision shall be made for their due execution; and all religious societies or bodies of men, that have or may be hereafter united and incorporated, for the advancement of religion and learning, or for other pious and charitable purposes, shall be encouraged and protected in the enjoyment of the privileges, immunities and estates which they, in justice ought to enjoy, under such regulations, as the General Assembly of this State shall direct.

2. *Constitution of* 1787

Chap. II, Sec. 38. Laws for the encouragement of virtue, and prevention of vice and immorality, ought to be constantly kept in force, and duly executed; and a competent number of schools ought to be maintained in each town for the convenient instruction of youth; and one or more grammar schools be incorporated, and properly supported in each county in this State. And all religious societies, or bodies of men, that may be hereafter united or incorporated, for the advancement of religion and learning, or for other pious and charitable purposes, shall be encouraged and protected in the enjoyment of the privileges, immunities, and estates, which they in justice ought to enjoy under such regulations as the General Assembly of this State shall direct.

This section was also incorporated in the constitution of 1793 unchanged, and is still in force.

MASSACHUSETTS, *Constitution of* 1780
(Part II, chap. V, The University at Cambridge, and Encouragement of Literature, etc.)

SECTION I. *The university*

ART. I. Whereas our wise and pious ancestors, so early as the year 1636, laid the foundation of Harvard College, in which university many persons of great eminence have, by the blessing of God, been initiated in those arts and sciences which qualified them for public employments, both in church and state; and whereas the encouragement of arts and sciences and all good literature, tends to the honor of God, the advantage of the Christian religion, and the great benefit of this and the other United States of America, it is declared, that the president and fellows of Harvard College, in their corporate capacity, and their successors in their capacity, their officers and servants, shall have, hold, use, exercise, and enjoy all the powers, authorities, rights, liberties, privileges, immunities, and franchises which they now have, or are entitled to have, hold, use, exercise, and enjoy; and the same are hereby ratified and confirmed unto them, the said president and fellows of Harvard College, and to their successors, and to their officers and servants respectively, forever.

Art. 2. And whereas there have been, at sundry times, by divers persons, gifts, grants, devises of houses, lands, tenements, goods, chattels, legacies, and conveyances heretofore made, either to Harvard College, in Cambridge, in New England, or to the president and fellows of Harvard College, or to the said college by some other description, under several charters successively, it is declared that all the said gifts, grants, devises, legacies, and conveyances are hereby forever confirmed unto the president and fellows of Harvard College, and to their successors, in the capacity aforesaid, according to the true intent and meaning of the donor or donors, grantor or grantors, devisor or devisors.

Art. 3. And whereas by an act of the general court of the colony of Massachusetts Bay, passed in the year 1642, the governor and deputy governor, for the time being, and all the magistrates of that jurisdiction, were, with the president, and a number of the clergy, in the said act described, constituted the overseers of Harvard College, and it being necessary, in this new constitution of government, to ascertain who shall be deemed successors to the said governor, deputy governor, and magistrates, it is declared that the governor, lieutenant-governor, council, and senate of this commonwealth, are, and shall be deemed, their successors; who, with the president of Harvard College, for the time being, together with the ministers of the Congregational churches in the towns of Cambridge, Watertown, Charlestown, Boston, Roxbury, and Dorchester, mentioned in the said act, shall be, and hereby are, vested with all the powers and authority belonging or in anyway appertaining to the overseers of Harvard College: *Provided*, That nothing herein shall be construed to prevent the legislature of this Commonwealth from making such alterations in the government of the said university as shall be conducive to its advantage and the interest of the republic of letters, in as full a manner as might have been done by the legislature of the late province of the Massachusetts Bay.

Section 2. *The encouragement of literature*

Chap. v, Sec. 2. Wisdom and knowledge, as well as virtue, diffused generally among the body of the people, being necessary for the preservation of their rights and liberties; and as these depend on spreading the opportunities and advantages of education in the various parts of the country, and among the different orders of the people, it shall be the duty of the legislatures and magistrates, in all future periods of this Commonwealth, to cherish the interests of literature and the sciences, and all seminaries of them; especially the university at Cambridge, public schools, and grammar-schools in the towns; to encourage private societies and public institutions, by rewards and immunities, for the promotion of agriculture, arts, sciences, commerce, trades, manufactures, and a natural history of the country; to countenance and inculcate the principles of humanity and general benevolence, public and private charity, industry and frugality, honesty and punctuality in their dealings; sincerity, good humor, and all social affections and generous sentiments among the people.

NEW HAMPSHIRE, *Constitution of* 1784, *and* 1792

(The constitution of 1776 had been silent on the subject)

Sec. 83. Knowledge and learning generally diffused through a community being essential to the preservation of a free government, spreading the opportunities and advantages of education through the various parts of the country being highly conducive to promote this end, it shall be the duty of the legislatures and magistrates, in all future periods of this government, to cherish the interest of literature and the sciences, and all seminaries and public schools; to encourage private and public institutions, rewards and immunities for the promotion of agriculture, arts, sciences, commerce, trade, manufactures, and natural history of the country; to countenance and inculcate the principles of humanity and general benevolence, public and private charity, industry and economy, honesty and punctuality, sincerity, sobriety, and all social affections and generous sentiments among the people.

PENNSYLVANIA, 1. *Constitution of* 1776

Sec. 44. A school or schools shall be established in every county by the legislature, for the convenient instruction of youth, with such salaries to the masters, paid by the public, as may enable them to instruct youth at low prices; and all useful learning shall be duly encouraged and promoted in one or more universities.

Sec. 45. Laws for the encouragement of virtue, and prevention of vice and immorality, shall be made and constantly kept in force, and provision shall be made for their due execution; and all religious societies or bodies of men heretofore united or incorporated for the advancement of religion or learning, or for other pious and charitable purposes, shall be encouraged and protected in the enjoyment of the privileges, immunities, and estates which they were accustomed to enjoy, or could of right have enjoyed, under the laws and former constitution of this State.

2. *Constitutions of* 1790 *and* 1838

Sec. 1. The legislature shall, as soon as conveniently may be, provide, by law, for the establishment of schools throughout the State, in such manner that the poor may be taught *gratis*.

Sec. 2. The arts and sciences shall be promoted in one or more seminaries of learning.

DELAWARE, *Constitution of* 1792
(The constitution of 1776 had been silent on the subject)

ART. VIII, Sec. 12. The Legislature shall, as soon as conveniently may be, provide by law for . . . establishing schools, and promoting arts and sciences. (Continued unchanged in the Constitution of 1831.)

NORTH CAROLINA, *Constitution of* 1776

41. That a school or schools shall be established by the legislature, for the convenient instruction of youth, with such salaries to the masters, paid by the public, as may enable them to instruct at low prices; and all useful learning shall be duly encouraged, and promoted, in one or more universities. (Continued unchanged in the Constitution of 1835)

GEORGIA, 1. *Constitution of* 1777

ART. 54. Schools shall be erected in each county, and supported at the general expense of the State, as the Legislature shall hereafter point out.

2. *Constitution of* 1798

ART. IV, Sec. 13. The arts and sciences shall be promoted, in one or more seminaries of learning; and the legislature shall, as soon as conveniently may be, give such further donations and privileges to those already established as may be necessary to secure the objects of their institution; and it shall be the duty of the general assembly, at their next session, to provide effectual measures for the improvement and permanent security of the funds and endowments of such institutions.

260. Educational Provisions of the First Ohio Constitution
(Constitution of Ohio, 1803. Poore, B. P., *Charters and Constitutions*, vol. II, pp. 1461–63. Washington, 1877)

The first constitution of Ohio, framed by a convention meeting at Chillicothe, November 1–29, 1803, the year after its admission as a State, contained two sections which were noteworthy, for the time, for the strong stand taken for religious freedom and against any discrimination against children of the poor in the new schools to be provided by the State. These sections read:

ARTICLE VIII

That the general, great, and essential principles of liberty and free government may be recognized, and forever unalterably established, we declare —

Sec. 3. That all men have a natural and indefeasible right to worship Almighty God according to the dictates of their conscience; that no human authority can, in any case whatever, control or interfere with the rights of conscience; that no man shall be compelled to attend, erect, or support any place of worship, or to maintain any ministry, against his consent; and that no preference shall ever be given by law to any religious society or mode of worship; and no religious test shall be required as a qualification to any office of trust or profit. But religion, morality, and knowledge being essentially necessary to the good government and the happiness of mankind, schools and the means of instruction shall forever be encouraged by legislative provision, not inconsistent with the rights of conscience.

Sec. 25. That no law shall be passed to prevent the poor in the several counties and townships within this State, from an equal participation in the schools, academies, colleges, and universities within this State, which are endowed, in whole or in part, from the revenues arising from the donations made by the United States for the support of schools and colleges; and the doors of the said schools, academies, and universities shall be open for the reception of scholars, students, and teachers of every grade, without any distinction or preference whatever, contrary to the intent for which the said donations were made.

261. Educational Provisions of the First Indiana Constitution

(Constitution of Indiana, 1816. Poore, B. P., *Charters and Constitutions*, vol. 1 pp. 508–9. Washington, 1877)

The first constitution of Indiana, adopted by the constitutional convention meeting at Corydon, on June 29, 1816, was noteworthy for its broad and generous provisions regarding the matter of education and the advancement of human welfare by the State. The article relating to education reads as follows:

SECTION 1. Knowledge and learning generally diffused through a community being essential to the preservation of a free government, and spreading the opportunities and advantages of education through the various parts of the country being highly conducive to this end, it shall be the duty of the general assembly to provide by law for the improvement of such lands as are, or hereafter may be, granted by the United States to this State for the use of schools, and to apply any funds which may be raised from such lands, or from any other quarter, to the accomplishment of the grand object for which they are or may be intended. But no lands granted for the use of schools or seminaries of learning shall be sold, by authority of this State, prior to the year eighteen hundred and twenty; and the moneys which may be raised out of the sale of any such lands, or otherwise obtained for the purposes aforesaid, shall be and remain a fund for the exclusive purpose of promoting the interest of literature and the sciences, and for the support of seminaries and the public schools. The general assembly shall, from time to time, pass such laws as shall be calculated to encourage intellectual, scientifical, and agricultural improvement by allowing rewards and immunities for the promotion and improvement of arts, sciences, commerce, manufactures, and natural history; and to countenance and encourage the principles of humanity, industry, and morality.

Sec. 2. It shall be the duty of the general assembly, as soon as circumstances will permit, to provide by law for a general system of education, ascending in a regular graduation from township schools to a State university, wherein tuition shall be gratis, and equally open to all.

Sec. 3. And for the promotion of such salutary end, the money which shall be paid as an equivalent by persons exempt from military duty, except in times of war, shall be exclusively, and in equal proportions, applied to the support of county seminaries; also, all fines assessed for any breach of the penal laws shall be applied to said seminaries, in the counties wherein they shall be assessed. .

Sec. 4. It shall be the duty of the general assembly, as soon as circumstances will permit, to form a penal code, founded on the principles of reformation, and not of vindictive justice; and also to provide one or more farms to be an asylum for such persons who, by reason of age, infirmity, or other misfortunes, may have a claim upon the aid and beneficence of society, on such principles that such persons may therein find employment and every reasonable comfort, and lose by their usefulness the degrading sense of dependence.

Sec. 5. The general assembly, at the time they lay off a new county, shall cause at least 10 per cent to be reserved out of the proceeds of the sale of town-lots in the seat of justice of such county for the use of a public library for such county; and at the same session they shall incorporate a library company, under such rules and regulations as will best secure its permanence and extend its benefits.

262. Early American State School Legislation

(Digest of legislation, compiled from state histories)

The States making the best provision for schools early in their national history were the four Calvinistic-Puritan States in New England, and the State of New York, which early became a virtual westward extension of New England. Beside supporting the three colony colleges — Harvard, Dartmouth, and Yale — and maintaining grammar schools and academies, the laws of these five States made, for the time, good provisions for the management and support of a state system of elementary schools. Summarized briefly by States the laws enacted provided as follows:

Vermont. First general state school law in 1782. District system authorized. Support of schools by district tax or rate bill on parents optional. State aid granted. 1797 — Districts failing to provide schools to receive no state assistance. Reading, writing, and arithmetic to be taught in all schools. 1810 — Town school tax obligatory, and gradually increased from 1 per cent to 3 per cent by 1826. 1825 — State school fund created. 1827 — New school law required towns to build school buildings; required certificates of teachers; made the beginnings of school supervision; and added spelling, grammar, history, geography, and good behavior to the list of required school subjects.

New Hampshire. First general state school law in 1789. Town tax required, and rate fixed; teachers' certificates required: English schools and Latin schools required in the larger towns. 1791 — Town taxes for schools increased. 1821 — State school fund created. 1827 — Poor children to be provided with schoolbooks free.

Massachusetts. First general state school law in 1789. This legalized the practices in education of the past hundred and fifty years, and changed them into state requirements. A six-months elementary school required in every town, and twelve-months if having 100 families. Also a six-months grammar school required of every town having 150 families, and twelve-months if 200 families. All teachers to be certificated, and all grammar school teachers to be college graduates or certificated by the minister as skilled in Latin. These laws also applied to Maine, which was a part of Massachusetts until 1820.

Connecticut. Laws of 1700 and 1712 required all parishes or school societies operating schools to maintain an elementary school for from six to eleven months a year, varying with the size of the parish. Law of 1714 required inspection of schools and teachers. These laws continued in force by the new State. A permanent school fund had been created in 1750 by the sale of some Connecticut lands, and in 1795, on the sale of the Western Reserve in Ohio for $1,200,000, this was added to the permanent school fund. 1798 — School visitors and overseers ordered appointed.

New York. Little of an educational nature had been done in this State before the Revolution, except in the matter of church charity schools. In 1795 a law, valid for five years, was enacted which distributed $100,000 a year to the counties for schools. By 1798 there were 1352 schools in 16 of the 23 counties, and 59,660 children were enrolled. On the expiration of the law, in 1800, it could not be reënacted. By 1812, when the first permanent school law was enacted, New England immigration into the State had counter balanced the private-parochial-charity-school attitude of New York City. The Massachusetts district system was instituted, local taxation required, state aid distributed on the basis of school census, and the first State Superintendent of Schools provided for. 1814 — Teachers to be examined. By 1820 New York schools probably the best of any State in the Union.

263. Jefferson's Plan for Education in Virginia

(Jefferson, Thomas, *Notes of the State of Virginia*, pp. 243–49)

In 1799 Jefferson, then a member of the Virginia Legislature, submitted to that body a comprehensive bill "For the more general diffusion of knowledge" in the State, through the organization of a complete state system of schools. The plan[1] was not approved, but in the following statement Jefferson gives the more important provisions of his bill.

FIG. 64. THOMAS JEFFERSON
(1743–1826)

This bill proposes to lay off every county into small districts of five or six miles square, called hundreds, and in each of them to establish a school for teaching reading, writing, and arithmetic. The tutor to be supported by the hundred, and every person in it entitled to send their children three years gratis, and as much longer as they please, paying for it. These schools to be under a visitor, who is annually to chuse the boy, of best genius in the school, of those whose parents are too poor to give them further education, and to send him forward to one of the grammar schools, of which twenty are proposed to be erected in different parts of the country, for teaching Greek, Latin, geography, and the higher branches of numerical arithmetic. Of the boys thus sent in any one year, trial is to be made at the grammar schools one or two years, and the best genius of the whole selected, and continued six years, and the residue dismissed. By this means twenty of the best geniuses will be raked from the rubbish annually, and be instructed, at the public expence, so far as the grammar schools go. At the end of six years' instruction, one half are to be discontinued (from among whom the grammar schools will probably be supplied with future masters); and the other half, who are to be chosen for the superiority of their parts and

---

[1] This plan, commonly known as Jefferson's First Plan, may be found in full in the *Biennial Report of the Superintendent of Public Instruction of Virginia*, 1900–01, pp. lxx–lxxv.

disposition, are to be sent and continued three years in the study of such sciences as they shall chuse, at William and Mary college, the plan of which is proposed to be enlarged, . . . and extended to all the useful sciences. The ultimate result of the whole scheme of education would be the teaching of all the children of the state reading, writing, and common arithmetic: turning out ten annually of superior genius, well taught in Greek, Latin, geography, and the higher branches of arithmetic: turning out ten others annually, of still superior parts, who, to those branches of learning, shall have added such of the sciences as their genius shall have led them to: the furnishing to the wealthier part of the people convenient schools, at which their children may be educated, at their own expense. . . . Of all the view of this law none is more important, none more legitimate, than that of rendering the people safe, as they are the ultimate guardians of their own liberty. For this purpose the reading in the first stage, where they will receive their whole education, is proposed, as has been said, to be chiefly historical. History by apprising them of the past will enable them to judge of the future.

CHAPTER XXI
NEW THEORY AND SUBJECT-MATTER FOR THE ELEMENTARY SCHOOL

THE Readings of this chapter deal with the work of Rousseau, Basedow, Pestalozzi, and Fellenberg, and the influence of their work in redirecting and reshaping the elementary vernacular school. Largely out of their labors, coming at a time when the democratic theory of education was fast superseding the religious, the elementary school of the nineteenth century was given form and direction.

The first selection (264) gives a series of illustrative extracts from the *Émile* of Rousseau, extracts which are characteristic of Rousseau's thought and form of treatment. The second and third selections deal with the work of the German educational reformer, Basedow. The second (265) outlines the course of instruction given to each class in the institution he established at Dessau, and the third (266) being a page from his famous *Elementarwerk*.

The remainder of the Readings deal with the work of the more celebrated German-Swiss reformer, Pestalozzi. The first of these (267) is an explanation from Pestalozzi's own pen, made to a Society supporting his work, in which he tells them the objects he had in mind in his work. The three selections which follow are appreciative estimates of Pestalozzi's labors. The first (268) is by Professor John Griscom, of New York; the second (269) by the New England educator, Woodbridge; and the third, (270) by the English Dr. Mayo. The Reading following these (271) is a careful comparison of the work of Basedow and Pestalozzi, pointing out the comparative merits of the work of each.

The final selection of the chapter (272) is a description and estimate of the agricultural and mechanical and literary Institute of Emmanuel Fellenberg, at Hofwyl, the prototype of all such institutions in the nineteenth century.

264. The *Émile* of Jean-Jacques Rousseau

(Rousseau, Jean-Jacques, *Émile*. Paris, 1762. Trans. in Barnard's *American Journal of Education*, vol. v)

In 1762 there appeared in Paris, from the pen of a man who had declared war on organized society, two of the most influential books of the eighteenth century. One was the *Contrat social* (**R. 249**), and the other the *Émile*. The first dealt with the conditions under which organized government should continue, and the second with the education of an imaginary boy and his future wife. The *Émile* was divided into five books, as follows:

Book   I.   Infancy, or education to the age of five.
Book   II.   Childhood, or education from five to twelve.
Book III.   Boyhood, or education from twelve to fifteen.
Book IV.   Adolescence, or education from fifteen to eighteen.
Book   V.   Youth, or education from eighteen to twenty, and the education of his future wife, Sophie.

The volume was written in charming literary style, but presented no workable plan for education. Instead it set forth Rousseau's criticisms of the education of his time and his ideas, largely drawn from the *Thoughts* of John Locke (**Rs. 216, 217, 228, 229**), as to needed reforms in educational procedure. He popularized the best ideas of Locke and scattered them over Europe, thus awakening an interest in the education of children before unknown.

The following extracts from the *Émile* give some idea as to Rousseau's style, method of treatment, and ideas.

(a) The Preface.

The book was originally written for a thoughtful mother. Even if the thoughts contained in it are of no value in themselves, they ought to serve to awaken valuable thoughts in others. Every body writes and cries out against the usual methods of instruction, but no one suggests a better one. The knowledge of our century serves much more for destroying than for building up.

Childhood is not understood. The most judicious, in their teaching, confine themselves to that which it is necessary for a man to know; without considering what children are fit to learn. They are always seeking for a man in the child, without ever thinking what the child is before it becomes a man.

My system is nature's course of development. This term will be mistaken by many of my readers. They will take my book to be, not a work upon education, but the dreams of a visionary. I do not see as others do; but can I give myself others' eyes? I can not change my views; I can only suspect them. It has been often said to me, Propose only what can be accomplished. This means, propose something which is done now; or, at least, something good, of such a kind that it will come into agreement with prevalent evils. Such a collocation would destroy the good without healing the bad. I would rather adhere entirely to what is already received than to try any half measures.

(b) *The Three Teachers of Men.*

We come weak into the world, and need strength; bare of every thing, and need assistance. All which we have not at our birth, and have when we grow up, we acquire by education. This education we receive either from nature, from man, or from things. The inner development of our powers and organs is the education of nature; the use which we are taught to make of this development, is education by man; and what we learn by our own experience of the circumstances which have an influence over us, the education by things.

. . . .

The natural man is complete within himself; his is the numerical unity; an absolute whole; which has relations only with itself, or with its like. The man of society is only a fraction, which depends on its denominator, and whose value is determined by its relations to the whole; to the social body. Those modes of education are best for society, which are most efficient in perverting man from nature; in robbing him of his absolute existence, in giving him the relative one, such that after it he will feel and act only as a member of society.

This opposition between education for a citizen and for a man, corresponds with the opposition between public education together, and private education in the family. The former existed in Sparta; but exists no longer, for there is no longer any fatherland, or any citizens.

Thus, there remains for us only private education, or that of nature. But what would the man educated only for himself become afterward, among others? To know this, it is necessary to know the completely educated man; and also the natural man. This book is intended to assist in gaining such knowledge.

What now is necessary to be done to educate the natural man? Much, no doubt; chiefly in order to hinder any thing from being done.

The child should be educated for the common human vocation, not for any special situation; he must merely live, in good or evil, as life should bring them; and should learn more by experience than by teaching. Considering the instability of human affairs, and the restless, rebellious spirit of the present century, which is overturning every thing, no more unnatural method of education could be devised than that which deals with a child as if he were never to leave home, or the companionship of his own friends. As soon as the unhappy pupil has gone a step away, he is lost.

(c) *Handling Children properly.*

Ever since children have been instructed, no other means have been invented of managing them, but emulation, energy, jealousy, covetousness, and debased fear; those easily-excited, most dangerous and soul-destroying passions. At every injudicious lesson, you plant a vice deep within the heart. Foolish teachers think they have done wonders, when they have made the children bad, in order to communicate to them the idea of goodness. Then they say gravely, "Such is human nature." Such is your discipline, rather.

. . . .

Let children be children. If we choose to reverse the order of things, we shall get premature and flavorless fruits, which soon decay; we shall have young doctors and old children. We might as well expect children to be five feet high, as to have judgment in their tenth year.

(d) *Education Negative to the Twelfth Year.*

The usual education is such as if children leaped, at one bound, from the mother's breast to the age of reason. An entirely opposite method is the necessary one; an entirely negative one; which does not teach virtue and truth, but seeks to preserve the heart from vices, and the understanding from error. If you can bring your pupil to his twelfth year healthy and strong, even if he could not distinguish his right hand from his left, the eyes of his understanding would open to your first lesson in reason; for he would have no prejudices, habits, or any thing to stand in the way of the efficacy of your efforts. He would soon become, under your hands, the wisest of men; and although you began with doing nothing, you would have accomplished a wonder of education.

Do the opposite of what is usual and you will almost always do right.

From the efforts to make the child not a child, but a doctor, come the multiplied fault-findings, flatteries, threats, and reasonings of fathers and teachers. Be reasonable enough not to reason with your pupil. Make him practice his body, his limbs, his senses, his faculties; but keep his soul as inactive as possible; let the character of childhood ripen in the child. By such delay you gain time to learn the gradually developing character of your pupil, before you undertake to guide it, and make precipitate mistakes.

(e) *Émile's Character at the Age of Twelve.*

His exterior indicates self-possession and ease; he speaks with simplicity, and does not talk unnecessarily. His ideas are confined and clear; he knows nothing by rote, but much by experience. If he does not read so well in books, he reads better in the book of nature; he has less memory than power of judgment; he speaks but one language, but understands what he says. If he does not speak so well as others, he is much more capable of doing. He knows nothing of routine, custom, or habit; and what he did yesterday does not indicate what he will do to-day. Neither authority nor example impose upon him; he does and says only what seems good to him. He knows nothing of study, speech, or manners; but his language corresponds with his ideas, and his behavior arises from his wishes.

He has few moral ideas, but they are such as correspond to his age. Speak to him of duty or obedience, he does not know what you mean; order him, he does not understand you; but say to him, if you will do this to please me, I will sometime do something to please you, and he will instantly exert himself to comply with your wish; for nothing will please him more than to add to his legitimate influence over you, which he holds inviolable.

If he needs help himself, he makes use of the first that comes to hand, whether it be a king or a servant; for all men are alike to his sight. He shows to him whom he asks, that he does not consider any one bound to grant his request. He is simple and laconic in his expressions, and neither servile nor arrogant. Grant his request, and he does not thank you, but feels that he is your debtor; refuse it, and he does not complain nor urge you, but lets the matter drop.

Lively, active, he undertakes nothing too great for his powers, but which he has tried and understands. He has an observing and intelligent eye; and asks no useless questions about what he sees, but examines it himself. As his imagination is yet inactive, and nothing has been done to stimulate it, he sees only what really exists, does not overestimate danger, and is always cool.

Business and play are the same to him, his play is his business; he finds no difference between them. Among city children, there is none more dextrous than he, and all are weaker; he is equal to country children in strength, and surpasses them in dexterity. He is fit to lead his companions, by his talent and experience, without any other authority, without wishing to command; he is at the head of the rest, and they obey him without knowing it.

He is a mature child, and has lived a child's life; his happiness has not been exchanged for his education. If he dies young, his death is to be mourned, but not his life.

Ordinary men would not understand a boy so trained; they would see in him nothing but a scapegrace. A teacher could make no parade with him, could ask him no show questions; and those are the chief of the education of the day.

(f) *Émile in his Fifteenth Year.*

Being obliged to learn by means of himself, he uses his own understanding, not that of other men; and yields nothing to authority. For most of our errors come less from ourselves than from others. By this continual practice, his mind has acquired a strength like that which is given to the body by labor and hardship. For the same reason his powers develop themselves only in proportion to his growth. He remembers only what has commended itself to his understanding. Thus he has little knowledge, but no half knowledge. He knows that his knowledge is not great; his mind is open, decided, and, if not instructed, at least capable of instruction. Of all that he does he knows the use, and of all he believes, the reason. He proceeds slowly, but thoroughly. He possesses only natural knowledge; none of history; and none of mathematics and ethics. He knows little of generalizing and forming abstractions; he observes properties common to many bodies, without reasoning upon the existence of these properties. What is strange to him he values only by its relations to himself, but this valuation is sufficient and certain. What is most useful to him he values most, and cares nothing for opinion.

Émile is laborious, moderate, patient, persevering, and courageous. His fancy, not heated in any way, never magnifies danger; he can endure sorrow with fortitude, for he has not been trained to oppose himself to fate. What death is, he does not rightly know, but, being accustomed to submit without resistance to the laws of necessity, he will die, when he must, without sighing and without pretense. Nature does not require more of us, in that moment, so abhorred by all. To live free, to set the heart as little as possible upon human things, is the surest means of learning to die.

Émile is destitute of the social virtues. He acts without respect to others; and it is right in his eyes that others should have no regard to him. He makes no demands upon others, he thinks himself under no obligation to any one. Standing alone in society, he counts only upon himself, and is capable of more than others at his age. He has no errors or vices, except such as are unavoidable. His body is healthy, his members are disciplined, his understanding correct and without prejudices, his heart free and without passions. Self-esteem, first and most natural of all the passions, has scarcely awakened in him. Without destroying the peace of any one, he has lived as peacefully, happily, and freely as nature will permit. Do you find that the child, thus educated to his fifteenth year, has wasted his earliest years?

(g) Émile, a Natural Man.

Émile now for the first time appears upon the theater of the world; or rather he stands behind the scenes, sees the players dress and undress themselves; and by what coarse means the spectators are deceived. It will elevate him to see how the human race makes sport of itself. Educated in entire freedom, he will sorrow over the misery of kings, those slaves of all those who obey them; false wise men, in the chains of their vain honors; rich fools, the martyrs to their own luxury. He will be in danger of thinking himself wise, and all others fools; and only mortifying experience can protect him from such vanity.

I shall be thought a visionary, and Émile a phantasy, because he is so different from ordinary youths. It is overlooked that he is a natural man, but that other youths are brought up according to the notions of men.

Others, at Émile's age, are already philosophers and theologians; while he does not know yet what philosophy is, and even has not yet heard God spoken of.

I am no visionary; my pedagogy is based upon experience; since without regard to rank, nation, &c., I have found what is proper to all men, and have educated Émile according to that; not as a savage for the woods, but as a man who will have to maintain himself independent in the whirlpool of society.

(h) Religious Instruction.

We are brought up in close connection with the natural world; and for the abstract, the purely intellectual, we have scarcely any comprehension. God withdraws our senses from themselves; the word mind has a meaning only for the philosophers. Monotheism has come, by a process of generalization, from material polytheism.

In his fifteenth year, Émile does not yet know that he has a soul; and perhaps he will find it out too early in his eighteenth.

A child, it is said, must be brought up in the religion of his father; and he must be taught that this alone is true; and that others are absurd. But if the power of this instruction extends only so far as the country in which it is given, and depends only upon authority, for which Émile has been taught to have no regard, what then? In what religion shall we educate him? To this there is only the simple answer, in none; we will only put him in a condition to choose for himself, that to which the best use of his own reason may bring him.

(i) The Approaching Revolutions in Society.

Your education of men should be adapted to what they are in themselves; not to any thing external. By training him exclusively for one condition, you make him unfit for any other, and unfortunate, if his situation should ever change. How ridiculous is a great lord who has become a beggar, and who holds in his misery to the prejudices of his birth; how contemptible the rich man become poor, who feels himself completely degraded!

You acquiesce in the social order of the present, without considering that this order is subject to unavoidable changes; and that it is impossible for you to foresee or to prevent the revolution which may come upon your children. The great will become small, the rich poor, the monarch a subject. We are approaching a crisis; the century of revolutions. It is impossible that the great monarchies of Europe can last long. And who can say what shall then happen to you? What men have made, men can destroy; only the character given by nature is indestructible; and nature makes neither princes, nor rich men, nor great lords. What will the satrap do in his debasement, who has been educated only for his high position? What will the farmer-general do, in his poverty, who lives only upon his money? Happy will he be, then, who shall understand how to leave the condition which has left him, and to remain a man in spite of fate.

265. The Instruction in Basedow's "Philanthropinum"

(Karl von Raumer, *Geschichte der Pädagogik;* trans. in Barnard's *American Journal of Education*, vol. v, pp. 519–20)

In 1774 there was opened, in the town of Dessau, in the duchy of Anhalt, in northern Germany, and through the patronage of

the prince of the village, a new type of school which was christened the "Philanthropinum." The school was provided and endowed by the prince to enable a German by the name of Johann Bernard Basedow to put into actual practice certain ideas he had for some time been advocating as to a new method in education; the ideas being based largely on the work of Rousseau. The school opened with Basedow and three assistants as teachers, and four-teen children in attendance, though in

FIG. 65. BASEDOW (1723–90)

a few years it came to have boarders drawn from long distances. The school was organized on a plan of four class divisions, small group instruction, and the following outline of work.

For the First Class of Younger Scholars

8–9   Reading German, with Jahn; the books being Von Rochow's and Weissen's *Children's Friend*, Campe's *Manual of Morals for Children of the Educated Classes*, Feddersen's *Examples of Wisdom and Virtue*, Funk's *Little Occupations for Children*, and *First nourishment for the sound human understanding*.

9–10   Writing, with Vogel, alternately with the second class, all the week; and instructive conversation with Rector Neuendorf, at his room, or during walks.

10–11   Latin, with Feder; from *Phædrus*, Büsching's *Liber Latinus*, and select parts of Basedow's *Liber Elementaris*, and *Chrestomathia Colloquiorum Erasmi*.

11–12   French, with Jasperson.

1–2 Music, and recreation, under care of Feder.

2–3 Drawing, with Doctor Samson, under charge, alternately, of Jasperson, Vogel, and Spener.

3–4 Dancing, with the master, under care of Vogel.

4–5 French, with Spener; from select portions of Basedow's *Manuel d'éducation*.

5–6 Latin, with Feder; from select portions of the Latin *Elementary Book*.

6–7 For walking, under the care of Neuendorf.

For the Second Class of Younger Pupils

8–9 Writing, with Vogel.

9–10 Writing and walking, alternately with the first class.

10–12 Latin, with Wölke.

1–2 As the first class.

2–3 Drawing, as in first class.

3–4 Dancing, as in first class.

4–5 French, with Jasperson; from select parts of the *Manuel d'éducation*.

5–6 Instructive reading, with Jahn, in his room.

6–7 Conversation with Neuendorf. On the first and fifteenth of each month, letter-writing was practiced. Walks were taken two afternoons a week.

For the First Class of Older Boarders

8–9 Instruction in taste, and in German style, by Professor Trapp, from Ramler's *Batteux*, Schützen's *Manual for Training the Understanding and the Taste*, and Sulzer's *First Exercises* (*Vorübungen*).   This for the first three days of the week.   In the other three, Professor Trapp instructed in natural religion and morals, from Basedow's *Natural Wisdom for those in Private Stations*.

9–10 Dancing, with a master; riding, with riding-master Schrödter, under the inspection of Feder and Hauber; alternately, every day, except Wednesday and Saturday.   Dancing was taught in the fourth auditorium, riding in the prince's riding-school.

10–12 Instruction by Basedow, at his house, in Latin; either in ancient history (with accompanying studies), or in practical philosophy, from Cicero's *De Officiis*.

12–1 Dinner.

1–2 Moderate exercise; as, turning, planing, and carpentry, in the rooms of Prince Dietrich's palace, granted for that purpose by the prince.

2–3 Monday and Tuesday, Geography, by Hauber, from Pfennig's *Geography*.   Wednesday, knowledge of the human body, and a partial course in Chemistry, by the prince's privy councilor and private physician, Kretzschmar, at his house, where the preparations and instruments were at hand. On the other three days of the week, mathematical drawing, by Professor Wölke.

3–5 French and universal history, by Professor Trapp, from Schröckh's *Universal History*, and Millot's *Histoire Universelle*, during five days. Saturday, a news-lecture, by Hauber, to make the elder pupils gradually acquainted with public transactions and remarkable occurrences.

5–6 Mathematics, by Busse, from Ebert's *Further Introduction to the Philosophical and Mathematical Sciences*, during the first three days of the week; in the other three, physics, from Erxleben's *Natural Philosophy*.

6–7 Knowledge of the heavens and earth, by Wölke, from Schmid's *Book of the Celestial Bodies*, twice a week; and the other four days, Greek, by Danner, from Rector Stroth's *Chrestomathia Græca*, Lucian's *Timon*, and Xenophon's *Memorabilia*.

For the Second Class of Elder Scholars

8–9 Similar to the studies of the first class; by Professor Trapp.

9–10 Riding and dancing, interchangeably with the first class. Arithmetic for some of them, with Professor Trapp.

10–11 Latin, with Hauber; from Basedow's *Chrestomathia in historia antiqua*.

11–12 Latin, with Danner; from Basedow's *Chrestomathia*.

1–2 Turning and planing; in alternation with the first class.

2–3 Drawing, with Doctor Samson. Some were instructed with the first class; and some study arithmetic, with Busse.

3–5 Same exercises as the first class.

5–6 Mathematics, with Danner, three days; on the other days, some were taught with the first class, and others received various kinds of private instruction.

6–7 English, from the *Vicar of Wakefield*, with Professor Trapp.

266. Basedow's *Elementarwerk*

The same year that Basedow was enabled to open his Philanthropinum at Dessau, he published two books upon which he had been at work for years, and the publication of which had been heralded throughout northern Europe. One was a *Method-Book for Fathers and Mothers*, and the second his famous *Elementarwerk mit Kupfern*, or illustrated *Elementary Book* for children. The latter was the first illustrated textbook prepared for the use of children since the publication (1654) of the *Orbis Pictus* (**R. 221**) of Comenius. It contained a hundred pictures, and was issued in four volumes. Written in German, it was translated into Latin, and later into Russian, in which form it enjoyed an extended popularity.

It was intended to be a veritable encyclopædia for young people of all that was most worth knowing about natural objects, mor-

FIG. 66. A LESSON IN NATURAL HISTORY
(Reproduced from the *Elementarwerk* of Basedow)

als, commerce, and social duties, and was claimed to provide "an incomparable method, founded on experience, of teaching children to read without weariness or loss of time." It became the *Orbis Pictus* of the eighteenth century for German lands.

The above illustration, reproduced from a copy of this celebrated work, is quite typical.

267. Pestalozzi explains his Work

(*The Method;* a Report by Pestalozzi. Aix-la-Chapelle, 1828)

One does not get a very good idea of Pestalozzi's work from his own writings. His impractical character showed in his attempts at writing as in his management of schools. Instead, it is from the writings of contemporaries that one gets the best picture of his work and his ideas. His *How Gertrude Teaches her Children* is perhaps the best exponent of his work.

In 1800 Pestalozzi made a Report in writing to a Society of Friends of Education, which had been formed to support his efforts at the time of his return from Stanz to Burgdorf. In this he gave a systematic statement of his conceptions as to method in education. The Report remained unprinted until 1828, when it was edited and published. The opening pages state the general outline of his method, and are reproduced below; the remainder of the Report goes into detail as to the application.

I am trying to psychologize the instruction of mankind; I am trying to bring it into harmony with the nature of my mind, with that of my circumstances and my relations to others. I start from no positive form of teaching, as such, but simply ask myself: —

"What would you do, if you wished to give a single child all the knowledge and practical skill he needs, so that by wise care of his best opportunities he might reach inner content?"

I think to gain this end the human race needs exactly the same thing as the single child.

I think, further, the poor man's child needs a greater refinement in the methods of instruction than the rich man's child.

Nature, indeed, does much for the human race, but we have strayed away from her path. The poor man is thrust away from her bosom, and the rich destroy themselves both by rioting and by lounging on her overflowing breast.

The picture is severe. But ever since I have been able to see I have seen it so; and it is from this view that the impulse arises within me, not merely to plaster over the evils in schools which are enervating the people of Europe, but to cure them at their root.

But this can never be done without subordinating all forms of instruction to those eternal laws by which the human mind is raised from physical impressions on the senses to clear ideas.

I have tried to simplify the elements of all human knowledge according to these laws, and to put them into a series of typical examples that shall result in spreading a wide knowledge of Nature, general clearness of the most important ideas in the mind, and vigorous exercises of the chief bodily powers, even among the lowest classes.

I know what I am undertaking; but neither the difficulties in the way, nor my own limitations in skill and insight, shall hinder me from giving my mite for a purpose which Europe needs so much. And, gentlemen, in laying before you the results of those labors on which my life has been spent, I beg of you but one thing. It is this: — Separate those of my assertions that may be doubtful from those that are indisputable. I wish to found my conclusions entirely upon complete convictions, or at least upon perfectly recognized premises.

The most essential point from which I start is this: —

Sense-impression of Nature is the only true foundation of human instruction, because it is the only true foundation of human knowledge.

All that follows is the result of this sense-impression, and the process of abstraction from it. Hence in every case where this is imperfect, the result also will be neither certain, safe, nor positive; and in any case, where the sense-impression is inaccurate, deception and error follow.

I start from this point and ask: — "What does Nature itself do in order to present the world truly to me, so far as it affects me? That is, — By what means does she bring the sense-impressions of the most important things around me to a perfection that contents me?" And I find, — She does this through my surroundings, my wants and my relations to others.

Through my surroundings she determines the kinds of sense-impressions I receive. Through my wants she stimulates my activities. Through my relations to others she widens my observation and raises it to insight and forethought. Through my surroundings, my wants, my relations to others, she lays the foundations of my knowledge, my work, and my right-doing.

And now I ask myself: — "What general method of the Art of Teaching has the experience of ages put into the hands of humanity to strengthen this influence of Nature in developing intelligence, energy, and virtue in our race?" And I find these methods are speech, the arts of drawing, writing, reckoning, and measuring.

And when I trace back all these elements of the human Art to their origin, I find it in the common basis of our mind, by means of which our understanding combines those impressions which the senses have received from Nature, and represents them as wholes, that is, as concepts.

.   .   .   .

And when I ask again: — What are the unmistakable consequences of thus rudely despising these laws, I cannot conceal from myself the physical atrophy, one-sidedness, warped judgment, superficiality, and presumptuous vanity that characterize the masses in this generation, are the necessary consequences of despising these laws, and of the isolated, unpsychological, baseless, unorganized, unconnected teaching, which our poor race has received in our lower schools.

Then the problem I have to solve is this: — How to bring the elements of every art into harmony with the very nature of my mind, by following the psychological mechanical laws by which my mind rises from physical sense-impressions to clear ideas.

Nature has two principal and general means of directing human activity towards the cultivation of the arts, and these should be employed, if not before, at least side by side with any particular means. They are singing, and the sense of the beautiful.

With song the mother lulls her babe to sleep; but here, as in every thing else, we do not follow the law of Nature. Before the child is a year old, the mother's song ceases; by that time she is, as a rule, no longer a mother to the weaned child. For him, as for all others, she is only a distracted, over-burdened woman. Alas! that it is so. Why has not the art of ages taught us to join the nursery lullabies to a series of national songs, that should rise in the cottages of the people from the gentle cradle song to the sublime hymn of praise? But I cannot fill this gap. I can only point it out.

It is the same with the sense of the beautiful. All Nature is full of grand and lively sights, but Europe has done nothing to awaken in the poor a sense for these beauties, or to arrange them in such a way as to produce a series of impressions, capable of developing this sense. The sun rises for us in vain; in vain for us he sets. In vain for us do wood and meadow, mountain and valley spread forth their innumerable charms. They are nothing to us.

Here, again, I can do nothing; but if ever popular education should cease to be the barbarous absurdity it now is, and put itself into harmony with the real needs of our nature, this want will be supplied.

I leave these means of directing the Art generally, and turn to the forms by which special means of education, speaking, reading, drawing, and writing should be taught.

268. A Visit to Pestalozzi at Yverdon

(Griscom, John, *A Year in Europe*, vol. i, pp. 415-20. New York, 1823; 2 vols.)

In 1818-19 Professor John Griscom (1774-1852), manager of a private school in New York City, and who later became a professor in Queen's (now Rutgers) College in New Jersey, visited Europe and made a study of the schools, colleges, and charitable institutions of Great Britain, France, Sweden, Italy, and Holland, and on his return published his observations in *A Year in Europe* (1819). This book had an important influence in the United States on the development of reformatory schools and institutions for the training of defectives. The following extract from the report of his visit to Pestalozzi's school at Yverdon gives an insight into the work and personal side of the school.

Breakfast finished, our first and chief concern here was to visit the celebrated Institute of Pestalozzi. This establishment occupies a large castle the use of which was granted to Pestalozzi by the Canton of Berne, when the town of Yverdon was included in that Canton, and the government of the Pays de Vaud, to which it now belongs, continues the grant. On entering the castle, we were invited into a private room. I gave my letters to the person in attendance, who took them immediately to the chief. The good old man soon came in, seized me warmly by the hand, and seeing my hat on my head, he pointed to it in a sort of ecstacy, with his eyes almost filled with tears. I hardly knew how to interpret this emotion, and asked him if he wished me to take it off. He answered very earnestly, "No, no, no; keep it on; you are right." He seemed very glad to see us, and as he speaks French very imperfectly, and with an indistinct accent, he said he would call Monsieur Greaves to talk with us. This gentleman soon came and entered immediately into a detail of the institution, its principles, its spirit, its arrangement, etc. He is an Englishman, and as I found upon inquiry, brother to the lady I had seen at Lausanne. He has been some weeks with Pestalozzi, for the purpose of understanding his system thoroughly, in order to aid a sister in England in the education of her children. He enters warmly into its concern, and will be useful in making it better known. He explained to us very clearly the leading ideas and views of human nature which induced Pestalozzi to become an instructor of youth. . . .

His school consists at present of about 90 boys, — German, Prussian, French, Swiss, Italian, Spanish, and English. It is divided into four principal classes, according to the attainments of the pupils. These classes are subdivided into others. There are seven schoolrooms in the castle, and twelve teachers or professors. . . .

We spent most of the day in the different schoolrooms witnessing the exercises of the scholars. Very few books are used, as it is expected the children can read well before they come there. But to describe the modes of teaching, so as to render them clearly intelligible, would require much more time and space than I can possibly allot to it, were I ever so competent to make it known. We saw the exercises of arithmetic, writing, drawing, mathematics, lessons in music and gymnastics, something of geography, French, Latin, and German. To teach a school, in the way practiced here, without book, and almost entirely by verbal instruction, is extremely laborious. The teacher must be constantly with the child, always talking, questioning, explaining, and repeating. The pupils, however, by this process, are brought into very close intimacy with the instructor. Their capacities, all their faculties and propensities, become laid open to his observation. This gives him an advantage which can not possibly be gained in the ordinary way in which schools are generally taught. The children look well, appear very contented, and apparently live in great harmony one with another; which, considering the diversity of national character and temper here collected, can be attributed only to the spirit of love and affection which sways the breast of the principal of the institution, and extends its benign influence throughout all the departments.

The success of this mode of instruction greatly depends upon the personal qualifications of those who undertake to conduct it. There is nothing of mechanism in it, as in the Lancastrian plan; no laying down of precise rules for managing classes, etc. It is all mind and feeling. Its arrangements must always depend on the ages, talents, and tempers of the scholars, and require on the part of the teachers the most diligent and faithful attention. Above all, it requires that the teacher should consider himself as the father and bosom friend of his pupils, and to be animated with the most affectionate desires for their good. Pestalozzi himself is all this. His heart glows with such a spirit that the good old man can hardly refrain from bestowing kisses on all with whom he is concerned. He holds out his hands to his pupils on every occasion, and they love him as a child loves its mother. His plan of teaching is just fit for the domestic fireside, with a father or mother in the center, and a circle of happy children around them. He is aware of this, and wishes to extend the knowledge of his plan to every parent. Pestalozzi is 72 years of age. It is quite unfortunate for the progress of his system on the continent, that he pays so little attention to exteriors, regarding dress, furniture, etc., as of no moment whatever, provided the mind and heart be right.

269. An Estimate of Pestalozzi's Work

(Woodbridge, Wm. C., *American Annals of Education and Instruction*, vol. vii, p. 14. January, 1837)

William C. Woodbridge was a New England educator who spent the year 1820 and the years 1825–29 in Europe. In a series of letters he first really brought the work of Pestalozzi and Fellenberg to the attention of American teachers. In closing an article comparing the work of Basedow and Pestalozzi (271) he offers the following estimate of Pestalozzi's work and influence.

. . . as one of his admirers observed, it was his province to educate ideas and not children. He combated, with unshrinking boldness and untiring perseverance, through a long life, the prejudices and abuses of the age in reference to education, both by his example and by his numerous publications. He attacked with great vigor, and with no small degree of success, that favorite maxim of bigotry and tyranny that obedience and devotion are the legitimate offspring of ignorance. He denounced that degrading system, which considers it enough to enable man to procure a subsistence for himself and his offspring — and in this manner, merely to place him on a level with the beast of the forest; and which deems every thing lost whose value can not be estimated in money. He urged upon the consciences of parents and rulers, with an energy approaching that of the ancient prophets, the solemn duties which Divine Providence had imposed upon them, in committing to their charge the present and future destinies of their fellow-beings. In this way, he produced an impulse, which pervaded the continent of Europe, and which, by means of his popular and theoretical works, reached the cottages of the poor and the palaces of the great. His institution at Yverdon was crowded with men of every nation; not merely those who were led by the same impulse which inspired him, but by the agents of kings and noblemen, and public institutions, who came to make themselves acquainted with his principles, in order to become his fellow-laborers in other countries.

270. Doctor Mayo on Pestalozzi

(From a pamphlet issued by the Reverend Charles Mayo. London, 1826)

The Reverend Charles Mayo (1792–1846), who, with his sister Elizabeth (1793–1865), did more than any one else to introduce Pestalozzian ideas and methods into England, spent the years 1819–22 at Yverdon as a worker with Pestalozzi. In 1826 he delivered several lectures on the principles of the Pestalozzian system of education, and later published a summary of these in a pamphlet for more general distribution. The following on Pestalozzi's school is an extract from this pamphlet.

Some years ago an Irish gentleman, traveling through Yverdon, in the Pays de Vaud, was prevailed on to spend a couple of hours in the Institution of Pestalozzi. The first class he inspected was carried on in a language not familiar to him, yet was he much struck with the intelligence and vivacity portrayed in the features of the pupils. But when, the following hour, he witnessed the power of the method in its application to arithmetic, he discovered in the scholars a clear conception of number and its relations, a precision and rapidity in mental calculation, and an animation and interest in their employment, which convinced him that a secret had been discovered by Pestalozzi, and he was resolved, if possible, to penetrate it. The proposed visit of two hours terminated at the expiration of three years; nor was his admiration of the method confined to a bare speculative reception of the principles; he transplanted into his own country the practical truths he had learned in Switzerland, and though Providence has interrupted the course of his more extended labors, he still, in the bosom of his own family, applies the lessons of Pestalozzi, and teaches his children to revere his name. It was not a theoretical examination of the method that effected this conviction and animated to these exertions; it was a personal view of the practical influence of the system, in scenes lit up by the genius and warmed with the benevolence of Pestalozzi himself. Could I transport you in thought to the scenes where Pestalozzi lived, and taught, and suffered with his scholars, the heart would feel even before the understanding discerned the beauty, the truth of his principles. A skeleton view of his system might lead you to a cold approbation of his views, but it must be the living, the breathing portraiture of the man, that must awaken your love, and dispose you to imitate what you have learned to admire. I have seen him surrounded by his pupils, have marked the overflowings of his tenderness; I have read in a thousand traits of good-nature the confirmation of his history. I have witnessed the affecting simplicity, the *abandon* with which he speaks of all he has done and essayed to do for humanity. Could I convey to others the sentiments I feel for him, Pestalozzi would be loved and honored as he deserves. Three years of intimate connection with him, every day marked with some proof of his affection, may well have knit my heart to his; and among the most cherished recollections of the past is, that Pestalozzi honored me with his friendship, and thanked me for cheering his decline.

271. Work of Pestalozzi and Basedow compared

(Woodbridge, Wm. C., *American Annals of Education and Instruction*, vol. VII, pp. 8-11. January, 1837)

In the article previously referred to (**269**) Woodbridge gives a comparative estimate of the work and principles of Basedow and Pestalozzi, as follows:

As the result of his investigations, Pestalozzi assumed, as a fundamental principle, that education, in order to fit man for his destination, must proceed according to the laws of nature. To adopt the language of his followers — that it must not act as an arbitrary mediator between the child and nature, between man and God, pursuing its own artificial arrangements, instead of the indications of Providence — that it should assist the course of natural development, instead of doing it violence — that it should watch and follow its progress, instead of attempting to mark out a path agreeably to a preconceived system.

I. In view of this principle, he did not choose, like Basedow, to cultivate the mind in a material way, merely by inculcating and engrafting every thing relating to external objects, and giving mechanical skill. He sought, on the contrary, to develop, and exercise, and strengthen the faculties of the child by a steady course of excitement to self-activity, with a limited degree of assistance to his efforts.

II. In opposition to the haste, and blind groping of many teachers without system, he endeavored to find the proper point for commencing, and to proceed in a slow and gradual, but uninterrupted course, from one point to another — always waiting until the first should have a certain degree of distinctness in the mind of the child, before entering upon the exhibition of the second. To pursue any other course would only give superficial knowledge, which would neither afford pleasure to the child, nor promote its real progress.

III. He opposed the undue cultivation of the memory and understanding, as hostile to true education. He placed the essence of education in the harmonious and uniform development of every faculty, so that the body should not be in advance of the mind, and that in the development of the mind, neither the physical powers, nor the affections, should be neglected; and that skill in action should be acquired at the same time with knowledge. When this point is secured, we may know that education has really begun, and that it is not merely superficial.

IV. He required close attention and constant reference to the peculiarities of every child, and of each sex, as well as to the characteristics of the people among whom he lived, in order that he might acquire the development and qualifications necessary for the situation to which the Creator destined him, when he gave him these active faculties, and be prepared to labor successfully for those among whom he was placed at his birth.

V. While Basedow introduced a multitude of subjects of instruction (**R. 265**) into the schools, without special regard to the development of the intellectual powers, Pestalozzi considered this plan as superficial. He limited the elementary subjects of instruction to Form, Number and Language, as the essential condition of definite and distinct knowledge; and believed that these elements should be taught with the utmost possible simplicity, comprehensiveness, and mutual connection.

VI. Pestalozzi, as well as Basedow, desired that instruction should commence with the intuition or simple perception of external objects and their relations. He was not, however, satisfied with this alone, but wished that the *art of observing* should also be acquired. He thought the things perceived of less consequence than the cultivation of the perceptive powers, which should enable the child to observe completely, — to exhaust the subjects which should be brought before his mind.

VII. While the Philanthropinists attached great importance to special exercises of reflection, Pestalozzi would not make this a subject of separate study. He maintained that every subject of instruction should be properly treated, and thus become an exercise of thought; and believed that lessons in Number, and Proportion and Size, would give the best occasion for it.

VIII. Pestalozzi, as well as Basedow, attached great importance to Arithmetic, particularly to Mental Arithmetic. He valued it, however, in the limited view of its practical usefulness, but as an excellent means of strengthening the mind. He also introduced Geometry into the elementary schools, and the art connected with it, of modeling and drawing beautiful objects. He wished, in this way, to train the eye, the hand, and the touch, for that more advanced species of drawing which had not been thought of before. Proceeding from the simple and intuitive, to the more complicated and difficult forms, he arranged a series of exercises, so gradual and complete, that the method of teaching this subject was soon brought to a good degree of perfection.

IX. The Philanthropinists introduced the instruction of language into the common schools, but limited it chiefly to the writing of letters and preparation of essays. But Pestalozzi was not satisfied with a lifeless repetition of the rules of grammar, nor yet with mere exercises for common life. He aimed at a development of the laws of language from within — an introduction into its internal nature and construction and peculiar spirit — which would not only cultivate the intellect, but also improve the affections. . . .

X. Like Basedow, Rochow, and others, Pestalozzi introduced vocal music into the circle of school studies, on account of its powerful influence on the heart. But he was not satisfied that the children should learn to sing a few melodies by note or by ear. He wished them to know the rules of melody and rhythm, and dynamics — to pursue a regular course of instruction, descending to its very elements, and rendering the musical notes as familiar as the sounds of the letters. The extensive work of Nageli and Pfeiffer has contributed very much to give this branch of instruction a better form.

XI. He opposed the abuse which was made of the Socratic method in many of the Philanthropinic and other schools, by attempting to draw something out of children before they had received any knowledge. He recommends, on the contrary, in the early periods of instruction, the established method of dictation by the teacher and repetition by the scholar, with a proper regard to rhythm, and at a later period, especially in the mathematical and other subjects which involve reasoning, the modern method, in which the teacher merely gives out the problems in a proper order, and leaves them to be solved by the pupils, by the exertion of their own powers.

XII. Pestalozzi opposes strenuously the opinion that religious instruction should be addressed exclusively to the understanding; and shows that religion lies deep in the hearts of men, and that it should not be enstamped from without, but developed from within; that the basis of religious feeling is to be found in the childish disposition to love, to thankfulness, to veneration, obedience and confidence toward its parents; that these should be cultivated and strengthened and directed toward God; and that religion should be formally treated of at a later period in connection with the feelings thus excited. As he requires the mother to direct the first development of all the faculties of her child, he assigns to her especially the task of first cultivating the religious feelings.

XIII. Pestalozzi agreed with Basedow, that mutual affection ought to reign between the educator and the pupil, both in the house and in the school, in order to render education effectual and useful. He was, therefore, as little disposed as Basedow, to sustain school despotism; but he did not rely on artificial excitements, such as those addressed to emulation. He preferred the children should find their best reward in the consciousness of increased intellectual vigor; and expected the teacher to render the instruction so attractive, that the delightful feeling of progress should be the strongest excitement to industry and to morality.

XIV. Pestalozzi attached as much importance to the cultivation of the bodily powers, and the exercise of the senses, as the Philanthropinists, and in his publications, pointed out a graduated course for this purpose. But as Gutsmuths, Vieth, Jahn, and Clias treated this subject very fully, nothing further concerning it was written by his immediate followers.

Such are the great principles which entitle Pestalozzi to the high praise of having given a more natural, a more comprehensive and deeper foundation for education and instruction, and of having called into being a method which is far superior to any that preceded it.

272. Hofwyl as seen by an American

(Griscom, John, *A Year in Europe*, vol. 1, pp. 382–98. New York, 1823; 2 vols.)

The chief influence of Griscom's book, previously referred to in the introduction to **R. 268,** was along the lines of reformatory and charitable education and the development of manual-labor schools, in both of which we were then just making a beginning. His description of his visits to Pestalozzi also awakened some interest. The following is selected from a rather long description of his visit to Fellenberg's Institutions, at Hofwyl.

Fellenberg, and his Principles of Education

I was introduced to Mr. Fellenberg by three letters — two from Paris and one from Geneva, and was cordially received, having recorded my name and residence in a book in the office, and sent in my card and letters. He is a man of middle age, of a mild and agreeable countenance, and of polite and genteel manners. He seated me on a sofa, and entered upon an explanation of the principles of his establishment, and the particular views of education, which had induced him to engage in it. He considers society as divisible into three distinct parts; the higher (comprehending the noble and wealthy), the middling, and the poor. The greatest defects of education he supposes to exist in the two extreme classes, and that these distinctions or classes among men would always prevail in every civilized country he believed to be incontrovertible; and, of course, any attempt to break down the distinction would be fruitless. It is, therefore, of consequence that they should be each educated in a manner conformable to their situations, but in such a way as to develop, to the highest extent, the best faculties of their nature; and, while it preserves the proper relation between them, it should, at the same time, encourage the feelings of kindliness and sympathy on the one part, and of respect and love on the other. This, he thought, could be effected upon no plan so effectually as bringing them up side by side, so that they should have each other constantly in view, without any necessity whatever of mixing or associating. The rich, by observing the industry, the skill, and the importance of the laboring classes, would learn to entertain just sentiments respecting them, and the poor, by feeling and experiencing the kindly influence of the rich, would regard them as benefactors.

With respect to the best means of cultivating the faculties which, in their due operation, are to promote the permanent happiness of men, he considers agriculture as affording opportunities and advantages of the greatest importance, and next to this, the mechanic arts. Agreeably to these leading views, his establishment consists of two distinct parts: a boarding-school of the sons of noblemen and gentlemen, in which no pains are spared to provide them with teachers in every useful science; and of a school of boys, taken from the poorest class, who are clothed and fed in a very plain, coarse, and farmer-like style, and who work diligently in the fields at employments adapted to their strength and skill. During two hours in the day in summer, and more in winter, these boys are instructed in letters, and in music. They are likewise introduced into the workshops, and taught the business of a blacksmith, a carpenter, a wheelwright, a cabinet-maker, a turner, a shoemaker, or a worker in brass, according as a particular talent for any of these may manifest itself. The produce of the labor of these boys bears no inconsiderable proportion of the expense of their maintenance and instruction.

The School for Poor Boys

In the evening the Count conducted us to the farm-house, where the class of the poor boys are lodged, fed, and instructed. . . . Their teacher (Vehrly) is a young man of very extraordinary qualifications. He received his early education from his father, who filled, in a distinguished manner, the office of schoolmaster for thirty years. . . . He lives with them, eats, sleeps, and works with them, dresses as they do, and makes himself their friend and companion, as well as their instructor. He is eminently fitted for such an occupation by his genius, his address, his temper and disposition, and above all, by his religious principles. The school-room serves also for a shoemaker's shop, and probably accommodates, occasionally, the tailor and harness-maker. The boys always take a lesson of one hour between supper and bed. This lesson is frequently confined to music. . . . The boys of this class appear to be very healthy and contented. They are taught to pay the utmost attention to cleanliness. Their clothing in summer is of coarse cotton, and, in winter, of woolen cloth. They go barefooted, except when they work in the fields, or when the state of the weather requires them to wear shoes and stockings; but their heads always remain uncovered. . . . In summer they rise at five, and in winter at six; and after having dressed themselves and said their prayers, they receive instruction for an hour. They then breakfast, after which they go to work until half-past eleven. They then have half an hour for dinner; after which Vehrly gives them a lesson of one hour. They work out till six, and after eating their supper, receive further instruction, which concludes with prayer, and they are generally in bed between eight and nine o'clock. But this distribution of time varies according to the seasons. In winter five or six hours a day are devoted to sedentary instruction. The morning of the first day of the week is always devoted to exercises of piety, and after dinner some hours are given to instruction in sacred history. But their lessons are by no means confined to the school-room. Vehrly takes pleasure in questioning them on subjects of natural history, geography, religion, morals, or any other useful topic, while they are at work in the fields or shops; and it may readily be conceived, that, with this devotion to the improvement of his pupils, occasions will perpetually present themselves of conveying instruction in every kind of knowledge calculated to expand the minds of children and to cultivate their best affections.

Pestalozzian Methods

With regard to the most effective means of eliciting the powers of the mind, and of conducting the literary exercises of young people, great credit is due to Pestalozzi, whose veteran labors, as one of the most enlightened teachers of the age, were well known and acknowledged long before the commencement of the Hofwyl Institution. His plans of communicating knowledge are in a great measure practiced by Vehrly. Much pains are taken to impress on the minds of the pupils a deep sense of the importance of time, and of habits of industry; and from the reports that have been published by commissioners appointed to examine the establishment, it is evident that the most favorable results have attended these endeavors. . . . In a few years, or even in less time, they learn to read, write, and calculate with and without the use of pencil or pen; the elements of drawing become familiar to them; and they acquire good notions of geometry, especially in its relation to field surveying, and its application to descriptive drawing. Botany and mineralogy constitute part of their amusements. They become well acquainted with all the plants of Hofwyl, and their different qualities, both the sanitary and noxious. Of the minerals also, they acquire the names and principal uses, and they make collections of all that is valuable and curious in minerals and vegetables. But the most admirable trait in the character of this school is the tone of religious feeling which, it is said, pervades it. This could not be accomplished were not Fellenberg and Vehrly both strongly imbued with a sense of religious obligation and unremittingly attentive to awaken those sentiments in the minds of the pupils. . . .

It will readily be conceived that a plan of instruction so admirable, and constantly directed to the best and purest affections of the mind and heart, can scarcely fail to redeem from indolence and vice those whose habits have been the most degraded. And it has accordingly happened that, notwithstanding the boys under Vehrly's charge have been taken from the very lowest ranks, and some of them the children of beggars, but one instance has occurred of such inveterate vice as to render it eventually necessary to abandon the culprit to his corrupt propensities, and expel him from the school.

In the religious exercises, which take place on the first day of the week, the boys of the poor school assemble with the superior class, but on no other occasion.

The Schools for the Well-to-do

The Hofwyl establishment, as I have before remarked, consists of two classes, the rich and the poor. The class of the rich contains at present about eighty. Twenty of these, consisting of children under ten years of age, are placed under the care of a respectable gentleman and his wife, in a house belonging to Fellenberg, situated about a mile from his own residence. A teacher or two have the charge of their instruction both in and out of the house. . . .

The other sixty, constituting the most prominent part of the Hofwyl institution, are provided with more than twenty teachers, or professors. Among the pupils are several princes and the sons of ministers of state, &c. The price of board and tuition varies from £100 to £300 sterling, per annum. We were not admitted to the interior of the building occupied by these students. We saw none of the performances of their schools, or their exercises. . . .

Besides the three schools already mentioned, he has another about half a mile from Hofwyl, where young men attend, during the winter, to courses of instruction in those subjects which relate to agriculture, and he lectures himself, I believe, on the practical operations of farming. It is here, too, that the professor of chemistry has his laboratory and lecture-room. We were introduced to him (Dr. Strobe), and judged him to be a good chemist. He is also the physician of the establishment, and his laboratory indicates an attachment to his profession, and judgment in its practical details. . . .

The Superior School

The superior class consisted of nearly 100 pupils, taught by upward of thirty professors. The course of instruction embraces the Greek, Latin, German, and French languages and literature; history, civil and sacred; geography, mathematics, pure and mixed; natural and mental philosophy; chemistry; music; drawing; gymnastics, including riding, swimming, dancing, &c.; natural history in all its branches; and religious instruction.

The pupils rise at six in winter and five in summer; they breakfast at seven, eat a little at ten, dine at noon, take a luncheon at five, and sup at eight. Five hours are appropriated to study in the forenoon and four in the afternoon; the rest of the day being devoted to their gymnastic, agricultural, and mechanical exercises. This arrangement, however, is not absolutely restrictive, but is made to conform to the varying circumstances of the establishment, the health and genius of the pupils, etc. The greatest pains are taken to cultivate their moral and religious sensibilities. The language chiefly spoken is the German. The internal or civil government (if it may be so called) of the school is regulated by a constitution and by-laws administered by the pupils themselves, and for which object they have their legislative and executive officers, under the supervision of the principal. The motives of emulation, as they are ordinarily excited by rewards, medals, honors, etc., or by a division into classes in the numerical order of first, second, third, etc., form no part of the Fellenberg system. His aim is to address his instructions to the more reasonable and noble principles of their nature, and by the number of his professors (for he has had as many as thirty-five with less than 100 pupils), to unite all the advantages of private with those of public instruction.

Unpopularity of Hofwyl at Home

From the information we received from others, as well as from the statements of Fellenberg himself, it is evident that his plans have ever been regarded with jealousy by a great number of his most influential neighbors and fellow-countrymen. He was at first condemned as a visionary, but when he had fairly demonstrated the practicability and utility of his schemes for the improvement of education, they accused him of sinister views, and alleged against him that his motives were mercenary, having an eye chiefly to the profits of the establishment. This narrow-minded spirit has not been content with mere expressions of disapprobation and condemnation. The government of the canton has gone so far as to lay positive obstructions in his way, and to threaten him with the weight of their aristocratical authority. He had a few years ago devised a plan for diffusing some of the benefits of his experience in the government of youth, throughout the canton. He invited the teachers of schools to repair to Hofwyl during the period of their vacation, and there to avail themselves of such information as the institution would afford, and their time would admit of. This offer was gladly accepted; but the next season the teachers of the canton were most arbitrarily interdicted by the government from resorting to Hofwyl. Fellenberg, thus very ungenerously thwarted in his wishes to do good, opened his establishment for the benefit of other cantons, and has thus had it in his power to extend still more widely the advantages of his system. His great desire is to introduce a taste for agricultural pursuits connected with an amelioration of the indigent classes.

General Impression

I have no hesitation in saying that, from all that I have read and all that I have seen of this establishment, it does appear to me to be conducted upon principles which are calculated to afford the very best kind of education which it is possible to confer upon a young man, whatever may be the situation he is to fill in active life. As it regards the poor, it is difficult to conceive how they could be brought up in a way which would better prepare them for filling the stations of industrious, skillful, and intelligent laborers. With respect to the rich, while they are cheerfully pursuing an excellent course of literary and scientific instruction, they are effectually preserved, by the principles of this institution, from those idle and vicious habits which so commonly result from the vacant time of colleges and universities. By turning their attention to agriculture and the mechanic arts; by inspiring them with a love of labor, or at least of a useful application of their strength and muscular activities; by exercising their ingenuity in the use of tools and instruments; by familiarizing them to an attentive observance of nature in her different kingdoms, and in the revolution of seasons, — a foundation is laid for those more expanded feelings and generous sympathies which bind the upper to the lower classes of the community, and eventually tend to exalt the condition of humanity.

The greatest recommendation of the Pestalozzian and Fellenberg plan of education is the moral charm which is diffused throughout all its operations. It cannot but happen (all other things being equal) that pupils thus educated will become not only more intelligent men and better philosophers, but also more moral and dignified members of society. I cannot but cherish the hope that this scheme of education, of combining agricultural and mechanical with literary and scientific instruction, will be speedily and extensively adopted in the United States. . . .

CHAPTER XXII
NATIONAL ORGANIZATION IN PRUSSIA

THE Readings of this chapter deal with the transfer of education from the Church to the State in Prussia, which took place in the century between the coming of King Frederick William I to the throne, in 1713, and the outbreak of the War of Liberation, in 1813; the early School Codes promulgated; and the type of state school systems finally created.

The first selection (273) describes the preparatory work of the Prussian King, Frederick William I, between 1713 and 1740. On the basis of the work done by this king, his son and successor, Frederick the Great (1740–86), laid the firm foundation of state control, though still working through the church authorities as agents for the State. These foundations he laid through his two detailed School Codes — that of 1763 for Prussia (274) and that of 1765 for the new Catholic province of Silesia (275). What he did was closely copied by Maria Theresa in her general Austrian School Code of 1774, which follows (276). A comparison of the three codes reveals a common plan for them all.

In 1806 Napoleon routed the Prussian armies, took possession of Berlin, took from Prussia all her territory west of the Elbe, and completely humiliated the State. In the winter of 1807–08 the philosopher Fichte, in a series of Addresses, appealed to the leaders to regenerate the State, urging that the road to this lay through education. Selection 277 gives an illustration of his appeals, and shows the importance the leaders soon came to attach to education as a reconstructive agent. His advice was followed; the State was regenerated; in the War of Liberation (1813–15) Napoleon was vanquished, and the Prussian territories were restored.

That the work of transforming the teaching force into a capable and efficient body required hard work may be inferred from Dinter's description (279) of the conditions he found existing in East Prussia, as late as 1819. The work accomplished in a century in providing elementary education was well summarized in the abortive law of 1819, as described by Cousin (280).

In 1843 the American, Horace Mann, visited the schools of Prussia and wrote a report of his observations of them. From this Report two extracts are taken. The first (278) reveals the nature of the selection and training of the Prussian elementary teacher, from which we may infer the reason for the regeneration of the State. In the second (281) Mr. Mann points out the evils of militarism, then clearly evident in the schools, along with their many excellent qualities.

273. The Organizing Work of Frederick William I

(From Henry Barnard's "Public Instruction in Prussia"; in Barnard's *American Journal of Education*, vol. xx, pp. 338–42. 1870)

In 1870 Henry Barnard, while acting as United States Commissioner of Education, prepared a comprehensive Report on National Education in Europe. To the article on education in each country he prefixed a brief historical account. That for Prussia gives a good statement of the work done by the early kings in organizing schools, and from it we take the following account of the work of Frederick William I, who reigned from 1713 to 1740.

The reign of Frederic William I. was a period of collecting, preparing, trying. The thrifty king did not only collect money and soldiers for the future great prince of battle, but he also bequeathed to the future great prince of peace a population, trained to be obedient to government, to fear God, to be industrious and thrifty. He alone had established eighteen hundred schools. . . .

Having found during his frequent journeys through Prussia and Lithuania that the peasants, particularly in Lithuania, "were in a most deplorable state of ignorance" he directed the authorities at Königsberg (July 2, 1718), to assist each other in their efforts, "in order to relieve this ignorance at last." He himself sent for this purpose several commissioners to Lithuania, provided the larger villages with schoolmasters, and gave to each of them some land "free of rent and taxes"; he renewed his orders from time to time, and desired the increase of schools still more emphatically after having induced colonists from different countries, particularly from Salzburg, to settle in his dominions. A long time, however, passed, before he could publish and execute his "*principia regulativa*," which were henceforth the fundamental laws of the province of Prussia. On their publication (February 21, 1737) it was announced "that the King had not only seen with great pity the infidelity and darkness in which the youths in some portions of the kingdom had been living and grown up to their temporal and eternal danger, but that he had also issued instructions from time to time, how to remedy it. Having been unable to attain this end as yet, he had found it necessary to do all in his power to place the youths every where under the guidance of able individuals, and to order that the latter should be provided with the necessaries of life; and that he had been therefore most graciously pleased to give fifty thousand thalers, for all time to come, to be employed without diminution for the maintenance of the empire of God." The interests of this capital were to be employed for the proper assistance of those schools which could not raise the money necessary for the sustenance of a schoolmaster, or which from accidents were temporarily unable to do so, and lastly, for the purpose of rendering assistance in the rebuilding of schoolhouses, destroyed by fire. The administration of this foundation, known by the designation *mons pietatis*, was in the hands of trustees presided over by a minister of State. The interests were distributed by parochial and school commissioners. The *Principia* embraced detailed instructions for those who had to contribute to the building of schoolhouses, others concerning the schoolmaster's income, and some remarks directed to the nobility and clergy, stating that they were expected to assist in providing for the sustenance of the schoolmaster; from this it may be inferred that those great social interests did not so heartily support the royal intentions as would have been becoming in them. . . .

It is certainly not necessary to demonstrate the importance of these school regulations, if properly carried out, being issued at a time when the government of scarcely any state of Europe had as yet given impulse to the awakening of an interest in public schools. It is clear, however, that a general and effective execution of these instructions could not be thought of, seeing the utter ignorance of the country people at that period, which prevented them from appreciating public instruction. Innumerable obstacles were to be removed; money was to be raised, to which both people and nobility were opposed; well qualified teachers were required, who could not be found; and hence the regulation allowed their selection to be made from among the tradesmen, who, at that time, possessed very rarely the proper qualifications. Public education could, therefore, only gradually assert its claims by conquering the prejudices and the ignorance of the people, and an unceasing and energetic attention on the part of the government was required to avoid suspension and to render progress possible.

Frederic William I, having taken possession of an important portion of Pomerania, showed equal solicitude for this country; he provided by special orders for the salary of the schoolmasters; desired that a more regular attendance at school should be enforced; sent several teachers from the Berlin Real-School, and gave even some directions concerning the subject of instruction. "The clergyman shall regulate the method of instruction by the advice of the *præpositus*." "The schoolmaster shall diligently rehearse the minister's catechism at school, and the minister may cause him to catechise the children in his presence, if he considers him able to do so." The instruction for visitations of town-schools in Pomerania directed the visitors to make such inquiries as would show an active interest in the improvement of the schools. Among others: "Whether unnecessary private primary schools were suffered to exist to the detriment of public schools?" "What suggestions for the improvement of the system of instruction might be offered?" "Whether the vacations were unnecessary and too long?" The "*præpositus*" was required to make all necessary arrangements for the improvement of the system of instruction.

The King issued at the request of the city authorities of Berlin, on October 16, 1738, a circular of instructions for the private schools in that town and its suburbs, which, having been approved by the highest dignitaries of the church, gives the most correct idea of the condition of schools in cities in that period. This circular is subdivided into five sections: the first treats on the method of instituting schoolmasters; the second on the requisite abilities and qualifications of schoolmasters; the third on their duties; the fourth on their salaries; the fifth on the relation of parents to schools. The ordinances of this able, well-meaning and often misapprehended prince are always in perfect harmony with the immediate wants of the young, with the pecuniary condition of the communities, and with the habits and customs of the country; they fix the salary of the teachers according to the pretensions which, in his life-time, they could have, as a recompense for their probably very moderate accomplishments. The price of a teacher must be necessarily low, when there is no strong popular inclination for learning, as was the case in that time.

Though the King has shown so much earnest and well-meaning solicitude, and though the number of schools had been greatly increased, yet a real development of the system of instruction was not yet effected. The strict decrees of government had, however, accustomed the people to accommodate themselves in the matter of education to the expressed will of their sovereign, and to have a certain respect for schools. But the teachers, as a class, did their work mechanically, following, as it were, a beaten track, so easily made; there was no genius as yet in the mechanism of school management.

274. The Prussian School Code of 1763

(Translation in Barnard's *American Journal of Education*, vol. XXII, pp. 861–68)

September 23, 1763, King Frederick the Great issued for Prussia, what is known as the *General-Land-Schül-Reglement* or General Regulations for Elementary Schools and Teachers in Prussia. This famous document was prepared under the King's direction, and was the first general School Code for the whole kingdom. It marks the real beginning of the Prussian state elementary-school system. The following quotations, and digest of sections, give the general nature of the Code.

GENERAL REGULATIONS OF ELEMENTARY SCHOOLS AND TEACHERS
August 12, 1763

We Frederick, *by the grace of God, King*, etc.:

Whereas, to our great displeasure, we have perceived that schools and the instruction of youth in the country have come to be greatly neglected, and that by the inexperience of many sacristans (*custos*) and schoolmasters, the young people grow up in stupidity and ignorance, it is our well-considered and serious pleasure, that instruction in the country, throughout all our provinces, should be placed on a better footing, and be better organized than heretofore. For, as we earnestly strive for the true welfare of our country, and of all classes of people; now that quiet and general peace have been restored, we find it necessary and wholesome to have a good foundation laid in the schools by a rational and Christian education of the young for the fear of God, and other useful ends. Therefore, by the power of our own highest motive, of our care and paternal disposition for the best good of all our subjects, we command hereby, all governors, consistories and other collegiates of our country; that they shall, on their part, contribute all they can, with affection and zeal, to maintain the following GENERAL SCHOOL REGULATIONS, and in future to arrange all things in accordance with the law to the end that ignorance, so injurious and unbecoming to Christianity, may be prevented and lessened, and the coming time may train and educate in the schools more enlightened and virtuous subjects.

1. *School attendance age.* First, it is our pleasure that all our subjects, parents, guardians or masters, whose duty it is to educate the young, shall send their children to school, and those confided to their care, boys and girls, if not sooner, certainly when they reach the age of five years; and shall continue regularly to do so, and require them to go to school until they are thirteen or fourteen years old, and know not only what is necessary of Christianity, fluent reading and writing, but can give answer in everything which they learn from the schools book, prescribed and approved by our consistory.

2. *Apprentices to be taught.* Masters to whom children in Prussia, by custom are bound to render work for certain years, are seriously advised not to withdraw such children from school until they can read well, and have laid a good foundation in Christian knowledge; also made a beginning in writing, and can present a certificate from the minister and schoolmaster to this effect to the school-visitors. Parents

and guardians ought much more to consider it their bounden duty that their children and wards receive sufficient instruction in the necessary branches.

3. *Leaving certificates.* If children, by their own aptitude or by the care of the teacher are sufficiently advanced in the common studies before they attain their thirteenth or fourteenth year, even then the parents or guardians are not at liberty to retain them at home, but can do so only when the superintendents or inspectors, after a notice from the minister and a testimonial of the schoolmaster, that the pupil has acquired a sufficient knowledge, have issued a regular dismissal based on the above testimonial. Still such children must attend the Repetition School, not only on Sundays, at the minister's, but also on weekdays at the schoolmaster's.

4. *Attendance required.* As in many towns, parents do not send their children to school in summer, on the plea that they have to guard the cattle; our magistrates and judges in the districts containing towns and communes, shall see that a special shepherd is engaged, rather than allow the children to be kept from school. . . .

5. *School hours.* In order to regulate definitely the summer and winter schools, we decree that winter schools must be held on all the six days of the week, from 8 to 11 o'clock in the forenoon, and from 1 to 4 o'clock in the afternoon, except Wednesday and Saturday afternoons. The winter school must be continued from Michaelmas to the Easter-days. But the summer schools shall be open only in the forenoon or, if necessary by the location of the place, during three hours every week-day, when the ministers can best decide at what hour to commence. No vacations are to be given, not even during harvest time; the schools shall be kept in the prescribed manner, with this distinction, that in summer each lesson is to be of half an hour's duration, and in winter of a full hour.

6. *Sunday instruction.* On Sundays, beside the lesson of the Catechism or repetition school by the minister given in the Church, the schoolmaster shall give in the school a recapitulary lesson to the unmarried people of the township. They shall there practice reading and writing. Reading should be from the New Testament or some other edifying book, and as an exercise in writing, the young people should write some passages, or the Epistle, or Gospel of the day. In towns where the schoolmaster is not likewise sexton, and not obliged to travel through the parish with the clergyman, he shall be bound to sing with the children in Church, either morning or afternoons, to hear them recite the catechism and address to them easy questions on the order of salvation. If the sacristan or schoolmaster has no experience in catechising, the minister shall write down for him the questions he must ask, that in this manner, together with their children, the people may be edified and improved in scriptural knowledge.

7. *Tuition fees.* In regard to tuition fee, every child, until it can read, shall pay in winter six pennies, after it can read, nine pennies, and when it can write and read, one groschen a week. For the months of summer, however, they shall pay only two-thirds of this fee, so that those who paid six pennies in winter, after his proportion shall pay four; those who paid nine pennies shall pay six; and those who paid one groschen will pay eight pennies. If, in any place the schoolmaster has been paid better, he must continue to receive the customary fees.

8. *Children of the poor.* Parents too poor to pay the tuition fee of their children, and orphan children who can not pay, must petition the magistrate, patron, minister or church-council for an allowance from any funds of the church or town at their disposal, that the schoolmaster may get his income, and teach the children of the poor and rich with equal diligence and fidelity.

9. [*Annual school sermon and collection.* Provides for the general delivery of an annual sermon, on Saint Michael's Sunday, on the subject of Christian education and edification of youth. After the sermon, the collection to provide textbooks for the children of the poor.]

10. *Compulsory attendance.* Having made good and sufficient provision for the instruction of the young, all parents, guardians, and others, having children to educate, who act contrary to this ordinance, by withholding them from school, shall still be obliged to pay the common school-fee for the term; and guardians shall not be permitted to charge the money thus paid to the account of their wards. And if, after earnest exhortation of the minister, they do not send their children regularly to school, then the magistrate of the town, in the last resort, shall direct execution against them. It is made the duty of the school-visitors to impose on such parents as have not made their children attend school regularly, a fine of sixteen groschen, to be paid into the school-treasury.

We therefore command all officers and magistrates to ascertain without delay, after receiving notice from the schoolmaster, of the nonattendance of any child, from the parent or guardian of the same the cause of such absence, and if it is for other reason than sickness, they shall employ proper legal means to secure that child's attendance.

11. *School census.* To this end, and to enable him the better to control the matter, the schoolmaster shall receive, from the register of the church or the town in which they are engaged, a list of all children of school age, that they may know who are due to the school; and the teacher shall also keep a monthly register, in which the children are enrolled as follows: (1) By their name and surname; (2) their age; (3) the names of their parents; (4) their residence; (5) the date when they enter school; (6) the lessons they study; (7) the degree of their diligence or negligence; (8) their abilities of mind; (9) their morals and conduct; (10) the day when they leave school.

This register, which no child should be suffered to read, is sent to the school-visitor before his annual inspection, and inspected by the minister during his weekly visits that he may know the delinquent children, and exhort them to greater diligence, and speak with their parents in this regard.

12. *Requisities for a teacher.* Since the chief requisite in a good school is a competent and faithful teacher, it is our gracious and earnest will, that one and all, who have the right of appointment, shall take heed to bring only well-qualified persons into office as teachers and sacristans. A schoolmaster should not only possess the necessary attainments and skill in instruction, but should be an example to the

FIG. 67. A GERMAN LATE EIGHTEENTH-CENTURY SCHOOL

children, and not tear down by his daily life what he builds up by his teaching. He should therefore strive after godliness, and guard against everything which might give offence or temptation to parents or children. Above all things, he should endeavor to obtain a correct knowledge of God and of Christ, thereby laying a foundation to honest life and true Christianity, and feeling that they are entrusted with their office from God, as followers of the Saviour, and in it have an opportunity, by diligence and good example, not only to render the children happy in the present life, but also to prepare them for eternal blessedness.

13. *Teacher's habits.* Though we intend to leave undiminished the privileges of the nobility and other patrons to select and appoint their sacristans and teachers, yet our superintendents, inspectors, and the clergy must see that no incompetent, unsuitable, nor reckless and wicked person is employed or continued in office. . . . All teachers are forbidden to keep tavern, to sell beer or wine, to engage in any other occupation by which their labor may be hindered or the children lured by their example into habits of idleness and dissipation, such as the hanging around taverns or making music at dinners and balls, which is prohibited under high fine and punishment.

14. *Examination of teachers.* No sacristan or teacher can be installed into office before his qualifications, ascertained by actual examination, are certified to by the Inspector. No clergyman can admit any person to such position in church or school who does not produce said certificate of a successful examination. . . .

15. *License to teach.* No person shall assume to teach in any school of the country, village, or town, who has not regularly obtained a license to teach; and all schools, whether kept by man or woman, not duly authorized, are entirely prohibited. But parents of wealth may, as heretofore, engage private teachers for their children, provided that the children of others who cannot yet be taught the higher branches, are not induced to withdraw from the regular school in order to share the private elementary instruction.

16. *Attendance to duty.* As a schoolmaster is not permitted to employ his pupils for his own work during school hours, neither shall he attend to his trade or other business during such hours, or entrust his wife with the duties of the school-room; though he may employ her or another person to assist when the school is too large for his personal instruction. If for any cause he neglects to teach the prescribed hours, the clergyman shall remind him of his duty; and, in case of persistent neglect, notice must be sent to the inspector that such irregularities may be corrected or punished.

17. [*School to open with prayer.* Nature of.]

18. [*School hours.* Eight to eleven, and one to four, unless ordered otherwise.]

19. [*Course of study.* Rather detailed provision made as to each hour of instruction. Summarized, it is as follows:

Morning.

1st Hour — Singing of a hymn, a different hymn to be learned each month. This followed by a prayer, and this in turn by instruction in the Catechism. Luther's "Smaller Catechism" for younger children; the larger for the older. Saturday lesson to be preparatory for Sunday, the Epistle for that day being read and written.

2d Hour — A B C class; reading from Old and New Testament; spelling; finding passages in the Scriptures; and memorizing verses from the Bible and learning Biblical names.

3d Hour — Reading, writing, spelling; writing in copybooks; rules of reading.   School closes with prayer, and reading of psalm.   On Saturday children exhorted to behave well on Sunday; to be quiet in church; and to treasure up the word of God for their salvation.

Afternoon.

4th Hour — Pupils sing verses, read a psalm, and are taught Biblical history from Rochow's "Manual for the Instruction of Children in Country Schools."

5th Hour — Catechism, after method given in the "Berlin Reader."   Pupils commit to memory, reading it with the teacher.   Interpretations for the larger children. Children to learn a Bible verse weekly.   During second half of hour, larger children to learn to read; middle class to spell; and lower class to learn their letters, as in second hour.

6th Hour — Upper class write and cipher; middle class spell; and lower class study their A B C.

In cities, where schools had more than one class, the local consistory could regulate the order of the lessons, and the method of instruction.]

20. *Uniform textbooks.*   As the country has hitherto been deluged with all sorts of school-books, especially with interpretations of the Catechism, and so-called "orders of salvation," because every preacher selects the books after his own pleasure, or writes some himself and has them printed, by which children, especially if parents change their residence, are much confused, it is our will, that henceforth no other books, than such as have been approved by our consistory, shall be used in any country-schools over which we have the right of patron.   These books include, according to the wants of the country, the New Testament, the book called "Exercise in Prayer," in which not only are the contents of each book in the Bible, but the main subject of each chapter is framed into a prayer, to assist the young in expressing their invocations in the words of divine truths.   Also the Halle or Berlin Bible, both of which agree in their divisions into paragraphs and pages; next the small and large Catechism of Luther; the Index of the books of the Bible; the Christian Doctrines in their connection; the Berlin Spelling-book and Reader; the General Attributes of God, of the world and man; and the Little Book for children in the country, on all sorts of necessary and useful things.

21. *Each pupil to have a book.* Each class must not only have the same books, but the clergyman and teacher must see that every child has his own book, so that two pupils need not look over the same book. Children, whose books are furnished from the funds of the church or the commune, are not allowed to take them home, but will deliver them to the master, at the close of the lessons, who will take charge of them as the property of the school.

22. [*Discipline.* Lays down rules for.]

23. [*Church attendance.* Parents on Sunday to send children to schoolmaster, who shall escort them to church and note conduct and absences, and on Monday question them on the sermon.]

24. *Relations of schoolmaster and clergyman.* In all other affairs of the school, the teacher must avail himself of the advice and suggestions of the clergyman, as his superior officer, and by his school-regulation the teachers are so directed. Of all that regards their office they must, on demand, give an account, and accept directions in reference to the prescribed method and discipline, because we have confidence in our ministers and bind it upon their consciences that in their towns they will earnestly endeavor to abolish all abuses and defects, and improve the condition of the schools. In case however one or the other of the schoolmasters should neglect the duties of his office, after he is engaged, and be found unreliable, the pastor's duty will be, earnestly to remind him of his duty, with kindness once or twice, and if he still continues in his negligence, to apply for a remedy to the nearest justice; at the same time to inform the Superintendent or Inspector, and if their warning is not heeded, make a report to the consistory, that, according to the circumstances, they may decree a suspension or removal.

25. *Clerical supervision.* Especially is it our pleasure, that clergymen in villages and towns shall visit the schools of their place, generally twice a week, sometimes in the morning and sometimes in the afternoon, and shall not only take the information of the sacristans or schoolmaster, but themselves examine the children in the Catechism and question them after other schoolbooks. They shall hold a monthly conference with the schoolteachers *in matre*, and designate to them the portion of the Catechism, the hymn, the psalm and Bible-verses which the children shall learn during the next month. Then he instructs them how to observe the principal divisions of the sermon and how to examine the children; he also points out the defects of their instruction in school, their method, discipline, and gives them other information, that the schoolteachers may fulfil their duties. If a clergyman, against our expectation, should be careless in his visits to the schools, or in the performance of other duties enjoined upon him in these regulations, and not labor earnestly to effect an exact observance of this law on the part of custos and teachers, he shall if convicted of the non-fulfilment of these instructions, be suspended *cum effectu*, for a time, or, as the case

may be, removed from office: because the care for the instruction of the young and the supervision thereof, belong to the most important duties of the ministry, as we always desire them to be considered.

26. *Annual inspection.* The Superintendents and Inspectors of every district are hereby commanded, in the most expressive manner, annually to inspect every country-school in their jurisdiction, and with due attention to inquire into the condition of the schools, and examine whether parents and school authorities have held their children to regular attendance at school or have been negligent; whether the clergymen have done their duty in the observance of these regulations, by visiting the schools and superintending the teacher; especially whether the schoolmaster has the ability required or is not competent, and whatever else is in need of improvement. About all this the said Superintendents and Inspectors shall remit a dutiful report, every year, to our High Consistory in this city, for further examination and disposition. . . .

Conclusion. In general we here confirm and renew all wholesome laws, published in former times, especially, that no clergyman shall admit to confirmation and the sacrament, any children not of his commune, nor those unable to read, or who are ignorant of the fundamental principles of evangelical religion.

275. The Silesian School Code of 1765

(Translation in Barnard's *American Journal of Education,* vol. XXII, pp. 869–77)

In 1748, as a result of an eight-year war known as the War of the Austrian Succession, Frederick the Great of Prussia succeeded in wresting by force from Maria Theresa of Austria the Province of Silesia. It was an arbitrary act of spoliation, similar to the "divisions" of Poland which soon followed. Silesia was a Catholic province, and in 1765 the King issued a long General Regulations (Code) for the Schools of Silesia, much like the previous (1763) Code for Prussia. In three particulars — (a) training of teachers, (b) regulation of conditions under which teachers lived and worked, and (e) the supervision of instruction by clergymen and inspectors — the Code embodied new directions, and these are reproduced below. The nature of the instruction required (c) and the regulations dealing with compulsory attendance (d) are also reproduced for comparison with similar regulations of the earlier Prussian Code. (**R. 274,** §§ 19, 20; 10, 11.) While still working through the Church authorities, the strong arm of the State is becoming increasingly evident.

REGULATIONS FOR CATHOLIC SCHOOLS IN SILESIA
November 3, 1765

We, Frederick, *by the grace of God, King of Prussia*, &c.,

Make known hereby that, as in our paternal care for the welfare of our faithful subjects, we were led to issue the order of August 12, 1763, for the better organization of the ill-managed country-schools, we have thought proper to proclaim a similar order in regard to our Roman Catholic subjects of Silesia and the county of Glatz, for the organization of the common elementary schools in towns and villages. That we may make our Roman Catholic subjects more useful citizens, we hereby ordain:

(a) *The training of teachers for the Catholic schools*

1. To strike at the source of all poor instruction, no schoolmaster, or by whatever name teachers in cities and villages may be designated, shall be anywhere engaged if he cannot prove, in the manner described below, that, with skill in singing and playing the organ sufficient to perform the services in the Church, he has acquired the art of instructing the young in the German language, after the manner approved by Catholic school authorities.

2. And that every one who desires to be employed in schools may have the opportunity for learning all that is needed by a good teacher, we have thought it best to establish here and there certain schools, in which not only the young will have the best instruction, but where adults, also, may be taught how to teach and manage youth. For this purpose we have selected the following schools: for Lower Silesia, the school of the Breslau Cathedral *ad Saint Joannem*, the school of the second Cistercians at the convents of Leubus, Grussau, and the Augustines of Sagan; for upper Silesia, the school in the city of Ratibor and of the Cistercians at the convent of Rauden; and for the county of Glatz, the school of the city of Habelschwerdt.

3. We command that the above-named schools, which are to serve as seminaries for future teachers, shall not only be constantly provided with skillful teachers, but each shall also have a well-informed director, who shall devote himself to maintaining and improving the condition of his school, and especially to training and instructing those who are preparing to teach. The director must observe the following:

4. He should aim at having everything in his school taught and learned thoroughly, and in reference to the needs of common life, which will be further described below. He should show the teachers how to give their pupils the reasons for everything, that they may obtain an understanding thereof, and become themselves able, on being questioned, to give these reasons. His object should not be to load the memory of the pupil, but to enlighten and train his mind.

5. And, since the method in which the first teachers of the above-named schools were instructed is such that, by retaining it, all those advantages may be reached, it is our will that it should be introduced everywhere, especially the essential part of the method of letters, tables, questions, and answers, as well as the books written for this purpose.

6. The directors should not omit to employ such other advantages as they or others may discover in connection with this popular mode of teaching; and to this end they should correspond among themselves, and read the best works on schools and education. That such writings may become known to them, we commend the publisher of the privileged Breslau literary periodical to notice and criticise such books and treaties as are new or reprinted.

(b) *Regulation of conditions under which teachers live and work*

13. It is well known how much children are hindered in their studies and become distracted when, in the room in which the school is kept,

FIG. 68. THE SCHOOL OF A HAND-WORKER

the wife and children and frequently even the relatives of the schoolmaster, work at their trade or domestic duties. In order to remove this evil, the school-room must be separated from the living room, in all new schoolhouses erected in cities and villages, and shall be convenient, well lighted, and large enough to accommodate all the children. In cities where schools have several teachers, a separate room must be constructed for every teacher, which shall not be used for any other than school purposes. These schools are to be erected at the expense of the commune, if it is mainly Catholic, with concurrence of the proprietors, without distinction of religion; because it is important to masters of every denomination that subordinates be made useful through the training of the school; and all necessary furniture, blackboards, inkstands, and books for children of destitute parents they shall furnish also.

14. In places where the salary of a teacher is so small that he cannot subsist on it, our Council of War and Domains shall see that the proprietors and Catholic subjects raise a sufficient support for him and pay it promptly. In places where the number of Catholic inhabitants is very small, and consequently a living salary for the teacher cannot be made up without oppressing the people, we will permit the teacher to practice a trade for his better subsistence, like that of a tailor or stocking weaver; but he shall not be permitted to work in the school room or during school hours. Any traffic in beer or liquor, or attendance at fairs with music, shall not be included in the lawful trades of a teacher. Experience shows that the first distracts a teacher and entices him from his duties; and by music and taverns the best schoolmasters are ruined, and reduced to drinking and idleness.

15. Therefore all teachers are forbidden to keep a tavern, or to wait on weddings and other occasions; and we permit them to labor in any trade that will be no hindrance to the work of teaching.

16. With the same intent of guarding schools against interruptions, we release teachers from the customary duty of carrying messages from the archbishop to the neighboring clergy, and we command that such should be done in future by other messengers from the commune, since these messages generally concern our war orders.

(c) Nature of the instruction

19. As schools in large cities have frequently two or three teachers, we ordain that one of them — he who writes the best hand — shall teach the smaller children in the first elements; the others the more advanced pupils.

20. Instruction to beginners includes: 1st, the letters, spelling, and simple reading. The letters must be learned in a month; and since, in cities, new children are coming in every month, the course is to be repeated. Every month the children should spell the six different classes of syllables in the spelling book; in the third month the children, who began with the letters the first month, should commence to read, but the difficult words must still be spelled and the rules be inquired into.

Every month they must go over the tables belonging to the subject, as they are found in the school books for children. 2d, in writing, the teacher should first acquaint the pupils with the rules of penmanship after the printed instructions, and they should then practice them until they have a correct German current handwriting, and can also write Latin letters according to the rules contained in the above instructions. He should go over the tables of calligraphy every month, taking the general principles during the first two weeks and the current letters; in the third week, Latin and current handwriting; and in the fourth week whatever is necessary to write words and sentences. In correcting, he should not omit to point at the tables, and proceed after the instructions printed on the same. 3d, in arithmetic he must likewise proceed after the tables on the five simple operations prepared for the Silesian schools; also in the rule of three with simple numbers, and he must endeavor to bring the children to do quick cyphering. During the first month he is to finish the table of enumeration, and the children should know how to pronounce and write any given number of not above eight or nine figures. Addition and multiplication should be completed in two months, and the remaining three months of the semi-annual term given to subtraction and division and recapitulating the other operations.

21. The children thus prepared are to be further instructed by the second teacher. When they are able to read the larger tables with fluency, they should be taught how to pronounce correctly the French words which occur frequently in German papers. In writing, the teacher should show them the law style and *fractura*, and the current letters which they learned from the first teacher need not conform to his own handwriting, and he need not make copies for them, but should cause them to copy select portions from books or other useful matters, he seeing that all they write is in agreement with the rules given in the tables of calligraphy. He should instruct them in orthography, not only by copying, but by dictating to them from time to time, in order that the pupils acquire a fluency in writing, and also to see how far they apply the rules of orthography. He should teach the older scholars to write compositions of various kinds, especially letters and forms which occur most frequently in common life. He should observe the mistakes in the use of language in the modifications or combinations of words, for which purpose he should use Gottsched's grammar. In arithmetic the pupils should learn the four operations in simple numbers and with fractions, the rule of three in all its applications, and the Italian practice, if any desire it. Oftentimes, especially to those who are about to leave the school and gain a living by the pen, the teacher should give them various bills and accounts, and show them how to draw these up correctly, and what must be done in revising accounts.

22. If, as in almost all large cities, the school has a third teacher, he

should instruct in the first elements of the French and Latin languages, in general and special history, in understanding and using a map, in studying geography from tables printed for this purpose, and in finding places on the map by means of the *Lexicorum*. We shall also, in order to give the young an idea of those things which render a State prosperous and the subjects contented, cause to be published a short textbook, containing the most useful knowledge of physics and some preliminary knowledge of the objects which are of importance in arts, trades, and manufactures. The duty of making the contents of such a book known to youth belongs, also, in larger cities, to the third teacher.

(d) Compulsion to attend

25. All these regulations, intended for the welfare of our faithful subjects, will create but little effect if, as has been the case heretofore, the schools are empty, where it is left to the will of the parents to send their children to school or not. We ordain, therefore, by this present, that all children in cities and villages, without distinction, whether the parents are able to pay for tuition or not, shall be sent to school as soon as they complete their sixth year, and shall attend the same until they are thirteen years old.

26. Parents and guardians who retain their children at home against this order shall, unless notoriously known as unable, pay double the tuition fee to the school teacher; the guardians from their own means, without any right of charging it to their wards' account; this to be levied by the justice of the court of the district; and the poor, who cannot pay this forfeiture, shall be compelled to two days' work for the commune, without pay, for every week they neglect to send their children to school. Children of less than eight years must attend school in summer and winter; in summer only in the forenoon.

27. As regards older children, whom the parents need for guarding the cattle and for other farm work, we permit that such, because the young now learn faster and more thoroughly by the new method introduced, be free from school from Saint George's day to Saint Martin's.

28. They shall be required, however, during this time, to attend the instruction in Christianity every Sunday afternoon, and after that to participate for two hours in the lessons in reading and writing given in school; which lessons the teachers shall give under direction of the pastor, that they may become useful to the young. Those, also, who have left school, and are not yet twenty years of age, must attend these lessons, though they may be in service on a domain or with a farmer, for their employers are bound to send them to school at such time, that they may recapitulate what they learned before, and prevent the utter lack of necessary knowledge. . . .

(e) The supervision of instruction by clergymen and the State

43. It is the duty of the clergyman to see that the young of his parish are well taught in school. We therefore command earnestly all clergymen in cities and villages to take care that these regulations are faithfully observed.

44. Clergymen who, on account of age or professional engagements, have been provided with one or more chaplains, may transfer the care of the schools over to one of them, but they shall be responsible for their delegate.

45. At least once every two weeks the clergyman or his chaplain shall visit every school during school hours, of which the teacher shall make a note in his register, by placing a V, for visitation, on that day.

46. The clergyman, during his visitation, shall observe: *a*, whether the prescribed school-hours are kept; *b*, whether the improved method is practiced; *c*, whether the catalogue and list is in order; *d*, whether punishments are too severe; *e*, whether the school utensils and books are well kept; *f*, whether the school room is clean, and used for no other than school purposes, those cases excepted where no other room is provided for the teacher.

47. In regard to the children, the clergyman should see — *a*, whether all persons, who, according to law, should attend the day school, or Sunday and repetition school, are regular in their attendance; *b*, whether the scholars are divided into classes on the basis of their abilities as well as age; *c*, whether they are benefited by the instructions and have made progress; *d*, whether the teacher advances them too rapidly before they have well learned the preceding lessons; *e*, whether the teacher employs children at his private work during school hours, and excuses them on this account from learning their lessons.

48. The clergyman shall also see whether the schoolhouse and furniture are in good condition, and whether a copy of the school regulations and everything necessary has been provided; and if not, he should notify the magistrate, the nobleman, or the justice; also expostulate with parents who neglect to send their children, and endeavor to remove all defects and impediments as much as is in his power; and where he cannot remedy them himself, he should notify the bishop and the school inspector. He should preserve the monthly statements of the teacher, and prepare an abstract of them, which he should be able to present to the bishop or school visitor.

49. He should remonstrate with the teacher for his faults, but not in presence of the children, only when alone, and endeavor to instruct him in those matters wherein he is deficient. He must never employ him for other purposes during school hours, especially not in his own interest. When ministerial duties, like the visitation of the sick, call him away, he must not take the schoolmaster along; but may take one of the larger boys. He should also exhort his people on the advantages of instruction, before taking up the collections for school purposes.

51. In order to render as permanent as possible this reform of schools, which lies near our heart, we cannot be satisfied with committing the care of schools to the clergy only. We find it necessary that our bureau of War and Domain, the bureau of the Episcopal Vicariate, and the dioceses in our Silesian and Glatz districts, as well as all special school inspectors, give all due attention to this subject, so important to the State.

71. The office of a Vicariate General, and the vicars and deacons of outside dioceses, must make a semi-annual report on the condition of schools, from the reports of school inspectors, to our royal Council of War and Domain, namely: at the end of May and at the end of November, and inform in regard to —

72. 1st, all neglect of these general school regulations, by magistrates, landholders, or subjects, which cannot be reached by the head priests and inspectors; 2d, impediments of any kind; 3d, when schoolhouses are out of repair, or the teachers are not paid; 4th, important observations and discoveries which may serve to a better arrangement of the school system; 5th, clergymen and teachers who distinguish themselves by their zeal and diligence in promoting education, that we may remove them to better benefices within our patronage; 6th, incorrigible schoolmasters in our domain or villages, that they may be removed from office.

73. We command our Council of War and Domain to see that all defects brought to their notice are remedied; all obstacles removed; all incorrigible teachers expelled and good ones put in their places; that all zealous school inspectors, directors of seminaries, clergymen and chaplains, who deserve reward for their exertions in the cause of education, are provided with better benefices whenever vacancies occur, and thus others may be encouraged to like zeal. To the Episcopal Vicariate General, the vicars and deacons of outside dioceses, to the magistrates, landholders, and to all our subjects, clergy or laity, whom these regulations concern, especially to all Roman Catholic school inspectors, head priests, directors of seminaries, clergymen, chaplains and schoolmasters, do we command, in the most serious manner, under pain of our disfavor and of due punishment, to superintend with all attention the fulfilment of these regulations to their full extent, and the duties made thereby obligatory on each and all.

Given at Potsdam, the 3d day of November, 1765.

FREDERICK

276. The Austrian School Code of 1774

(Translation in Barnard's *American Journal of Education*, vol. XXII, pp. 879–84)

In 1770 the Empress Maria Theresa of Austria, a ruler deeply in sympathy with the progressive movements then stirring in

Europe, took up in real earnest the education of her subjects. Her first act was to create a School Commission for lower Austria (1770), and the year following the first Austrian normal school was established in Vienna. In 1774 she promulgated a General School Code for all the provinces of Austria, of which the more important points are reproduced below.

GENERAL LAW FOR THE SCHOOLS OF AUSTRIA
December 6, 1774

MARIA THERESA, etc.

Having nothing more at heart than the true welfare of the countries which God has confided to us, and having always attentively considered whatever might contribute to this end, we have observed that the education of both sexes, the basis of the real happiness of nations, requires our especial care. This very important object has the more attracted our attention, inasmuch as the future destiny of man, the genius and thought of entire nations, depend mainly on the good instruction and right training of children from their tenderest years. Such an object, however, can never be attained if the darkness of ignorance is not dispelled by well-regulated instruction and education, so that every individual can acquire knowledge according to his ability and condition. These necessary ends, the utility of which is generally acknowledged, we desire to reach by the following regulation for all schools in our kingdoms and hereditary states:

1. *Creation of a school commission in every State.* In each State of the monarchy shall be formed a school-commission, composed of two or three counselors of the government, one under-delegate, and a secretary, associated with the inspector-general of normal schools.

This commission is charged with the supervision of all school interests, school-officers as well as school material, and they shall assure themselves that the method prescribed by ordinance is employed. . . . Frequent reports on the condition of schools must be rendered.

2. *Grades of schools, and where.* Schools are of three classes: Normal schools, Principal schools (superior primary schools), and Trivial schools (primary).

There shall be one normal (pattern or model) school in each province. All other establishments must conform to this school. The corps of teachers shall consist of a director and four or five teachers, one of whom shall be a catechist.

Every capital of a canton must possess a Principal school.

Finally, shall be established Trivial schools in all the small cities or boroughs in the country, and in all villages where exists a parish or a filial church, distant from the centre.

3. *Rules for the establishment of schools.* It is not intended to estab-

lish new schools everywhere, but to improve existing schools. In future no teacher shall be admitted, unless he knows the prescribed method of teaching, and has been found capable, on examination before the teachers of the Normal school.

The right of keeping school or teaching the young shall continue to all laymen and ecclesiastics, who at present are engaged in the profession of teachers; but they must, as soon as possible, make themselves familiar with the new method, and conform to the principles of this ordinance.

New schools shall be created only where none exist, and only as many as are necessary; also in those places where the young are too numerous for the existing schools to accommodate all, or for the teachers to bestow the necessary care upon them. When the insufficiency is proved to exist, new schools must be erected, or the old ones repaired, as appears necessary, at the expense of the communes, who draw direct profit therefrom, unless the nobility, who have the advantage of drawing from these schools employees of good character, take upon themselves the expense, or other means are devised.

The school-commission is charged with stating the real wants, and to determine what portion of the expenses each party shall contribute.

4. [*Rules for the construction of schoolhouses.* General details as to construction, lighting, and equipment.]

5. *Branches of instruction. In each of the three classes of schools the instruction shall be:*

I. NORMAL SCHOOL. **A. Religion.** Instruction in religion is to be given:

1st. From the Catechism specially introduced by the bishop of the diocese, or from the Vienna Catechism for normal schools, approved by the bishops.

2d. In a systematic manner, for which purpose the Reader is arranged.

3d. As history, that the pupils may learn under what circumstances and in what periods the divine revelations took place; what lessons man should draw from them, relative to his own conduct, etc.

4th. By means of interpretation of passages in the Reader, which treat of the principles of morality and the condition of man.

B. Reading. Reading, writing, and orthography; arithmetic and its application; and, in general, all that can contribute to inspire a well-regulated conduct, and be conducive to good manners.

C. Language and science. Subjects which serve to prepare pupils for the study of Latin, or those who intend to pursue the career of political economy, and especially those who will devote themselves to agriculture and the arts and trades, should be introduced. The mother language should be taught by exercises in composition; and the pupils should obtain a sufficient knowledge of Latin to be able to begin the *humanitas*, to learn surgery and pharmacy, or to take up the profession of a writer. The best principles of economy, and especially of domestic economy, should be taught; also the history of arts and trades, as well as natural history, within the limits of utility and necessity. Also the elements of history and geography, especially of their own country; also the principles of surveying and mechanics; drawing by means of compass, ruler, and instruments.

D. Methods of instruction. Those who aspire to the profession of teaching, shall be specially made to know, and have explained, what are the duties and qualifications of a good teacher; the methods and practical means by which order and discipline are maintained in classes; how the school registers must be kept, and in what manner they should question the pupils in an examination; finally, what is required of public, and of private teachers.

II. PRINCIPAL SCHOOLS. The programme of the Principal schools comprises the subjects indicated under A and B, and as much as possible, those under C, as the number and ability of the teachers and the time prescribed permit.

III. TRIVIAL SCHOOLS. The subjects of instruction in the schools of small cities, boroughs, and villages, are:

(*a*) Religion and its history; morals drawn from the Bible and reading.

(*b*) Reading printed and written type; current handwriting; the four rules of arithmetic, with the rule of simple proportions.

(*c*) In the country a little book is to be used, which has been written to form "an honest citizen," and to teach him thrift and management.

6. *Who shall teach the different branches of instruction.* Ecclesiastics alone may teach the Christian doctrine. The Normal and Principal schools have a professor specially charged with giving every day, at least one hour, lessons on the catechism, on sacred history and morality, and explaining the epistles and gospels. It shall be the duty of the vicar to catechise twice, or at least once a week, in the Trivial schools. If the vicars are not sufficient to teach religion in the schools of small towns, burghs, and the country, friars may be appointed, with the approval of the bishops, by the superiors of the neighboring convents. The schoolmasters shall be present during the lessons in the catechism, and pay good attention, that they may be able to repeat to the children the explanations which have been made. If the vicar or clergyman is prevented, the teachers themselves shall be obliged to question the children on what they have learned by heart, for instances, on verses from the Holy Scriptures, etc., or on what they have studied in the Reader relative to religion. Other subjects can be taught by laymen or ecclesiastics, provided they have passed their examination. The

teachers of the Principal schools consist of the director and four or five assistant teachers.

7. [*On school books.* Charts and school books to be uniform.]

8. *On the manner of teaching.* Instruction must be given simultaneously to all pupils of the same class. The teacher should take special care that all pupils read together. He will punctually conform to the directions given in the books on method, and aim less at crowding the memory of children than at developing their mind by clear and precise explanations. He should accustom the children to express themselves with facility and exactitude on things which have been explained to them.

9–11. [*Division of classes; school hours; duration of studies.*]

12. *Duty of school-attendance.* In cities, all children of both sexes, for whom parents or guardians cannot or will not take a special teacher, must, without exception, attend the public schools from the age of six years until they are sufficiently instructed to choose a trade or profession. As they hardly attain this degree of instruction before the age of twelve years, we shall see with satisfaction, if parents send them to school during six or seven years, and permit them to attend even longer.

Children who desire to enter a Latin school before their twelfth year, must submit to a public examination, and obtain a certificate from the school-inspector that they possess the required knowledge.

Where distinct schools exist, girls shall be taught separately, and they shall be instructed also in sewing, and all work suitable for their sex. If no distinct schools are organized, the girls shall attend the mixed school, but seated on separate benches.

13. *Duty of parents and guardians to send children to school.* As the education and instruction of youth has a very great influence on the general well-being, we will not let the good success of our maternal care, in this regard, be endangered by the carelessness of parents and guardians. Consequently we ordain, that they send their children to school at the proper age, or have them instructed at home. We recommend to magistrates and superiors to watch over the execution of this ordinance, to reprimand, and if necessary, to enforce obedience on the part of parents or guardians who neglect this duty.

After the necessary measures have been taken to train capable teachers in the Normal schools, no person shall be permitted to follow the work of teaching, if he possesses no certificate of ability, signed by the authorities of a Normal or Principal school, and for want of such certificate he shall be excluded from the profession.

14. *Orphans to be instructed.* That the service of orphans may not be an obstacle to their instruction, it shall not be lawful for magistrates to put them out to service before their thirteenth year; or at least those who have not reached that age must be permitted to attend school in Winter. Other persons, who take into their service orphans below

thirteen years of age, will be obliged to send them to school morning and afternoon, and if they are not insolvent, they shall pay half tuition fees for them.

15. *Continuation schools.* In the country, as well as in cities, the young people who have ceased to belong to primary schools, and particularly those who are apprentices, must, especially in Summer, on Sundays after divine service, if possible, congregate at the common school, where, for two hours, the teacher will recapitulate with them, under the inspection of the curate or vicar. They shall attend these exercises till they are twenty years old. First, they will read the epistle or gospel of the day; then have an exercise in reading, writing, arithmetic, that they may revise the knowledge acquired at school. For these repetitions, passages will be selected from standard works, treating on religion, morality, and all subjects that tend to cultivate honest principles and domestic and simple tastes. The young should be frequently questioned on various important themes.

The obligation of apprentices to take part in these repetitions shall be such, that their apprenticeship cannot be declared ended, until they have obtained from the school-inspector a certificate, stating that they have fruitfully attended the repetition-school, after making good progress in religion, reading, writing, and arithmetic, in the ordinary course.

16. [*School register, and pupil records.*]

17. *Ordinary inspectors charged with examining the condition of schools.* In order that the present regulation shall be observed, the authorities shall appoint in every village some special inspectors, whose reports, addressed to the Commission of Studies, shall contain their names. In the Normal and principal schools the director has the superintendence; moreover, a citizen of the place, a friend of education, shall be nominated by the magistrate, to watch the progress of the schools, and to assure himself that the regulations are faithfully carried out. This inspector will keep account of the children that are diligent, and of those who are not regular in their attendance. He shall state whether the teacher proves zealous or negligent, or conforms to the ordinance. The inspectors should not make their visits at stated periods, but whenever they think proper, without notifying the teachers.

In cities, burghs, or the country, the curate of the parish shall be appointed inspector, one of the magistracy and a prudent man from the inhabitants of the commune. They shall conform to what has been ordained in regard to the inspectors in larger cities. Every inspector addresses a report to the Inspector-General of Normal schools, on the condition of the schools in his jurisdiction.

18. *Nomination of Inspector-Generals.* The School-Commissions shall elect as Inspector-Generals only persons perfectly capable. A certain district will be assigned to each Inspector-General, in which to make his visits and institute schools. These Inspectors shall make

themselves acquainted with the deficiencies of schools; examine the children in presence of the teacher, and receive the reports of the local inspectors, rendered at Easter and Saint Michel's.   These reports the Inspector-Generals forward to the government, which refers them to the School-Commission.   They add an abstract of their observations, as well as their remarks on the following objects:

1. In what place and point do magistrates, gentry, and inhabitants, act against the ordinance.
2. What are the obstacles to the success of schools.
3. In what places are school-buildings not in order, or need repair; how are the school servants salaried.
4. What measures should be taken to improve instruction.
5. What curates, vicars, catechisers, and schoolmasters have distinguished themselves by diligence and zeal in teaching, and deserve to be rewarded.
6. What teachers neglect their duty and should be punished; or are incorrigible, and should consequently be discharged.

19–20. [*Introducing reforms, and ecclesiastics to learn school methods.*]

21. *Prohibition to teachers to keep a tavern.*   Though we are well disposed to permit teachers in the country to exercise an honest trade, provided it does not form an obstacle to their special duties, yet we order and ordain hereby, that no teacher who receives a sufficient salary and enjoys an honest subsistence, shall keep a tavern, under pain of removal.

Neither can we permit school teachers to make music or play at a fair, wedding, or other occasion, in taverns or similar houses.   This in future they are strictly forbidden to do, likewise, under pain of removal.   We also forbid curates to be accompanied by the teacher in their visits to the sick; they should address themselves to other persons.

22–24. [*Examinations, records, reports, inspection.*]

Given in our capital and residence, city of Vienna, December 6, 1774.

277. Fichte's Addresses to the German Nation

(Fichte, J. G., *Reden an die deutsche Nation.*   Berlin, 1808; trans. in Barnard's *American Journal of Education*, vol. IV, pp. 150–51)

To the thoughtful intellectual leadership of Johann Gottlieb Fichte (1762–1814), for a time professor of philosophy at the University of Jena, and afterwards Rector of the new University of Berlin, perhaps more than to any other one man, were the Prussian people indebted for their regeneration during the first two decades of the nineteenth century.   During the winter of 1807–08 he delivered a series of lectures in Berlin to the German people (*Reden an die deutsche Nation*), which stirred the leaders as they had not been stirred since the days of the Reformation. The following selection from one of these lectures gives a good idea as to the importance he attached to education in connection with national welfare.

Would that the State would look its present peculiar condition steadily in the face, and acknowledge to itself what that condition really is; would that it could clearly perceive that there remains for it no other sphere in which it can act and resolve as an independent State, except the education of the rising generation; that, unless it is absolutely determined to do nothing, this is now all it can do; but that the merit of doing this would be conceded to it undiminished and unenvied. That we are no longer able to offer an active resistance, was before presupposed as obvious, and as acknowledged by every one. How then can we defend our continued existence, obtained by submission, against the reproach of cowardice and an unworthy love of life? In no other way than by resolving not to live for ourselves, and by acting up to this resolution; by raising up a worthy posterity, and by preserving our own existence solely in order that we may accomplish this object. If we had not this first object of life, what else were there for us to do? Our constitutions will be made for us, the alliances which we are to form, and the direction in which our military resources shall be applied, will be indicated to us, a statute-book will be lent to us, even the administration of justice will sometimes be taken out of our hands; we shall be relieved of all these cares for the next years to come. Education alone has not been thought of; if we are seeking for an occupation, let us seize this. We may expect that in this occupation we shall be left undisturbed. I hope (perhaps I deceive myself, but as I have only this hope still to live for, I shall not cease to hope), that I convince some Germans, and that I shall bring them to see that it is education alone which can save us from all the evils by which we are oppressed. I count especially on this, as a favorable circumstance, that our need will have rendered us more disposed to attentive observation and serious reflection than we were in the day of our prosperity. Foreign lands have other consolations and other remedies; it is not to be expected that they would pay any attention, or give any credit to this idea, should it ever reach them; I will much rather hope that it will be a rich source of amusement to the readers of their journals, if they ever learn that any one promises himself so great things from education.

278. The Prussian Elementary Teacher and his Training

(Mann, Horace, *Seventh Annual Report, Massachusetts State Board of Education.* Boston, 1843)

In the spring of 1843 Horace Mann, then Secretary of the newly created (1837) State Board of Education for Massachusetts, went on a short trip to Europe, and visited schools in England, Ireland, Scotland, Prussia, Saxony, the south German States, Holland and Belgium. Of the schools he saw he ranked those of Prussia first, those of Saxony second, those in the western and southern German States third, and those of Holland fourth.

He was much impressed by what he saw of the Prussian seminaries for the training of teachers, the careful selection of pupils for training, the course of instruction given, and the transformation which had taken place in the elementary-school teaching by reason of the training given. The teachers and their training he describes in the following selection from his *Report*.

I speak of the teachers whom I saw, and with whom I had more or less of personal intercourse; and, after some opportunity for the observation of public assemblies or bodies of men, I do not hesitate to say, that if those teachers were brought together, in one body, I believe they would form as dignified, intelligent, benevolent-looking a company of men as could be collected from the same amount of population in any country. They were alike free from arrogant pretension and from the affectation of humility. . . .

Whence came this beneficent order of men, scattered over the whole country, molding the character of its people, and carrying them forward in a career of civilization more rapidly than any other people in the world are now advancing? This is a question which can be answered only by giving an account of the Seminaries for Teachers.

From the year 1820 to 1830 or 1835, it was customary, in all accounts of Prussian education, to mention the number of these Seminaries for Teachers. This item of information has now become unimportant, as there are seminaries sufficient to supply the wants of the whole country. The stated term of residence at these seminaries is three years. Lately, and in a few places, a class of preliminary institutions has sprung up — institutions where pupils are received in order to determine whether they are fit to become candidates to be candidates. As a pupil of the seminary is liable to be set aside for incompetency, even after a three years' course of study; so the pupils of these preliminary institutions, after having gone through with a shorter course, are liable to be set aside for incompetency to become competent.

Let us look for a moment at the guards and securities which, in that country, environ this sacred calling. In the first place, the teacher's profession holds such a high rank in public estimation, that none who have failed in other employments or departments of business, are encouraged to look upon school-keeping as an ultimate resource. Those, too, who, from any cause, despair of success in other departments of business or walks of life, have very slender prospects in looking forward to this. These considerations exclude at once all that inferior order of men who, in some countries, constitute the main body of the teachers. Then come, — though only in some parts of Prussia, — these preliminary schools, where those who wish eventually to become teachers, go, in order to have their natural qualities and adaptation for school-keeping tested; for it must be borne in mind that a man may have the most unexceptionable character, may be capable of mastering all the branches of study, may even be able to make most brilliant recitations from day to day; and yet, from some coldness or repulsiveness of manner, from harshness of voice, from some natural defect in his person or in one of his senses, he may be adjudged an unsuitable model or archetype for children to be conformed to, or to grow by; and hence he may be dismissed at the end of his probationary term of six months. At one of these preparatory schools, which I visited, the list of subjects at the examination, — a part of which I saw, — was divided into two classes, as follows: 1. Readiness in thinking, German language, including orthography and composition, history, description of the earth, knowledge of nature, thorough bass, calligraphy, drawing. 2. Religion, knowledge of the Bible, knowledge of nature, mental arithmetic, singing, violin-playing, and readiness or facility in speaking. The examination in all the branches of the first class was conducted in writing. To test a pupil's readiness in thinking, for instance, several topics for composition are given out, and, after a lapse of a certain number of minutes, whatever has been written must be handed in to the examiners. So questions in arithmetic are given, and the time occupied by the pupils in solving them, is a test of their quickness of thought, or power of commanding their own resources. This facility, or faculty, is considered of great importance in a teacher. In the second class of subjects the pupils were examined *orally*. Two entire days were occupied in examining a class of thirty pupils, and only twenty-one were admitted to the seminary school; — that is only about two-thirds were considered to be eligible *to become eligible*, as teachers, after three years further study. Thus, in this first process, the chaff is winnowed out, and not a few of the lighter grains of the wheat.

It is to be understood that those who enter the seminary directly, and without this preliminary trial, have already studied, under able masters in the Common Schools, at least all the branches I have above described. The first two of the three years, they spend mainly in reviewing and expanding their elementary knowledge. The German language is studied in its relation to rhetoric and logic, and as æsthetic literature; arithmetic is carried out into algebra and mixed mathematics; geography into commerce and manufactures, and into a knowledge of the various botanical and zoölogical productions of the different quarters of the globe; linear drawing into perspective and machine drawing, and the drawing from models of all kinds, and from objects in nature, &c. The theory and practice, not only of vocal, but of instrumental music, occupy much time. Every pupil must play on the violin; most of them play on the organ, and some on other instruments. I recollect seeing a Normal class engaged in learning the principles of Harmony. The teacher first explained the principles on which they were to proceed. He then wrote a bar of music upon the blackboard, and called upon a pupil to write such notes for another part, or accompaniment, as would make *harmony* with the first. So he would write a bar with certain intervals, and then require a pupil to write another, with such intervals as, according to the principles of musical science, would correspond with the first. A thorough course of reading on the subject of education is undertaken, as well as a more general course. Bible history is almost committed to memory. Connected with all the seminaries for teachers are large Model or Experimental Schools. During the last part of the course much of the students' time is spent in these schools. At first they go in and look on in silence, while an accomplished teacher is instructing a class. Then they themselves commence teaching under the eye of such a teacher. At last they teach a class alone, being responsible for its proficiency, and for its condition as to order, &c., at the end of a week or other period. During the whole course, there are lectures, discussions, compositions, &c., on the theory and practice of teaching. The essential qualifications of a candidate for the office, his attainments, and the spirit of devotion and religious fidelity in which he should enter upon his work; the modes of teaching the different branches; the motive-powers to be applied to the minds of children; dissertations upon the different natural dispositions of children, and consequently, the different ways of addressing them, of securing their confidence and affection, and of winning them to a love of learning and a sense of duty; and especially the sacredness of the teacher's profession, — the idea that he stands for the time being, in the place of a parent, and therefore that a parent's responsibilities rest upon him, that the most precious hopes of society are committed to his charge, and that on him depends, to a great extent, the temporal and perhaps the future well-being of hundreds of his fellow-creatures, — these are the conversations, the ideas, the feelings, amid which the candidate for teaching spends his probationary years. This is the daily atmosphere he breathes. These are the sacred, elevating, invigorating influences constantly pouring in upon his soul. Hence, at the expiration of his course, he leaves the seminary to enter upon his profession, glowing with enthusiasm for the noble cause he has espoused, and strong in his resolves to perform its manifold and momentous duties.

Here, then, is the cause of the worth and standing of the teachers, whom I had the pleasure and the honor to see. As a body of men, their character is more enviable than that of either of the three, so-called, 'professions.' They have more benevolence and self-sacrifice than the legal or medical, while they have less of sanctimoniousness and austerity, less of indisposition to enter into all the innocent amusements and joyous feelings of childhood, than the clerical. They are not unmindful of what belongs to men while they are serving God; nor of the duties they owe to this world while preparing for another.

279. Some Prussian Schools and Teachers as Dinter found them

(Dinter, G. F., *Dinter's Leben von ihm selbst beschrieben;* trans. in Barnard's
American Journal of Education, vol. XXII, pp. 833–34)

Gustavus Friedrich Dinter was a distinguished clergyman, normal school director in Saxony, and State School Inspector for East Prussia. In his Autobiography he has left some interesting pictures as to the conditions he found in the elementary schools there when he took up his duties as inspector (1819) for the province. The following are illustrative.

In an examination of a school in East Prussia, which was taught by a subaltern officer dismissed from the army, the teacher gave Dinter a specimen of his skill in the illustration of a Scripture narrative. The passage was Luke VII, the miracle of raising the widow's son at Nain.

FIG. 69
GUSTAVUS FR. DINTER
(1760–1831)

"See, children (says the teacher), Nain was a great city, a beautiful city; but even in such a great, beautiful city, there lived people who must die. *They brought the dead youth out.* See, children, it was the same then as it is now — dead people couldn't go alone — they had to be carried. *He that was dead began to speak.* This was a sure sign that he was alive again, for if he had continued dead he couldn't have spoken a word."

In a letter to the King, a dismissed schoolmaster complained that the district was indebted to him 200705 dollars. Dinter supposed the man must be insane, and wrote to the physician of the place to inquire. The physician replied that the poor man was not insane, but only ignorant of the numeration table, writing 200 70 5 instead of 275. Dinter subjoins, "By the help of God, the King, and good men, very much has now been done to make things better."

In examining candidates for the school-teacher's office, Dinter asked one where the Kingdom of Prussia was situated. He replied, that he believed it was somewhere in the southern part of India.   He asked another the cause of the ignis-fatuus, commonly called Jack-with-the-lantern.   He said they were specters made by the devil.   Another being asked why he wished to become a school-teacher, replied, that he must get a living somehow.

A military man of great influence once urged Dinter to recommend a disabled soldier, in whom he was interested, as a school-teacher. "I will do so," says Dinter, "if he sustains the requisite examination." "Oh," says the Colonel, "he doesn't know much about school-teaching, but he is a good, moral, steady man, and I hope you will recommend him to oblige me."   *D.* — Oh yes, Colonel, to oblige you, if you in your turn will do me a favor.   *Col.* — What is that?   *D.* — Get me appointed a drum-major in your regiment.   True, I can neither beat a drum, nor play a fife; but I am a good, moral, steady man as ever lived.

A rich landholder once said to him, "Why do you wish the peasant children to be educated?   It will only make them unruly and disobedient."   Dinter replied, "If the masters are wise, and the laws good, the more intelligent the people, the better they will obey."

Dinter complained that the military system of Prussia was a great hinderance to the schools.   A nobleman replied that the young men enjoyed the protection of the government, and were thereby bound to defend it by arms.   Dinter asked if every stick of timber in a house ought first to be used in a fire-engine, because the house was protected by the engine? or whether it would be good policy to cut down all the trees of an orchard to build a fence with, to keep the hogs from eating the fruit?

280. Cousin's Report on Education in Prussia

(Cousin, Victor, *Rapport sur l'état de l'instruction publique en Prusse.*   Paris, 1831; trans. by Sarah Austin; London, 1834, pp. 105–08)

When the restored monarchy of France (1815–30) was overthrown by the revolution of July, 1830, and a more progressive government, supported by the leading thinkers of France came into power, one of their first acts was to begin the establishment of a state system of primary schools for France.   To this end one of the first things done was to send (1831) M. Victor Cousin, director of the Superior Normal School at Paris, to Prussia to study what was then regarded as the best school system of Europe.   His *Report on the State of Public Instruction in Prussia*, made that same year, carried conviction throughout France, and resulted in the Law of 1833, creating primary and superior primary schools for the nation.

In a summary of his Report he gives an interesting picture of the system of organization and administration, and shows how this was the result of a long local evolution.

The six Points,[1] Sir, which I have now gone over in succession, embrace the entire organization of primary instruction in Prussia. There is not a single article which is not translated from the text of the law of 1819. This law, without going into detail with relation to any particular branch, omits no topic of interest, and is the most extensive and complete law on primary instruction of which I have any knowledge.

It is impossible not to be struck with its profound wisdom. No inapplicable general principles, no spirit of system, no partial or exclusive views govern the legislator. He avails himself of all the means that can conduce to his end, however widely these means may differ. It is a king, and an absolute king, who issued this law; it is an irresponsible minister who advised or who digested it; and yet we find no injudicious spirit of centralization or of official despotism (*bureaucratie ministérielle*); almost everything is left to the parochial, departmental, or provincial authorities; little more than the general supervision and direction are reserved to the minister. The clergy have a great share in the management of popular instruction, and householders are also consulted in the towns and villages. In a word, all persons or classes who have an interest in the subject, find their appropriate place in this organization, and concur, each in his own manner and degree, to the common end, which is, the civilization of the people.

On these grounds the Prussian law of 1819 appears to me excellent; nor is it to be imagined that such a law could be conceived and matured by the wisdom of an individual. Baron von Altenstein rather digested than created it. Indeed, we may almost say that it already existed in a vast number of partial and detached ordinances, and in the manners and customs of the country. There is, perhaps, not a single article of this long law to which numerous anterior regulations did not serve as a groundwork; and, in a paper on the history of primary instruction in Prussia inserted in the first number of the second volume of the Journal of Primary Instruction, by Councillor von Beckedorff, I find rules as old as the years 1728 and 1736 which comprise a number of the provisions of the law of 1819. The obligation of parents to send their children to school is of great antiquity in Prussia. The powerful and active superintendence exercised by the Church over the education

---

[1] The six points, or titles of chapters in his Report, to which he refers, were:

    I. Duty of parents to send their children to the primary schools.

    II. Duty of each parish to support a primary school.

    III. General objects and different gradations of primary instruction.

    IV. Training, appointment, promotion, and discipline of primary teachers.

    V. The superintendence of primary instruction.

    VI. Of private schools.

of the people, dates from the origin of Protestantism, of which it is an inherent characteristic. It is evident that the authors of a revolution effected in the name of liberty of conscience must necessarily labour at the emancipation of the popular mind, and the diffusion of knowledge, as the only secure means of defending their cause and rooting it in the minds of the people. Unquestionably the law of 1819 raises education to a sufficiently high pitch in the elementary schools and those for the middle classes; but if the course of instruction seems somewhat too full for some places or districts, it must be remembered that it was already acted up to, and even surpassed, in many others. The boldest measure was the establishment of a grand primary normal school for each department; but there were already similar establishments in most of the old provinces of the monarchy.   In short, this law does little more than methodize what already existed, not only in Prussia, but throughout Germany.

It is not, then, a metaphysical, arbitrary and artificial abstraction, like the greater part of our laws on primary instruction; it is founded on reality and experience, and has, for that reason, been carried into execution, and produced the happiest results with extraordinary rapidity.   Having taken care to ascertain that it was everywhere practicable, the Prussian minister peremptorily required that it should everywhere be practiced; leaving the details to the authorities appointed to execute them, and reserving to himself only the general guidance and supervision. This guidance has been so firm, this supervision has been so vigilant, and the parochial, departmental and provincial authorities ... entrusted with the management of schools have displayed so steady and well-directed a zeal, that in almost every part of the kingdom the reality actually goes beyond the law; and, on all points at least where zeal alone is required, even more is done than is commanded.

281. The Military Aspect of Prussian Education

(Mann, Horace, *Seventh Annual Report, Massachusetts State Board of Education.*
Boston, 1843)

This is another selection from the same *Report* as Reading **278,** and deals with the military and obedience aspect of the schools as Mann saw them.   At the time of his visit (1843) the forces of reaction following the victory over Napoleon were fast reaching a climax, though Pestalozzian normal schools and methods were still permitted.   That he saw the weaknesses of the Prussian schools, as well as their points of strength, may be seen from the following.

Among the nations of Europe, Prussia has long enjoyed the most distinguished reputation for the excellence of its schools.   In reviews, in speeches, in tracts, and even in graver works devoted to the cause of education, its schools have been exhibited as models for the imitation of the rest of Christendom.   For many years, scarce a suspicion was breathed that the general plan of education in that kingdom was not sound in theory and most beneficial in practice.   Recently, however, grave charges have been preferred against it by high authority.   The popular traveler, Laing, has devoted several chapters of his large work on Prussia to the disparagement of its school system.   An octavo volume, entitled "The Age of Great Cities," has recently appeared in England, in which that system is strongly condemned; and during the pendency of the famous "Factories Bill" before the British House of Commons, in 1843, numerous tracts were issued from the English press, not merely calling in question, but strongly denouncing, the whole plan of education in Prussia, as being not only designed to produce, but as actually producing, a spirit of blind acquiescence to arbitrary power, in things spiritual as well as temporal — as being, in fine, a system of education adapted to enslave, and not to enfranchise, the human mind.   And even in some parts of the United States — the very nature and essence of whose institutions consist in the idea that the people are wise enough to distinguish between what is right and what is wrong — even here, some have been illiberal enough to condemn, in advance, everything that savors of the Prussian system, because that system is sustained by arbitrary power.

.   .   .   .

But allowing all these charges against the Prussian system to be true, there were still two reasons why I was not deterred from examining it.

In the first place, the evils imputed to it were easily and naturally separable from the good which it was not denied to possess.   If the Prussian schoolmaster has better methods of teaching reading, writing, grammar, geography, arithmetic, &c., so that, in half the time, he produces greater and better results, surely we may copy his modes of teaching these elements without adopting his notions of passive obedience to government, or of blind adherence to the articles of a church. By the ordinance of nature, the human faculties are substantially the same all over the world, and hence the best means for their development and growth in one place, must be substantially the best for their development and growth everywhere.   The spirit which shall control the action of these faculties when matured, which shall train them to self-reliance or to abject submission, which shall lead them to refer all questions to the standard of reason or to that of authority, — this spirit is wholly distinct and distinguishable from the manner in which the faculties themselves ought to be trained; and we may avail ourselves of all improved methods in the earlier processes, without being contaminated by the abuses which may be made to follow them.   The best style of teaching arithmetic and spelling has no necessary or natural connection with the doctrine of hereditary right; and an accomplished lesson in geography or grammar commits the human intellect to no particular dogma in religion.

In the second place, if Prussia can pervert the benign influences of education to the support of arbitrary power, we surely can employ them for the support and perpetuation of republican institutions. A national spirit of liberty can be cultivated more easily than a national spirit of bondage; and if it may be made one of the great prerogatives of education to perform the unnatural and unholy work of making slaves, then surely it must be one of the noblest instrumentalities for rearing a nation of freemen. If a moral power over the understandings and affections of the people may be turned to evil, may it not also be employed for the highest good?

Besides, a generous and impartial mind does not ask whence a thing comes, but what it is. Those who, at the present day, would reject an improvement because of the place of its origin, belong to the same school of bigotry with those who inquired if any good could come out of Nazareth; and what infinite blessings would the world have lost had that party been punished by success! Throughout my whole tour, no one principle has been more frequently exemplified than this, — that wherever I have found the best institutions, — educational, reformatory, charitable, penal, or otherwise, — there I have always found the greatest desire to know how similar institutions were administered among ourselves; and where I have found the worst, there I have found most of the spirit of self-complacency, and even an offensive disinclination to hear of better methods.

CHAPTER XXIII

NATIONAL ORGANIZATION IN FRANCE

THE Readings in this chapter have been selected to illustrate the founding of the centralized state school system of France, and cover the period from the reign of Napoleon to the beginnings of modern educational organization under the Third Republic.

The first selection (282) gives the story of the founding of the National School of Arts and Trades by Napoleon, and is illustrative both of his interests and his methods of work. The second (283) reproduces the Statutes for the refounding of the Superior Normal School at Paris, and indicates the type of school intended to be created. The next (284) is a selection from the Report of M. Victor Cousin on the Prussian school system, a report that not only led to the Law of 1833 in France, but was influential in England and the United States as well. The organizing Law of 1833 for France was presented to the Chamber of Deputies by the Minister of Public Instruction, M. Guizot, and selection 285 contains three extracts from his address on that occasion. In 286 M. Guizot gives an interesting picture of the framing of the Law, by a group of progressive conservatives, and 287 is an important extract from his detailed letter to the teachers of France on the inauguration of the Law. Selection 288 is an appreciation of the work of M. Guizot from the pen of an English School Inspector.

After the reversion to the Second Empire, education went back in part to clerical control. At the same time an agitation was continued for lay and secular schools. The extract from M. Edgar Quinet (289) presents an excellent argument on the question. After the establishment of the Third Republic the desires of earlier theorists and workers found realization, and the extract from the address of M. Jules Ferry (290) to the teachers of France, on moral and civic education, forms an interesting contrast with the letter of M. Guizot and pictures well the changes which had taken place in French thinking and French educational practices.

282. Founding of the National School of Arts and Trades

(Report of Inspector M. Le Brun; trans. in Barnard's *American Journal of Education*, vol. XXI, pp. 451–52)

The story of the founding of the French School of Arts and Trades, by Napoleon, in 1803, is characteristic of the interest in practical education taken by him. In 1800 he had used the endowments of the old *Collège Louis le Grande* (founded in 1567 as a humanistic school) to create three military colleges. Most of the pupils were sent to these at public expense, and were taught French, the classical languages, ancient history, geography, drawing, mathematics, and military drill. One day Napoleon, while still First Consul, visited the military college at Compiègne, and questioned the older pupils as to what they intended to do on leaving it. He was so dissatisfied with the answers that he said:

The Government pays considerable sums to educate these young men, and when their studies are ended, none of them, except those who enter the army, are of any use to the country. Nearly all of them remain at home, a burden to their families, which they ought to aid. This shall continue no longer. I have just visited the great manufacturing establishments in the north and the larger workshops of Paris. I everywhere found foremen clever in the manual labor of their trades, but scarcely one among them able to draw the outlines or make the most simple calculations of a machine to convey his ideas by a sketch or a written description. This is a great defect, and I will here provide the means for remedying it. There must be no more Latin here; that will be learned in the lyceums about to be organized; but the study of trades, with so much theory as is necessary for their progress; by this course we shall obtain well-taught foremen for our manufactories.

A few days later (February 25, 1803), the following decision was printed in the official *Moniteur:*

From and after the month of Germinal, year XI (March, 1803), the teaching in the College of Compiègne shall have for its object the training of workmen and managers of shops.

The work of the school was now rearranged on the following plan:

The pupils under twelve years of age were divided into three classes, in which they received an elementary education: 1. Reading, writing, and the rudiments of French grammar. 2. Continuation of the same studies, with the four rules of arithmetic. 3. The same studies, with the elements of geometry and first principles of drawing. From this college the pupils passed to the School of Arts and Trades, where, according to the occupations which they were to pursue, and qualifications, they were distributed among the different workshops, as — 1. Smiths, filers, fitters, turners in metal.   2. Founders.   3. Carpenters, joiners for buildings, furniture, and machines.   4. Turners in wood.   5. Wheel-wrights.   In these shops they worked eight hours a day.   There were six classes, according to the proficiency and aptitude of the pupils. Only two hours per day were devoted to study and to theory, including geometry, descriptive geometry applied to the arts, drawing and tinting of plans and machines.   It was also arranged that those who should make great progress and display extraordinary talents should receive a more advanced education.   They were to continue the same studies and were also to be instructed in the application of the principles of mechanics to the practice of the industrial arts.

283. Refounding of the Superior Normal School

Report of M. Charles Jourdain; trans. in Barnard's *American Journal of Education*, vol. xx, p. 324)

In 1794 the National Convention had created a higher normal school (*école normale supérieure*) for the training of professors for the higher institutions of learning in France.   The school opened in 1795, with great expectations, but closed in a few months from apparent failure.   When Napoleon created the Imperial University of France, in 1808, he re-created the normal school, and it began work in 1810.   The following selections from the University of France decree relate to the normal school, and reveal the nature of the institution created.

Art. 110.   There shall be established, at Paris, a Normal Boarding-School, prepared to receive at least three hundred young men, who shall be educated in the art of teaching letters and science.

111. The inspectors of the academy shall select, each year, from the lyceums, after due examination and competition, a certain number of pupils, of seventeen years of age or over, whose good conduct and progress have been most marked, and who shall have shown aptitude for governing and instructing.

112. Those who present themselves for examination shall be authorized by their father or guardian to pursue the university course.   They shall be received into the normal school only on engaging to continue in the profession of teaching for at least ten years.

113. These candidates shall pursue their studies at the College of France, or the Polytechnic School, or the Museum of Natural History, according as they intend to teach letters, or the different sciences.

114. Besides their regular lessons, there shall be tutors, chosen from the older and more talented pupils, under whose direction they shall

review the subjects taught in the special schools before mentioned, and have laboratory practice in natural philosophy or chemistry.

115. The pupils shall not remain at the normal boarding-school more than two years. They shall then be supported at the expense of the university, and be bound out to their profession.

116. The normal school shall be under the supervision of one of the counselors for life, who shall reside at the institution, and have under him a director of studies.

117. The number of candidates for the normal school shall be regulated by the condition and needs of the colleges and lyceums.

118. The candidates, during their course of two years, or at the close of it, must take their degrees at Paris, in the department of letters, or in that of science. They will then be called upon, in regular order, to fill vacant places in the academies, as they may occur.

284. Cousin's Recommendations for Education in France

(Cousin, Victor, *Rapport sur l'état l'instruction publique en Prusse.* Paris, 1831; trans. by Sarah Austin. London, 1834, pp. 111–33)

This selection is a continuation of Reading **280.** The *Report* was addressed to Count de Montalivet, Minister of Public Instruction and Ecclesiastical Affairs for France. After describing primary (*Volksschule*) education in Prussia in some detail (see footnote, page 486, for chapter titles), he makes a summary of recommendations to the Minister for the drawing up of a Law for primary education in France. The following selections represent the more important portions of the *Report.*

FIG. 70. VICTOR COUSIN (1792–1867)

(*a*) *Previous neglect of primary education.* Without question, Sir, in the present state of things, a law concerning primary instruction is indispensable in France; the question is, how to produce a good one, in a country where there is a total absence of all precedent and all experience in so grave a matter. The education of the people has hitherto been so neglected — so few trials have been made, or those trials have succeeded so ill, that we are entirely without those universally received notions, those predilections rooted in the habits and the mind of a nation, which are the conditions and the bases of all good legislation. I wish, then, for a law; and at the same time I dread it; for I tremble lest we should plunge into visionary and impracticable projects again, without attending to what actually exists. . . .

(*b*) *Compulsion to attend.* The idea of compelling parents to send their children to school is perhaps not sufficiently diffused through the nation to justify the experiment of making it law; but everybody agrees in regarding the establishment of a school in every *commune* as necessary. It is also willingly conceded that the maintenance of this school must rest with the *commune;* always provided that, in case of inability through poverty, the *commune* shall apply to the department, and the department to the state. This point may be assumed as universally admitted, and may therefore become law. . . .

(*c*) *Normal schools.* You are likewise aware, Sir, that many of the councils of departments have felt the necessity of securing a supply of schoolmasters, and a more complete education for them, and have, with this view, established primary normal schools in their departments. Indeed, they have often shown rather prodigality than parsimony on this head. This, too, is a most valuable and encouraging indication; and a law ordaining the establishment of a primary normal school in each department, as well as of a primary school in each *commune*, would do little more than confirm and generalize what is now actually doing in almost all parts of the country. Of course this primary normal school must be more or less considerable according to the resources of each department.

(*d*) *The collèges* (*Lycées*). Here we have already two most important points on which the country is almost unanimously agreed. You have also, without doubt, been struck with the petitions of a number of towns, great and small, for the establishment of schools of a class rather higher than the common primary schools; such as, though still inferior in classical and scientific studies to our royal and communal *collèges*, might be more particularly adapted to give that kind of generally useful knowledge indispensable to the large portion of the population which is not intended for the learned professions, but which yet needs more extended and varied acquirements than the class of day-labourers and artisans. Such petitions are almost universal. Several municipal councils have voted considerable funds for the purpose, and have applied to us for the necessary authority, for advice and assistance. It is impossible not to regard this as the symptom of a real want, — the indication of a serious deficiency in our system of public instruction.

You, Sir, are sufficiently acquainted with my zeal for classical and scientific studies; not only do I think that we must keep up to the plan of study prescribed in our *collèges*, and particularly the philological part of that plan, but I think we ought to raise and extend it, and thus, while we maintain our incontestable superiority in the physical and mathematical sciences, endeavour to rival Germany in the solidity of our classical learning. . . . Classical studies keep alive the sacred tradition of the moral and intellectual life of the human race. To curtail or enfeeble such studies would, in my eyes, be an act of barbarism, a crime against all true and high civilization, and in some sort an act of high treason against humanity.

(e) *Middle-class schools.* Let our royal *collèges* then, and even a great proportion of our communal *collèges*, continue to lead the youth of France into this sanctuary; they will merit the thanks of their country. But can the whole population enter learned schools? or, indeed, is it to be wished that it should? Primary instruction with us, however, is but meagre; between that and the *collèges* there is nothing; so that a tradesman, even in the lower ranks of the middle classes, who has the honourable wish of giving his sons a good education, has no resource but to send them to the *collège.* . . . Our *collèges* ought, without doubt, to remain open to all who can pay the expense of them; but we ought by no means to force the lower classes into them; yet this is the inevitable effect of having no intermediate establishments between the primary schools and the *collèges*. Germany, and Prussia more especially, are rich in establishments of this kind. I have described several in detail, at Frankfort, Weimar, and Leipsig. The Prussian law of 1819 sanctions them. You perceive, Sir, that I allude to the schools called tradesmen's or burghers' schools, or schools for the middle classes (*Bürgerschulen*), *écoles bourgeoises,* — a name which it is perhaps impossible to transplant into France, but which is accurate and expressive, as contradistinguishing them from the learned schools (*Gelehrteschulen*), called in Germany *Gymnasia,* and in France *collèges* (in England "grammar-schools") — a name, too, honourable to the class for whose especial use and benefit they are provided, — honourable to those of a lower class, who by frequenting them can rise to a level with that above them. The burgher schools form the higher step of primary instruction, of which the elementary schools are the lower step. . . . The Prussian law, which fixes a minimum of instruction for the elementary schools, likewise fixes a minimum of instruction for the burgher schools; and there are two kinds of examination, extremely distinct, for obtaining the brevet of primary teacher for these two gradations. . . . In Prussia this class of schools has, accordingly, very different gradations, from the minimum fixed by the law, with which I have already made you acquainted, to that point where it becomes closely allied with the *Gymnasium,* properly so called. At this point it sometimes has the name of Progymnasium.

. . . In general, the German burgher schools, which are a little inferior to our communal *collèges* in classical and scientific studies, are incomparably superior to them in religious instruction, geography, history, modern languages, music, drawing, and national literature.

In my opinion, it is of the highest importance to create in France, under one name or another, burgher schools, or schools for the middle classes, which give a very varied education; and to convert a certain number of our communal *collèges* into schools of that description. I regard this, Sir, as an affair of state. . . .

(*f*) *Local control for the schools.* I regard as another incontestable point, the necessary intervention of the municipal and departmental councils in the management of public instruction. As there ought to be a school in every *commune*, so there ought to be for every communal school a special committee of superintendence, which ought to be formed out of the municipal council, and presided over by the *maire*. . . .

After the administrative authorities, it is unquestionably the clergy who ought to occupy the most important place in the business of popular education. How is it possible they could neglect, nay, even repugn, such a mission? But that they have done so is a fact, which, however deplorable, we are bound to acknowledge. The clergy in France are generally indifferent, or even hostile, to the education of the people. Let them blame themselves if the law does not give them great influence over primary instruction; for it was their duty to anticipate the law, and to take up a position which they must necessarily have continued to occupy. The law, offspring of facts, will therefore place small reliance on the clergy; but if it rejected them altogether, it would commit an egregious fault; for it would set the clergy in decided opposition to primary instruction, and would engage in a conflict, open, scandalous, and perilous. The rational middle course is to put the *curé* or the pastor, and if need be both, on every communal committee; and the highest dignitary of the church in each department, on the departmental committee. . . .

(*g*) *Private teachers and schools.* As to private teachers, and what people are pleased to call liberty of primary tuition, I can only repeat what I have said elsewhere, — we must neither oppose it, nor reckon upon it. There are branches of the public service which must be secured against all casualties by the state, and in the first rank of these is primary instruction. It is the bounden duty of government to guarantee it against all caprices of public opinion, and against the variable and uncertain calculations of those who would engage in it as a means of subsistence. On this principle are founded our primary normal schools in each department, bound to furnish annually the average number of schoolmasters required by the department. We must rely exclusively on these normal schools for the regular supply of communal teachers.

But if, in the face of our primary communal schools, there are persons who, without having passed through the normal schools, choose to establish schools at their own risk and peril, it is obvious that they ought not only to be tolerated, but encouraged; — just as we rejoice that private institutions and boarding-schools should spring up beside our royal and communal *collèges*. This competition cannot be otherwise than useful, in every point of view. If the private schools prosper, so much the better; they are at full liberty to try all sorts of methods, and to make experiments in teaching, which, on such a scale, cannot be very perilous. At all events, there are our normal schools. Thus all interests are reconciled, — the duties of the state, and the rights of individuals; the claims of experience, and those of innovation. Whoever wishes to set up a private school must be subject to only two conditions, from which no school, public or private, can on any pretext be exempt, — the brevet of capacity, given by the commission of examination, and the supervision of the committee of the *commune* and of the inspector of the department. I would very readily give up the certificate of moral character, as illusory, and as implicitly contained in that of fitness. . . .

(*h*) *The law to represent experience.* All these measures, on which I will not enlarge, are more or less founded on existing facts; they have the sanction of experience; it would be simply advantageous to add that of law. On all the points concerning which the law is silent, experiments might be made. Among these experiments some would probably be successful; when sufficiently long practice had confirmed them, they might be inserted in a new law; or *ordonnances* and instructions, maturely weighed by the royal council, would convert them into general and official measures. Nothing must pass into a law which has not the warranty of success. Laws are not to be perilous experiments on society; they ought simply to sum up and to generalize the lessons of experience.

285. Guizot on the Law of 1833

(M. Guizot, An *Address* made on introducing the Law in the French Chamber of Deputies, 1833; trans. in Barnard's *Am. Jour. of Education*, vol. xx, pp. 236–37)

On the experience of Prussia as a basis (**Rs. 280, 284**), M. Guizot, Minister of Public Instruction from 1832 to 1837, prepared and had enacted the famous Law of 1833, organizing primary and higher primary instruction for France. In introducing the bill he made a lengthy Address, from which the following extracts, which give the general nature of the bill, are taken.

(*a*) *History of primary education up to 1832.* In framing this bill, it is experience, and experience alone, that we have taken for our guide. The principles and practices recommended have been supplied to us by facts. There is not one part of the mechanism which has not been worked successfully. We conceive that, on the subject of the education of the people, our business is rather to methodize and improve what exists, than to destroy for the purpose of inventing and renewing upon the faith of dangerous theories. It is by laboring incessantly on these maxims, that the Administration has been enabled to communicate a firm and steady movement to this important branch of the public service; so much so, that we take leave to say, that more has been done for primary education during the last two years (1831, 1832), and by the Government of July, than during the forty years preceding, by all the former Governments.   The first Revolution was lavish of prom-

ises, without troubling itself about the performance.   The Imperial Government exhausted itself in efforts to regenerate the higher instruction, called secondary; but did nothing for that of the people.   The restored Dynasty, up to 1828, expended no more than 50,000 francs annually upon primary instruction.   The Ministry of 1828 obtained from the Chamber a grant of 300,000 francs.   Since the revolution of July, 1830, a million has been voted annually — that is, more in two years than the Restoration in fifteen.   Those are the means, and here are the results.   All of you are aware that primary instruction depends altogether on the corresponding Normal Schools.   The prosperity of

FIG. 71. M. GUIZOT
(1787–1874)

these establishments is the measure of its progress.   The Imperial Government, which first pronounced with effect the words, Normal Schools, left us a legacy of one.   The Restoration added five or six. Those, of which some were in their infancy, we have greatly improved within the last two years, and have, at the same time, established thirty new ones; twenty of which are in full operation, forming in each department a vast focus of light, scattering its rays in all directions among the people.

(b) *The two grades of primary instruction.*   The first degree of instruction should be common to the country and the towns; it should be met with in the humblest borough, as well as in the largest city, wherever a human being is to be found within our land of France.   By the teaching of reading, writing, and accounts, it provides for the most essential wants of life; by that of the legal system of weights and measures, and of the French language, it implants, enlarges, and spreads everywhere the spirit and unity of the French nationality; finally, by moral and religious instruction, it provides for another class of wants quite as real as the others, and which Providence has placed in the hearts of the poorest, as well as of the richest, in this world, for upholding the dignity of human life and the protection of social order.   The first degree of instruction is extensive enough to make a man of him who will receive it, and is, at the same time, sufficiently limited to be everywhere realized.   It is the strict debt of the country toward all its children.

But the law is so framed that by higher elementary schools, primary instruction can be so developed, so varied, as to satisfy the wants of those professions which, though not scientific, yet require to be acquainted with "the elements of science, as they apply it every day in the office, the workshop, and field."

(c) *The training of the teacher*. All the provisions hitherto described would be of no effect, if we took no pains to procure for the public school thus constituted an able master, and worthy of the high vocation of instructing the people. It can not be too often repeated, that it is the master that makes the school. . . . A bad schoolmaster, like a bad parish priest, is a scourge to a *commune;* and though we are often obliged to be contented with indifferent ones, we must do our best to improve the average quality. We have, therefore, availed ourselves of a bright thought struck out in the heat of the Revolution, by a decree of the National Convention in 1794, and afterward applied by Napoleon, in his decree, in 1808, for the organization of the University, to the establishment of his central Normal School at Paris. We carry its application still lower than he did in the social scale, when we propose that no schoolmaster shall be appointed who has not himself been a pupil of the school which instructs in the art of teaching, and who is not certified, after a strict examination, to have profited by the opportunities he has enjoyed.

286. Principles underlying the Law of 1833

(M. Guizot, *Mémoires pour servir à l'histoire de mon temps*. 8 vols., Paris, 1858–61; trans. of chapter in Barnard's *Amer. Jour. of Education*, vol. xx, pp. 266–67)

M. François Pierre Guillaume Guizot (1787–1874), in the *Mémoires* which he wrote to illustrate the history of his life, devoted a chapter to his work as Minister of Public Instruction for France, a position he held during the constructive period from 1832 to 1837. In this he describes the formation of the important Law of 1833, and the principles which guided his action and that of his colleagues. The following extract is interesting as illustrating the tender feeling still existing toward religious education, and also toward the rights of parents to educate their own children in their own way, or not at all, as they saw fit, on the part of the conservative statesmen of the time.

The first point, and the one which, not only in my estimation, but in that of many sound thinkers, still remains undecided, whether the elementary instruction of all children should be an absolute obligation imposed by the law on their parents, and supported by specific penalties in case of neglect, as adopted in Prussia and in the greater portion of the German States. I have nothing to say in respect to the countries where this rule has been long established, and acknowledged by national sentiment. There it has certainly produced beneficial results. But I must observe that it is almost exclusively confined to nations hitherto exacting little on the question of liberty, and that it has originated with those with whom, through the Reformation of the sixteenth century, the civil power is also in matters of religion, or touching upon religious interests, the sovereign authority. The proud susceptibility of free peoples, and the strong mutual independence of temporal and spiritual power, would accommodate themselves badly to this coercive action of the state on the domestic economy of families: where not sanctioned by tradition, the laws would fail to introduce it, for either they would be confined to an empty command, or to compel obedience they would have recourse to proscriptions and inquisitorial searches, hateful to attempt, and almost impossible to execute, especially in a great country. The National Convention tried, or rather decreed this, in 1793, and amongst all its acts of tyranny, this, at least, remained without effect.

Popular instruction is at present, in England, whether on the part of national and municipal authorities, or of simple citizens, the object of persevering zeal and exertion. No one proposes to enforce the obligation on parents by law. The system prospers in the United States of America, where local governments and private societies make great sacrifices to increase and improve the schools; but no efforts are attempted to intrude into the bosoms of families to recruit the scholars by compulsion. It forms a characteristic and redounds to the honor of a free people, that they are at the same time confiding and patient; that they rely on the empire of enlightened reason and well-understood interests, and know how to wait their results. I care little for regulations that bear the impress of the convent or the barrack room. I therefore decidedly expunged constraint from my bill on elementary education, and none of my fellow-laborers insisted on its being retained, not even those who regretted the omission.

Next to the question of compulsory elementary education, came that of free primary instruction. Here, indeed, there could be no doubt. The charter had promised liberty on this point, and it was not in regard to the first principles of instruction that this promise could give rise to opposite interpretations or lengthened disputes. No one thought of demanding that elementary education should be entirely committed to private industry, evidently incapable of furnishing the necessary supply, and little tempted to undertake it. The labor is immense, and without brilliant perspectives. The interference of the State here becomes indispensable. A free competition between the government and private individuals, private and public schools opened side by side, and under the same regulations, comprised all that the most exacting liberals required, and produced no opposition from the stanchest supporters of power.

A third question gave rise to more discussion. In the public schools, should elementary instruction be absolutely gratuitous, and supplied by the State to all children of the soil? This was the dream of generous spirits. Under the constitution of 1791, the Constituent Assembly had decreed that "a system of public instruction should be created and organized, common to every citizen, and gratuitous with regard to those branches of education indispensable to all men." The National Convention, while maintaining this principle, fixed the salaries of the tutors at a *minimum* of 1200 francs. Experience has proved the vanity of these promises, as irrational as they were impracticable. The State is bound to offer elementary instruction to all families, and to give it to those who have not the means of paying for it; and thus it does more for the moral life of the people than it can effect for their material condition. This I consider the true principle of the question, and this I adopted in my bill.

These general and in some degree preliminary points being disposed of, there remained others of a more special character, the solution of which formed the text and scope of the bill. What were to be the objects and limits of elementary instruction? How were the public institutions to be formed and recruited? What authorities were to be charged with the superintendence of the elementary schools? What should be the means and securities for the effective execution of the act?

France, in company with all progressive modern nations, has since abandoned these positions. Popular education in France was made wholly free in 1881, and compulsory in 1882, while the supplanting of religious by lay teachers was begun in 1891, and in 1904 all religious schools were closed.

287. Guizot's Letter to the Primary Teachers of France

(*Official Circular*, Minister of Public Instruction for France; trans. in Barnard's *American Journal of Education*, vol. xx, pp. 278–80)

The following extracts from an Official Circular, sent out by M. Guizot to the 39,300 primary teachers of France, of all kinds, accompanying a copy of the new Law of June 28, 1833, establishing primary instruction in France under the aid and control of the State, reveal the spirit with which M. Guizot worked. The beginning and closing of the Circular are reproduced; the central part was a statement as to the duties of the teachers as regarded the children, morals, religious instruction, etc.

SIR: I send you herewith the law of the 28th of June last, on elementary education; together with a statement of the reasons that led to its enactment when, in obedience to the orders of the King, I had the honor of presenting it, on the 2d of January, to the Chamber of Deputies.

The law is, in reality, the charter of elementary education; and for that reason I am anxious that it should directly reach the knowledge, and remain in the possession of every tutor.   If you study it carefully, and reflect with attention on its provisions, as well as on the motives which develop its true spirit, you may be assured of thoroughly comprehending your duties and privileges, together with the new position assigned to you by our institutions.

Do not deceive yourself.   Although the career of an elementary teacher may be unostentatious; although his life and labors may, for the most part, be consumed within the boundary of a single township, — those labors interest society at large, and his profession participates in the importance of public duties.   It is not for a particular district, of tor any interest exclusively local, that the law desires every Frenchman to acquire, if possible, the knowledge indispensable to social existence, without which intelligence languishes, and sometimes becomes brutified.   The law is for the state at large, and for public advantage; and because liberty can neither be assured nor regular, except with a people sufficiently enlightened to listen, under all circumstances, to the voice of reason.   Universal elementary education will become henceforward a guarantee for order and social stability.   As all the principles of our government are sound and rational, to develop intellect and propagate light is to confirm the empire and durability of our constitutional monarchy.

. . . .

In conclusion, I have no occasion to dwell on your relations with the special authorities which watch over the schools, and with the University itself.   You will obtain from them general advice, all necessary directions, and frequently a support against local difficulties and incidental enmity.   The administration has no other interests than those of elementary education, which are, in fact, your own.   It only requires of you to understand thoroughly and progressively the spirit of your mission.   While, on its part, it will carefully protect your rights, your interests, and your future, do you, in turn, maintain by unremitting vigilance the dignity of your position.   Do not disorder it by unseasonable speculations, or by employments incompatible with instruction.   Keep your eyes fixed on every possible method of improving the instruction you disperse around you.   Assistance will not be wanting.   In the greater number of large towns, advanced classes are opened; in the normal schools, places are reserved for such tutors as may feel desirous of going there to improve their teaching.   Every day it becomes easier for you to obtain, at a trifling cost, a library sufficient for your requirements.   Finally, in some districts and cantons, conferences have already been established between the teachers.   By these means, they can unite their common experience and encourage each other by mutual aid.

At the moment when, under the auspices of a new legislation, you are about to enter on a new career, when elementary education is destined to become the object of the most extensive practical experience that has ever yet been attempted in our country, I have felt it my duty to detail to you the principles which govern the administration of public instruction, and the hopes founded on your exertions. I rely on your utmost endeavors to insure the success of our undertaking.

288. Guizot's Work as Minister of Public Instruction

(Arnold, Matthew, *Popular Education in France.* London, 1861)

Mr. Arnold was an Inspector of Schools for the English government. He made careful studies on education on the continent of Europe, and wrote Reports on his work for his home government. In one of these he gives the following very interesting picture of the work of M. Guizot, Minister of Public Instruction for France from 1832 to 1837. At the time he wrote the earlier zeal for popular education had largely died out.

Such was the Law of 1833, not more remarkable for the judgment with which it was framed than for the energy with which it was executed. As if he had foreseen the weak point of his law, the inadequacy of the local authorities to discharge the trust committed to their hands, M. Guizot multiplied his efforts to stimulate and to enlighten them. In successive circulars to prefects, to rectors, to directors of normal schools, to inspectors, he endeavored to procure the active coöperation of all his agents in the designs of the Government, and to inspire in all of them the zeal with which he himself was animated. On behalf of the elementary schools, he strove to awaken that spirit of local interest and independent activity which he and his friends have never ceased to invoke for their country, and the want of which has, since the Revolution, been the great want of France. He succeeded imperfectly in inspiring his countrymen with a faith in habits of local exertion; but he succeeded at last in founding the elementary schools of France, and in inspiring faith in his own zeal for them. In the chamber of the Frère Philippe or of the Père Étienne, as among the Protestant populations of Nismes and of Strasbourg; in the palaces of bishops and in the manses of pastors; in the villages of Brittany and in the villages of the Cevennes — everywhere I found M. Guizot's name held in honor for the justice and wisdom of his direction of popular education when it was in fashion, for his fidelity to it now that it is no longer talked of. Singular confidence inspired in quarters the most various upon the most delicate of questions, which insincere ability can never conciliate, which even sincere ability can not always conciliate; only ability united with that heartfelt devotion to a great cause, which friends of the cause instinctively recognize, and warm towards it because they share it.

289. A Lay School for a Lay Society

(Quinet, Edgar, *L'enseignement du peuple*.   Paris, 1850; trans. in Buisson and Farrington *French Ideals of Today*.   World Book Company, Yonkers, New York, 1919.   Reproduced by permission)

Edgar Quinet (1803–75) was a professor at the Collège de France, and was forced into exile after the establishment of the Second Empire because of his republican protests. The nineteen years of his exile (1851–70) he devoted to the awakening of the French conscience in matters of lay education, and by his writings did much to prepare France for the complete national system of education adopted after 1870.   His book on the "Instruction of a People" states clearly the principles of republican and national education, as the following extract shows.

FIG. 72. EDGAR QUINET (1803–75)

No particular church being the soul of France, the teaching which diffuses this soul should be independent of every particular church.

The teacher is not merely the priest's assistant; he teaches what no priest can teach, the alliance of churches in the same society.

The teacher has a more universal doctrine than the priest, for he speaks to Catholic, Protestant, and Jew alike, and he brings them all into the same civil communion.

The teacher is obliged to say: "You are all children of the same God and of the same country; take hold of each others' hands until death." The priest is obliged to say: "You are the children of different churches, but among these mothers there is but one who is legitimate.   All those who do not belong to her are accursed; they shall remain orphans.   Be, then, separated in time, since you must be separated in eternity."

Do you think it would be a misfortune for your child thus to be born to civil life with any feeling of concord, peace, and union toward his brethren?   Is the first smile that heaven has given him, given him to curse?   Must his first lisping be an anathema?

The intention of the sacerdotal castes has always been that they are the only power capable of giving a foundation to civil and political institutions. Look at them wherever they have held sway, among the Hindus or in the states of Rome.   While they reigned, each detail of the civil state, its administration, even the police, were things sacred; in the theocracy of Moses the smallest hygienic or agricultural regulation came from the wisdom on high. Every prescription of the priest is of divine institution; the thought of heaven permeates the whole body of laws.

As soon as lay society frees itself from the rule of the priests, it is considered to have broken off all relation with the eternal order. The same laws which formerly were filled with the spirit of God are now but the caprices of chance. From the moment that this State, which was said to be of divine institution, dispenses with the priest, it is proclaimed atheistic. Yesterday it was eternal wisdom, manifested and written in the laws. To-day it is a blind person who pushes away his guide. It knows nothing, it sees nothing. Separated from the priest, what remains for it to teach? Not even the wisdom which the ant teaches the ant.

If society without the priest does not believe in justice, why does it seek from century to century to come nearer to justice in the development of law? If it does not believe in truth, why does it pursue truth in science? If it does not believe in order, why does it pursue order in the succession of its institutions and revolutions?

Justice, truth, absolute order, what are they but the eternal source of divine ideas; in other words, that essence of the God on which the customs of the State are ordered? This God of order and of justice, this eternal geometer who descends by degrees into the very groundwork of the laws of all civilized peoples, is not the one who pleases the sacerdotal castes. Is this a reason for conceding that a society contains no principle outside its Church, no moral teaching outside its clergy, or that all light dies out if it is not lighted at the altar?

People repeat incessantly that lay society has no fundamental principle and consequently nothing to teach. At least you must admit that better than any one else it can teach itself, and that is precisely the point in lay teaching.

For my part I have always claimed that society possesses a principle which it alone is in a position to profess, and that on this principle is founded its absolute right to teach in civil matters. That which forms the foundation of this society, makes its existence possible, and prevents it from falling to pieces, is precisely a point which cannot be taught with equal authority by any of the official cults. This society lives on the principle of the love of citizens for one another, independently of their beliefs.

Do you wish to free lay teaching? Dare affirm what three centuries have affirmed before you, that it is sufficient unto itself, that it exists of itself, that it itself is belief and science.

How has modern science been constituted? By breaking away from the science of the Church. The civil law? By breaking away from canon law. The political constitution? By breaking away from the religion of the State. All the elements of modern society have developed by emancipating themselves from the Church. The most important of all — education — remains to be emancipated. By a conclusion deduced from all that precedes, is it not clear that we can regulate it only on condition that it be completely separated from ecclesiastical education?

290. Moral and Civic Instruction replaces the Religious

(Ferry, Jules, Letter to the Primary Teachers of France, November 17, 1883; trans. in Buisson and Farrington, *French Ideals of Today*. World Book Company, Yonkers, New York, 1919. Reproduced by permission)

Jules Ferry (1832–93) was mayor of Paris during the trying period of 1870–71; later a member of the French legislature; and from 1879 to 1885 was several times Minister of Public Instruction. From his letter to the teachers of France, in 1883, the following extract relative to moral and civic education, which now replaced the religious, is taken. This expresses well the spirit of the new government, and of the state system of education it created.

The academic year just opened will be the second since the Law of March 28, 1882, went into effect. At this time I cannot refrain from sending you personally a few brief words which you will probably not

FIG. 73. JULES FERRY
(1832–93)

find inopportune, in view of the experience you have just had with the new régime. Of the diverse obligations it imposes upon you, assuredly the one nearest your heart, the one which brings you the heaviest increase of work and anxiety, is your mission to instruct your pupils in ethics and citizenship. You will be grateful to me, I am sure, for answering the questions which preoccupy you at present, by trying to determine the character and the purpose of this teaching. In order to succeed more surely I shall, with your permission, put myself in your place for an instant to show you by examples borrowed from your everyday experience how you can do your duty, and your whole duty, in this respect.

The Law of March 28 is characterized by two provisions which supplement each other and harmonize completely: on the one hand it excludes the teaching of any particular dogma; on the other it gives first place among required subjects to moral and civic teaching. Religious instruction is the province of the family; moral instruction belongs to the school.

Our legislators did not mean to pass an act that was purely negative. Doubtless their first object was to separate the school from the Church, to assure freedom of conscience to both teachers and pupils, in short, to distinguish between two domains too long confused; the domain of beliefs, which are personal, free, and variable; and that of knowledge, which, by universal consent, is common and indispensable to all. But there is something else in the law of March 28. It states the determination of the people to found here at home a national education, and to found it on the idea of duty and of right, which the legislator does not hesitate to inscribe among the fundamental truths of which no one can be ignorant.

It is on you, Sir, that the public has counted to realize this all-important part of education. While you are relieved from religious teaching, there never was a question of relieving you from moral teaching. That would have deprived you of the chief dignity of your profession. On the contrary, it seemed quite natural that the master, while teaching the children to read and write, should also impart to them those simple rules of moral conduct which are not less universally accepted than the rules of language or of arithmetic.

CHAPTER XXIV

THE STRUGGLE FOR NATIONAL ORGANIZATION IN ENGLAND

THE Readings in this chapter have been selected to illustrate the long struggle to create a national system of education in England. They cover the early beginnings, the period of the charitable-voluntary conception of education, the period of philanthropic effort to provide schools, and the long struggle to secure national support and national organization.

The first selection (291) reproduces the testimony of a witness, called before one of the many parliamentary commissions of inquiry, as to educational conditions among the poor of London, and the maintenance of a charity-school. It is typical of volumes of evidence collected in the course of a half-century by such means. The next (292) is a bookkeeping statement as to the early cost for a charity-school, and what was provided each pupil. In 1780 Sunday Schools were begun, as a means of helping solve the problem of educating and bettering the condition of the children of the poor, and in selection 293 Robert Raikes tells of the beginnings of the movement. Another form of charitable and philanthropic effort was the Ragged School, and 294 gives the Constitution and Rules for one of these, showing how they were organized and supported, for whom they were intended, and what they taught.

At about the same time that the French Revolutionary theorists were stating their theories as to education being an affair of the State, Adam Smith's celebrated book appeared, and selection 295 gives his reasoning as to why general education becomes especially necessary as society becomes more highly organized. A little later Rev. T. R. Malthus added to the argument for national education (296) by pointing out the wastefulness of poor relief, and the advantages of teaching people to help themselves.

The introduction of monitorial or mutual instruction, which was evolved near the beginning of the nineteenth century, gave a great impetus to the development of schools by making education for all for the first time seem possible. Selections 297 and 298 give good descriptions of the organization and instruction given in the monitorial schools organized and directed by Lancaster.

In 1833 the first parliamentary grant for elementary education was made, and the conditions under which this was voted are described in **299**. Now ensued a battle to extend the aid, and to enact a law organizing elementary education. This continued unsuccessfully until 1870. Selection **300** gives an extract from a speech of Lord Macaulay, declaring it the duty of the State to act in the matter. This speech is typical of many such made in both houses of Parliament. The evils of the existing conditions were pointed out in many official reports, of which **301,** on the apprenticing of the children of paupers, is given as an example.

All these efforts met with much opposition, and selection **302** is introduced to show a typical conservative attitude. In 1858 a new Parliamentary Commission was appointed to review progress and to analyze needs, and a summary of the principles and recommendations of this body are given in **303**. Finally the Education Act of 1870 was attained, the fundamental features of this being given in **304**. It provided that children in the state schools need not attend religious instruction, and the same year another law (**305**) exempted students and candidates for degrees at the old English universities from similar requirements. Selection **306** is an excellent brief statement of the outstanding events in a century of English educational progress, and gives a good review of the efforts made to create a national system.

291. Charity-School Education described

(*Report from Select Committee of the House of Commons, appointed to inquire into the Education of the Lower Orders in the Metropolis. Minutes of Evidence, II.* London, 1816)

This Commission was appointed, on motion of Henry Brougham (later Lord Brougham), to take evidence as to educational conditions in London, Westminster, and Southwark, and to report to the House of Commons "what may be fit to be done with respect to the children of Paupers." The Commission found one hundred and thirty thousand children without school accommodations, and recommended that Parliament should take "proper measures for supplying the deficiency of the means of Instruction which exist at present, and for extending this blessing to the Poor of all descriptions."

The following evidence, given by the first witness examined, is both typical of the evidence and descriptive of the work and means of support of a charity-school.

Monday, June 3rd, 1816.
HENRY BROUGHAM, Esq. in the Chair.
Mr. GEORGE GRIFFITHS called in, and examined.

Where do you live? — Saint Katherine's, near the Tower.

Are you a schoolmaster in the neighbourhood? — Yes.

Of what school? — Saint Katherine's charity-school.

Upon what foundation is that school? — It is supported by voluntary contributions.

Have you any other funds? — There is a fund established by the contributions, which is placed in the bank.

To what does it amount? — The last purchase that was made has made it up to £1550.

What is the amount of annual subscriptions? — It has varied very much within the last seven or eight years; it formerly used not to amount to more than sixty or seventy pounds, it has in the last six or seven years amounted to upwards of £100 by subscriptions and donations.

What is the whole amount of the yearly income? — I am not prepared to state that exactly.

Is it £200? — Yes, it must be that, because our expenses amount to that.

How many children are educated there? — Fifty.

Boys and girls? — Yes.

What are they taught? — Reading, writing, and arithmetic, and clothed.

What is the master's salary? — The master and mistress, £60 a year between them.

Are there any other salaries than the master's and mistress's? — Nothing more than a trifling salary, for teaching psalmody, of four guineas a year.

Have the master and the mistress any perquisite? — None.

A house? — A house to live in, and coal, but no candle.

Are there ever fewer children than fifty? — No.

How long have you been master? — About eight years.

How many were there when you came? — Fifty.

Have there never been fewer, at any one time of the year, since the time you have been there? — There may have been so for a month or six weeks; the committee meet the first Tuesday in every month, and if there is a vacancy they admit whatever child is next in rotation to come in.

How long has the school been established? — Since the year 1707.

Had it never any more property, besides the money in the funds? — The chapter of Saint Katherine's has made it a present, at several times, of the leases of three houses towards its support.

Have they that leasehold property at present? — They have.

At what are the houses underlet? — Sixty pounds a year, the three.

Then the school has this £60 a year in addition to the interest of £1550 in the funds, and £100 a year subscriptions? — The increase of stock has doubled since I have been schoolmaster, owing to a lady who died and left us £500.

In what stock is it? — Navy 5 per cents.

Then instead of nearly £200, it appears the income of the school is above £250 a year? — I was not aware of any question of the kind being asked, or I would have been prepared to answer it.

Is there any other property whatever belonging to the establishment? — None.

How are the children clothed? — They are completely clothed at Midsummer, and extra shoes, stockings, and linen, at Christmas.

Any other salary paid, besides the master and mistress's ? — None.

Do the premises belong to the institution? — During the lease; the schoolhouse is a gift of the chapter of Saint Katherine's, during their pleasure, for which no rent is paid; there is a ground-rent paid for the other property.

Are there any occasional contributions and donations, besides the annual subscriptions? — I include those in the annual subscriptions.

Any charity sermons? — Yes, we have about one a year.

Is that included in the former account of £100? — No, that is not, so that the produce of this is to be added to the former sum.

What are the hours of teaching? — From nine to twelve, and from two to five; six hours a day.

Have you any other occupation than schoolmaster? — I am parish clerk.

Any other occupation? — As parish clerk, I do a little business in the undertaking line, which I employ other people to do.

Any other? — I do make a trifle as a musician; I am chorus singer to his Majesty's ancient concert of music in Hanover-square.

Have you any other employment? — No.

Do you teach any other scholars besides those in the school? — I am allowed to take a few, as they offer, such as sixpenny scholars per week; and very often I give several children their education, without charging them any thing.

Do the fifty children upon the foundation pay any thing? — Nothing.

Are they in general children of very poor people? — In general very poor.

Are there many poor children in the neighbourhood in which you reside, destitute of instruction? — The generality of the children are poor people's children; the neighbourhood is a very poor neighbourhood.

Have those children the means of instruction? — Not till they are placed in our establishment, or other establishments in the neighbourhood.

. . . .

Is there any indisposition among the lower orders to send their children to those schools? — None; the parents are very anxious to get their children on the establishment.

In all those schools do they clothe? — In all the schools I have mentioned.

They do not board them? — No.

292. Cost of and Support of Charity-Schools

(Allen, W. O. B., and McClure, Edm., *History of the Society for Promoting Christian Knowledge*, pp. 140–42. London, 1898)

In their history of two hundred years' work of the S.P.C.K., the two secretaries of the Society give the following statement as to the cost for clothing and education, in 1710, and the means whereby the schools were provided. They say:

In 1704 the ordinary charge in London of a "School for 50 Boys Cloathed comes to about £75 p. Ann., for which a School-Room, Books, and Firing are provided, a Master paid, and to each Boy is given yearly, 3 Bands, 1 Cap, 1 Coat, 1 pair of Stockings and 1 pair of Shooes." A girls' school of the same size then cost £60 per annum, which paid for the room, books, firing, and mistress, and provided for each girl, "2 Coyfs, 2 Bands, 1 Gown and Petticoat, 1 Pair of knit Gloves, 1 pair of Stockings, and 2 pair of Shooes."

In 1706 the cost of "cloathing a Poor Boy" was stated to be 9s. 9 1/2d. and of a girl 10s. 7d. This had increased in 1710, and the following detailed statement may be of interest:

The Charge of Cloathing a Poor Boy of a Charity-School in London

	£	s.	d.
1 Yard and half quarter of Grey *Yorkshire* Broad Cloth, 6 quarters wide, makes a Coat	00	03	00
Making the Coat, with Pewter Buttons and all other Materials	00	01	00
A Waistcoat of the same Cloth, lined	00	03	06
A pair of Breeches of Cloth or Leather, lined	00	02	06
1 Knit Cap, with Tuft and String, of any Colour	00	00	10
1 Band	00	00	02
1 Shirt	00	01	06
1 Pair of Woolen Stockings	00	00	08
1 Pair of Shoes	00	01	10
1 Pair of Buckles	00	00	01
	00	15	01

The Charge of Cloathing a Poor Girl of a Charity-School in London

	£	s.	d.
3 Yards and half of blue long Ells, about Yard wide, at 16d.			
p. Yard, makes a Gown and Petticoat..................	00	04	08
Making thereof, Strings, Body-lining, and other Materials..	00	01	00
A Coif and Band of Scotch Cloth, plain with a Border.....	00	00	09
A Shift...	00	01	06
A pair of Leather Bodice and Stomacher..................	00	02	06
1 Pair of Woolen Stockings.............................	00	00	08
1 Pair of Shoes.......................................	00	01	08
1 pair of Buckles.....................................	00	00	01
	00	12	10

This zeal for the education of the children of the poor was widely spread, and some of the earliest parochial and ward schools arose under the auspices of our Society. A yearly account of all the charity-schools was printed and published, as an appendix to the sermon preached on the anniversary service attended by the charity children. Even in small villages where it was impossible to collect sufficient money to start a charity-school, a plan was proposed and adopted for opening day schools. Some discreet and sober person was to be pitched upon in each parish, and to be paid by *results*. So soon as the child could name and distinguish all the letters in the alphabet, the teacher was to receive *2s. 6d.* "A like payment was to be made when the child could spell well; and *5s.* more when such child could read well and distinctly, and say the Church Catechism. By which means Poor Children may be taught to read for *Ten shillings;* and the additional Charge for Books will be very inconsiderable."

The clergy were specially noted for their zeal in this good work. In some places they taught the children *gratis.* In others persons were made parish clerks, on condition they would teach a certain number of children gratis. At Warwick a charity box, set up in the church, with this inscription, *"For the use and increase of the Charity-School,"* had so good an effect that several children were taught and clothed by what was put in it. In some places effigies or statues of charity children were placed at the church or school doors, with a poor's box near them, and suitable texts of Scripture, to excite the alms of people resorting thither.

In another place (Ewhurst in Surrey), where the minister of the parish was at the whole expense of educating the children, he "had provided two palls, the one of which is let out for *2s. 6d.* and the other for *1s.* a time, for the more decent funerals of the dead; and the money so arising bears a good part of the charge of teaching the poor children there." In a few cases the parents contributed something. In the account for 1717, "At Winleton in the County of Durham, the workmen of an iron-work, who are about 400 or 500, allow one farthing and a half per shilling, per week, which together with their master's contribution, maintains their poor, and affords about £17 per annum for teaching their children to read, etc."

293. Raikes' Description of the Gloucester Sunday School

(*Gentleman's Magazine*, June, 1784; *Gloucester Journal*, May 24, 1784)

The following letter, written by Robert Raikes to Colonel Townley, of Sheffield, describes the origin and work of the Gloucester Sunday Schools, under the direction of Raikes.

Gloucester, *November 25th*, 1783.

SIR, — My friend, the Mayor (Mr. Colborne) has just communicated to me the letter which you have honoured him with, enquiring into the nature of Sunday Schools. The beginning of this scheme was entirely owing to accident. Some business leading me one morning into the suburbs of the city, where the lowest of the people (who are principally employed in the pin manufactory) chiefly reside, I was struck with concern at seeing a group of children, wretchedly ragged, at play in the streets. I asked an inhabitant whether those children belonged to that part of town, and lamented their misery and idleness. "Ah! sir," said the woman to whom I was speaking, "could you take a view of this part of the town on a Sunday, you would be shocked indeed; for then the street is filled with multitudes of these wretches, who, released on that day from employment, spend their time in noise and riot, playing at 'chuck,' and cursing and swearing in a manner so horrid as to convey to any serious mind an idea of hell rather than any other place. We have a worthy clergyman (said she), curate of our parish, who has put some of them to school; but on the Sabbath day they are all given up to follow their own inclinations without restraint, as their parents, totally abandoned themselves, have no idea of instilling into the minds of their children principles to which they themselves are entire strangers."

This conversation suggested to me that it would be at least a harmless attempt, if it were productive of no good, should some little plan be formed to check the deplorable profanation of the Sabbath. I then enquired of the woman, if there were any decent well-disposed women in the neighbourhood who kept schools for teaching to read. I presently was directed to four: to these I applied, and made an agreement with them to receive as many children as I should send upon the Sunday, whom they were to instruct in reading and in the Church Catechism. For this I engaged to pay them each a shilling for their day's employment. The women seemed pleased with the proposal. I then waited on the clergyman before mentioned, and imparted to him my plan; he was so much satisfied with the idea, that he engaged to lend his assistance, by going round to the schools on a Sunday afternoon, to examine the progress that was made, and to enforce order and decorum among such a set of little heathens.

This, sir, was the commencement of the plan. It is now about three years since we began, and I could wish you were here to make enquiry into the effect. A woman who lives in a lane where I had fixed a school told me, some time ago, that the place was quite a heaven on Sundays, compared to what it used to be. The numbers who have learned to read and say their Catechism are so great that I am astonished at it. Upon the Sunday afternoon the mistresses take their scholars to church, a place into which neither they nor their ancestors had ever before entered, with a view to the glory of God. But what is yet more extraordinary, within this month these little ragamuffins have in great numbers taken it into their heads to frequent the early morning prayers, which are held every morning at the Cathedral at seven o'clock. I believe there were nearly fifty this morning. They assemble at the house of one of the mistresses, and walk before her to church, two and two, in as much order as a company of soldiers. I am generally at church, and after service they all come around me to make their bow; and, if any animosities have arisen, to make their complaints. The great principle I inculcate is, to be kind and good natured to each other; not to provoke one another; to be dutiful to their parents; not to offend God by cursing and swearing; and such little plain precepts as all may comprehend. As my profession is that of a printer, I have printed a little book, which I gave amongst them; and some friends of mine, subscribers to the Society for Promoting Christian Knowledge, sometimes make me a present of a parcel of Bibles, Testaments, &c., which I distribute as rewards to the deserving. The success that has attended this scheme has induced one or two of my friends to adopt the plan, and set up Sunday Schools in other parts of the city, and now a whole parish has taken up the object; so that I flatter myself in time the good effects will appear so conspicuous as to become generally adopted. The number of children at present thus engaged on the Sabbath are between two and three hundred, and they are increasing every week, as the benefit is universally seen. I have endeavoured to engage the clergy of my acquaintance that reside in their parishes; one has entered into the scheme with great fervour, and it was in order to excite others to follow the example that I inserted in my paper the paragraph which I suppose you saw copied into the London papers.

. . . With regard to the rules adopted, I only require that they may come to the school on Sunday as clean as possible. Many were at first deterred because they wanted decent clothing, but I could not undertake to supply this defect. I argue, therefore, if you can loiter about without shoes, and in a ragged coat, you may as well come to school and learn what may tend to your good in that garb. I reject none on that footing. All that I require are clean hands, clean face, and their hair combed; if you have no clean shirt, come in what you have on.

The want of decent apparel at first kept great numbers at a distance, but they now begin to grow wiser, and all pressing to learn. I have had the good luck to procure places for some that were deserving, which has been of great use. You will understand that these children are from six years old to twelve or fourteen. Boys and girls above this age, who have been totally undisciplined, are generally too refractory for this government. A reformation in society seems to me to be only practicable by establishing notions of duty, and practical habits of order and decorum, at an early age. . . .

I have the honour to be, Sir, yours, &c.,

R. RAIKES.

In his *Gloucester Journal* for May 24, 1784, Raikes printed the following item regarding the good effects of the schools in Gloucester, and of their establishment elsewhere.

The good effects of Sunday Schools established in this city are instanced in the account given by the principal persons in the pin and sack manufactories, wherein great reformation has taken place among the multitudes whom they employ. From being idle, ungovernable, profligate, and filthy in the extreme, they say the boys and girls are become not only cleanly and decent in their appearance, but are greatly humanized in their manners — more orderly, tractable, and attentive to business, and, of course, more serviceable than they ever expected to find them. The cursing and swearing and other vile expressions, which used to form the sum of their conversation, are now rarely heard among them.

Such, we are well assured, is the fact. The *London Chronicle* of Tuesday last mentions that the plan of Sunday Schools is taken up with such general concurrence in Leeds and Yorkshire that the spirited inhabitants of that place have them in all quarters of their populous town, and have already admitted near 2000 poor children!

294. The Organization, Support, and Work of a Ragged School

("CONSTITUTION AND RULES of the Association for the Establishment of Ragged Industrial Schools for Destitute Children in Edinburgh." Guthrie, Thomas, *Seed Time and Harvest of Ragged Schools*, Appendix II. Edinburgh, 1860)

The following Constitution and Rules for a Scotch Ragged School are illustrative of the humanitarian origin and support of such a school, and of the nature of the instruction given in it.

1. It is the object of this Association to reclaim the neglected and destitute children of Edinburgh, by offering them the benefits of a good common and Christian Education, and by training them to habits of regular industry, so as to enable them to earn an honest livelihood, and fit them for the duties of life.

2. With this view the Association shall establish and maintain one or more schools for such children, in such parts of the city or suburbs as may be found most desirable.

3. The following classes of children shall be excluded: — 1st, Those who are already attending Day-Schools; — 2d, Those whose parents are earning a regular income, and able to procure education for their children; — 3d, Those who are receiving, or entitled to receive, support and education from the Parochial Boards; — with this declaration, that it shall be in the power of the Acting Committee to deal with special cases, although falling under any of these classes, having regard always to the special objects of the Association.

4. The Association shall consist of all Subscribers of Ten Shillings per annum and upwards, and of all Donors of Five Pounds and upwards.

5. It shall be governed by a General Committee, consisting of fifty Members (fifteen being a quorum), and an Acting Committee, consisting of twenty-five Members (five being a quorum), with a Secretary and Treasurer. The Acting Committee shall be entitled to be present and vote at all Meetings of the General Committee.

FIG. 74. A RAGGED-SCHOOL PUPIL

(From a photograph of a boy on entering the school; later changed into a respectable tradesman. From Guthrie)

6. A Meeting of the Association shall be held annually, in April, when a Report of the proceedings shall be read, and the Committees and Office-Bearers elected for the ensuing year. The Acting Committee shall meet at least once every month.

7. The Acting Committee shall have power to elect the Office-Bearers, to appoint Local Committees, and to make laws and regulations to be observed in conducting the business of the Association; and all Schools to be established by the Association shall be subject to such laws and regulations; but no school shall be established without the consent of the General Committee.

8. The Appointment of Teachers, and other officers, shall be made by the Acting Committee.

9. The general plan upon which the Schools shall be conducted shall be as follows, viz. —

To give the children an allowance of food for their daily support.

To instruct them in reading, writing, and arithmetic.

To train them in habits of industry, by instructing and employing them daily in such sorts of work as are suited to their years.

To teach them the truths of the gospel, making the Holy Scriptures the groundwork of instruction.

On Sabbath the children shall receive food as on other days, and such religious instruction as shall be arranged by the Acting Committee.

295. Adam Smith on the Instruction of the Common People

(Smith, Adam, *An Inquiry into the Nature and Causes of the Wealth of Nations*, book v, chap. I, part III, art II. [1776.] Reprint of second edition; Edited by Rogers, Oxford, 1880)

In 1776 there was published one of those epoch-making books which from time to time appear to mould human thinking anew. The author, Adam Smith, was a Scotchman by birth who had

FIG. 75. ADAM SMITH (1723–90)

studied at Glasgow and Oxford. It was a long and rather exhaustive treatment as to what constitutes the real wealth of nations, and, among other things, he included two chapters on the "Expense of the Institutions for Education." From one of these chapters the following selection, relating to state support of elementary education, has been taken.

Ought the public, therefore, to give no attention, it may be asked, to the education of the people? Or if it ought to give any, what are the different parts of education which it ought to attend to in the different orders of the people? and in what manner ought it to attend to them?

In some cases the state of the society necessarily places the greater part of individuals in such situations as naturally form in them, without any attention of government, almost all the abilities and virtues which that state requires, or perhaps can admit of. In other cases the state of the society does not place the greater part of individuals in such situations, and some attention of government is necessary in order to prevent the almost entire corruption and degeneracy of the great body of the people.

In the progress of the division of labour, the employment of the far greater part of those who live by labour, that is, of the great body of the people, comes to be confined to a few very simple operations; frequently to one or two. But the understandings of the greater part of men are necessarily formed by their ordinary employments. The man whose whole life is spent in performing a few simple operations, of which the effects too are, perhaps, always the same, or very nearly the same, has no occasion to exert his understanding or to exercise his invention in finding out expedients for removing difficulties which never occur. He naturally loses, therefore, the habit of such exertion, and generally becomes as stupid and ignorant as it is possible for a human creature to become. The torpor of his mind renders him not only incapable of relishing or bearing a part in any rational conversation, but of conceiving any generous, noble, or tender sentiment, and consequently of forming any just judgment concerning many even of the ordinary duties of private life. Of the great and extensive interests of his country, he is altogether incapable of judging. . . .

The education of the common people requires perhaps, in a civilized and commercial society, the attention of the public more than that of people of some rank and fortune. People of some rank and fortune are generally eighteen or nineteen years of age before they enter upon that particular business, profession, or trade, by which they propose to distinguish themselves in the world. They have before that full time to acquire, or at least to fit themselves for afterwards acquiring, every accomplishment which can recommend them to the public esteem, or render them worthy of it. Their parents or guardians are generally sufficiently anxious that they should be so accomplished, and are, in most cases, willing enough to lay out the expense which is necessary for that purpose. If they are not always properly educated, it is seldom from want of expense laid out upon their education; but from the improper application of that expense. . . .

It is otherwise with the common people. They have little time to spare for education. Their parents can scarce afford to maintain them even in infancy. As soon as they are able to work, they must apply to some trade by which they can earn their subsistence. That trade, too, is generally so simple and uniform as to give little exercise to the understanding; while, at the same time, their labour is both so constant and so severe, that it leaves them little leisure and less inclination to apply to, or even think of anything else.

But though the common people cannot, in any civilised society, be so well instructed as people of some rank and fortune, the most essential parts of education, however, to read, write, and account, can be acquired at so early a period of life, that the greater part even of those who are to be bred to the lowest occupations have time to acquire them before they can be employed in those occupations. For a very small expense the public can facilitate, can encourage, and can even impose upon almost all the whole body of the people, the necessity of acquiring those most essential parts of education.

The public can facilitate this acquisition by establishing in every parish or district a little school, where children may be taught for a reward so moderate, that even a common labourer may afford it; the master being partly, but not wholly paid by the public; because if he was wholly, or even principally paid by it, he would soon learn to neglect his business. In Scotland the establishment of such parish schools has taught almost the whole common people to read, and a very great proportion of them to write and account. In England the establishment of charity-schools has had an effect of the same kind, though not so universally, because the establishment is not so universal. If in those little schools the books, by which the children are taught to read, were a little more instructive than they generally are, and if, instead of a little smattering of Latin, which the children of the common people are sometimes taught there, and which can scarce ever be of any use to them, they were instructed in the elementary parts of geometry and mechanics, the literary education of this rank of people would perhaps be as complete as it can be. There is scarce a common trade which does not afford some opportunities of applying to it the principles of geometry and mechanics, and which would not therefore gradually exercise and improve the common people in those principles, the necessary introduction to the most sublime as well as the most useful sciences.

The public can encourage the acquisition of those most essential parts of education by giving small premiums, and little badges of distinction, to the children of the common people who excel in them.

The public can impose upon almost the whole body of the people the necessity of acquiring those most essential parts of education, by obliging every man to undergo an examination or probation in them before he can obtain the freedom in any corporation, or be allowed to be set up in any trade either in a village or town corporate.

.   .   .   .

. . . Though the state was to derive no advantage from the instruction of the inferior ranks of people, it would still deserve its attention that they should not be altogether uninstructed. The state, however, derives no inconsiderable advantage from their instruction. The more they are instructed, the less liable they are to the delusions of enthusiasm and superstition, which, among ignorant nations, frequently occasion the most dreadful disorders. An instructed and intelligent people besides are always more decent and orderly than an ignorant and stupid one. They feel themselves, each individually, more respectable, and more likely to obtain the respect of their lawful superiors, and they are therefore more disposed to respect those superiors. They are more disposed to examine, and more capable of seeing through, the interested complaints of faction and sedition, and they are, upon that account, less apt to be misled into any wanton or unnecessary opposition to the measures of government. In free countries, where the safety of government depends very much upon the favourable judgment which the people may form of its conduct, it must surely be of the highest importance that they should not be disposed to judge rashly or capriciously concerning it.

296. Malthus on National Education

Malthus, Rev. T. R., *An Essay on the Principles of Population*, book IV, chap. IX. [1798.] Reprint of the sixth edition, London, 1890)

The *Essay* by Malthus, a work of over six hundred octavo pages, which appeared in 1798, was another of the great books of all time. The ideas it contained underlay some of the work of Darwin more than a half-century later. On the question of poor relief and education he wrote:

We have lavished immense sums on the poor, which we have every reason to think have constantly tended to aggravate their misery. But in their education and in the circulation of those important political truths that most nearly concern them, which are perhaps the only means in our power of really raising their condition, and of making them happier men and more peaceable subjects, we have been miserably deficient. It is surely a great national disgrace, that the education of the lower classes of people in England should be left merely to a few Sunday Schools, supported by a subscription from individuals, who can give to the course of instruction in them any kind of bias which they please. And even the improvement of Sunday Schools (for, objectionable as they are in some points of view, and imperfect in all, I cannot but consider as an improvement) is of very late date.

FIG. 76. THE REVEREND T. R. MALTHUS (1766–1834)

The arguments which have been urged against instructing the people appear to me to be not only illiberal, but to the last degree feeble; and they ought, on the contrary, to be extremely forcible, and to be supported by the most obvious and striking necessity, to warrant us in withholding the means of raising the condition of the lower classes of people, when they are in our power. Those who will not listen to any answer to these arguments drawn from theory, cannot, I think, refuse the testimony of experience; and I would ask, whether the advantage of superior instruction which the lower classes of people in Scotland are known to possess, has appeared to have any tendency toward creating a spirit of tumult and discontent amongst them. . . . The quiet and peaceable habits of the instructed Scotch peasant, compared with the turbulent disposition of the ignorant Irishman, ought not to be without effect upon every impartial reasoner.

The principal argument which I have heard advanced against a system of national education in England is, that the common people would be put in a capacity to read such works as those of Paine, and that the consequences would probably be fatal to government. But on this subject I agree most cordially with Adam Smith in thinking, that an instructed and well-informed people would be much less likely to be led away by inflammatory writings, and much better able to detect the false declamation of interested and ambitious demagogues, than an ignorant people. One or two readers in a parish are sufficient to circulate any quantity of sedition; and if these be gained to the democratic side, they will probably have the power of doing much more mischief, by selecting the passages best suited to their hearers, and choosing the moments when their oratory is likely to have the most effect, than if each individual in the parish had been in a capacity to read and judge of the whole work himself; and at the same time to read and judge of the opposing arguments, which we may suppose would also reach him.

But in addition to this, a double weight would undoubtedly be added to the observation of Adam Smith, if these schools were made the means of instructing the people in the real nature of their situation; if they were taught, what is really true, that without an increase of their own industry and prudence no change of government could essentially better their condition; that, though they might get rid of some particular grievance, yet in the great point of supporting their families they would be but little, or perhaps not at all benefited; that a revolution would not alter in their favour the proportion of the supply of labour to the demand, or the quantity of food to the number of the consumers; and that if the supply of labour were greater than the demand, and the demand for food greater than the supply, they might suffer the utmost severity of want, under the freest, the most perfect, and best executed government, that the human imagination could conceive.

A knowledge of these truths so obviously tends to promote peace and quietness, to weaken the effect of inflammatory writings and to prevent all unreasonable and ill-directed opposition to the constituted authorities, that those who would still object to the instruction of the people may be fairly suspected of a wish to encourage their ignorance, as a pretext for tyranny, and an opportunity of increasing the power and the influence of the executive government.

297. The School of Lancaster described

(Sidney Smith, in *Edinburgh Review*, vol. XI, pp. 62–65. 1807)

The following description of Lancaster's school, in South London, gives a sympathetic account of and a very good idea as to the kind of work done in the monitorial schools. The monitorial system was both improved in organization and extended in scope after its introduction into the United States.

The first or lower class of children are taught to write the printed alphabet, and to name the letters when they see them. The same with the figures used in arithmetic. One day the boy traces the form of a letter, or figure; the next he tells the name, when he sees the letter. These two methods assist each other. When he is required to write H, for example, the shape of the letter which he saw yesterday assists his manual execution — when he is required to say how that letter is named, the shape of the letter reminds him of his manual execution; and the manual execution has associated itself with the name. In the same manner he learns syllables and words; writing them one day — reading them the next. The same process for writing the common epistolary character, and for reading it.

(A) This progress made, the class go up to the master to read — a class consisting perhaps of 30. While one boy is reading, the word, e.g. Ab-so-lu-ti-on, is given out with a loud voice by the monitor, and written down by all the other 29 boys, who are provided with slates for the purpose; which writing is looked over by monitors, and then another word called, and so on; whoever writes a word, spells it of course at the same time, and spells it with much more attention than in the common way. So that there is always one boy reading, and twenty-nine writing and spelling at the same time; whereas, in the ancient method, the other twenty-nine did nothing.

(B) The first and second classes write in sand; the middle classes on slates; only a few of the upper boys on paper with ink. This is a great

Fig. 77. Monitor inspecting Written Work at Signal, "Show Slates"

saving point of expense, — in books the saving is still greater. Twenty or thirty boys stand around a card suspended on a nail, making a semi-circle. On this card are printed the letters in very large characters; —

these letters the boys are to name, at the request of the monitor. When one spelling class have said their lessons in this manner, they are despatched off to some other occupation, and another spelling class succeeds. In this way one book or card may serve for two hundred boys, who would, according to the common method, have had a book each. In the same manner, syllables and reading lessons are printed on cards and used with the same beneficial economy.

(C) In arithmetic, the monitor dictates a sum, ex. gr. in addition, which all the boys write down on their slates, for example,

$$
\begin{array}{r}
724 \\
378 \\
\hline
946 \\
\hline
\end{array}
$$

He then tells them, aloud, how to add the sum. First column — 6 and 8 are 14, and 4 are 18; set down 8 and carry 1 to the next column; and so on. In this manner, the class acquire facility of writing figures, and placing them; and, by practicing what the monitor dictates, insensibly acquire facility in adding. Again they are placed around arithmetical cards, in the same manner as in paragraph (B), and required to add up the columns. This method evinces what progress they have made from the preceding method of dictating; and the two methods are always used alternately.

It is obvious that a school like this of Mr. Lancaster's, consisting of from 700 to 800 boys, would soon fall into decay, without very close attention to order and method. In this part of his system, Mr. Lancaster has been as eminently successful as in any other; contriving to make the method and arrangement, so necessary to his institution, a source of amusement to the children. In coming into school, in going out, and in moving in their classes from one part of the school to another, the children move in a kind of a measured pace, and in known places, according to their number, of which every boy has one. Upon the first institution of the school, there was great loss and confusion of hats. After every boy has taken his place there, they all stand up expecting the word of command, "Sling your hats!" upon which they immediately suspend their hats round their necks by a string provided for that purpose. When the young children write in sand, they all look attentively to their monitor, waiting for the word, and instantly fall to work, with military precision, upon receiving it. All these little inventions keep children in a constant state of activity, prevent the listlessness so observable in all other institutions for education, and evince (trifling as they appear to be) a very original and observing mind in him who invented them.

The boys assembled round their reading or arithmetical cards take places as in common schools. The boy who is at the head of the class wears a ticket, with some suitable inscription, and has a prize of a little picture. The ticket-bearer yields his badge of honour to whoever can excel him; and the desire of obtaining and the fear of losing the mark of distinction, create, as may easily be conceived, no common degree of enterprize and exertion. Boys have a prize when they are moved from one class to another, as the monitor has also from whose class they are removed. Mr. Lancaster has established a sort of paper currency of tickets. These tickets are given for merit — two tickets are worth a paper kite; three worth a ball; four worth a wooden horse, etc.

It is no unusual thing for me to deliver one or two hundred prizes at the same time. And at such times the countenances of the whole school exhibit a most pleasing scene of delight; as the boys who obtain prizes commonly walk around the school in procession, holding the prizes in their hands, with a herald proclaiming before them, "These good boys have obtained prizes for going into another class." The honour of this has an effect as powerful, if not more so, than the prizes themselves.

A large collection of toys, bats, balls, pictures, kites, is suspended above the master's head beaming glory and pleasure upon the school beneath. Mr. Lancaster has also, as another incentive, an order of merit. No boys are admitted to this order but those who distinguish themselves by attention to their studies, and by their endeavours to check vice. The distinguishing badge is a silver medal and plated chain hanging from the neck. The superior class has a fixed place in the school; any class that can excel it may eject them from this place and occupy it themselves. Every member, both of the attacking and defending classes, feels of course the most lively interest in the issue of the contest.

Mr. Lancaster punishes by shame rather than pain; varying the means of exciting shame, because as he justly observes, any mode of punishment long continued loses its effect.

The boys in the school appointed to teach others are called monitors; they are in the proportion of about one monitor to ten boys. So that, for the whole school of one thousand boys, there is only one master; the rest of the teaching is all done by the boys themselves. Besides the teaching monitors, there are general monitors, such as, inspectors of slates, inspectors of absentees, etc.

298. Automatic Character of the Monitorial Schools

(The Philanthropist, vol. i, p. 83. 1811)

The following description is taken from an article in an issue of the above-mentioned magazine, entitled "On the Importance of Promoting the General Education of the Poor." It shows well the automatic nature of the school, and also reveals the organizing genius of Lancaster.

One of the peculiar features of this plan is the extraordinary manner in which the talents of boys are drawn forth, and many instances may be given, where young lads, acting upon this system, have evinced energies which are rarely to be met with in mature age. In the Royal Free School, at the Borough Road, a little boy of twelve or thirteen years of age often commands the whole school, and that with the same ease to himself, and with equal obedience from the many hundred children of which the school is composed, as a military officer would experience with a body of well-disciplined troops; the firmness, promptness and decision attendant on military order are interwoven into the school discipline, but without the least severity; a constant activity is maintained, by which the minds of the children are amused; they acquire the more important habit of fixing their attention; their duties are made a pleasure, and their progress in learning is proportionally rapid.

In Shropshire and Staffordshire in the space of only eight months a boy scarcely seventeen has lately organized schools and instructed schoolmasters for above one thousand children; the affectionate and mild but firm conduct of this amiable lad rendered each school a scene of pleasure and delight, in which his steady application of the system of order proved its utility and excellence. When he took leave of one school, in order to open another at a different place, it was a most delightful sight to behold the whole school of children lamenting his departure, as they would the loss of their nearest friend. He introduced the system so completely into one school that the children required very little attention to execute the plan, and thereby teach themselves; to a person not an eye-witness it would scarcely seem credible, but it is a fact, that the master, who was a shoe-maker, would sit at the head of the school with his last and leather, and alternately work and overlook the tuition of the school; he had no occasion to exert himself to prevent confusion, for the order of the system was so far introduced into the habits of the children, that they would themselves be the first to correct the smallest disorderly movement; the success of this boy's labour was so great in one instance as to induce a countryman to go to the clergyman of the parish, who was the patron of the school, to complain that his children learned so much and so fast that, as he did not get on at such a rate when he was a child at school, he thought witchcraft alone could produce such an effect upon his children. The worthy clergyman, though scarcely able to refrain from laughter, was obliged to put on a grave countenance, and assure his parishioner that neither magic, incantation, nor witchcraft had anything to do in the business.

There are other young men who, before they were eighteen years of age, have organized schools for more than two thousand children.

299. The First Parliamentary Grant for Elementary Education

(Montmorency, J. E. G. de, *State Intervention in English Education*, pp. 239–40.
Cambridge, 1902)

From 1807 to 1833 was a period of investigation and discussion as to the need for state aid for elementary education, and the year 1833, when the first grant of parliamentary funds to help build schoolhouses was made, is a dividing point between the old condition of affairs and the new. This grant of aid, small as it was, formed a precedent from which the House of Commons has never turned back. The following description of the passage of the Act making the grant reveals something of the attitude of many Englishmen toward the question of public education.

On Saturday, August 17th, 1833, in a very empty House of Commons, a vote of £20,000 for the purposes of education was passed after a hot debate by 50 votes to 26 votes. Mr. T. B. Macaulay voted with the majority in favour of the grant. Lord Althorp explained that the object of the grant was to build schools where there already existed the means of carrying on such schools. In the debate Lord John Russell pointed out, in answer to a complaint that no ground for the experiment had been shown, that in the Report of the Education Committee in 1818 there were cases referred to of parishes which, if they could have been assisted in the first outlay, would afterwards have supported their own schools. This was still the case in 1833, and justified a vote for building grants. Mr. William Cobbett, the Member for Oldham, opposed the grant on the ground that education was not improving the condition of the country. In the country districts, he said, the father was a better man and a better labourer than his son. Reports on the table of the House proved, he declared, that men became more and more immoral every year. Then what had become of the benefits of education? Education had been more and more spread; but to what did it all tend? "Nothing but to increase the number of schoolmasters and schoolmistresses — that new race of idlers. Crime, too, went on increasing. If so, what reason was there to tax the people for the increase of education? It was nothing but an attempt to force education — it was a French — it was a Doctrinaire — plan, and he should always be opposed to it." It is difficult to realize that Mr. Cobbett — a praiser of times past, a hater of State intervention, a despiser of French philosophy — was the advanced reformer of his day. One does not usually couple such opinions with the conceptions of reform. Mr. Joseph Hume opposed the grant on the somewhat reasonable ground that it was too small to constitute a national system, and without such a system there was no justification for the grant. In the division on the grant he acted as one of the tellers for the Noes. The form of vote was as follows: "That a Sum, not exceeding Twenty thousand pounds, be granted to His Majesty, to be issued in aid of Private Subscriptions for the Erection of School Houses, for the Education of the Children of the Poorer Classes in *Great Britain*, to the 31st day of March 1834; and that the said sum be issued and paid without any fee or other deduction whatsoever." The vote of £20,000 appears in the Revenue Act, 1833, as a grant for the erection of school houses in Great Britain.

300. Lord Macaulay on the Duty of the State to provide Education

(Extract from an Address in the House of Commons, in 1847. Reported in Barnard's *National Education in Europe*, p. 747. Hartford, 1854)

Among the early champions of a general state system of education for the masses was Thomas Babington Macaulay. In defending the minutes of the Committee of Council on Education relative to nationalizing education, he said, in part:

I hold that it is the right and duty of the State to provide for the education of the common people. I conceive the arguments by which this position may be proved are perfectly simple, perfectly obvious, and the most cogent possible. . . . All are agreed that it is the sacred duty of every government to take effectual measures for securing the persons and property of the community; and that the government which neglects that duty is unfit for its situation. This being once admitted, I ask, can it be denied that the education of the common people is the most effectual means of protecting persons and property? On that subject I can not refer to higher authority, or use more strong terms, than have been employed by Adam Smith; and I take his authority the more readily, because he is not very friendly to State interference; and almost on the same page as that I refer to, he declares that the State ought not to meddle with the education of the higher orders; but he distinctly says that there is a difference, particularly in a highly civilized and commercial community, between the education of the higher classes and the education of the poor. The education of the poor he pronounces to be a matter in which government is most deeply concerned; and he compares ignorance, spread through the lower classes, neglected by the State, to a leprosy, or some other fearful disease, and says that where this duty is neglected, the State is in danger of falling into the terrible disorder. He had scarcely written this than the axiom

FIG. 78.
LORD T. B. MACAULAY
(1800–59)

was fearfully illustrated in the riots of 1780. I do not know if from all history I could select a stronger instance of my position, when I say that ignorance makes the persons and property of the community unsafe, and that the government is bound to take measures to prevent that ignorance. On that occasion, what was the state of things? Without any shadow of a grievance, at the summons of a madman, 100,000 men rising in insurrection — a week of anarchy — Parliament besieged — your predecessor, sir, trembling in the Chair — the Lords pulled out of their coaches — the Bishops flying over the tiles — not a sight, I trust, that would be pleasurable to those who are now so unfavorable to the Church of England — thirty-six fires blazing at once in London — the house of the Chief Justice sacked — the children of the Prime Minister taken out of their beds in their night clothes, and laid on the table of the horse guards — and all this the effect of nothing but the gross, brutish ignorance of the population, who had been left brutes in the midst of Christianity, savages in the midst of civilization. . . . Could it have been supposed that all this could have taken place in a community were even the common laborer to have his mind opened by education, and be taught to find his pleasure in the exercise of his intellect, taught to revere his maker, taught to regard his fellow-creatures with kindness, and taught likewise to feel respect for legitimate authority, taught how to pursue redress of real wrongs by constitutional methods?

. . . Take away education, and what are your means? Military force, prisons, solitary cells, penal colonies, gibbets — all the other apparatus of penal laws. If, then, there be an end to which government is bound to attain — if there are two ways only of attaining it — if one of those ways is by elevating the moral and intellectual character of the people, and if the other way is by inflicting pain, who can doubt which way every government ought to take? It seems to me that no proposition can be more strange than this — that the State ought to have power to punish and is bound to punish its subjects for not knowing their duty, but at the same time is to take no step to let them know what their duty is.

301. Evils of apprenticing the Children of Paupers

(Report of the Reverend H. Mosely, Inspector, to the Committee of Council on Education for England. In a *Report on Kneeler Hall Training School*, 1851)

Kneeler Hall Training School, twelve miles from London, was established in 1846 to train teachers for service in workhouse and penal schools, and was under the direct control of the Committee of Council on Education. The *Report of the Poor-Law Board* for 1850 showed that there were, on January 1, 1851, 43,138 children in the workhouses of England and Wales, and 838 teachers employed in their instruction. This was about one child in eight for whom poor-relief was being extended, and for whom the State stood more or less *in loco parentis*. For these children, the Report held, "every dictate of humanity and wise economy demands that the State should make immediate and thorough provision in schools and teachers of the right kind."

Of the system of apprenticing the children of paupers, Mr. Mosely wrote :

The system of education under the old poor law was that of parish apprenticeship. Pauper children were bound apprentices to such persons as were supposed capable of instructing them in some useful calling. In some cases this was by compulsion, the apprentices being assigned to different rate-payers, who render themselves liable to fines if they refuse to receive them, which fines sometimes went to the rates, and in other cases were paid as premiums to persons who afterward took these apprentices. Another method of apprenticeship was by premiums paid from the rates to masters who, in consideration of such premiums, were contented to take pauper children as apprentices.

The evils of this system were manifold: —

1st. As it regarded the independent laborer, whom, by its competition, it prevented "from getting his children out, except by making them parish paupers, he having no means of offering the advantages given by the parish," and in whom it discouraged that which in a parent is the strongest motive to self-denial, forethought, and industry — a desire to provide for his children.

2dly. As it regards those to whom the children were apprenticed; who, when they took them on compulsion, took them at an inconvenience and a disadvantage — to whom these parish apprentices "were much worse servants and less under control than others," — who often found them "hostile both in conduct and disposition, ready listeners, retailers of falsehood and scandal of the family affairs, ready agents of mischief of the parents and other persons ill disposed to their employers," — who "not infrequently excited the children to disobedience, in order to get their indentures cancelled," — they were the unwilling servants of unwilling masters; they could not be trusted, and yet could not be dismissed. The demoralization of the apprentices made them undesirable inmates. They disseminate in the parish the morals of the workhouse.

3dly. As it regards the children themselves: —

1. They were often apprenticed to "needy persons, to whom the premium offered was an irresistible temptation to apply for them," and "after a certain interval had been allowed to elapse, means were not unfrequently taken to disgust them with their occupation, and to render their situations so irksome as to make them abscond."

2. They were looked upon by such persons as "defenseless, and deserted by their natural protectors," and were often cruelly treated. So that to be treated "worse than a parish apprentice" has passed into a proverb.

3. Not only was their moral culture neglected, but their moral well-being was often totally disregarded. The facts under this head are fearful. There was a mutual contamination. The system appears, says Mr. Austin, to have led directly to cruelty, immorality, and suffering, although, in some cases, apprenticeship was not unproductive of certain beneficial results to both master and apprentice.

4. Their instruction in any useful calling was for the most part neglected, because their masters were often unfit to teach them, and because they were obstinately unwilling to learn. The position which the parish apprentice occupied in the house was therefore commonly that of the household drudge.

It is scarcely to be wondered at, that among a race thus born in pauperism, and educated to it, pauperism became *hereditary*.

.   .   .   .

When the Poor Law Board abolished the system of education by apprenticeship, they took upon themselves the responsibility of providing some better form of education. Every workhouse was accordingly required to provide a schoolmaster who should educate the children. For which purpose they were to be completely separated from the adults, and instructed for at least three hours every day.

Lest the guardians should be tempted to employ inefficient schoolmasters, that they might not have to pay them high salaries, it was afterward provided that the salaries of workhouse schoolmasters should be paid out of a grant voted specially for that purpose by Parliament; and, later still, these salaries were ordered to be determined by your Lordships, upon examination by Her Majesty's Inspectors.

302. Typical Reasoning in Opposition to Free Schools

(Kay-Shuttleworth, Sir James, *Public Education as affected by the Minutes of the Committee of Privy Council, 1846–52*. London, 1853)

The following brief extract from the above volume is typical of much of the reasoning of the time in favor of supporting schools by public grants, coupled with tuition fees, in preference to the creation of a system of national education based on taxation.

A weekly payment from the parents of scholars is that form of taxation, the justice of which is most apparent, to the humbler classes. Every one who has even an elementary knowledge of finance is aware that no tax can be largely productive from which the great mass of the people are exempt.

The moral advantage of a tax on the poor in the form of school pence is, that it appeals to the sense of paternal duty. It enforces a lesson of domestic piety. It establishes the parental authority, and vindicates personal freedom. The child is neither wholly educated by religious charity, nor by the State. He owes to his parents that honor and obedience, which are the source of domestic tranquillity, and to which the promise of long life is attached. Let no one rudely interfere with the bonds of filial reverence and affection. Especially is it the interest of the State to make these the primal elements of social order. Nor can the paternal charities of a wise commonwealth be substituted for the personal ties of parental love and esteem, without undermining society at its base.

The parent should not be led to regard the school as the privilege of the citizen, so much as another scene of household duty. Those communities are neither most prosperous, nor most happy, in which the political or social relations of the family are more prominent than the domestic. That which happily distinguishes the Saxon and Teutonic races is, the prevalence of the idea of "*home*." To make the households of the poor, scenes of Christian peace, is the first object of the school. Why then should we substitute its external relation for its internal — the idea of the citizen, for that of the parent — the sense of political or social rights, for those of domestic duties — the claim of public privilege, for the personal law of conscience?

303. The Duke of Newcastle Commission Report

(Summary by Macnamera, J. T. In Binn's *A Century of Education*, pp. 268-69.
London, 1898)

In 1858 a new parliamentary Commission of Inquiry, commonly known as the Duke of Newcastle's Commission, was appointed to review educational conditions, progress, and needs, and to report on the same to Parliament. The Commission reported in 1861. The following is a good brief summary of its findings and recommendations. It was this Commission which proposed the "payment by results" plan, adopted in 1862.

a. Summary of Findings.

1. One in every eight of the population was at some time in some school or other.

2. Of the estimated number of two and a half millions who ought to be at school, only 1,675,000 were in public schools of any sort.

3. Of the pupils in public schools only one-half were in schools receiving any grant, or under any sort of inspection.

4. The attendance in inspected schools was estimated at only 74.35 per cent of the scholars on the books.

5. The number of assisted schools amounted to 6897, containing 917,255 scholars; while 15,750 denominational schools, and about 317

others, containing together 691,393 scholars, were outside the range of the operations of the department.

6. Of the pupils in the inspected schools not more than one-fourth of the children were receiving a good education, the instruction given being too much adapted to the elder scholars to the neglect of the younger ones.

b. Chief Recommendations.

1. That all assistance given to the annual maintenance of schools should be simplified and reduced to grants of two kinds. The first of these grants should be paid out of the general taxation of the country, in consideration of the fulfilment of certain conditions by the managers of the schools. Compliance with these conditions was to be ascertained by the inspectors. The second was to be paid out of the county rates, in consideration of the attainment of a certain degree of knowledge by the children in the school during the year preceding the payment. The existence of this degree of knowledge would be ascertained by examiners appointed by county and borough boards of education hereinafter described.

2. That no school should be entitled to these grants which did not fulfil the following general conditions: — The school would have to be registered at the office of the Privy Council, on the report of the inspector, as an elementary school for the education of the poor. The school would have to be certified by the inspector to be healthy and properly drained and ventilated, and supplied with offices; and the principal school-room must contain at least eight square feet of superficial area for each child in average daily attendance.

With a view to making the teaching in schools more effective and more evenly distributed among the scholars, the Commission recommended what has since been known as "payment by results." "There is only one way," the Commission reported, "of securing this result, which is to institute a searching examination by competent authority of every child in every school to which grants are to be paid, with a view to ascertaining whether these indispensable elements of knowledge are thoroughly acquired, and to make the prospects and position of the teacher dependent, to a considerable extent, on the results of this examination."

Of these recommendations, that one which proposed that education should be supported partly by means of a local rate bore no immediate fruit. The other main suggestions, viz., that the Parliamentary grant should be paid directly to the managers, who should arrange all questions of stipend with their teachers, and that this grant should be made to depend largely on the record of individual examination of the scholars, formed the backbone of Mr. Lowe's Revised Code.

The bedrock principle of this famous code, the principle of "payment by results," was bitterly challenged by educationists; but it held the field for thirty years. In recent years, however, it has been steadily departed from, with, as I think, the most salutary effects upon the permanent value and fruitfulness of the teaching given.

304. The Elementary Education Act of 1870

(Elementary Education Act; 33 and 34 Victoria, chap. 75)

In 1870 the culmination of over sixty years of struggle to secure the beginnings of national organization for education was reached, and the Act providing for the organization of elementary education to supply deficiencies, and further providing that the Board Schools should be free from religious compulsion, was secured.

The essential features of the Act of 1870 were:

There shall be provided for every school district a sufficient amount of accommodation in public elementary schools (as hereinafter defined) available for all the children resident in such district for whose elementary education efficient and suitable provision is not otherwise made; and where there is an insufficient amount of such accommodation, in this act referred to as "public school accommodation," the deficiency shall be supplied in the manner provided by this act.

Where the education department, in the manner provided by this act, are satisfied and have given public notice that there is an insufficient amount of public school accommodation for any school district, and the deficiency is not supplied as hereinafter required, a school board shall be formed for such district and shall supply such deficiency, and in case of default by the school board the education department shall cause the duty of such board to be performed in the manner provided by this act.

Every elementary school which is conducted in accordance with the following regulations shall be a public elementary school within the meaning of this act; and every public elementary school shall be conducted in accordance with the following regulations (a copy of which regulations shall be conspicuously put up in every such school); namely, (1) it shall not be required, as a condition of any child being admitted in or continuing in the school, that he shall attend or abstain from attending any Sunday School or any place of religious worship, or that he shall attend any religious observance or any instruction in religious subjects in the school or elsewhere, from which observance or instruction he may be withdrawn by his parent, or that he shall, if withdrawn by his parent, attend the school on any day exclusively set apart for religious observance by the religious body to which his parent belongs: (2) the time or times during which any religious observance is practiced or instruction in religious subjects is given at any meeting of the school shall be either at the beginning, or at the end, or at the beginning and the end of such meeting.

305. The Abolition of Religious Tests for Degrees at the English Universities

(The Universities Tests Act of 1871; 34 and 35 Victoria, chap. 26)

Queen Elizabeth did much to foster and advance learning in the English universities, but she felt the necessity of keeping these institutions free from popery. Accordingly, in 1558, she imposed on all graduates the oath of supremacy, in all temporal and spiritual matters, to prevent non-conformists from receiving university degrees. Under the requirements every student, fellow, and lecturer was compelled to take certain oaths, and to conform in religious matters in a way that none but members of the Church of England could possibly do. In time this came to be a heavy burden on the English nation, in that it prevented many bright minds from attendance on the universities. Finally, as part of the educational and political awakening of the nation which took place after 1850, Parliament, in 1871, repealed this burdensome statute of 1558, and opened the universities to dissenters as well as churchmen. The chief points in this law, abolishing religious tests for degrees, are contained in the following extract.

Whereas, it is expedient that the benefits of the universities of Oxford, Cambridge, and Durham, and of the colleges and halls now subsisting therein, as places of religion and learning, should be rendered freely accessible to the nation:

And whereas, by means of divers restrictions, tests, and disabilities, many of Her Majesty's subjects are debarred from the full enjoyment of the same:

And whereas, it is expedient that such restrictions, tests, and disabilities should be removed, under proper safeguards for the maintenance of religious instruction and worship in the said universities and the colleges and halls now subsisting within the same. . . .

No person shall be required, upon taking or to enable him to take any degree (other than a degree in divinity) within the universities of Oxford, Cambridge, and Durham, or any of them, or upon exercising or to enable him to exercise any of the rights and privileges which may heretofore have been or may hereafter be exercised by graduates in the said universities or any of them, or in any college subsisting at the time of the passing of this act in any of the said universities, or upon taking or holding, or to enable him to take or hold any office in any of the said universities or any such college as aforesaid, or upon teaching or to enable him to teach within any of the said universities or any such colleges as aforesaid, or upon opening or to enable him to open a private hall or hostel in any of the said universities for the reception of students, to subscribe any article or formulary of faith, or to make any declaration or take any oath respecting his religious belief or profession, or to conform to any religious observance, or to attend or abstain from attending any form of public worship, or to belong to any specified church, sect, or denomination; nor shall any person be compelled, in any of the said universities or any such college as aforesaid, to attend the public worship of any church, sect, or denomination to which he does not belong.

306. The Educational Traditions of England

(London *Times*, Educational Supplement, September, 1917)

The following is reproduced as an excellent summary of a century of English educational history.

Mr. Fisher's Education Bill, which was read for the first time on Friday last, is the legitimate successor of a series of educational impulses dating from the very end of the eighteenth century, when Joseph Lancaster and Andrew Bell realized, almost simultaneously, the straits to which the introduction of machinery into labor had reduced the children of the land.

At that moment the universities of Oxford and Cambridge were stirring in their eighteenth-century sleep, but in all other directions a profound coma lay upon national education. The Charity-Schools had definitely failed; the endowment schools were for the most part out of action; the children of a Christian land had no facilities for the simplest form of education despite the efforts of the leaders of the new Sunday-school movement that had reached London in 1780. The monitorial movement initiated by Bell and Lancaster revived similar expedients necessitated by the lack of teachers in the thirteenth and the sixteenth centuries. It was at once crowned with an embarrassing success, and it was clear in the dawn of the nineteenth century that the tradition of education was but asleep, that the people of the land were as hungry for education as in any past age. . . .

From 1802 to 1832 many stalwart efforts were made to secure a universal system of education. Mr. Whitbread in 1807 introduced a bill for the establishment of schools throughout the land to supply machinery by which all children were to be entitled to two years' schooling between the ages of seven and fourteen years. Public opinion has been or was being stimulated by the keenest minds: Blackstone, Adam Smith, Bentham demanded in no uncertain tones education for all. In 1816 a Select Committee of the Commons was directed to report on the subject of the education of the lower orders. In 1818 it proclaimed "the anxiety of the poor for education," and dwelt on their meager opportunities. The committee recommended a universal conscience clause, the establishment of rate-supported free parochial schools in very poor districts — the goal which was achieved in 1870 — and Parliamentary building grants in richer districts — the principle adopted in 1833. A full century ago, the true principles of advance were advocated by Parliament, but nothing was done.

In 1820 Brougham took up that subject of national education which he was destined ceaselessly to pursue until his last speech of July, 1864. The persistence of his efforts gave a certain continuity to the whole struggle for progress. He was often wrong in his dogmatism, but never in his optimism and in his determination to secure educational justice for the people of England. Mr. Fisher's measure of 1917 is a direct descendant of Brougham's measure of 1820, when he recommended the universal establishment of undenominational parochial schools with efficient teachers supported out of local rates supplemented by the old endowments. In 1828 Brougham passionately declared in the house that "the schoolmaster was abroad, and he trusted more to the schoolmaster armed with his primer than he did to the soldier in full military array for upholding and extending the liberties of his country." In 1825 he published his pamphlet, "Observations on the Education of the People," which within a year ran through twenty editions. The desire for a national system had spread through England, and in 1833 there were already over a million children in the schools of the education societies. On Saturday, August 17, 1833, in a house as empty as that addressed by Mr. Fisher on Friday, August 10, 1917, the House of Commons voted the sum of £20,000 "in aid of private subscriptions for the erection of schoolhouses for the education of the children of the poorer classes." State intervention in English education had begun at last, and this little grant was the first rivulet of the great river of to-day on which so many national argosies are floating.

Lord Althorp's government placed the administration of the grant in the hands of the Treasury. The response to the grant showed that the country was hungering for education, and applications for grants poured in with ample voluntary funds. A great scheme was then possible, but the Treasury refused to recommend any increase in the grant. The first "fine careless rapture" of the reformers died away, and though Parliament made a grant of £10,000 for training colleges in 1834, it remained unused until 1839. Parliament in 1837 refused leave to introduce a bill to establish a national system, and Brougham had to abandon his educational charities bills in the same year, while a proposal to form a board to distribute the grant was flatly defeated in the house in 1838. But three successive Select Committees produced the gloomiest reports as to national educational conditions, and as to the dreadful state of child labor. The committee of 1837–38 was forced by Gladstone and others to reject a proposal for a Board of Education. In 1839 Queen Victoria personally intervened with a protest at a lack of education "not in accordance with the character of a civilized and Christian nation." This brought a new figure into the field, Lord John Russell, and suddenly the formation of a Committee of Council on Education gathered to a head slumbering political excitement. Gladstone, Disraeli and Peel all attacked the new departure, which by a bare majority in a crowded house was confirmed, and became the basis of all subsequent developments.

From 1839 to 1870 the Education Committee (which by statute in 1856 was combined with the Department of Science and Art into the Education Department) carried on the heavy work of administering a rapidly growing grant under the Regulations, first issued in 1839, that later became the well-known Code. The work of inspection was carried out with great thoroughness, and the reports of the inspectors are some of the most valuable documents extant for the social history of the mid-nineteenth century. Macaulay, Brougham and Russell fought with herculean energy to destroy the "empire of ignorance." On April 19, 1847, grants were extended from school buildings to education itself, and then the long struggle for compulsory education began. Russell proposed in 1842 that rates should be made available for education. The proposal was part of a great scheme dealing with all grades of education. Bill after bill followed; bill after bill disappeared, while the conditions of childhood grew rapidly worse. It seemed as if the state itself could never enfranchise the slave-children of the people. Gladstone was bitterly opposed even to the increase of the grant, which in 1856 was nearly half a million. Two years later a Royal Commission was appointed. Robert Lowe came upon the scene, and in 1859 introduced education estimates approaching one million. The report of the commission in 1861 proposed the introduction of rate grants as well as state grants, and hoped to secure local administration by county and borough boards. But nothing came of the report, and Mr. Lowe introduced his famous Revised Code to meet a position which was rapidly getting worse. The average of attendance was lower than ten years earlier. His remedy was a single grant dependent on examinations, coupled with attendance, efficient buildings and efficient teaching. It was only to apply to children up to the age of twelve. A tremendous Parliamentary struggle followed, the Code was accepted, and it seemed successful, since the numbers inspected increased with lower estimates. But the system left half the children of the country without education, and the end of efforts that now seem to us puerile was at hand. Bills were introduced in 1867 and 1868 intended to strengthen the voluntary system, but they were clearly inadequate. It is true that in 1869 a million children were at school, and a million and a half on the registers, but of these 400,000 were under six and only 640,000 were examined; while there were a million children between six and ten and half a million between ten and twelve not on the registers at all. Compulsory attendance and compulsory rating were beyond all doubt essential, and with the Act of 1870 the new system was inaugurated.

When we gaze into the perspective of the history before 1870 we are able to see more signs of hope than the generation actually engaged in the struggle could detect. In seventy years the school-going habit of English childhood had been reëstablished. Parents throughout the country had come to recognize that school was the place for children, and though compulsion involved loss of wages it was gladly accepted by the industrial classes. We do not realize to-day what a wonderful achievement this was. . . . That was one gain. Another was the religious training of the schools, which was excellent throughout the period and kept alive one of the most important of the English educational traditions. A third gain was the deep basis of voluntary effort that had been laid. It was prophesied that when compulsion came voluntary effort would cease. Instead it multiplied, and it flourishes to-day in every grade of education. But the pre-compulsion period did more than all this. It laid the basis for reform in all other grades of education. Organized state effort in respect to science and art began in 1836; a long struggle for the re-creation of our secondary system of endowed schools reached its goal in 1868 and 1869 and restored to English education the full current of mediæval and Elizabethan humanism, and this was supplemented by the brilliant awakening of the old universities, the birth of many new places of higher education, and the creation of a living relation from 1856 onwards (when Oxford started the local examinations) between the universities and the people. By 1870 the threefold tradition of English education — religion, humanism, and science — was again in full operation.

The period from 1870 to 1917 was occupied with one long struggle, the effort to give this tradition full operative value in the life of the people as a whole. In order to do this it was essential to correlate once again our educational and our local government systems. The weakness of the school-board system was that it did not adequately fit into a system of local government. . . . Until the two were related real progress was scarcely possible, though the great school boards in the teeth of the law did much to press forward the claims of democracy to full educational facilities. The evils of child labor, of exemptions from school, of lack of facilities for higher education, of lack of health through evil social conditions, could not be grasped while local government itself was invertebrate. That ceased to be the case in 1888, when the county councils and borough councils were formed. From that moment educational reform became possible once more. The demand for reform began at once. Compulsory fees for schooling ceased in 1891, though in fact the system of fees with alternative free schools is only now to be abolished. The abolition of fees was followed by growing demands for efficiency, and from 1897 necessitous schools received special grants. But it had become clear enough that national education required drastic reorganization; that the efforts for higher education must not be blighted by a technical definition of elementary education; that secondary and elementary and technical education must be coördinated, and that while a new centralization at Whitehall was necessary a new decentralization was equally essential, and that the position of the teacher must be placed on a higher stage. So in 1899 the Education Department and the Science and Art Department were amalgamated in the Board of Education, to which new body was transferred the powers of the Charity Commissioners in relation to educational trusts. . . . But the creation of a real Board of Education . . . only achieved one aspect of reform. It was left to Mr. Balfour, in his great Act of 1902, to graft the educational system into the new (or rather revived) local government system, and create committees of the local authorities to take over not only the work of the School Boards, but also many duties, with more or less adequate rating powers, in relation to higher education. This Act was extended to London in 1903. In the 15 years since education once more passed into the hands of local authorities responsible for all the other social work of the district a new aspect has come over the whole subject. The great School Medical Service was introduced in 1907. A numerous class of skilled educational administrators with immense technical knowledge has grown up; a deep sense of educational responsibility in the local authorities has developed; the interrelation of education and public health has become obvious; the dependence of industry on education has become almost as obvious, and with this recognition the claims of higher education have advanced and have been recognized and especially in the regions of technical studies. In 1887 national education seemed at a standstill; real progress seemed impossible. Thirty years later we see, in the midst of the greatest war that Europe has known, progress with gigantic strides not only possible but indubitable.

During the progress of the Bill of 1902 the attention of the public was chiefly fixed on the clauses relating to religious teaching, and Mr. Balfour had to devise ways and means to meet the conflicting claims of the voluntary and the provided schools. Not only was attention riveted on this side of the case, but for ten years after, the Act suggesting legislation to amend these clauses occupied the attention of Parliament and roused the bitterest feeling among the leaders of various denominations. But all this while wider views were growing; the clauses in question in the vast majority of schools were seen in fact not to work unjustly, and the local authorities and educationists devoted themselves to the great difficulties of actual education standing in the way of a national system that should give to every child the means of freely developing his or her own peculiar gifts. The questions of child labor, of child health, of adequate teaching, smaller classes, better school-houses, able and contented teachers, the coördination of grades of education, continuously occupied the attention of the Board of Education, of the local authorities, and of educationists at large. When the war came in 1914 it looked for a moment as if the labors of a decade were to be cast aside. But a trumpet call for an educational revolution came, and after more than two years of continuous effort a really great Minister of Education has been able to bring forward a measure of reform that crowns the efforts of men like Whitbread, Brougham, Macaulay, Russell, Forster, and certainly not least Mr. Balfour, who may claim to have created machinery that coördinated the ancient traditions of English education and made possible the revolution of to-day.

CHAPTER XXV

AWAKENING AN EDUCATIONAL CONSCIOUSNESS IN THE UNITED STATES

THE Readings of this chapter have been selected to illustrate educational conditions and movements during the first half-century of American national existence, during the period of transition from colonial conditions, and before any clear educational consciousness on the part of the people had been awakened.

The first group of selections describes early schools. The first of these (**307**) is a characterization of the schools of Boston during the period of about 1790 to 1815, by the celebrated teacher and textbook writer, Caleb Bingham. His description of the origin of the double elementary-school system of Boston is important, as is also that of the instruction and the textbooks used. In Rhode Island, the first and for long the only city to maintain schools was Providence, and selection **308** reproduces the first course of study (1800); selection **309** is a reprint of the early rules and regulations for the schools; and **310** is a memorial to the City Council from a very important society of the city praying for better schools, and giving facts as to attendance and costs.

Among the many charitable and philanthropic undertakings begun to found schools, the School Societies for day and infant schools, and the Lancastrian monitorial organizations, were the most important. Selection **311** is an appeal to the people of New York City by the newly founded Public School Society, and represents the beginnings of public education there. Selection **312** is from a Report made to the School Committee of Boston, stating the advantages of the monitorial plan of instruction over the older individual plan, and supplements the descriptions of the plan previously reproduced (**297, 298**). Selection **313** is the Report of the Boston School Committee which resulted in the creation of primary schools in that city. The selection which follows (**314**) describes the Boston elementary-school system of 1823, as reorganized early in the century and with the new infant schools added. This description is continued for the secondary schools in **327**.

After about 1825 the newly formed workingmen's associations began to take a prominent part in the agitation for schools, and from New York to Maryland they were particularly active. Many resolutions were adopted and reports made, of which **315,** a Report of the Workingmen's Committee of Philadelphia, is reproduced as typical.

307. The Schools of Boston about 1790–1815

(Fowle, Wm. B., Memoir of Caleb Bingham. Barnard's *American Journal of Education*, vol. v, pp. 325–34)

Caleb Bingham (1757–1817) enjoyed an enviable reputation as a teacher in Boston during the last decade of the eighteenth century, and later became a notable textbook writer and publisher of schoolbooks. In this *Memoir* the writer gives an excellent picture of the schools of Boston, as reorganized by the School Committee in 1789, and as they continued for more than a quarter of a century.

(a) *Schools for girls.* The main object of Mr. Bingham in coming to Boston was to establish a school for girls; and the project was of the most promising description, for the town of Boston had even then become eminent for its wealth and intelligence, and, strange to say, was deficient in public and private schools for females. It certainly is a remarkable fact, that, while the girls of every town in the state were allowed and expected to attend the village schools, no public provision seems to have been made for their instruction in the metropolis, and men of talents do not seem to have met with any encouragement to open private schools for this all important class of children. The only schools in the city to which girls were admitted, were kept by the teachers of public schools, between the forenoon and afternoon sessions, and how insufficient this chance for an education was, may be gathered from the fact, that all the public teachers who opened private schools, were uneducated men, selected for their skill in penmanship and the elements of arithmetic. The schools were called writing schools; and, although reading and spelling were also taught in them, this instruction was only incidental, being carried on, we cannot say "attended to," while the teachers were making or mending pens, preparatory to the regular writing lesson.

This had probably been the state of things for more than a century, and at the advent of Mr. Bingham, there were only two such schools, while there were two others devoted exclusively to the study of Latin and Greek, although the pupils of these latter schools hardly numbered one tenth of the others. Of course, the proposal of Mr. Bingham to open a school, in which girls should be taught, not only writing and arithmetic, but, reading, spelling and English grammar, met with a hearty reception, and his room, which was in State street, from which schools and dwelling houses had been banished nearly half a century, was soon filled with children of the most respectable families. There does not seem to have been any competition, and Mr. Bingham had the field to himself for at least four years before any movement was made to improve the old public system, or to extend the means of private instruction.

(b) *The public writing schools.* At that time, and for more than a century and a half, the public schools of Boston, and indeed, those of the state had been under the control and supervision of the selectmen, three to nine citizens, elected annually to manage the financial and other concerns of the several towns, without much, if any, regard to their literary qualifications. The selectmen of Boston were generally merchants, several of whom, at the time under consideration, had daughters or relatives in the school of Mr. Bingham. It was natural that the additional expense thus incurred, for they were taxed to support the public schools, from which their daughters were excluded, should lead them to inquire why such a preference was given to parents with boys; and the idea seemed, for the first time, to be started, that the prevailing system was not only imperfect, but evidently unfair. The simplest and most natural process would have been to open the schools to both sexes, as the spirit of the laws required, but this would have left the instruction in the hands of the incompetent writing masters, when a higher order of teachers was required; or it would have involved the dismission of all the writing masters, a bold step, which the committee dared not to hazard, because many citizens were opposed to any innovation, and the friends of the masters were so influential, that no change was practicable which did not provide for their support. After much consultation, therefore, there being some complaint of the insufficient number of the schools, the school committee proposed the only plan which seemed to secure the triple object — room for the girls, employment for the old masters, and the introduction of others better qualified.

(c) *Origin of the reading schools.* The new plan was to institute three new schools, to be called READING SCHOOLS, in which reading, spelling, grammar and perhaps geography, should be taught by masters to be appointed; the two old writing schools to be continued, a new one established; and one of the Latin schools to be abolished. As no rooms were prepared, temporary ones were hired, so that the same pupils attended a writing school in one building half the day, and a reading school in a different building, at a considerable distance, and under a different and independent teacher, the other half. Each reading school had its corresponding writing school, and while the boys were in one school, the girls were in the other, alternating forenoon and afternoon, and changing the half day once a month, because, Thursday and Saturday afternoons being vacation, this arrangement was necessary to equalize the lessons taught in the separate schools. This system afterwards acquired the name of the double-headed system, and it was continued, essentially, for more than half a century, in spite of all the defects and abuses to which it was exposed. Even when the town built new schoolhouses, the upper room was devoted to the reading school, and the lower to the writing, the masters never changing rooms, and the boys and girls alternating as before. The points gained, however, were very important, the girls were provided for, better teachers were appointed, and the sexes were separated into different rooms. . . .

(d) *The Latin schools.* Another evil in the new system also held its ground for many years. Boys had been admitted into the Latin school at the early age of seven years, on the mistaken idea, that the very young are best qualified to learn a dead language, as they undoubtedly are to learn a spoken one. The age was increased to ten years by the new system, but, as before, no provision was made in the Latin school for their instruction in English, in penmanship, or in any of the common branches. To remedy this serious defect, the Latin scholars were *allowed* to attend the writing schools two hours, forenoon or afternoon, and about thirty availed themselves of the privilege, although they were obliged to neglect one school to attend the other, and unpunctuality and disorder, in all the schools, were the natural consequence. . . .

(e) *Books used; Methods of instruction.* The books used in the reading schools were, the Holy Bible, Webster's Spelling Book, Webster's Third Part, and the Young Lady's Accidence. The Children's Friend and Morse's Geography were allowed, not required; and "Newspapers were to be introduced, occasionally, at the discretion of the masters." . . .

Furthermore, it was ordered that, in the writing schools, the children "should begin to learn arithmetic at eleven years of age; that, at twelve, they should be taught to make pens." Until eleven years old, all the pupils did, in a whole forenoon or afternoon, was to write one page of a copy book, not exceeding ten lines. When they began to cipher, it rarely happened that they performed more than two sums in the simplest rules. These were set in the pupil's manuscript, and the operation was there recorded by him. No printed book was used. Such writing and ciphering, however, were too much for one day, and the boys who ciphered, only did so every other day. If it be asked, how were the three hours of school time occupied? The answer is, in one of three ways, — in mischief; in play; or in idleness. . . .

In the reading schools, the course was for every child to read one verse of the Bible, or a short paragraph of the Third Part. The master heard the first and second, that is, the two highest classes, and the usher heard the two lowest. While one class was reading, the other studied the spelling lesson. The lesson was spelled by the scholars in turn, so that, the classes being large, each boy seldom spelled more than one or two words. In grammar, the custom was to recite six or more lines once a fortnight, and to go through the book three times before any application of it was made to what was called parsing. No geography was prepared for the schools until Mr. Bingham left them. Morse's abridgment began to be a reading book about the year 1800, and soon after, Mr. Bingham prepared his little Catechism, which was probably based upon it. When Mr. B.'s American Preceptor was published, it displaced Webster's Third Part. His Child's Companion superseded Webster's Spelling Book in the lower classes, and the Columbian Orator was the reading book of the upper class, to the displacement of the Bible, which, instead of being read by the children, was read by the reading masters as a religious exercise, at the opening of school in the morning, and at its close in the afternoon. The writing masters were not required to read or pray for fifteen or twenty years after the great reform.

308. Petition for Free Schools in Rhode Island

(Petition of Mechanics and Manufacturers Association, of Providence, 1799. Reproduced in Carroll, Charles, *Public Education in Rhode Island*, pp. 77–78. Providence, 1918)

One of the very influential associations which did effective propaganda work for free schools, in the early days of American national life, was the Providence Association of Mechanics and Manufacturers, in the educational work of which a barber of Providence, John Howland by name, was the leading spirit. He is commonly designated as the founder of the free schools of Providence.

In 1799 this Association addressed the following petition to the General Assembly of Rhode Island:

A Petition for Free Schools. To the Honorable General Assembly of the State of Rhode Island and Providence Plantations, to be holden at Greenwich, on the last Monday of February, A.D. 1799:

The Memorial and Petition of the Providence Association of Mechanics and Manufacturers respectfully presents —

That the means of education which are enjoyed in this state are very inadequate to a purpose so highly important.

That numbers of the rising generation whom nature has liberally endowed, are suffered to grow up in ignorance, when a common education would qualify them to act their parts in life with advantage to the public and reputation to themselves.

That in consequence of there being no legal provision for the establishment of schools, and for want of public attention and encouragement, this so essential part of our social duty is left to the partial patronage of individuals, whose cares do not extend beyond the limits of their own families, while numbers in every part of the state are deprived of a privilege which is the common right of every child to enjoy.

That when to that respect which as individuals we feel ourselves bound to render to the representatives of the people we add our public declaration of gratitude for the privilege we enjoy as a corporate body, we at the same time solicit this Honorable Assembly to make legal provision for the establishment of free schools sufficient to educate all the children in the several towns throughout the state; with great confidence we bring this, our earnest solicitation before this Honorable Assembly, from the interest we feel in the public welfare and from the consideration that our society is composed of members not originally of any particular town, but assembled mostly in our early years from almost every town in the state.

That we feel as individuals the want of that education which we now ask to be bestowed on those who are to succeed us in life, and which is so essential in directing its common concerns. That we feel a still greater degree of confidence from the consideration that while we pray this Honorable Assembly to establish free schools, we are at the same time advocating the cause of the great majority of children throughout the state, and in particular of those who are poor and destitute — the son of the widow and the child of distress.

Trusting that our occupations as mechanics and manufacturers ought not to prevent us from adding to these reasons an argument which cannot fail to operate on those to whom is committed the guardianship of the public welfare, and that is, liberty and security under a republican form of government depend on a general diffusion of knowledge among the people.

In confiding this petition and the reasons which have dictated it to the wisdom of the Legislature, we assure ourselves that their decision will be such as will reflect on this Honorable General Assembly the praise and the gratitude, not only of the youth of the present generation, but of thousands the date of whose existence has not commenced.

Respectfully submitted by John Howland, Joel Metcalf, William Richmond, Peter Grinnell, Richard Anthony, Grindall Reynolds, Samuel Thurber, Jr., and Nathan Foster, committee.

The petition was referred to a committee, which reported favorably, and the General Free School Act of 1800 was the result. Providence at once organized free schools under the Act, as did two or three other towns, but in 1803 the Act was repealed, and no further general legislation took place until 1828.

309. The Schools of Providence in 1820

(Report of the Committee for revising the School Regulations, June 20, 1820;
in *Centennial Report School Committee*, 1899–1900, pp. 42–43)

Until 1825 the schools of Providence remained almost the only schools in Rhode Island. The following documents describe the first schools established, and the regulations for their government. In 1800 a set of rules and regulations was drawn up, and in 1820 these were revised by re-wording but without materially changing their character. The 1820 regulations are reproduced below as describing the schools at a little later date, though they are substantially the same as those for 1800.

*Regulations for the instruction and government of the publick schools
in the Town of Providence*

The Publick Schools are established for the general benefit of the community; And all children, of both sexes, having attained the age of six years, shall be received therein and faithfully instructed, without preference or partiality.

The Instruction shall be uniform in the several schools, and shall consist of spelling, Reading, the use of Capital letters and Punctuation, Writing, English Grammar & Arithmetick.

The Pronunciation shall be uniform in the several schools & the standard shall be the Critical Pronouncing Dictionary of John Walker.

The following Books, and none others, shall be used in the several schools, viz: Alden's Spelling Book, first & second part, New Testament, American Preceptor, Murray's Sequel to the English Reader, Murray's Abridgement of English Grammar and Dabols Arithmetick.

The scholars shall be put in separate classes according to their several improvements, each sex by itself.

The Schools are statedly to begin and end as follows: From the first Monday in October to the first Monday in May to begin at 9 o'clock A.M. and end at 12 ock. M.: and half past one ock P.M. & end at half past four ock. P.M.   From the first Monday in May to the first Monday in October, to begin at 8 ock. A.M. & end at 11 ock A.M.; And at 2 ock. P.M. and end at 5 ock P.M.

The Scholars shall be excused from attending the schools on Saturdays, on Christmas day, on the 4th day of July, on public Fasts and Thanksgiving, on the last Monday in April, on the day of Regimental Training; on the day succeeding each quarterly visitation and during the whole of Commencement Week.   But on no other days shall the Preceptors dismiss the Schools without permission obtained from the Town Council.

As Discipline and Good Government are absolutely necessary to improvement it is indispensible that the scholars should implicitly obey the Regulations of the Schools.

The good morals of the Youth being essential to their own comfort & to their progress in useful knowledge, they are strictly enjoined to avoid idleness and profaneness, falsehood and deceitfulness, and every other wicked & disgraceful practice; and to conduct themselves in a sober, orderly & decent manner both in & out of school. If any scholar should prove disobedient & refractory, after all reasonable means used by the Preceptor to bring him or her to a just sense of duty, such offender shall be suspended from attendance & instruction in any School, until the next visitation of the committee. Each Scholar shall be punctual in attendance at the appointed hour and be as constant as possible in daily attendance and all excuses for absence shall be by note, from the Parent or Guardian of the scholar.

It shall be the duty of the Preceptors to report at each quarterly visitation the names of those scholars who have been grossly negligent in attending School or inattentive to their Studies.

It is recommended to the Preceptors, as far as practicable, to exclude corporal punishment from the schools, and particularly that they never permit it to be inflicted by their ushers in their presence, or at any time by a scholar.

That they inculcate upon the scholars the necessity of good behaviour during their absence from school. That they endeavor to convince the children by their treatment that they feel a parental affection for them, and never make dismission from school at an early hour a reward for good conduct or diligence, but endeavor to teach the scholars to consider being at school as a privilege & dismission from it as a punishment.

That they endeavor to impress on the minds of the scholars a sense of the Being & Providence of God & their obligations to love & reverence Him, — their duty to their parents & preceptors, the beauty & excellency of truth, justice & mutual love, tenderness to brute creatures, the happy tendency of self government and obedience to the dictates of reason & religion; the observance of the Sabbath as a sacred institution, the duty which they owe to their country & the necessity of a strict obedience to its Laws, and that they caution them against the prevailing vices.

310. A Memorial for Better Schools

(*Centennial Report School Committee*, Providence, R.I., 1899–1900, pp. 55–56)

The "Providence Association of Mechanics and Manufacturers," to which belongs the credit for starting the schools in Providence by petitioning the Legislature (**R. 308**), in 1799, "praying for the establishment of free schools throughout the State," sent the following resolutions to the City Council, in 1837. The Council at that time was also the School Committee or Board of Education for the city.

TO THE CITY COUNCIL OF THE CITY OF PROVIDENCE:

The undersigned, in behalf of the Providence Association of Mechanics and Manufacturers, respectfully represent: That

At a meeting of the Association, held on Monday evening, January 30, 1837, the accompanying resolutions were unanimously adopted:

RESOLVED, That no subject can be of more importance to the inhabitants of this city, than the education of the rising generation.

RESOLVED, That as the members of this association were the pioneers in the establishment of the public schools, they manifested a most laudable zeal on that subject.

RESOLVED, That the public schools of this city come far short of the wants of the community, and are much inferior in their character to the public schools in neighboring cities.

RESOLVED, That the public schools can and ought to be made equal to the private schools, so far as relates to the common branches now taught.

RESOLVED, That two of the greatest evils now existing, as respects public school instruction are the great number of scholars in each school, and the small salaries paid to the teachers.

RESOLVED, That an increased number of public schools ought to be established in this city as soon as practicable.

RESOLVED, That a committee be appointed to draft a memorial to the City Council, on the subject of public schools, in conformity with the recommendation of the Select Committee, to report at an adjourned meeting, to be held on Saturday evening next.

Accompanying the above resolutions was a Memorial, from which the following statistical statement is taken:

In evidence of these statements, it is found that the number attending public schools in this city, in 1836, was 1,456
Private schools 3,235
Attending no school 1,604
Amount actually paid for public schools from June, 1835, to June, 1836, by the City $5,936.34
Total cost for schools 7,461.99
Amount paid for private school instruction, over $20,000.00
Number attending public schools in Boston in 1836 8,847
Number attending private schools 4,000
Amount paid for public schools $88,000.00
Amount paid for private schools 100,000.00

There are about 50 per cent more attending private-school instruction than public, in this city; while in Boston, *three fifths* of the whole number, 12,848, are attending the public schools.

Boston, containing a population of about 80,000, pays $88,000; and Providence, whose population is about 20,000, pays $7,461. Should Providence pay $22,000, instead of the sum above stated, her public schools might then be equal in standing, and perhaps nearly adequate to the actual wants of the community.

311. The Beginnings of Public Education in New York City

("Address" published in New York City papers of May, 1805. Reproduced in Bourne, Wm. O., *History of the Public School Society of the City of New York.* New York, 1870)

In 1800 New York City had a population of 60,489, but no school facilities other than those provided by private and church schools. In February, 1805, a body of public-spirited citizens formed an Association, and applied to the legislature for a charter to establish a School Society. The legislature approved the request and chartered the Society, under the name given in the following "Address" to the Public. To secure funds to erect the first building the Society issued this appeal, asking for subscriptions. The "Address" states well the conditions existing at the time, and reveals the philanthropic origin of the society and of the public schools.

TO THE PUBLIC

Address of the Trustees of the "Society for Establishing a Free School in the City of New York, for the Education of such Poor Children as do not Belong to, or are not Provided for by, any Religious Society."

While the various religious and benevolent societies in this city, with a spirit of charity and zeal which the precepts and example of the Divine Author of our religion could alone inspire, amply provide for the education of such poor children as belong to their respective associations, there still remains a large number living in total neglect of religious and moral instruction, and unacquainted with the common rudiments of learning, essentially requisite for the due management of the ordinary business of life. This neglect may be imputed either to the extreme indigence of the parents of such children, their intemperance and vice, or to a blind indifference to the best interests of their offspring. The consequences must be obvious to the most careless observer. Children thus brought up in ignorance, and amidst the contagion of bad example, are in imminent danger of ruin; and too many of them, it is to be feared, instead of being useful members of the community, will become the burden and pests of society. Early instruction and fixed habits of industry, decency, and order, are the surest safeguards of virtuous conduct; and when parents are either unable or unwilling to bestow the necessary attention on the education of their children, it becomes the duty of the public, and of individuals, who have the power,

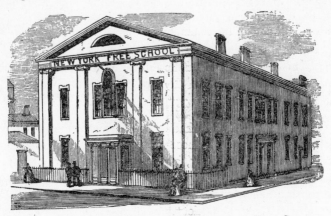

FIG. 79. THE FIRST SCHOOLHOUSE BUILT BY THE FREE SCHOOL
SOCIETY IN NEW YORK CITY

Built in 1809, in Tryon Row. Cost, without site, $13,000

to assist them in the discharge of this important obligation. It is in vain that laws are made for the punishment of crimes, or that good men attempt to stem the torrent of irreligion and vice, if the evil is not checked at its source; and the means of prevention, by the salutary discipline of early education, seasonably applied. It is certainly in the power of the opulent and charitable, by a timely and judicious interposition of their influence and aid, if not wholly to prevent, at least to diminish, the pernicious effects resulting from the neglected education of the children of the poor.

Influenced by these considerations, and from a sense of the necessity of providing some remedy for an increasing and alarming evil, several individuals, actuated by similar motives, agree to form an association for the purpose of extending the means of education to such poor children as do not belong to, or are not provided for, by any religious society. After meetings, numerously attended, a plan of association was framed, and a Memorial prepared and addressed to the legislature, soliciting an Act of Incorporation, the better to enable them to carry into effect their benevolent design. Such a law the Legislature, at their last session, was pleased to pass; and at a meeting of the Society, under the Act of Incorporation, on the sixth instant, thirteen Trustees were elected for the ensuing year.

The particular plan of the school, and the rules for its discipline and management, will be made known previous to its commencement. Care will be exercised in the selection of teachers, and, besides the elements of learning usually taught in schools, strict attention will be bestowed on the morals of the children, and all suitable means be used to counteract the disadvantages resulting from the situation of their parents. It is proposed, also, to establish, on the first day of the week, a school, called a Sunday School, more particularly for such children as, from peculiar circumstances, are unable to attend on the other days of the week. In this, as in the Common School, it will be a primary object, without observing the peculiar forms of any religious Society, to inculcate the sublime truths of religion and morality contained in the Holy Scriptures.

This Society, as will appear from its name, interferes with no existing institution, since children already provided with the means of education, or attached to any other Society, will not come under its care. Humble gleaners in the wide field of benevolence, the members of this Association seek such objects only as are left by those who have gone before, or are fellow-laborers with them in the great work of charity. They, therefore, look with confidence for the encouragement and support of the affluent and charitable of every denomination of Christians; and when they consider that in no community is to be found a greater spirit of liberal and active benevolence than among the citizens of New York, they feel assured that adequate means for the prosecution of their plan will be easily obtained. In addition to the respectable list of original subscriptions, considerable funds will be requisite for the purchase or hire of a piece of ground, and the erection of a suitable building for the school, to pay the teachers, and to defray other charges incident to the establishment. To accomplish this design, and to place the Institution on a solid and respectable foundation, the Society depend on the voluntary bounty of those who may be charitably disposed to contribute their aid in the promotion of an object of great and universal concern.

DE WITT CLINTON, *President.*
JOHN MURRAY, JR., *Vice-President.*
LEONARD BLEEKER, *Treasurer.*
B. D. PERKINS, *Secretary.*

New York, May (5th Month) 18. 1805.

312. Advantages of the Monitorial System

(*Report on Monitorial Instruction to the Boston School Committee,* 1828)

In 1828 the Boston School Committee (Board of Education) investigated the much-talked-of Lancastrian monitorial system, then in use in New York and other central cities, and the committee reported as below. The selection contrasts well the monitorial and the individual plans.

The advantages of the monitorial system, in comparison with the old system, may briefly be thus stated. To the student it makes learning less irksome, by simplifying and facilitating his progress, it gives to instruction more interest, by alternation and variety of exercise, in which physical and intellectual action are combined; it keeps attention awake and interested, by permitting no moment of idleness or listlessness; its effects on the habits, character and intelligence of youth are highly beneficial; disposing their minds to industry, to readiness of attention, and to subordination thereby creating in early life a love of order, preparation for business, and acquaintance with the relative obligations and duties both of pupils and instructor. To the master also, it renders teaching less irksome and more interesting, giving an air of sprightliness and vivacity to his duties, exciting the principles of emulation among his scholars, aiding him by the number of assistants he can thus employ, and, by relieving him from the constant necessity of direct supervision of every individual, capacitates him to concentrate his mind and efforts on doings and objects of the most importance, difficulty, and responsibility. To all which it may be added, though a consideration less important yet not to be overlooked, that it is an immense saving both of time and money, in consequence of the far greater numbers which can be taught as well by this mode, as a smaller number can by the former. It will be sufficient under this head to state that in New York, masters, in three distinct schools, teach fifteen hundred and forty-seven boys, being an average of upwards of five hundred each. In our schools the same number of boys require seven schools and fifteen instructors. In New York a female teaches a school, on this principle, of four hundred. In our schools the average number to an instructress is fifty-six. The success and progressive advancement in those schools, is asserted by men deemed competent judges, to be not less than ours.

313. The Establishment of Primary Schools in Boston

(Wightman, Jos. M., *Annals of the Boston Primary School Committee*, pp. 33–34. Boston, 1860)

In Boston, as in a number of other cities, children were supposed to learn to read in private dame schools before being admitted to the public schools. This produced friction and agitation, and, in 1817, a petition was presented to the Selectmen of Boston asking for the establishment of public primary schools. The matter was considered in town meeting, and referred to the School Committee, which in time reported adversely on the question.

This produced more agitation, many articles on the matter appeared in the newspapers, a new and larger petition was drawn up and presented, and, in 1818, the School Committee reversed itself and established the first primary schools in the city.

The report of the Committee, to whom the second petition was referred, and who recommended action, is interesting for the light it throws on primary education in Boston and in the State at that time. It reads:

The Committee appointed at the Town meeting on the 25th of May, to consider the subject of the petition of a number of the inhabitants, for the establishment by the town of schools for children under seven years of age, having attentively considered the same, ask leave respectfully to report.

That, in their opinion, the opening for such schools for children under the age of seven years, is highly expedient and necessary; that several hundred children of that age do not attend any school, because the Charity-Schools are, in most instances, provided only for *female* children, being under the inspection of ladies, their founders; and the private schools are so expensive that many parents find it difficult to defray that expense; that the examination of the circumstances of the several parts of the town in this respect, made last July, presented a return by which it was found that two hundred and eighty-three, between the ages of four and seven years, did not attend any school; but from inquiry of some of the gentlemen who made the returns, the Committee are satisfied that many children of that age were omitted, their parents or guardians being unwilling to acknowledge that they were sent to no school. That the Committee, with greater confidence, recommend the adoption of such a course, because most of the towns in this Commonwealth provide schools for children four years old equally with others, and particularly is this adhered to in the large towns of Salem, Newburyport, and Portland; that the best mode of providing such schools, seems to them to be by the guidance and direction of three gentlemen from each ward, of sufficient activity, firmness, discretion and energy, to be nominated by the School Committee.

314. The Boston School System in 1823

(Selected from *The System of Education pursued at the Free Schools in Boston*, 56 pp. Boston, 1823)

The following description of the primary schools of Boston, in 1823, gives a good picture of the type of elementary education provided in one of the leading American cities of the time.

(*a*) *The Primary Schools.* The basis of free education in Boston is laid in the *Primary Schools*, kept by women the year round, for instructing, at the public expense, all children, of either sex, between four and seven years of age, who may be duly sent to them. . . .

The object of these schools is to teach children to spell and read well, and thereby to prepare them so thoroughly for admission to the free reading and writing schools, which they are permitted to enter at seven, that the character and rank of these schools may be gradually raised, and thus the whole system of public instruction in the city improved from its foundations. Their number is so considerable, both because it is found that more than fifty or sixty children of this age cannot be well managed by one person, and because it is expedient to have such schools as near as possible to the homes of their pupils, who, at so tender an age, could not conveniently go far, under the most favorable circumstances, and would necessarily be prevented from attendance in bad weather. It is, in short, their object to bring the first rudiments of knowledge so near to the doors of those who need it, and make instruction in them so thorough, that all who are not determined to keep their children in ignorance, shall have no excuse for neglecting to begin the work of their education so soon and so well, as to have it afterwards successfully accomplished in the higher free schools of the city. . . .

(b) *The old Writing Schools.* It has already been stated that the object of the primary schools is to qualify children for entering the English Grammar Schools, to which they are admissible at seven years of age. By the laws of the Commonwealth it is required, that "no youth shall be sent to such Grammar Schools, unless they shall have learned in some other school, or in some other way, to read the English language, *by spelling the same.*" The laws likewise provide for the establishment of preparatory schools where grammar is not taught, but for many years, previous to the establishment of the primary schools, there were no public schools of this description in Boston, and children, without much regard to age or qualifications, were received into what should have been grammar schools. Writing, reading, and arithmetic were taught in one room, by the same master, who, being selected for his skill in writing, was usually incompetent to teach any thing else. Grammar was not attempted, and the only reading book was the Bible. No provision was made for the education of females at the public expense; although in the other towns no such distinction was made. At the close of the last century, an unusual interest was excited on the subject of education, and several important changes were effected in the schools; which, as no material alterations in the system have since taken place, will be understood by a description of the present state of the schools.

(c) *The reformed school plan.* These schools are separated into two rooms, the upper being occupied for the reading, and the lower for the writing department, the two branches being kept entirely distinct.

Each room is provided with a master and assistant, and is calculated to accommodate about 300 children. From the middle of April till the middle of October, the girls are permitted to attend these schools; half the day being spent in the reading, and half in the writing room, the boys changing in like manner to accommodate them. It being supposed that females would not attend during the inclement season, they are excluded from October to April, when the boys are divided between the two rooms, the highest and lowest classes being separated from the two intermediate ones. As writing and arithmetic only are taught at the writing schools, the masters are selected with special reference to their qualifications in these branches; but the law requires that the master of the grammar or reading school, shall have been "educated at some college or university, and be a citizen of the United States by birth or naturalization."

(d) *The Reading Schools.* The reading schools are subdivided into four classes, of which the first is the highest. The two upper classes are under the care of the master, and the two lower under his assistant; but they are overlooked and frequently examined by the master. These are generally the most numerous, and attend to nothing but reading and spelling. The second class commit the grammar to memory, and the first apply it to practice; in some schools the second class are sufficiently advanced to do this. Geography is taught only to the highest class, but as the schools are not furnished with any apparatus, less is effected in this study than might be with more facilities. The most promising children are from time to time advanced, and finally reach the first class; from which there is annually made a selection of the best boys, who are transferred to the English Classical, or to the Latin Grammar School to perfect what they have already begun, and to pursue more advanced studies.

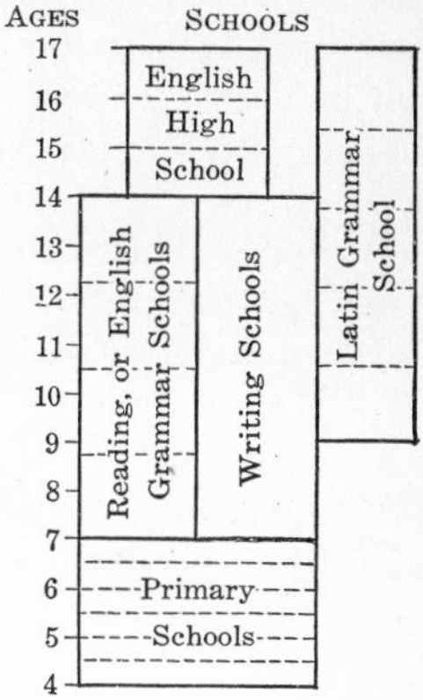

FIG. 80. THE BOSTON SCHOOL SYSTEM IN 1823

(e) *The Writing Schools.* In the writing school the exercises are few and simple. The master and his assistant usually set the copies and make the pens at home, or at school out of school hours. In a few minutes after the school commences, the classes in arithmetic, which consist of about one third of the school, begin to write. The scholars bring out their writing books, and present their exercise for examination, and themselves for instruction two or three times before their exercise is completed. If the exercise be not satisfactory when finished, another is required, and so on till one is accepted. After the arithmeticians have done writing, which is generally about an hour from the opening of the school, their books are closed, and the residue of their time is devoted to arithmetic. While the two first classes are thus employed in writing, the teachers are engaged in examining their exercises, mending their pens, or hearing the boys, *who do not cipher*, repeat the tables and rules in arithmetic. For as soon as the upper classes begin to write, the lower classes are taken out to commit to memory such tables and rules in arithmetic as are proper to prepare them for that study. These take their turn at writing when the upper classes have done. Thus all have employment for the whole of school hours. Some use of the system of mutual instruction is also made in the writing schools. On the first Tuesday of each month it is customary for the scholars to take places according to merit. The first scholar has the privilege of choosing a seat for the month, and likewise of selecting two or more *young scholars* to sit near, whose studies he overlooks, and for whose improvement and good conduct in school he is responsible. The next scholar does the same, and so on, as far as they are qualified to teach others. When we consider how many children are under the care of each master, we are naturally led to fear that but little attention can be shown to each individually, and consequently little progress made; but the greater number of distinguished citizens, who have received no other education than our public schools afforded, is the best proof of their utility.

. . . .

The number of children varies in the different schools, but by the returns made to the Committee, in July, 1823, the average number of boys in each school exceeded two hundred, and the girls one hundred and seventy. The salary of the master is twelve hundred dollars, and that of the assistant six hundred; making the expense of tuition alone, about nine dollars a year for each child.

For the continuation of this description, as it related to the secondary schools, see **R. 327.**

315. Report of the Working-Men's Committee of Philadelphia

(*Working-Man's Advocate*, of New York, March 6, 1830. Copied from the *Mechanics' Free Press*, of Philadelphia)

This committee, appointed by the working-men to consider the Pennsylvania situation, after nearly five months' investigation and deliberation, made a long report on the matter. After three evenings spent in considering the Report, it was adopted, February 11, 1830. This Report is typical of many similar documents of the period from 1828 to 1840. The reasoning of the latter part of the Report as to the need for free schools in a republic is thoroughly typical of the reasoning in many other similar documents of this period. Pertinent extracts from the Report hold:

With the exception of this city and county, the city and incorporated borough of Lancaster, and the city of Pittsburg, erected into "school districts" since 1818, it appears that the entire state is destitute of any provisions for public instruction, except those furnished by the enactment of 1809. This law requires the assessors of the several counties to ascertain and return the number of children whose parents are unable, through poverty, to educate them; and such children are permitted to be instructed at the most convenient schools at the expense of their respective counties.

The provisions of this act, however, are incomplete and frequently inoperative. They are, in some instances, but partially executed; in others, perverted and abused — and in many cases entirely and culpably neglected. The funds appropriated by the act, have, in some instances, been embezzled by fraudulent agents; and in others, partial returns of the children have been made, and some have been illegally and intentionally excluded from participating in the provisions of the law. From a parsimonious desire of saving the county funds, the cheapest, and consequently the most inefficient schools have been usually selected by the commissioners of the several counties.

The elementary schools throughout the state are irresponsible institutions, established by individuals, from mere motives of private speculation or gain, who are sometimes destitute of character, and frequently, of the requisite attainments and abilities. From the circumstance of the schools being the absolute property of individuals, no supervision or effectual control can be exercised over them; hence, ignorance, inattention, and even immorality, prevail to a lamentable extent among their teachers.

. . . .

But the principles on which these "school districts" are founded, are yet, in the opinion of the committees, extremely defective and inefficient. Their leading feature is pauperism! They are confined, exclusively, to the children of the poor, while there are, perhaps, thousands of children whose parents are unable to afford for them, a good private education, yet whose standing, professions or connexions in society effectually exclude them from taking the benefit of a poor law. There are great numbers, even of the poorest parents, who hold a dependence on the public bounty to be incompatible with the rights and liberties of an American citizen, and whose deep and cherished consciousness of independence determines them rather to starve the intellect of their offspring, than submit to become the objects of public charity.

. . . .

Another radical and glaring defect in the existing public school system is the very limited amount of instruction it affords, even to the comparatively small number of youth, who enjoy its benefits. It extends, in no case, further than a tolerable proficiency in reading, writing, and arithmetic, and sometimes to a slight acquaintance with geography. Besides these, the girls are taught a few simple branches of industry. A great proportion of scholars, however, from the causes already enumerated, acquire but a very slight and partial knowledge of these branches.

. . . .

The original element of despotism is a monopoly of talent, which consigns the multitude to comparative ignorance, and secures the balance of knowledge on the side of the rich and the rulers. If then the healthy existence of a free government be, as the committee believe, rooted in the will of the American people, it follows as a necessary consequence, of a government based upon that will, that this monopoly should be broken up, and that the means of equal knowledge (the only security for equal liberty) should be rendered, by legal provision, the common property of all classes.

In a republic, the people constitute the government, and by wielding its powers in accordance with the dictates, either of their intelligence or their ignorance, of their judgment or their caprices, are the makers and the rulers of their own good or evil destiny. They frame the laws and create the institutions, that promote their happiness or produce their destruction. If they be wise and intelligent, no laws but what are just and equal will receive their approbation, or be sustained by their suffrages. If they be ignorant and capricious, they will be deceived by mistaken or designing rulers, into the support of laws that are unequal and unjust.

It appears, therefore, to the committees that there can be no real liberty without a wide diffusion of real intelligence; that the members of a republic should all be alike instructed in the nature and character of their equal rights and duties, as human beings, and as citizens; and that education, instead of being limited as in our public poor schools, to a simple acquaintance with words and cyphers, should tend, as far as possible, to the production of a just disposition, virtuous habits, and a rational self-governing character.

CHAPTER XXVI
THE AMERICAN BATTLE FOR FREE STATE SCHOOLS

THE Readings of this chapter deal with the struggle that took place in the American States east of the Mississippi River and north of the Ohio and Potomac Rivers, between about 1820 and 1850, and which resulted there in the creation of state school systems. The strategical points in this American struggle were the battles for tax support, for the elimination of the pauper-school idea and of the rate-bill, the prohibition of support for sectarian schools, the establishment of the American high school, and the addition of the state university to crown the educational ladder created.

The first Reading (316), from one of Horace Mann's famous Annual Reports, states well the necessary financial basis for school support. After schools had been established they frequently experienced many difficulties, and Readings 317 and 318 illustrate such. The two relate to the repeal of the Connecticut School Law and the abolition of the State Board of Education and its Secretary, after these had been provided for by the State. The next selection (319) also illustrates the kind of controversies frequently aroused by the free-school proposal, and shows how important it often was to allow the opposition to talk itself out, before progress could be made in establishing schools.

Reading 320 is typical of many "Addresses" made to the people of the States urging legislative action, this one being an eloquent and convincing appeal for the abolition of the pauper-school idea in New Jersey. The following Reading (321) is a reproduction of a typical "rate-bill," with a warrant for its collection.

The next three Readings are illustrative of the controversy over the elimination of sectarian instruction from the schools. The first (322) is a clear statement, by Horace Mann, of the fundamental principles involved in the question, he being one of the earliest schoolmen to have to meet the religious issue publicly. The two following (323, 324) are illustrative of the petitions and counter-petitions to legislatures for and against a division of the school funds of the different States, once these had been created. This question was finally settled by the general adoption of state constitutional amendments, between 1842 and 1885, which forbade any diversion of the state school funds to the support of sectarian schools.

The next half-dozen Readings relate to the early struggle to establish the American high school as an integral part of our state school systems. The first (325) gives the Act of Incorporation of one of the precursors of the high school — the American Academy. The second (326) describes the founding of the first American high school at Boston, in 1821. The third (327) describes the secondary schools of Boston, as they were in 1823, and is a continuation of Reading 314. In 1827 Massachusetts enacted the first general state law providing for and requiring high schools, and this is reproduced in Reading 328. Many, probably most, of the early high schools met with bitter local opposition, and Reading 329 gives an example of such in Norwich, Connecticut. In a number of States the establishment of the high school as a part of the common-school system was contested in the courts, and one of the most comprehensive and complete of the supreme court decisions rendered on this subject came in Michigan, in what is known as the Kalamazoo case. In Reading 330 the most important portions of this decision are reproduced.

The last two Readings relate to the completed state school system, 331 describing the instruction, in 1843–44, in one of the earliest of our state universities to get under way; and 332 describing the state system as completed, by 1855, in an important Western State.

316. The Ground of the Free-School System

(Mann, Horace, *Tenth Annual Report* as Secretary of the Massachusetts State Board of Education. Boston, 1846)

Horace Mann (1796–1859) was the great leader in the Common-School Revival in New England in the middle of the nineteenth century. The Massachusetts State Board of Education was created in 1837, and he was elected its first Secretary. This office he held until 1848. In each of his Annual Reports he discussed some topic of importance. In the one for 1846 he took up the basis of the free-school system, and the following extract is typical of his reasoning.

The Pilgrim Fathers, amid all their privations and dangers, conceived the magnificent idea, not only of a universal, but of a free education for the whole people. To find the time and the means to reduce this grand conception to practice, they stinted themselves, amid all their poverty, to a still scantier pittance; amid all their toils, they imposed upon themselves still more burdensome labors; and, amid all their perils, they braved still greater dangers. Two divine ideas filled their great hearts — their duty to God and to posterity. For the one they built the church, for the other they opened the school. Religion and knowledge — two attributes of the same glorious and eternal truth, and that truth the only one on which immortal or mortal happiness can be securely founded!

It is impossible for us adequately to conceive the boldness of the measure which aimed at universal education through the establishment of free schools. As a fact, it had no precedent in the world's history; and, as a theory, it could have been refuted and silenced by a more formidable array of argument and experience than was ever marshalled against any other institution of human origin. But time has ratified its soundness. Two centuries of successful operation now proclaim it to be as wise as it was courageous, and as beneficent as it was disinterested. Every community in the civilized world awards it the meed of praise; and states at home and nations abroad, in the order of their intelligence, are copying the bright example. What we call the enlightened nations of Christendom are approaching, by slow degrees, to the moral elevation which our ancestors reached at a single bound. . . .

. . . .

In later times, and since the achievement of American independence, the universal and ever-repeated argument in favor of free schools has been that the general intelligence which they are capable of diffusing, and which can be imparted by no other human instrumentality, is indispensable to the continuance of a republican government. This argument, it is obvious, assumes, as a *postulatum*, the superiority of a republican over all other forms of government; and, as a people, we religiously believe in the soundness both of the assumption and of the argument founded upon it. But, if this be all, then a sincere monarchist, or a defender of arbitrary power, or a believer in the divine right of kings, would oppose free schools for the identical reasons we offer in their behalf. . . .

Again, the expediency of free schools is sometimes advocated on grounds of political economy. An educated people is always a more industrious and productive people. Intelligence is a primary ingredient in the wealth of nations. . . . The moralist, too, takes up the argument of the economist. He demonstrates that vice and crime are not only prodigals and spendthrifts of their own, but defrauders and plunderers of the means of others, that they would seize upon all the gains of honest industry and exhaust the bounties of Heaven itself without satiating their rapacity; and that often in the history of the world whole generations might have been trained to industry and virtue by the wealth which one enemy to his race has destroyed.

And yet, notwithstanding these views have been presented a thousand times with irrefutable logic, and with a divine eloquence of truth which it would seem that nothing but combined stolidity and depravity could resist, there is not at the present time [1846], with the exception of the States of New England and a few small communities elsewhere, a country or a state in Christendom which maintains a system of free schools for the education of its children. . . .

I believe that this amazing dereliction from duty, especially in our own country, originates more in the false notions which men entertain *respecting the nature of their right to property* than in anything else.   In the district school meeting, in the town meeting, in legislative halls, everywhere, the advocates for a more generous education could carry their respective audiences with them in behalf of increased privileges for our children, were it not instinctively foreseen that increased privileges must be followed by increased taxation.   Against this obstacle, argument falls dead.   The rich man who has no children declares that the exaction of a contribution from him to educate the children of his neighbor is an invasion of his rights of property.   The man who has reared and educated a family of children denounces it as a double tax when he is called upon to assist in educating the children of others also; or, if he has reared his own children without educating them, he thinks it peculiarly oppressive to be obliged to do for others what he refrained from doing even for himself.   Another, having children, but disdaining to educate them with the common mass, withdraws them from the public school, puts them under what he calls "selecter influences," and then thinks it a grievance to be obliged to support a school which he contemns.   Or, if these different parties so far yield to the force of traditionary sentiment and usage, and to the public opinion around them, as to consent to do something for the cause, they soon reach the limit of expense at which their admitted obligation or their alleged charity terminates.

It seems not irrelevant, therefore, in this connection, and for the purpose of strengthening the foundation on which our free-school system reposes, to inquire into the nature of a man's right to the property he possesses, and to satisfy ourselves respecting the question whether any man has such an indefeasible title to his estates or such an absolute ownership of them as renders it unjust in the government to assess upon him his share of the expenses of educating the children of the community up to such a point as the nature of the institutions under which he lives, and the well-being of society, require.

.   .   .   .

I bring my argument on this point, then, to a close; and I present a test of its validity, which, as it seems to me, defies denial or evasion.

In obedience to the laws of God and to the laws of all civilized communities, society is bound to protect the natural life of children; and this natural life cannot be protected without the appropriation and use of a portion of the property which society possesses. We prohibit infanticide under penalty of death. We practice a refinement in this particular. The life of an infant is inviolable, even before he is born; and he who feloniously takes it, even before birth, is as subject to the extreme penalty of the law as though he had struck down manhood in its vigor, or taken away a mother by violence from the sanctuary of home where she blesses her offspring. But why preserve the natural life of a child, why preserve unborn embryos of life, if we do not intend to watch over and to protect them, and to expand their subsequent existence into usefulness and happiness? As individuals, or as an organized community, we have no natural right, we can derive no authority or countenance from reason, we can cite no attribute or purpose of the divine nature, for giving birth to any human being, and then inflicting upon that being the curse of ignorance, of poverty, and of vice, with all their attendant calamities. We are brought, then, to this startling but inevitable alternative, — the natural life of an infant should be extinguished as soon as it is born, or the means should be provided to save that life from being a curse to its possessor; and, therefore, every State is morally bound to enact a code of laws legalizing and enforcing infanticide or a code of laws establishing free schools.

The three following propositions, then, describe the broad and everduring foundation on which the common-school system of Massachusetts reposes:

The successive generations of men, taken collectively, constitute one great commonwealth.

The property of this commonwealth is pledged for the education of all its youth, up to such a point as will save them from poverty and vice, and prepare them for the adequate performance of their social and civil duties.

The successive holders of this property are trustees, bound to the faithful execution of their trust by the most sacred obligations; and embezzlement and pillage from children and descendants have not less of criminality, and have more of meanness, than the same offences when perpetrated against contemporaries.

317. Repeal of the Connecticut School Law

(Message of Governor Cleveland to the Connecticut Legislature, in May, 1842. In Barnard's *American Journal of Education*, vol. i, p. 677)

In 1837 the first American State Board of Education was created by the Legislature of Massachusetts, and in 1838 the Legislature of Connecticut, under the inspiration of Henry Barnard, one of its members, created a similar board. Henry Barnard was appointed its first Secretary, and from 1838 to 1842 gave his best efforts to the creation of an educational sentiment and to the establishment and improvement of schools in Connecticut, for the munificent salary of $3.00 a day. What promised to be the beginning of a new era in education in that State was soon cut short by a succeeding Legislature, acting under the inspiration of a Governor opposed to the new ideas. In his message to the Connecticut Legislature, in May, 1842, Governor Cleveland said:

An opinion was advanced some years since, calling in question, to some extent, the beneficial influence of the School Fund, as it has been applied; and the Legislature, by way of experiment, established a Board of Commissioners of Common Schools; and, under the belief that some essential improvements might be made, an officer has been employed, at considerable expense, to visit the various schools in the State with reference to their improvement. As a part of the same plan, provision was subsequently made by law for paying the visitors of the district schools one dollar a day for their services. The reason for the imposition of this tax, which, when the number of districts and committee-men is considered, will appear to be a considerable sum, has never been apparent. From time immemorial, it has been deemed a part of the obligations which competent men owed to society, to attend to these duties; and no inconvenience had ever been experienced. Until the spirit of benevolence and good-will to men shall cease to burn in the hearts of our people, I anticipate no difficulty in following, in this respect, in the path of our fathers. Without questioning the motives of those by whom these experiments were suggested and adopted, I think it obvious, that the public expectations, in regard to their consequences, have not been realized; and that to continue them, will be only to entail upon the State a useless expense. In conformity with this opinion, and in obedience to what I believe to be the public sentiment, I recommend the repeal of these laws.

In addition the Governor successfully used his personal influence with the members of the Legislature, and secured the repeal of the law creating the Board, the abolition of the Union-Schools law, and other progressive legislation. The Union-Schools law was regarded as a "dangerous innovation," because it "created by law schools of a higher order."

318. Horace Mann on the Repeal of the Connecticut Law

(*Massachusetts Common School Journal*, 1846. Reproduced in Barnard's
American Journal of Education, vol. i, p. 719)

After commenting on the progress of education in Rhode Island, Vermont, New Hampshire, Maine, and Massachusetts, Mann has the following to say of Connecticut.

One only of the New England States proves recreant to duty in this glorious cause — the State of Connecticut. Favored for half a century, in the munificence of her endowments, beyond any of her New England sisters, she is the only one which, for the last few years, has not merely been stationary, but has absolutely retrograded; and now, if she promises to be useful at all, it is as a warning and not as an example. A common ancestry, an identity of general interests and pursuits, a similar position in regard to the other States of the Union, and a similar duty to furnish them with high example and encouragement, has led us all to expect that we should have, not only the sympathy, but the active coöperation, of Connecticut, in this common cause. We not only expected it, we *believed* it. Events seemed auspicious. The year after the Massachusetts Board of Education was established, an organization almost identical in its form, and entirely so in its object, was created in Connecticut. For carrying out its measures of reform and improvement, an agent was selected — Henry Barnard, Esquire — of whom it is not extravagant to say that, if a better man be required, we must wait, at least, until the next generation, for a better one is not to be found in the present. This agent entered upon his duties with unbounded zeal. He devoted to their discharge his time, talents, and means. The cold torpidity of the State soon felt the sensations of returning vitality. Its half-suspended animation began to quicken with a warmer life. Much and most valuable information was diffused. Many parents began to appreciate more adequately what it is to be a parent. Teachers were awakened. Associations for mutual improvement were formed. System began to supersede confusion. Some salutary laws were enacted. All things gave favorable augury of a prosperous career. And it may be further affirmed, that the cause was so administered as to give occasion of offence to no one. The whole movement was kept aloof from political strife. All religious men had reason to rejoice that a higher tone of religious and moral feeling was making its way into the schools, without giving occasion of jealousy to the one-sided views of any denomination. But all these auguries of good were delusive. In an evil hour the whole fabric was overthrown. The Educational Board was abolished. Of course, the office of its devoted and faithful Secretary fell with it. As if this were not enough, the remedial laws which had been enacted during the brief existence of the Board, and which might have continued and diffused their benefits without the Board, were spitefully repealed.

The whole educational movement in Connecticut, or rather, the body in which the vital movement had begun, was paralyzed by this stroke. Once or twice, since, it has attempted to rise, but has fallen back prostrate as before.

319. The Struggle for Free Schools in Norwich, Connecticut

(Address by the Reverend J. P. Gulliver, at the inauguration of the Norwich Free Academy. In *Annual Report of the Superintendent of Common Schools of Connecticut*, 1856)

The following selection is illustrative of the slow and patient struggle that had to be carried on by those favoring the establishment and improvement of schools, often allowing the opposition to talk itself out before any substantial progress in developing or improving schools could be made. What was true for Norwich was true for many other places, in the middle of the nineteenth century.

Movements were commenced about twenty years since, for a re-organization of the public schools of the Second School Society of Norwich. The usual opposition, originated by a few narrow-minded tax-payers, and fanned into life by ambitious demagogues, was arrayed against the measure, and it was finally defeated. The whole community had, however, been agitated with the subject, and much good seed had been sown, which has since borne beautiful fruit. For ten years the citizens of Norwich made the best they could of a set of disjointed schools, thrown together with scarcely any attempt at gradation, governed by six independent districts, and some forty school officers, and supported entirely without taxation. Good men labored hard; but almost in vain, to secure for the people, under the existing system, good schools.

An effort was then made, with still greater earnestness, to improve the schools, without any attempt at re-organization. They were regularly visited. A monthly meeting of the visitors was held, at which the condition of each school was minutely reported. Every possible effort was made to elevate the schools. The success was, however, but partial. After a trial of two years, the gentlemen, whose valuable time had been given to the effort, came unanimously to the conclusion that without a consolidation of at least the more central school districts, and the thorough grading of the schools, and the taxation of property for the support of schools, this labor would be thrown away. The board, accordingly laid before the school society a proposition for inaugurating such a change. This was the signal for a storm! A few (but only a few) of the heavy tax-payers were the first to smell treason. They passed the word to a set of men, who flourish in their own esteem, by exhibiting their powers in thwarting what others attempt to do. The usual cry was raised, "a school for the rich!" The prejudices of poor men were appealed to. This class, who were to be most benefited by the change, were excited to oppose it. Men who had been paying rate bills for years, clamored against the proposition to support schools by taxing property. Parents, who had bitterly complained that their children could not be as well educated as those of the wealthy, refused to accept a plan which was to bring the highest order of schools within their reach, at a mere nominal expense. The intelligent portion of the community were, however, thoroughly aroused. Meeting after meeting was held. Crowds attended and listened to the discussions. Light was rapidly diffused. The opposition became desperate. All manner of offensive personalities were made use of to intimidate those who were inclined to be champions of the good cause. Still, it was apparent, by incidental votes, that a large and an increasing majority were in favor of the proposed change. This majority, however, forbore to press the question to a decisive vote. They publicly avowed their intention to postpone final action, until the whole community should have fully examined the question, and arrived at an intelligent decision upon it.

This concession was taken advantage of. At an adjourned meeting where it was generally understood no decisive action was to take place, the opposition collected a large force, very many of whom were not legal voters, and, in the absence of the great body of the friends of the measure, voted the indefinite postponement of the whole subject. No sooner had this been accomplished than a general regret was expressed at the result, even among those who had boisterously aided in the movement. Many declared, that had they expected to succeed, they would not have opposed the measure. Their leaders, instead of receiving the coveted meed of applause from their followers, for the victory, were overwhelmed with reproaches. In these circumstances, the friends of reform judged it wise to cease all further agitation of the subject, and to leave the responsibility of the consequences upon those who had chosen to assume it. The administration of the schools was accordingly left in their hands. They appointed such officers as they chose, and no attempt was made in any form, for two years, to interfere with their wishes. During this time, the schools sunk to a lower level than ever. Even the most ignorant and prejudiced could not fail to see and feel the evil. The attendance constantly diminished, until it was ascertained that only about one-third of the children, between the ages of four and sixteen, attended school at all. The feeling of the community on the subject was becoming intense. The attention of the people having been so thoroughly aroused by previous discussion, every defect was seen as in a focal light.   Those who had been distinguished as the leaders in the effort to defeat the proposed reforms, found themselves in a most uncomfortable position.   They were daily reproached as the authors of all the mischief.

The first fruit of this ripened public sentiment, was a movement for the endowment of a free high school.   Every attempt to improve the lower schools had been met by the cry, "You want a high school!   You want a school for the rich, and mean to tax the poor to pay for it!" Some thirty-five individuals accordingly determined that they would unite and establish a high school and endow it, which should be open, free of all charge, to all classes.   This effort was successful, some eighty-five thousand dollars having been subscribed for that purpose.   It was generally understood that as soon as this subscription was complete, a new appeal was to be made to the school society to acknowledge this magnificent donation, by re-organizing their lower schools on the plan previously rejected.   Before this plan could be carried out, it was ascertained that the leaders in the former opposition were moving in the same direction, and were about to propose the same thing!   Most gladly the friends of reform left the business in their hands.   The result was, that a consolidation of the two central districts of the city was effected, a vote was passed, *unanimously*, to purchase one of the most valuable lots in the city, and to erect a noble structure three stories in height.   Soon after, the provisions of the new school law were accepted, a Board of Education was appointed, the ablest teachers were engaged at liberal salaries, a perfect gradation of schools established, and every provision made for the institution of the very best system of public education.

320. "The State and Education"

(An "Address to the People of New Jersey," adopted by the Convention assembled in Trenton, January 27 and 28, 1838)

Written by the Right Reverend George W. Doane, of the Protestant Episcopal Church, chairman of a committee of nine appointed to draft the "Address," by "the most notable convention of the friends of the common schools ever held in the State." This "Address" so aroused the people that a new law establishing a partial school system was secured, and six years later a new state constitution made provision for the creation of a non-pauper state school system.   Two important features of the Address attract attention, — the emphasis upon education for state ends, and the utter repudiation of the pauper-school idea which had characterized New Jersey education since 1830.

We were appointed by the convention of your own delegates to address you on the subject of common schools.   We approach you with solicitude, as deeply sensible of the great importance of the interest intrusted to us, yet, as freemen speaking to freemen, with prevailing confidence.

The points which we propose for your attention, and, if we might, would press into every heart, are few, simple, and practical; the necessary consequences, it seems to us, from principles which all admit. We say that knowledge is the universal right of man, and we need bring no clearer demonstration than that intellectual nature, capable of it, thirsting for it, expanding and aspiring with it, which is God's own argument in every living soul; we say that the assertion for himself of this inherent right, to the full measure of his abilities and opportunities, is the universal duty of man, and that whoever fails of it thwarts the design of his Creator, and, in proportion as he neglects the gift of God, dwarfs and enslaves and brutifies the high capacity for truth and liberty which he inherits. And all experience and every page of history confirm the assertion, in the close kindred which has everywhere been proved of ignorance and vice with wretchedness and slavery. And we say, further, that the security of this inherent right to every individual, and its extension, in the fullest measure, to the greatest number, is the universal interest of man; so that they who deny or abridge it to their fellows, or who encourage, or, from want of proper influence, permit them to neglect it, are undermining the foundations of government, weakening the hold of society, and preparing the way for that unsettling and dissolving of all human institutions which must result in anarchy and ruin, and in which they who have the greatest stake must be the greatest sufferers. . . .

If the truth of these positions be established their application is self-evident, and there never was a nation since the world was made in which their obligation was so clear or its application so important. In the theory of our Constitution the people are the governors. In practice they ought to be. And is ignorance the qualification for good government? Would you select a man to make your laws who can not read, or one who can not write to execute them? Yet the authority which they exercise and the abuses of which they are capable are nothing in comparison with theirs from whom all power proceeds, and without whose permission no wrong can be done. Fellow-citizens, we are republicans. Our country is our Commonwealth. We all have an equal share in her. Her laws are alike for the protection of all. Her institutions are alike for the advantage of all. Her blessings are our common privilege. Her glory is our common pride. But common privileges impose a common responsibility, and equal rights can never be disjoined from equal duties. The Constitution, which under God secures our liberties, is in the keeping of us all. It is a sacred trust which no man can delegate. He holds it for himself not only, but for his children, for posterity, and for the world, and he who can not read it, who does not understand its provisions, who could not on a just occasion assert its principles, no more sustains the character of an American citizen than the man who would not seal it with his blood.

It is in vain to say that education is a private matter, and that it is the duty of every parent to provide for the instruction of his own children. In theory it is so. But there are some who can not and there are more who will not make provision. And the question, then, is, Shall the State suffer from individual inability or from individual neglect? When the child who has not been trained up in the way in which he ought to go commits a crime against the State, the law, with iron hand, comes in between the parent and his offspring and takes charge of the offender. And shall there be provision to punish only and none to prevent? Shall the only offices in which this State is known be those of jailer or executioner? Shall she content herself with the stern attributes of justice and discard the gentler ministries of mercy? It was said of Draco's laws that they were writ with blood. Is it less true of any State which makes provision for the whipping post, the penitentiary, the scaffold, and leaves the education of her children to individual effort or precarious charity? . . .

If the positions be maintained that the education of the people is indispensable to the preservation of free institutions, and that it is therefore the duty of every free State to provide for the education of her children, we are prepared, fellow-citizens, for the inquiry, How far has provision been made for the discharge of this duty in the State with which we are most intimately connected, — the State of New Jersey? That the duty of making some provision for this end has long been recognized, the twenty-one years which have elapsed since the passage of the first act "to create a fund for the support of free schools" sufficiently attest. That what has been done is insufficient, you have yourselves borne witness. . . .

Omitting all considerations . . . of what has been or of what may be legislative enactments on the subject, we address you as the sovereign people, and we say that it is your duty and your highest interest to provide and to maintain, within the reach of every child, the means of such an education as will qualify him to discharge the duties of a citizen of the Republic, and will enable him, by subsequent exertion, in the free exercise of the unconquerable will, to attain the highest eminence in knowledge and in power which God may place within his reach. We utterly repudiate as unworthy, not of freemen only, but of men, the narrow notion that there is to be an education for the poor as such. Has God provided for the poor a coarser earth, a thinner air, a paler sky? Does not the glorious sun pour down his golden flood as cheerily upon the poor man's hovel as upon the rich man's palace? Have not the cotter's children as keen a sense of all the freshness, verdure, fragrance, melody, and beauty of luxuriant nature as the pale sons of kings? Or is it on the mind that God has stamped the imprint of a baser birth, so that the poor man's child knows with an inborn certainty that his lot is to crawl, not climb? It is not so. God has not done it. Men can not do it. Mind is immortal. Mind is imperial. It bears no mark of high or low, of rich or poor. It needs no bound of time or place, or rank or circumstance. It asks but freedom. It requires but light. It is heaven born, and it aspires to heaven. Weakness does not enfeeble it. Poverty can not repress it. Difficulties do but stimulate its vigor. And the poor tallow chandler's son that sits up all the night to read the book which an apprentice lends him, lest the master's eye should miss it in the morning, shall stand and treat with kings, shall add new provinces to the domain of science, shall bind the lightning with a hempen cord and bring it harmless from the skies. The common school is common, not as inferior, not as the school for poor men's children, but as the light and air are common. It ought to be the best school because it is the first school. . . .

Fellow-citizens, it is for you to say what shall be the present character, what shall be the future destiny of New Jersey. We have indeed a goodly heritage, but it has been long and shamefully neglected. We have undervalued our privileges. We have overlooked our duties. We have been content to be a pendent merely, when we ought to be an independent State. There is now, thank God, the sound as of a trumpet in the land that stirs the old heroic blood. We feel the remnant sparks of the forgotten fire which warmed our fathers' hearts. The spirit of the elder day is breathing on us with its quickening and invigorating power. Let us accept the omen. Let us obey the noble impulse. Let us arise to duty and to glory. Men of New Jersey, it is you that are to rise. You are the State. You create and you control the legislature. You enact and you sustain the laws. Yours are the means. Yours is the influence. Yours is the work. You make, you are the State. Go on as you have now begun. The system of common schools which shall be adopted by the present legislature, take it into your own hands. If it is not what it should be, see that the next legislature make it such. Act together. Act with system. Act like men. The organization for the purpose is complete. The general committee, the committees of correspondence for the counties, the committees of the townships — there is not an inch of ground that is not reached; there is not a citizen of New Jersey whose heart may not be roused by this electric chain.

321. A Rate-Bill and a Warrant for Collection

(Gregory, J. M., *School Funds and School Laws of Michigan*, 1859, pp. 290–93)

The following forms were used in Michigan, and these may be considered as typical of all the New England States and of the

States to the westward to which New England people emigrated. That the collection of these small amounts was exceedingly vexatious must be evident.

Form of Rate-Bill and Warrant

Rate-Bill containing the name of each person liable for teachers' wages in District No......., in the township of........., for the term ending on......day of........, A.D. 18.., and the amount for which each person not exempted from the payment thereof is so liable, with the fees of the assessor thereon.

Names of inhabitants sending to school	Whole number of days sent	Amount of school bill	Assessor's fees thereon	Amount for fuel	Whole amount to be raised
James Emerson......	104	$1.04	$.05	*	$1.09
John L. Barney......	416	4.16	.21	$1.25	5.62
William Jones........	313	3.13	.16	*	3.29
Peter Parley........	54	.54	.03	*	.57
S. C. Goodrich.......	104	1.04	.05	.50	1.59
M. Barney..........	104	1.04	.05	*	1.09
F. Sawyer..........	416	4.16	.21	*	4.37

* Exemption from fuel bill because fuel was furnished to school.

Warrant

You are hereby commanded to collect from each of the persons in the annexed rate-bill named, the several sums set opposite their respective names in the last column thereof, and within sixty days after receiving this warrant, to pay over the amount so collected by you (retaining five percent for your fees) to the order of the Director of said District, countersigned by the Moderator; and in case any person named therein, shall neglect or refuse, on demand, to pay the amount set opposite his name as aforesaid, you are to collect the same by distress and sale of goods and chattels of such persons wherever found, within the county or counties in which said District is situated, having first published such sale at least ten days, by posting up notices thereof in three public places in the townships where such property shall be sold.

At the expiration of this warrant, you will make a return thereof in writing, with the rate-bill attached, to the Director; stating the amount collected on said rate-bill, the amount uncollected, and the names of the persons from whom collections have not been made.

Given under our hands this..... day of ...., in the year of our Lord, one thousand eight hundred and ......

A. B., Director
C. D., Moderator.

322. Horace Mann on Religious Instruction in the Schools

(Mann, Horace, *Sequel to the so-called Correspondence between the Rev. M. H. Smith and Horace Mann.* Boston, 1847)

In 1846 a Reverend Mr. Smith attacked the Massachusetts State Board of Education and its Secretary, Mr. Mann, in a sermon entitled "The Ark of God on a New Cart." In this sermon he claimed that the increase in crime and immorality was due to the "Godless schools," sponsored by Mr. Mann and the State Board. Mr. Mann and the Reverend Mr. Smith exchanged two letters each on the question, and then Smith published the sermon and the correspondence in a book entitled *The Bible, the Rod, and Religion in Common Schools*. To this Mann published a *Sequel*, etc., of fifty-six pages, in which he judiciously examined the question at issue. He said he stood firmly for the reading of the Bible in the schools, but without comment; examined the matter in its different aspects; and in the concluding portion of the pamphlet said:

It is easy to see that the experiment would not stop with having half a dozen conflicting creeds taught by authority of law in the different schools of the same town or vicinity. Majorities will change in the same place. One sect may have the ascendency to-day; another to-morrow. This year there will be three Persons in the Godhead; next year but one; and the third year the Trinity will be restored to hold its precarious sovereignty until it shall be again dethroned by the worms of the dust it has made. This year, the everlasting fires of hell will burn to terrify the impenitent; next year, and without any repentance, its eternal flames will be extinguished, to be rekindled forever, or to be quenched forever as it may be decided at annual town meetings. This year, under Congregational rule, the Rev. Mr. So and So and the Rev. Dr. So and So will be on the committee; but next year these reverends and reverend doctors will be plain misters, never having had apostolic consecration from the bishop. This year the ordinance of baptism is inefficacious without immersion; next year one drop of water will be as good as forty fathoms. Children attending the district school will be taught one way; going from the district school to the high school they will be taught another way. In controversies involving such momentous interests, the fiercest party spirit will rage, and all the contemplations of heaven be poisoned by the passions of earth. Will not town lines and school district lines be altered, to restore an unsuccessful or to defeat a successful party? Will not fiery zealots move from place to place, to turn the theological scale, as it is said is sometimes now done to turn a political one? And will not the godless make a merchandise of religion by being bribed to do the same thing? Can aught be conceived more deplorable, more fatal to the interests of the young than this? Such strifes and persecutions on the question of total depravity as to make all men depraved at any rate; and such contests about the nature and the number of persons in the Godhead in heaven, as to make little children atheists on earth.

If the question, "What theology shall be taught in school?" is to be decided by districts or towns, then all the prudential and the superintending school committees must be chosen with express reference to their faith; the creed of every candidate for teaching must be investigated; and when litigations arise — and such a system will breed them in swarms — an ecclesiastical tribunal, some star chamber, or high commission court must be created to decide them. If the governor is to have power to appoint the judges of this spiritual tribunal, he also must be chosen with reference to the appointments he will make, and so, too, must the legislators who are to define their power, and to give them the purse and sword of the State, to execute their authority. Call such officers by the name of judge and governor, or cardinal and pope, the thing will be the same. The establishment of the true faith will not stop with the schoolroom. Its grasping jurisdiction will extend over all schools, over all private faith and public worship, until at last, after all our centuries of struggle and of suffering, it will come back to the inquisition, the faggot, and the rack.

Let me ask here, too, where is the consistency of those who advocate the right of a town or a district to determine, by a majority, what theology shall be taught in the schools, but deny the same right to the State? Does not this inconsistency blaze out into the faces of such advocates so as to make them feel, if they are too blind to see? This would be true, even if the State had written out the theology it would enforce. But ours has not. It has only said that no one sect shall obtain any advantage over other sects by means of the school system, which, for purposes of self-preservation, it has established.

323. Petition for a Division of the School Funds

(*Report of the Superintendent of Public Instruction for Michigan*, 1853, pp. 190–91)

The following petition to the Legislature of Michigan, in 1853, by the Catholics of Detroit, is typical of petitions of the time to Legislatures in other States. This petition contains an interesting sectarian definition of free schools and liberty in instruction. It was met with a counter-petition from the Protestant Episcopal Bishop for the Diocese of Michigan (**R. 324**), and the matter was threshed out before the Legislature. Committees of both the Senate and the House made reports opposing division, and the Legislature took no further action on the request.

Memorial to the Legislature relative to a division of the School Fund

We, the undersigned, citizens of Michigan, respectfully represent to your Honorable Body, that we have labored, and are still laboring under grievances to which neither Justice nor Patriotism require longer submission on our part, without an effort for their removal.

We, your petitioners, wish to represent to your Honorable Body, that notwithstanding the Constitution guarantees liberty of conscience to every citizen of the State, yet our Public School laws compel us to violate our conscience, or deprive us unjustly of our share of the Public School Funds, and also impose on us taxes for the support of schools, which, as a matter of conscience, we cannot allow our children to attend.

To convince your Honorable Body of the magnitude of these grievances, we have but to refer you to the fact, that in the cities of Monroe and Detroit alone, there are educated at the expense of their parents, and charitable contributions, some 2500 of our children. Your petitioners might bear longer their present grievances, hoping that our fellow-citizens would soon discover the injustice done to us by the present School laws, and that the love of public justice for which they are distinguished, would prompt them to protest against laws which are self-evidently a violation of liberty of conscience, a liberty which is equally dear to every American citizen; but, as the new Constitution requires that free schools be established in every district of our State, and as the present Legislature will be called upon to act upon the subject, your petitioners consider that their duty to themselves, their duty to their children, and their duty to their country, the liberties of which they are morally and religiously bound to defend, as well as their duty to their God, require that they apprise your Honorable Body of the oppressive nature of our present School laws, the injustice of which is equalled only by the laws of England, which compel the people of all denominations to support a church, the doctrines of which they do not believe.

Your petitioners would not wish to be understood as being opposed to education; on the contrary they are prepared to bear every reasonable burden your Honorable Body are willing to impose on them, to promote the cause of education, providing that our schools be free indeed. But they do not consider schools free when the law imposes on parents the necessity of giving their children such an education as their conscience cannot approve of. But that your Honorable Body may not be ignorant of what they understand by free schools, your petitioners wish to say that in their opinions, schools can be free only, when the business of school teaching be placed on the same legal footing as the other learned professions, when all may teach who will, their success depending, as in other cases, on their fitness for their profession, and the satisfaction that they may render to the public; that in all cases the parent be left free to choose the teacher to whom he will entrust the education of his child, as he is left to choose his physician, his lawyer, etc.; that each person teaching any public school in the State should be entitled to draw from the public school fund, such sums as the law might provide for every child so taught by the month, quarter, or otherwise, on producing such evidence as the law might require in such cases. Schools established on such principles are what your petitioners understand by free schools.

Your petitioners, therefore, respectfully urge that the public school system for our State, be based on these broad democratic principles of equal liberty to all, allowing freedom of conscience to the child, who also has a conscience, as well as to the instructor and parent. And your petitioners will ever pray.

324. Counter-Petition against Division

(*Report of the Superintendent of Public Instruction for Michigan*, 1853, p. 205)

To the preceding petition for a division of the school funds, Samuel A. McCoskry, Bishop of the Protestant Episcopal Church in the Diocese of Michigan, entered the following counter-petition:

The undersigned is the Bishop of the Protestant Episcopal Church in the Diocese of Michigan: He has learned from the public newspapers, and from petitions about to be presented to your honorable bodies, that an application is to be made for a division of the school fund of this State, so that "in all cases the parent be left free to choose the teacher to whom he will entrust the education of his child." Such application (if granted) he considers as giving the right not only to parents, but to every religious body, to select teachers who will teach the peculiarities of the religious views of opinions they may hold. It will place the school fund of this State in the hands of religious bodies or sects, and entrust to them the education of the children of the State; for the right, if given to one, will be claimed by each and all. Whatever opinion the writer may entertain in reference to the system and effects of the common-school education, he begs leave to say, that he has no wish or desire to interfere with, or in any way alter, or abridge the system which has been the pride of the State, and which has furnished to so many thousands of her children the means of obtaining a high secular education; nor does he wish that the fund so generously granted to the people of the State, and so carefully guarded by her Legislature, and so highly prized by her citizens, should be used for the promotion of sectarian strife and bitterness.

It is one of the distinguishing features of our free institutions, and which lies at the foundation of happiness and freedom of the people, that neither religious tests nor religious preferences form any part of our legislation. All religious bodies are placed on precisely the same footing, and whatever may be the exclusive claims of each and all, they can be settled only by an appeal to a higher and different authority than State legislatures. But if your honorable bodies see fit to over-turn and destroy that system which has been heretofore so carefully guarded, and which has introduced into every occupation and profession, some of the most distinguished men of the State, and which has brought to the door of the poor man the means of educating his children; and if the Priests and Clergymen of every religious body are to take the place of the common-school teacher, and the State is to assume the duty, through them, of extending and building up religious differences, and of fomenting strife and contention, then, the undersigned (most reluctantly) would claim to have a share in this work. If then such a change is to be made in our common-school law, so as to allow parents to choose teachers for their children, the undersigned would respectfully ask for his proportion of the common-school fund, so that the people entrusted to his spiritual oversight may employ such teachers as will fully carry out their religious preferences. He would freely and frankly state to your honorable bodies that the amount thus granted, shall be carefully used in teaching the principles and doctrines of the Protestant Episcopal Church, and that the services of as many clergymen and laymen of the Church will be secured and used, so that no other principles and doctrines shall find any place in the different schools.

Detroit, January 19th, 1853.

325. Act of Incorporation of the Norwich Free Academy

(Laws of Connecticut, 1854)

The following is typical of many acts incorporating free academies in towns and cities. A body of citizens was constituted the "corporation," with power to establish and conduct the school. Some of these school corporations still exist, though most of them have been turned over to the towns or cities and merged with or become the public high schools.

Act of Incorporation

Upon the petition of Russell Hubbard and others of Norwich, county of New London, praying for an act of incorporation for a free Academy, in said town of Norwich, as per petition on file, dated May 5th, 1854:

Resolved by this Assembly, That Russell Hubbard, (35 others here named) and their successors, be, and they hereby are constituted a body corporate and politic, by the name of "The Norwich Free Academy," and by that name shall have perpetual succession, and be capable in law to purchase, receive, hold and convey all kinds of property requisite and convenient for the purposes of a school; to sue and to be sued; defend and be defended, in all courts and places whatsoever; may have a common seal, and change and alter the same at their discretion; appoint proper officers and agents; elect residents of said town of Norwich, to fill the vacancies occurring in their number by death, resignation, or removal from said town, so that hereafter the number of said corporators shall be maintained at twenty-five, when from any of these causes it shall be reduced below that number; and make such regulations, rules and by-laws, as they shall deem expedient, to carry out the objects of the corporation, not inconsistent with the laws of this State or of the United States.

Provided always, that this resolve may be altered, amended, or repealed by the General Assembly.

326. The Establishment of the First American High School

(Report of the School Committee to the Town Meeting of Boston, January, 1821)

In 1818 Boston had extended its school system downward to include Primary Schools, and in 1820 steps were taken to extend it upward for those not destined for the Latin Grammar School and College. In October, 1820, the School Committee voted "that it is expedient to establish an English Classical School in the Town of Boston." The matter was submitted to a town meeting in January, 1821, in the form of the Report which follows, and by an almost unanimous vote the School Committee was instructed to establish the school. The school opened in May, 1821, as the *English Classical School*, and in 1824 the name was changed to that of the *English High School*. The report, as adopted, reads:

Fig. 81. The First High School in the United States

Established in Boston in 1821.

Though the present system of public education, and the munificence with which it is supported, are highly beneficial and honorable to the town; yet, in the opinion of the Committee, it is susceptible of a greater degree of perfection and usefulness, without materially augmenting the weight of the public burdens. Till recently, our system occupied a middle station: it neither commenced with the rudiments of Education, nor extended to the higher branches of knowledge. This system was supported by the Town at a very great expense, and to be admitted to its advantages, certain preliminary qualifications were required at individual cost, which have the effect of excluding many children of the poor and unfortunate classes of the community from the benefits of a public education. The Town saw and felt this inconsistency in the plan, and have removed the defect by providing Schools (Primary) in which the children of the poor can be fitted for admission into the public seminaries.

The present system, in the opinion of the Committee, requires still further amendment. The studies that are pursued at the English grammar schools are merely elementary, and more time than is necessary is devoted to their acquisition. A scholar is admitted at seven, and is dismissed at fourteen years of age; thus, seven years are expended in the acquisition of a degree of knowledge, which with ordinary diligence and a common capacity, may be easily and perfectly acquired in five. If then, a boy remain the usual term, a large portion of the time will have been idly or uselessly expended, as he may have learned all that he may have been taught long before its expiration. This loss of time occurs at that interesting and critical period of life, when the habits and inclinations are forming by which the future character will be fixed and determined. This evil, therefore, should be removed, by enlarging the present system, not merely that the time now lost may be saved, but that those early habits of industry and application may be acquired, which are so essential in leading to a future life of virtue and usefulness.

Nor are these the only existing evils. The mode of education now adopted, and the branches of knowledge that are taught at our English grammar schools, are not sufficiently extensive nor otherwise calculated to bring the powers of the mind into operation nor to qualify a youth to fill usefully and respectably many of those stations, both public and private, in which he may be placed. A parent who wishes to give a child an education that shall fit him for active life, and shall serve as a foundation for eminence in his profession, whether Mercantile or Mechanical, is under the necessity of giving him a different education from any which our public schools can now furnish. Hence, many children are separated from their parents and sent to private academies in this vicinity, to acquire that instruction which cannot be obtained at the public seminaries. Thus, many parents, who contribute largely to the support of these institutions, are subjected to heavy expense for the same object, in other towns.

The Committee, for these and many other weighty considerations that might be offered, and in order to render the present system of public education more nearly perfect, are of the opinion that an additional School is required.   They therefore recommend the founding of a seminary which shall be called the English Classical School, and submit the following as a general outline of a plan for its organization and of the course of studies to be pursued.

1st. That the term of time for pursuing the course of studies proposed, be three years.

2ndly. That the School be divided into three classes, and one year be assigned to the studies of each class.

3rdly. That the age of admission be not less than twelve years.

4thly. That the School be for Boys exclusively.

5thly. That candidates for admission be proposed on a given day annually; but scholars with suitable qualifications may be admitted at any intermediate time to an advanced standing.

6thly. That candidates for admission shall be subject to a strict examination, in such manner as the School Committee may direct, to ascertain their qualifications according to these rules.

7thly. That it be required of every candidate, to qualify him for admission, that he be well acquainted with reading, writing, English grammar in all its branches, and arithmetic as far as simple proportion.

8thly. That it be required of the Masters and Ushers, as a necessary qualification, that they shall have been regularly educated at some University.

First Class: Composition; reading from the most approved authors; exercises in criticism, comprising critical analyses of the language, grammar, and style of the best English authors, their errors and beauties; Declamation; Geography; Arithmetic continued.

Second Class: Composition, Reading, Exercises in Criticism, Declamation; Algebra; Ancient and Modern History and Chronology; Logic; Geometry; Plane Trigonometry, and its application to mensuration of heights and distances; Navigation; Surveying; Mensuration of Surfaces and Solids; Forensic Discussions.

Third Class: Composition; Exercises in Criticism; Declamation; Mathematics; Logic; History, particularly that of the United States; Natural Philosophy, including Astronomy; Moral and Political Philosophy.

The Report was followed by a financial statement, showing that the school was to employ a master, a sub-master, and two ushers (assistant teachers), and would cost $4000 for maintenance the ensuing year.

327. The Boston Secondary-School System in 1823

(Selected from *The System of Education pursued at the Free Schools in Boston*,
56 pp. Boston, 1823)

This is a continuation of the Report given in Reading 314, and describes the new High School, and the old Latin Grammar School.

The English Classical School
(In 1824 renamed as the English High School)

Public opinion and the wants of a large class of citizens of this town have long been calling for a school in which those, who have either not the desire or the means of obtaining a classical education, might receive instruction in many branches of great practical importance which have usually been taught only at the Colleges. This led to the establishment of the English Classical School.

This school was established by a vote of the town in 1820, expressly for the purpose of affording to lads, intending to become merchants or mechanics, better means of instruction than were provided at any of the public schools. A large building was erected, in a central part of the town, and an appropriation made of $2500, to furnish a philosophical apparatus. It was provided that there should be four instructors, viz. one Principal, one Sub-master, and two Ushers. A plan was reported for the studies of the course, including three years. This, however, was only an outline, and intended for the general guidance, rather than the particular direction of the instructors, as to the order in which the studies should be introduced, and the time which should be devoted to each. The instructors, accordingly, while they have adhered to the general intention, have, with the concurrence of the school committee, deviated from the plan in the disposition of the studies, and have introduced some studies not originally included.

The school went into operation in May, 1821; since which time, one hundred and seventy-six boys have been admitted, of which number nearly one hundred are now in the school. The annual examination for admission is in August.

For admission, boys are examined in those branches which are taught at the Grammar schools, viz. Reading, Writing, English Grammar, and Arithmetic; and, as they are allowed to remain in the Grammar schools until fourteen, none are admitted to this school under twelve. Fourteen was fixed as the other limit, but it was found that this would operate unjustly on those boys who were just fourteen, and this had consequently not been strictly insisted on.

As there are many lads who cannot continue at school during a complete course, nor even remain long after they have become able to do something for their own support, it is desirable to arrange the studies in such a manner that those branches should fall in the first year, which are of the most essential importance. The course for the first year includes Intellectual and Written Arithmetic, Geography and the use of the Globes, exercises in Grammar, General History, and History of the United States, Book-keeping by single entry, Elements of some Arts and Sciences, Composition and Declamation. That for the second and third year embraces Geometry, Algebra, Trigonometry and its applications, Book-keeping by double entry, various branches of Natural Philosophy, Natural History, Chemistry, Moral Philosophy and Natural Theology, Rhetoric, Evidences of Christianity, Intellectual Philosophy, Political Economy, and Logic.

. . . .

The establishment of this school forms an era in the history of Free Education in Boston. Its present high reputation and growing importance, while they render it an object of increasing interest, promise extensive and lasting utility; and furnish a gratifying proof of the wisdom of that policy which brings forward to places of high responsibility *young men* of talents and learning, who have a reputation and fortune to gain.

The Latin Grammar School

This ancient and venerable institution, so intimately connected with the early history of Boston, and of its learned men in generations that are past, seems to demand a moment's pause: *Res ipsa hortari videtur, quoniam de moribus civitatis tempus admonuit, supra repetere, ac, paucis, instituta majorum disserere.* It is grateful to look back on the picture of primitive, but enlightened simplicity exhibited in the early history of New England, and to arrest, as far as possible, the progress of decay by which its already indistinct lines are rapidly fading from our view.

. . . .

The whole school house in School Street, is now appropriated to this school. The last catalogue contains *two hundred and twenty-five* scholars. These are distributed into six separate apartments, under the care of the same number of instructors; viz. a Principal, or head master, a sub-master, and four assistants. For admission, boys must be at least nine years old; able to read correctly and with fluency, and to write running hand; they must know all the stops, marks, and abbreviations, and have sufficient knowledge of English Grammar to parse common sentences in prose. The time of admission is the Friday and Saturday next preceding the Commencement at Cambridge, which two days are devoted to the examination of candidates. The regular course of instruction lasts five years; and the school is divided into five classes, according to the time of entrance.

When a class has entered, the boys commence the Latin Grammar all together, under the eye of the principal; where they continue until he has become in some degree acquainted with their individual characters and capacities. As they change their places at each recitation, those boys will naturally rise to the upper part of the class, who are most industrious, or who learn with the greatest facility. After a time a division of from twelve to fifteen boys is taken off from the upper end of the class; after a few days more, another division is in like manner taken off; and so on, till the whole class is separated into divisions of equal number; it having been found that from twelve to fifteen is the most convenient number *to drill* together.

In this way boys of like capacities are put together, and the evil of having some unable to learn the lesson which others get in half the time allowed, is in some measure obviated. The class, thus arranged for the year, is distributed among the assistant teachers, a division to each . . . as writing is not taught in the school, the younger classes for the first two or three years are dismissed at eleven o'clock, an hour before school is done, that they may attend a writing school. . . .

. . . .

Thus we have endeavoured to give a view of the means, provided at the public expense, for the gratuitous instruction of the children of all classes of the citizens of Boston. They are offered equally to all. The poorest inhabitant may have his children instructed from the age of four to seventeen, at schools, some of which are already equal, if not *superior* to any private schools in our country; and *all* of them may be made so.

Indeed if a child be kept at a Primary School from four to seven, and then at one of the Grammar Schools until nine, and from that time till seventeen at the Latin, and the English Classical School, there is no question but he will go through a more *thorough* and *complete* course of instruction, and in *reality* enjoy greater advantages than are provided at many of the respectable colleges in the Union.

328. The Massachusetts High-School Law of 1827

(*Laws of Massachusetts*, January Session, 1827, chapter CXLIII)

This is the first American law requiring the establishment of high schools, and is important as a landmark in the history of the evolution of the high school. It is also significant in that its provisions are mandatory, whereas legislation in most of the States, for decades thereafter, was merely permissive.

Be it enacted by the Senate and House of Representatives in General Court assembled and by the authority of the same. That each town or district within this Commonwealth, containing fifty families, or householders, shall be provided with a teacher or teachers, of good morals, to instruct children in orthography, reading, writing, English grammar, geography, arithmetic, and good behavior, for such term of time as shall be equivalent to six months for one school in each year; and every town or district containing one hundred families or householders, shall be provided with such teacher or teachers, for such term of time as shall be equivalent to eighteen months, for one school in each year. And every city, town, or district, containing five hundred families, or householders, shall be provided with such teacher or teachers for such term of time as shall be equivalent to twenty-four months, for one school in each year, and shall also be provided with a master of good morals, competent to instruct, in addition to the branches of learning aforesaid, the history of the United States, bookkeeping by single entry, geometry, surveying, algebra; and shall employ such master to instruct a school, in such city, town, or district, for the benefit of all the inhabitants thereof, at least ten months in each year, exclusive of vacations, in such convenient place, or alternately at such places in such city, town, or district, as the said inhabitants, at their meeting in March, or April, annually, shall determine; and in every city, or town, containing four thousand inhabitants, such master shall be competent in addition to all the foregoing branches, to instruct the Latin and Greek languages, history, rhetoric, and logic.

329. An Example of the Opposition to High Schools

(Gulliver, John P., *Norwich* (Connecticut) *Weekly Courier*, November 25, 1856)

The following extract from an Address is illustrative of the difficulties experienced in establishing high schools, likewise of the arguments advanced against taxation for them, not only in Connecticut, but in other States as well.

. . . The lower schools up to the grade of the grammar school were well sustained. Men were to be found in all our communities who had been themselves educated up to that point, and understood, practically, the importance of such schools, in sufficient numbers to control popular sentiment, and secure for them ample appropriations and steady support. But the studies of the high school, Algebra, Geometry, Chemistry, Natural Philosophy, Ancient History, Latin, Greek, French and German, were a perfect "terra incognita" to the great mass of the people. While the High School was a new thing and while a few enlightened citizens had the control of it, in numerous instances it was carried to a high state of perfection. But after a time the burden of taxation would begin to be felt. Men would discuss the high salaries paid to the accomplished teachers which such schools demand, and would ask, "To what purpose is this waste?" Demagogues, keen-scented as wolves, would snuff the prey. "What do we want of a High School to teach rich men's children?" they would shout. "It is a shame to tax the poor man to pay a man $1,800, to teach the children to make x's and pot-hooks and gabble parley-vous." The work would go bravely on; and on election day, amid great excitement, a new school committee would be chosen, in favor of retrenchment and popular rights. In a single day the fruits of years of labor would be destroyed.

330. The Kalamazoo Decision

(Charles E. Stuart *et al.* *vs.* School District No. 1 of the Village of Kalamazoo, 30 *Michigan*, p. 69)

This is a famous decision, as settling the rights of a community to maintain a high school by taxation. The decision was of importance as a precedent in many other States. The School Board of Kalamazoo, Michigan, decided to open a high school and employ a superintendent of schools. A citizen, Charles E. Stuart, brought suit to prevent the collection of the tax levied therefor. The case was taken to the Supreme Court of the State of Michigan, and the decision was written by Chief Justice Thomas M. Cooley. The decision was emphatic that the State had the right to establish a complete system of schools, including a non-teaching Superintendent, and was not limited to the so-called "common schools."

The bill in this case is filed to restrain the collection of such portion of the school taxes assessed against complainants for the year 1872, as have been voted for the support of the high school in that village, and for the payment of the salary of the superintendent. While, nominally, this is the end sought to be attained by the bill, the real purpose of the bill is wider and vastly more comprehensive than this brief statement would indicate, inasmuch as it seeks a judicial determination of the right of school authorities, in what are called union school districts of the state, to levy taxes upon the general public for the support of what in this state are known as high schools, and to make free by such taxation the instruction of children in other languages than the English.

.   .   .   .

The more general question which the record presents we shall endeavor to state in our own language, but so as to make it stand out distinctly as a naked question of law, disconnected from all considerations of policy or expediency, in which light alone we are at liberty to consider it. It is, as we understand it, that there is no authority in this state to make the high schools free by taxation levied on the people at large. The argument is that while there may be no constitutional provision expressly prohibiting such taxation, the general course of legislation in the state and the general understanding of the people have been such as to require us to regard the instruction in the classics and in the living modern languages in these schools as in the nature not of practical and therefore necessary instruction for the benefit of the people at large, but rather as accomplishments for the few, to be sought after in the main by those best able to pay for them, and to be paid for by those who seek them, and not by general tax. And not only has this been the general state policy, but this higher learning of itself, when supplied by the state, is so far a matter of private concern to those who receive it that the courts ought to declare it incompetent to supply it wholly at the public expense. This is in substance, as we understand it, the position of the complainants in this suit.

When this doctrine was broached to us, we must confess to no little surprise that the legislation and policy of our state were appealed to against the right of the state to furnish a liberal education to the youth of the state in schools brought within the reach of all classes. We supposed it had always been understood in this state that education, not merely in the rudiments, but in an enlarged sense, was regarded as an important practical advantage to be supplied at their option to rich and poor alike, and not as something pertaining merely to culture and accomplishment to be brought as such within the reach of those whose accumulated wealth enabled them to pay for it. As this, however, is now so seriously disputed, it may be necessary, perhaps, to take a brief survey of the legislation and general course, not only of the state, but of the antecedent territory, on the subject.

Here follows a review of the educational history of the State, from the Ordinance of 1787 to the new state constitution of 1850, to show the intention to establish "a complete system of education." Of the constitution of 1850 the court says:

The instrument submitted by the convention to the people and adopted by them provided for the establishment of free schools in every school district for at least three months in each year, and for the university. By the aid of these we have every reason to believe the people expected a complete collegiate education might be obtained. . . . The inference seems irresistible that the people expected the tendency towards the establishment of high schools in the primary-school districts would continue until every locality capable of supporting one was supplied. And this inference is strengthened by the fact that a considerable number of our union schools date their establishment from the year 1850 and the two or three years following.

The final opinion of the court as to the legality of the high school is stated as follows:

If these facts do not demonstrate clearly and conclusively a general state policy, beginning in 1817 and continuing until after the adoption

of the present constitution, in the direction of free schools in which
education, and at their option the elements of classical education,
might be brought within the reach of all the children of the state, then,
as it seems to us, nothing can demonstrate it.   We might follow the
subject further and show that the subsequent legislation has all con-
curred with this policy, but it would be a waste of time and labor.   We
content ourselves with the statement that neither in our state policy, in
our constitution, or in our laws, do we find the primary-school districts
restricted in the branches of knowledge which their officers may cause
to be taught, or the grade of instruction that may be given, if their
voters consent in regular form to bear the expense and raise the taxes
for the purpose.

331. Program of Studies in the University of Michigan, 1843-44

(Joint Documents of the Legislature of Michigan, 1852, p. 388)

The following program of studies of the University of Michigan,
for the academic year 1843–44, reveals the meager scope, from a
modern point of view, of the leading western state university of
that time.   The institution at that date had a faculty of three
professors, one tutor, one assistant in science, and one visiting
lecturer, and there were fifty-three students in attendance.   The
following program of studies shows that this faculty then offered
all told, in the entire four-year course, fifty term courses (of one-
third of a year each), twenty-six of which were in Greek, Latin,
and mathematics; nine in natural science; five in intellectual science; three in morals and religion; three in political science; and
four in English.   The program of studies for 1850, when the university had come to have 72 students, shows but slight change
from that for 1843.

Each class was required to attend three recitations daily, with
Bible Study on Monday mornings and Elocution on Saturday
mornings as extras, making a 17-hour week.   These extras are
also found in the 1850 program.   The instruction throughout was
the same for all.

The program of studies offered is interesting both as showing
the long continuance of the early conception of an English
teaching college, and by way of illustrating the very remarkable
transformation in American higher education which took place
in the half-century between 1850 and 1900.

PROGRAM OF STUDIES, UNIVERSITY OF MICHIGAN, 1843–44

Year	Term	Languages and Literatures	Mathematics and Science	Intellectual and Moral Sciences
I	1	Folsom's *Livy* Xenophon's *Cyropædia* and *Anabasis*	Bowdon's *Algebra*	
	2	Livy finished, Horace begun Roman Antiquities Thucydides, Herodotus	Algebra finished, Legendre's *Geometry* begun, and Botany	
	3	Horace finished Homer's *Odyssey*	Geometry finished; Mensuration, Applications of Algebra to Geometry	
II	1	Cicero's *de Senectute* and *de Amicitia* Lysias, Isocrates, and Demosthenes	Plane and Spherical Trigonometry	
	2	Cicero's *de Oratore* Greek tragedy, and Antiquities Newcomb's *Rhetoric*	Davies' *Descriptive and Analytical Geometry*	
	3	Tacitus' *Vita Agricolæ* and *Germanii* Greek tragedy	Analytic Geometry completed, Bridge's *Conic Sections*	
III	1	Cicero's *de Officiis* Greek poetry	Olmstead's *Natural Philosophy*, and Zoölogy	Abercrombie's *Intellectual Power* Paley's *Natural Theology*
	2	Terence Greek poetry, general grammar	Natural Philosophy, and Chemistry	
	3	Whiteley's *Rhetoric*	Olmstead's *Astronomy*, Chemistry continued, and Mineralogy	

PROGRAM OF STUDIES, UNIVERSITY OF MICHIGAN, 1843–44 (*continued*)

Year	Term	Languages and Literatures	Mathematics and Science	Intellectual and Moral Sciences
IV	1	Lectures on the Greek and Latin languages and literatures	Calculus, and Geology	Stuart's *Intellectual Philosophy*, and Cousin's *Psychology*
	2			Whiteley's *Logic* Wayland's *Moral Science* Political Grammar
	3			Studies of the Constitution Wayland's *Political Economy* Butler's *Analogy*

332. The Michigan System of Public Instruction

(Tappan, Henry P., "Report to the Regents of the University of Michigan, 1856"; in *Report of Superintendent of Public Instruction*, Michigan, 1855–56–57, pp. 155–84)

The report of President Tappan to his Board of Regents, from which the following extract is taken, describes the system of public instruction in Michigan, as it had then been developed and conceived, and shows the unity of the state school system from the primary school to the university.

An entire system of public education comprises three grades and can comprise but three grades: the primary, the intermediate, and the university. . . . The primary school comes first. . . . All human learning begins with the alphabet.

The second grade occupies the period of youth — of adolescence or growth. This is the period when the foundations of knowledge and character can be most amply and securely laid. . . .

But let it be remembered that the intermediate grade embraces only the apprenticeship of the scholar. . . . Hence the necessity of universities, as the highest form of educational institutions. . . .

The highest institutions are necessary to supply the proper standard of education; to raise up instructors of the proper qualifications; to define the principles and methods of education. . . .

Nothing is more evident than that the three grades of education — the primary, the intermediate, the university — are all alike necessary. The one cannot exist, in perfection, without the others; they imply one another. . . .

It is to the honor of Michigan that she has conceived of a complete system of public education running through the three grades we have discussed above. Nor do these grades exist merely in name. She has established the primary grade of schools and made them well-nigh free. She has laid the foundation of an institution which admits of being expanded to a true university. In former days she had her "branches" belonging to the intermediate grade; and now we see rising up those invaluable institutions, the "union schools," belonging to the same grade. We say not that legislation has adequately reached the entire system, or made provision for its development; but the idea of the entire system is abroad among the people; it has not been absent from our legislation; it has appeared in the reports of superintendents and visitors, and in other documents; and the people, at this moment, unaided by any special appropriation, are organizing above the district school, the best schools of the intermediate grade, less than a college, which have yet existed among us; and are erecting large, tasteful, and convenient edifices for their accommodation. These ideas, spontaneously working in the minds of the people, these spontaneous efforts to create schools of a higher grade, must determine future legislation and indicate the grand point to which our educational development is tending.

CHAPTER XXVII
EDUCATION BECOMES A NATIONAL·TOOL

THE Readings in this chapter relate to the spread of the state-control-of-education idea among the nations of the earth; the scientific advances of the nineteenth century; the Industrial Revolution; and the use made by nations of education for national ends.

The first Reading (333) reproduces those parts of the Swiss Federal Constitution which relate to the maintenance of education, and the relations of churches and religious orders thereto — education in Switzerland, as in the United States, being left to the twenty-two different cantons to control. This is a type of what modern constitutions have ordered that governments provide, though the best examples of such constitutional provisions are found in new lands, and not among the older nations of Europe. The second Reading (334) reproduces the basic documents for Japanese education, from which both the character and the state purpose of the school system may easily be inferred. The third (335) deals with the remarkable transformation which has taken place since the beginning of the twentieth century in China. The fourth (336) is an extract from one of the celebrated *Annual Reports* of Horace Mann, still readable and pertinent, as to the relation between the promotion of education and the advancement of the national welfare.

The three Readings which follow the above relate to the wonderful advancement of science, invention, and intercommunication which have characterized the nineteenth century. The first (337) is an extract from Huxley's celebrated *Essay;* the second (338) gives a good statement as to why the human inventive faculty lay dormant for so long, and then flowered so wonderfully; and the third (339) describes a lack of world intercourse a century ago that seems almost unbelievable to-day.

The three Readings which follow deal with the use of education to promote nationality. The first (340) is an excellent statement of the influence of the struggle for nationality on educational practice; the second (341) reveals how intelligently the French have used education as a constructive national tool; while the third (342) is a good description of the narrowly-national ends which the Germans have made it serve.

The final Reading of the chapter (343) relates to the work of the American teacher in the Philippines, and the transformation which has been effected there during the past quarter of a century.

333. The Swiss Constitution on Education and Religious Freedom

(Federal Constitution of the Swiss Confederation, 1874)

In Readings 260 and 261 the early constitutional mandates relating to education in two American States were given, and in the following a similar extract from the Swiss Constitution is reproduced.

In the Name of Almighty God

The Swiss Confederation, desiring to confirm the allegiance of the Confederates, to maintain and to promote the unity, strength, and honor of the Swiss nation, has adopted the Federal Constitution following:

Chapter I. General Provisions

Art. 27. The Confederation has the right to establish, besides the existing Polytechnic School, a Federal University and other institutions of higher instruction, or to subsidize institutions of such nature.

The Cantons provide for primary instruction, which shall be sufficient, and shall be placed exclusively under the direction of the secular authority. It is compulsory and, in the public schools, free.

The public schools shall be such that they may be frequented by the adherents of all religious sects, without any offense to their freedom of conscience or of belief.

The Confederation shall take the necessary measures against such Cantons as shall not fulfill these duties.

Art. 50. The free exercise of religious worship is guaranteed within the limits compatible with public order and good morals.

The Cantons and the Confederation may take suitable measures for the preservation of public order and of peace between the members of different religious bodies, and also against encroachments of ecclesiastical authorities upon the rights of citizens and of the State.

Contests in public and private law, which arise out of the formation or the division of religious bodies, may be brought by appeal before the competent federal authorities.

No bishopric shall be created upon Swiss territory without the consent of the Confederation.

Art. 51. The order of the Jesuits, and the societies affiliated with them, shall not be received into any part of Switzerland; and all action in church and school is forbidden to its members.

This prohibition may be extended also, by federal ordinance, to other religious orders, the action of which is dangerous to the state or disturbs the peace between sects.

Art. 52. The foundation of new convents or religious orders, and the reëstablishment of those which have been suppressed, are forbidden.

334. The Basic Documents for Japanese Education

(Baron D. Kikuchi, Article on "Education in Japan"; in Monroe's *Cyclopedia of Education*, vol. iii)

The following selections set forth well the spirit of Japanese popular education. The first (*a*) is the Preamble to the first Education Code of the Empire (1872). This provides for a two-class type of educational system, though based on the very democratic principle of the equality of all in the lower school. The second (*b*) is a Rescript issued by the Mikado, in 1890, and forms the basis for the moral education of the people. A copy of this is to be found in every schoolroom in Japan, those in the public schools being actually signed by the Mikado himself. Based on this Rescript, textbooks on moral education have been prepared by a special commission, and the following instructions (*c*) to schools have been issued by the Ministry for Education. Two hours a week are given to moral instruction in all primary schools in Japan.

(a) Preamble to the Education Code of 1872

It is intended that henceforth universally without any distinction of class or sex, in a village there shall be no house without learning (education), and in a house no individual without learning. Fathers and elder brothers must take note of this intention, and, bringing up their children or younger brothers (or sisters) with warm feeling of love, must not fail to let them acquire learning. As for higher learning, that depends upon the capacity of individuals, but it shall be regarded as a neglect of duty on the part of fathers or elder brothers, should they fail to send young children to primary schools at least without distinction of sex.

(b) Imperial Rescript on Moral Education

Know ye, Our Subjects:

Our Imperial Ancestors have founded our Empire on a basis broad and everlasting, and have deeply and firmly implanted virtue; Our subjects ever united in loyalty and filial piety have from generation to generation illustrated the beauty thereof: This is the glory of the fundamental character of Our Empire, and herein also lies the source of our Education. Ye, Our Subjects, be filial to your parents, affectionate to your brothers and sisters; as husbands and wives be harmonious, as friends true; bear yourselves in modesty and moderation; extend your benevolence to all; pursue learning and cultivate arts, and thereby develop intellectual faculties and perfect moral powers; furthermore, advance public good and promote common interests; always respect the Constitution and observe the laws; should emergency arise, offer yourself courageously to the State; and thus guard and maintain the prosperity of Our Imperial Throne, coeval with heaven and earth. So shall ye not only be Our good and faithful subjects, but render illustrious the best traditions of your forefathers.

The Way here set forth is indeed the teaching bequeathed by Our Imperial Ancestors, to be observed alike by Their Descendants and the subjects, infallible for all ages and true in all places. It is Our wish to lay it to heart in all reverence, in common with you, Our subjects, that we may all attain to the same virtue.

The 30th day of the 10th month of the 23rd year of Meiji (October 30th, 1890).

Imperial Sign Manual, Imperial Seal.

(c) Instructions to Schools as to Lessons on Morals

The teaching of morals must be based on the Imperial Rescript on education, and its aim should be to cultivate the moral nature of children and to guide them in practices of virtue.

In the ordinary primary course, easy precepts appropriate for practice concerning such virtues as filial piety and obedience to elders, affection and friendship, frugality and industry, modesty, courage, etc., should be given, and then some of the duties toward the State and society, with a view to elevate their moral character, strengthen their will, increase their spirit of enterprise, make them value public virtues, and foster the spirit of loyalty and patriotism.

In the higher primary course, the above must be further extended and training given made still more solid.

In the teaching of girls, special stress must be laid on the virtues of chastity and modesty.

Encouragement and admonition should be given by means of wise sayings and proverbs and by tales of good deeds, so that children may lay them to heart.

335. The Transformation of China by Education

(Ping Wen Kuo, *The Chinese System of Public Education*, pp. 163–64.
New York, 1915)

The following brief statement as to the relation between education and national progress, as seen by a distinguished Chinese, is interesting also for the comparison made between ancient Chinese and European Renaissance learning.

The history of Chinese education forms an excellent example of the important relation of school training to national progress. For many centuries Chinese education was purely literary, philosophical in character. There was little that could be called concrete or practical in the modern sense of the word, neither was there anything requiring the knowledge of the experimental method or of inductive reasoning. Education strongly resembled the form of training which prevailed in Europe for two centuries after the revival of Greek learning. This peculiar quality of Chinese education produced a prodigious effect on the career of the nation. It accounts for the present comparatively backward condition of China, explaining why the country made little progress in the arts of modern life and in the modern sciences until the last decade.

Since her contact with the western nations, her educational system has undergone a radical change through the introduction of modern subjects of study and the education of many of her students in foreign lands. The effect of this change upon her national life has been marvelous. It set the country on the high road of progress and reform. A great revolution, at once political, industrial, and social, is taking place under our very eyes. Educational reform in China now forms the very pivot around which all other reforms turn, for it is to education that China is looking for the men to steer the ship of state into the haven of safety. This close relationship between education and national progress should be an argument for the introduction of a more practical training in the public schools of China.

336. Education and National Prosperity

(Mann, Horace, *Twelfth Annual Report*, as Secretary of the Massachusetts State
Board of Education. Boston, 1848)

Each year, Mr. Mann, in his Annual Report as Secretary, discussed some topic of general interest. In his Report for 1848 he chose the relation of education to national prosperity, and some of the paragraphs of this Report make good reading, even to-day. The following have been selected to show Mr. Mann's conception of the importance of education for national welfare.

A cardinal object which the government of Massachusetts, and all the influential men in the State, should propose to themselves, is the physical well-being of all the people, — the sufficiency, comfort, competence, of every individual in regard to food, raiment, and shelter. And these necessaries and conveniences of life should be obtained by each individual for himself, or by each family for themselves, rather than accepted from the hand of charity or extorted by poor-laws. It is not averred that this most desirable result can, in all instances, be obtained; but it is, nevertheless, the end to be aimed at. True statesmanship and true political economy, not less than true philanthropy, present this perfect theory as the goal, to be more and more closely approximated by our imperfect practice. The desire to achieve such a result cannot be regarded as an unreasonable ambition; for, though all mankind were well fed, well clothed, and well housed, they might still be but half civilized.

According to the European theory, men are divided into classes, — some to toil and earn, others to seize and enjoy. According to the Massachusetts theory, all are to have an equal chance for earning, and equal security in the enjoyment of what they earn. The latter tends to equality of condition; the former, to the grossest inequalities. Tried by any Christian standard of morals, or even by any of the better sort of heathen standards, can any one hesitate, for a moment, in declaring which of the two will produce the greater amount of human welfare, and which, therefore, is the more conformable to the divine will? The European theory is blind to what constitutes the highest glory as well as the highest duty of a State.

. . . .

Our ambition as a State should trace itself to a different origin, and propose to itself a different object. Its flame should be lighted at the skies. Its radiance and its warmth should reach the darkest and the coldest abodes of men. It should seek the solution of such problems as these: To what extent can competence displace pauperism? How nearly can we free ourselves from the low-minded and the vicious, not by their expatriation, but by their elevation? To what extent can the resources and powers of Nature be converted into human welfare, the peaceful arts of life be advanced, and the vast treasures of human talent and genius be developed? How much of suffering, in all its forms, can be relieved? or, what is better than relief, how much can be prevented? Cannot the classes of crimes be lessened, and the number of criminals in each class be diminished?

. . . .

Now two or three things will doubtless be admitted to be true, beyond all controversy, in regard to Massachusetts. By its industrial condition, and its business operations, it is exposed, far beyond any other State in the Union, to the fatal extremes of overgrown wealth and desperate poverty. Its population is far more dense than that of any other State. It is four or five times more dense than the average of all the other States taken together; and density of population has always been one of the proximate causes of social inequality. According to population and territorial extent there is far more capital in Massachusetts — capital which is movable, and instantaneously available — than in any other State in the Union; and probably both these qualifications respecting population and territory could be omitted without endangering the truth of the assertion.

. . . .

Now surely nothing but universal education can counterwork this tendency to the domination of capital and the servility of labor. If one class possesses all the wealth and the education, while the residue of society is ignorant and poor, it matters not by what name the relation between them may be called: the latter, in fact and in truth, will be the servile dependants and subjects of the former. But, if education be equally diffused, it will draw property after it by the strongest of all attractions; for such a thing never did happen, and never can happen, as that an intelligent and practical body of men should be permanently poor. Property and labor in different classes are essentially antagonistic; but property and labor in the same class are essentially fraternal. The people of Massachusetts have, in some degree, appreciated the truth that the unexampled prosperity of the State — its comfort, its competence, its general intelligence and virtue — is attributable to the education, more or less perfect, which all its people have received; but are they sensible of a fact equally important, — namely, that it is to this same education that two-thirds of the people are indebted for not being to-day the vassals of as severe a tyranny, in the form of capital, as the lower classes of Europe are bound to in the form of brute force?

Education, then, beyond all other devices of human origin, is the great equalizer of the conditions of men, — the balance-wheel of the social machinery. I do not here mean that it so elevates the moral nature as to make men disdain and abhor the oppression of their fellow-men. This idea pertains to another of its attributes. But I mean that it gives each man the independence and the means by which he can resist the selfishness of other men. It does better than to disarm the poor of their hostility towards the rich: it prevents being poor. Agrarianism is the revenge of poverty against wealth. The wanton destruction of the property of others — the burning of hay-ricks and corn-ricks, the demolition of machinery because it supersedes hand-labor, the sprinkling of vitriol on rich dresses — is only agrarianism run mad. Education prevents both the revenge and the madness. On the other hand, a fellow-feeling for one's class or caste is the common instinct of hearts not wholly sunk in selfish regards for person or for family. The spread of education, by enlarging the cultivated class or caste, will open a wider area over which the social feelings will expand; and, if this education should be universal and complete, it would do more than all things else to obliterate factitious distinctions in society.

.   .   .   .

For the creation of wealth, then, — for the existence of a wealthy people and a wealthy nation, — intelligence is the grand condition. The number of improvers will increase as the intellectual constituency, if I may so call it, increases. In former times, and in most parts of the world even at the present day, not one man in a million has ever had such a development of mind as made it possible for him to become a contributor to art or science. Let this development precede, and contributions, numberless, and of inestimable value, will be sure to follow. That political economy, therefore, which busies itself about capital and labor, supply and demand, interest and rents, favorable and unfavorable balances of trade, but leaves out of account the element of a wide-spread mental development, is naught but stupendous folly. The greatest of all the arts in political economy is to change a consumer into a producer; and the next greatest is to increase the producer's producing power, — an end to be directly attained by increasing his intelligence. For mere delving, an ignorant man is but little better than a swine, whom he so much resembles in his appetites, and surpasses in his powers of mischief. . . .

337. The Recent Progress of Science

(Huxley, T. H., *Methods and Results*, Essay II.   London, 1893)

In an Essay, dated 1887, on "The Progress of Science," the English scientist Thomas Huxley begins with the following striking statement as to nineteenth-century scientific advances.

The most obvious and the most distinctive feature of the History of Civilisation, during the last fifty years, is the wonderful increase of industrial production by the application of machinery, the improvement of old technical processes and the invention of new ones, accompanied by an even more remarkable development of old and new means of locomotion and intercommunication. By this rapid and vast multiplication of the commodities and conveniences of existence, the general standard of comfort has been raised; the ravages of pestilence and famine have been checked; and the natural obstacles, which time and space offer to mutual intercourse, have been reduced in a manner, and to an extent, unknown to former ages. The diminution or removal of local ignorance and prejudice, the creation of common interests among the most widely separated peoples, and the strengthening of the forces of the organisation of the commonwealth against those of political or social anarchy, thus effected, have exerted an influence on the present and future fortunes of mankind the full significance of which may be divined, but cannot, as yet, be estimated at its full value.

This revolution — for it is nothing less — in the political and social aspects of modern civilisation has been preceded, accompanied, and in a great measure caused, by a less obvious, but no less marvellous, increase of natural knowledge, and especially of that part of it which is known as Physical Science, in consequence of the application of scientific method to the investigation of the phenomena of the material world. Not that the growth of physical science is an exclusive prerogative of the Victorian age. Its present strength and volume merely indicate the highest level of a stream which took its rise alongside of the primal founts of Philosophy, Literature,

FIG. 82.

THOMAS H. HUXLEY
(1825–95)

and Art, in ancient Greece; and, after being dammed up for a thousand years, once more began to flow three centuries ago.

. . . .

In the early decades of the seventeenth century, the men of the Renaissance could show that they had already put out to good interest the treasure bequeathed to them by the Greeks. They had produced the astronomical system of Copernicus, with Kepler's great additions; the astronomical discoveries and the physical investigations of Galileo; the mechanics of Stevinus and the *De Magnete* of Gilbert; the anatomy of the great French and Italian schools and the physiology of Harvey. In Italy, which had succeeded Greece in the hegemony of the scientific world, the *Accademia dei Lyncei* and sundry other such associations for the investigation of nature, the models of all subsequent academies and scientific societies, had been founded: while the literary skill and biting wit of Galileo had made the great scientific questions of the day not only intelligible, but attractive, to the general public. In our own country, Francis Bacon had essayed to sum up the past of physical science, and to indicate the path which it must follow if its great destinies were to be fulfilled. . . .

The progress of science, during the first century after Bacon's death, by no means verified his sanguine prediction of the fruits which it would yield. For, though the revived and renewed study of nature had spread and grown to an extent which surpassed reasonable expectation, the practical results — the "good to men's estate" — were, at first, by no means apparent. Sixty years after Bacon's death, Newton had crowned the long labours of the astronomers and the physicists, by coördinating the phenomena of molar motion throughout the visible universe into one vast system; but the *Principia* helped no man to either wealth or comfort. Descartes, Newton, and Leibnitz had opened up new worlds to the mathematician, but the acquisitions of their genius enriched only man's ideal estate. Descartes had laid the foundations of rational cosmogony and of physiological psychology; Boyle had produced models of experimentation in various branches of physics and chemistry; Pascal and Torricelli had weighed the air; Malpighi and Grew, Ray and Willoughby had done work of no less importance in the biological sciences; but weaving and spinning were carried on with the old appliances; nobody could travel faster by sea or by land than at any previous time in the world's history, and King George could send a message from London to York no faster than King John might have done. Metals were worked from their ores by immemorial rule of thumb, and the center of the iron trade of these islands was still among the oak forests of Sussex. The utmost skill of our mechanicians did not get beyond the production of a coarse watch.

. . . .

But, a little later, that growth of knowledge beyond imaginable utilitarian ends, which is the condition precedent of its practical utility, began to produce some effect upon practical life; and the operation of that part of nature we call human upon the rest began to create, not "new natures," in Bacon's sense, but a new Nature, the existence of which is dependent upon men's efforts, which is subservient to their wants, and which would disappear if man's shaping and guiding hand were withdrawn. Every mechanical artifice, every chemically pure substance employed in manufacture, every abnormally fertile race of plants, or rapidly growing and fattening breed of animals, is a part of the new Nature created by science. Without it, the most densely populated regions of modern Europe and America must retain their primitive, sparsely inhabited, agricultural or pastoral condition; it is the foundation of our wealth and the condition of our safety from submergence by another flood of barbarous hordes; it is the bond which unites into a solid political whole, regions larger than any empire of antiquity; it secures us from the recurrence of the pestilences and famines of former times; it is the source of endless comforts and conveniences, which are not mere luxuries, but conduce to physical and moral well-being. During the last fifty years, this new birth of time, this new Nature begotten by science upon fact, has pressed itself daily and hourly upon our attention, and has worked miracles which have modified the whole fashion of our lives.

338. Scientific Knowledge must precede Invention

(Editorial in the *San Francisco Chronicle*, October, 1919)

The following selection, which appeared as an editorial in a Sunday edition of the above-mentioned newspaper, offers so good an explanation as to why the human inventive faculty waited so long, and then within a century has borne such abundant fruit, that it is reproduced here in its entirety as furnishing good collateral reading for the subject-matter of the corresponding chapter in the text.

When one casts a backward look over the multitude of inventions that have been given to the world in the last hundred years, and then a farther look back over the long barren centuries that went before, there rises a natural feeling of amazement that the world should have lived so long without the simple devices that now are part of our lives and that invention, so long delayed, should have come in such a flood.

Though the time when man first learned to use fire was so far back that we have no account of it except in myth, it was not until our grandmothers' days that man had safety matches; though the arrow goes so far back that we cannot find on the face of the earth a savage so isolated that he has it not, we had no airplanes until the present decade; though history does not take us back far enough to find a time when geometry and arithmetic were not fairly well understood, it was not until comparatively modern times that the discovery of the zero made arithmetic a supple servant and made possible the great modern development of mathematics; though the cart is found on the earliest monuments, it was only within the last twenty years that we produced the first practical automobile.

We are quite apt to conclude that the human race has been without mechanical ideas for the greater part of its life, and acquired them only a hundred or so years ago.   Such a conclusion, though natural enough, must be dismissed as erroneous.   A more correct conclusion is that the mechanical faculties of the race lay dormant for long centuries.   They must have existed from the very beginning of intelligence, for the fundamental inventions and discoveries from which civilization has arisen were made so far back that we cannot give them date.   Fire, the cooking pot, the bow, the wheel, the lever, the knife, all came before the dawn of civilization.   These are simple inventions, you say; but they are no more simple than the lamp chimney, the cotton gin, or even the phonograph.

There are other reasons for the thousands of years barren of invention, followed by a sudden flowering.   Undoubtedly the fact that in the ancient civilizations labor was almost exclusively slave labor stifled the inventive faculty. The slave had no incentive to better the devices he worked with, or to work out new ones. Then, too, mankind did not have the constantly widening circle of needs that began to expand only with the development of ocean commerce and the discovery of the new world. There was another thing; there were no patent laws, and no organization of industry to ensure a reward for the man who worked overtime to devise a better clock or some new convenience.

But the chief reason is that the vast majority of modern inventions had to wait for the invention of the steam power-plant and the development of modern science. The steam engine brought in its train a host of inventions that would have been either impossible or useless before. The locomotive, the steam-hammer, are examples of those impossible; the screw propeller is an example of one that would have been useless. The discoveries of modern science have been responsible for a huge number of inventions. Without a knowledge of electricity, the telegraph and telephone, simple as they are, were impossible. The old alchemy gave us gunpowder, but only modern chemistry could give us the aniline dye, dynamite, high-speed steel, aluminum, the Bessemer process, gasoline, usable rubber, and oleomargarine.

The bicycle had to wait for the discovery of rubber gum, and then for the invention of the vulcanizing process. The automobile had to wait not only for that, but for the development of the gasoline engine. The airplane was impracticable before the internal combustion engine had reached a high stage of perfection.

Once started by the invention of the steam engine and the development of science, modern invention has proceeded in geometrical progression, each new invention or discovery making possible a dozen, or a hundred, more. Though example and the increase of possibilities has spurred the inventive faculty, it is perhaps no greater now than it ever was.

339. Lack of Intercommunication illustrated by Ticknor

(Life, Letters, and Journals of George Ticknor, vol. i, pp. 11–12. Boston, 1825)

George Ticknor (1791–1871) was the fourth American who went to a German university for the purpose of study, and the first who left an account of his journey and residence there. He studied at the University of Göttingen, 1815–17. Two other American students preceded him by a few years; one having gone there from Philadelphia to study medicine as early as 1789. Germany, though, before the days of railways, telegraphs, and fast steamships, was almost as unknown to Americans as was China. In 1813 Madame de Staël's book on Germany (*De l'Allemagne*) was published in England. This opened up a new world to Ticknor, a

Boston boy who had been graduated from Dartmouth and had opened a law office in Boston, as it did to many other English and American readers. Of his efforts to learn something about the German universities, then the most celebrated in Europe (**R.** 359), and to study the German language, he wrote:

The first intimation I ever had on the subject was from Mme. de Staël's work on Germany, then just published. My next came from a pamphlet, published by Villers, to defend the University of Göttingen from the ill intentions of Jerome Bonaparte, the King of Westphalia, in which he gave a sketch of the university and its courses of study. My astonishment at these revelations was increased by an account of its library, given by an Englishman who had been at Göttingen, to my friend, the Rev. Samuel C. Thacher. I was sure that I should like to study at such a university, but it was in vain that I endeavored to get further knowledge upon the subject. I would gladly have prepared for it by learning the language I should have to use there, but there was no one in Boston who could teach me.

At Jamaica Plain there was a Dr. Brosius, a native of Strasburg, who gave me instruction in mathematics. He was willing to do what he could for me in German, but he warned me that his pronunciation was very bad, as was that of all Alsace, which had become a part of France. Nor was it possible to get books. I borrowed Meidinger's Grammar, French and German, from my friend Mr. Everett, and sent to New Hampshire, where I knew there was a German dictionary, and procured it. I also obtained a copy of Goethe's Werther in German (through Mr. William S. Shaw's connivance) from among Mr. J. Q. Adams's books, deposited by him on going to Europe in the Athenæum, under Mr. Shaw's care, but without giving him permission to lend them. I got so far as to write a translation of Werther, but no further.

340. The Struggle for National Realization

(Monroe, Paul, Introduction to "Teachers College Syllabi, No. 9," on *Democracy and Nationalism in Education*. New York, 1919. Reproduced by permission)

In an Introduction to a brief syllabus of lectures by Professor Reisner, as given above, Professor Monroe has given such an excellent statement of the struggle for nationality which has characterized modern history, and the use by nations of education as a tool to that end, that permission has been secured to reproduce the Introduction in full, which is done in the following Reading.

The growth of nations has been the conspicuous political feature of modern times, and the problems of the relation of education to this development have become obvious during the nineteenth century.

The earliest stage of political development occurred with the fixing of tribal groups in a definite habitat. The earliest form of this was the city state with its environing dependencies. These early states looked upon all other groups as hostile and unworthy of existence, except as they became subordinated. This incorporation was usually accomplished by force, which process tended to destroy the distinctive cultural features of the minor groups. In other words, the groups expanding by military power led by dynastic ability and ambition looked upon political organization as all-inclusive. With the Roman Empire this tendency became substantially a reality. With the Christianization of the Roman Empire the ecclesiastical ideal and pretension paralleled the political one and both became coterminous with civilization. This belief in the universal scope of political organization constituted in form the world's political theory long after the actual conditions were changed. The Holy Roman Empire which expressed this theory in the early modern period was only destroyed by Napoleon in 1804. The chief force in rendering this organization a mere form was that of growing nationalism.

From very early days certain groups, especially the English, had grown up in isolation. Over these the Holy Roman Empire had possessed only the most nebulous authority. From the twelfth to the sixteenth century both the English and the French groups, and to a less extent the German and Italian, through internal conflict, developed a local consciousness which more and more gave a distinctive character to each group. The original tribal groups which had entered into the composition of these dawning national groups were marked by distinct racial characteristics. Through internal conflicts, through migration, through conquest and the merging of conqueror and conquered, in time these developing national groups came to represent the accomplished amalgamation of many tribal or racial strains. In fact, the strongest of these early nationalities, the English and French, represented the fusion of most diverse elements.

Thus early became distinct the three great factors determining modern nationalities, namely, blood relationship or race, habitat or geographical environment, and culture. Culture in this sense means common ideals, common traditions, habits and aspirations. A number of other specific characteristics are often urged as essential to nationality, such as common language, common religion, common laws, but there is no one characteristic except that of a common culture which may be posited but what exceptions may be found. The one most commonly given, that of race, cannot be accepted, for every European nation represents a great mixture, and the United States has become the greatest mixture of all. Nor, on the other hand, can such great admixture of racial groups be made an essential, for there are illustrations of the opposite as in the case of Japan. A compact habitat is a usual characteristic, but there are exceptions as in the case of Greece, now struggling for national realization, or that of the British Empire. It cannot be maintained that common language is an essential, for there is the case of Switzerland with its three languages. Common religion, for a period believed to be essential, was responsible for the many wars of the sixteenth and seventeenth centuries; but strong national states have developed in spite of internal differences of religious belief. Common laws cannot be held as essential, for federal states are based on the recognition of a diversity of laws.

Modern history since the fifteenth century has been essentially the story of the struggle for national realization. This long struggle has brought a growing recognition that a common culture, that composite of common habits, ideals and purposes, is the one essential characteristic of nationality. Most modern wars, especially of Europe, have been caused by the violation of this principle. This was particularly true during the nineteenth century, because most international settlements, particularly those made by the Congress of Vienna in 1816 and by the Congress of Berlin in 1878, resulted in gross violations of that principle, in favor of other principles usually based on arbitrary force. In a very true sense, then, the great war is but a readjustment of the evils produced by the imperfect and unjust settlements made at the close of the Napoleonic struggle.

From the late eighteenth century the element of common culture has become the dominating one in the conception of nationality. This has resulted in the recognition of two fundamental and correlated truths: First, common culture is a trait which transcends social, religious, and economic distinctions, and its recognition transfers the seat of national existence from dynasties or bureaucratic legal institutions supported by military force to the masses of the people. Second, the discovery was made that common culture was an artificial product and could be manufactured. The process of this manufacture is by education. From one point of view then the nineteenth century is the period of national development, working towards the democratic interpretation of the problem of nationality and using education as a means.

The first people consciously to apply this method of education to the determination of nationality was the German. Beginning near the middle of the eighteenth century, or even earlier, with special groups, and after 1809 very definitely for the whole group, this people before the Napoleonic wars organized into more than one hundred independent nations has gradually amalgamated into one. The limitation to this development of a German nation as we see it now is that the Germans retained along with this democratic conception of nationality the old dynastic and predatory one. The latter has now been eliminated, in part at least, and it remains to be seen what the former may accomplish.

Other European nations, more favorably situated in regard to other factors in nationality, or relying more upon the older interpretations of national strength, recognized more tardily the importance of education as a means of developing national unity and power.   Even the United States has depended more on geographical environment, racial selection, political institutions and common language than upon consciously developed cultural unity.   While in the early national period the importance of education to the successful workings and perpetuation of free institutions was commonly recognized, yet a wholly individualistic interpretation of education was practised.

Practically all modern nations are now awake to the fact that education is the most potent means in the development of the essentials of nationality.   Education is the means by which peoples of retarded cultures may be brought rapidly to the common level.   Education is the means by which small or weak nations may become so strong through their cultural strength and achievements that their place in the political world may be made secure.   Education is the means by which nations, strong in the strength of the past, may go through the perilous transition to the modern world, as has Japan and as will Russia.   Education is the only means by which the world can be "made safe" for the national type of organization.

Thus the history of nationality during the nineteenth century is closely bound up with the problems of education.   And, on the other hand, the education of the present may find an interpretation of all of its problems, whether of purpose, of subject-matter, of organization, or even of method in terms of nationality.

341. The French Teacher and the National Spirit

(Buisson, Ferdinand, "The Schoolmaster as a Pioneer of Democracy"; in *Manuel général*, September 28, 1909.   Reproduced by permission from Buisson and Farrington's *French Educational Ideals of Today*.   World Book Company, Yonkers, 1919)

The following address to the teachers of France, printed in the principal educational journal of France, in 1909, by its Editor — at that time a member of and chairman of the Committee on Education of the French Chamber of Deputies — is so expressive of the French use of education for national ends, and likewise so expressive of the French educational spirit, that a good portion of the address is here reproduced.

In the eyes of the world, France is attempting what some one has called an "unheard-of experiment."   She has pledged herself to establish a new social order founded upon reason and justice.   She has proclaimed the rights of man, enunciated the principal of universal liberty, and suppressed all caste privileges. Since escaping as if by a miracle from all forms of reaction and starting again on her march with the Third Republic, she is building up step by step the new type of society that she conceived — a society in which each individual will not only encounter no obstacle but will be sure to receive the support of society in the free and complete development of his personality.

Wishing to realize this ideal, the Republic needed to interest the entire nation. In a democracy nothing is done unless the people wish it, and then only to the extent that the people wish.

The Republic found a man in each village who was very close to the people, one possessing the confidence of the citizens, and enjoying a situation at once modest and independent, whose profession removed him from petty local quarrels, but left him capable of exerting an incalculable influence, through the children upon the family, and through the family upon the district. It was natural, it was inevitable, that the Republic

FIG. 83
FERDINAND BUISSON
(b. 1841)

in its propaganda should have made of the schoolmaster its first national agent, the sower of republican ideas.

Thus the schoolmaster's social rôle evolved, not a product of faint ambition, nor of vain presumption, but of the very force of circumstances.

To the sons of working men and peasants whose education the Republic confides to them, they are bound to give a course in civic instruction which will enable these children to live in the twentieth century and not in the eighteenth, in a democratic republic and no longer under a king or an emperor. They are bound to teach their pupils that the Republic wishes all men to "be born and to remain free and in rights equal"; that it will be neither a blameworthy nor a chimerical hope on their part to desire to see this ideal realized; that this realization depends in great measure upon themselves; that the political, economic, and intellectual emancipation of the workers will be the act of the workers themselves; that it suffices for them to agree, to organize, to teach themselves to apply the perfectly legal means of political action which universal suffrage offers them, the syndicate and economic coöperation; that to this end there is need of having recourse neither to rioting, nor to dynamite, nor to sabotage, nor to any form of violence; and finally that the lesson of these last years, not only in France, but in Belgium, Germany, and England, proves that through association the proletariat can become a power, capable of treating with other powers as their peer. All this, they are bound to teach. Such being the case, they can show only a cordial sympathy and a fraternal spirit to all efforts toward organization on the part of the working class.

On the other hand, they can no longer believe that war is an institution forever necessary and inevitable. They belong to a people who have always passed for brave men and who have one of the richest heritages of military glory that history records, but who also treasure in their family inheritance the persistent idea of abolishing war and of substituting for bloody violence between peoples and between men the rational law of arbitration. They will not hide from these French youths that a Frenchman of the twentieth century dare no longer have the mental attitude of the soldiers of Louis XIV or of the "growlers" of Napoleon. They will not leave the youth ignorant of the fact that we send statesmen to The Hague to write line by line with labored pen, but none the less surely, the charter of a civilization to come, which some day perhaps will solve by simple and peaceful arbitration the conflicts that are so tragically and sometimes so wrongly decided to-day by the massacre of millions of men.

On these two points the teacher of 1909 is obliged by his profession to act in sympathy with his time and his country.

. . . .

What, then, is the difficulty? And why is the schoolmaster of our time wrestling with practical problems that his predecessors did not have and that are not known to the same extent by his colleagues in other countries?

We have just seen the reason. It is because he is being asked what has never before been asked of a teaching body: to teach at the same time for both the present and the future.

The French schoolmaster is the servant of a republic and of a democracy that does not insult him by believing him neutral, indifferent, or skeptical. This republic, this democracy, wishes him to speak for her, to act openly for her, to make her understood, to make her loved, to furnish her with generations of men inspired with principles of republican and democratic faith. He must, therefore, give these new generations a twofold education, the one they need immediately and the one that they will doubtless need later, for the democracy is constantly advancing, and the young must be able to advance with her. They are not destined to live indefinitely the life of the present, this transitional moment which is no longer the monarchy and which is not yet the perfect democracy.

A twofold education, then, for our children when they become citizens will entail a twofold duty. Whether they consider national or foreign policy, social relations or international relations, they will have constantly to harmonize the vision of the future with the good of the present, the hope of to-morrow with the obligation of to-day.

From the social point of view our pupils can not only hope for, but they should support vigorously with their votes and with their united efforts a demand for, a state of affairs more and more in conformity to the principles of justice. The teacher should inspire in them the spirit of association and coöperation. Thus he will arm them against the so-called revolutionary methods, which can only retard the real economic revolution, against the revolutionary general strike, against sabotage, "that affront to the conscience of work," against illegal and violent action, which is but one more disorder added to others — in short, against all forms of anarchy, which would do more harm to the democratic and social republic than they would to any other society.

Where the military question is concerned, we have the same twofold duty.

That which makes the task of the teacher both unique and noble is that as he awakens in the souls of the young people the idea of one of the greatest advances humanity can make, he will tell them that the best means of hastening this great reform is to support with all their energy the country that has conceived this reform and may some day have the honor of carrying it through triumphantly. Far, then, from lessening the duty these young citizens owe the country, this outlook can only strengthen it, since it gives them additional reasons for shedding their blood for their country if such a sacrifice becomes necessary. . . . True patriotism is like all other virtues; an honest man does not make a display of it. The teacher prefers acts to words. The conduct of his pupils will prove that they know how to serve their country like men, assuming if necessary all possible sacrifices. In suggesting this conduct he no longer appeals to hatred of the foreigner, or love of glory, or blind chauvinism, or the intoxication of battle. His pupils will find an equally strong incentive in the clear notion of duty and in the vivid feeling of the devotion they owe to France; for is not serving France the surest way of serving humanity?

. . . .

The moment through which modern civilization is passing imposes upon the teacher two functions, two tasks, which seem to contradict each other, but which nevertheless he is expected to perform simultaneously.

He is a pioneer in all the new ideas which are the very soul of democracy. Nevertheless he should keep himself and his pupils from digressions, from excesses, and from impatience. In speaking to the young, he should appeal frankly to all the generosity that youth possesses, to faith in progress, to enthusiasm for the good. At the same time he should dissuade from employing methods that appear the most expeditious, but which are brusque and brutal. He should inspire a determination to urge society forward by reason and not by force.

Commissioned to propagate the spirit of solidarity, the love of liberty, the thirst for justice, the will to progress, the schoolmaster should perform his function as magistrate of civic education while at the same time binding himself to neutrality in everything that does not concern the very principles of democracy itself.

He is both a militant and a man of peace. At heart he is in sympathy with the people, yet he must not teach class hatred. He is the servant of the nation, and at the same time he is conscious of an international duty. He says openly, "Have a horror of war!" But he prepares his pupils to be good soldiers, capable some day of being heroes.

We readily acknowledge that such a task is less simple than that of the schoolmaster of a bygone day. But it is to the honor of the teachers, men and women, such as the Republic has made them, that one should consider putting into their hands the moral direction of a whole people, not determining exactly what is expected of them, but leaving them to act freely, with reason for a guide and conscience as judge.

Are we not justified in saying that rarely in history has a bolder, a more delicate and difficult enterprise been confided, not to a carefully chosen élite, but to a corps of more than one hundred thousand persons taken from the lower strata of the nation?

.   .   .   .

342. The German Emphasis on National Ends

(Fr. de Hovre, *German and English Education*, pp. 23–29.   London, 1916)

The following selection is from a very interesting little book, comparing German and English education, by a *Maître de Conférences* on the Philosophy of Education at the Higher Institute of Philosophy, of Louvain University, which appeared in London, written by a Belgian exile, during the World War. In the chapter from which this is taken the author defines German *Kultur*, and declares it to be "The Soul of Modern Germany."

What is meant by Kultur? The best way to grasp what it means is to go back to its origin. Kultur is something German; it is an historical product of their life, and therefore it is only by noting its development that we shall come to see its full and cumulative meaning.

Being the real soul of the new Germany, Kultur is really the foundation-stone upon which the German Empire has been built. It is as old as the very idea of the German nation, with which it is most closely bound up.

.   .   .   .

It was in those dark days (1806–13) that the national idea ripened in the German mind. The noise of battle had scarcely ceased before the man arose who was to give voice to the sentiments which had gradually matured in the German heart.   This apostle of German nationalism was Fichte.   In 1808, two years after the defeat of Jena, he delivered in Berlin his famous "Discourses to the German Nation" which are the gospel of German nationalism and contain the very pith and substance of their Kultur.

.   .   .   .

Fichte found the highest expression of the German nation in the German language.   The German language, says Fichte, must be loved not only as the expression of the German mind, but also because it is the only purely original language in Europe.   All others have been corrupted by Latin and Greek.   German alone has remained pure.   Continuing, he maintains that a nation with such an original language must trace its descent from the birth of humanity.   It must be a primitive nation.   And in this way it comes about that the German nation is the oldest people in Europe.   Moreover such a language must have been fashioned by a people with an original mind; therefore the German mind must be the only one which is truly original.   The German mind, on the other hand, must be original not only in the elaboration of its language, but also in the expression of its feelings and thoughts, in all the provinces of its activity, namely, in its religion, philosophy, poetry, science, art, industry, social organization, education, etc.   Such a nation, in short, must have its own idiosyncracy in all departments of life.   It must have its own Kultur.   Thus Fichte laid the national foundation-stone of German Kultur.

The nation warrants the originality of Kultur; the State assures its consolidation.   Though the idea of the Kultur-State was already revolving in the mind of Fichte, it was by Hegel that the political foundation of Kultur was laid.

According to Hegel, the State is previous to the individual, previous to all social institutions; it existed before the family, before society, before the nation and the Church.   Just as the premises imply the conclusion, just as the Absolute dominates the contingent and the universal includes the particular and the class, in the same way the State implies the individual and the social institutions.   The State is the source of all existence, the creator of all rights, the highest power on earth, the "realization of the moral idea," the "divine will," the "earthly divinity."

By his view that "the rational is real and the real is rational," Hegel very soon came to regard the German State as the truest embodiment of his State-idea.   The organism of Germany, with him, is the German State; the individuals are only its cells; the social institutions are merely its organs.   The German State stands supreme over and rests under no obligation to any other State.   The German State is a closed system, bound by no power on earth, absolute, omnipotent.   Its own life, its own existence is its one concern.

The place to be assigned to Kultur is thus clearly indicated: it will be but another subservient element in the German State. Kultur is the spiritual capital of the nation, the German State is its owner; Kultur is the soul, the State is the body of Germany; Kultur is the heart, the State is the protecting thorax of the national organism: Kultur is the marrow, the State is the backbone of Germany. On this so intimate connection between the two is founded the idea of the German Kultur-State.

Fichte and Hegel were the spiritual fathers of Germany, the two pioneers of the German Kultur idea. Later on their work was developed by others. The political basis of Kultur, established by Hegel, was afterwards indebted for development, firstly, on the side of history to Treitschke; secondly, in the realm of practical politics to Bismarck; thirdly, in the realm of matters military to men like Scharnhorst, Hardenberg, to writers like Clausewitz, Moltke, Bernhardi. The national basis of Kultur, conceived and laid by Fichte, was later developed in the various liberal sciences and other departments; so, for instance, in economic theory by the National-Economists, in practice by the Zollverein (Customs-Union).

If we take both its national and its political basis into consideration, German Kultur may thus be defined: "the whole of the creations and achievements of the German nation; its language, science, art, literature, industry, army, education, etc., organized and controlled by the German State for the German State."

343. The Landing of the Pilgrims at Manila

(Stuntz, Homer C., in *Journal of Education*, vol. 75, p. 66. January 18, 1912)

The following brief article, by one of the earliest American teachers in the Philippines, gives well the spirit with which the United States went about helping the Filipino people to help themselves.

Ten years ago to-day (viz. August 23, 1901), the famous shipload of American teachers landed in Manila. There is no parallel to that event in the history of nations, and certainly not in the history of colonization in Asia or Africa. A strong nation finds itself in control of eight million weak and belated people. This control comes after two years of war, with rifle and gunboat and cannon, bringing public order out of chaos and insurrection.

All the precedents set America by pioneers in Asiatic colonization may be scrutinized in vain to find a suggestion of the course taken by Governor Taft and his advisers. They passed "Act number 74," — a free public school act. Then they set scores of college presidents in the United States to work securing teachers, and on this date, ten years ago, the army transport Thomas took five hundred and fifty graduates of our universities, colleges, and normal schools to the Philippines to begin that education of all the people which must precede the establishment there of a government of the Philippines by the Filipinos.

It was a great day. I can never forget that I was not only a witness, but a participant in an event that had no precedent and can never be duplicated. No salute was fired; but tons of powder burned in "shameless shocks of senseless sound" could not have made more significant the "landing of the Pilgrims" in Philippine pedagogy — the layers of sure foundation principles for hosts unborn to build upon. We were Americans. Over our heads floated free the stars and stripes. The yellow flag of Spain was gone. With it should go illiteracy, intolerance, monarchy, and that ruthless disregard of the individual's welfare which goes with the unruly trinity named.

England had ruled parts of the East for more than a century, and, in the main, ruled it well. Germany, the Netherlands, Portugal, and France had each colonized parts of the vast continent of Asia and some of its islands, but no one of these nations had ever let an official drag-net down among the graduates of her institutions of higher education and seined up over five hundred young men and women, and then chartered a ship and sent them "to the uttermost parts of the earth" to lift their belated wards up to a plane upon which they could hope to stand as a self-respecting and a self-governing people. That America did, and every patriot's pulse should beat a bit more rapidly when he recalls this notable anniversary from year to year — August 23.

These teachers and their successors have wrought wonders in the decade which closes to-night. Over half a million Filipino children and youth are now in school. Five hundred thousand Filipino young men and women are now teaching English to their own people, and none of them knew English ten years ago. More Filipinos can now speak English than could ever speak Spanish, and our less than ten years of actual school work seems a very brief period when compared with three hundred years during which Spain could have taught her tongue.

Splendid new intermediate and high school buildings are being built, costing up to $50,000. each. The new building for the Manila Normal School is about completed, at a cost of $250,000. The University of the Philippines is fast taking on the proportions of a great state university. Trade schools are receiving special attention. A group of twenty new and fully-equipped buildings is being planned for this one phase of the new educational era in the Philippines.

The *Report of the Superintendent of Education for the Philippine Islands*, for 1918, contains information which supplements the above in an interesting manner. The following is a digest of certain portions of this Report.

The steady progress of the people of the Philippine Islands toward preparedness for unassisted self-government is reflected in the change in the character of the teaching force, and the new interest in education shown by the Filipino people themselves. In 1913 the percentage of American teachers in the intermediate schools of the Islands was 20; in 1918 but 2.7 per cent; in the secondary schools the reduction was from 97.5 to 67 per cent; and among the supervisors of education the reduction was from 64 to 22 per cent. In 1918 the Filipino legislature appropriated $1,500,000 for an educational program extending over the following ten years, with a view to placing free elementary instruction within the reach of every child of school age on the Islands. To do this twelve thousand additional teachers will need to be trained, and thousands of new school buildings will have to be erected. The six hundred thousand pupils in English-speaking schools in 1918 will be doubled by 1923, and by 1921 a majority of the Filipino legislature will be English-speaking. The Spanish language is steadily giving way to the English, and the general adoption of the latter as the official language of the Islands is only a matter of a short time.

CHAPTER XXVIII

NEW CONCEPTIONS OF THE EDUCATIONAL PROCESS

THE Readings of this chapter relate largely to the rise of teacher-training and the normal school, the grading of instruction, and the new theories as to the educational purpose and process which have come in during the latter part of the nineteenth century.

The first nations to organize special institutions for the training of teachers were the German States and France, the former taking the lead. Still later came England and the United States. These four were the leading nations in the movement, up to beyond the middle of the nineteenth century, and from these four the teacher-training idea has spread over the world. Selections **344** and **345** relate to the German teachers' seminaries, as early travelers abroad found them, the first describing their work in general terms, and the second a specific institution. Selection **346** describes a French normal school of the same period. Selections **347** and **348** relate to beginnings in England, the first describing the origins of the training-college system, and the second the pupil-teacher system which was introduced later on. All these descriptions were influential in getting under way the early American development. Selection **349** reproduces the recommendation of Governor Clinton, of New York, for the inauguration of teacher-training in the academies, a recommendation which was at once adopted by the New York legislature. The next, **350 a-c,** describes the real beginnings of the state normal school idea in the United States — **350 a** reproducing the first Massachusetts law, **350 b** the first admission regulations and course of instruction, and **350 c** Horace Mann's conception of the importance of the normal school in a state system of public instruction, as expressed at the dedication of the first building erected in the United States for the specific purpose of training teachers.

The next group of selections relates to the transformation in the instruction of the school produced by the coming of professional training and the industrial and social revolutions of the nineteenth century. Selection **351** reproduces a number of extracts from popular early American school textbooks, to illustrate the old type of subject-matter instruction.   Selection 352 reproduces a typical teacher's contract of the same period, which also is illustrative of the early textbook and fact-instruction type of school. The next selection (353) is introduced to show the partly ungraded character and subjects of study of the schools of the city of Berlin, at about the same time.   The next selection (354) describes the process of grading American schools which took place during the first half of the nineteenth century — the evolution at Providence, Rhode Island, being taken as a type of early American development.

The remaining selections of the chapter relate to nineteenth-century educational theory and practice. Selections 355 and 356 give good statements as to the nature and importance of the work done by Herbart.   Selection 357 is a good brief statement of scientific progress and of the changes in psychology during the century, while selection 364 compares the psychology of Pestalozzi and his followers with that of more recent educational workers.   Selection 358 gives a good brief exposition of Froebel's educational ideas, by his most important interpreter and propagandist.

Selections 359 to 363 relate to the movement for the introduction of science study.   Selection 359 contrasts the English and German universities of the mid-nineteenth century in the matter of scientific research.   Selections 360 and 361 describe the English elementary and secondary education at the same time, revealing the dearth of modern studies.   Selections 362 and 363 give the argument and the conclusions of Herbert Spencer on the question he raised as to "What Knowledge is of Most Worth?"

Selections 365 and 366 describe the recent transformation of school instruction from the older textbook type (351) to instruction which tries to relate the work of the school to life outside. The first (365) shows the difficulties experienced in transforming a school system of the old type into the new, as illustrated by China; and the second (366), illustrates, from the teaching of history, the modern attempt to socialize all school work.

344. The German Seminaries for Teachers

(Bache, Alexander D., *Report on Education in Europe*, pp. 325–26. Philadelphia, 1839)

In 1836 the trustees of the newly founded Girard College, at Philadelphia, an institution for the education of orphans, sent

Professor A. D. Bache "to visit all establishments in Europe re-
sembling Girard College." On his return, in 1839, his *Report on
Education in Europe* was printed. He devoted much space to an
enthusiastic description of the Pestalozzian methods, as he had
seen them in the schools of Holland and the German States, and
had the following to say with reference to the German system for
training teachers.

When education is to be rapidly advanced, Seminaries for Teachers
offer the means of securing this result. An eminent teacher is selected
as Director of the Seminary; and by aid of competent assistants, and
while benefiting the community by the instruction given in the schools
attached to the Seminary, trains, yearly, from thirty to forty youths
in the enlightened practice of his methods; these, in turn, become
teachers of schools, which they are fit at once to conduct, without the
failures and mistakes usual with novices; for though beginners in name,
they have acquired, in the course of two or three years spent at the
Seminary, an experience equivalent to many years of unguided efforts.
This result has been fully realized in the success of the attempts to
spread methods of Pestalozzi and others through Prussia. The plan
has been adopted, and is yielding its appropriate fruits in Holland,
Switzerland, France, and Saxony; while in Austria, where the method
of preparing teachers by their attendance on the primary schools is
still adhered to, the schools are stationary, and behind those of Northern and Middle Germany.

These Seminaries produce a strong *esprit de corps* among teachers,
which tends powerfully to interest them in their profession, to attach
them to it, to elevate it in their eyes, and to stimulate them to improve
constantly upon the attainments with which they may have commenced its exercise. By their aid a standard of examination in the
theory and practice of instruction is furnished, which may be fairly
exacted of candidates who have chosen a different way to obtain access
to the profession.

345. A German Teachers' Seminary described

(Bache, Alexander D., *Report on Education in Europe*, pp. 237–40. Philadelphia, 1839)

The preceding selection deals with the German Teachers' Seminaries in general, and the following describes the work of one of
the best of the time (1838), located at Weissenfels, in Saxony.

This seminary, for the education of teachers for the elementary
schools, is one of four belonging to the province of Saxony, and was last
organized in 1822. It combines within its premises, or in the neighborhood, so as to be subject to the control of the same director, the follow-

ing establishments: 1. The normal school, or seminary for teachers, a government institution. 2. A preparatory school, subsidiary to the former, and established by the enterprise of its teachers. 3. A seminary school, or burgher school, of four hundred pupils already described. 4. An elementary school for poor children, of two hundred pupils. 5. A school for the deaf and dumb, of twenty-five pupils, established in 1828, and supported by the government. The last three mentioned schools afford practice to the students of the seminary.

The government of these establishments is confided to a director, who is responsible immediately to the provincial school-board in Magdeburg. He has the personal charge of the seminary in which he gives instruction, and of which he superintends the domestic economy, discipline, and policy. He is assisted in the seminary by three teachers, who meet him once a week in conference, to discuss the progress and conduct of the pupils, the plans of instruction, and other matters relating to the school. There are also seven assistant teachers, five for the seminary school, and two for the deaf and dumb institution, who also assist in the seminary itself. Once a month there is a general meeting of the teachers of all the schools just enumerated, for similar purposes.

Applicants for admission are required to produce certificates of baptism, of moral conduct, and of health, besides an engagement on the part of their parents or guardians to pay an annual sum of fifty thalers (thirty-seven dollars) for maintenance. These papers must be forwarded to the director a fortnight before the day of examination. The candidates are examined at a certain time of the year (after Easter), in the presence of all the teachers of the school, and their attainments must prove satisfactory in Bible and church history, the Lutheran Catechism, reading, writing, German grammar, especially the orthography of the language, the ground-rules of arithmetic (mental and written), geography and history, and natural history and philosophy, of the grade of the highest class of a burgher school. They must also be able to play, at sight, easy pieces of music upon the violin. The usual age of admission is eighteen; and the lowest at which they are admissible, seventeen. On entrance they are entitled to free lodging and instruction, and, if their conduct and progress are satisfactory, in general, receive a yearly allowance of twenty-five dollars, which is equivalent, nearly, to the cost of their maintenance. Their clothing and school books are provided by the pupils. The modes of preparation judged most appropriate by the authorities of the seminary are, the attendance on a burgher school, with private lessons from a competent teacher, or entrance into the preparatory establishment at Weissenfels. A gymnasium is considered by no means a proper place for the preparation of pupils, its courses, discipline, and mode of life having a different tendency from that required by the future teacher of a common school.

The admission of new pupils takes place with some ceremony, in presence of the teachers and pupils. The director gives a charge, in which he makes them acquainted with the rules of the school, chiefly those relating to moral conduct, to obedience to the authorities, punctuality, regular attendance at study, school, church, and, in general, on the appointed exercises, due exertion, neatness in their habits, and exactness in the payment of dues to the tradesmen with whom they may deal. They bind themselves to serve for three years after leaving the school, in whatever situation may be assigned them by the regency of Merseburg, or to pay the cost of their education and maintenance. During their stay at the seminary, they are exempted from military service, except for six weeks. . . .

The courses of instruction are, — morals and religion, German, arithmetic and geometry, cosmology, pedagogy, terraculture, hygiene, theory and practice of music, drawing and writing. Cosmology is a comprehensive term for geography, an outline of history and biography, the elements of natural history and natural philosophy, all that relates to the world (earth) and its inhabitants. Pedagogy includes both the science and art of teaching. The courses just enumerated are divided among the masters, according to the supposed ability of each in the particular branches, the whole instruction being given by the four teachers. The director, as is customary in these schools, takes the religious instruction, and the science and art of teaching, as his especial province, and adds lectures on the theory of farming and gardening (terraculture), and of health.

The duration of the course of studies has been reduced from three years to two, on account, it is alleged, of the necessity for a more abundant supply of teachers. There are, probably, other reasons, such as the expense, and the fear of over-educating the pupils for their station, which have been influential in bringing about this reduction. There are two classes corresponding to the two years of study. The first year is devoted entirely to receiving instruction; and in the second, practice in teaching is combined with it. In the preparatory school there is likewise a course of two years, and the pupils are divided into two classes. . . .

346. A French Normal School described

(Bache, Alexander D., *Report on Education in Europe*, pp. 349–53. Philadelphia, 1839)

The following description gives a good idea of a typical French normal school for the training of elementary teachers of the time (1837) of Guizot.

The Primary Normal School of Versailles is for the Department of Seine and Oise. It comprises within its ample premises several establishments for the instruction and practice of teachers. The school itself contains eighty pupils under regular instruction throughout the year, and furnishes a two months' course to adult schoolmasters. The establishments for practice begin with the infant school, and rise through the primary to the grade of primary superior. Of the elementary schools, one affords the young teacher an example of the method of mutual, and another of simultaneous instruction. The primary superior school had been recently established, at the date of my visit, in 1837. There is, besides, an evening department for the elementary instruction of adults, taught by the pupils of the Normal School, and also a school of design, which is established here rather for convenience than as properly belonging to the range of the institution.

. . . The age of admission is, by rule, between sixteen and twenty-one, but the former limit is considered too early for profitable entrance. The qualifications for admission consist in a thorough knowledge of the subjects taught in the elementary schools.

The period of instruction is two years. The first year is devoted to the revision of elementary studies, and the second to an extension of them, and to theoretical and practical instruction in the science and art of teaching. The subjects of revision or instruction are, reading, writing, linear drawing, geography, history, the drawing of maps, morals and religion, vocal music, arithmetic, elementary physics, terra-culture, and pedagogy.

The religious instruction is given by an ecclesiastic, who is almoner to the school; it includes lessons on the doctrines and history of the church, given twice per week. Protestants are not required to attend these lessons, but receive instruction out of the institution from a minister of their own confession.

. . . .

Besides the more usual school implements, this institution has a library, a small collection of physical and chemical apparatus, of technological specimens, already of considerable interest, and of models of agricultural implements. There are also two gardens, one of which is laid out to serve the purposes of systematic instruction in horticulture, the other of which contains specimens of agricultural products, and a ground for gymnastic exercises. The pupils work by details of three at a time, under the direction of the gardener, in cultivating flowers, fruits, vegetables, etc. They have the use of a set of carpenters' and joiners' tools, with which they have fitted up their own library in a very creditable way. In the second year they receive lectures on the science and art of teaching, and in turn give instruction in the schools, under the direction of the teachers. Their performances are subsequently criticised for their improvement.

The order of the day in summer is as follows:

The pupils rise at five, wash, make up their beds, and clean their dormitories, in two divisions, which alternate; meet in the study hall at half past five for prayers, breakfast, engage in studies or recitation until one; dine and have recreation until two; study or recite until four; have exercises or recreation, sup, study, and engage in religious reading and prayers; and retire at ten, except in special cases. Before meals there is a grace said, and during meals one of the pupils reads aloud.

In distributing the time devoted to study and recitation, an hour of study is made to precede a lesson, when the latter requires specific preparation; when, on the contrary, the lesson requires after-reflection to fix its principles, or consists of a lecture, of which the notes are to be written out, the study hour follows the lesson. The branches of a mechanical nature are interspersed with the intellectual. The students of the second year are employed, in turn, in teaching, and are relieved from other duties during the hours devoted to the schools of practice.

On Sunday, after the morning service, the pupils are free to leave the walls of the institution. The same is the case on Thursday afternoon. The director has found, however, bad results from these indiscriminate leaves of absence.

347. The Beginnings of Teacher Training in England

(Barnard, Henry, *National Education in Europe*, p. 751. Hartford, 1854)

The following brief historical account is descriptive of the beginnings of teacher training in England and Scotland.

The germ of all the institutions for training teachers for elementary schools in England, must be found in the model school and teachers' class of the British and Foreign School Society in the Borough-road, London. So early as 1805, the "training of schoolmasters," in the methods of this school, was made the ground of a subscription in its behalf, and in 1808, it was set forth as one of the cardinal objects of the society. From that time, persons have been admitted every year to the school to observe, learn, and practice the methods of classification and instruction pursued there. Its accommodations as a normal school were insufficient even on the plan of observation and practice pursued there, until 1842, when the present building was completed at an expense of £21,433, toward which the Committee of Council extended a grant of £5000. In the mean time the National Society was pursuing a similar plan in its model school at Westminster; and the necessity of training well-qualified teachers by means of a special course of instruction and practice was ably discussed, and the mode and results of such training as exhibited on the continent, and especially in Prussia, were ably advocated in parliament, pamphlets, reviews, and the daily press. The *Quarterly Journal of Education*, and the publications of the Central Society of Education, and especially the Prize Essay of Mr. Lalor, set forth this necessity, and the experience of other countries in a very able manner. Lord Brougham, in his whole public life the early and eloquent advocate of popular education, in a speech in the House of Lords on the education of the people on the 23d May, 1835, remarked:

"These seminaries for training masters are an invaluable gift to mankind and lead to the indefinite improvement of education. It is this which above all things we ought to labor to introduce into our system. . . . Place all normal schools — seminaries for training teachers — in a few such places as London, York, Liverpool, Durham, and Exeter, and you will yearly qualify five hundred persons fitted for diffusing a perfect system of instruction all over the country. These training seminaries will not only teach the masters the branches of learning and science in which they are now deficient, but will teach them what they know far less, the didactic art — the mode of imparting the knowledge they have, or may acquire — the best method of training and dealing with children, in all that regards temper, capacity, and habits, and the means of stirring them to exertion, and controlling their aberrations."

The speaker, though he failed in this, as well as in former, and subsequent efforts in parliament, to establish a system of national education, according to his own views, has lived long enough to see thirty-six normal schools, or training colleges in England and Wales, four in Scotland, and one in Ireland, in successful operation; and both the quantity and quality of elementary instruction greatly improved. These results have been realized mainly through the action of the Board, or Committee of Council on Education, first appointed in 1839.

One of the first objects proposed for the consideration of the Board, was a normal, or model school, in organizing which they were advised that "it is her Majesty's wish, that the youth of this kingdom should be religiously brought up, and that the right of conscience should be respected." The committee experienced so much difficulty in devising the plan of a normal school, under their direction, and in reconciling conflicting views of religious communions, that the subject was postponed, and the sum of £10,000 granted by parliament in 1835 toward the erection of such a school, was distributed in equal proportions to the National Society, and the British and Foreign School Society, to be applied by them for this purpose.

With the aid of this grant, the British and Foreign School Society proceeded to provide suitable accommodations for a class of eighty normal pupils, in connection with the model schools in the Borough-road. The building was completed in 1842, at an expense of £21,433. The National Society commenced, in 1840, the erection of a training college for seventy-four masters of schools in connection with that Society, at Stanley Grove, in Chelsea, two miles from Hyde Park Corner. . . .

The success of these experiments dissipated the vague apprehensions, which the first announcement of normal schools, as a foreign institution, had created, and inspired general confidence in their tendencies, and conviction of their necessities. The different religious communions, by whose exertions and jealousies the plan of the Committee of Council had been defeated in 1839, now came forward to found Training Colleges for teachers of schools in their several connections. The Committee of Council encouraged the erection of suitable buildings by grants of money, and contributed toward their support and usefulness by the establishment of the system of pupil teachers, and Queen's scholarships, by which young men and young women of the right character are prepared for these institutions, and enabled to remain in them for a sufficient length of time to profit by the extended course of instruction, and practice prescribed.

.   .   .   .

In 1852, there were thirty-four Normal Schools or Training Colleges in England and Wales, erected at an expense in building alone of over £350,000 of which sum the government contributed about one half. These institutions provide the means of residence for about 1000 males and seven hundred females, at an annual outlay of about £80,000, of which the government will contribute, in grants for Queen's scholars, about one half.

.   .   .   .

In Scotland, the first attempt to train teachers in the principles and practice of their art, was made by the Education Committee of the Church of Scotland, in 1826, by placing a few teachers appointed to their schools in the Highlands, for a short course of observation, instruction and practice, in one of their best-conducted schools in Edinburgh. This plan was enlarged and improved in 1838; and, in 1846, a building was erected for a Normal School in Castle Place, in Edinburgh, at an expense of £10,000. In the mean time, Mr. Snow, in 1836, commenced at Glasgow, a similar enterprise at his own risk to exemplify, and finally, to train teachers on a system of instruction somewhat peculiar. He was subsequently aided by a voluntary society, and finally the building was completed by the General Assembly Committee in 1840. The disruption of the Church of Scotland, and the organization of the free church, has led to the establishment of two other Normal Schools, one at Edinburgh, in 1849, and the other at Glasgow, in 1852, at an aggregate expense of over £20,000. The buildings for Normal Schools, in Scotland, have cost over £45,000 ($225,000.), and will accommodate about 300 resident pupils, besides the schools of practice.

Of the forty Training Colleges in England and Scotland, twenty-seven are connected with the Church of England, two with the established Church of Scotland, two with the Free Church of Scotland, one with the Roman Catholic Church, one with the Wesleyan, one with the Congregational denomination; and in the six others, the Church of England has a virtual ascendency.

348. The Pupil-Training System described

(Barnard, Henry, *National Education in Europe*, p. 753.   Hartford, 1854)

In 1846 the English educational authorities, in an effort to secure more trained teachers for the schools, instituted an apprenticeship form of teacher training.   Under this system pupils were apprenticed, usually from thirteen to eighteen years of age, to learn the art of teaching, after which they might be eligible to enter a training college.   The following is a brief description of the plan.

To stimulate and aid the elementary schools, and to prepare pupils for the Training Schools, stipends from £10 to £18, increasing from year to year for five years, are allowed to a certain number of the most vigorous, intelligent, well-behaved and proficient scholars in any school, subject to the inspection of the government, who shall pass in a satisfactory manner, the examination prescribed by the Committee of Council, for an apprenticeship to the office of teaching.   These *pupil teachers*, as they are called, receive daily one hour and a half of separate instruction from the master of the schools, to which they belong (who receives an annual addition to his salary according to the number of such pupils), besides spending about the same time in diligent preparation; and during five hours each day, are familiarized with the management and instruction of an elementary school, by having charge of one of its classes.   After spending five years in this way, and passing satisfactorily the annual written and oral examination on subjects presented by the committee, these pupil teachers are then allowed to enter on a vigorous competition for admission in any of the Training Schools, as *Queen's scholars*.   In all of the Training Schools, aided and inspected by the Committee of Council, the government allows £25 for the first year, £20 for the second, and £30 for the third year, towards the cost of maintenance and education of a given number of pupil teachers who can pass in a satisfactory manner the examination prescribed by the committee.   Each Training School receives a grant, varying from £20 to £30 on each Queen scholar instructed during the year. . . . This system of an annual and strict examination, and of an annual grant to deserving pupils to aid them in obtaining the requisite knowledge of the principles and practice of teaching, before entering on the responsibilities of a school, and of rewarding afterwards those who prove faithful and successful, is changing the whole aspect of elementary education in England.   The full results will not be seen, until after the 5000 pupil teachers, who have served an apprenticeship of five years in the best elementary schools of the kingdom, have spent three years in the Training Colleges, and having gained the certificates of merit, are actively engaged as teachers.

349. Governor Clinton on Teacher-Training Schools

(Randall, S. S., *Common School System of the State of New York*, p. 27. Troy, 1851)

In 1827 Governor DeWitt Clinton, in his message to the legislature, thus recommends the establishment of academies in the different counties of the State, in large part to train teachers for schools.

The great bulwark of republican government is the cultivation of education; for the right of suffrage cannot be exercised in a salutary manner without intelligence. It is gratifying to find that education continues to flourish. We may safely estimate the number of our common schools at 8000; the number of children taught during the last year, on an average of eight months, at 430,000; and the sum expended in education at 200,000 dollars. It is, however, too palpable that our system is surrounded by imperfections which demand the wise consideration and improving interposition of the legislature. In the first place, there is no provision made for the education of competent instructors. Of the eight thousand now employed in this state, too many are destitute of the requisite qualifications, and perhaps no considerable number are able to teach beyond rudimental instruction. Ten years of a child's life, from five to fifteen, may be spent in a common school; and ought this immense portion of time to be absorbed in learning what can be acquired in a short period? Perhaps one-fourth of our population is annually instructed in our common schools; and ought the minds and morals of the rising, and perhaps the destinies of all future generations, to be entrusted to the guardianship of incompetence? The scale of instruction must be elevated; the standard of education ought to be raised, and a central school on the monitorial plan ought to be established in each county for the education of teachers, and as exemplars for other momentous purposes connected with the improvement of the human mind.

350. Organization of the First Massachusetts Normal Schools

(*Tenth Annual Report Massachusetts State Board of Education*. Boston, 1846)

From 1825 on, James Carter and others had been trying to get a state normal school established in Massachusetts. In 1839 a citizen of Boston, Mr. Edmund Dwight, authorized Horace Mann, then Secretary of the Massachusetts State Board of Education, to say to the legislature that he would personally give $10,000 for the project, if the State of Massachusetts would appropriate a similar sum. This was done, by the following:

(a) The Organizing Law

RESOLVES

Relative to qualifying teachers for common schools

Whereas, by letter from the Honorable Horace Mann, Secretary of the Board of Education, addressed, on the 12th of March current, to the President of the Senate, and the Speaker of the House of Representatives, it appears, that private munificence has placed at his disposal the sum of ten thousand dollars, to promote the cause of popular education in Massachusetts, on condition that the Commonwealth will contribute from unappropriated funds, the same amount in aid of the same cause, the two sums to be drawn upon equally from time to time, as needed, and to be disbursed under the direction of the Board of Education in qualifying teachers for our Common Schools; therefore,

Resolved, That his Excellency, the Governor, be, and he is hereby authorized and requested, by and with the advice and consent of the Council, to draw his warrant upon the Treasurer of the Commonwealth in favor of the Board of Education, for the sum of $10,000, in such installments and at such times, as said Board may request: *provided*, said Board, in their request, shall certify, that the Secretary of said Board has placed at their disposal an amount equal to that for which such application may by them be made; both sums to be expended, under the direction of said Board, in qualifying teachers for the Common Schools in Massachusetts.

Resolved, That the Board of Education shall render an annual account of the manner in which said moneys have been by them expended.

The State Board of Education, after mature deliberation, decided to establish three state normal schools, rather than give the money to the Academies, as New York had done. This was done, and the first three state normal schools in the United States opened at Lexington, July 3, 1839; Barre, September 4, 1839; and Bridgewater, September 9, 1840. For these schools the Board established admission requirements and a course of study, as follows:

(b) Admission and Instruction

As a prerequisite to admission, candidates must declare it to be their intention to qualify themselves to become school teachers. If they belong to the State, or have an intention and a reasonable expectation of keeping school in the State, tuition is gratis. Otherwise, a tuition-fee is charged, which is intended to be about the same as is usually charged at good academies in the same neighborhood. . . .

If males, pupils must have attained the age of seventeen years complete, and of sixteen, if females; and they must be free from any disease or infirmity, which would unfit them for the office of school teachers.

They must undergo an examination, and prove themselves to be well versed in orthography, reading, writing, English grammar, geography, and arithmetic.

They must furnish satisfactory evidence of good intellectual capacity and of high moral character and principles.

Examinations for admission take place at the commencement of each term, of which there are three in a year.

Term of study.

. . . The minimum of the term of study is one year, and this must be in consecutive terms of the schools. . . .

Course of study.

The studies first to be attended to in the State Normal Schools are those which the law requires to be taught in the district schools, namely, orthography, reading, writing, English grammar, geography, and arithmetic. When these are mastered, those of a higher order will be progressively taken.

For those who wish to remain at the school more than one year, and for all belonging to the school, so far as their previous attainments will permit, the following course is arranged:

1. Orthography, reading, grammar, composition, rhetoric, and logic.
2. Writing and drawing.
3. Arithmetic, mental and written, algebra, geometry, bookkeeping, navigation, surveying.
4. Geography, ancient and modern, with chronology, statistics and general history.
5. Human Physiology, and hygiene or the Laws of Health.
6. Mental Philosophy.
7. Music.
8. Constitution and History of Massachusetts and of the United States.
9. Natural Philosophy and Astronomy.
10. Natural History.
11. The principles of piety and morality, common to all sects of Christians.
12. The science and art of teaching, with reference to all the above-named studies.

Religious exercises.

A portion of the Scriptures shall be read daily, in every State Normal School.

To these new schools Mr. Mann gave most hearty support, and helped them to weather legislative storms for a decade before they became firmly established as parts of the school system of the State.   Probably nowhere else in the Union could the normal school have been established at so early a date, or, if established, been allowed to remain.   Speaking at the dedication of the first building for normal school purposes erected in the United States, at Bridgewater, in 1846, Mr. Mann showed the deep interest he felt in the establishment of normal schools, when he said:

(c) *Importance of the Normal School*

I believe the Normal schools to be a new instrumentality in the advancement of the race.   I believe that without them free schools themselves would be shorn of their strength and their healing power, and would at length become mere charity-schools, and thus die out in

FIG. 84. THE FIRST NORMAL SCHOOL BUILDING IN THE
UNITED STATES
At Bridgewater, Massachusetts. Dedicated by Horace Mann, in 1846

fact and in form. Neither the art of printing, nor the trial by jury, nor a free press, nor free suffrage, can long exist to any beneficial and salutary purpose without schools for the training of teachers; for if the character and qualifications of teachers be allowed to degenerate, the free schools will become pauper schools, and the pauper schools will produce pauper souls, and the free press will become a false and licentious press, and ignorant voters will become venal voters, and through the medium and guise of republican forms an oligarchy of profligate and flagitious men will govern the land; nay, the universal diffusion and ultimate triumph of all-glorious Christianity itself must await the time when knowledge shall be diffused among men through the instrumentality of good schools.   Coiled up in this institution, as in a spring, there is a vigor whose uncoiling may wheel the spheres.

351. Examples of Instruction from Early Textbooks

To illustrate the type of instruction that was common in our early educational history, a few typical pages from two popular early textbooks are here reproduced. With such subject-matter, and with small texts, almost entirely devoid of illustrations, the work of the teacher was largely confined to keeping order and hearing the pupils recite what they had memorized from the text.

CHAPTER VII.

COMMENCEMENT OF HOSTILITIES.

Q. What occasioned the battle of Lexington?
A. In April 1775, Col. Smith and Major Pitcairn were sent with a body of troops to destroy the military stores which had been collected at Concord, about twenty miles from Boston. At Lexington, the militia were collected to oppose the incursion of the British troops.

Q. Were the Lexington corps successful in their opposition?
A. No: they were dispersed, and some of their number killed.

Q. When did the battle of Lexington take place? A. On the 19th of April 1775: here was shed the first blood in the American Revolution.

Q. By whom, was Delaware first settled?
A. Swedes and Finlanders.
Q. In what year, did the Swedes and Finlanders purchase the country from the Indians?
A. In 1627.
Q. What name did they give to it?
A. New Sweden.
Q. Did this territory become the property of William Penn? A. Yes.
Q. By whom, was it conveyed to him?
A. The Duke of York.
Q. In what year, was Georgia founded?
A. In the year 1732.
Q. From whom, did it derive its name?
A. George II.; under whose authority it was established.
Q. Who is mentioned as the promoter of Georgia? A. General Oglethorpe.
Q. Which is the oldest British settlement in Georgia? A. Savannah.
Q. How is Savannah situated?
Q. Of what country, was general Oglethorpe?
A. England.

FIG. 85. TWO PAGES FROM DAVENPORT'S "HISTORY OF THE UNITED STATES"

These show the catechetical form of the volume

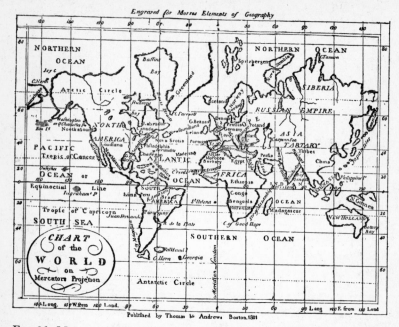

FIG. 86. MAP OF THE WORLD, PRINTED OPPOSITE TITLE-PAGE OF MORSE'S
"ELEMENTS OF GEOGRAPHY"

This was one of the two maps the volume contained, the other being a rough drawing of the eastern part of the United States, but not showing state lines

The first selection, given on page 631, reproduces two pages
from a *History of the United States*, by B. Davenport, published in
Philadelphia, in 1831. This was a little book, three and a half by
five and a half inches in size, which contained eighty-one pages
of questions and answers covering American history, arranged in
catechism form, to which was added the Declaration of Independence, the Federal Constitution, and a Table of Chronology of
thirty-two pages, extending from the creation of the world (4004
B.C.) to 1830. The entire book contained a hundred and forty-
four pages.

The second selection (pages 632, 633) reproduces the main map,
as well as the title-page and one page of text, of a very popular
early *Geography*. This was also a volume of a hundred and forty-
four pages, three and a half by five and a half inches in size. It
contained two maps, but no illustrations.

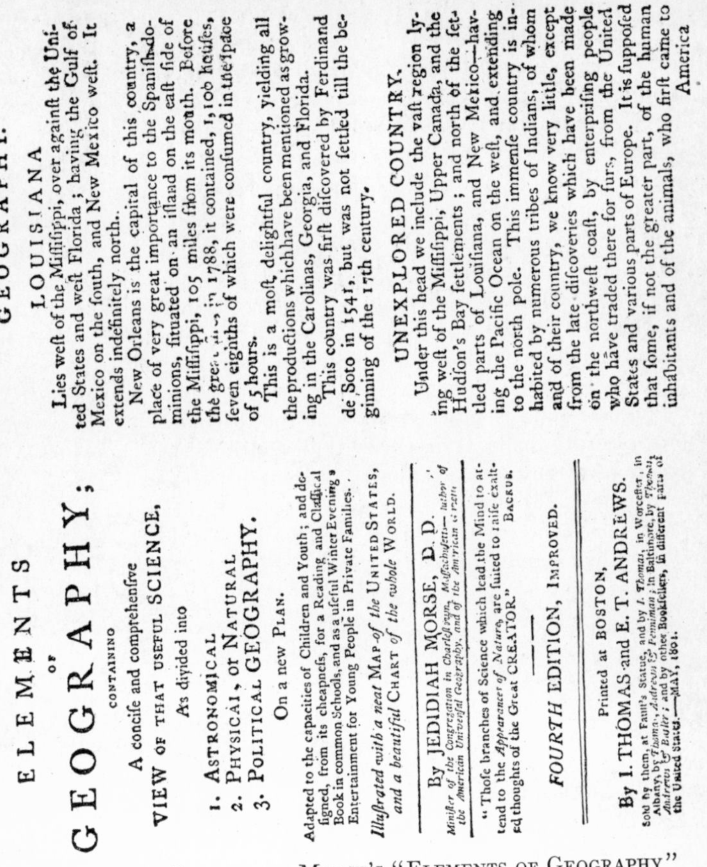

ELEMENTS
OF
GEOGRAPHY;

CONTAINING

A concise and comprehensive

VIEW OF THAT USEFUL SCIENCE,

As divided into

1. ASTRONOMICAL,
2. PHYSICAL, or NATURAL,
3. POLITICAL GEOGRAPHY.

On a new PLAN.

Adapted to the capacities of Children and Youth; and designed, from its cheapness, for a Reading and Classical Book in common Schools, and as a useful Winter Evening Entertainment for Young People in Private Families.

Illustrated with a neat Map of the UNITED STATES, and a beautiful CHART of the whole WORLD.

By JEDIDIAH MORSE, D. D.
Minister of the Congregation in Charlestown, Massachusetts— author of the American Universal Geography, and of the American Gazetteer.

"Those branches of Science which lead the Mind to attend to the Appearances of Nature, are suited to excite exalted thoughts of the Great CREATOR."   BACKUS.

FOURTH EDITION, IMPROVED.

Printed at BOSTON.

By I. THOMAS and E. T. ANDREWS.
Sold by them, at Faust's statue, and by J. Thomas, in Worcester; in Albany by Thomas, Andrews & Penniman; in Baltimore, by Thomas, Andrews & Butler; and by other Booksellers, in different parts of the United States.—MAY, 1801.

GEOGRAPHY.

LOUISIANA

Lies west of the Mississippi, over against the United States and west Florida; having the Gulf of Mexico on the south, and New Mexico west. It extends indefinitely north.

New Orleans is the capital of this country, a place of very great importance to the Spanish dominions, situated on an island on the east side of the Mississippi, 105 miles from its mouth. Before the grec...in 1788, it contained, 1,100 houses, seven eighths of which were confumed in the space of 5 hours.

This is a most delightful country, yielding all the productions which have been mentioned as growing in the Carolinas, Georgia, and Florida.

This country was first discovered by Ferdinand de Soto in 1541, but was not settled till the beginning of the 17th century.

UNEXPLORED COUNTRY.

Under this head we include the vast region lying west of the Mississippi, Upper Canada, and the Hudson's Bay settlements; and north of the settled parts of Louisiana, and New Mexico—having the Pacific Ocean on the west, and extending to the north pole. This immense country is inhabited by numerous tribes of Indians, of whom and of their country, we know very little, except from the late discoveries which have been made on the northwest coast, by enterprising people who have traded there for furs, from the United States and various parts of Europe. It is supposed that some, if not the greater part, of the human inhabitants and of the animals, who first came to America

FIG. 87. TWO PAGES FROM MORSE'S "ELEMENTS OF GEOGRAPHY"
These reveal the nature of the subject-matter of the text

352. A Typical Teacher's Contract

(Murray, David, *History of Education in New Jersey*, pp. 141. Washington, 1889)

The following teacher's contract, executed in New Jersey, in 1841, is typical of thousands of contracts of this period. It is interesting as showing the subjects taught, the ungraded character of the school, and the fact-type of instruction which the school of the time was supposed to give.

Joseph Thompson hereby agrees to teach a common English day school for the term of thirteen weeks of five days in each week (or an equivalent) in the Center schoolhouse, being District No. 8, of Bridgewater, to which is attached a part of Readington Township. He will give instruction to all the youth of the district that may be placed under his care in some or all of the following branches, as their capacities may reach, viz: Orthography, reading, writing, arithmetic, English grammar, geography, history, composition, and bookkeeping by single entry. And we, the trustees of said school, do hereby agree to furnish said teacher with fuel and all necessaries for the comfort and convenience of said school, and at the expiration of the term pay to him or his order in compensation for his services the sum of sixty-five dollars. The said teacher shall have the privilege of instructing his own children in said school and not be required to pay any proportional part of the above sum. All pupils which do not belong in the district and attend this school to learn any of the above-named branches, one half of their schooling shall belong to the teacher, and the other half to go into the funds of the school. The excess of charge for higher branches (if any are taught) shall belong exclusively to the teacher. If circumstances should occur to render it necessary to discontinue the school before the expiration of the term, a majority of the trustees or the teacher may discontinue, and he receive pay for the time then taught.

In witness whereof the parties have to these presents interchangeably set their hands this thirtieth day of October, in the year of our Lord 1841.

JOSEPH THOMPSON, *Teacher.*

ABRAHAM A. AMERMAN,
PETER Q. BROKAW,
ABRAHAM AMERMAN,

Trustees.

353. The Elementary Schools in Berlin in 1838

(Bache, Alexander D., *Report on Education in Europe*, pp. 231–35. Philadelphia, 1839)

At the time of Professor Bache's visit (1838) the elementary schools of Berlin were divided into two classes, the first covering instruction from six to ten, and the second from ten to fourteen. He gives the subjects of study, for both boys and girls, for each class, to be as follows:

Subjects of Instruction

For the first class:

1. For religion: the Bible, Catechism, the positive truths of Christianity.
2. For the German language: language considered as the expression of thought; the most general rules of grammar, clear and intelligible pronunciation, reading and orthography.
3. Writing.
4. Arithmetic, to fractions and the rule-of-three, inclusive.
5. Singing, and particularly exercises in sacred choral music.

For the second class:

(a) *Boys:* The most general elements of the natural sciences, of geography, and national history, as well as the elements of geometry and linear drawing should be added.

For the second class:

(b) *Girls:* Instruction in needle-work, knitting, &c. School hours, for both boys and girls, eight to twelve, and two to four, daily.

Time distribution — Boys' School

First class, 6–10 years of age.

3 hours for religious instruction (principally narratives from the Bible).

12 hours for the German language, pronunciation, reading, orthography, &c.

5 hours for arithmetic; 3 for the slate as far as division, and 2 for mental arithmetic.

4 hours for writing.

2 hours for singing (without counting the verses sung at the beginning and end of each day).

__

26 hours per week.

Second class, 10–14 years of age.

6 hours for religion, instruction in the Bible and Catechism.

10 hours for the German language, reading, grammar, intellectual exercises.

5 hours for arithmetic, on the slate and in the head.

4 hours for writing.

2 hours for geometry, and linear drawing.

3 hours for natural philosophy, geography, and history, &c.

2 hours for singing (not including the verses sung morning and evening).

__

32 hours per week

Time Distribution — Girls' School

First class, 6–10 years of age.

3 hours for religion (narratives from the Bible).

7 hours for the German language.

3 hours for arithmetic, on the slate and mentally.

3 hours for writing.

2 hours for singing.

8 hours for needle-work, &c.

__

26 hours per week

Second class, 10–14 *years of age.*

   6 hours for religion.

   8 hours for the German language.

   4 hours for arithmetic.

   3 hours for writing.

   3 hours for singing.

   8 hours for needle-work, &c. (in the afternoon).

  32 hours per week.

354. Grading the Schools of Providence

(Regulations of the School Committee, 1800, 1827, 1828, and Ordinance of the City Council of Providence, Rhode Island, of April 9, 1838; in *Centennial Report School Committee*, 1899–1900, pp. 49, 51–52, 58, 72)

In 1799 the "Providence Association of Mechanics and Manufacturers" petitioned the Legislature to "establish free schools throughout the State." In response a law was passed under which Providence began schools, in 1800.

The original course of study for the schools, adopted at the time of their origin, is reproduced below. It is noteworthy for its brevity and simplicity, and reveals an ungraded, individual-instruction school. It reads:

The principal part of the Instruction will consist in teaching Spelling, Accenting and Reading both Prose and Verse with propriety and accuracy, and a general knowledge of English Grammar and Composition: Also writing a good hand according to the most approved Rules, and Arithmetic through all the previous Rules, and Vulgar and Decimal Fractions, including Tare and Tret, Fellowship, Exchange, Interest, &c.

The books to be used in carrying on the above Instruction are Alden's Spelling Book, 1st and 2d part, the Young Ladies' Accidence, by Caleb Bingham, The American Preceptor, Morse's Geography, abridged, the Holy Bible in select portions and such other Books as shall hereafter be adopted and appointed by the Committee. The Book for teaching Arithmetic shall be agreed on by the Masters.

In 1827 Primary Schools were added below, to the ungraded schools organized in 1800, and the course of study was changed to read as follows: —

2d. The branches taught in the Primary Schools shall be reading and spelling; and the books used for instruction therein shall be the following and no other: viz. the New York Primer; Alden's Spelling Book, first and second parts; Easy Lessons and the New Testament.

3d. Children of both sexes of the age of four years and upwards may attend the primary schools in their respective districts and no other until they are transferred to the writing schools as is herein after prescribed.

4th. The branches taught in the writing schools shall be spelling, reading, the use of capital letters and punctuation, writing, arithmetic, the rudiments of book keeping, English grammar, geography and epistolary composition; and the books used shall be the following and no other, viz. Alden's Spelling Book, second part, the new Testament, the American Preceptor, the Brief Remarker, Murray's Sequel to the English reader, Smith's Arithmetic, Murray's Abridgement of English grammar and Woodbridge's small Geography.

Some attempt at the grading of the Writing or Grammar Schools was introduced at about this same time, by a resolution of July 23, 1827, which read:

RESOLVED that it be recommended to the Committee of the Council appointed to set off a portion of the 4th District School for a female School, and to make enquiry whether a sufficient attention be paid to the study of Arithmetic in said School. —

RESOLVED that it be recommended by this Committee that no male pupil in the public schools shall commence the study of Geography until he shall have pursued the Study of Arithmetic as far as practice, nor shall any female pupil study Geography until she shall have pursued the Study of Arithmetic as far as Compound Division.

In 1838 a higher school was voted, and organized in 1843, to complete the system upward, and a City Superintendent of Schools was ordered employed. At this time the City Council fixed the scope of the school system by an ordinance providing for one High School, six Grammar or Writing Schools, and ten Primary Schools, and made the following provisions concerning them:

Sec. 2. That each Primary School shall be under the care of a principal and one assistant teacher and the rudiments of an English education shall be taught therein. That each Grammar and Writing School shall be under the care of a Master and at least two female assistant teachers, or one male assistant teacher, at the discretion of the school committee; and the ordinary branches of an English education shall be taught therein. That the High School shall be under the care of a Preceptor and one or more Assistant teachers, and thorough instruction shall be given therein in all the branches of a good English education; and instruction shall also be given therein, to all the pupils whose parents or guardians may desire it, in all the preparatory branches of a classical education.

Sec. 3. The High School shall not at any time contain more than two hundred pupils, of which number not more than one hundred shall be females, except when the number of male pupils shall be less than one hundred; in which case, an additional number of females may be admitted, until the School shall be filled, under such conditions as the School Committee may prescribe.

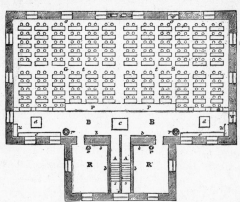

FIG. 88. EXTERIOR AND INTERIOR OF A PROVIDENCE, RHODE ISLAND
SCHOOL

This was the typical grammar-school building of about 1840. Each floor seated 228 pupils, and was conducted as a separate school. Boys and girls were here seated on opposite sides of the central aisle, though the usual plan was to give one floor to each sex. In Boston the upper floor was used by the writing school and the lower floor by the reading school. Two small recitation rooms are shown leading off the main room, for the use of the assistant teachers

Sec. 5. That the School Committee be and they are hereby authorized and requested to appoint annually a Superintendent of the Public
Schools, who shall perform such duties in relation to the public schools
as said Committee may from time to time prescribe, said Superintendent to be subject to removal at any time by the School Committee in
case of inability or mismanagement.

By 1844 the schools were re-divided into Primary, Intermediate, Grammar, and High Schools, and then the yearly grading was
further applied to perfect the system.

355. Herbart's Educational Ideas

(Felkin, Henry M. and Emmie. Translator's "Introduction" to Herbart's
Science of Education. London, 1891)

The following extracts from a long Introduction to an English
translation of Herbart's "The Æsthetic Revelation of the World"
and his "General Principles of the Science of Education," give a
fairly good idea as to the philosophy and principles worked out by
Herbart, and the relation of his psychology to that of his predecessors.

The significance of Herbart's life and work for the teacher arises from
the fact that education with him was the starting point and end of
all his investigations. He was the only modern thinker who has not
treated education casually in his works, or looked at it, as Fichte did,
mainly from a political standpoint, but has allowed the whole weight
of his philosophy and ethics to operate on it, and construct it into a
scientific system. He not only sought, found, and explained its psychological basis, but he did this in the light of his larger philosophy.
"I for my part," he writes, "have for twenty years called to my aid
metaphysics and mathematics, besides self-observation, experience,
and experiments, in order only to find the foundation of true psycho-
logic knowledge."

.   .   .   .

Philosophers before Herbart (Wolff, Kant, and his disciples) adhered to Aristotle's principle, but slightly modified, that the soul is the
dwelling-place of higher and lower capacities, entirely separate from
each other. According to this theory, mental processes lying open to
the observation of experience were classified into smaller and larger
divisions, according to their similitude. All phenomena of one kind
were regarded as effects of a single capacity, originally inherent in the
soul. Three chief capacities were assumed — knowledge, feeling, and
will, each of which was again separated into its sub-capacities, the result being a system which was nothing more than a classification of so-
called capacities. Given these as the material for their work, the old

school of teachers set before itself a corresponding diversity of aims, each of which was to be reached by a separate road, and imagined an all-round perfection of the single capacity would follow from its concentration on one object. Herbart proved not only the falsity of this theory, but also that, were it true, education in its noblest conception would be but an empty word.

Educational problems first directed him to the study of psychology, and, convinced of its supreme importance not only for them but for natural philosophy, and the philosophy of history, ethics, and politics, he pursued it with never-failing energy for the rest of his life. Relegating in its light the "capacities" to the region of myth, he may be said to have created, as the result of his long and deep research, a natural history of the human mind. He proved how vain was the attempt to deduce from the capacities, the conformity of mental activity to law, or to reconcile with their multiplicity the simple nature of the soul and the unity of consciousness, how irrational to consider as original those endowments of the soul, which are the result of a long process of development. . . .

The proposition, then, which forms the basis of his psychology is, — that presentations (*Vorstellungen*) are the elements of mental life, and their combinations, permutations, and interactions cause all the rest of the manifold forms of consciousness. They are to psychology what the elements are to chemistry, and cells to physiology. By a presentation, Herbart means not only the complex idea presented to the mind through sense, to which the term is usually applied (for instance the idea of a chain), but the numerous elementary ideas to the furthest extremity of thought of which it is composed. . . .

The masses of presentations which the teacher finds already existent in the child's mind have two main sources, experience and intercourse. It is the teacher's work to create from the former *knowledge*, from the latter *sympathy*, by means of an educating instruction.

. . . .

If, then, the mind be built up of presentations, and consequently is inherently neither good nor bad, but develops one way or the other, under external influences and guidance of the teacher, it follows necessarily that *what* it receives in the form of presentations and their mode of combination, that is to say the work of education, is of infinite importance. It is, in Herbart's own words, "the formation of the circle of thought" (*Gedankenkreis*), upon which depends the *good*, that is the *enlightened will* — the source of the one and only aim of education — *morality*. His insistence on the circle of thought as the seat of the good will, and its result, the formation of a moral character, as the whole and sole end of the teacher's work, and the strictly logical method by which *on the basis of his psychology* he showed the absolute dependence of the aim to be attained, upon the enlightenment of the will, is the *greatest* service which Herbart rendered to education. Morality depends on the *good will*, this again on the enlightenment of the whole man. Cultivate in the pupil this enlightenment, *i.e.* a "large and, in all its parts, interconnected circle of thought, which possesses the power of overcoming what is unfavorable in the environment, as well as of dissolving and absorbing from it what is good," for "he only wields the full force of education who does so." The fundamental thought and aim of the *Pädagogik* is thus to aid the pupil to form his moral character by *his own power* — by "'a making' he himself discovers when choosing the good and rejecting the bad." To place the power already existent and in its nature trustworthy under such conditions that it must surely and infallibly accomplish this rise, is the work of the teacher, and the means to its accomplishment as elaborated in Herbart's system of education are government, instruction, and discipline.

. . . .

The immeasurable service Herbart rendered to education by the new light he threw on the laws of mind, indicates his distinct advance in one direction on his predecessors. Comenius and Pestalozzi, insisting that education should follow the course of the child's natural development and be based on the psychological laws of human nature, had advanced far in the same direction. But the knowledge of those laws in their day was too vague to allow of any but the most general expression of the vital truth they saw and proclaimed. Herbart himself made no pretension to possess a complete science of mind; no one was more penetrated than he by the conviction that this science was in its earliest beginning, leaving an immeasurable field for future investigators. But his wide knowledge, his power of analytic and abstract thought, and incorruptible love of truth enabled him to gain a more accurate insight into the origin and process of mental activity, and with it the possibility of marking out a systematic course of education, which in the employment of definite means would attain sure results and compass its appointed end. Such a course of education, together with its means and their employment, is developed in the *General Principles of the Science of Education*. The system of education it contains is, as the title of the book sets forth, deduced from its aim — morality, which in the *Æsthetic Revelation of the World* Herbart presents as the highest aim of humanity, and consequently of education. . . .

356. Application of Herbart's Ideas to Instruction

(Felkin, Henry M. and Emmie. In Translator's "Introduction" to Herbart's *Science of Education*. London, 1891)

The following is a continuation of the preceding selection, and applies Herbart's educational ideas to the process of instruction.

We have seen that Herbart founded his pedagogy on ethics and psychology, the former supplying the aim of education, and the latter the means thereto. On its ethical side, pedagogy is purely specula-tive; but on its psychological side it must take counsel with experience. Viewed, then, in relation to ethics, it is a science (that which is known); in its relation to psychology — to experience, it is an art (that which is done). Education as an art is classified as government, instruction, and discipline.

1. *Government.* The highest and necessary aim of education is morality. But the boy when grown to manhood will set other aims beside this before himself; therefore the teacher must consider not only the necessary, but these other possible aims of his pupil also — aims which will answer to his talents, dispositions, and inclinations. Since the teacher cannot know what these aims will be, he must qualify the pupil to attain them by preparing inward power, and this can only be done by giving a general stimulus to the mind.

The starting point of education is individuality, — what the pupil is and has. The idiosyncrasies of the individual are to be re-spected, for in them lies the strength of individuality, which is to be maintained as unimpaired as possible, that the child may not become a mere type of the race.

The sole object of government, the first division of education, is to create order and keep the child within bounds; it therefore deals with the present alone. Authority and love support its measures, which are occupation, supervision, threatening and punishment. These must gradually be made dispensable and then withdrawn.

2. *Instruction.* Instruction, the second division of education, is the most important. Education must determine the will towards virtue. But both will and wisdom have their roots in the circle of thought, that is to say, in the combination and coöperative activity of the presenta-tions acquired, and the true cultivation of that circle instruction alone can give. The more immediate aim of instruction on its way to its ultimate aim is a balanced, *many-sided interest;* that is, an intellectual activity prompted by instruction, and directed towards many objects, in which no single effort preponderates, but all are as far as possible of equal strength. Interest as such depends immediately upon its object, and is thereby differentiated from *desire*, which strives toward some-thing in the future. When the mind becomes concentrated on the future more than the present, interest passes into desire. Observa-tion and expectation are conditions of interest, demand and action of desire. . . .

Interest, whose object is to create a many-sided activity, is directed first to the natural already-existent presentations, i.e., those which have been given by experience and intercourse. Since experience leads to knowledge of nature, and intercourse to the disposition toward human beings (sympathy), instruction must be brought to bear on both in order that it may correct and complete them.

. . . To place all in balanced action is to create the perfect many-sided culture of the mind.

. . . .

The course of instruction is determined accordingly. It will be analytical in so far as it separates and dissects, moreover corrects and completes; in it the chief work will fall on the pupil. Or it will be synthetical in so far as the elements are given and combined; in this the teacher will determine the order of connection. Both analytical and synthetical instruction are classified in conformity with the six classes of interest, and the two must naturally support each other. Instruction must universally point out, connect, teach, philosophise; the first is productive of Clearness, the second of Association, the third leads to System, the last to Method. In matters appertaining to sympathy, instruction is observing, continuous, elevating, active in the sphere of reality. And these conditions are again in like manner productive in order of clearness, association, system, and method.

3. *Discipline.* Discipline, the third division of education, consists in direct action on the child, with intent to form him. This cannot be accomplished, however, by merely exciting the feelings. Through the influence of discipline, the circle of thought itself must receive additions, and the desires be transformed into action. Therefore its work is indirect, so far as it prepares the way for instruction to determine the circle of thought, and direct so far as it transforms the contents of that circle into action, and thus lays the foundation for character. The aim of discipline is *moral strength of character*, that is steadfastness in progress to virtue. Character consists in uniformity and firmness of will, as these are exhibited both in what the man will, and what he will not do. . . .

The attitude which the teacher assumes toward the pupil is the most important aid to discipline — his expressed satisfaction or dissatisfaction, freedom granted or restraint imposed, etc., — throughout which, the pupil's susceptibility is to be observed, made use of carefully, and not over-stimulated.

The book on discipline closes with suggestions as to its method of procedure. It is the formation of character by the light of psychology. Special stress is laid on the importance of keeping the mind as a whole tranquil and clear, so that the æsthetic judgments may form, and the character become moral. In proportion as the pupil has gained trust in his opinions and principles, discipline must retreat and allow room for self-education.

357. Herbart and Modern Psychology

(Titchener, E. B., in *Journal of Education*. Boston, May 19, 1898)

The following is not only a good brief statement of the origin of modern psychology, but also a good brief presentation of the larger stages in the history of the progress of science.

The history of science is a history of differentiation. When the human race first began to reflect upon the universe, it took the universe in the large; early Greek "science" is cosmic philosophy. Little by little, the sciences have split off from philosophy, far more recently than one is apt to believe. Descartes (1596–1650) included both medicine and mechanics under philosophy; Wolff (1679–1754) thought that physics was as much a part of philosophy as was empirical psychology. Even to-day we find physical apparatus catalogued under the title of "philosophical instruments."

The first thing that a science has to do, then, in order to be a science, is to shake itself free of philosophy, of speculation about the ultimate nature of the universe. It must assert its independence, and declare itself lord and master over a certain range of facts. But many a "science" has made this assertion, and yet fallen back again under philosophical dominion. If the revolt is to be successful, it must be carried out with method. Method, a definite and fruitful way of arranging and discovering facts, is the *conditio sine qua non* of a science.

The nineteenth century has witnessed a long series of victories for science over philosophy. We have the new biology of Darwin; the new physiology of Ludwig; the new pathology of Virchow; the new chemistry of Liebig; the new physics of Maxwell and Helmholtz and Thomson. There are some bodies of knowledge — ethics, æsthetics, sociology, for instance — that have not yet succeeded in freeing themselves from metaphysical influence; but no one can doubt that they are well on their way to become sciences. And the place of philosophy has undergone a corresponding change. So far from dictating to science what it shall teach and what it shall refrain from teaching, metaphysics now follows in the train of the special sciences, and shapes its own doctrines in accordance with scientific results.

Psychology has played its part in this revolution. At the beginning of the century it was an integral part of philosophy; at the end it is a science of the sciences, a "laboratory" science. Let us compare the two points of view for a moment, and see precisely wherein the difference consists:

The change from philosophy to science was mediated very largely by the work of one man — Johann Friedrich Herbart (1776–1841). Herbart dealt the power theory of mind its deathblow. So far, he may be accounted a "new" psychologist. Nevertheless, he still based his psychology directly upon metaphysics. The system of competing ideas which he substituted for the older faculties is meaningless and unsubstantial unless it is backed by his metaphysical system. The "new psychology" proper, psychology as natural science, is the combined work of four other men: Hermann Lotze (1817–1881), Ernst Heinrich Weber (1795–1878), Gustav Theodor Fechner (1801–1887), and Wilhelm Maximilian Wundt (1832).

358. Froebel's Educational Views

(Marenholtz-Bülow, Baroness Bertha von, *Child and Child Nature.*
Berlin, 1878; trans. by Alice M. Christie. London, 1879)

Froebel's writings are so mystical and religious in character that they convey but little idea of the kindergarten as it is to-day developed, and the best conception as to his educational theory is found in the writings of those who have interpreted him, rather than in his own books. His greatest interpreter and propagandist was the Baroness Bertha von Marenholtz-Bülow (-Wendhausen) (1810–1893), who expounded his ideas in the leading countries of Europe, and, after 1870, in a training college in Dresden. The following extract from her "Contributions to the Understanding of Froebel's Educational Theories" gives a fairly good idea as to his educational ideas.

"The purpose of nature is development. The purpose of the spiritual world is culture. The problem of this world is an educational one, the solution of which is proceeding according to fixed divine laws." — Froebel.

EDUCATION is emancipation — the setting free of the bound-up forces of the body and the soul. The inner conditions necessary to this setting free or development all healthily-born children bring with them into the world, the outer ones must be supplied through education.

. . . .

LAW OF DEVELOPMENT

Everything in the kingdom of nature, however different the stages of progress may be, comes under one universal law, and development means the same as *progress according to law*, — systematic going on from the unformed to the formed, from chaos to cosmos.

And as does the physical so also must the spiritual development proceed in systematic fashion, or education would be impossible. For what we call education is influencing the development of the child, guiding and regulating it as well in its spiritual as in its physical aspect.

But how common a thing it is to hear people maintain that during the instinctive, unconscious period of a child's life, it should be left to follow its impulses entirely, and no attempt made to deal with it systematically. But, as the soul undoubtedly begins to unfold and form itself in the period of unconsciousness in the same systematic manner as in later periods, any such assertion must be erroneous and based on false premises. Spiritual development must proceed in as regular and systematic a course as organic development, seeing that the physical organs are intended to correspond as implicitly to the soul, which they serve, as cause corresponds to effect. Psychology has determined the order of the development of the soul, as has physiology that of the circulation of the blood, but the former science has chiefly concerned itself with the already more or less formed soul of the adult, which, through self-will and voluntary deflection from the path of order, is always to a certain extent the slave of arbitrariness and the growth of the soul in the period of childhood has been little studied or observed.

Froebel used to say constantly when lecturing: "If you want to understand clearly the regular working of nature you must observe the common wild plants, many of which are designated as weeds: it is seen more clearly in these than in the complexity of cultivated plants." For this purpose he grew different species of wild plants in pots.

The same holds true of the human plant. The young child's soul, while yet in its primitive and instinctive stage, without forethought and without artificiality, exhibits to the really seeing and understanding observer the systematic regularity, the *logic* of nature's dealings in her development process, in spite of the variety of individual endowment.

.   .   .   .

CORRESPONDENCES — INDIVIDUAL — THE RACE

Froebel says: "There is a continuous connection in the spiritual life as a whole, as there is universal harmony in nature." And certainly it cannot be otherwise: the eternal law of order, which reigns throughout the universe, must also determine the development of the human soul. But the educator who would supply the human bud in right manner with light and warmth, rain and dew, and so induce it to emancipate itself from its fettered condition, and through the unfolding of all its slumbering forces to blossom into worthy life, must not only understand the law but must also possess the means of acting in accordance with the law: i.e., his method of education must follow the same systematic plan as nature does, and the outward practical means must correspond.

No one will dispute the assertion that *instruction* is only worthy of the name when it is methodical. Instruction of such kind is a branch of education: but branch and stem spring from the same root. However much may have been done, from the days of antiquity up to the present day, to improve educational and instructional systems, and to adapt them more closely to the natural process of development, and thus attain the result aimed at — *knowledge* — in the best and quickest manner, the laws of development of the infant mind are, nevertheless, still veiled in obscurity. No infallible chart has yet been found, which, as the magnet to the mariner, will show the educator invariably the right direction to steer in, spite of all ebbs and flows, spite of all the thousand different courses that each vessel, each character, according to its individual destination, has to strike into. But so long as some such fixed method of education remains undiscovered, so long will even the best education be more or less an arbitrary work.

It was also Pestalozzi's chief endeavor to discover and apply that which he called "the principle of the organic," and to him, and his educational forerunners, are we indebted for our first knowledge of the course of child development, and for the means by which education and instruction have been more systematically organized. Without their preliminary efforts Froebel might not, perhaps, have discovered the method whereby he built upon the foundations laid by them, and brought their, and especially Pestalozzi's, practical endeavors to completion. In like manner will Froebel's successors be called upon to develop further what he has laid the foundation of.

In one of his letters to me, Froebel says: "As motion in the universe depends on the law of gravitation, so do movements in the life of humanity depend on the law of the unity of life." — And further: "As the laws of the fruit are developments of the laws of the flower, and the laws of the flower developments of the laws of the bud, and the laws of the bud, flower, and fruit, are at the same time one with the laws of the whole tree or plant; so are the laws of the development of the spiritual life higher outcomes, or developments, of the laws of the solar and planetary system of the universe. Were this not the case man could not understand the latter, for he can only understand that which is homogeneous to him. And, according to this, the laws of the development of life, in the region of the spiritual, must be apprehended, demonstrated, and built upon, in the same manner as the laws of the formation of the world. It will be the work of the Kindergarten to point out the application of these laws, as one stage of progressive human cultivation."

Froebel's aim and efforts may, I think, be summed up thus: he was striving to hit on a regular course or method of *education*, corresponding to the method of *instruction* long ago established by pedagogic science.

. . . .

Whether it has happened to Froebel by a lucky hit to give a new basis to education, experience and the application and carrying out of his method must show. A written exposition can do no more than represent the matter in its general outlines, and thus awaken the desire to understand it better, and to test its merits by application.

The most difficult of all difficult tasks is without doubt to give a universally enlightening definition to a new truth — great or small — for new truths always lie outside the general mental horizon.   Even Froebel himself, therefore, has had little success in describing his educational theory in its full compass, and he is, perhaps, even more justified than Hegel and other thinkers in complaining that he has not been understood.   Far be it from us to pretend here to expound this idea in its whole breadth and depth — we would only attempt by means of the following short statements to open up the way to an understanding of it:

The process of spiritual development goes on according to fixed laws.

These laws correspond to the general laws which reign throughout the universe, but are at the same time higher, because suited to a higher stage of development.

This system of laws must be able to be traced back to a fundamental law, however much the latter may vary in its formulæ.

. . . .

FROEBEL'S THEORY OF EDUCATION

As a result of the foregoing we find the first general educational requisites to be:

Assistance of spontaneous development which shall accord with the laws of nature;

Considerations for the outward conditions of life of each epoch, and for each personality;

Understanding and application of the universal laws of spiritual development.

With regard to the special services rendered by Froebel, let me here repeat what I have already mentioned, that Froebel has discovered the method and practical means of disciplining, or of developing, body, soul and mind, will, feeling and understanding according to the systematic laws of nature.

In the practical application of the positive and individual portion of it, the simplicity and naturalness of Froebel's method stand out markedly, and at once do away with any idea of its being pedantic or artificial, and in opposition to the natural free development of the child.

. . . .

359. English and German Universities contrasted

(Huxley, T. H., *Science and Education*, pp. 104–07.   Collected Essays, vol. III. London, 1893)

The ablest English writer and speaker who forcefully supported the general line of argument advanced by Herbert Spencer, as to the importance of a revision of existing school instruction and the introduction of science teaching, was the English scientist, Thomas Henry Huxley (1825–1895).

In an address delivered, in 1868, to the South London Working Men's College on "A Liberal Education; and Where to find it," Huxley stated so clearly the defects of existing educational conditions in England, and gave such a good definition as to what in his judgment constituted a liberal education, that this address may be taken as one of the most important expressions of the period of the new interest in England in educational reform. Contrasting the English and German universities, he said:

I believe there can be no doubt that the foreigner who should wish to become acquainted with the scientific, or the literary, activity of modern England, would simply lose his time and his pains if he visited our universities with that object.

And, as for works of profound research on any subject, and, above all, in that classical lore for which the universities profess to sacrifice almost everything else, why, a third-rate, poverty-stricken German university turns out more produce of that kind in one year, than our vast and wealthy foundations elaborate in ten.

Ask the man who is investigating any question, profoundly and thoroughly — be it historical, philosophical, philological, physical, literary, or theological; who is trying to make himself master of any abstract subject (except, perhaps, political economy and geology, both of which are intensely Anglican sciences), whether he is not compelled to read half a dozen times as many German as English books? And whether, of these English books, more than one in ten is the work of a fellow of a college, or a professor of an English university?

Is this from any lack of power in the English as compared with the German mind? The countrymen of Grote and of Mill, of Faraday, of Robert Brown, of Lyell, and of Darwin, to go no further back than the contemporaries of men of middle age, can afford to smile at such a suggestion. England can show now, as she had been able to show in every generation since civilisation spread over the West, individual men who hold their own against the world, and keep alive the old tradition of her intellectual eminence.

But, in the majority of cases, these men are what they are in virtue of their native intellectual force, and of a strength of character which will not recognize impediments. They are not trained in the courts of the Temple of Science, but storm the walls of that edifice in all sorts of irregular ways, and with much loss of time and power, in order to obtain their legitimate positions.

Our universities not only do not encourage such men; do not offer them positions, in which it should be their highest duty to do, thoroughly, that which they are most capable of doing; but, as far as possible, university training shuts out of the minds of those among them, who are subjected to it, the prospect that there is anything in the world for which they are specially fitted.   Imagine the success of the attempt to still the intellectual hunger of any of the men I have mentioned, by putting before him, as the object of existence, the successful mimicry of a Greek song, or the roll of Ciceronian prose!   Imagine how much success would be likely to attend the attempt to persuade such men that the education which leads to perfection in such elegances is alone to be called culture; while the facts of history, the process of thought, the conditions of moral and social existence, and the laws of physical nature are left to be dealt with as they may be by outside barbarians.

It is not thus that the German universities, from being beneath notice a century ago, have become what they now are — the most intensely cultivated and the most productive intellectual corporations the world has ever seen,

The student who repairs to them sees in the list of classes and of professors a fair picture of the world of knowledge.   Whatever he needs to know there is some one ready to teach him, some one competent to discipline him in the way of learning; whatever his special bent, let him but be able and diligent, and in due time he shall find distinction and a career.   Among his professors, he sees men whose names are known and revered throughout the civilised world; and their living example infects him with a noble ambition, and a love for the spirit of work.

The Germans dominate the intellectual world by virtue of the same simple secret as that which made Napoleon the master of old Europe. They have declared *la carrière ouverte aux talents*, and every Bursch marches with a professor's gown in his knapsack.   Let him become a great scholar, or man of science, and ministers will compete for his services. In Germany, they do not leave the chance of his holding the office he would render illustrious to the tender mercies of a hot canvass, and the final wisdom of a mob of country parsons.

In short, in Germany, the universities are exactly what the Rector of Lincoln and the Commissioners tell us the English universities are not; that is to say, corporations "of learned men devoting their lives to the cultivation of science, and the direction of academical education." They are not "boarding schools for youths," nor clerical seminaries; but institutions for the higher culture of men, in which the theological faculty is of no more importance, or prominence, than the rest; and which are truly "universities," since they strive to represent and embody the totality of human knowledge, and to find room for all forms of intellectual activity.

360. Mid-Nineteenth Century Elementary Education in England

(Huxley, T. H., *Science and Education*, pp. 87–91. Collected Essays, vol. III.
London, 1893)

Continuing still further on English education of the time
(1868), Huxley draws the following picture as to the nature and
value of the instruction then provided in the elementary schools
of the people:

. . . Consider our primary schools and what is taught in them.   A
child learns:

1. To read, write, and cipher, more or less well; but in a very large
proportion of cases not so well as to take pleasure in reading, or to be
able to write the commonest letter properly.

2. A quantity of dogmatic theology, of which the child, nine times
out of ten, understands next to nothing.

3. Mixed up with this, so as to seem to stand or fall with it, a few of
the broadest and simplest principles of morality.   This, to my mind, is
much as if a man of science should make the story of the fall of the apple
in Newton's garden an integral part of the doctrine of gravitation, and
teach it as of equal authority with the law of the inverse squares.

4. A good deal of Jewish history and Syrian geography, and perhaps a little something about English history and the geography of the
child's own country.   But I doubt if there is a primary school in England in which hangs a map of the hundred in which the village lies, so
that the children may be practically taught by it what a map means.

5. A certain amount of regularity, attentive obedience, respect for
others: obtained by fear, if the master be incompetent or foolish; by
love and reverence, if he be wise.

So far as this school course embraces a training in the theory and
practice of obedience to the moral laws of Nature, I gladly admit, not
only that it contains a valuable educational element, but that, so far,
it deals with the most valuable and important part of all education.
Yet, contrast what is done in this direction with what might be done;
with the time given to matters of comparatively no importance; with
the absence of any attention to things of the highest moment; and one
is tempted to think of Falstaff's bill and "the halfpenny worth of bread
to all that quantity of sack."

Let us consider what a child thus "educated" knows, and what it
does not know.   Begin with the most important topic of all — morality, as the guide of conduct.   The child knows well enough that some
acts meet with approbation and some with disapprobation.   But it has
never heard that there lies in the nature of things a reason for every
moral law, as cogent and as well defined as that which underlies every
physical law; that stealing and lying are just as certain to be followed

by evil consequences, as putting your hand in the fire, or jumping out of a garret window. Again, though the scholar may have been made acquainted, in dogmatic fashion, with the broad laws of morality, he has had no training in the application of those laws to the difficult problems which result from the complex conditions of modern civilisation.

.   .   .   .

Again, the child learns absolutely nothing of the history or the political organization of his own country. His general impression is, that everything of much importance happened a very long while ago; and that the Queen and the gentlefolks govern the country much after the fashion of King David and the elders and nobles of Israel — his sole models. Will you give a man with this much information a vote? In easy times he sells it for a pot of beer. Why should he not? It is of about as much use to him as a chignon, and he knows as much what to do with it, for any other purpose. In bad times, on the contrary, he applies his simple theory of government, and believes that his rulers are the cause of his sufferings — a belief which sometimes bears remarkable practical fruits.

Least of all, does the child gather from this primary "education" of ours a conception of the laws of the physical world, or of the relations of cause and effect therein. And this is the more to be lamented, as the poor are especially exposed to physical evils, and are more interested in removing them than any other class of the community. If any one is concerned in knowing the ordinary laws of mechanics one would think it is the hand-labourer, whose daily toil lies among levers and pulleys; or among the other implements of artisan work. And if any one is interested in the laws of health, it is the poor workman, whose strength is wasted by ill-prepared food, whose health is sapped by bad ventilation and bad drainage, and half whose children are massacred by disorders which might be prevented. Not only does our present primary education carefully abstain from hinting to the workman that some of his greatest evils are traceable to mere physical agencies, which could be removed by energy, patience, and frugality; but it does worse — it renders him, so far as it can, deaf to those who would help him, and tries to substitute an Oriental submission to what is falsely declared to be the will of God, for his natural tendency to strive after a better condition.

What wonder, then, if very recently an appeal has been made to statistics for the profoundly foolish purpose of showing that education is of no good — that it diminishes neither misery nor crime among the masses of mankind? I reply, why should the thing which has been called education do either the one or the other? . . .

361. Mid-Nineteenth Century Secondary Education in England

(Huxley, T. H., *Science and Education*, pp. 92–101.   Collected Essays, vol. III.
London, 1893)

After describing English elementary education, as given in the
preceding selection, Huxley proceeds, as follows, to point out the
defects of English secondary education of his time.

It may be said that all these animadversions may apply to primary
schools, but that the higher schools, at any rate, must be allowed to
give a liberal education.   In fact they professedly sacrifice everything
else to this object.

Let us inquire into this matter.   What do the higher schools, those
to which the great middle class of the country sends its children, teach,
over and above the instruction given in the primary schools?   There
is a little more reading and writing of English.   But, for all that, every
one knows that it is a rare thing to find a boy of the middle or upper
classes who can read aloud decently, or who can put his thoughts on
paper in clear and grammatical (to say nothing of good or elegant)
language.   The "ciphering" of the lower schools expands into elementary mathematics in the higher; into arithmetic, with a little algebra, a
little Euclid.   But I doubt if one boy in five hundred has ever heard
the explanation of a rule of arithmetic, or knows his Euclid otherwise
than by rote.

Of theology, the middle class schoolboy gets rather less than poorer
children, less absolutely and less relatively, because there are so many
other claims upon his attention.   I venture to say that, in the great
majority of cases, his ideas on this subject when he leaves school are of
the most shadowy and vague description, and associated with painful
impressions of the weary hours spent learning collects and catechism
by heart.

Modern geography, modern history, modern literature; the English
language as a language; the whole circle of the sciences, physical,
moral, and social, are even more completely ignored in the higher than
in the lower schools.   Up till within a few years back, a boy might
have passed through any one of the great public schools with the
greatest distinction and credit, and might never so much as heard of
one of the subjects I have just mentioned.   He might never have
heard that the earth goes round the sun; that England underwent a
great revolution in 1688, and France another in 1789; that there once
lived certain notable men called Chaucer, Shakespeare, Milton, Voltaire, Goethe, Schiller.   The first might be a German and the last an
Englishman for anything he could tell you to the contrary.   And as
for Science, the only idea the word would suggest to his mind would be
dexterity in boxing.

· · · · · · · · · · · · · ·

Now let us pause to consider this wonderful state of affairs; for the time will come when Englishmen will quote it as the stock example of the stolid stupidity of their ancestors in the nineteenth century. The most thoroughly commercial people, the greatest voluntary wanderers and colonists the world has ever seen, are precisely the middle classes of this country. If there be a people which has been busy making history on the great scale for the last three hundred years — and the most profoundly interesting history — history which, if it had happened to be that of Greece or Rome, we should study with avidity — it is the English. If there be a people, which during the same period, has developed a remarkable literature, it is our own. If there be a nation whose prosperity depends absolutely and wholly upon their mastery over the forces of Nature, upon their intelligent apprehension of, and obedience to the laws of the creation and distribution of wealth, and of the stable equilibrium of the forces of society, it is precisely this nation. And yet this is what these wonderful people tell their sons:

"At the cost of one to two thousand pounds of our hard-earned money, we devote twelve of the most precious years of your lives to school. There you shall toil, or be supposed to toil; but there you shall not learn one single thing of all those you will most want to know directly you leave school and enter upon the practical business of life. You will in all probability go into business, but you shall not know where, or how, any article of commerce is produced, or the difference between an export and an import, or the meaning of the word 'capital.' You will very likely settle in a colony, but you shall not know whether Tasmania is a part of New South Wales, or *vice versa*.

"Very probably you may become a manufacturer, but you shall not be provided with the means of understanding the working of one of your own steam-engines; and, when you are asked to buy a patent, you shall not have the slightest means of judging whether the inventor is an imposter who is contravening the elementary principles of science, or a man who will make you as rich as Crœsus.

"You will very likely get into the House of Commons. You will have to take your share in making laws which may prove a blessing or a curse to millions of men. But you shall not hear one word respecting the political organisation of your country; the meaning of the controversy between free-traders and protectionists shall never have been mentioned to you; you shall not so much as know that there are such things as economical laws.

"The mental power which will be of most importance in your daily life will be the power of seeing things as they are without regard to authority; and of drawing accurate general conclusions from particular facts. But at school and at college you shall know of no source of truth but authority; nor exercise your reasoning faculty upon anything but deduction from that which is laid down by authority.

"You will have to weary your soul with work, and many a time eat your bread in sorrow and in bitterness, and you shall not have learned to take refuge in the great source of pleasure without alloy, the serene resting-place for worn human nature, — the world of art."

Said I not rightly that we are a wonderful people? I am quite prepared to allow, that education entirely devoted to these omitted subjects might not be a completely liberal education. But is an education which ignores them all a liberal education? Nay, is it too much to say that the education which should embrace these subjects and no others would be a real education, though an incomplete one; while an education which omits them is really not an education at all, but a more or less useful course of intellectual gymnastics?

For what does the middle-class school put in the place of all these things which are left out? It substitutes what is usually comprised under the compendious title of the "classics" — that is to say, the languages, the literature, and the history of the ancient Greeks and Romans, and the geography of so much of the world as was known to these two great nations of antiquity. . . .

. . . What is to be said of classical teaching at its worst, or in other words, of the classics of our ordinary middle-class schools? It means getting up endless forms and rules by heart. It means turning Latin and Greek into English, for the mere sake of being able to do it, and without the smallest regard to the worth, or worthlessness, of the author read. It means the learning of innumerable, not always decent, fables in such a shape that the meaning they once had is dried up into utter trash; and the only impression left upon a boy's mind is, that the people who believed such things must have been the greatest idiots the world ever saw. And it means, finally, that after a dozen years spent at this kind of work, the sufferer shall be incompetent to interpret a passage in an author he has not already got up; that he shall loathe the sight of a Greek or Latin book; and that he shall never open, or think of, a classical writer again, until, wonderful to relate, he insists upon submitting his sons to the same process.

These be your gods, O Israel! For the sake of this net result (and respectability) the British father denies his children all the knowledge they might turn to account in life, not merely for the achievement of vulgar success, but for guidance in the great crises of human existence. This is the stone he offers to those to whom he is bound by the strongest and tenderest ties to feed with bread.

362. What Knowledge is of Most Worth?

(Spencer, Herbert, *Education*, chap. 1. London, 1861)

In the *Westminster Review* for July, 1859, Herbert Spencer (1820–1903) published an article under the above title which challenged in forceful terms the old ideas as to education. He had previously published three other articles on phases of the question of education — namely, on "Intellectual Education" (1854), "Moral Education" (1858), and "Physical Education" (1859), to all of which the July, 1859, article formed an introduction. In 1861 the four essays were published in book form under the general title of *Education; Intellectual, Moral, and Physical.*

The book represented the best ideas of the sense-realists and educational reformers since the days of Francis Bacon, stated anew in clear and forceful English, and was of importance in starting anew a discussion of relative values.

The following selections from the first chapter give a good idea of Spencer's forceful style, his fundamental educational theses, and the nature of the challenge he made to the educational practices of his time.

It has been truly remarked that in order of time decoration precedes dress. Among people who submit to great physical suffering that they may have themselves handsomely tattooed, extremes of temperature are borne with but little attempt at mitigation. Humboldt tells us that an Orinoco Indian, though quite regardless of bodily comfort, will yet labor for a fortnight to purchase pigment wherewith to make himself admired; and that the same woman who would not hesitate to leave her hut without a fragment of clothing on, would not dare to commit such a breach of decorum as to go out unpainted. Voyagers uniformly find that colored beads and trinkets are much more prized by wild tribes than are calicoes or broadcloths. And the anecdotes we have of the ways in which, when shirts and coats are given, they turn them to some ludicrous display, show how completely the idea of ornament predominates over that of use.

FIG. 89
HERBERT SPENCER
(1820–1903)

．　　．　　．　　．　　．　　．　　．　　．　　．　　．　　．

It is not a little curious that the like relations hold with the mind. Among mental as among bodily acquisitions, the ornamental comes before the useful. Not only in times past, but almost as much in our own era, that knowledge which conduces to personal well-being has been postponed to that which brings applause. In the Greek schools, music, poetry, rhetoric, and a philosophy which, until Socrates taught, had but little bearing upon action, were the dominant subjects; while knowledge aiding the arts of life had a very subordinate place. And in our own universities and schools at the present moment the like antithesis holds.

We are guilty of something like a platitude when we say that throughout his after-career a boy, in nine cases out of ten, applies his Latin and Greek to no practical purposes. The remark is trite that in his shop, or his office, in managing his estate or his family, in playing his part as director of a bank or a railway, he is very little aided by this knowledge he took so many years to acquire — so little, — that generally the greater part of it drops out of his memory; and if he occasionally vents a Latin quotation, or alludes to some Greek myth, it is less to throw light on the topic in hand than for the sake of effect. If we inquire what is the real motive for giving boys a classical education, we find it to be simply conformity to public opinion. Men dress their children's minds as they do their bodies, in the prevailing fashion. As the Orinoco Indian puts on his paint before leaving his hut, not with a view to any direct benefit, but because he would be ashamed to be seen without it, so a boy's drilling in Latin and Greek is insisted on, not because of their intrinsic value, but that he may not be disgraced by being found ignorant of them — that he may have "the education of a gentleman" — the badge marking a certain social position, and bringing a consequent respect.

This parallel is still more clearly displayed in the case of the other sex. In the treatment of both mind and body the decorative element has continued to predominate in a greater degree among women than among men. . . .

In their education, the immense preponderance of "accomplishments" proves how here, too, use is subordinated to display. Dancing, deportment, the piano, singing, drawing — what a large space do these occupy! If you ask why Italian and German are learnt, you will find that, under all the sham reasons given, the real reason is, that a knowledge of those tongues is thought ladylike. It is not that the books written in them may be utilized, which they scarcely ever are, but that Italian and German songs may be sung, and that the extent of attainment may bring whispered admiration. The births, deaths, and marriages of kings, and other like historic trivialities, are committed to memory, not because of any direct benefits that can possibly result from knowing them, but because society considers them parts of a good education — because the absence of such knowledge may bring the contempt of others. When we have named reading, writing, spelling, grammar, arithmetic, and sewing, we have named about all the things a girl is taught with a view to their actual uses in life; and even some of these have more reference to the good opinion of others than to immediate personal welfare.

The question which we contend is of such transcendent moment is, not whether such and such knowledge is of worth, but what is its *relative* worth. When they have named certain advantages which a given course of study has secured them, persons are apt to assume that they have justified themselves; quite forgetting that the adequateness of the advantages is the point to be judged.

.   .   .   .

In education, then, this is the question of questions, which it is high time we discussed in some methodic way. The first in importance, though the last to be considered, is the problem — how to decide among the conflicting claims of various subjects on our attention. Before there can be a rational *curriculum*, we must settle which things it most concerns us to know; or, to use a word of Bacon's, now unfortunately obsolete — we must determine the relative values of knowledges. To this end, a measure of value is the first requisite. And happily, respecting the true measure of value, as expressed in general terms, there can be no dispute.

How to live? — that is the essential question for us. Not how to live in the mere material sense only, but in the widest sense. The general problem which comprehends every special problem is — the right ruling of conduct in all directions under all circumstances. In what way to treat the body; in what way to treat the mind; in what way to manage our affairs; in what way to bring up a family; in what way to behave as a citizen; in what way to utilize all those sources of happiness which nature supplies — how to use all our faculties to the greatest advantage of ourselves and others — how to live completely? And this being the great thing needful for us to learn is, by consequence, the great thing which education has to teach. *To prepare us for complete living* is the function which education has to discharge; and the only rational mode of judging of an educational course is to judge in what degree it discharges such function.

.   .   .   .

Doubtless the task is difficult — perhaps never to be more than approximately achieved. But, considering the vastness of the interests at stake, its difficulty is no reason for pusillanimously passing it by, but rather for devoting every energy to its mastery. And if we only proceed systematically we may very soon get at results of no small moment.

Our first step must obviously be to classify, in the order of their importance, the leading kinds of activity which constitute human life. They may be naturally arranged into:

1. Those activities which directly minister to self-preservation.

2. Those activities which, by securing the necessaries of life, indirectly minister to self-preservation.

3. Those activities which have for their end the rearing and discipline of offspring.

4. Those activities which are involved in the maintenance of proper social and political relations.

5. Those miscellaneous activities which fill up the leisure part of life, devoted to the gratification of the tastes and feelings.

That these stand in something like their true order of subordination it needs no long consideration to show.

.   .   .   .

Of course the ideal of education is — complete preparation in all these divisions.   But failing this ideal, as in our phase of civilization every one must do more or less, the aim should be to maintain *a due proportion* between the degrees of preparation in each.   Not exhaustive cultivation in any one, supremely important though it may be; not even an exclusive attention to the two, three, or four divisions of greatest importance; but an attention to all; greatest where the value is greatest, less where the value is less, least where the value is least. For the average man (not to forget the cases in which peculiar aptitude for some one department of knowledge rightly makes pursuit of that one the bread-winning occupation) — for the average man, we say, the desideratum is, a training that approaches nearest to perfection in the things which most subserve complete living, and falls more and more below perfection in the things that have more and more remote bearings on complete living.

.   .   .   .

363. Spencer's Conclusions as to the Importance of Science

(Spencer, Herbert, *Education*, chap. 1.   London, 1861)

After classifying knowledge in the order of relative importance, as given in the preceding selection, Spencer enters into quite a discussion as to the question he has raised, and under the following headings:

A. Knowledge for Guidance.
    I. Self-Preservation.
    II. Self-Maintenance.
    III. Parental Duties.
    IV. Good Citizenship.
    V. The Refinements of Life.
B. Knowledge for Discipline.

Under each he points out what knowledge is of most worth, and then summarizes his conclusions, as follows:

We conclude, then, that for discipline, as well as for guidance, science is of chiefest value.   In all its effects, learning the meanings of things is better than learning the meanings of words. Whether for intellectual, moral, or religious training, the study of surrounding phenomena is immensely superior to the study of grammars and lexicons.

Thus to the question with which we set out — What knowledge is of most worth? — the uniform reply is — Science. This is the verdict on all the counts. For direct self-preservation, or the maintenance of life and health, the all-important knowledge is — Science. For that indirect self-preservation which we call gaining a livelihood, the knowledge of greatest value is — Science. For the due discharge of parental functions, the proper guidance is to be found only in — Science. For that interpretation of national life, past and present, without which the citizen cannot rightly regulate his conduct, the indispensable key is — Science. Alike for the most perfect production and highest enjoyment of art in all its forms, the needful preparation is still — Science. And for purposes of discipline — intellectual, moral, religious — the most efficient study is, once more — Science.

The question which at first seemed so perplexed, has become, in the course of our inquiry, comparatively simple. We have not to estimate the degrees of importance of different orders of human activity, and different studies as severally fitting us for them, since we find that the study of Science, in its most comprehensive meaning, is the best preparation for all these orders of activity. We have not to decide between the claims of knowledge of great though conventional value, and knowledge of less though intrinsic value; seeing that the knowledge which we find to be of most value in all other respects, is intrinsically most valuable; its worth is not dependent upon opinion, but is as fixed as is the relation of man to the surrounding world. Necessary and eternal as are its truths, all Science concerns all mankind for all time. Equally at present, and in the remotest future, must it be of incalculable importance for the regulation of their conduct that men should understand the science of life, physical, mental, and social, and that they should understand all other science as a key to the science of life.

And yet the knowledge which is of such transcendent value is that which, in our age of boasted education, receives the least attention. While this which we call civilization could never have arisen had it not been for science, science forms scarcely an appreciable element in what men consider civilized training. Though to the progress of science we owe it that millions find support where once there was food only for thousands, yet of these millions but a few thousands pay any respect to that which has made their existence possible. Though this increasing knowledge of the properties and relations of things has not only enabled wandering tribes to grow into populous nations, but has given to the countless members of those populous nations comforts and pleasures which their naked ancestors never even conceived, or could have believed, yet is this kind of knowledge only now receiving a grudging recognition in our highest educational institutions. To the slowly growing acquaintance with the uniform co-existences and sequences of phenomena — to the establishment of invariable laws, we owe our emancipation from the grossest superstitions. But for science we should be still worshipping fetishes; or, with hecatombs of victims, propitiating diabolical deities. And yet this science, which, in place of the most degrading conceptions of things, has given us some insight to the grandeurs of creation, is written against in our theologies and frowned upon from our pulpits.

Paraphrasing an Eastern fable, we may say that in the family of knowledges, Science is the household drudge, who, in obscurity, hides unrecognized perfections. To her has been committed all the work; by her skill, intelligence, and devotion, have all the conveniences and gratifications been obtained; and while ceaselessly occupied in ministering to the rest, she has been kept in the background, that her haughty sisters might flaunt their fripperies in the eyes of the world. The parallel holds yet further. For we are fast coming to the *dénouement*, when the positions will be changed; and while these haughty sisters sink into merited neglect, Science, proclaimed as highest alike in worth and beauty, will reign supreme.

364. The Old and the New Psychology contrasted

(Dewey, John, "The Psychology of the Elementary Curriculum"; in *The Elementary School Record*, pp. 222–25. Chicago, 1900)

The foremost American interpreter of the social and industrial changes of a century in terms of education has been Professor John Dewey. His work, both experimental and theoretical, has stated a new social psychology for the educational process. While at the University of Chicago he conducted an experimental elementary school, the important results of which were published in 1900, in nine monographs, under the title of *The Elementary School Record*. In the last of the series he contrasted the old and the new psychology, as it applies to the education of the child, in the following words:

What, then, are the chief working hypotheses that have been adopted from psychology? What educational counterparts have been hit upon as in some degree in line with the adopted psychology?

The discussion of these questions may be approached by pointing out a contrast between contemporary psychology and the psychology of former days. The contrast is a triple one. Earlier psychology regarded mind as a purely individual affair in direct and naked contact with an external world. The only question asked was of the ways in which the world and the mind acted upon each other. The entire process recognized would have been in theory exactly the same if there were one mind living alone in the universe. At present the tendency is to conceive individual mind as a function of social life, — as not capable of operating or developing by itself, but as requiring continual stimulus from social agencies, and finding its nutrition in social supplies. The idea of heredity has made familiar the notion that the equipment of the individual, mental as well as physical, is an inheritance from the race: a capital inherited by the individual from the past and held in trust by him for the future. The idea of evolution has made familiar the notion that mind cannot be regarded as an individual monopolistic possession, but represents the outworkings of the endeavor and thought of humanity; that it is developed in an environment which is social as well as physical, and that social needs and aims have been most potent in shaping it, — that the chief difference between savagery and civilization is not in the naked nature which each faces, but the social heredity and social medium.

.   .   .   .

In the second place, the older psychology was a psychology of knowledge, of intellect. Emotion and endeavor occupied but an incidental and derivative place. Much was said about sensations, — next to nothing about movements. There was discussion of ideas and of whether they originated in sensations or in some innate mental faculty; but the possibility of their origin in and from the needs of action was ignored. Their influence upon conduct, upon behavior, was regarded as an external attachment.

.   .   .   .

The third point of contrast lies in the modern conception of the mind as essentially a process — a process of growth, not a fixed thing. According to the older view mind was mind, and that was the whole story. Mind was the same throughout, because fitted out with the same assortment of faculties, whether in child or adult. If any difference was made it was simply that some of these ready-made faculties — such as memory — came into play at an earlier time, while others, such as judging and inferring, made their appearance only after the child, through memorizing drills, had been reduced to complete independence upon the thought of others. The only important difference that was recognized was one of quantity, of amount. The boy was a little man and his mind was a little mind, — in everything but size the same as that of the adult, having its own ready-furnished equipment of faculties of attention, memory, etc. Now we believe in the mind as a growing affair, and hence as essentially changing, presenting distinctive phases of capacity and interest at different periods. These are all one and the same in the sense of continuity of life, but all different in that each has its own distinctive claims and offices. "First the blade, then the ear, and then the full corn in the ear."

365. Difficulties in Transforming the School

Ping Wen Kuo, *The Chinese System of Public Instruction*, pp. 161–62.
New York, 1915)

The transformation of a nation's schools from institutions for formal training in book knowledge to institutions which give real life experience and prepare for intelligent living in modern society has everywhere been difficult. The following description of the difficulties experienced recently in China gives a picture of conditions not particularly different from those in other lands.

(a) *Relating Education to Life*

There is at least one more educational problem of importance deserving special mention, namely, the problem of effectively relating education to the life of those who receive it. In the western countries the conflict so long waged between formal book training and the newer, more practical forms of education centering in the social and industrial needs of children, may be said to have been settled theoretically, at least, in favor of the latter, but in China the conflict has only just begun. For not until recent years has there been felt the need of bringing about a closer adjustment of school work to the changing social and industrial demands of the time, and of making the curriculum a means of preparing the pupils to solve the problems of their daily life. True enough, most of the modern school subjects, such as geography, civics, and the like, have been introduced into the regular course of study, but these subjects are often taught without much reference to the daily life of the pupil or that of the community.

As a result, a serious doubt has arisen in the minds of many of the Chinese as to the efficacy of modern education in solving the perplexing problems of the country. There is a feeling on the part of some that both the subjects taught in school and the method used in teaching those subjects do little good to the children. Indeed, a loud cry has already been raised against this form of education as failing to do what is expected of it. The charge is made that from the moment a child enters school, he begins to alienate himself from the life of the family and that of the community, and that by the time he graduates he is fit neither to be a farmer nor to be a merchant. This serious charge against new education, although it is not true of all schools, is yet not made without grounds. The root of the trouble lies, as already suggested, in the fact that much of the school work consists of merely imparting knowledge without reference either to the purposes which brought the children to school, or to the needs of the community in which they live. To remedy the evil something fundamental needs to be done, both in the selection of material for the curriculum and in the method of teaching the various subjects of study. Fortunate it is for the new republic that these two problems are beginning to receive the serious attention of her more progressive leaders in education.

(b) The Old Teacher and the New System

The facts that China went into this work of educating a quarter of the population of the globe without a sufficient body of teachers and that the growth of the new educational system has been probably more rapid than was anticipated, would not have made the problem of supplying teachers so serious had China been able to recruit teachers from the old schools. This she has not been able to do, although many of the old teaching staff did find their way into modern schools. Chinese scholars there were, and many of them too, but they lacked the knowledge and the skill demanded of the teachers of modern schools. Under the old educational system any one could set up as a school teacher, and a great many scholars who had attained the first degree in the examination, to say nothing of the host of others who had failed, made this their chief means of obtaining a living. No certificate was required for teaching, and no book or curriculum was compulsory, except that which was universally established by tradition or usage. The instruction was usually imparted either in the home of the children or in that of the teacher. Such private schools seldom comprised more than twenty children. The kind of teaching tended to develop memory rather than reasoning power.

Under the new system of education, the situation which the teacher has to face is entirely different. He must know more than mere Chinese classics and composition. He has to teach students in classes instead of individually. Again, the teacher in a modern school is expected to develop in the pupils the power of reasoning, instead of only mere memory. And the old-time teacher does not easily lend himself to the new order. He is by training conservative, inclined to cling to the methods to which he is accustomed. He is himself so wedded to the old that he confesses to a sort of intellectual awkwardness when he tries to use the new learning and new methods. In his fear of making mistakes, he confines himself closely to textbooks. Consciously or unconsciously he still over-emphasizes the value of memory. He himself is not trained to think, and of course is not inclined to adopt methods which quicken thought in his student. Modern pedagogy is to him so new a science that either he has little appreciation of its worth, or, if he is able to appreciate, he is not able to use it with facility and efficiency.

366. Socialization of School Work illustrated by History

(Dewey, John, "The Aim of History in Elementary Education"; in *The Elementary School Record*, pp. 199–200. Chicago, 1900)

To illustrate how Professor Dewey attempted to socialize the elementary school subjects, the following extract from his introduction to the monograph on History Teaching is given.

If history be regarded as just the record of the past, it is hard to see any grounds for claiming that it should play any large rôle in the curriculum of elementary education. The past is the past, and the dead may be safely left to bury its dead. There are too many urgent demands in the present, too many calls over the threshold of the future, to permit the child to become deeply immersed in what is forever gone by. Not so when history is considered an account of the forces and forms of social life. Social life we have always with us; the distinction of past and present is indifferent to it. Whether it was lived just here or just there is a matter of slight moment. It is life for all that; it shows the motives which draw men together and push them apart, and depicts what is desirable

FIG. 90. CONSTRUCTIVE ACTIVITY IN THE STUDY OF HISTORY

Dewey's Experimental School, Chicago

and what is hurtful. Whatever history may be for the scientific historian, for the educator it must be an indirect sociology — a study of society which lays bare its process of becoming and its modes of organization. Existing society is both too complex and too close to the child to be studied. He finds no clues into its labyrinth of detail, and can mount no eminence whence to get a perspective of arrangement.

If the aim of historical instruction is to enable the child to appreciate the values of social life, to see in imagination the forces which favor and let men's effective coöperation with one another, to understand the sorts of character that help on and that hold back, the essential thing in its presentation is to make it moving, dynamic. History must be presented not as an accumulation of results or effects, a mere statement of what happened, but as a forceful, acting thing. The motives, that is, the motors, must stand out. To study history is not to amass information, but to use information in constructing a vivid picture of how and why men did thus and so; achieved their successes and came to their failures.

When history is conceived as dynamic, as moving, its economic and industrial aspects are emphasized. These are but technical terms which express the problem with which humanity is unceasingly engaged; how to live, how to master and use nature so as to make it tributary to the enrichment of human life. The great advances in civilization have come through those manifestations of intelligence which have lifted man from his precarious subjection to nature, and revealed to him how he may make its forces coöperate with his own purposes. The social world in which the child now lives is so rich and full that it is not easy to see how much it cost, how much effort and thought lie back of it. Man has a tremendous equipment ready at hand. The child may be led to translate these ready-made resources into fluid terms; he may be led to see man face to face with nature, without inherited capital, without tools, without manufactured materials. And, step by step, he may follow the processes by which man recognized the needs of his situation, thought out the weapons and instruments that enabled him to cope with them; and may learn how these new resources opened new horizons of growth and created new problems. The industrial history of man is not a materialistic or a merely utilitarian affair. It is a matter of intelligence. Its record is the record of how man learned to think, to think to some effect, to transform the conditions of life so that life itself becomes a different thing. It is an ethical record as well; the account of the conditions which men have patiently wrought out to serve their ends.

The question of how human beings live, indeed, represents the dominant interest with which the child approaches historic material. It is this point of view which brings those who worked in the past close to the beings with whom he is daily associated, and confers upon him the gift of sympathetic penetration.

The child who is interested in the way in which men lived, the tools they had to do with, the new inventions they made, the transformations of life that arose from the power and leisure thus gained, is eager to repeat like processes in his own action, to remake utensils, to reproduce processes, to rehandle materials. Since he understands their problems and their successes only by seeing what obstacles and what resources they had from nature, the child is interested in field and forest, ocean and mountain, plant and animal. By building up a conception of the natural environment in which lived the people he is studying, he gets his hold upon their lives. This reproduction he cannot make excepting as he gains acquaintance with the natural forces and forms with which he is himself surrounded. The interest in history gives a more human coloring, a wider significance, to his own study of nature. His knowledge of nature lends point and accuracy to his study of history. This is the natural "correlation" of history and science.

CHAPTER XXIX
NEW TENDENCIES AND EXPANSIONS

THE Readings of this chapter have been selected with a view to illustrating a few of the more important new tendencies in educational organization — political, scientific, vocational, and sociological — which have characterized educational progress in recent decades.

The first (367), dealing with the environmental influence of the State, sets forth the new state needs and the different attitudes toward education which the State may legitimately assume. The second (368) is introduced to show how governments, interested in the promotion of national welfare, may turn the school into new directions the better to serve national ends. The third (369) states well the position of the university as the head and crown of the state's educational system, and the relation of university thinking and teaching to national welfare and progress.

The next three selections relate to applied science and vocational training in the schools. The first of the group (370) describes the work of the Folk High Schools in Denmark, a little nation that had been made over by agricultural education since its spoliation at the hands of Prussia, in 1864. The second (371) describes the extended work done by the Germans in developing vocational training, before the World War. The third (372) states well the intimate relation existing, under modern industrial conditions, between the vocational education of a people and national prosperity.

The three selections which close the chapter have been chosen to illustrate some of the new attitudes toward child care and child welfare which have characterized the late nineteenth century. From the first (373), one may obtain a good idea of the change in attitude toward child labor and child welfare. The second (374) states simply and clearly the new problem of child labor. The third (375) describes briefly the reasons for the school undertaking a better supervision of child health than parents are usually able to provide.

367. The Environmental Influence of the State

(McKechnie, W. S., *The State and the Individual*, pp. 363-64.   Glasgow, 1896)

The duty of the State in the matter of training the young for citizenship in the State, and the positions toward such training which it may legitimately assume, are well stated in the following selection.

The child comes into the world a bundle of undeveloped potentialities, void of experience and thought.   The environment and external circumstances necessary for the growth of his mind and body are all supplied by the State.   This is true, although not all nor even the chief part of them are imparted to the child directly by the officials of the government or by the laws or other organs of the State.   The immediate environment depends on the influence of the family and of other institutions and agencies included in and controlled by the State. The child may have "innate ideas" in the sense of that *a priori* element which is one of the prerequisites of all conscious existence; but the equally necessary *a posteriori* element can be got only from experience; and the sphere of the State, or of various parts of the State, is the only school where experience is possible for him.   He is born into the commonwealth, and from the day of his birth the rights of citizenship, which he cannot actually enjoy till he has acquired full age, are held in trust for him by the State.   It is true that it is the family whose influences at first surround him, molding his earliest tendencies and aspirations after its traditions, but the family itself would be empty of content except for what flows into it from society and the State.   The community as a whole, then, is the environment of the individual.   It is the State which fills him with its own ideas and molds him after its own pattern.   The English youth grows up with habits and ideas quite absent in the Zulu or even in the Frenchman.   Allowing all claims for heredity — though this too has been indirectly supplied by the State through ancestors who were themselves its members — his environment has made him what he is.

The State then — using the word in its widest sense — puts its stamp on the young individuality before he has reached manhood and acquired the ability to choose his own surroundings.   Willingly or unwillingly, it educates the individual and so has a terrible responsibility thrust upon its shoulders.   The young mind as well as the young body is thrown upon its care during the important and impressionable years fated to mold the development of an immortal soul for time and for eternity.   This trust, burdensome and disquieting as it is, is yet one which the State dare not decline.

Its duty to the young cannot be brushed aside or lightly treated. But it has also a duty to itself.   In each helpless child lies a future citizen who will form an organic portion of the commonwealth, and may exercise a deep and lasting influence on its destinies. All children cannot become great statesmen, but all great statesmen once were children.

On these two grounds the State has both a right and a duty to include the education of the young within its proper province. Indeed it must educate whether it will or no. The only question is whether it will do so consciously or unconsciously, systematically or at random, well or ill. Government need not undertake the work of education, but the supreme legislative sovereign is forced to assume some attitude towards that all-important question.

There are three positions, any one of which Parliament may adopt. (I) It may repudiate all direct responsibility, leaving each child to scramble for itself. (II) It may compel parents to educate their offspring at their own expense. (III) It may enforce education upon all, and pay for it out of the national purse. Each of these three courses has its adherents.

368. German Secondary Schools and National Needs

(Address of Emperor William II, at Berlin Conference of 1890. Translated in *Report United States Commissioner of Education*, 1889-90, vol. I, pp. 359-63)

In 1890, after some previous discussion, a call was issued for a conference on problems relating to the German secondary schools. At this conference the then young German Emperor, William II, gave the main opening address, demanding that the instruction be changed to serve better the national ends. His speech created widespread discussion among German secondary schoolmasters, and is important as revealing new national conceptions as to the place and purpose of the secondary school. He said, in part:

GENTLEMEN: I desire to address a few words to you at the outset because it seemed to me important that you should know from the first what I think about this matter. Naturally there will be many things discussed that cannot be decided, and I believe that many points will remain cloudy and obscure. I have considered it proper not to leave the gentlemen in doubt as to my own views.

In the first place I wish to observe that we have to do here above all not with a political school question, but entirely with technical and pedagogical measures which we must adopt in order to fit the growing generation for the demands of the present, for the position of our Fatherland and of our life in the world at large. . . .

This cabinet order, which the honorable minister has had the goodness to mention before, would perhaps not have been necessary if the schools had stood in the position where they ought to have stood. I should like to observe in the outset that if I should be somewhat sharp I have reference to no one personally, but to the system, to the entire situation. If the schools had done that which we demand of them, and I can speak to you as one who is initiated, for I have also attended the gymnasium and know what goes on there, then they would of necessity have taken upon themselves from the very outset the fight against social democracy. The teaching faculties would have taken firm hold of the matter unitedly, and would have so instructed the growing generation that those young people who are of about the same age as myself, that is to say, about thirty years of age, would voluntarily offer the material with which I could work in the State in order the more rapidly to become master of the movement. This has, however, not been the case. The last period in which our school was still a standard for our whole national life and of our development was in the years 1864, 1866 to 1870. Then the Prussian schools and the Prussian teaching faculties were the bearers of the idea of unity that was preached everywhere. Every graduate who came out of the school and began his voluntary military service or entered upon active life, all were united upon this one point: The German Empire shall be again established, and Alsace and Lorraine won back again. That ceased with the year 1870. The Empire is united; we have that which we wishéd to gain, and there the matter rested.

Starting from the new basis, the school ought now to animate the youth and make clear to them that the new political condition exists, that it may be preserved. Nothing of this kind has been observed, and in the short time that the Empire has existed centrifugal tendencies have already developed themselves. I can surely judge that accurately, because I stand at the top and all such questions come to me. The reason is to be sought in the education of the young. Where is the lack there? The lack is surely in many places. The chief reason is that since the year 1870 the philologists as *beati possidentes* have sat in the gymnasia and have laid their chief emphasis on the subject that was taught, upon learning and knowing, but not upon the formation of character and the needs of the life of to-day. You, Mr. Privy Councilor Hinzpeter, will pardon me — you are an enthusiastic philologist; but none the less in my opinion the matter has reached a height where finally it can go no farther. Less emphasis has been placed upon the *can* than upon the *ken;* that is shown in the requirements that are made in examinations. One proceeds from the axiom that above all things the scholar must know as much as possible; whether that is suitable for life or not is a secondary consideration. If one should converse with one of the gentlemen concerned and seek to explain to him that the young man must, after all, to a certain extent, receive a practical preparation for life and its problems, the answer is ever, that is not the task of the schools; the chief object is the gymnastics of the intellect, and if these gymnastics were properly pursued the young man would be in a condition to accomplish with these gymnastics all that was necessary for life. I believe that we can be no longer deluded from this standpoint.

If I now return to the schools themselves, and especially to the gymnasium, I know very well that in many circles I am considered a fanatical opponent of the gymnasium, and that I have been represented in favor of other kinds of schools. Gentlemen, that is not the case. Whoever has been in the gymnasium himself and has caught a glimpse behind the scenes knows what is lacking there. Above all, the national basis is lacking. We must take the German as the foundation for the gymnasium; we ought to educate national young Germans and not young Greeks and Romans. We must depart entirely from the basis that has existed for centuries, — from the old monastic education of the Middle Ages, where the standard was Latin with a little Greek added. That is no longer the standard; we must make German the basis. The German exercise must be the central point about which all turns. . . .

In like manner I should like to see the national sentiment further advanced with us in questions of history, geography, and traditions. Pray let us begin at home. After, when we are perfectly acquainted with our own rooms and chambers, then can we go to the museum and look about there also. But first of all we must be perfectly at home in the history of the Fatherland. The great elector was only a misty specter in my school days; the Seven Years' War already lay outside of all consideration, and history closed with the end of the preceding century, with the French Revolution. The wars for freedom, which are the most important for the young citizen, were not gone through, and only through supplementary and very interesting lectures of Mr. Privy Councilor Hinzpeter was I in a position, thank Heaven, to learn these things. But that is precisely the *punctum saliens*. Why are our young people misled? Why do so many confused muddled reformers of the world appear? Why is our government continually growled about and foreign lands referred to? Because the young people do not know how our conditions have developed themselves, and that the roots lie in the time of the French Revolution; and therefore I am firmly convinced that if we explain to the young people in its chief traits this transition from the French Revolution to the nineteenth century, they will get quite a different understanding for the questions of to-day from that which they have hitherto had. They are then in a position to improve and increase their knowledge through the supplementary lectures which they will hear in the university. . . .

These, gentlemen, are in general the matters I wished to bring before you, things that have touched my heart, and I can only give you this assurance. The innumerable petitions, requests, and wishes that I have received from parents, although we fathers were declared in the preceding year by my honored Mr. Hinzpeter to be a party that had nothing to say concerning the education of children, place me, as the common father of the country, under the obligation of declaring it can go no further so. [Gentlemen, men are not to look at the world through spectacles, but with their own eyes, and are to find pleasure in that which they have before them, their native land and its institutions. To this end you are now to help.]

369. The University and the State

(Van Hise, Chas. R., Commencement Address, University of Wisconsin, 1910)

The following extracts from an able commencement address state well the position of a modern state university as the crowning feature of the educational system of a State.

The strength of the state university lies in its close relations to the State. The State demands of it service; the university feels a peculiar obligation to the State in which it is situated. It is the duty of the state university to instruct young men and women; it is its duty to advance knowledge, and especially those lines of knowledge which concern the development of the State. It is the duty of the staff of the state university to be at the service of the State along all lines in which their expert knowledge will be helpful; it is their duty to assist in carrying knowledge to the people.

These relations between the university and the State bind them closely together. The growth of the university is dependent upon the State. The State owns the university; and every citizen feels himself to be a stockholder in that ownership.

It has been said that the university should be the soul of the State; this is not my phrase, but I shall be proud of the University of Wisconsin, just in proportion as it becomes the soul of the State. Every man of high ideals is a part of that soul. Every institution which works for the upbuilding of humanity, be it church or prison, is a part of the soul of the State. Every school and college is a part of that soul, and it should be the aim of each to be as large a part as possible. The university, the culmination of the educational system of the State, would be a miserable institution indeed if it could not justly claim to be a large segment of the soul of the State.

The unrest which has characterized the first decade of this twentieth century has led to many new proposals in all fields. The conservatives have sometimes been disturbed because questions have arisen which in the past have been regarded as settled.

With reference to such questions it has sometimes been said that the university should keep off; that it should take no part in their consideration; that it should let the battle be fought out by others without any attempt at leadership. This position the university authorities and its friends must firmly resist. At times of unrest when new and important issues are arising, when old convictions are being questioned, is a time when the men of learning who know history, who should know the facts broadly and who have no purpose but the greatest good of the greatest number, should be absolutely free. If at such times those who should be leaders do not throw their intellect and influence in the right direction, there is danger that demagoguery and passion may lead in wrong directions with resulting disaster. It is because of the present general unrest that I again formulate the principles in reference to a free university, well established for a hundred years, lest by any deviation from that at this critical time the University of Wisconsin shall fail to do its full duty to the State and to the Nation.

The progress of the Nation and the State will continue. The old ideas and ideals will be modified. The human race is ever moving upward and onward; but such movement always involves vexation, strife, dissension, often pain on the part of those who are disturbed in their convictions. No advance has ever been made without suffering; such is the cost of progress. This is alike true of the labor-saving machine and of the forward intellectual or spiritual step. In order that the suffering and pain of advance shall be reduced to a minimum; in order that the benefactions of the advance shall be a maximum; and far outweigh the cost, it is incumbent that the universities play their part in leadership. Times of unrest, of changing ideas and ideals, are above all the times when the university should be most effective in the guidance of public opinion.

Times of unrest and change are not the times for the university to trim; they are the times to set every sail from the main course to the sky sails so that all may draw. If at a time of stress the university furls its sails the people will lose confidence in the institution that remains supinely in the harbor when the State is confronted with vital questions in reference to which assistance should be given. The State has a right to demand of the university expert service in valuing a public utility; it has equally the right to demand expert service in politics and sociology.

370. What the Folk High Schools have done for Denmark

(Friend, L. L., *The Folk High Schools of Denmark*, pp. 15–17. Washington, 1914)

The following description of the work of the folk and agricultural high schools of Denmark gives an interesting sidelight on the work of these essentially democratic institutions, and of the services they have rendered in the regeneration of Denmark.

Intellectually the Danes are the equal of any people in the world. The Danish peasantry is said by many to be the most intelligent in the world.   Agriculture, which is the principal industry in Denmark, has since the war with Germany in 1864 raised the nation from practical bankruptcy to a position of independence and self-respect, in spite of the fact that there are conditions in Denmark which make successful farming more difficult than in some other countries.   This has been accomplished by the intelligence of the Danish farmer.   He is constantly a student of his task, experimenting, testing, trying always to get better returns from the soil and from his dairy, and endeavoring to improve the products of his farm so that more people in England and other countries that buy them will want them.   He reads more newspapers, agricultural papers, and magazines than any other farmer in the world. For this intelligence and its consequent prosperity, the folk high schools and the agricultural schools which have grown from them receive a large share of credit from the Danish people.   The folk high schools have given them inspiration, and the agricultural schools have given them definite preparation for their work.   The work of these institutions in the education of their students does not end when they leave their halls, nor is it confined to their students alone.   The high schools, in addition to their regular courses of instruction, maintain lecturing societies and hold annual high-school meetings for the intellectual improvement of all the rural population.   The agricultural schools, besides giving short practical courses for farmers and farmers' wives, prepare specialists whose business it is to advise farmers and give them assistance in working out their experiments and agricultural problems.

The influence of the high schools on the civic life of rural Denmark is easily discovered.   They have raised the standard of intelligence of the people, and the people are therefore well informed in regard to questions of politics and government and are able to do their own thinking on such questions. . . .

On the economic side of Danish life the influence of the high schools also stands out conspicuously.   The higher standard of intelligence established by the high schools has improved the condition of the Danish farmer amazingly, and has made him the chief factor in Danish life. Though as a rule his farm is small, it almost invariably produces a good living for its owner and usually contributes something to the export trade of the nation.   The export trade of Denmark consists chiefly in butter, cheese, bacon, and eggs.   These go largely to the markets of England, and are produced and marketed usually under the direction of the Danish coöperative agricultural societies.   Coöperation is the watchword in all rural activities in Denmark.   In coöperation in agriculture this little country has become an example for the rest of the world.   In 1912 there were marketed, through the coöperative societies, eggs, butter, bacon, and meats to the value of $121,000,000.

371. The German System of Vocational Education

(Report of the Commission on National Aid to Vocational Education, vol. 1,
Appendix A. Washington, 1914)

The following selection offers a very interesting description of the system of vocational education which the German Empire developed, after 1871, to enable the nation to overcome its handicaps in natural resources and provide for a rapidly increasing population.

Vocational education in Germany undertakes to meet the requirements of every occupation, however simple, in so far as these have been accurately determined, and to give precisely that instruction and training which will develop in the worker the greatest efficiency. The vocational schools of Germany are, therefore, almost as diverse in character as are the occupations of her workers, and this very diversity in character renders any detailed account of them impossible in a brief statement The object has been not simply to develop a national system of education, but rather to provide in each locality, and for each group of workers, schools adapted to the special needs of the locality and occupations of the workers. . . .

The Industrial Schools. The system of vocational industrial schools embraces the following general types of institutions:

1. The technical universities, which are similar to our best technological colleges, and are intended to train students for leadership in industrial enterprises.

2. The middle technical schools, which "aim to train managing officers for the greater industries, and persons who initiate and manage the lesser industrial undertakings.". . .

3. The lower technical schools. The requirements for admission to these schools are briefly summed up as follows:

   (a) A preliminary general education, such as is given in a good elementary school.

   (b) The training given in the continuation schools, or the preparatory course of the technical schools.

   (c) Several years' practical experience in a trade, and generally the completion of apprenticeship.

4. The industrial continuation schools. The requirement for admission to these schools is completion of the elementary school course. The instruction in these schools commonly does not occupy more than 8 or 10 hours a week, in the evening on week days and on Sunday afternoons, and is intended to "give all the workers in the industries and handicrafts, whether apprentices or journeymen, an opportunity to acquire, without giving up their practical work in the shop, a knowledge and skill in drawing, which is absolutely necessary for efficiency in their occupations." . . .

In some respects the most significant feature of the German system of industrial education is found in the systematic effort, through the continuation schools and other agencies, to rehabilitate the apprenticeship system and to provide for the continued development of the boy during his period of apprenticeship. The school retains for several years its hold upon the boy who has entered the factory or shop, and provides for him an open way for improvement in efficiency. . . .

In general, the types of schools described above are found more or less clearly differentiated, in the field of mining and industrial production, covering the mechanical, the chemical, and the building trades, the art trades, and handicrafts. Recently the technical training of women in industrial and commercial pursuits and in domestic economy has been undertaken.

The control of these schools is commonly entrusted to the ministries of commerce and industry, or to commissions representing these ministries, and the ministry of education.

Commercial Technical Education. The differentiation of the commercial technical schools is less well defined than it is in the case of the industrial schools, and the development of the commercial schools has come at a later date. There are, however, excellent advanced commercial schools for the thorough training of business managers. The courses of study cover national economics, commercial law, foreign languages, commercial geography, and accounting. The middle and lower commercial technical schools and the commercial continuation schools, which give instruction of a lower grade, vary greatly in character and efficiency, but in general render the services with reference to training for commercial pursuits which is rendered by industrial schools of corresponding grade for industrial pursuits.

Results of Vocational Training. Relatively to other countries, the only conditions more favorable in Germany to industrial and commercial development, in 1871, were a greater poverty of her people, less abundant natural resources, and a greater necessity of providing at home for the employment and maintenance of a rapidly increasing population. France, with a richer soil, had not the stimulus of an increasing population, and England, with abundant supplies of coal and iron available for domestic manufactures, possessed in her colonial empire an outlet for her surplus population. While, however, other European peoples whose necessities and poverty were equally as great as were those of Germany have not found in their necessities a stimulus to economic advancement, Germany has risen, within the lifetime of the present generation, from a position of commercial and industrial insignificance to a position of dominance in the markets of the world, largely as a direct consequence of the work of her vocational, technical, and technological schools.

At the close of the Franco-Prussian War, in 1871, not only were Germany's manufactures and commerce relatively insignificant and poorly conditioned, but the habits and occupations of her people were domestic and agricultural. Her natural resources and the economic capacity of her people, who had given no evidence of possessing any peculiar genius for industrial activities, seemed inadequate to provide for an increasing population. Under these conditions the individual genius of Bismarck, through direction of the ministry of commerce and industry, undertook the achievement of economic prosperity, and in this work he relied principally upon the institution and development of a system of practical education which should embrace the entire working population of Germany.

In the four decades which measure the period of her rise as an industrial and commercial nation, Germany has demonstrated that nations which depend upon convention, established prestige, or superior natural resources, can not compete successfully against a nation which systematically develops the intelligence and efficiency of her laborers, and regards the farm, the shop, and the factory as laboratories for the application of science to economic processes. "It can not be doubted," declares a recent writer, "that under equal conditions the competition of German manufactured goods with English manufactured goods would be impossible anywhere outside of Germany, owing to the unfavorable geographical position of Germany's coal fields and industrial centers. Germany is competing largely on account of her system of industrial education."

While in other countries the development of science has been academic, in Germany every new principle elaborated by science has revolutionized some industry, modified some manufacturing process, or opened up an entirely new field of commercial exploitation. In the chemical industries of Germany, it is stated that there is one university trained chemist for every forty work people. It is important to realize that the development of Germany's manufactures and commerce has depended not upon the establishment of any monopoly in the domain of science, nor upon any advancement of science within her boundaries more aggressive and rapid than that which has taken place in other countries, but primarily upon the practical utilization of the results of scientific research in Germany and in other countries. In this whole process of bringing science into practice industrial education is an important factor.

372. Vocational Education and National Prosperity

(*Report of the Commission on National Aid to Vocational Education*, vol.1, pp. 22–23. Washington, 1914)

In this selection from the *Report* the Commission states well the new dependence of commercial and industrial nations on vocational education for their workers for national prosperity.

Our National Prosperity is at Stake

We have become a great industrial as well as a great agricultural nation. Each year shows a less percentage of our people on the farms and a greater in the cities.

Our factory population is growing apace. Our future as a nation will depend more and more on the success of our industrial life, as well as upon the volume and quality of our agricultural products. It has repeatedly been pointed out that the time is not far distant when our rapidly increasing population will press hard upon an improved agriculture for its food supply, and force our industries to reach out over the entire world for trade wherewith to meet the demands for labor of untold millions of bread winners.

In volume of output the United States leads the four great manufacturing nations of the world. More than a billion and a half of people outside of these four countries are largely dependent upon them for manufactured articles. "The rewards offered in this world trade are beyond comprehension. They are to be measured in money, in intellectual advancement, in national spirit, in heightened civilization." Yet we have only begun to invade this market, where we find our competitor too often in possession of the field and strongly entrenched against us.

It is true that we have a large foreign trade in manufactured articles, but of our exports a very large proportion consists of crude materials. German, French, and English exports represent on the average a much greater value in skill and workmanship than do those from our own ports. Less than one-third of the volume of our foreign commerce is made up of manufactures ready for consumption. A very large proportion consists of raw and semi-raw materials, such as lumber, cotton, meat, coal, oil, and copper bar, to secure which we have robbed our soil and the earth beneath our feet of the riches we have been foolish enough to regard as inexhaustible. The statistics of our foreign commerce show that the proportion of these raw products, in the total volume of our exports, has been declining during the past three decades, and that the maintenance and development of our foreign trade is coming to depend each year to a greater extent upon our ability to compete with foreign nations in the products of skilled labor, — upon our ability to "sell more brains and less material."

The volume of our foreign trade has in the past depended upon the exploitation of a virgin soil and of our other natural resources. In this crude work we have had no competitors. Our profit has been the profit of the miner working in a rich soil. The volume and profitableness of our trade in the future, however, must depend much more largely upon the relative skill and efficiency of the vocationally-trained artisans of England, France, and Germany. Our products will find a market in foreign countries only in those lines of industrial activity in which the labor is as efficient and as well trained as the labor of the countries with which we must compete.

The battles of the future between nations will be fought in the markets of the world. That nation will triumph, with all that its success means to the happiness and welfare of its citizenship, which is able to put the greatest amount of skill and brains into what it produces. Our foreign commerce, and to some extent our domestic commerce, are being threatened by the commercial prestige which Germany has won, largely as the result of a policy of training its workers begun by the far-seeing Bismarck almost half a century ago.

France and England, and even far-off Japan, profiting by the schools of the Fatherland, are now establishing national schools of vocational education. In Germany, within the next few years, there will probably be no such thing as an untrained man. In the United States probably not more than 25,000 of the eleven or twelve million workers in manufacturing and mechanical pursuits have had an opportunity to acquire an adequate training for their work in life.

373. English Conditions before the first Factory Labor Act

(Montmorency, J. E. G. de, *The Progress of Education in England*, pp. 66–68. London, 1904)

The following extract describes the pitiable conditions surrounding child life in England after the rise of manufacturing and before the passage of the first factory control legislation, and gives the more significant provisions of this pioneer law.

. . . Parliament, during the eighteenth century, had taken an intermittent interest in education, and had created, at any rate, a certain distinct power to charge the rates with the education of the destitute. But the closing years of the century saw the gradual reopening of a new social problem. The invention and introduction of machinery into certain districts of the North of England, involved the aggregation of large masses of people in those districts. This broke down the parochial school system, and, moreover, in the end, did away with all education, for parents and employers rapidly discovered the value of child labour in mechanical production. Not only were all available children drafted into the mills, but the destitute children of the great towns were purchased, under a system of indenture, by the manufacturers from the poor-law authorities. Sir Samuel Romilly declared, in the House of Commons, in 1806, that parish apprentices were often sent by contract from London to the Lancashire cotton mills "in carts, like so many negro slaves." Until the year 1816, pauper children under the age of nine years could be compulsorily apprenticed in pursuance of statute 43 Eliz., c.2, s.5. It was not until 1833 that it became unlawful generally to employ in mills children who had not completed their ninth year, and this age was actually lowered by a year in 1844. Moreover, the Statute of 1833 reserved the case of silk mills, and until the year 1879 children from the age of eight years could be employed in such mills. This seems almost unbelievable. But the fact remains, and through half of the nineteenth century the country was face to face with the knowledge that an immense number of children were growing up as parts of a great industrial machine, without any knowledge of either religion or letters, — human beings brought up as beasts of burden; housed, fed, and worked. Old Mr. Bonwick, in his "Reminiscences" before referred to, tells us that when he was a boy it was pitiful "to see the boy chimney-sweep, shivering and half-starved as a work-house apprentice, driven by a brutal master to clamber up the steep. What dreadful stories I then heard of the poor factory children, forced, as mere babes in the wintry darkness, breakfastless, to the mill!" The intolerable character of the evil — an evil of so profitable a character that both masters and parents rejoiced at its existence — awakened the conscience of, at any rate, certain minds in Parliament. It was felt that a generation was growing up that had no knowledge or appreciation of the forces that bind society together, — no knowledge of home life, of religion, of morality. The future depends on the children of the present, and the outlook for the nineteenth century looked dark enough in the year of grace 1802.

On April 13th, 1802, a Bill was introduced into the House of Commons "for the preservation of the health and morals of apprentices and others, employed in cotton and other mills, and cotton and other factories." This Bill, slightly amended and improved, received the Royal assent on June 22nd, 1802. The state of the factory children may be guessed from the provisions of the Act. It directed the mill rooms to be whitewashed twice a year, and to be ventilated; it ordered an apprentice to have one suit of clothes a year, and not to work more than twelve hours a day, exclusive of meal times; it forbade work between nine at night and six in the morning; it provided that male and female apprentices should sleep in separate rooms, and not more than two apprentices should sleep in one bed; it made medical attendance compulsory in the case of infectious disease; it directed the mills to be inspected by visitors appointed by the justices, and ordered the children to be taught the elements of learning and the principles of Christianity. The sixth section of the Act runs as follows: "Every such apprentice shall be instructed, in some part of every working day, for the first four years at least of his or her apprenticeship. . . . in the usual hours of work, in reading, writing, and arithmetic, or either of them, according to the age and abilities of such apprentice, by some discreet and proper person, to be provided and paid by the master or mistress of such apprentice, in some room or place in such mill or factory to be set apart for that purpose; and that the time hereby decided to be allotted for such instruction as aforesaid, shall be deemed and taken on all occasions as part of the respective periods limited by this Act during which any such apprentice shall be employed or compelled to work." Section 8 provided that "Every apprentice or (in case the apprentices shall attend in classes) every such class shall, for the space of one hour at least every Sunday, be instructed and examined in the principles of the Christian religion, by some proper person, to be provided and paid by the master or mistress of such apprentice." Church of England children were to be examined at least once a year by the clergyman of the parish, and presented to the Bishop for confirmation between the ages of fourteen and eighteen years. Moreover, divine service was to be attended every Sunday, and not less than once a month at an Established Church.

This reformatory measure was petitioned against in the following year by manufacturers and parents, and it was never enforced. Many generations of little seven-year old slaves were to be worn away in the mills before effective relief came.

374. The New Problem of Child Labor

(Giddings, F. R., From an Address on "The Social and Legal Aspect of Compulsory Education and Child Labor," before the National Education Association, at Asbury Park, in 1905)

The following short extract from the above cited address states both simply and clearly the new problem of child labor, as it has arisen since the coming of the Industrial Revolution and the factory system.

The educational problem and the industrial problem of child labor cannot be separated. This is true, whether every parent is permitted to deal as he will with his child, or whether he is compelled, as in most American Commonwealths, to withhold his child from gainful employment and to keep him in a school, or otherwise to provide systematic instruction for him, during certain weeks of each year. Child labor itself is a kind of education which, according to its nature and extent, may be consistent or altogether inconsistent with other kinds. The labor that American boys and girls had to perform on the farm a generation and more ago was often an invaluable discipline of mind and character, fitting them for self-reliant and useful careers quite as effectively as their meager school training did. Such labor did not necessarily unfit the child for the enjoyment of the highest educational advantages. Exhausting confinement in stores, sweat-shops and factories is child labor of an altogether different sort. It is antagonistic to the child's mental and physical development and it cannot be combined with any sound educational policy.

Compulsory education by the State and the prohibition of child labor are policies undoubtedly socialistic in character. They assert the supremacy of the State's interest in the child as against any opposing interest of the parent. The American people have never been afraid of socialism to this extent, and within the last ten years it has greatly extended both compulsory education and the prohibition of the labor of children.

375. Health Work in the Schools

(Hoag, E. B., and Terman, L. M., *Health Work in the Schools*, pp. 1–5. Boston, 1914)

The following selection, taken from the introductory chapter of a standard text on health supervision as a phase of the work of public education, gives a good idea as to the spread of health work in the schools, and of the responsibility of society for such attention to child needs.

The health supervision of schools is not a passing fad. The conservation of the child is a problem which, like that of world peace, is bound to take possession of the minds of all humanitarian people. To the ethical principle of humanitarianism is added the stern counsel of biological laws, which teach us that an elaborate scheme of mental culture which proceeds without regard to the needs of the body is but a house built upon the sands.

It is significant for the future of the movement that, with minor exceptions, all civilized countries have almost simultaneously taken it up. Its universal development is inevitable. Progress has been remarkably uniform in different countries, though naturally there are some differences in the details of procedure and in the points of emphasis. Germany has forged ahead with her dental clinics and open-air schools. France, with her school lunches and vacation colonies; while England has set the whole world an example in the earnest way in which she has undertaken to ameliorate the evils which medical inspection of schools has revealed. Our own country, on the whole, is behind most of the nations of Europe in the practice of school hygiene, but is making progress rapidly. But the doctor has not been brought into the school without opposition, and it is therefore desirable to inquire further into the justification for this new assumption of responsibility on the part of organized society.

.   .   .   .

If all parents were wise in regard to health matters, it would not be so necessary for schools to make a special study of the physical conditions of the children entrusted to their care. All that could then be fairly required would be the guaranty of a healthful school environment, correct methods of lighting and heating, sanitary plumbing, the control of contagious diseases, frequent recesses, sufficient physical training, and the proper sort of health instruction. But it is a fact and not a theory that not all parents possess the special knowledge which is necessary for the hygienic supervision of physical and mental development. Even intelligent parents may be unable to detect the early symptoms of physical disorder, just as they may be unable to decide upon the best methods or texts for teaching history or geography. They do not see the defects in their own children because they are used to them. Many are so superstitious as to prefer to treat adenoids by suggestion, others so ignorant as to interpret *pediculosis capitis* as a sign of good health. Plainly, therefore, it becomes the duty of the school department to furnish not only a healthful school environment, but also a health guardianship over its pupils.

The children of to-day must be viewed as the raw material of a new State; the schools as the nursery of the Nation. To conserve this raw material is as logical a function of the State as to conserve the natural resources of coal, iron, and water power. To investigate exhaustively the evils which exist, and to remedy all that may be remedied without transgressing unduly upon the jealous precincts of parental responsibility, is a plain matter of duty. Theoretically, it matters little how the State performs this duty, whether by a house-to-house census of the children, or in some other way. Practically, however, there is no effective or convenient way except to do the work in connection with the public schools. In many of our best towns and cities the people themselves are demanding such supervision on the principle that it is one of the important functions of the public-school system.

The argument that the health supervision of schools invades the rights of the home has precisely the same value as the corresponding argument against compulsory school attendance and prescribed courses of study. The school does not claim anything more than the right to make an examination of the child's physical and mental condition in order that the work of the school may be properly adjusted to his health and growth needs, and, further, to notify and advise parents regarding such defects as are found to exist. This is not an unwarranted assumption of power. The responsibility for remedial action is left entirely with the parents. The school has not undertaken forcibly to subject children to surgical operations, nor is there at present any legal method of compelling parents to perform their duty in this respect. We can invoke the law for wanton neglect of a broken bone, but there is no way to punish the neglect of discharging ears, adenoids, or astigmatism, any one of which may prove more serious in the long run than a fractured bone.

It is interesting to conjecture how far present practice in this regard is likely to be modified. Compulsory public education itself is so recent that only a few decades ago it was considered by a majority of people as a species of meddlesome paternalism. According to the old conception the child was the parents' child; if they questioned the value of an education there was no recourse in the child's behalf. There are a million or more illiterate adults in the United States to-day who are victims of this mistaken social theory. The theory, happily, has been discarded. We know now that the interests of society demand an elaborate scheme of educational processes under social control. Some time we shall understand, just as clearly, that the child's physical growth also stands in need of more expert supervision than the average parent is capable of exercising.